CLASSICAL PRESENCES

General Editors

LORNA HARDWICK   JAMES I. PORTER

CLASSICAL PRESENCES

Attempts to receive the texts, images, and material culture of ancient Greece and Rome inevitably run the risk of appropriating the past in order to authenticate the present. Exploring the ways in which the classical past has been mapped over the centuries allows us to trace the avowal and disavowal of values and identities, old and new. Classical Presences brings the latest scholarship to bear on the contexts, theory, and practice of such use, and abuse, of the classical past.

Classics and Irish Politics, 1916–2016

Edited by

ISABELLE TORRANCE AND
DONNCHA O'ROURKE

OXFORD
UNIVERSITY PRESS

OXFORD
UNIVERSITY PRESS

Great Clarendon Street, Oxford, OX2 6DP,
United Kingdom

Oxford University Press is a department of the University of Oxford.
It furthers the University's objective of excellence in research, scholarship,
and education by publishing worldwide. Oxford is a registered trade mark of
Oxford University Press in the UK and in certain other countries

First Edition published in 2020

Impression: 1

Published in the United States of America by Oxford University Press
198 Madison Avenue, New York, NY 10016, United States of America

British Library Cataloguing in Publication Data
Data available

Library of Congress Control Number: 2020933776

ISBN 978-0-19-886448-6

Printed and bound by
CPI Group (UK) Ltd, Croydon, CR0 4YY

Acknowledgements

This edited collection is based in part on some of the papers presented at a conference of the same name at the Royal Irish Academy and Trinity College Dublin in June 2016. That conference was generously sponsored by the University of Notre Dame, and it is a pleasure to acknowledge the extensive financial support received from the University's various units and initiatives including the Keough-Naughton Institute for Irish Studies, the Nanovic Institute for European Studies, the Office of the Vice President for Research, the Department of Classics, the Henkels conference fund, and the Global Collaboration Initiative. We are indebted to the original speakers and audience members for a stimulating and inspiring conference. To those whose papers have been revised for publication here, and to the authors commissioned thereafter (Chapters 5, 6, 11, 12, 17, 19, 21), we express our deepest gratitude for their patience during the long processes of editing and review that this manuscript has undergone. Our thanks also go to the anonymous reviewers for insightful and constructive feedback, to the editors of the Classical Presences series for their encouragement, and to the OUP editorial staff for all their assistance. A particular debt is owed, finally, to Fiachra Mac Góráin, who has generously been on call throughout the preparation of this volume to advise on details of Irish language and culture.

A number of other institutions have supported the publication of this book and we are most grateful to have the opportunity to acknowledge that support. The work of Isabelle Torrance on this book has been completed during a Marie Skłodowska-Curie Co-Fund Research Fellowship at the Aarhus Institute of Advanced Studies. The Institute has also contributed significantly to permissions and reproductions expenses, and Aarhus University's School of Communication and Culture has covered the costs of indexing. Donncha O'Rourke's work on this project has been facilitated by a period of research leave sponsored by the School of History, Classics and Archaeology at the University of Edinburgh, which has also contributed generously to the costs of permissions and reproductions. For permissions expenses related to Chapters 8, 9, and 20, we acknowledge the support of the University of Toronto, the Leverhulme Trust, and the Department of Classics at Trinity College Dublin, respectively.

Isabelle Torrance, Aarhus
Donncha O'Rourke, Edinburgh

Contents

List of Illustrations   xi

List of Contributors   xv

1. Classics and Irish Politics: Introduction   1
   Isabelle Torrance and Donncha O'Rourke

I: RECEPTION AND REJECTION OF THE CLASSICS IN IRELAND

2. The Use and Abuse of Classics: Thoughts on Empire, Epic, and Language   27
   Declan Kiberd

3. Greece, Rome, and the Revolutionaries of 1916   43
   Brian McGing

4. Classics in the Van of the Irish Revolt: Thomas MacDonagh, 'alien to Athens and Rome'?   60
   Eoghan Moloney

II: LANGUAGE POLITICS

5. Translating into Irish from Greek and Latin in the Early Years of the Irish State   83
   Síle Ní Mhurchú

6. Classics through Irish at University College, Galway, 1931–78   100
   Pádraic Moran
   Appendix A to Chapter 6: Report from George Thomson to the Academic Council, 1933   120
   Appendix B to Chapter 6: Unpublished Irish Translations of Classical Texts Archived at NUI Galway   122
   Appendix C to Chapters 5 and 6: Irish Translations and Editions of Greek and Latin Texts and Related Works (to 1978)   125

7. Dinneen's Irish Virgil   137
   Fiachra Mac Góráin

8. Classics, Medievalism, and Cultural Politics in Myles na gCopaleen's *Cruiskeen Lawn* Columns   156
   Cillian O'Hogan

III: BETWEEN SCHOLARSHIP AND LITERATURE

9. Abjection and the Irish-Greek Fir Bolg in Aran Island Writing   173
   Arabella Currie

10. Sinn Féin and *Ulysses*: Between Professor Robert Mitchell Henry
    and James Joyce   193
    Edith Hall

11. Yeats and Oedipus: The Dark Road   218
    Chris Morash

IV: GENDER, SEXUALITY, AND CLASS

12. Wilde, Classicism, and Homosexuality in Modern Ireland   237
    Eibhear Walshe

13. Trojan Women and Irish Sexual Politics, 1920–2015   254
    Isabelle Torrance

14. Irish Didos: Empire, Gender, and Class in the Irish Popular
    Tradition to Frank McGuinness's *Carthaginians*   268
    Siobhán McElduff

V: CLASSICAL POETRY AND NORTHERN IRELAND

15. Elegies for Ireland: W. B. Yeats, Michael Longley, and the
    Roman Elegists   291
    Donncha O'Rourke

16. Michael Longley's 'Ceasefire' and the *Iliad*   308
    Maureen Alden

17. Post-Ceasefire Antigones and Northern Ireland   326
    Isabelle Torrance

VI: MATERIAL CULTURE AND (DE)COLONIALISM

18. Classicism and the Making of Commemorative Monuments in
    Newly Independent Ireland   349
    Judith Hill

19. The Politics of Neoclassicism in Belfast and Dublin: A Tale of
    Two Buildings   374
    Suzanne O'Neill

20. The Classical Themes of Irish Coinage, 1928–2002: Images
    from a Usable Past   393
    Christine Morris

21. Epilogue   407
    Richard P. Martin

Bibliography   419
Index   455

List of Illustrations

4.1. The first page of Joyce Kilmer's article on the Easter Rising, published in
The New York Times magazine 7 May 1916. 61

4.2. MS 10,851/6/8 from the collection of 'Thomas MacDonagh Papers,
1898–1916', National Library of Ireland. Page presenting Thomas
MacDonagh's handwritten translations of Catullus 5 (top centre), Catullus
85 (bottom centre), and Catullus 58 (top left). Image and permission to
reproduce provided courtesy of the National Library of Ireland. 72

4.3. MS 10,851/6/2 from the collection of 'Thomas MacDonagh Papers,
1898–1916', National Library of Ireland. Manuscript draft of Catullus 8,
written on the reverse of a partial letter concerning public action on
behalf of the Irish Self-Government Alliance (both sides shown). Images
and permission to reproduce provided courtesy of the National Library of
Ireland. 74

7.1. Foreign names translated into Irish and printed in Gaelic typeface. Ua
Duinnín (1929: 99). 143

10.1. Caricature of R. M. Henry, Papers of R. M. Henry, McClay Library,
Queen's University, Belfast. Image reproduced courtesy of Special
Collections, McClay Library, Queen's University, Belfast. 196

10.2. Petition against Mission of the Ulster Volunteers, Papers of R. M. Henry,
McClay Library, Queen's University, Belfast. Image reproduced courtesy
of Special Collections, McClay Library, Queen's University, Belfast. 202

10.3. Page from Henry's 'Suggested Gaelic Reading List', Papers of
R. M. Henry, McClay Library, Queen's University, Belfast. Image
reproduced courtesy of Special Collections, McClay Library, Queen's
University, Belfast. 204

10.4. Portrait of Kuno Meyer, 1903. Image courtesy of the National Library of
Ireland (ref. NPA POLF211). 207

13.1. Programme cover for the 1920 production of *Trojan Women* by the
Dublin Drama League. Artist not credited. Held by the Bodleian Library,
Papers of Gilbert Murray 507, fol. 92r. Permission to reproduce comes
courtesy of the Keeper of Special Collections, Bodleian Libraries,
supported by an Orphan Works Licence. 256

18.1. Irish National War Memorial, 1929–38, view of Great War Stone and
cross. Photograph and copyright Judith Hill, 2018.   361

18.2. Irish National War Memorial, 1929–38, view of sunken garden to the
west, looking past the pavilions to the enclosed lawn with the Wellington
Testimonial in the background. Photograph and copyright Judith Hill, 2018.   362

18.3. The temporary cenotaph, Leinster Lawn, 1922–3. Fergus O'Connor
Collection, OCO 227. Image and permission to reproduce provided
courtesy of the National Library of Ireland.   366

18.4. Drawing of the proposed permanent cenotaph for Leinster Lawn, Harold
Leask, 1939. National Archives of Ireland, S 5734B. Image and permission
to reproduce provided courtesy of the National Archives of Ireland.   369

18.5. Permanent cenotaph, Leinster Lawn, 1948–50. Photograph and copyright
Judith Hill, 2018.   371

19.1. The Northern Ireland Parliament Building (Stormont) designed by Sir
Arnold Thornely and opened in 1932. Photograph and copyright Suzanne
O'Neill, 2019.   375

19.2. Statue group in the tympanum of Stormont's pediment depicting Ulster
presenting a flame of loyalty to Britain and the Commonwealth.
Photograph and copyright Suzanne O'Neill, 2019.   379

19.3. The Dublin General Post Office (GPO) designed by Francis Johnston and
opened in 1818. Photograph and copyright Suzanne O'Neill, 2019.   384

19.4. The tomb of Sir James Craig at Stormont. The sarcophagus is decorated
with the Craigavon coat of arms supported by a constable of the Ulster
Special Constabulary and a soldier of the Royal Ulster Rifles. Photograph
and copyright Suzanne O'Neill, 2019.   387

20.1. Carolyn Mulholland's bronze sculpture for 'Keen for the Coins', new
version cast in 2018, 33 × 20 cm. Image and permission to reproduce
provided courtesy of the artist.   394

20.2. The eight animals of the new Irish coinage (1928, designed by Percy
Metcalfe): horse (half-crown); salmon (florin); bull (shilling); hound
(sixpence); hare (threepence); hen and chicks (penny); pig and piglets
(halfpenny); woodcock (farthing). Image personally held by Christine Morris.   395

20.3. Greek coins from southern Italy. Left: coin depicting a bull from Thurii,
c.400–350 BCE. Right: coin depicting a hare from Sicilian Messana, fifth
century BCE. Images personally held by Christine Morris.   398

20.4. Plaster models of Percy Metcalfe's original designs. Left to right:
halfpenny pig and ram (two alternate designs); bull; horse.
Images and permission to reproduce provided courtesy of the
National Museum of Ireland.   400

20.5. Bull designs submitted by other invited artists. Left to right: Paul
Manship; Carl Milles; Publio Morbiducci. Images and permission to
reproduce provided courtesy of the National Museum of Ireland.   401

20.6. Percy Metcalfe with his lion sculpture for the Palace of Industry at the
British Empire Exhibition of 1924. Image and permission to reproduce
provided courtesy of the Brent Museum and Archives.   403

List of Contributors

Maureen Alden is Senior Honorary Research Fellow in Ancient Greek at Queen's University, Belfast. She is author of *Homer Beside Himself: Para-Narratives in the* Iliad (Oxford, 2000) and *Para-Narratives in the* Odyssey: *Stories in the Frame* (Oxford, 2017). She has also published widely on Greek literature and on the poetry of Michael Longley.

Arabella Currie is a Leverhulme Early Career Research Fellow at the University of Exeter's English Department. She holds a doctorate in Classics from the University of Oxford and an MPhil in Theatre and Performance from Trinity College Dublin. In 2016, she co-curated an exhibition at the Bodleian Library, Oxford, to mark the centenary of the 1916 Easter Rising.

Edith Hall is Professor of Classics at King's College London. She has published more than twenty books on ancient Greece, Rome, and their reception. In 2015 she was awarded both the Erasmus Medal of the European Academy in recognition of her impact on international research, and a Goodwin Award from the American Society for Classical Studies for her book *Adventures with Iphigenia in Tauris* (Oxford, 2013). One of her most recent books, *A People's History of Classics: Class and Greco-Roman Antiquity in Britain and Ireland 1689 to 1939* (London, 2020), is co-authored with Henry Stead.

Judith Hill is a Visiting Research Fellow at Trinity College Dublin (2020–23). An architectural historian and author, she holds a PhD in Architectural History from Trinity College Dublin and has published extensively on Irish art and architecture. Her books include *The Building of Limerick* (Cork and Dublin, 1991), *Irish Public Sculpture: A History* (Dublin, 1998), *Lady Gregory: An Irish Life* (Stroud, 2005), *In Search of Islands: A Life of Conor O'Brien* (Cork, 2009), and *An Introduction to the Architectural Heritage of County Limerick* (Dublin, 2011). She is currently writing a book on Gothic revival architecture, investigating its use as a vehicle to assert political and social status in post-Union Ireland.

Declan Kiberd is Donald and Marilyn Keough Professor of Irish Studies and Professor of English and Irish language and literature at the University of Notre Dame. Among his many publications are *Men and Feminism in Modern Literature* (New York, 1985), *Synge and the Irish Language* (London, 1993), *Inventing Ireland: The Literature of a Modern Nation* (Cambridge MA, 1995), *Irish Classics* (London, 2000), *The Irish Writer and the World* (Cambridge, 2005), *Ulysses and Us: The Art of Everyday Life in Joyce's Masterpiece* (New York, 2009), *Handbook of the Irish Revival: An Anthology of Irish Cultural and Political Writings 1891–1922* (Dublin, 2015, with P. J. Mathews), and *After Ireland: Writing from Beckett to the Present* (Cambridge MA, 2017). Awards include the Oscar Wilde Award for Literary Achievement and the *Irish Times* Literature Prize for Non-Fiction (both for *Inventing Ireland*) and the Truman Capote Prize for Best Work of Literary Criticism in the English-Speaking World (for *Irish Classics*).

Fiachra Mac Góráin studied Classics at Trinity College Dublin and at the University of Oxford, and is now Associate Professor of Classics at University College London. He is editor of *Dionysus and Rome: Religion and Literature* (Berlin and New York, 2020) and co-editor (with Charles Martindale) of *The Cambridge Companion to Virgil. Second Edition* (Cambridge, 2019). He has published articles on Virgil, including on the reception of Virgil in Ireland, and is preparing a monograph entitled *Virgil's Dionysus*. He is a native Irish speaker.

Richard P. Martin is Antony and Isabelle Raubitschek Professor of Classics at Stanford University and was trained in classical and Celtic philology at Harvard. His many publications include *The Language of Heroes: Speech and Performance in the* Iliad (Ithaca NY, 1989), *Bulfinch's Mythology* (New York, 1991), *Myths of the Ancient Greeks* (New York, 2003), *Classical Mythology: The Basics* (London, 2016), *Mythologizing Performance* (Ithaca NY, forthcoming), and numerous articles and book chapters on topics ranging from the performance of ancient poetry to the reception of Homer in Ireland. Martin has also collaborated with Paul Muldoon on a translation of Aristophanes' *Birds* (Philadelphia, 1999).

Siobhán McElduff is Associate Professor of Latin Language and Literature at the University of British Columbia. Her books include *Cicero: In Defense of the Republic* (London, 2011), *Complicating the History of Western Translation: The Ancient Mediterranean in Perspective* (Manchester, 2011), and *Roman Theories of Translation: Surpassing the Source* (London, 2013). She is currently preparing a monograph on Classics among the working classes in eighteenth- and nineteenth-century Ireland, England, and Scotland.

Brian McGing is Emeritus Regius Professor of Greek at Trinity College Dublin. His books include *The Foreign Policy of Mithradates Eupator IV, King of Pontus* (Leiden, 1986), *Greek Papyri from Dublin* (Bonn, 1995), *The Limits of Ancient Biography* (Swansea, 2006), *Polybius'* Histories (Oxford, 2010) and the new Loeb edition and translation of *Appian: Roman History* (Cambridge MA, 2019–20; six volumes).

Eoghan Moloney is Senior Lecturer in Classical Studies at the University of Winchester. Publications include *Peace and Reconciliation in the Classical World*, co-edited with M. S. Williams (London, 2017) and articles on the kingdom of Macedon in the classical period. He is currently completing a monograph on the cultured court of the Argead kings.

Pádraic Moran is Lecturer in Classics and Head of Discipline at the National University of Ireland, Galway. He specializes in the history of education and scholarship in antiquity and the early Middle Ages, and in the transmission and reception of classical texts in Ireland and across Europe. Publications include *De Origine Scoticae Linguae (O'Mulconry's Glossary): An early Irish linguistic tract, edited with a related glossary, Irsan* (Turnhout, 2019), *Early Medieval Ireland and Europe: Chronology, Contacts, Scholarship: A Festschrift for Dáibhí Ó Cróinín*, co-edited with I. Warntjes (Turnhout, 2015), and numerous articles on the study of classical languages in Ireland.

Chris Morash is the inaugural Seamus Heaney Professor of Irish Writing and was formerly Vice Provost at Trinity College Dublin. He has published widely on Irish literature, especially theatre, and on Irish media. In addition to numerous edited volumes, books include *Writing the Irish Famine* (Oxford, 1995), *A History of Irish Theatre, 1601–2000* (Cambridge, 2002), the first Irish book to win the Theatre Book Prize, *A History of the Media in Ireland* (Cambridge, 2009), and *Mapping Irish Theatre: Theories of Space and Place* (Cambridge, 2013) co-authored with Shaun Richards. He is currently writing a book on Yeats and theatre.

Christine Morris is the Andrew A. David Senior Lecturer in Greek Archaeology and History at Trinity College Dublin. Her books include *Ancient Goddesses: The Myths and the Evidence* (Madison, 1998), *The Lure of Greece: Irish Involvement in Greek Literature, History, Culture and Politics* (Dublin, 2007), and *Archaeology of Spiritualities* (New York, 2012).

Síle Ní Mhurchú is Lecturer in Modern Irish at University College Cork. She publishes on the Ossianic lays, the Finn Cycle (*an fhiannaíocht*), Irish love poetry (na dánta grá), and on Irish manuscripts. She is currently preparing an edition of *Agallamh Oisín agus Phádraig*.

Cillian O'Hogan is Assistant Professor of Medieval Latin at the University of Toronto. Publications include *Prudentius and the Landscapes of Late Antiquity* (Oxford, 2016), *Codex Sinaiticus: New Perspectives on the Ancient Biblical Manuscript*, co-edited with S. McKendrick, D. Parker, and A. Myshrall (London, 2015), and articles on topics ranging from Latin literature in late antiquity to classical reception in medieval and modern Ireland.

Suzanne O'Neill completed her PhD in the Department of Classics at Trinity College Dublin, where she is now a lecturer. She teaches on several programmes in the School of Histories and Humanities and on the Trinity College Access Programme. She has published on classical architecture in Northern Ireland and her research interests include both the reception of ancient Greek material culture and Ireland's engagement with Classics in its education system. She is currently writing a book on the reception of the Temple of Apollo at Bassai.

Donncha O'Rourke is Senior Lecturer in Classics at the University of Edinburgh. He is author of *Propertius and the Virgilian Sensibility* (Cambridge, forthcoming) and of various articles principally on Roman elegiac and didactic poetry. His other edited collections are *Approaches to Lucretius: Traditions and Innovations in Reading the* De Rerum Natura (Cambridge, 2020) and, with L. G. Canevaro, *Didactic Poetry of Greece, Rome and Beyond: Knowledge, Power, Tradition* (Swansea, 2019).

Isabelle Torrance is Professor of Classical Reception at Aarhus University and Principal Investigator on the project 'Classical Influences and Irish Culture' (CLIC) funded by the European Research Council (2019–24). Her publications include *Aeschylus: Seven against Thebes* (London, 2007), *Metapoetry in Euripides* (Oxford, 2013), *Oaths and Swearing in Ancient Greece* (Berlin, 2014; co-authored with Alan Sommerstein and other contributors), *Euripides* (London, 2019), *Euripides: Iphigenia among the Taurians* (London, 2019), an edited volume *Aeschylus and War: Comparative Perspectives on Seven Against Thebes* (London, 2017), and numerous articles on Greek tragedy and its reception.

Eibhear Walshe is Senior Lecturer in English at University College Cork and Director of Creative Writing. He has published extensively in the areas of modern Irish fiction and drama with a focus on literary criticism, biography and cultural history, including pioneering work in the field of gay and lesbian studies. He has published three monographs, a memoir, two novels, and nine edited volumes, as well as numerous articles and book chapters on Irish writers. Recent books include *Oscar's Shadow* (Cork, 2011), *A Different Story: The Fictions of Colm Tóibín* (Dublin, 2013), *The Diary of Mary Travers* (Cork, 2014), and *The Trumpet Shall Sound* (Cork, 2019).

1

Classics and Irish Politics

Introduction

Isabelle Torrance and Donncha O'Rourke

There has been much work done in recent years on the tensions associated with the exploitation of classical models in postcolonial societies, where the classical, normatively associated with imperial powers, is reappropriated and repurposed for an indigenous nationalist agenda.[1] Ireland very rarely features in such discussions;[2] and what has not been clearly articulated in scholarship to date is that Ireland is a unique case as the only postcolonial culture with native pre-colonial expertise in classical languages and literature dating back to the sixth century.[3] Classical sources, then, are indigenous to Ireland in a way that does not apply to other colonized nations. Moreover, as a divided island, part of which still belongs to the United Kingdom, Ireland retains a particularly complex relationship with Britain—one that in recent years achieved unprecedented cordiality in the reciprocal visits of their heads of state, but which latterly has experienced renewed strain following the United Kingdom's 2016 referendum vote to terminate its membership of the European Union (a 56-per-cent majority in the United Kingdom's province of Northern Ireland voted to remain in the EU). At the time of writing, the issue of the Irish border continued to impede the UK government's implementation of Brexit. Against a backdrop of political stalemate and the stalling of Northern Ireland's devolved political institutions, fears of a renewed escalation of political violence intensified, with republican paramilitaries threatening any border infrastructure as a 'legitimate target'.[4]

---

[1] E.g. Goff (2005), Hardwick and Gillespie (2007), Bradley (2010), Hall and Vasunia (2010), Stephens and Vasunia (2010), Vasunia (2013), Parker (2017).

[2] Wilmer (2007) and Allen (2010) are rare exceptions. The former suggests a continuity of colonial preoccupations in his analysis of Seamus Heaney's 2004 *The Burial at Thebes*, a version of Sophocles' *Antigone*. The latter underlines the vernacular classicism of twentieth-century Irish authors, including Heaney, in relation to legacies of colonization. Hardwick (2002), (2003: 102–7), (2005: 110–11) also references Heaney within broader postcolonial contexts.

[3] Stanford (1976) charts the classical tradition in Ireland dating back to Columbanus.

[4] In an interview with Channel 4 News on 16 October 2019 a masked spokesman for the New IRA stated that any border infrastructure and personnel would be considered legitimate targets for attack by the organization. The interview followed a number of paramilitary attacks by the New IRA, including an attack which resulted in the death of 29-year-old Lyra McKee. A journalist and gay rights activist from Belfast who wrote on the lasting impact of political violence in Northern Ireland, McKee was

Isabelle Torrance and Donncha O'Rourke, *Classics and Irish Politics: Introduction* In: *Classics and Irish Politics, 1916–2016*. Edited by: Isabelle Torrance and Donncha O'Rourke, Oxford University Press (2020).
© Oxford University Press.
DOI: 10.1093/oso/9780198864486.003.0001

As it happens, the year of the Brexit vote in the United Kingdom coincided with the centenary anniversary of the 1916 Easter Rising in Ireland. The rebellion of Irish nationalists against British imperial forces in 1916 became almost instantly mythologized in Irish political memory as a turning point in the nation's development towards the independent Irish Republic that it is today.[5] The 1916 Rising has been the most heavily commemorated of the many centenaries marked by the Irish government's official 'Decade of Centenaries' programme. Launched in 2012 by the Department of Culture, Heritage and the Gaeltacht, the programme aims to commemorate landmark historical events from the centenary of the introduction of the Third Home Rule Bill in 1912, which proposed self-governance for Ireland, to one hundred years of Irish independence since 1922.[6] It is within this interrogation of Irish political history that the present collection seeks to position itself in revealing how models from Greek and Roman antiquity have permeated and mediated Irish political discourse over the last century.

Many scholars have illuminated how classical sources have functioned as points of *literary* inspiration for the titans of twentieth-century Irish literature across the genres of poetry, drama, and the novel.[7] With the exception of litera-ture alluding to the Northern Irish Troubles, however, little attention has been paid to the political implications specific to Irish engagement with classical models.[8] This collection aims to reframe our understanding of classical influences in the last one hundred years of Irish culture along sociopolitical lines and from fresh perspectives. Important studies of earlier periods have shown how Irish exiles in the sixteenth and seventeenth centuries, during periods of colonial conquest justified by a particular reading of the Classics, sought to make Ireland 'Roman'

---

shot dead on 19 April 2019 while reporting on a riot in the Cleggan area of Derry (violence had escal-ated following police raids on the homes of dissident republicans ahead of parades commemorating the 1916 Rising). The New IRA acknowledged responsibility for her death.

[5] The equivalent iconic historical event for Ulster unionists is the 1916 battle of the Somme, with commemorations celebrating the heroism of the Ulstermen who fought and sacrificed their lives for Britain during World War I. Illuminating analyses of the memorialization of both the 1916 Rising and the battle of the Somme, across the political divides in Ireland, have been published in Grayson and McGarry (2016).

[6] A timeline of events commemorated, along with detailed information, can be found on the programme's official website: https://www.decadeofcentenaries.com/ (accessed 5 December 2019).

[7] The bibliography is vast. References here are confined to book-length studies. On classical influ-ences in Irish poetry see, e.g., Arkins (1990), Liebregts (1993), Impens (2018), Harrison, Macintosh, and Eastman (2019). On Greek tragedy and Irish drama see, e.g., Macintosh (1994), Younger (2001), M. McDonald and Walton (2002), Arkins (2010a), Wallace (2015). On James Joyce's debt to classical literature see, e.g., Schork (1997) and (1998), and Arkins (1999). Arkins (2005) examines Greek and Roman themes in a broad survey of modern Irish literature.

[8] Classical influences on Northern Irish literature are given political texture in the discussions of, e.g., Roche (1988: 221–9), M. McDonald (1996), Teevan (1998), Denard (2000), P. McDonald (2000), Paulin (2002), Vendler (2002), Arkins (2009), Heaney (2009), Cieniuch (2010), Pelletier (2012), Hardwick (2016: 292–302). In a different context, Pogorzelski (2016), who proposes a political reading of Joyce's *Ulysses* alongside Virgil's *Aeneid* as a mediating source of inspiration on nationalism and imperialism, is a rare example of a politically oriented analysis of Irish intertextuality with classical sources.

by expressing Irish cultural and Catholic identity through Latin as the medium of contemporary European intellectual exchange.[9] Many less affluent Irish people were versed in the classical languages, too, as Laurie O'Higgins has shown in an extraordinary study of the dissemination of classical learning in eighteenth- and nineteenth-century Ireland.[10] Shifting the focus to the twentieth century and beyond, our volume aims to continue in the vein of reflecting on the deep complexities of Ireland's relationship with classical Greece and Rome. Now a breakaway colony of an empire that identified strongly with a Roman 'SPQR mentality' (Ch. 2), Ireland could read Latin literature and Roman culture as a cipher for imperialism and elitism, and it is perhaps no surprise that Irish authors of the past hundred years have tended to identify more commonly with classical Greece, which fended off would-be colonizers from Persia, than with ancient Rome.

Yet this is only part of the story. As the studies of earlier periods have shown, Ireland's Roman Catholicism was a pathway to an alternative discourse of 'Roman' identity: distinct from historically Protestant colonizers, who had repeatedly legislated punitively against the perceived threat of Irish Catholicism, a Roman (Catholic) identity could also be construed as *anti*-imperial. In the twentieth century, this confluence of Catholicism and anti-colonial sentiment continued and contributed to the legacy of classical learning in Ireland. Members of the Irish clergy were instrumental in disseminating classical texts through Irish in the years after independence, and one such cleric, Patrick Dinneen, marshals the Roman poet Virgil to the Irish nationalist cause in a most arresting fashion, as Fiachra Mac Góráin documents (Ch. 7). At the same time, a fuller account of twentieth-century Irish Hellenism would point out that it is heir to European literary movements such as the Romanticism embraced by W. B. Yeats and the Modernism which characterizes the work of James Joyce, and that the English had their fair share of such Hellenism, too. Classical material has thus given twentieth-century Irish authors a distinctly European voice,[11] but also access to a third space, so to speak, in which to communicate between the antagonistic (yet internally complex) positions of 'Gaelic' or 'English', a space that is indigenous because of its pre-colonial roots, yet also available to other traditions. On a narrow 'nativist' view of Irish culture, of the kind espoused by Daniel Corkery, this proposition would not be accepted, and the present volume acknowledges that significant figures on the Irish political and intellectual stage, such as Patrick Pearse and Thomas MacDonagh, struggled under pressures both internal and external in promoting Gaelic literature above the classical literature which they greatly admired (Ch. 3 and Ch. 4).[12] Yet the volume also demonstrates that, in

---

[9] See the essays collected in Harris and Sidwell (2009).   [10] O'Higgins (2017).

[11] See Impens (2018: 11–43 and *passim*).

[12] For consistency of language and spelling, the English Patrick Pearse is used throughout this volume rather than the Irish Pádraig Mac Piarais or the hybrid Pádraig Pearse.

spite of certain academic and nationalist debates, classical models have been remarkably flexible and inclusive media for the expression of Ireland's social and political complexities over the course of the past century.

Taking this complex backdrop into consideration, our collection considers the intellectual struggle among Irish revolutionaries and nationalists in prioritizing Gaelic over classical material (or vice versa) during the turbulent years leading up to independence (Section I); it scrutinizes how Irish language publications impacted the politicized dissemination of classical texts and ideas (Section II); it examines how politically-rooted scholarship in the fields of Classics and Celtic Studies hovered at the margins of influential literary works (Section III); it excavates the recourse of Irish writers and public figures to classical models in underlining political inequalities regarding gender, sexuality, and class (Section IV); it makes new observations on the well-known tendency of Northern Irish authors to adapt classical literature for reflection on political violence (Section V); it looks to the influence of classical architecture and material culture in Ireland as media through which colonialism can be asserted or rejected (Section VI); finally, a concluding Epilogue offers an analysis on the themes of contiguity, affinity, and chance that bind the essays together. The arrangement of essays along thematic lines aims to highlight some of the principal ways in which the polyvalent legacy of classical material in Ireland can be traced, without making any claim to being definitive or exhaustive. There are no subdivisions, for instance, separating Greek material from Roman material, or tracing explicitly how classical reception in Ireland has been coopted for challenging elites, or focusing on the differences between translation and literary adaptation. Nevertheless, these topics do not go unobserved in the volume and our introduction here aims to highlight significant aspects of individual contributions that speak to each other across the different sections.

The analysis of material culture is an important feature in a collection which otherwise focuses primarily on literature and scholarship. Classically influenced architecture was a central part of the British imperial project, as Phiroze Vasunia has discussed, for instance, in relation to colonial India.[13] Unlike those aspects of Ireland's classical heritage which precede its colonial experience, Irish neoclassical art and architecture are not pre-colonial, and in this respect Ireland resembles other postcolonial nations. The classically influenced equestrian statue of William III, for instance, was unveiled in Dublin's College Green in 1701. Modelled on the statue of Marcus Aurelius from the Capitoline Hill in Rome, this William III—clad in Roman armour and crowned with a laurel wreath—was a conspicuous symbol of Protestant Ireland and imperialism. As Judith Hill has observed, the statue was 'of a different order from anything else in its vicinity', and 'conveyed a more

---

[13] Vasunia (2013: 157–92).

aggressive image than the Roman original' in a manner aimed, she suggests, at 'making the figure appear more classical' through a deeper sense of gravitas.[14] For over two centuries the statue was a site both for celebration by an increasingly sectarian Protestantism and for nationalist dissent expressed through its vandalism. It was finally toppled and decapitated (with the head stolen) in 1929. Similarly, the dramatic equestrian statue of George II in Roman dress, erected in Dublin's St Stephen's Green in 1758, became a target for nationalists. It was bombed twice, first in 1928 causing minor damage, and then more conclusively in 1937, leading to its removal.[15] The best-known example of a classically inspired imperial landmark to be destroyed by Irish nationalists was Nelson's column, constructed in imitation of Roman models and unveiled in central Dublin in 1809 to celebrate Nelson's victory at Trafalgar four years earlier. From its inception the monument generated opposition from nationalists and finally met its end when it was bombed by the IRA in 1966 on the fiftieth anniversary of the 1916 Rising (illustrated in the photograph on the jacket of this book). Many more neoclassical structures and buildings became sites for the expression of political rebellion during the twentieth century throughout Ireland, although the largest concentration of such activity was in Dublin where imperial building projects had been intimately connected with the creation of an impressive colonial outpost.[16]

Architecture associated with political supremacism can, however, be reframed within new narratives. Such is the case, for instance, with South Africa's Freedom Park in Pretoria: 'a new memorial… [e]ncompassing all battles for human rights in South Africa, its message trumps British imperialism at the Union Buildings and Afrikaner power at the [Vootrekker] Monument.'[17] Colonial buildings, divested of their imperial insignia, have been reanimated with national significance in Ireland. Both The Customs House and The Four Courts, which were significantly damaged in the early 1920s, were rebuilt and remain significant landmarks in Dublin. The most exceptional example of a politically revivified neoclassical building, however, is Dublin's General Post Office (GPO). Originally an imperial building, it is now a symbol, if not *the* symbol, of Irish independence as headquarters of the 1916 nationalist fighters and the site of their accompanying proclamation of independence. As Suzanne O'Neill demonstrates, however, the legacy of Dublin's GPO stands in stark contrast to the Northern Irish parliament buildings at Stormont (Ch. 19). Erected after independence was granted to

---

[14] Hill (1998: 42–3).

[15] The equestrian statue of George I, also modelled on the Roman Marcus Aurelius and erected in Dublin in 1722 on Essex (now Grattan) Bridge, the most easterly of the River Liffey's bridges, was less conspicuous. Removed in 1753 when the bridge was condemned, the statue was later erected in the precincts of the Mansion House, and was eventually sold, in 1937, to the Barber Institute of Fine Arts at the University of Birmingham. See Hill (1998: 44–6 and 48–51) on the statue of George II.

[16] See Hill (1998: 41–83).   [17] Rankin and Schneider (2017: 209).

twenty-six of Ireland's thirty-two counties, Stormont was constructed as a neoclassical bastion of unionism for the six counties of Northern Ireland under the leadership of Sir James Craig, one of whose idiosyncratic stipulations was that the entire project be completed in English Portland stone imported at great expense while the local Irish granite quarries at Newry lay idle. The intimidating appropriation of classical architecture at Stormont, constructed in 'imperial' stone sourced from the seat of power, as O'Neill documents, means that the location remains a physically unwelcoming landscape for nationalist politicians.

Within the newly independent Irish Free State, and in the subsequent Republic of Ireland, architectural classicism could be coopted for new purposes, as Judith Hill shows in her discussion of commemorative monuments commissioned and completed after Irish independence (Ch. 18). Despite the tradition of Celtic revivalism and a general nationalist antipathy to classicism as an imperial aesthetic, it remained possible to transcend political divisions through classically inspired monuments such as the National War Memorial, dedicated to those who died in World War I, and the Cenotaph (first temporary and then permanent) erected in memory of Irish nationalists Michael Collins, Arthur Griffith, and, latterly, Kevin O'Higgins. As Hill's chapter reveals, architectural classicism lent itself to timeless commemoration and non-partisan reconciliation in a manner that was aesthetically connected to the existing urban landscape of Dublin. In fact, sculptural classicism did have a nationalist legacy also in Ireland. The nationalist hero Daniel O'Connell, who campaigned tirelessly for Catholic emancipation in the first half of the nineteenth century, had been represented as a Roman orator in a celebrated marble statue by John Hogan which has resided in Dublin's City Hall since the 1840s; other neoclassical monuments to O'Connell were erected in Limerick and Ennis, while John Henry Foley's O'Connell, unveiled in 1882, remains a central monument in Dublin's contemporary landscape at the head of O'Connell Street in the heart of the city. The figure of O'Connell is set on a large drum carved with representations of his labours, below which again are seated four winged victories.[18] Another example is Oliver Sheppard's critically acclaimed bronze statue *The Death of Cúchulainn*, placed in the GPO in 1935 as a memorial to 1916. Sculpted in the classical tradition of the heroic male nude, the figure marries the aesthetics of classicism with Celtic mythology, thus instantiating a tension evident also in the works of Patrick Pearse (cf. Ch. 3), with whom Sheppard had been associated.

An aesthetic link between the classical and the national was asserted still more emphatically through the design of new coinage for the Irish Free State, as Christine Morris shows (Ch. 20). Signifiers of the newly independent nation, the Irish coins first minted in 1928 were radical in avoiding the representation of

---

[18] On the classically inspired O'Connell statues and monuments, see Hill (1998: 89–97).

figureheads and establishing instead an iconography of Irish fauna. Three of the animals depicted on the Irish coins—the horse, the bull, and the hare—were directly inspired by coins from the ancient Greek world. As Morris underlines in her examination of the 'biography' of this originally controversial though subsequently much-loved 'barnyard set', the cultural alignment of Ireland with classical Greece was a politicized move. Replacing a British coinage that had featured the monarch's head, Latin inscriptions, the crown atop the Irish harp, and other symbols inspired by imperial Rome, the new set freed the harp from the colonial crown on the obverse of all coins, used Irish text and scripts for the legend, and rejected Roman imperial models in favour of an agrarian aestheticism rooted in ancient Greece.

The fact that W. B. Yeats, in his role as Senator, was Chairman of the Coinage Committee established by the 1926 Coinage Act, as Morris points out, is directly related to the committee's decision to appropriate Greek models for the new national coinage. As a poet, it is well known that Yeats frequently aligned nationalist Ireland with classical Greece.[19] After Irish independence, as Chris Morash demonstrates (Ch. 11), the gravitas of Sophocles allowed Yeats to avoid censorship at the hands of the new Committee on Evil Literature created in 1926. In a clear act of censor-baiting, Yeats staged his version of Sophocles' *Oedipus the King*, toning down the most gratuitous aspects of the play's incest so that a ban on the production would seem ridiculous. Accessing the play through the translation of Irish classical scholar Richard Claverhouse Jebb, Yeats also incorporated references that would resonate with his audience, alluding for instance to the Great Famine of 1845–9. The resounding success of the play thoroughly thwarted its potential censors. However, Yeats's collision with conservatism also continued under the Catholic hierarchy of the Irish Free State, traced here by Morash in his analysis of *A Vision*, where the poet's engagement with classical Greek philosophy informed his conception of cyclical transformations in relation to the broader political landscape of Europe between World Wars I and II. Morash notes that Plotinus features significantly among Yeats's highly selective readings from classical literature. It would seem, then, to be no accident that Yeats was an admirer of the nationalist Stephen MacKenna, whose monumental and highly acclaimed English translation of Plotinus' *Enneads* was completed in 1930, with the dedication 'Do chum glóire Dé agus onóra na h-Éireann' ('Composed for the glory of God and the honour of Ireland').[20]

---

[19] In one example among many, observed by Macintosh (1994: 14), Yeats links the 1916 rebels to the Greeks at the battle of Salamis in his poem 'The Statues', implying a symbolic victory of (Irish/Greek) civilization over (British/Persian) imperial barbarism. Arkins (1990) and Liebregts (1993) give detailed surveys of Yeats's engagement with classical material.

[20] Yeats (1966a: 230). Cf. Stanford (1976: 97) and Arkins (1990: 36) for Yeats' familiarity with MacKenna's translation of Plotinus. The phrasing of MacKenna's dedication is identical to the inscription on the Cenotaph for Collins, Griffith, and O'Higgins; cf. Hill n. 107 (Ch. 18).

Beyond the newly independent Ireland, Yeats's *King Oedipus* has had an extraordinary reception history, as Fiona Macintosh has documented elsewhere, and continues to inspire new performances to this day.[21] Similarly, Yeats's personal insistence on Greek models for Irish coinage has had an unexpectedly far-reaching influence on international coin design, which Morris traces from 1930s Greece and Fiji to 1970s Tonga (Ch. 20). As Morris also discusses, Seamus Heaney marked the demise of the Irish 'barnyard set' when Ireland entered the Eurozone in 2002 with his poem 'A Keen for Coins', a text subsequently immortalized in sculptural form by artist Carolyn Mulholland (Ch. 20). Like Yeats, Heaney was an Irish poet of global renown who frequently reworked classical literature and mythology for political expression. The Greeks are a significant presence, particularly in Heaney's reworkings of Greek tragedy: *The Cure at Troy* is a version of Sophocles' *Philoctetes*, 'Mycenae Lookout' was inspired by Aeschylus' *Oresteia*, and *The Burial at Thebes* is a version of Sophocles' *Antigone* (on which see Ch. 17). It is the Roman Virgil, however, who stands out as Heaney's primary classical inspiration.[22] An author studied in Heaney's boyhood Latin classes, Virgil secured a place in the Irish poet's oeuvre with the posthumous publication of his exquisite translation of *Aeneid* 6, in which the Trojan hero Aeneas visits the underworld and encounters the dead.[23]

Heaney was not the only nationalist Irish intellectual to find inspiration in Virgil. As noted above, the distinguished scholar of Irish and classical languages, Fr Patrick Dinneen, published a number of works on Virgil in the Irish language from the 1920s onwards. Fiachra Mac Góráin demonstrates how Dinneen's optic and strategies of appropriation suggest a native Irish ownership of the material, in particular through the translation of Latin names into Irish forms and through a complex interweaving of Irish culture with classical antiquity (Ch. 7). Dinneen saw himself as a latter-day Virgil, similarly dispossessed of his home but engaged in the creation of a national literature, and calling his fellow citizens back to the land, as he saw Virgil doing in the *Georgics*, after periods of strife. Here we might usefully compare the observations of Peter Fallon, whose own English translation of the *Georgics* was first published in 2004. For Fallon, who comes from an agrarian background, the hard work and peace to be found in farming during a period of civil war, as advocated in Virgil's *Georgics*, echoes strongly with the Irish experience.[24] Seamus Heaney, meanwhile, had looked to Virgil's *Eclogues* to

---

[21] Macintosh (2008). We may add Wayne Jordan's script for *Oedipus*, produced at the Abbey Theatre in 2015, which was heavily influenced by Yeats.

[22] Impens (2017) traces Heaney's engagement with Virgil throughout his career.

[23] Specifically, Heaney had studied *Aeneid* 9 at school, but his interest in *Aeneid* 6 had been piqued at this early age by his Latin teacher Fr Michael McGlinchey (cf. Heaney (2016: vii)). The young Heaney's annotations on J. W. Mackail's translation of the *Aeneid* (Books 7–12) are discussed by Hall (2019). For an appreciation of the translation see Harrison (2019: 252–61); see further n. 28 below.

[24] Fallon (2006: xxxiv); see also the insightful analysis by O'Hogan (2018: 406–11). Differently, the translation of the *Georgics* by Anglo-Irish poet Cecil Day-Lewis, first published in 1940, speaks to

reflect on displacement and the brutality of land confiscations, as well as the potential of the land to generate renewal in poems such as 'Bann Valley Eclogue', 'Virgil: Eclogue IX', and 'Glanmore Eclogue' in his 2001 collection *Electric Light*.[25]

Nevertheless, there remains a tension, to some extent acknowledged by Dinneen, between Irish nationalism and a favourable view of the Roman Empire. Dinneen attempts to reconcile this tension through a positive representation of the spread of Christianity and civilization under the Roman Empire, reading Anchises' exhortation 'to spare the vanquished and conquer the proud' (*parcere subiectis et debellare superbos*) in a famous passage at the end of *Aeneid* 6 (851–3) as a benign form of imperialism (Ch. 7). Heaney takes a different approach in dealing with the imperialist context of Virgil's poetic production. In a surviving fragment of the opening paragraph for an afterword to his *Aeneid VI*, Heaney had called it 'the best of books and the worst of books. Best because of its mythopoeic visions, the twilit fetch of its language, the pathos of the many encounters it allows the living Aeneas with his familiar dead. Worst because of its imperial certitude, its celebration of Rome's manifest destiny and the catalogue of Roman heroes....'[26] Heaney refers here to the culminating section of *Aeneid* 6, where the shade of Anchises reveals to his son Aeneas a procession of future descendants destined to found and rule over Rome. In his opening translator's note Heaney references the 'grim determination' required to translate this portion of *Aeneid* 6, putting on record his view that 'the roll call of generals and imperial heroes, the allusions to variously famous or obscure historical victories and defeats, make this part of the poem something of a test for reader and translator alike'.[27] Colin Burrow finds this section of Heaney's book 'marred by plain weariness', an indication that this 'prophecy of Roman heroes...was always at odds with Heaney's deliberately off-centre and counter-imperial view of the *Aeneid*'.[28] Heaney had evoked motifs from *Aeneid* 6 in his earlier poems: the spirits of the dead, victims of the Troubles, appear in 'Station Island' from his eponymous 1984 collection; the death of Heaney's own father in 1986 finds echoes in the exchange between Aeneas and his father's ghost evoked through the 1991 collection *Seeing Things*; the twelve-part

post-war sentiment in Britain, to which the Laois-born poet had since transferred his allegiance: see Thomas (2001).

[25] On 'Bann Valley Eclogue' see M. Tyler (2005: 50–60), Harrison (2008), Twiddy (2012); on 'Virgil: Eclogue IX' see O'Hogan (2018: 402–6); on 'Glanmore Eclogue' see M. Tyler (2005: 68–73); on the relationship between Heaney's eclogues and those of Virgil more generally see Putnam (2010) and Impens (2018: 70–4), and see O'Donoghue (2019) for Heaney's debt to Yeats in his eclogues. Virgil's own focus in the *Eclogues* on political turmoil, land redistribution, and the tensions between the disenfranchised and those in power can undermine colonial overtones in the poems' Irish reception, as Mac Góráin (2013) has demonstrated in his analysis of a 1701 Dublin eclogue. Written by a Dublin woman to welcome the new Lord Lieutenant of Ireland, the eclogue's attempt at unequivocal praise does not obscure profound political ironies.

[26] Heaney (2016: 95).   [27] Heaney (2016: viii).   [28] Burrow (2016: 14).

poem 'Route 110', from the 2010 collection *Human Chain*, was Heaney's most extensive engagement with *Aeneid* 6 prior to his translation.[29] The manner, as Burrow puts it, 'might be called a postcolonial parallax, in which a master text of a dominant civilization is deliberately transformed from the ostentatiously low perspective of an unheroic life'.[30]

Earlier allusions to *Aeneid* 6 in Heaney's poetry notably avoid engagement with its concluding 'imperial' section. Eavan Boland is another Irish poet whose reworking of *Aeneid* 6 is highly selective and who, like Heaney, came to Virgil through Latin classes in a Catholic school.[31] In undertaking a translation of the entire book, however, Heaney was forced to confront the 'imperial certitude' of the Roman heroes which he had evaded up to that point. While Burrow finds this to be the least successful passage in Heaney's translation, we might yet connect this paradoxical funeral procession of ancestors (from the perspective of the reader) who are yet to be born (as focalized through Aeneas) to the broader Irish patterns of encountering the past, of thinking about death, and—especially in Northern Ireland—of reading politicized funeral rituals through the lens of classical mythology. Torrance argues that Heaney's *The Burial at Thebes* is one in a series of an intense post-ceasefire interrogations of the Antigone myth in the context of the treatment of corpses in Northern Ireland, alongside adaptations by Stacey Gregg, Owen McCafferty, and Gerard Humphreys, in a tradition that dates back to the political and ideological collision between historian and journalist Conor Cruise O'Brien and playwright Tom Paulin at the height of the Troubles (Ch. 17). Building on the work of Fiona Macintosh, who has pointed out in a general sense how Sophocles' *Antigone* resonates with Irish authors because funeral rituals tend not to be hidden from public view in Ireland,[32] Torrance draws a distinction between Northern Ireland and the Republic: the legacy of the Troubles, the continuation of horrific instances of conflict-related violence (even after the signing of the Good Friday Agreement in 1998), a highly charged culture of politicized public and processional display, and the contested treatment of corpses in Northern Ireland (the disappeared, paramilitary funerals, bodies left out in the street) all help to explain why there have been so many Northern Irish Antigones during an ostensible period of peace.

In her analysis of Michael Longley's 'Ceasefire', which has a significant reception history in other conflict zones, Maureen Alden also stresses the continued presence of brutal violence and its toll on Northern Ireland (Ch. 16). Alden resituates

---

[29] Burrow (2016: 13) sketches out how *Aeneid* 6 manifested itself in Heaney's work throughout his career. For more detailed discussion of Virgil-reception in these poems see Putnam (2012), Impens (2018: 56–60, 70–8), Falconer (2019), McDonald (2019), Riley (2019).

[30] Burrow (2016: 13).

[31] Impens (2018: 38–9) notes how Boland's evocation of *Aeneid* 6 contrasts the vivacity of Virgil with the dull context of religious schooling.

[32] Macintosh (2011).

this famous poem both within the language of Homeric decorum (by which it was inspired) and in relation to real-life casualties of the Troubles. Like the old Trojan king Priam in *Iliad* 24, some parents bereaved in the Troubles wanted to meet with their children's murderers. Some of them showed forgiveness, but this ethic is in fact alien to the Iliadic model of Longley's poem. In Homer, Priam's act of courage in confronting Achilles, the murderer of his son, and his request for the return of his son's body, is the moral denouement of the *Iliad*, all the more so for the reader who knows that the war will shortly resume and claim the lives of Priam and Achilles themselves. A ceasefire, indeed, is not the end of the conflict, and when Longley's 'Ceasefire' is read alongside its companion poem 'All of these people' it becomes clear that the poet perceives the true opposite of warfare not to be peace (which is merely the absence of war), but civilization (the very impossibility of war).

Longley's ecumenical response to the Troubles is expressed through his encounters with many other classical sources, not least Roman love elegy. Donncha O'Rourke shows that this genre draws its pertinence to Ireland from its own genesis in the context of civil war, and from its eroticized optic on violence, human relations, and reconciliation (Ch. 15). As O'Rourke argues, Longley's recasting of Roman elegy against the backdrop of civil warfare in Northern Ireland has its roots in W. B. Yeats's appropriation of Propertius in the context of 1916, an Irish elegiac continuum that brings to light both the constant presence and changing shape of classical reception in the century since the Easter Rising. For both poets, this tradition is mediated by their modernist confrère Ezra Pound, who had read Propertius as an anti-imperialist in the context of World War I. Pound was a close associate of Yeats, and it was during their tour of Sicily in 1925 that the latter found inspiration for the new Irish coinage in the numismatics of the independent states of Magna Graecia (cf. Ch. 20). If Yeats's response to Propertius takes a similarly partisan and anti-imperial approach, albeit one also bound up in his personal affairs, Longley rather differently exploits the lyrical form of elegy in his anti-war appropriation of epic, drawing on Tibullus and Sulpicia, as well as on his 'soul mate' Propertius, in an erotic, gendered, and rustic exposé of cycles of violence in public and domestic space. In this way, Longley's poetry seems to offer a common ground between opposing traditions and to hope in a more pacific model of the elegiac woman than is found in Yeats's revolutionary muse.

In his famous poem 'No Second Troy', first published in 1916, Yeats had implicitly cast his muse Maud Gonne (MacBride) as the Greek Helen. By 1920, Maud Gonne had recast herself as the long-suffering Trojan queen Hecuba by starring in that role for a performance of Euripides' *Trojan Women* produced by the Dublin Drama League. As Torrance discusses, the production had an obvious political topicality in dealing with colonial aggression (Ch. 13). Yet the reception of this performance, and subsequent Irish adaptations of the *Trojan Women* tragedy, have highlighted instead women's lack of political agency. The topicality of the 1920 production is lost on its reviewer, who is enamoured with Helen's seductive character and expresses disappointment that the other female performers did not pour forth more passion 'in red-hot sentences'. This kind of conservatism, which objectifies women and denies them political agency, resurfaces in Brendan Kennelly's 1993 *Trojan Women*, where Hecuba and the other Greek women circle Helen in a shocking slut-shaming scene. Kennelly exposes the collusion of Irish women in sexist oppression for which men escape responsibility. In 2015, Marina Carr can present a sexually liberated Hecuba as the title character of her adaptation of the Trojan women's story (*Hecuba*). Torrance argues, however, that using sexuality to survive captivity is a largely illusory form of agency, particularly in a play where Carr has deprived Hecuba of her traditionally murderous revenge. Hecuba is humanized because of this, but all three of the Irish plays discussed connect female sexuality with disenfranchisement in various ways, a pointed message in light of the 2016 'Waking the Feminists' movement which underlined female disempowerment in the Irish theatre industry.

Recourse to classical sources for championing issues of sexual and gendered rights in Ireland has more commonly been associated with the gay community, dating back to Oscar Wilde's attempt, in his speech from the dock during his 1895 trial for gross indecency, to aestheticize and justify his homosexuality through the classical Greek ideal of male friendship. Eibhear Walshe traces the pervasive influence of Wilde on Irish authors, showing how he was perceived as a patriotic dissident against England by Joyce, for example, and as a champion and liberator for gay writers (Ch. 12). Despite the conservatism of the Republic of Ireland, where homosexuality was not decriminalized until 1993, Wilde continued to make his cultural presence felt in twentieth-century Irish culture. The writings of Brendan Behan, for instance, whose biography bears strong parallels to Wilde's, are permeated by Wilde's Hellenism. With liberalization and decriminalization, Wilde could be fully embraced as gay and Irish, a symbol of Irish modernity and postcolonialism. Jamie O'Neill's 2001 novel on homoerotic love in 1916, *At Swim Two Boys*, presents Wilde as an icon and symbol of patriotic rebellion, and Classics as a gay-friendly subject that Catholic hierarchies sought to 'sanitize'. Controversy continues nevertheless in the association of Hellenism with paedophilia, as witnessed in the contentious debates surrounding Irish-language poet Cathal Ó Searcaigh and senator David Norris. One elusive figure in this story is Patrick Pearse, leader of the 1916 Rising, whose sexuality has been the subject of significant speculation. Pearse never mentions Wilde but must have been influenced by him, Walshe argues, in the presentation of male martyrdom in his plays and in the parallels he draws between ancient Greek and Irish masculinity.

The audible silence of Pearse on Wilde's Hellenism is similar to the unacknowledged influence of classical oratory on Pearse's public speeches traced by Brian McGing (Ch. 3). In particular, Pearse's funeral speech for O'Donovan Rossa in

1915 bears comparison to Pericles' funeral oration in Thucydides through the intermediary of Lincoln's Gettysburg address, with which Pearse was familiar. As McGing shows, there is a tension between Pearse's commitment to the Gaelic and Catholic movement, which had eclipsed the classicism of earlier political rhetoric and popular culture in Ireland, and his obvious interest in classical culture throughout his essays. Thomas MacDonagh, another of the 1916 leaders, is comparable in ostensibly placing a higher value on Irish traditions over classical ones while, at the same time, being deeply influenced by classical literature. As Eoghan Moloney demonstrates in some detail, and with the support of archival material, MacDonagh's literary output is classically inflected in spite of his ties to the nativist movement (Ch. 4). The dominant nationalist narrative, which has romanticized the rebel leaders, has also tended to bury the significance of classical models. These were not, in fact, entirely overshadowed by native Irish literature for figures like MacDonagh, who was open to a wide range of cultural influences. That being said, MacDonagh did find classical culture distant, and his poem 'Barbara' constructs his daughter as unacquainted with Greece and Rome. MacDonagh himself, however, was not able to follow through on this paradigm, producing a surprising number of versions, both published and unpublished, of poems by Catullus informed by his own personal experience. Catullus seems to have enabled MacDonagh to find the consonance between past and present that was central to his theory of literary reception.

Thomas MacDonagh, like Patrick Dinneen, had been an important figure in the Irish Literary Revival, though they promoted different approaches. While MacDonagh advocated a distinctive form of Irish literature in the English language, Dinneen proposed the development of a national literature through Irish. Dinneen himself contributed to the translation of Greek and Latin texts and textbooks into Irish under the auspices of An Gúm's broader translation scheme in the early years of the Irish state. Síle Ní Mhurchú compiles details of individuals involved and of the works they translated, including Mairghréad Ní Éimhthigh (Margaret Heavey), Cormac Ó Cadhlaigh, Maoghnas Ó Domhnaill, Domhnall Ó Mathghamhna, Pádraic Ua Duinnín (i.e. Patrick Dinneen), and Peadar Ua Laoghaire, but focuses on two especially prolific contributors to the scheme: Pádraig de Brún and George Thomson (Ch. 5). The language politics of nativists versus progressives played into the place of translation in the scheme. Pádraig de Brún, like the nativists, saw Irish as untouched by the Renaissance, but he also saw this as a deficiency to be remedied rather than a virtue *tout court*. For this reason, de Brún championed Irish translations of classical literature, and in the 1920s and 1930s he himself produced beautiful renditions of Greek tragedies and of Plutarch's *Lives* in the Corca Dhuibhne dialect of the Dingle peninsula in Co. Kerry. By the 1930s, however, de Brún had become involved in a bitter public debate about the value of translating foreign works into Irish. His formidable opponent Daniel Corkery seemed to win public opinion, and this may well account for the fact that de Brún's translations of the *Iliad* and the *Odyssey* were not published as planned.[33] George Thomson, on the other hand, had a somewhat different agenda in promoting access to the study of Classics as a discipline through Irish. However, although highly productive, he too faced challenges and, ultimately, failures in bringing some of his work to publication.

George Thomson is the best known of all the scholars who sought to advance Classics through Irish. A Cambridge-educated professor of Greek, a Marxist philosopher, and active member of the Communist Party, Thomson had also mastered the Irish language through his long-standing connection with the inhabitants of the Blasket Islands. His experience of pre-capitalist society and of the tradition of oral poetry on the Blasket Islands deeply affected his conception of archaic and classical Greek culture.[34] Among the intellectuals influenced by Thomson's work is Kevin O'Nolan (brother of the Brian O'Nolan discussed by O'Hogan in Ch. 8), who taught Classics at University College Dublin during the 1960s, 1970s, and early 1980s, and whose research focused on issues of oral poetry and the bardic tradition.[35] At the same time, the work of earlier Celtic comparatists, including John Millington Synge, also left its mark on Irish intellectuals, as Arabella Currie discusses in relation to the Aran Islands (Ch. 9). The story of Thomson's accession in 1931 to the Greek post at the National University of Ireland, Galway (NUIG), however, has been unduly romanticized, as Pádraic Moran exposes (Ch. 6). Thomson's celebrity, moreover, has obscured the extraordinary work of his colleague Margaret Heavey, who was appointed at the same time. Both Thomson and Heavey produced their own teaching materials in Irish, some of which were subsequently published, though others remain in the NUIG archives. Thomson attempted to launch a programme of public engagement lectures, but was hampered by the church and other authorities. Citing various frustrations, including the challenges he had faced with the government's publications office, he resigned after three years. Heavey, on the other hand, continued to teach Classics through Irish at NUIG until the 1970s, and was by all accounts a talented and inspiring mentor. Declining numbers of students meant that teaching Classics through Irish was phased out at the institution during the 1970s. This fact is linked both to the failure of a broadscale Irish language revival, which meant that the teaching programme for Classics through Irish could only ever have a niche student base, and to the decline of interest in Greek and Latin after the 1960s following the promotion of scientific and vocational subjects as more promising career pathways.

The decline in teaching Greek and Latin at Irish schools and universities led W. B. Stanford to conclude his book *Ireland and the Classical Tradition*, published

---

[33] De Brún's Irish translation of the *Odyssey* was eventually published in 1990. His *Iliad* has yet to be published.
[34] Seaford (2014).   [35] See K. O'Nolan (1968), (1969), (1970), (1973).

in 1976, on a note of alarm. The downward trend in numbers of students with training in classical languages has continued into the twenty-first century. In Irish universities, as elsewhere, Classics departments have adapted to a new kind of student body, offering both *ab initio* intensive language courses along with newly designed courses in classical civilization for students without Greek and Latin. Queen's University Belfast closed the doors of its Classics Department amid fierce controversy, with its final undergraduate student intake of 2002 becoming its last cohort of graduating classicists in 2005. The closure was announced at a time when the department was ranked fifth in the United Kingdom for teaching standards; it was vociferously but unsuccessfully opposed.[36] Ancient historians were incorporated into what is now the School of History, Anthropology, Philosophy and Politics, and the classical languages programme was wound down. In spite of this terrible loss, the new Belfast Summer School in Latin and Classical Greek, founded in 2015 by Helen McVeigh, has been growing steadily, while the Classical Association of Northern Ireland continues to organize public events and outreach sessions for schools. The enormous influence of classical literature on contemporary Northern Irish writers remains evident (Chs. 15, 16, and 17), amply fulfilling a prophecy in which Stanford hoped in the final sentence of *Ireland and the Classical Tradition*: 'if future geniuses of the stature of...Joyce are moved to create brilliant masterpieces from their personal vision of ancient Greece and Rome, then the classical tradition will prove again...its power to inspire as well as to instruct.'[37]

No doubt Stanford would have welcomed the enlarging of this group in the decades following the publication of his book, but the theoretical framework which informs our collection here, namely reception studies, stands in contradistinction to Stanford's 'classical tradition' approach, which assumes that ancient culture can be accessed and appreciated primarily through an implicitly elite education system.[38] Placing a high emphasis on the value of certain kinds of education, investigations into the classical tradition can tend to undervalue diversity.[39] Symptomatic of this is the complete omission from *Ireland and the Classical Tradition* of any mention of classical language instruction through Irish, despite its three chapters devoted to education, with one specifically discussing universities and learned societies and tracing pertinent events down to 1970.[40] The material discussed by Ní Mhurchú and Moran, then, helps to revivify experiences that have been marginalized if not erased from the mainstream narrative (Ch. 5 and Ch. 6), and complements the extraordinary new work of Laurie O'Higgins in tracing the Irish-language material relevant to the education of the poor in eighteenth- and nineteenth-century Ireland.[41]

---

[36] For an overview of the debate see Unsworth (2002).   [37] Stanford (1976: 249).
[38] Cf. Silk, Gildenhard, and Barrow (2014: 5).   [39] Cf. Hardwick (2003: 2–3).
[40] Stanford (1976: 1–72, 45–72 on universities and learned societies).
[41] O'Higgins (2017).

This is not to say that Stanford's magisterial work has become redundant. His *Ireland and the Classical Tradition* remains the only attempt to give a broad historical overview of Irish classicism. The erudition of its author is evident on every page, and its scope is impressive, giving due attention to literature in Irish from the medieval period to the eighteenth century, as well as to art and architecture.[42] Stanford's instinct is inclusive, then, but he remains constrained by the boundaries of the discipline. This tension is felt, for example, in Stanford's conclusions on old, middle, and eighteenth-century Irish-language versions of classical tales: 'Gaelic nonchalance may seem irresponsible, even outrageous, to modern classical readers taught to venerate the ancient authors as supreme in their class...But what should be recognized...is that here we have a new literary fusion which is both scholarly and creative.' Even as Stanford nobly attempts to defend 'the Irish genius' in his final sentence, he concludes that, in these works, 'the conventional categories are broken down and new modes, *sometimes monstrous or barbaric by conventional standards*, come to birth.'[43] The language Stanford uses regrettably perpetuates the crypto-colonial notion of an acceptable stylistic norm against which the Irish example is viewed as barbaric, in spite of his efforts to push forward his own view of the Irish achievement. The weight of the classical tradition, with all its implications, is too heavy a burden for the Irish case.

Reception studies, on the other hand, emphasizes the interactive relationship between the source culture and the receiving culture with a focus on the cultural processes that shape these relationships.[44] It frees us from the constraints of assuming a singular normative view of classicism. When approached through the lens of reception studies, the meaning behind an engagement with classical models becomes dependent on cultural-historical processes, as our collection seeks to underline. Edith Hall, a pioneer in the field of reception studies, offers a composite interpretation of Sinn Féin viewed from the dual perspectives of Robert Mitchell Henry, Professor of Latin at Queen's University Belfast and author of *The Evolution of Sinn Féin* (1920), and James Joyce's Sinn Féiner 'Citizen' (Cyclops) Cusack in *Ulysses* Episode 12 (Ch. 10). Hall contextualizes Henry's nationalism alongside that of two other contemporary Irish Classicists. The first, Eric Roberston Dodds, also from Northern Ireland, would become a celebrated Oxford Classicist, but was almost expelled (or 'sent down') from that university as a student for his vocal support of the 1916 Rising. The second, Benjamin Farrington, a Marxist scholar of Classics from Cork, brought his revolutionary ideas to South Africa before moving to Britain in the 1930s. Within this nexus of associations between classicism and Irish nationalism, Hall reveals through

---

[42] Stanford (1976: 73–89 on literature in Irish, 113–30 on art and architecture).

[43] Stanford (1976: 87, emphasis added). It is notable that Stanford's phrasing here is reminiscent of the monstrous artistic hybrids criticized (with tongue in cheek) by Horace at *Ars Poetica* 1–23.

[44] Hardwick (2003: 5).

original archival research that Henry was on the ground in 1916 as a member of the Irish Volunteers. What has not been appreciated to date, moreover, is the connection between Henry's expertise in Roman historiography and his composition of *The Evolution of Sinn Féin*. Although it includes little overt classical reference, there is a biting Tacitean style in its representation of human failings related to colonial oppression, which effectively inverts the parallelism of Britain and Rome as imperial powers and generates thereby a critique of British colonialism.

Like Henry, Joyce espoused the ideal of an Ireland belonging to all its people, regardless of ethnic origin. This is evident, for instance, in his satires of a narrow-minded nationalism and of the British Empire in Episode 12 of *Ulysses*. These lively pages include a crew of Gaelic scholars and, Hall argues, a parody of the controversial figure Kuno Meyer. Originally celebrated for his expertise in Celtic philology and literature, his support for Germany at the outbreak of World War I lost him many former admirers. It was Meyer, however, who had produced the first English translation of the medieval 'Irish *Odyssey*', the *Merugud Ulix Maicc Leirtis* ('Wanderings of Ulysses son of Laertes'), in 1886. Meyer's translation, suggests Hall, cannot have failed to influence the young James Joyce, who must have been aware of this medieval tale. As an indigenous Irish *Odyssey*, it bears comparison to—and may well have inspired—the whole project of Joyce's own *Ulysses*.

An awareness of Irish medieval culture and its intersection with classical literature is not uncommon in Irish society. One rather more unusual index of this, presented by Cillian O'Hogan, is the *Cruiskeen Lawn* column published in *The Irish Times* several days a week between 1940 and 1966 (Ch. 8). Written by Brian O'Nolan under the pseudonym Myles na gCopaleen, the columns commented on current affairs, often in a humorous manner injected with the personal experiences of the fictional 'Myles'. As O'Hogan demonstrates, the columns occupy a marginal position in which allusion to medieval and classical culture plays a significant role, not least in witnessing changing attitudes to classical learning in mid-twentieth-century Ireland. O'Nolan himself was a liminal figure operating between intelligentsia and mob, modern and postmodern, Irish and English, classical and medieval. This ephemeral publication, which affectionately entered the Irish popular imagination, became gradually more politicized. 'Myles' puts the Irish language on an equal footing with Greek and Latin, and sometimes critiques Greek and Latin to the advantage of Irish, in response to the perceived tension between Irish and classical learning that is also a recurrent theme in this collection. Positioning himself on the margins of the 'nativist' debate in Celtic studies, 'Myles' code-switches between Latin and Irish, makes pointed use of the Gaelic typeface, and creates glosses on other items in the leader page through typographic markers reminiscent of medieval scribal practice. Rather like Dinneen (cf. Ch. 7), but in a more public arena, 'Myles' uses his oeuvre (and here also his allusions to medieval culture) to downplay English and to suggest that

Irish is learned not at the expense of Greek and Latin, but rather as a language intrinsically connected with its classical Indo-European cousins.

The immense popularity of the *Cruiskeen Lawn* columns is attested by the longevity of their run, which concluded only with O'Nolan's death in 1966. The fit of scholarship and cultural understanding, however, is not always so snug. Such is the case with the reception history of the Fir Bolg, a legendary people of Ireland who sought refuge in Greece, were enslaved there, rebelled and returned to Ireland, where they were driven west to the Aran Islands by invaders. Arabella Currie examines the complex scholarly and cultural appropriations of the Fir Bolg, whose origin was subject to heated debate and was mixed up more broadly with identity politics in Ireland (Ch. 9). The monumental forts attributed to the Fir Bolg on the Aran Islands encouraged parallels with Greek archaeological remains, thereby forging a Greek-Aran kinship. At the same time, the topos of the inhospitable rockface, common to island writing, contributed to a discourse of abjection, while notions of racial purity linked the Fir Bolg to the Greeks as reputedly dark-haired (regardless of scientific evidence to the contrary). Contrasting two main approaches to the Fir Bolg, Currie sees them either as abject and downtrodden, or as revolutionary, their abject status reclaimed as a means of resistance. A notable voice in this debate was nationalist historian and politician Eoin MacNeill, who rejected negative mid-seventeenth-century descriptions of the Fir Bolg as motivated by a colonial agenda. The loudest voices, however, promoted the abjection rather than the revolutionary potential of the Fir Bolg. Currie explains why this occurs by locating the Fir Bolg within the genre of Aran island writing. Primitivism uses antiquity in these writings not so much as a dialectical challenge but rather as an enshrinement into pastness. The antiquarian approach deadens the past/present confrontation, with the result that the Fir Bolg culture has always already run its course. Seeing the Fir Bolg not as historical but outside of time exempts those who control the discourse from moral responsibility, enables the packaging of the Fir Bolg for tourist consumption, and makes them apolitical. The Fir Bolg are fought for, not with, and so are never participants in history. All this stands in contrast to political engagement on the Aran Islands themselves. The islander and lifelong republican Bridget Dirrane, for instance, recalled in her memoir how she had served tea to Patrick Pearse and other rebel leaders. One glaring silence on the Fir Bolg, Currie argues, may nevertheless serve to activate their revolutionary potential. John Millington Synge, whose work was very much influenced by Greek literature, and who wrote extensively about the Aran Islands, makes virtually no mention of the Fir Bolg—except, as Currie uncovers, in his unpublished notes and drafts, which by contrast are full of speculation about them. In what may be a deliberate evasion, then, Synge's account of the Aran Islands was prescient in resisting the atemporality of the Fir Bolg to create a space in which they might become resurgent under erasure.

It emerges, then, that the ways in which ancient Greece and Rome have been interrogated in relation to Irish identity in the twentieth century and into the twenty-first are multiple and manifold, and that these interrogations are often rooted in earlier periods of Irish history. In this connection, one pertinent classical location remains to be mentioned—Carthage. This ancient Phoenician state located in North Africa had a long history of hostilities with the Greek colonies in Sicily and later with the Roman Republic, falling decisively to Rome in 146 BCE. Famous for its mythological founder, queen Dido (who, according to Virgil's account in *Aeneid* 4, falls in love with Aeneas and commits suicide on his departure), Carthage was identified with Ireland in the eighteenth century in a most remarkable fashion. In 1772, Charles Vallancey published his treatise *An Essay on the Antiquity of the Irish Language: Being a Collation of the Irish with the Punic Language*. The work presented a detailed case arguing for a fundamentally close relationship between the Irish and Punic (i.e. Phoenician) languages, claiming that Phoenicians had colonized Ireland in archaic prehistory and called it Thule, a name that survives in ancient sources as an unidentified location in the far north.[45] Siobhán McElduff takes us on an alternative path in tracing the shifting associations between Ireland and Carthage that ultimately lie behind Frank McGuinness's 1988 play *Carthaginians* (Ch. 14). In excavating the popular Irish ballad tradition of the eighteenth century, McElduff highlights how the persona of Dido figures prominently in different guises and in marked contrast to a palpable silence on the Trojan/Roman Aeneas. McGuinness's Dido is a gay Northern Irish man, a fluid figure in a way that would have been controversial in 1980s Irish culture (cf. Ch. 12). *Carthaginians*, like the ballad tradition, substitutes high culture with lower-class concerns. As McElduff draws out, the play's quiz motif levels all kinds of knowledge, highbrow and lowbrow, while McGuinness's Dido becomes a symbol of resilience in contrast to the despairing Dido of Virgil. McGuinness's Dido is the author of *The Burning Balaclava*, the play-within-the-play that presents a travesty of the events of Bloody Sunday in 1972, when British forces shot twenty-eight unarmed civilians, killing fourteen, during a protest against internment. *The Burning Balaclava* sees the characters of the play re-enacting their own oppression or the roles of their oppressors. Here, as throughout *Carthaginians*, the persecution of the downtrodden working class is a constant theme. A pyramid of rubbish constructed during the course of the play symbolizes a non-heroic paradigm according to which empire is relativized and history trivialized. In the end, it is by rejecting imperial models that these working-class characters survive. Survival is similarly a concern in Stacey Gregg's 2006 play *Ismene*, where the refusal to engage in paramilitary violence is what alone can allow working-class Northern Irish characters to survive (cf. Ch. 17).

---

[45] See Roling (2018) for further discussion.

Gregg and McGuinness both domesticate the 'high culture' of antiquity in their dramas. As Declan Kiberd shows, Joyce's *Ulysses* is likewise a domestication of epic reframed through a non-elitist optic (Ch. 2). T. S. Eliot, in his imperialist view of what constitutes a classic work of literature, could not comprehend that Joyce's *Ulysses*, far from imposing order, was about exposing disorder. Hall notes that Joyce had studied Latin along with Modern Languages and Logic at University College Dublin (Ch. 10), and Kiberd traces the complex and paradoxical associations of Latin in Ireland (Ch. 2). The instruction of Latin was in many ways coordinate with an imperial mentality which significantly downplayed the atrocities of empire in its implied parallels between Rome and Britain. Translation exercises from L. A. Wilding's *Latin Course for Schools*, for instance, emphasized how conquered natives were won over by 'justice and kindness', as Kiberd discusses. One might adduce further examples of imperialist self-satisfaction from the widely used *Latin Prose Composition for the Middle Forms of Schools* by M. A. North and Rev. A. E. Hillard, first published in 1895, and translated into Irish by Maoghnus Ó Dómhnaill in 1937 (cf. Appendix C to Chapters 5 and 6). Exercise 107 presents Irish rebels and their French allies being decisively scattered by cavalry sent out from Cork. Yet more prescient and, in retrospect, ironic is Exercise 163, in which a group of unrepentant Irishmen is brought to trial on the charge of stirring up revolution. As the exercise has it, 'They asserted that they had done nothing contrary to the law of nations, since the English were oppressing their land, and they themselves were only trying to free her from an unjust dominion.' The conclusion of the exercise was rather less prescient, however, in imagining that their 'words displeased many who were present; but since the prisoners were young, and had never before been accused of any crime, they were spared'.[46] Here in the classroom the magnanimity of the British Empire is demonstrated in the face of Irishmen who are 'not easy to govern', but whose insurgent nationalism might be tamed into past Latinity in the copybook exercise.

From the opposite perspective, the educational materials produced in Ireland after independence could, for their part, insinuate a domesticating and, on occasion, allegorical reading of Roman imperialism. The aforementioned appropriation of Virgil's experience by Dinneen, discussed by Mac Góráin (Ch. 7), expands to a wider parallel between the Irish and the Gauls as Celtic nations who suffered at the hands of imperialist invaders. Appendix C to Chapters 5 and 6 records no fewer than eleven Irish translations or editions of different parts of Caesar's *commentarii* on the Gallic war. The tenor of these can be appreciated also from James J. Carey's two-volume English-language commentary on *De Bello Gallico* I and II, which went to multiple reprints and was a staple for those studying Latin for the Certificate Examinations of the Department of Education between the

---

[46] North and Hillard (1904 [1895]: 84 and 126).

1940s and 1980s.[47] The introduction highlights various parallels between Gaul and 'Ireland before the Conquest' on the levels of social and political organization, religion and mythology, trade and commerce (e.g. 'the Latin *caballus* = "saddle horse" is clearly an adaptation of the Celtic word, of which the Modern Irish form is ᴄᴀᴩᴀʟʟ'),[48] and language, literature, and education. Carey necessarily points out to his students that '[w]hat has been said about the Gauls in the preceding section is true in the main of the race which inhabited Britain in Caesar's time', but following as it does an intervening assessment of the literary agenda of *De Bello Gallico*, which turns on the principle that '[t]o justify their actions, conquerors in all ages have endeavoured to discredit the conquered', the phrase 'in Caesar's time' ensures that the section on The Britons leaves the overarching parallel between the Gauls and the Irish intact.[49]

Perhaps it was Carey's edition, or one like it, that Irish novelist and critic Liam Mac Cóil remembers studying at school. His essay on the status of the Irish language within an increasingly globalized world begins with a reference to Latin as an imperial language, and to the well-known opening phrase of Caesar's *De Bello Gallico*, *Gallia est omnis divisa in partes tres* (*BGall.* 1.1 'Gaul is a whole divided into three parts').[50] Mac Cóil finds a useful metaphor for identifying the place of Irish among world languages in the concept of sending out scouts, a mainstay of Caesar's narrative, but openly acknowledges having been 'on the side of the brave, great-hearted Celts' during his days as a schoolboy, drawing clear distinctions between imperial and non-imperial languages throughout his discussion.[51]

A further element in this challenge to imperialism on the level of language comes in connection with use of Latin by the Catholic Church in Ireland after the Penal Laws, as Kiberd points out. The Catholic Church ensured the survival of Latin in an alternative framework that could be packaged as nationalist. The Irish clergy played a significant role in producing intellectually rigorous scholarship, translations, and textbooks for Irish speakers to study classical literature in both Greek and Latin. Patrick Dinneen (Ch. 7) and Pádraig de Brún (Ch. 5) were among the most prolific, but there were many other men of the cloth involved in the production of these materials, from John MacHale in the nineteenth century to numerous twentieth-century clerics: Art Mac Giolla Eoin, Cathal Mac Giobúin, Liam Mac Philibín, Micheál Ó Baoighill, Pádraic Ó Laoi, Peadar Ua Laoghaire, Seán Mac Craith, Seán Ó Catháin (see Appendix C to Chapters 5 and 6). Seamus Heaney's warmly remembered Latin teacher, who introduced him to Virgil, was a Catholic priest.

---

[47] Carey (1961 [1945]). The introduction is reprinted at pp. vi–xxiv in both volumes.
[48] Carey switches into the cló Gaelach (Irish typeface) for printing the Irish word ('capall'), a practice adopted also by Brian O'Nolan in his contemporaneous 'Cruiskeen Lawn' columns, as discussed by O'Hogan (Ch. 8).
[49] Quotations from Carey (1961 [1945]: xvii, xix).   [50] Mac Cóil (2003: 127).
[51] Mac Cóil (2003: *passim*, quotation at 127).

We return, then, to the point with which we opened our introduction, namely that Irish engagement with classical models raises a unique set of (post)colonial tensions. Unequivocally colonial within the British imperial project, classical languages and literature, particularly in the Latin and Roman tradition, could nevertheless be appropriated as indigenous by Irish nationalists through the centuries-old native Irish legacy of expertise and scholarship in the field. As a result, figures like Patrick Dinneen and Seamus Heaney could find ways to articulate nationalist concerns through Virgil, who in other contexts of British colonialism is identified as 'the poet of empire'.[52] Dinneen (Ch. 5), alongside de Brún (Ch. 7), championed classical literature at a time when Irish intellectuals were divided in their opinions on the value of non-Irish and non-Celtic material. Leaders of the 1916 Rebellion, including Patrick Pearse (Ch. 3) and Thomas MacDonagh (Ch. 4), were clearly conflicted on the issue, at once prioritizing native Irish models while at the same time being deeply influenced by classical modes of expression. Like Dinneen and de Brún, Pearse and MacDonagh were liberal, intellectually speaking, and these men realized that embracing classical literature, and indeed European literature more broadly, did not threaten the legitimacy of indigenous Irish literature.

We have seen how the opposition de Brún faced at the hands of Daniel Corkery led to the discontinuance of de Brún's publications of Greek texts in Irish. As Kiberd relates (Ch. 2), Corkery argued that importing the classical paradigm stifled national individualism when (on Corkery's view) Irish culture had been, and should remain, untainted by such foreign intrusions. On the other hand, professors at Trinity College Dublin, like John Pentland Mahaffy (Professor of Ancient History) and Robert Atkinson (Professor of Sanskrit and Comparative Philology), worked hard to undermine the development of Irish as a university subject. Their opposition to modern Irish was based on the notion that the language was disorganized, lacking standardized spelling, and that its literature was not worth studying. Kiberd highlights some ironies in this debate: Corkery's fetishization of tradition in fact worked to downplay individual talent; and when Irish did become a school subject, it suffered the fate of being codified like a classical language, although (as Kiberd points out) this codification might also be traced to the artificiality inherent in the classicizing form of bardic poetry stretching back to the collapse of Gaelic bardic culture in the 1600s.[53] After collapse new forms emerge—a pattern that holds also for the collapse of colonial culture in the twentieth century. One example of this, discussed in Kiberd's chapter, is Howard Brenton's 1981 play *The Romans in Britain*, which turns on a direct parallelism

---

[52] Vasunia (2013: 241).

[53] The *Rudimenta Grammaticae Hibernicae* (*c.*1600), composed by Bonaventura O'Hussey (*c.*1570–1614), who had trained as a bard before joining the Franciscan order, was 'written in Latin and based on the structures of Latin grammar' (O'Higgins (2017: 26)). On pre-revival codification of the Irish language see further Wolf (2012).

between the Roman conquest of Britain and the British military presence in Northern Ireland. The radical point being made is that the British, like the Irish, are intrinsically Celtic, and the play works persistently to undermine the dichotomy between the British and the Irish as enemies, even as the British soldiers, who mostly insist on tracing their lineage to King Arthur, fail to comprehend the self-contradictory nature of their country's colonial vision.

We have endeavoured, in this introduction, to avoid replicating the sequence of the sections and chapters of the volume, which we hope speaks for itself, in order to highlight alternative points of contact between chapters and to draw attention to issues, themes, and individuals that speak across the different subsections. We are aware that this collection merely scratches the surface of a vast reception history, but hope nevertheless that it will prove to be a valuable stepping stone for future research in this area. The recent allocation of a large grant from the European Research Council to support the project 'Classical Influences and Irish Culture' (2019–24), which will investigate the sociopolitical implications of Irish engagement with classical models from the medieval period to the present day across different fields (including literature in Irish and in English, history, philosophy, gender studies, material culture), is a promising development.[54]

[54] For further information on this project see http://clic.au.dk/ (accessed 5 December 2019).

I

RECEPTION AND REJECTION OF THE CLASSICS IN IRELAND

2

The Use and Abuse of Classics

Thoughts on Empire, Epic, and Language

Declan Kiberd

The classic is often jocularly described as a book which nobody reads but every-one wants to have read. This sounds suspiciously like a notorious wish: 'as for reading, our schoolkids can do that for us.' There are two ways of reading a classic. The first is the familiar-enough scholarly treatment, imagining how it was intended for its original readers by exploring how it captures the ideas, feelings, and language of the time and place from which it came. The second is to make the ancient work contemporary, showing how in reading it with reckless interpretative freedom, we allow it to read us. This is what artists do in high-profile retellings, but it is also the democratic right of the general reader. The best treatments may permit people to take X-rays of lost elements of the original work, thereby offering both kinds of interpretation in one, as I will argue later is the case with Joyce's reworking of Homer's *Odyssey*. Classic works of art are characterized by awesome beauty and rigour of arrangement, responsive to intensive analysis. They often generate mythical characters who can be so potent as to obscure the individual author or authors, carrying an impersonal, sometimes superhuman force. And quite a few serve to shape public policies based on their cultural explanations of the world.[1] It is under this third heading that I wish to consider the use and abuse of classics.

Empires and Ireland: Literary Approaches in Times of Conflict

In 1919 the American poet T. S. Eliot, exiled in London, praised order, empire, and racial purity, citing Rudyard Kipling as an artist who had protected these values from attack.[2] Eliot could see no admirable system emerging from the break-up of empires after World War I or from the Russian revolution of 1917. In his later years he turned to the British Empire and Anglican Church as forces which

---

[1] On the complexities of disentangling the terminology of 'Classics' and the 'classical' see Porter (2006a).
[2] Eliot (1919: 297).

Declan Kiberd, *The Use and Abuse of Classics: Thoughts on Empire, Epic, and Language* In: *Classics and Irish Politics, 1916–2016*. Edited by: Isabelle Torrance and Donncha O'Rourke, Oxford University Press (2020).
© Oxford University Press.
DOI: 10.1093/oso/9780198864486.003.0002

might stave off this ruin. 'I am all for empires,' he told Ford Madox Ford in 1924, 'especially the Austro-Hungarian Empire, and I deplore the outburst of artificial nationalities, constructed like artificial genealogies for millionaires all over the world.'[3] This may have been an occluded reference to Ireland, officially declared a Free State in 1922. In his signature poem of the same year, Eliot foretold hooded hordes swarming from the east to destroy European humanism:

Falling towers
Jerusalem, Athens, Alexandria,
Vienna, London
Unreal[4]

Eliot called for a European Christian empire to hold back the Bolsheviks and insisted that it should submit to the leadership of Britain, the only European empire which (he suggested) had established a global empire on the same lines as the old Roman one. In essays of the 1920s, Eliot sketched the lineaments of a European mind whose thinking might underwrite that order—a tradition reaching back from Goethe through Shakespeare and Dante all the way to Virgil, that linkman between ancient and modern worlds. Destiny for Virgil, wrote Eliot, 'means the *imperium romanum*'. But then, in a sudden, deft, and candid disclosure, Eliot admitted that this classic writer's empire was largely utopian. 'He set the ideal for Rome, and for empire in general, which was never realized in history...We are all, so far as we inherit the civilizations of Europe, still citizens of the Roman Empire.'[5] Honest enough to admit that the institution imagined by a gifted civil servant such as Virgil was not quite the sordid affair of scheming proconsuls and parasites that features in many history books, Eliot nonetheless saw the British Empire as a good thing and eventually became a British subject. By 1958 he was calling Kipling the greatest English man of letters of his generation. So the Joseph Conrad who had supplied key lines for *The Waste Land* and *The Hollow Men*[6] was forgotten and Kipling reaffirmed (among liberals, the reputation of that great writer took a long time to recover from this ringing endorsement).

English Studies, as practised under the sign of Eliot, had its origins in a crisis of empire—and in this last-ditch attempt by an immigrant American empire-lover to shore selected fragments of European tradition against the collapse of political systems in Europe. Yet an irony attended Eliot's efforts. The study of 'English' came slowly to displace that of 'Greek and Latin', as higher education ceased to be the sole preserve of wealthy gentlemen, much as 'cultural studies' have gradually

---

[3] Cited in Raskin (2009: 55).
[4] T. S. Eliot, *The Waste Land* (1922), quoted from North (2001: 17–18).
[5] Cited in Raskin (2009: 57).
[6] For the former, 'the horror, the horror' as epigraph to the poem; for the lead-in to the latter, 'Mistah Kurtz, he dead'.

displaced courses in modern literary classics in more recent decades. In the years following World War II, however, when an exhausted Britain was overtaken by the United States as the new world power, Eliot's account of literary culture remained relatively undisturbed, and he might, as an Anglo-American, have been taken to represent the growing rapport between the old imperialists and the new. Practical Criticism, though invented by English poets and critics, was perfected in the American academy, where it fitted well with the 'end of ideology' notions sponsored by establishment intellectuals in Washington.

In celebrating the classics, T. S. Eliot spoke of the mind of Europe as a unified thing, a transnational system of order. (In this, he was not altogether different from a naive Minnesotan who, shaking my hand after a heartfelt conversation, said, 'I do love to talk to someone with a European accent.') Yet most Europeans, now as through history, have scant inclination or ability to envisage a mind of Europe. Insofar as it has been codified, either with admiration or castigation, it has been done by *outsiders*. Some have been Americans, such as Eliot or Henry James, who wished to define a European mainstream which they might enter. Others have been anti-colonial Africans, such as Frantz Fanon or Aimé Cesaire, who conceived of it as a source of coercion and ruin for their peoples. There are other ways of doing this, of course, which avoid extremes of triumphalism or negation. In *Black Athena*, the scholar Martin Bernal pointed to the African (mostly Egyptian) roots of Greek civilization, a deft and unexpected manoeuvre which complicated received ideas of classical tradition. Bernal's book eventually drew forth an Irish equivalent, *Atlantean* by Bob Quinn, which argued for a North African rather than Euro-celtic basis of Irish civilization: for instance, he linked sean-nós (traditional Irish) singing in Connemara to the incantatory music of Berbers, and so on.[7]

There may be some truth in these dialogic models of ancient cultures, all based on the idea that the sea in olden days allowed for remarkable levels of mobility and cross-cultural influence. Nothing was ever as unidirectional as subsequent historians (in search of neat influences) often wanted to make it seem. Even some critiques of Europe, such as that produced by Toussaint L'Ouverture and the Black Jacobins, had definite roots in the philosophy of the Enlightenment, itself based to some degree on a notion of restoring certain meritocratic elements of Roman life.[8] Yet that version of Rome is not the same one of which Professor MacHugh speaks in James Joyce's *Ulysses*:

We think of Rome, imperial, imperious, imperative.... What was their civilization? Vast, I allow: but vile. Cloacae: sewers. The Jews in the wilderness and on

---

[7] Quinn (1986); see also https://www.dailymotion.com/video/xscgzc (accessed 5 December 2019) for Quinn's film on the same topic.
[8] See James (2001).

the mountain-top said: *It is meet to be here. Let us build an altar to Jehovah.* The Roman, like the Englishman who follows in his footsteps, brought to every new shore on which he set his foot (on our shores he never set it) only his cloacal obsession. He gazed about him in his toga and said: *It is meet to be here. Let us construct a water-closet.*[9]

All through Ulysses, from the moment when Stephen teaches a lesson about Pyrrhus in Roman History to the commentaries by Professor MacHugh in 'Aeolus', there is an implication that many Latin teachers in the Ireland of 1904 hate their jobs:

> We were always loyal to lost causes, the professor said. Success for us is the death of the intellect and of the imagination. We were never loyal to the successful. We serve them. I teach the blatant Latin language. I speak the tongue of a race the acme of whose mentality is the maxim: time is money. Material domination. *Dominus!* Lord! Where is the spirituality? Lord Jesus! Lord Salisbury! A sofa in a westend club. But the Greek![10]

You would never suspect, reading such passages, that the Greeks themselves had once colonized large tracts of southern Italy. By Joyce's time, the Greeks were (despite a certain coarseness) good guys—with whom the Irish could identify, as a people of greater culture than that possessed by their conquerors. Yet these revivalist sentimentalizations were promoted by people (such as Joyce) who did not know much Greek but had been force-fed Latin in schools.

Latin, Education, and the British Empire

The standard justification for educational policies on the study of Latin was that learning the language was character-forming. As late as 1969, according to the Irish Department of Education examination records, Latin was taken by over 70 per cent of secondary school students and was compulsory for matriculation at university. Latin provided the root-basis of many modern languages and their systems of grammar. But this was often a pretext for another agenda: the development in schoolchildren of an imperial, administrative mentality, as developed through a study of Caesar's writings and so on. The use of Roman numerals to describe a school XI or XV; the resort to nomenclature like 'Smith Major' or 'Smith Minor'; and the SPQR mentality accompanying these things was a way of initiating children in the rhetoric of empire; and the *virtus* displayed in establishing

---

[9] Joyce (1992 [1922]: 166).   [10] Joyce (1992 [1922]: 169).

the past empire might serve to strengthen the current British affair. For example, L. A. Wilding, in his *Latin Course for Schools, Part One*, comments in his 'Introduction to the Beginner':

> The study of a foreign language is an exciting matter; it is like a key that will open many doors...By a knowledge of Latin we are introduced to a great people, the Romans. The Romans led the world as men of action; they built good roads, made good laws, and organized what was in their time almost world-wide government and citizenship. At their best, too, they set the highest examples of honour, loyalty and self-sacrifice.[11]

In identifying modern Britain with ancient Rome, such commentators managed to overlook the squalid and barbaric realities which underlay the Roman conquest, just as people in Britain were spared too graphic accounts of the torture of African schoolboys or the shooting of Indian pacifists. However, Wilding's course is a perfect preparation for such negotiations:

> Exercise 65: By means of justice and kindness Agricola wins over the natives of Britain. He then hastens beyond Chester towards Scotland. He rouses his troops to battle and to victory. At first, Agricola wastes the land; then he displays to the natives his moderation.[12]

This is Tacitus and Wilding accepts his version. At the battle of Mons Graupius, ten thousand ancestors of the Scots died, but Wilding gives only a cursory summary of the speech of their leader Calgacus in AD 84 to his troops, which ended, according to Tacitus, with the words: 'To plunder, butcher, steal, these things they misname empire: they make a desolation and they call it peace' (*Agricola* 30).

All through the 1950s, 1960s, and 1970s, Scottish schoolchildren (like their English, Irish, and Welsh counterparts), studied textbooks like Wilding's, which went into new paperback reissues in 1995 and 2013, and which took it as a natural thing that the Romans slaughtered their ancestors in this way.[13] The implication of these texts was that in the 1,800 years between the Roman and British Empires, nothing of major value had befallen civilization. The fact that the Romans had slaves was glossed over, not just for the painful light which it might shed on the ancient heroes but more poignantly still because of the light it might shed on contemporary British class society.

It was up to a radical playwright, Howard Brenton, to restore the raw meaning of the analogy on which the British educational self-image was based. Throughout

---

[11] Wilding (1952: 9).   [12] Wilding (1952: 69).
[13] It is interesting to note, as well, that standard British Latin language school texts were translated into Irish after independence for instruction of Latin through Irish. See Ní Mhurchú (Ch. 5).

his 1981 play, *The Romans in Britain*, he elaborates the parallel. Children throwing stones at Roman legionaries in Part 1 become Northern Irish schoolchildren stoning British troops in Part 2. In Part 1 a tired Roman soldier complains that all he ever seems to do is build lavatories in other people's fields, the same complaint raised by British soldiers in Part 2. (The water closet, again...). The Celtic villagers in Part 1 who have never set eyes upon Romans—whom they can more easily demonize as men with the heads of hawks—are like those Irish farmers who have never met a British soldier up close in Part 2. And so on. It is no surprise, therefore, that the Envoy who warns the ancient Celts of the Roman arrival should sound at times like the school textbook: 'Understand. The Romans are different. They are – (He gestures, trying to find the word. He fails. He tries again). A nation. Nation. What? A great family? No. A people. No. They are one huge thing.' And it is no surprise either that a Celtic woman would say of the speaker: 'He's shit frightened.'[14]

Brenton's deeper point is that beneath this thin Roman overlay the British are fundamentally Celtic in their origins—in other words, like their current latter-day enemies, the Irish. If imperialism succeeds in turning former enemies into contemporary doubles, then it may also disclose the fact that current enemies were once doubles, so crazy and mixed up has the basic situation become. It is this confusion which unhinges the complex mind of the British soldier-spy Chichester who sees beneath mere surfaces, as does Brenton, and in consequence goes half-mad. 'It's Celts we're fighting in Ireland,' he explains to his comrades: 'We won't get anywhere till we know what that means... King Arthur was a Celtic warlord! Who fought twelve great battles against the Saxons. That is, us.'[15] Yet the British army sees itself in the tradition of knightly Arthur, seeking to restore his golden age of civilization in Ireland. Only Chichester can see how self-contradictory that vision has become: 'The Celts! Ha! Very fashionable, the Celts, with the arty-crafty. Ley-lines. Druids. But show them the real thing – an Irishman with a gun, or under a blanket in an H-block and they run a mile... If king Arthur walked out of those trees, now, know what he'd look like to us? One more fucking mick.'[16]

The Domestication of Epic

Howard Brenton has done with his Latin sources what Theodor Adorno and Max Horkheimer did with the *Odyssey* in their book *Dialectic of Enlightenment*, first published in 1944.[17] Adorno had always been aware of the danger of an uncritical identification with the figures in classical texts. He wrote once by way of warning

---

[14] Brenton (1980: 45).   [15] Brenton (1980: 73).   [16] Brenton (1980: 75).
[17] See the recent English translation by Edmund Jephcott: Adorno and Horkheimer (2002).

that 'whoever occupies a period house embalms himself alive',[18] a nice variant on Leopold Bloom's aphorism that 'the Irishman's house is his coffin'.[19] If Seamus Heaney, through a use of demotic language, sometimes takes his own covert revenge on Virgil by making him sound like a yard-boy, Adorno and Horkheimer offer their own account of the *Odyssey* as a very early example of what most critics still say began only with Cervantes, the domestication of epic. Its project, as they saw it, was to destroy mythical thinking and replace it with the rational order of a trading world. In the tale, Odysseus is treated often as a travelling salesman or barterer, and he is even taunted for being a profiteering merchant rather than an aristocratic athlete. His refusal to be seduced by the song of the Sirens is a rejection of myth by a prudent rationalist, for the bourgeois wins by doing nothing, by simply waiting, by deferring gratification. Odysseus refuses to eat the lotus-plant or the sacred cows and opts instead to be both sacrifice and priest, in what can be seen as an astonishing anticipation of the role of Jesus. So the bourgeois ego owes its existence to the sacrifice of the present to the future, much as the *Odyssey* deferred some of its gratifications until *Ulysses*. In the old story, Odysseus saves his life at one point by losing his very name, just as Jesus will offer a 'new' code by which whoever loses his life will save it. Bloom, too, will be divested of his proper name to become simply 'the man'. In all of these narratives, a passive but caring person achieves a sort of semi-divine status, at once victim and god, by a sort of anonymous celebrity.

Joyce seized on the anti-mythological element in the *Odyssey* to free his own generation from the cult of war. In lacerating the earlier, now-sacred text, Joyce was guilty of nothing more than a rigorous application of Homer's underlying logic. The modern translator is never merely an aggressor, for he or she also helps to create the aura of the *original*. But by setting a new text to vibrate with an ancient one, the translator also serves to decanonize the original. In this process Homer becomes a botched, incompletely imagined, ur-version of Joyce, much as Simon Dedalus is presented as an unsatisfactory father to Stephen. Every major work of art contains and reinforces our sense of the strangeness of its original, even as it shows how elements of the modern may be found in the pre-historical. The converse is also true: aspects of the pre-historical may sometimes be found in the modern, which is forever in danger of lapsing back into mythological mentalities, as in the anti-Semitic attacks on Bloom. Autocratic nationalities have often despised and feared seafarers, who are notoriously hybrid and innovative in their sense of cultural identity.

The author of *Ulysses* sensed that in his world the surviving shreds of premodern thought might yet become the basis for a common culture. That, after all, was the understanding upon which W. B. Yeats and his collaborators were basing

---

[18] Adorno (2005: 71).   [19] Joyce (1992 [1922]: 139).

the Irish Literary Revival. The difference was that Joyce tried to imagine past heroes in our space, rather than us in theirs. Read in this way, Joyce's *Ulysses* and its use of Homer is precisely *not* what T. S. Eliot said of it. Eliot praised Joyce's mythic method as a way of imposing some sort of control over the anarchy and disorder of modern life. In *The Waste Land* he evoked the splendour of classical Greece and Elizabethan England to mock the hollow men of the modern metropolis. In his essay 'Ulysses, Order and Myth', the analysis reads like a nervous apology for his own poem and an implicit denial that he has simply filched the method from Joyce: 'In using the myth, in manipulating a continuous parallel between contemporaneity and antiquity, Mr Joyce is pursuing a method which others must pursue after him. They will not be imitators, any more than the scientist who uses the discoveries of an Einstein, in pursuing his own, independent, further investigations.'[20]

But is that really how Joyce uses Homer? Does Eliot's analysis even capture Homer's use of Homer? Surely, the immense panorama of futility and anarchy is Homer's own world. After all, his traveller had gone beyond all known paradigms away out into uncharted waters, rather in the manner of those who enter the otherworld. He had entered into the zones of the unconscious, which somehow he had to survive and report with true clarity. It was he who, long before Joyce, was using his tale to put a semblance of order upon a world which had in fact been shattered by his hero's travels and by the knowledge which he had gained on those voyages. The *Odyssey* was, in Carol Dougherty's reading, 'trying to construct an interpretation of the worlds and peoples of its own mythic pasts in order to make sense of a tumultuous and volatile present'.[21] So his tale is about Odysseus's attempt to decode various alien cultures in order to recode them for his own, much as Joyce turned Homer's 'then' into his own 'now'.

Greek, Latin, and Irish

Approaches such as those described in the preceding section are based on a far less militaristic view of Greek than of Latin culture; and, of course, Joyce has chosen the more pacific *Odyssey* than *Iliad* (the former selling far more copies than the latter through the past century because of its perceived modernity and love of travel). According to Penguin Books' marketing department, it sold significantly more copies through each decade of the period. For those who studied Latin, the language of the Romans has many beauties, not only in the *fons Bandusiae* poetry of Horace, but also in the gorgeous rhythms of the Holy Week ceremonies, which Joyce knew by heart and recited in quiet synchrony with the officiating priest as he stood at the back of the church. Nevertheless, the Catholic Church

---

[20] Eliot (1923), cited in Kiberd (1992: xxx).   [21] Dougherty (2001: 9).

sought to mimic much of the SPQR mentality, all as it consolidated a different kind of Roman Empire. Its administrative structures were quasi-military and even the lay apostolate, the Legion of Mary, called its missionaries in Africa 'legion-aries', as if the whole show were an imitation of the British Empire. 'The most belated race in Europe'[22]—yet again.

There may be a further reason why Greek went largely unstudied in Irish sec-ondary schools, and Latin itself was rather sullenly embraced by the years of the cultural revival (1891–1922)—a conviction that the real classic literature available to the nation's children was to be found in the Irish language. The controversies in the first decade of the Irish Revival about whether or not to put the study of Irish on the syllabus of schools are tell-tale. The main opposition came from two pro-fessors at Trinity College Dublin, the ancient historian J. P. Mahaffy and the phil-ologist Robert Atkinson. They suggested that the major texts of Irish were often either 'silly or indecent' and could give an innocent reader a shock from which he or she might never recover.[23] The language itself was not settled in its grammar and thus doubly unsuitable for character-forming study. It was merely a patois, useful for a gentleman trying to talk to gillies as he fished for salmon in the west—but that was all. Soon a satiric verse was doing the rounds, referencing the eighteenth-century philosopher Bishop George Berkeley, who reportedly answered Johnsonian common sense by saying 'we Irish think otherwise':

The Irish language, Mahaffy said,
Is a couple of books, written clerkly,
A dirty word in a song or two.
Matter a damn, said Berkeley.

Atkinson also drew scorn from Gaelic Leaguers for errors in his analysis of Irish grammar:

Atkinson of TCD
Doesn't know the verb 'to be'[24]

Both men clearly feared—and rightly so, as things turned out—that the movement for the revival of Irish might become a plank in a more generally separatist, nationalist agenda. The Anglo-Irish ascendancy was already losing ground after the Land War of the 1870s and 1880s, and the ensuing Land Acts; and many of its leading members had studied Greek and Latin at university as a seal on their

---

[22] James Joyce, 'The Day of the Rabblement', in Mason and Ellmann (1964: 70).
[23] See Ó Fiaich (1972: 67–8).
[24] Ó Fiaich (1972: 68). For contemporary documentation see 'Dr Atkinson's evidence to the Royal Commission' in Kiberd and Mathews (2015: 115).

gentility. The campaign of cultural nationalists threatened a whole way of life; and, even more specifically, the jobs of classicists in colleges and schools. Divisions between the TCD Classics professors and the Irish revival movement ran deep. There had been a Chair of Irish language at TCD since 1840, and Douglas Hyde, the founder of the Gaelic League, applied for this position at his alma mater when it became vacant in 1896. He had the support of major scholars in the field, such as Kuno Meyer and Standish O'Grady, and was confident his application would be successful, but it was rejected, due in large part to interference from Atkinson, and this came as a bitter blow. In correspondence with W. B. Yeats, Hyde asserts his disdain for the man appointed (Rev. James W. H. Murphy) and his conviction that 'the worse the man [appointed] was the better pleased [TCD colleagues] were, so that no attention could be drawn to Gaelic studies by him'.[25] In 1907 the position of Lecturer in Celtic Languages was created at TCD and Edward John Gwynn was appointed. Gwynn supported the study of early Irish language and literature but found little or no academic value in modern Irish.[26] Mahaffy himself was a great wit as well as an intermittently astute thinker. He did foresee just how fetishized the study of Irish could become, for as far back as 1898 he had written: 'A famous Scotsman has said that, if he could control a people's songs, he cared not who made their laws. In the unfortunate twentieth century, the adage is likely to take another form: give me a nation's examination papers, and I defy the politicians to control its sentiments.'[27] A second wave of such fears assailed other Trinity dons in the aftermath of political independence in 1922: the great Berkeley scholar A. A. Luce feared that the compulsory study of Irish in state schools might result in the conversion of many Protestant children into Catholics.[28]

Ultimately, the Gaelic League won a victory, and Irish was recognized as a school subject by the colonial authorities as well as a valid subject for university matriculation.[29] However, it seems likely that the biting sarcasms voiced by Mahaffy and Atkinson so stung the Gaelic League that many of its leaders attempted to 'classicize' the study of Irish. Although this kind of process of codification was part of the history of Irish scholarship,[30] the language now came to be taught by many as—paraxodically for the revivalists—a sort of dead language, with complex declensions of the noun and conjugations of the verb. In those early decades of the Free State, when Catholicism in Ireland was being reconfigured as a rule-bound moralism, Irish too often attracted as teachers the sort of martinet who considered that there was a definite character-building element in the struggles of

---

[25] Cited by Robinson (1992: 22), who also comments on Atkinson's either ill-informed or malicious undermining of Hyde's linguistic competence (23).

[26] Robinson (1992: 24).   [27] Stanford and McDowell (1971: 110).

[28] Akenson (1976: 35–62).

[29] On education policies for the Irish language see Ó Buachalla (1984).

[30] See, e.g., Wolf (2012).

children to learn irregular verbs and to master a codified, regularized Gaelic, which was employed in sections of the civil service but had never actually been spoken on land or sea. None of this need ever have happened—after all, irregular verbs were also studied in French class, without the fire-and-brimstone theatrics which too often accompanied Irish, which came to be seen by most children as a threat rather than a gift. These strict methods were, to some degree, a response to the strictures of the TCD classicists (who themselves, in turn, had possibly been perturbed by the view of some late Victorian scholars that the Greeks themselves were a barbaric, ill-bred people—the strictures about Irish may have contained a strong element of 'projection'). The appallingly saccharine, improving nature of many Gaelic texts invented for study in schoolrooms was itself a panic response to allegations of bawdiness and decadence. The leading prose writer Máirtín Ó Cadhain wearily observed that most of these texts seem to have been crafted for an audience of credulous schoolchildren and pre-Vatican II nuns.

Irish Classicism

Some of us were luckier than the depressed majority and found inspiration in good teachers who really did believe in a more authentic Irish classicism. The stories of the Fianna warriors with their three signature virtues—'glaine inár gcroí, neart inár ngéag, is beart de réir ár mbriathar' ('cleanliness of heart, strength of limb, and keeping our word')—might furnish examples of what Samuel Beckett would laughingly call 'the Victorian Gael',[31] but they were told in a beautiful language that could be rousing. The bardic poetry produced by professional artists between 1200 and 1600 created a clear outline and disciplined form that remained as a precious legacy to modern writers in Irish—the aim was to say ordinary things with aphoristic force.

Like much classical poetry, the Irish bardic tradition had developed a specialized jargon and rigidity of form which caused most of its exponents to lose touch with the energies of everyday speech (an ironic failure in a poetry which prided itself on being recited). There must always be a tension between the language of poetry and of everyday life. If they grow too close, there is a loss of that imaginative challenge and redemptive strangeness, which are crucial to every good poem; but if these languages veer too far apart, as often occurs in the decadence of a classical tradition, 'poetry' can be constrained in a stilted, artificial, factitious dialect, disconnected from the pressures of felt experience. With the fall of the Gaelic earls in the early 1600s and the replacement of their society with the Elizabethan and Jacobean plantations, the bards lost their patrons. In truth, their fate is a

---

[31] Samuel Beckett, 'Recent Irish Poetry', quoted from the edition of Cohn (1984: 70).

warning that in systems of classical literature overdependence on patrons can leave an artist vulnerable when those patrons are toppled. In the aftermath of this collapse, Irish bards developed newer forms in a language more comprehensible to the multitude. There was a discernible literary revival in Irish between 1600 and 1650,[32] as there would be in the English language of Ireland three centuries later—and for much the same reasons. Because of sudden shifts in the social order, in both cases stripping aristocrats of land, the forms of art went into meltdown and works of surpassing brilliance emerged from traumatic transitional moments, versions of a kind of modernism *avant la lettre*.

Yet that is not how the controversial Daniel Corkery, advancing his nativist view of Gaelic poetry, configured these writings.[33] In *The Hidden Ireland* and in a famous essay 'Filíocht na Gaeilge: A Cineál', Corkery insisted that literature in Irish in the seventeenth, eighteenth, and nineteenth centuries remained classical in essence.[34] There is truth in that contention insofar as the writers often felt themselves to be articulating a social consensus. Ever since the first Irish-language translation of Virgil, *Imtheachta Aeniasa*, in the twelfth century, poetry had been filled with analogies between local beauties and Helen, between local scholars and Herodotus.[35] The collapse of bardic schools reinforced these tendencies, for in an occupied, colonized country versions of Greek or even Latin narrative could have a subversive edge. The assertion of a continuity with ancient Greece offered an exalted pedigree to an insulted, humiliated people; and that assertion was maintained even in the poetry of Anthony Raftery in the mid-nineteenth century:

> Tá pósaidh glégheal ar bhruach na céibhe,
>   Agus bhuail sí Deirdre le sgéimh, is gnaoi,
> Is dá nabrainn Helen an bhainríon Ghréagach
>   Ar thuit na céadta dá barr san Traoi.
>
> There's a lovely posy lives by the roadway,
>   Deirdre was nowhere beside my joy;
> Nor Helen who boasted of conquests Trojan,
>   For whom was wasted the town of Troy.[36]

---

[32] See Ó Maonaigh (1962) and Kiberd (2000a: 13–70).

[33] Corkery's views on Irish literature were not shared by all academics, but were nevertheless influential. His public denouncement of Pádraig de Brún's Irish translations of ancient Greek texts, for instance, on the grounds that such translations were foreign intrusions on the native Irish literary landscape, brought to a regrettable end de Brún's publications in this area, as Ní Mhurchú discusses (Ch. 5).

[34] On the intersection of classical and Irish languages in the eighteenth and nineteenth centuries see O'Higgins (2017).

[35] For discussion of the medieval Irish classicism in the *Imtheachta Aeniasa* see Poppe (2014).

[36] Hyde (1903: 43).

Perhaps Joyce's Professor MacHugh is invoking this tradition when he uses the Greeks as a code for the forces resisting domination in Ireland; and it may also be that the sedulous use of Latin in Catholic schools and diocesan colleges, after the relaxation of the Penal Laws in the later eighteenth century, was itself a none-too-coded challenge to the more directly imperial use of Latin made by the colonizers. If so, these Greek and Latin 'codes' eventually collapsed, like the Irish language, into an imitation of those very discourses they were supposed to contest. Yet Joyce might be said to have resuscitated the more radical potentials of the classical languages. Although *Ulysses* begins with the opening of the Latin Mass (*introibo ad altare Dei*, 'I will go to the altar of God'), and although the young men entering the brothel district of Nighttown invert the gender of the godhead in satiric response (*ad deam qui laetificat juventutem meum*, 'to the goddess who gives joy to my youth'), the main action commences with a warning against these toxic associations. It then delivers on Malachi Mulligan's promise of Hellenizing Ireland by presenting a Leopold Bloom who is, in Mulligan's words, 'Greeker than the Greeks'.[37]

What did critics like Corkery mean in asserting that literature in the Irish language is essentially classical? Corkery intended this word to denote a meaning never dreamed of by Mahaffy or Atkinson, for he considered classic authors to be poets of their people, not a stand-alone elite. Joyce's own celebration of the common man in a narrative derived from Homer, increasingly portrayed by radical analysts as a poet of his people, would be of a piece with this. That notion of a people's inherent classicism would move George Thomson to recognize it in the common culture of Blasket Islanders. In *The Prehistoric Aegean* (1949), Thomson wrote: 'The conversation of those ragged peasants, as soon as I had learned to follow it, electrified me. It was as though Homer had come alive. Its vitality was inexhaustible, yet it was rhythmical, alliterative, formal, artificial – always on the point of bursting into poetry.'[38]

All of this was founded upon a reaction against the subjectivity and individualism of the Romantic poets of the early nineteenth century. Modern Irish classicists were followers of Matthew Arnold who said that 'the great artist emphasizes not himself but his object – he sees the object as it really is, and subordinates expression to that which it is designed to express'.[39] The beauty of Celtic nature poets was classical in rigour: they gave the image which they received. In that respect, their work was far more Irish than the lyrics of Thomas Davis and Young Ireland, lyrics which could only ever constitute a subset of English Romanticism. Aware that the leading writers of High Modernism were returning to a more austere and classical sense of form, Corkery announced that this was, and had been

---

[37] Joyce (1992 [1922]: 279).
[38] Cited by Mac Conghail (1987: 154). For further discussion of George Thomson and his work of disseminating classical Greek texts, in particular, through the Irish language see Moran (Ch. 6).
[39] Arnold (1853: ix), cited in Ó Foghludha (1952: 13).

for centuries, the Irish way. Inevitably, his theory overlooked a great deal of writing, as overarching theories generally do; but it was an audacious way in which to fuse a defiant answer to the Mahaffy\Atkinson combination with the modes of High Modernism. No wonder that *The Hidden Ireland* was the bestselling work of literary criticism in the first decade of the Free State.

Corkery had to pass over the fact that the poetry written before his chosen period—the seventeenth and eighteenth centuries—was a product of the decadence of classicism, of a moment when living form lapsed into dead formula. He also ignored the fact that many Romantics shared his belief in connecting art with the energies of everyday speech. But he was playing on a far vaster field. His Greeks were 'dílis don dúchas', i.e. faithful to their ancestral culture, in ways that subsequent Renaissance imitators could never be. By virtue of imitating the Greeks, these mimic men failed to be themselves. The only classicism worth practising was a purely native, or (as Corkery believed) national, form. So his theory comes to a grand climax with the following utterances:

> Greek standards in their own time and place were standards arrived at by the nation – they were *national* standards. Caught up at second-hand into the art-mind of Europe, they became diffused and international and their effect was naturally to whiten the youthfully tender national cultures of Europe. That is, the standards of a dead nation killed in other nations those aptitudes through which they themselves had become memorable. Since the Renaissance there have been, strictly speaking, no self-contained national cultures in Europe.[40]

Literature in Irish, it was argued, was the one major literature not so corrupted by the Renaissance. Hence its continuing homeliness, directness, refusal of ornamentation. This is mostly poppycock, of course, but very interesting poppycock insofar as it helps us to understand what the revivalists meant by self-conquest. The task was not so much to become like the Greeks as to reproduce the ways in which the Greeks once had the courage to become and assume their own deepest, destined selves. Every literary movement should, as that of the Greeks did, grow out of the here and now, out of a feeling for immediate locality, out of a given time and place. The good critic is one who can see each text against its enabling context; and that is indeed a cornerstone of the neoclassic criticism practised by Samuel Johnson. The latter wrote: 'Every man's performance must be compared with the state of the age in which he lived and with his opportunities... There is always a silent reference of human works to human abilities, which has a dignity greater than in what rank we shall place any particular performance.'[41] The problem is that Corkery's refusal of any meaningful comparison between literatures

---

[40] Corkery (1924: 12).
[41] Samuel Johnson, 'Preface to Shakespeare', cited from Enright and de Chickera (1962: 123).

leaves each one helplessly marooned within its own space, submitting a literature only to a local franchise. Applying such criteria, Corkery always tended to fetishize tradition and to downplay the individual talent, whereas, for all his flaws, T. S. Eliot knew that literature required a perpetual balancing act between them.

In the end Corkery fetishized Gaelic tradition as classical for much the same reasons that Eliot fetishized Europe: because he grew up outside it and was like a boy with his nose pressed to the window, forever hoping that someone would invite him inside. In this, he was like most of his English-speaking readers. He wanted to believe in the existence of a singular Gaelic mind; and so he ignored the echoes of *amour courtois* in the 'dánta grá' (love poems), or of the Franco-Norman in a Munster word like *garsún* (boy). Classics, he asserted—and this some years after *Ulysses*—cannot be modelled on other classics: the only viable models must be from within a national tradition. For this reason, the only literature of Europe akin to the Irish was the Russian: 'That literature, born too late to share deeply in the scars of the Renaissance, is at once the most national and the most significant of all modern literatures.'[42] On this rather strange basis, Corkery announced in *The Hidden Ireland* that there were six qualities essential to classicism: (i) realism, (ii) homeliness, (iii) rigour, (iv) a sense of community, (v) pride in tribe and place, (vi) humour. These six qualities, he asserts, are notably lacking in most English literature. There was nothing left for Corkery to do, after writing this, than to become Professor of English at University College Cork. He was in truth the A. A. Zdhanov of Irish writing and would probably not have felt at all insulted by such a comparison. Twenty-eight years later, in his essay-preface to *Filí na Máighe* (1952), Corkery's epic list of classical traits remained virtually unchanged:

> Is iad na tréithe is dual do chlasaiceas – nádúrthacht, náisiúntacht, móráltacht, ábhair substintiúla, neamh-phearsantacht agus cothromaíocht.

> The features common to classicism are – nature, nationalism, morality, substantive content, impersonality and equilibrium.

The latter two have been sneaked in, perhaps in deference to Eliot and Pound, but being foreign classicists (and, worse still, Americans) they cannot be named. Nor can Corkery's own dirty little secret be mentioned—that his own most successful texts were written in English and that the Irish in 'Filíocht na Gaeilge' is pretty poor.

Like all who blind themselves to four fifths of reality, Corkery achieved some piercing insights into the one fifth that remained visible to him. He was right to lament the fact that the revival of Irish had by the 1920s fallen into the hands of grammarians. (The hobby of Osborn Bergin, a keen student of bardic poetry, was

---

[42] Corkery (1924: 12).

to walk the streets of Dublin, pencilling in corrections to misprints in the most recent novel by Agatha Christie.) Even in this sad fate, Irish shared something with the classics: it became a happy hunting ground for textualists and pedants (usually of the male persuasion). Corkery's own attempt to counter all this with a developed literary criticism might be seen as a tonic and early instance of postcolonial theory; but his codifying of an Irish classicism went too far, and was deformed by its production within a culture of censorious rule-keeping. Yet there was a kernel of truth in what he said. The Irish Revival was a new Republic of Letters, a new version of the Enlightenment; and in its wilder, earlier phase, just after the besting of Mahaffy and Atkinson, it let the weirdness in. Patrick Pearse's use of the Cúchulainn story, like Joyce's of Odysseus, found in these ancient tales anticipatory illuminations of the worlds out of which they wrote.

These were great moments, when creative artists could align a native modernism with the mind of Europe; and in excavating one, one rediscovers the other, without foolishly feeling the need to privilege either. F. Scott Fitzgerald once said that an artist writes for the youth of today, the critics of tomorrow, and the schoolmasters of ever afterward.[43] The problem with too many classics is that they have become overassociated with the educational process. The classroom is their inevitable destination, of course; but the longer a text avoids the classroom, the more likely it is to survive its eventual academic capture intact. Too many of today's poems (including many good ones), like too many works in the Irish language, have been conceived as if destined from the outset for the college seminar. There are real dangers in the ease with which the word 'modern' can now be so easily appended to the word 'classic'. Nevertheless, the tradition of excavating native modernism through classics has continued to flourish in Ireland in Seamus Heaney's *Aeneid*-inspired poetry or in Marina Carr's versions of Greek tragedies. The study of classical literature against its own backdrop is a worthy enterprise in many of the ways outlined by Corkery: but making a classic our own, making it vibrate again with a contemporary implication, is even more useful and beautiful.

---

[43] The remark was usually attributed to him by Edmund Wilson.

3

Greece, Rome, and the Revolutionaries of 1916

Brian McGing

Walking across College Green in Dublin through the Front Gate of Trinity College would impress on anyone that here was a place where the classical world had laid deep roots. The architectural vocabulary is above all classical, with the old parliament on the left and the facade of the College directly in front. Central to this space is John Foley's wonderful sculptural triumvirate of Trinity graduates: Edmund Burke, Cicero's reincarnation if ever there was one, and Oliver Goldsmith, author of a two-volume history of Rome alongside his more famous writings,[1] look across the Green to Henry Grattan, addressed by Charles James Fox as 'the Irish Demosthenes' (according to Justin McCarthy).[2] If these eighteenth-century Irishmen speak of the past, one does not have to dig very deeply into the contemporary works of Seamus Heaney, Peter Fallon, Michael Longley, Marina Carr, and others, to recognize that the classical strand is still a vigorous part of Irish literature[3]—even if it was not, for much of the twentieth century, part of the central political narrative that demanded the sidelining of anything other than the Gaelic and the Catholic. If Greek and Latin were accepted, it was probably mostly because they were the sacred languages of Catholicism, and hallowed as part of the resistance offered by the hedge schools.[4]

This tension between Ireland's classical and Gaelic heritage, between the legacy of the political past and new emphases more expedient to the present and future, can be felt, for example, in Patrick Pearse's oration for the Irish republican leader Jeremiah O'Donovan Rossa delivered at his funeral on 1 August 1915 in Glasnevin Cemetery (which will be discussed more fully below). It is striking that while the speech contains no hint of a reference to Greek or Roman history or literature, it is stylistically so full of the figures and tropes of Greek and Roman rhetoric that it could almost have been written by Gorgias, Demosthenes, or Cicero. This chapter will address the role played by Greece and Rome in the world of the 1916

---

[1] Goldsmith (1769).   [2] McCarthy (1903: 125).
[3] On the use made by modern Irish poets of classical works see Impens (2018).
[4] On the teaching of Greek and Latin in the hedge schools see Arkins (1991: 203–4), O'Higgins (2017), and also Mac Góráin (Ch. 7).

Brian McGing, *Greece, Rome, and the Revolutionaries of 1916* In: *Classics and Irish Politics, 1916–2016*. Edited by: Isabelle Torrance and Donncha O'Rourke, Oxford University Press (2020). © Oxford University Press.
DOI: 10.1093/oso/9780198864486.003.0003

revolutionaries, considering in particular how Patrick Pearse and Thomas MacDonagh, who worked closely together in the early days of St Enda's school in Ranelagh (and later Rathfarnham), reacted to the classical past.

If the Classics are in this way present 'under erasure' in the Ireland of 1916, this presents an instructive contrast with other revolutionary contexts. Declan Kiberd has valuable observations on the way that revolutionaries mask the newness of their message by wrapping it in old clothing.[5] The French rebels of 1789, for example, 'presented themselves not as revolutionary businessmen but as resurrected Romans, restoring ancient democratic rights'.[6] Some of them even dressed up in Roman togas to be painted. So, too, one might add the Founding Fathers in America. Carl Richard, in his classic study, has shown the deep penetration of classical literature and history into the lives and thinking of the Founding Fathers, and the deep influence, fully acknowledged by them, of the Classics on their political debates and decisions, and ultimately on the American constitution.[7] They, too, dressed their revolution in Greek and Roman clothing. In the Irish context, by contrast, as Kiberd notes, it was James Joyce who 'was learning how to gift-wrap the most subversive narrative of the modernist movement, *Ulysses*, in one of Europe's oldest tales, the *Odyssey* of Homer'.[8] What is interesting is that while the Classics might have been acceptable for literary modernism, in political discourse the gift-wrapping was not Greece or Rome, but Cúchulainn and the Gaelic past.

Shifting Relations: Classical Models in Irish Politics and Popular Culture before Independence

A century earlier, the classical past had been the model of choice, most famously for Edmund Burke. Burke's sustained attack on Warren Hastings, appointed governor-general of Bengal in 1774, impeached in 1787, and finally acquitted in 1795, was consciously modelled on Cicero's famous speeches prosecuting the governor of Sicily, Gaius Verres.[9] In 1800 there was no challenge to the validity of the classical model. In fact, Burke himself was openly supportive of the British imperial project (and conversely hostile to the French Revolution). What he objected to was not Britain's imperial presence in India, but rather the erosion of political sovereignty under the powers of rapacious and damaging mercantile

---

[5] Kiberd (2009: 67–70).   [6] Kiberd (2009: 69).   [7] Richard (1994).
[8] Kiberd (2009: 70).
[9] The importance to Burke of Cicero as a model, and the close correspondence between the Verrine speeches and Burke's against Hastings, have been carefully traced by modern scholars: see, for instance, Carnall (1989: 76–90); Canter (1914: 199–211).

interests (represented by Hastings).[10] At the same time, although the Act of Union deprived Ireland of a forum for its own political oratory, exempla from the classical world continued to appear in popular and political discourse, most famously in Thomas Davis' song *A Nation Once Again* from the 1840s:

> When boyhood's fire was in my blood
> I read of ancient freemen,
> For Greece and Rome who bravely stood,
> Three hundred men and three men.

The battle of Thermopylae in 480 BCE, where Leonidas and his 300 Spartans (and other troops) famously delayed the advance of King Xerxes and his Persian army, and Horatius and his two brothers defending Rome against the Etruscan king Lars Porsenna, were obvious examples of heroic resistance against imperialism for the classically educated Davis, who 'explicitly derived his politics from "the fountain of Greece" and made repeated use of classical models throughout his writings'.[11] In the editorial for 19 July 1848 in *The Nation*—the newspaper Davis founded with Charles Gavan Duffy and John Blake Dillon—Jane Francesca Elgee, the future mother of Oscar Wilde, wrote (in lieu of Davis himself, since he was under arrest at the time):[12]

> Oh, that my words could burn like molten metal through your veins and light up this ancient heroic daring which would make each man of you a Leonidas – each battlefield a Marathon – each pass a Thermopylae.

The battle of Marathon in 490 BCE, at which the Athenians and their allies repulsed the superior forces of the Persian king Darius, is one of the other great exemplars from the classical world that was part of public discourse. Marathon continued to be mentioned from time to time. On 3 December 1904, for instance, the *Kerry Sentinel* described the battle of Clontarf as 'the Marathon of Irish history'. In 1910, the *Strabane Chronicle* for 12 April compared Dr John Hall-Edwards, a pioneer in the use of X-rays who had lost his left arm and some of his right-hand fingers to cancer, to Cynegirus, the Athenian soldier and brother of the famous playwright Aeschylus, who lost both hands at the battle of Marathon (Herodotus 6.114). The *Connaught Telegraph* of 11 November 1905 offered a satire on the Shelbourne Society of Ballyhaunis, which assumed a substantial

---

[10] For further discussion of Burke's exploitation of Cicero, and of Virgil, in his prosecution speeches against Hastings see Vasunia (2013: 257–60).
[11] Dwan (2008: 51–2).   [12] See Bourke (2002: 62).

knowledge of Greek history.[13] And 'A Nation Once Again' remained permanently popular: on Sunday 31 March 1912, for example, it got 'many vigorous airings', when a huge crowd gathered in Dublin to celebrate the British Government's new Home Rule Bill.[14] In spite of occasional references like these, however, Greece and Rome very largely drop out of popular discourse in the second half of the nineteenth century.[15]

The later nineteenth-century decline in classical reference was coincident with the Gaelic Revival, whose influence grew stronger still with the foundation of the Gaelic League in 1893. In a renewed Gaelic world, free from Britain, the history and literature of Greece and Rome could be considered too representative of the British mode of thinking. This was particularly the case with Rome, itself an imperial power. Occasionally coopted for nationalist political purposes, Roman literature and history were more commonly rejected by Irish authors.[16] The hostility is evident in the 'Aeolus episode' of Joyce's *Ulysses*, quoted by Kiberd (Ch. 2), where imperial Rome is aligned with England, both powers being obsessed with water closets. The analogy between the Romans and the British is clear, and in due course that between the Greeks and the Irish also emerges, as Professor MacHugh continues:

KYRIE ELEISON!
A smile of light brightened his darkrimmed eyes, lengthened his long lips.

—The Greek! he said again. *Kyrios!* Shining word! The vowels the Semite and the Saxon know not. *Kyrie!* The radiance of the intellect. I ought to profess Greek, the language of the mind. *Kyrie eleison!* The closetmaker and the cloacamaker will never be lords of our spirit. We are liege subjects of the catholic chivalry of Europe that foundered at Trafalgar and of the empire of the spirit, not an *imperium,* that went under with the Athenian fleets at Ægospotami. Yes, yes. They went under. Pyrrhus, misled by an oracle, made a last attempt to retrieve the fortunes of Greece. Loyal to a lost cause.

He strode away from them towards the window.

—They went forth to battle, Mr O'Madden Burke said greyly, but they always fell.[17]

Mr O'Madden Burke here claims that Ireland is a descendant of the fifth-century BCE Athenian Empire, whose defeat by the Spartan admiral Lysander at the battle

---

[13] Perhaps somewhat strangely, in an editorial of 23 April 1910, the *Butte Independent* compared Irish and ancient Greek history in some detail. What the readers in the US state of Montana made of this would be difficult to say, but the editor was a certain J. B. Mulcahy, and the newspaper was clearly very Catholic and very Irish.
[14] Dooley (2015: 1).   [15] As noted in passing by Stanford (1976: 219).
[16] Dinneen is an exception to this general rule. See Mac Góráin (Ch. 7).
[17] Joyce (1992 [1922]: 169).

of Aegospotami in 405 BCE heralded the end of the Peloponnesian War. Somewhat bizarrely, he also regards the fourth-/third-century BCE Epirote adventurer Pyrrhus as belonging to the same tradition. Mr O'Madden Burke's last sentence, however, although applied to the Greeks, fits rather better in an Irish context. After all, the Athenians enjoyed a century of unprecedented military success and cultural brilliance before their defeat in the Peloponnesian War, and while Pyrrhus was killed in battle when an old lady threw a tile at him from a rooftop in Argos, he had also enjoyed a remarkable career. It was Irishmen, loyal to lost causes, who went forth to battle and always fell.

Gaelic, Greek, and Roman: Tensions in the Work of Pearse and MacDonagh

If the revolutionary generation were seeking to free themselves from Britain's empire, exempla from the Roman Empire could be problematic. But Greek literature, for Joyce (in Professor MacHugh's words) 'the language of the mind', posed a challenge for Patrick Pearse and Thomas MacDonagh. Both wrote works praising Gaelic literature, but felt compelled to confront the brilliance of Greek. Pearse is the more insistent on the superiority of Irish literature over Greek, particularly in his work, *Some Aspects of Irish Literature* (1912). At the start of this essay, Pearse ruminates on what would have happened if the fifteenth century had rediscovered not Greek and Roman literature but Gaelic:

> ...the Celtic would have become the classic and the Gael would have given laws to Europe. I do not say positively that literature would have gained, but I am not sure that it would have lost. Something it would have lost: the Greek ideal of perfection in form, the wise calm Greek scrutiny. Yet something it would have gained: a more piercing vision, a nobler, because a more humane, inspiration, above all a deeper spirituality.[18]

Gaelic superiority is emphasized: 'Now I claim for Irish literature, at its best, these excellences: a clearer than Greek vision, a more generous than Greek humanity, a deeper than Greek spirituality.' He goes on to outline these thoughts in more detail. What he meant was

> that the Irish chivalry and the Irish spirituality which would then have commenced to percolate the literatures of Europe was a finer thing than the spirit of the old classic literatures, more heroic, more gentle, more delicate and mystical.

---

[18] Pearse (1912, CELT edition: 132–3).

And it is remarkable that the most chivalrous inspiration in modern literature does in fact come from a Celtic source: that King Arthur and the Knights of the Round Table have meant more to modern men than the heroes who warred at Troy or than Charlemagne and his Paladins. But how much richer might European literature have been had the story of Cuchulainn become a European possession! For the story of Cuchulainn I take to be the finest epic stuff in the world: as we have it, it is not the most finely-finished epic, but it is, I repeat, the finest epic stuff. I mean not merely that Conor and Fergus and Conall and Cuchulainn are nobler figures, humaner figures, than Agammemnon and Hector and Ulysses and Achilles; not merely that Macha and Meadhbh and Deirdre and Emer are more gracious figures, more appealing figures, than Hecuba and Helen; I mean also that the story itself is greater than any Greek story, the tragedy as pitiful as any Greek tragedy, yet at the same time more joyous, more exultant.[19]

This is a bold statement of Ireland's superiority in the field of epic. Pearse is presumably yielding first place in terms of 'the most finely-finished' epic to Homer, but the story of Cúchulainn is nevertheless presented as more agreeable and successful on multiple levels. In his earlier essay on 'Gaelic Prose Literature' from *Three Lectures on Gaelic Topics*, published in 1898 when he was only 19 years old, Pearse was, perhaps not surprisingly, less confident and not sufficiently assured to claim superiority for Irish literature. There he had said that 'Ireland possesses a more ancient, a more extensive, and a better literature, *wholly of native growth*, than any other European country, with the single exception of Greece'.[20] If in this earlier text Pearse seems to yield pride of place to Greek literature, the association of the Greeks with the Irish is strong, as it is in his lecture, 'The Intellectual Future of the Gael', also published in *Three Lectures on Gaelic Topics*. 'What the Greek was to the ancient world the Gael will be to the modern; and in no point will the parallel prove more true than in the fervent and noble love of learning which distinguishes both races. The Gael, like the Greek, loves learning, and like the Greek, he loves it solely for its own sake.'[21] If Pearse was anxious to push the claims of Irish literature, however, it was not due to a narrow and chauvinistic approach to culture. On the contrary, his great appreciation of classical literature is evident from the appointment in 1910 to the staff of St Enda's, his school in Rathfarnham (Dublin), of Frank Nolan, who had taught Classics at Loreto College in

---

[19] Pearse (1912, CELT edition: 154–5).   [20] Pearse (1898, CELT Edition: 164).
[21] Pearse (1898, CELT Edition: 231).

St Stephen's Green.[22] Latin features every day on the weekly timetable for 1912–13 on display in the museum at St Enda's.[23]

Thomas MacDonagh in his *Literature in Ireland: Studies Irish and Anglo-Irish* (1916) also sets Gaelic literature against the great works of Greek and Latin literature. It would be difficult to imagine that he and Pearse did not discuss the subject, but MacDonagh pursues a different line from Pearse in arguing that the anonymity of Gaelic literature makes it fundamentally different from Greek and Latin. Taking Horace as his example, he argues that classical literature owes its success to convention and the known personality of the writer. 'Some odes of Horace,' he writes, 'with no philosophy and no emotional appeal, with nothing of the thrill of lyric singing are still traditionally admired.'[24] Literatures are judged by great names, and Horace is a great name:

> So we go to our Horace, so we go to our Villon, the scapegrace; so we go to some or other 'marvellous boy,' some 'sleepless soul.'[25] Consciously or unconsciously, we are influenced in reading Keats by the thought of his twenty-five years. The Gaelic Renaissance is only beginning. It can never be of just the same importance and influence as the Classic. It goes back to a literature of a different kind from the Greek and Latin, a literature almost entirely anonymous, a literature without epic or dramatic verse, a literature, as far as poetry is concerned, of fragments – little personal poems, nature poems, religious poems, short dramatic monologues and dramatic lyrics interspersed in prose tales. And yet it has been claimed for this remnant of literature, and claimed by the best authority in the matter, Doctor Kuno Meyer,[26] that as 'the earliest voice from the dawn of West

---

[22] See Walsh (2007: 236). In addition, Dr Patrick Doody taught Greek and Latin in St Enda's, although badly, according to an inspector's report, in spite of the fact that he was the only teacher on the staff who had a PhD; and Thomas MacDonagh also taught Latin: see Walsh (2007: 253–5). The Prospectus of Scoil Éanna in 1909 states that 'Latin is taught to all boys in the upper forms, and Greek and Old Irish to such as exhibit an aptitude for classical studies': see Ó Buachalla (1980: 318).

[23] It is instructive to note Pearse's comments in *The Murder Machine* (1916c, CELT Edition: 7–9) comparing British education in Ireland to ancient systems of slavery: 'Professor Eoin MacNeill has compared the English education system in Ireland to the systems of slave education which existed in the ancient pagan republics side by side with the systems intended for the education of freemen. To the children of the free were taught all noble and goodly things which would tend to make them strong and proud and valiant; from the children of the slaves all such dangerous knowledge was hidden. They were taught not to be strong and proud and valiant, but to be sleek, to be obsequious, to be dexterous: the object was not to make them good men, but to make them good slaves. And so in Ireland. The education system here was designed by our masters in order to make us willing or at least manageable slaves.'

[24] MacDonagh (1916: 104–5).

[25] Taken from Wordsworth's *Resolution and Independence*: 'I thought of Chetterton, the marvellous boy | the sleepless soul that perished in his prime.'

[26] Kuno Meyer (1858–1919) was a famous scholar of Celtic Studies, whose pro-German speech in August 1914 to Clan na Gael in America caused great scandal. For his brilliant and colourful career see Ó Lúing (1991). Hall (Ch. 10) argues that James Joyce may well have been influenced by Meyer's English translation of the medieval Irish version of Homer's *Odyssey*.

European civilization, it is the most primitive and original among the literatures of Western Europe.' Most original, and of not least intrinsic worth. It is a fragment. It must not be judged as if it were a fragment of a literature of the Hellenic kind. The difference between Greek and Gael is no fiction.

If MacDonagh was no great admirer of Horace, Greek and Latin did influence the poetry that he himself wrote. Even the title of his first collection, *Through the Ivory Gate* (1902), betrays a classical heritage, taken as it was originally from Penelope's account in Homer's *Odyssey* of false dreams coming through the gate of ivory, true dreams through the gate of horn (*Od.* 19.560–9). MacDonagh had a particular admiration for Catullus; and he also fashioned a fine poem around a line of Lucretius, *Luna dies et nox et noctis signa severa* (Lucr. 5.1190). In another poem entitled, 'Of a Greek Poem', MacDonagh seems to regret his 'far pursuing' investigation of the classics and neglect of 'the lamps of home'.[27]

Both Pearse and MacDonagh, then, embraced classical learning in their writing and approach to education, but in Pearse's case it also profoundly influenced his public speaking. Nowhere is this clearer than in his oration for O'Donovan Rossa.[28] I have drawn attention, by underlining, to the repeated use of classical rhetorical techniques: epanaphora (the repetition of the same words or phrases at the beginnings of successive cola); polysyndeton (the repeated use of conjunctions in close proximity); chiastic structure (i.e. ABBA); antithesis. Pearse opened his oration with an introduction in Irish, which is worth quoting here to highlight the combination of Irish and classicizing modes of expression present in the speech:

A Ghaedheala

Do hiarradh orm-sa labhairt indiu ar son a bhfuil cruinnighthe ar an láthair so agus ar son a bhfuil beo de Chlannaibh Gaedheal, ag moladh an leomhain do leagamar i gcré annso agus ag gríosadh meanman na gcarad atá go brónach ina dhiaidh.

A cháirde, ná bíodh brón ar éinne atá ina sheasamh ag an uaigh so, acht bíodh buidheachas againn inar gcroidhthibh do Dhia na ngrás do chruthuigh anam uasal áluinn Dhiarmuda Uí Dhonnabháin Rosa agus thug ré fhada dhó ar an saoghal so.

Ba chalma an fear thu, a Dhiarmuid. Is tréan d'fhearais cath ar son cirt do chine, is ní beag ar fhuilingis; agus ní dhéanfaidh Gaedhil dearmad ort go bráth na breithe.

---

[27] Moloney (Ch. 4) discusses the classical influences on MacDonagh's poetry in more detail. Latin also affected some of the poetry of Joseph Plunkett: see, for instance, his poem, 'Nomina sunt consequentia rerum' (a quotation from Justinian), and the Latin titles of others: 'Arbor vitae' and 'Occulta'.

[28] The Irish text is transcribed in roman typeface from Pearse (1917–22: 133); for assistance with the text and translation the editors are grateful to Fiachra Mac Góráin. The English section is reproduced as it appears in the manuscript version of the oration on display in St Enda's, which is slightly different from the CELT edition (133–7) available online at https://celt.ucc.ie/published/E900007-008/text001.html (accessed 11 March 2020).

Acht, a cháirde, ná bíodh brón orainn, acht bíodh misneach inar gcroidhthibh agus bíodh neart inar gcuisleannaibh, óir cuimhnighimís nach mbíonn aon bhás ann nach mbíonn aiséirghe ina dhiaidh, agus gurab as an uaigh so agus as na huaghannaibh atá inar dtimcheall éireochas saoirse Ghaedheal.

[Fellow Gaels

I was asked to speak today on behalf of those gathered in this place and on behalf of the living members of our Gaelic Clans, to praise the lion that we have buried here and to bolster the courage of the friends who grieve after him.

Friends, let no one grieve who is standing at this grave, but let us be thankful in our hearts to the God of grace who created the fine and noble spirit of Jeremiah O'Donovan Rossa and gave him a long span in this life.

A brave man you were, Jeremiah. Fiercely did you wage war for the rights of your race, and not a little did you suffer; and Gaels will never forget you.

But, friends, let us not grieve, but let there be courage in our hearts and strength in our veins, for let us remember that there is no death without resurrection after it, and that it is from this grave and the graves around us that the freedom of the Gaels will arise.]

It has been thought right, before we turn away from this place in which we have laid the mortal remains of O'Donovan Rossa, that one amongst us should, in the name of all, speak the praise of that valiant man, and endeavour to formulate the thought and the hope that are in us as we stand around his grave. And if there is anything that makes it fitting that I rather than another, I rather than one of the grey-haired men who were young with him, and shared in his labour and in his suffering, should speak here, it is, perhaps, that I may be taken as speaking on behalf of a new generation that has been re-baptised in the Fenian faith, and that has accepted the responsibility of carrying out the Fenian programme. I propose to you, then, that here by the grave of this unrepentant Fenian, we renew our baptismal vows; that here by the grave of this unconquered and unconquerable man, we ask of God, each one for himself, such unshakeable purpose, such high and gallant courage, such unbreakable strength of soul as belonged to O'Donovan Rossa.

Deliberately here we avow ourselves, as he avowed himself in the dock, Irishmen of one allegiance only. We, of the Irish Volunteers, and you others who are associated with us in to-day's task and duty, are bound together, and must stand together henceforth in brotherly union for the achievement of the freedom of Ireland. And we know only one definition of freedom: It is Tone's definition;[29] it is Mitchel's definition; it is Rossa's definition. Let no one

---

[29] Evidence of the tensions within Pearse's own thoughts on Ireland and the classical tradition may be seen in his Caesarian analogy for Tone as a democrat in *The Separatist Idea*, Pearse (1916b, CELT edition: 283–4): 'And Tone, the greatest of modern Irish Separatists, is the first and greatest of modern Irish democrats. It was Tone that said: "Our independence must be had at all hazards. If the men of property will not support us, they must fall: we can support ourselves by the aid of that numerous and respectable class of the community the men of no property." In this glorious appeal to Caesar modern Irish democracy has its origin.'

blaspheme the cause that the dead generations of Ireland served by giving it any other <u>name and definition</u> than their <u>name and definition</u>.

We stand at Rossa's grave, <u>not in sadness, but rather in exaltation</u> of spirit that it has been given us to come thus into so close a communion with that brave and splendid Gael. <u>Splendid and holy causes are served by men who are themselves splendid and holy</u>. O'Donovan Rossa was <u>splendid in</u> the proud manhood of him - <u>splendid in</u> the heroic grace of him, <u>splendid in</u> the Gaelic strength <u>and</u> clarity <u>and</u> truth of him. <u>And</u> all that splendour, <u>and</u> pride, <u>and</u> strength was compatible with a humility and a simplicity of devotion to Ireland, to all that was olden <u>and</u> beautiful <u>and</u> Gaelic in Ireland; the holiness and simplicity of patriotism of a Michael O'Clery or of an Eoghan O'Growney. The clear true eyes of this man almost alone in his day visioned Ireland as we to-day would surely have her – <u>not free merely but Gaelic as well; not Gaelic merely, but free as well.</u>

<u>In a closer spiritual communion</u> with him now than ever before, or perhaps ever again, <u>in spiritual communion</u> with those of his day living and dead, who suffered with him in English prisons, <u>in communion of spirit too</u> with our own dear comrades who suffer in English prisons to-day, and speaking on their behalf as well as our own, <u>we pledge to Ireland our love, and we pledge to English rule in Ireland our hate</u>. This is a place of peace, sacred to the dead, where men should speak with all charity and with all restraint; but I hold it a Christian thing, as O'Donovan Rossa held it, <u>to hate evil, to hate untruth, to hate oppression</u>, and hating them, to strive to overthrow them. Our foes are <u>strong, and wise, and wary</u>; but <u>strong and wise and wary</u> as they are, they cannot undo the miracles of God, Who ripens in the hearts of young men <u>the seeds sown by the young men</u> of a former generation. And <u>the seeds sown by the young men</u> of '65 and '67 are coming to their miraculous ripening to-day. Rulers and Defenders of Realms had need to be wary if they would guard against such processes. <u>Life springs from death, and from the graves of patriot men and women spring live nations</u>. The defenders of this realm have worked well <u>in secret and in the open</u>. <u>They think that they have pacified</u> Ireland. <u>They think that they have</u> purchased half of us, and intimidated the other half. <u>They think that they have</u> foreseen everything. <u>They think that they have</u> provided against everything; but <u>the fools, the fools, the fools</u>! They have left us our Fenian dead, and while Ireland holds these graves, Ireland unfree shall never be at peace.

I am not qualified to comment on the quality and rhetoric of Pearse's Irish, but it does him a great disservice to omit the Irish opening of this oration (as many online versions do). His speech was a remarkable fusion of Irish, English, and the classical. How did he learn to write in such a classical mode? In the past, there had been rhetorical handbooks. In the eighteenth century, works by two Trinity Professors of Oratory had been particularly influential: Thomas Leland's *A Dissertation on the Principles of Human Eloquence* (1764) and John Lawson's

Lectures Concerning Oratory (1758). They were responding to pressure that Trinity College provide practical training for use in the parliament across the road.[30] Both Leland and Lawson taught Burke. Leland's translation of the orations of Demosthenes was also much used for oratorical education, becoming 'the model for the Anglo-Irish tradition of parliamentary speaking'.[31] In America one of the most influential handbooks for the eighteenth and nineteenth centuries was Hugh Blair's *Lectures on Rhetoric and Belles-Lettres* (Edinburgh 1783), adopted as a standard text in Harvard and Yale in the 1780s and thereafter by numerous American colleges.[32] Were any of these works used by Pearse? Joost Augusteijn claims that Pearse 'was known to study rhetoric actively, in particular through Yeats', and Ruth Dudley-Edwards talks of Pearse speaking at the school debating society in Westland Row in what a fellow student described as 'the grand manner', 'a style,' she writes, 'which from then on would characterize all his oratorical endeavours'.[33] For someone steeped in classical literature and the oratory of Burke, Grattan, and other Irish parliamentarians, perhaps there was no need of special rhetorical training or handbooks, and the oration for O'Donovan Rossa just flowed naturally from his pencil.[34]

If it is not possible to trace exactly how Pearse acquired his classical style of public speaking, neither did he have an obvious model for the content of the O'Donovan Rossa oration. Pat Cooke has argued for the influence of both Thomas Carlyle and English literary romanticism on Pearse's writings in general, and in particular of Shelley on the line, 'Life springs from death, and from the graves of patriot men and women spring live nations'.[35] Pearse himself, he points out, had written, 'Life springs from death, life lives on death', in the 1910 issue of *An Macaomh*, the school magazine of St Enda's; and in his pamphlet, *The Sovereign People* (1916), Pearse quotes from John Mitchel's discussion of the relationship between destruction and construction, death and birth, in which Mitchel quotes a line from Shelley's poem, *Lines Written on Hearing of the Death of Napoleon*: 'the quick spring like weeds out of the dead'. It is not clear whether Pearse recognizes the line of Shelley, but it is clear that Mitchel, and Pearse's justification of Mitchel's message of hate, are echoed in parts of the O'Donovan Rossa oration. In *The Sovereign People*, Pearse responds to the accusation that Mitchel's gospel of hate was 'barren':

---

[30] Bullard (2011: 52–3; 67–71).   [31] Welch (1996: 306).

[32] For the widespread use of Blair's *Lectures* see Horner (1993: 176).

[33] Augusteijn (2009: 8); Dudley-Edwards (1977: 16).

[34] My colleague, Patrick Geoghegan, of the Department of History at Trinity College Dublin informs me by email that Daniel O'Connell, the nineteenth-century Irish politician who campaigned for Catholic emancipation, knew his classical texts well, Cicero and Demosthenes among them. He says that 'his actual oratory training came from attending debates in the British House of Commons, some debating societies, and studying voice projection at the theatre'.

[35] Cooke (2009: 49–50).

The answer to this is – first, that love and hate are not mutually antagonistic but mutually complementary; that love connotes hate, hate of the thing that denies or destroys or threatens the thing beloved: that love of good connotes hate of evil, love of truth hate of falsehood, love of freedom hate of oppression; that hate may be as pure and good a thing as love, just as love may be as impure and evil a thing as hate; that hate is no more ineffective and barren than love, both being as necessary to moral sanity and growth as sun and storm are to physical life and growth. And, secondly, that Mitchel, the least apologetic of men, was at pains to explain that his hate was not of English men and women, but of the English thing which called itself a government in Ireland...[36]

In the Rossa oration, Pearse is careful to observe what he regards as Mitchel's distinction between English men and women, and English government in Ireland: 'we pledge to Ireland our love, and we pledge to English rule in Ireland our hate.' In both works we find repeated the hatred of evil, falsehood, and oppression, and the same idea that the people of Ireland have either been bought or intimidated (with the exception, in *The Sovereign People*, of the common people, who have for the most part remained 'unbought and unterrified'). There are similar sentiments in the address Pearse delivered at the Emmet Commemoration in the Aeolian Hall, New York, on 9 March 1914:

> When England thinks she has trampled out our battle in blood, some brave man rises and rallies us again; when England thinks she has purchased us with a bribe, some good man redeems us by a sacrifice...There can be no peace between right and wrong, between truth and falsehood, between justice and oppression, between freedom and tyranny. Between them it is eternal war until wrong is righted, until the true thing is established, until justice is accomplished, until freedom is won.[37]

The repetition of 'England thinks' they have defeated us, 'England thinks' they have bought us, is surely echoed in the oration's famous ending, 'they think they have pacified Ireland. They think they have purchased half of us...'; and there is another variation on the theme of defeating evil and oppression, and achieving freedom. It seems, then, that Pearse found the details for the oration in his own ideas, experiences, and words. But are there, perhaps, other inspirations? Two other famous funeral speeches come to mind—Pericles' speech for the first Athenian casualties of the Peloponnesian War reported in Thucydides (2.34–46), and Abraham Lincoln's Gettysburg address, which was itself to some extent modelled on the paradigm of Thucydides.[38]

---

[36]   Pearse (1916a, CELT edition: 366).
[37]   Published in Pearse (1915, CELT edition: 76–7).
[38]   I am grateful to Ciaran Brady, another of my colleagues from the History Department at Trinity College Dublin, for drawing my attention to the possibility of Lincoln's speech as an inspiration for Pearse. For a discussion of Thucydides' influence on Lincoln see Wills (1992: 41–62).

Thucydides, Lincoln, and Pearse

Pearse visited the United States for three months in 1914. He was mostly based in New York, but also gave lectures in Wilmington, Delaware and Philadelphia.[39] This was all very much Civil War territory, and Irish participation in the war, and the recruitment of Irish veterans to the Fenian cause in America and Ireland, are well attested.[40] The Fenian proclamation of the Irish Republic in 1867 includes the words, 'All men are born with equal rights', and although this could be an echo of the American Declaration of Independence in 1776 ('We hold these truths to be self-evident, that all men are created equal, that they are endowed by their creator with certain inalienable rights…'), it might also reflect a familiarity with Lincoln's more recent, and widely celebrated, expression of the same sentiment in his Gettysburg address ('Four score and seven years ago our fathers brought forth on this continent a new nation, conceived in Liberty, and dedicated to the proposition that all men are created equal…'). O'Donovan Rossa was in America in June and July 1863, and he recalls on the day after the battle of Gettysburg (1–3 July) meeting Captain William O'Shea, of the 42nd New York Regiment, the Tammany Regiment. O'Shea, who was known to Rossa as a fellow inmate some years earlier in Cork gaol, was wounded in the battle, along with many other Fenian casualties.[41] Rossa refers to the battle of Gettysburg six times in his *Recollections*,[42] all mentioning the Irish casualties he knew. One of Pearse's main promoters in America was the famous Fenian John Devoy, a close friend of Rossa, and although Devoy did not go into exile in the United States until 1871, he had already developed close associations with the Irish veterans of the American Civil War who had come over to Ireland to take part in the planned Fenian rising.[43] The extensive association of Irishmen with the Civil War, including the battle of Gettysburg, the fame of Lincoln's address, and Pearse's evident interest in oratory, make it very unlikely that Pearse was not familiar with Lincoln's speech at Gettysburg. This is not, of course, proof that he was influenced by it, but certain elements of Pearse's oration recall Lincoln's words at Gettysburg:

> Four score and seven years ago our fathers brought forth on this continent, a new nation, conceived in Liberty, and dedicated to the proposition that all men are created equal.

---

[39] See Dudley-Edwards (1977: 184–97) for detailed coverage of Pearse's trip to in the United States.

[40] Among many studies see especially Bruce (2006); Callaghan (2006); Gleeson (2013). For American officers in the Fenian uprising of 1867 see Ó Cathaoir (2018: 141–5).

[41] O'Donovan Rossa (1898: 382–3). For further coverage of O'Shea and other Fenians at the battle of Gettysburg see ' "Fearless Captain Billy O'", Forgotten Fenians of the American Civil War', 9 March 2018, on the excellent website, *Irish in the American Civil War*, at https://irishamericancivilwar.com/ (accessed 15 February 2020).

[42] O'Donovan Rossa (1898: 144, 174, 219, 258, 318, 382).   [43] See Golway (2015: 33–45).

Now we are engaged in a great civil war, testing whether that nation, or any nation so conceived and so dedicated, can long endure. We are met on a great battlefield-field of that war. We have come to dedicate a portion of that field, as a final resting place for those who here gave their lives that that nation might live. It is altogether fitting and proper that we should do this.

But, in a larger sense, we can not dedicate – we can not consecrate – we can not hallow – this ground. The brave men, living and dead, who struggled here, have consecrated it, far above our poor power to add or detract. The world will little note, nor long remember what we say here, but it can never forget what they did here. It is for us the living, rather, to be dedicated here to the unfinished work which they who fought here have thus far so nobly advanced. It is rather for us to be here dedicated to the great task remaining before us – that from these honored dead we take increased devotion to that cause for which they gave the last full measure of devotion – that we here highly resolve that these dead shall not have died in vain – that this nation, under God, shall have a new birth of freedom – and that government of the people, by the people, for the people, shall not perish from the earth.[44]

Abraham Lincoln
November 19, 1863

Lincoln and Pearse were both standing in a cemetery when delivering their orations. For Lincoln, it was 'altogether fitting and proper' that they dedicate a part of the Gettysburg battlefield as a final resting place for those who died. For Pearse, 'it has been thought right' to praise O'Donovan Rossa on behalf of those who stand around his grave, and it is 'fitting' that it should be Pearse. Lincoln praises those who died in the battle. Rossa died of old age and illness in hospital, but Pearse describes him (in the Irish introduction) as someone who 'fiercely waged war'. So, like the Gettysburg dead, Rossa is also, in some sense, a warrior. For Lincoln, it is the living who must complete the work of the soldiers who died, and resolve that they did not die in vain and that the nation shall have a new birth of freedom. This was a bold restatement of the Declaration of Independence, and Lincoln consciously had in mind the freedom of slaves. Freedom (from the slavery of British rule) was also Pearse's main concern. For him, the freedom of Ireland will rise from Rossa's grave, but it is those who stand around his grave who must achieve the freedom of Ireland: like Lincoln, Pearse's whole emphasis is on the duty of the living to complete the work of the dead. And perhaps most striking of all is the notion of the dead giving life to the nation: at Gettysburg, the combatants 'gave their lives that the nation might live' (Lincoln used the word 'nation' five times in his address), while for Pearse 'Life springs from death, and from the

---

[44] I quote the Bliss version.

graves of patriot men and women spring live nations.' These are sufficiently close similarities to think that somewhere on his American trip, or through American connections, Pearse had encountered Lincoln's famous words, and that some of the president's language and ideas had, even subconsciously, filtered into the oration for O'Donovan Rossa.

Pearse and the Greek Funeral Oration

In his various references to Greek literature, Pearse nowhere speaks of Greek historians. When considering which races have contributed most to the intellectual advancement of mankind, he certainly thinks first of the Greeks, 'the pioneers of intellectual progress in Europe', and he identifies them as giving us 'the world's greatest epic poet, the world's greatest orator, several of the world's greatest lyric poets, dramatists and philosophers'.[45] Presumably by 'the world's greatest orator' he means Demosthenes, and thus reveals his interest in oratory, but neither here nor anywhere else does Pearse discuss the famous Greek historians Herodotus, Thucydides, and Xenophon, or classical Athens and its history. While there is no specific detail in the Rossa oration that immediately recalls the speech of Pericles, it is unlikely that Pearse did not know it, given his close interest in Greek literature. But if Pearse was familiar with Demosthenes, as he implies, he would have known Demosthenes' funeral speech (Dem. 60), and perhaps that of Lysias, too, and there are certainly close similarities between his oration for O'Donovan Rossa and Greek funeral orations (*epitaphioi*) in terms of style, type of content, and purpose.[46]

Standard elements in the *epitaphioi* include the following:[47] the difficulty of composing adequate praise for the fallen; praise of ancestors; episodes of Athens' mythic and historical past; Athens' cultural leadership and championing of Greek freedom; consolation and exhortation for the living. Pearse does not make the famous distinction of the *epitaphioi* between word and deed (*logos* and *ergon*)— he does not explicitly draw attention to the inadequacy of his words to describe the deeds of the fallen in the way Pericles, other Greek orators, and Lincoln did— but he does begin, as they did, with the task of the orator, and there is perhaps a hint of the inadequacy of words in his description of that task: the speaker can only 'endeavour to formulate the thoughts and hopes that are in us all'. He then goes on to praise the dead man and mentions some of the glorious personalities and moments of Irish history, and although he does not quite reproduce the formal consolation of *epitaphioi*, he does describe his purpose, in the Irish introduction,

---

[45] 'The Intellectual Future of the Gael', from *Three Lectures on Gaelic Topics*, Pearse (1898, CELT edition: 222).

[46] The standard work on Athenian funeral oratory is Loraux (1986). On Lysias' funeral oration, and the form of the *epitaphios* in general, see Grethlein (2010: 105–25).

[47] See, for instance, Usher (1999: 350).

as consolatory—to give courage to the friends who mourn O'Donovan Rossa. In its overall function, this is recognizably a relative of the Greek funeral oration. As Chris Carey has observed, 'Though its obvious function is to praise the dead, which it does, like all funerary activity the *epitaphios logos* is more for the living than the dead. While commemmorating the achievements of the specific hono-randi, it locates them in a larger tradition and, in the process, defines the group present at the event... It thus becomes an act of collective self-definition and self-assertion.'[48] This is surely, above all, what Pearse's oration is—an act of collective self-definition and self-assertion for the living.

The Tenacity of Classical Models: Conclusions

Ireland in the early twentieth century was a land in which the classical past was still a substantial part of Irish identity. In 1871 in the 574 'superior' schools of the state, that is, schools in which a foreign language was taught, 9,440 students were enrolled in Latin, 6,605 in Greek.[49] That sort of enrolment must have produced a very large number of people in the revolutionary generation who knew their clas-sical authors and history. In the face of a new Gaelic past, popular and political discourse may have had a tense relationship with the classical past, but neither Pearse nor MacDonagh attempted to abandon their classical heritage. They both embraced it warmly, MacDonagh in his poetry, and both of them in their writings on Gaelic literature. If Patrick Pearse went to the well of Irish history for the contents of his oration at the funeral of O'Donovan Rossa, the style and form of the speech were thoroughly Greek. Moreover, he was surely aware, as Declan Kiberd has argued, of the classical setting for the reading of the Proclamation of Independence in 1916, standing as he was between the great Ionic columns of the General Post Office (GPO).[50] Pearse and his colleagues may not have dressed their revolution in classical clothing, but underneath their green uniform, the classical toga still showed through. I do not mean to imply that it was intention-ally hidden. While his major intellectual engagement with the Classics was with Greek literature because of the challenge it posed to his championing of Gaelic literature, Pearse had no difficulty in making use of the Latin language in his thinking. His assessment of Thomas Davis is a fitting place to end:

> The highest form of genius is the genius for sanctity, the genius for noble life and thought. That genius was Davis's. Character is the greatest thing in a man; and Davis's character was such as the Apollo Belvidere is said to be in the physical order – in his presence all men stood more erect.

---

[48] Carey (2010: 243).   [49] Coolahan (1981: 59–60).
[50] Kiberd (1995: 206–7), who notes Michael Collins's comment on the events of Easter 1916 as having 'the air of a Greek tragedy'. On the significance of the GPO's classical architecture in narratives of Irish independence see O'Neill (Ch. 19).

The Romans had a noble word which summed up all moral beauty and all private and civic valour: the word *virtus*. If English had as noble a word as that, it would be the word to apply to the thing which made Thomas Davis so great a man.[51]

It is striking that Latin is the language of choice here to describe a great champion of Irish nationalism.

[51] *The Spiritual Nation*, Pearse (1916d, CELT edition: 328–9).

4

Classics in the Van of the Irish Revolt

Thomas MacDonagh, 'alien to Athens and Rome'?

Eoghan Moloney

Thomas MacDonagh and the 1916 Rebels

Shortly after the tumultuous events of April 1916, in the days after the execution of Patrick Pearse, Thomas Clarke, and Thomas MacDonagh, Joyce Kilmer's 'Poets Marched in the Van of the Irish Revolt' was published in *The New York Times* magazine (Fig. 4.1). Kilmer's article is an often-noted contemporary response to the events of the Easter Rising. Offering a series of idealized biographies of those involved at the 'highest levels' of the recent action back in Ireland, it demonstrates just how quickly the ideal of a 'rally of the bards to the 1916 standard' came about.[1] The playwright and poet Padraic Colum, based in New York at the time, was Kilmer's key source for the piece and it is his distinctive vision of a nationalist movement and rebellion led by authors and artists—many old colleagues of Colum's—that is presented to readers. Consequently, the Rising is recast as 'A poetic revolution—indeed, a poets' revolution—that is what has been happening in Ireland during the last two weeks'.[2] In a memorable image, the rebels are presented as 'almost without exception, men of literary tastes and training, who went into battle, as one of the dispatches from Dublin phrased it, "with a revolver in one hand and a copy of Sophocles in the other"'.[3]

The picture painted in the 'Dublin dispatches' is a striking one. Perhaps we might have expected that the leaders of this revolution would keep copies of W. B. Yeats's nationalist drama *Cathleen ni Houilhan* as a close companion, rather than the work of an ancient Athenian playwright. Of course, invoking the classical here brought a certain gravitas to the piece and its presentation of the key figures in

---

[1] Martin (1967: 17). On this long-standing tendency to refashion the Rising as a cultural and religious act, downplaying the politics and violence involved, see Allen (2016: 156–7) and O'Malley-Younger (2016: 455–67).

[2] Murray (2016: 105–17) reviews Colum's attempts to shape the public impression of the rebellion. On the presentation of the rebel leaders in Irish nationalist journals see Murphy (2017: 47–56), who suggests that the broader consideration of 'non-political qualities' in their portraits was, in part, a consequence of official restrictions on the discussion of recent events.

[3] As quoted in Kilmer (1916: 3).

Eoghan Moloney, *Classics in the Van of the Irish Revolt: Thomas MacDonagh, 'alien to Athens and Rome'?* In: *Classics and Irish Politics, 1916–2016.* Edited by: Isabelle Torrance and Donncha O'Rourke, Oxford University Press (2020).
© Oxford University Press.
DOI: 10.1093/oso/9780198864486.003.0004

Fig. 4.1. The first page of Joyce Kilmer's article on the Easter Rising, published in *The New York Times* magazine 7 May 1916.

the Rising as 'serious thinkers and writers', and it was part of a considered response by Colum to contemporary criticism of the rebels.[4] His vision of the rebel leaders presents men inspired by both the spiritual and the intellectual, by both ancient and modern ideals, as we see in the series of articles and interviews he produced

---

[4] Schmuhl (2016: 49). We must note that not all of *The New York Times* accounts of the trouble in Ireland were quite so positive. See Foley (2016: 7–8): 'However generous and romantic the Joyce Kilmer article was, much of the coverage in *The New York Times* was in the main anti the rising and even anti-Irish.'

through 1916.[5] For example, in his defence of Sir Roger Casement in the *Gaelic American* (6 May), Colum looks to Casement's sonnet 'Hamilcar Barca' when describing the man who thought of himself as one 'such as the ancient Punic champion' in his defence of the Irish people and a 'Celtic faith'.[6] Similarly, in his introduction to the collection *Poems of the Irish Revolutionary Brotherhood* (published in July 1916), Colum notes of his friend Thomas MacDonagh:

> ...His dream was always of action – of a man dominating a crowd for a great end. The historical figures that appealed straight to him were the Gracchi and the Irish military leader of the seventeenth century, Owen Roe O'Neill. In the lives of these three there was the drama that appealed to him – the thoughtful man become revolutionist; the preparation of the crowd; the fierce conflict and the catastrophe. Many things Thomas MacDonagh said and wrote were extraordinarily prophetic. Most prophetic of all was his mental dramatization of the end of Tiberius Gracchus. At last he, too, had the ascendancy over the crowd; he saw the conflict in the city, and he faced the vengeance of the capitalists and the imperialists.[7]

However, Colum's colourful defence of the rebel leaders in such terms, and particularly this vision of Thomas MacDonagh, is somewhat at odds with some later evaluations. The most distinguished of the Easter Poets, MacDonagh was later recast in popular rhetoric as 'the perfect, tragic fusion of literature and politics in Ireland',[8] and, as is the case with so many of those involved in the insurrection, his role in the Rising has tended to overshadow all else in the consideration of his life. Idealized as *the* Irish 'poet-martyr', the 'hyper-nationalist impulse' of subsequent decades marginalized the broader cultural inclusiveness evident in MacDonagh's literary output and also the particular influence of the classical tradition on his work.[9]

Of course, in pursuing that narrower vision of the writer's work, and in discounting the classical influences that also shaped it, later commentators would develop key themes first presented in the discourse of the Irish Literary Revival

---

[5]   See Murray (2016: 110): as early as an interview published in *The New York Times* on 30 April, Colum was sure to characterize the leaders of the rebellion as 'no mere hot-headed fanatics, but resolute, thoughtful men'.

[6]   Colum (1916: 4–5). On this 'Celtic faith', Colum notes that it is 'the faith that Ireland has a separate destiny, and has the right to create a culture and a competence for herself' (4).

[7]   Colum and O'Brien (1916: xxx–xxxi). Colum would again compare MacDonagh to 'one of the Gracchi' in *The Irish Rebellion of 1916 and its Martyrs: Erin's Tragic Easter*, published at the end of 1916.

[8]   Storey (1988: 8). In June 1916, *Studies: An Irish Quarterly Review* began a series considering the literary work of the 'Poets of the Insurrection'; the first of these, an anonymous article by 'X. Z.' (actually Fr George O'Neill, Professor of English Language at University College Dublin) focuses on MacDonagh as the most established writer of the group.

[9]   Bullock (2014: 184–5) on that 'imagined afterlife' of MacDonagh; see Smyth (2000: 48) and Smyth (1998: 82–3) on the narrow focus of many later nationalist presentations.

itself, where we can see an ambiguous engagement with, and consideration of, antiquity.[10] From George Siegerson down to W. B. Yeats, there were many who maintained that the eminent position and influence of classical culture represented a rival to the revived Irish, Celtic, Gaelic literature.[11] We might note, briefly, Patrick Pearse's essay 'Some aspects of Irish literature', and the boast there that early Irish writers

> ...saw certain gracious things more clearly and felt certain mystic things more acutely and heard certain deep music more perfectly than did men in ancient Greece. And it is from Greece that we have received our standards...
>
> Now I claim for Irish literature, at its best, these excellences: a clearer than Greek vision, a more generous than Greek humanity, a deeper than Greek spirituality. And I claim that Irish literature has never lost those excellences: that they are of the essence of Irish nature and are characteristic of modern Irish folk poetry even as they are of ancient Irish epic and of mediaeval Irish hymns.[12]

As McGing shows in the previous chapter, however, these claims for the superiority of the Irish tradition over the classical are not straightforward, and Pearse's works reveal an uneasy rivalry between Irish and classical models as sources for inspiration. Moreover, while the contest of cultures that played out during the Revival could produce strident rejections of the hegemonic status of the classical tradition, these did not represent a standard response to the classical world.[13] Even beyond any test of authoritative traditions, there was often no standard response to 'classics' across the work of individuals.[14] Consequently, whether offering a challenge to classical literature or acknowledging affinities between Gael and Greek, it is not the case that 'appeals to classical precedents became rarer' in the cultural discourse of the period.[15] Instead, a dual dialogue with the ancient past

---

[10] Lloyd (2011: 52).

[11] See Richards (1991: 120–4), particularly his discussion of Yeats's 'The Literary Movement in Ireland' (1899). For notes on various contemporary responses to the classical—from J. P. Mahaffy to Patrick Pearse—consider the opening chapter of Fiona Macintosh's *Dying Acts* (1994: 2–14), still an essential starting point for those interested in this topic.

[12] Pearse (1924: 132–3). This passage is noted by both Stanford (1976: 218) and Macintosh (1994: 8–9).

[13] The clear distinctions drawn by Hall and Stead (2015: 1–19) are useful, distinguishing 'between "Classics" as an educational discipline and "classics" as the cultural products of ancient Greece and Rome' (3). Even in an age where 'the classical student is bred to the purple', as Louis MacNeice put it, the rejection of Classics' elite connotations by cultural nationalists did not necessarily require abandoning key texts and narratives.

[14] Crucial observations made by Macintosh (1994: 2–4). Even Pearse would urge students in St Enda's to harden their minds by reading Plato (see Murphy 2017: 132–4), and we find classical allusions in the few examples of verse he composed (e.g. in 'The World Hath Conquered, The Wind Hath Scattered Like Dust'). On Pearse's debts to classical oratory see McGing (Ch. 3).

[15] As Stanford (1976: 219) would have it, a view rightly challenged by Macintosh (1994: 3): 'Stanford, it appears, has fallen victim to nationalist rhetoric in taking a public disavowal of the classical tradition as fact, and has consequently failed to note that Irish independence was fuelled by classical example no less than other nationalist movements.'

continued and those who saw themselves both as a part of, or apart from, the Literary Revival still produced classicizing works. And yet while the influence of Greece and Rome on the work of some notables such as Yeats or Synge has been well noted previously,[16] there is still much to consider. What of the engagement of the other 'insurgent intellectuals' with classical culture, for example?[17] MacDonagh's writings certainly present an illuminating case study of a nationalist's engagement with classical themes in the years up to 1916.

To focus on MacDonagh is to consider the varied life of an enigmatic figure. Poet, playwright, teacher, and revolutionary, he was 'a man of contrasting extremes'.[18] Yeats in his commemorative poem 'Easter 1916' remembered the young man as a writer of promise who 'might have won fame',[19] but MacDonagh's enduring literary legacy is the critical work *Literature in Ireland: Studies Irish and Anglo-Irish* (1916). Published posthumously, this collection of essays has become, as Kelly notes, 'one of the foundational texts of Irish literary criticism'.[20] MacDonagh's great study of Anglo-Irish literature considers the influence and impact of 'the Irish mode' on English verse and seeks to define the special character of an inclusive Anglo-Irish literature. That advocacy of a distinctive form of Irish writing in the English language was prescient, and reflected the breadth of MacDonagh's enduring engagement with English and European literature. But as has been well noted, those proposals for a high culture that was *not* limited to the 'national genius' were contrary to the ambitions of many contemporaries in the Revival, who sought a cultural separatism and wanted to 'purify' the Irish tradition of 'alien' influences.[21] Such attitudes were not shared by MacDonagh, who taught English, French, and Latin literature in his career, who wrote his Masters thesis on Thomas Campion, who co-founded the Irish Theatre Company, and presented Chekhov, Strindberg, and Ibsen to Dublin audiences. MacDonagh sought to retain a broader mentality throughout his life and an approach open enough even to accommodate an ongoing dialogue with the classical past in his literary work.[22]

---

[16] For example, see Arkins (1990) and Liebregts (1993) on Yeats, Sullivan (1969) and Lloyd (2011) on Synge.

[17] To borrow from Murphy (2017: 132).

[18] White (2009b); for Norstedt (1980: 144), MacDonagh was a man of 'too many parts'.

[19] Yeats writes that MacDonagh, 'Was coming into his force; | He might have won fame in the end, | So sensitive his nature seemed, | So daring and sweet his thought.' Yeats notes the death of MacDonagh again in the ballad 'Sixteen Dead Men'. By the time of his death, MacDonagh was less kind in return: although he did dedicate his first volume of poetry, *Through the Ivory Gate* (1902), to Yeats, MacDonagh's *Metempsychosis: Or a Mad World: A Play in One Act* (1912) presents a blatant satire of Yeats and his mannerisms. See Ryan (1961: 715–19) and Newell (2011: 38–86) for different takes on this relationship.

[20] Aaron Kelly (2008: 30). On this 'epoch-making' study see Kiberd (1979: 16) and Goek (2014: 22–36).

[21] As Gibbons (1991: 562–3) notes: 'MacDonagh sought an accommodation with the English language and literature, and was the first to propose systematically that Irish literature in the English language was no less authentic than the native Gaelic mode. "Irishness" was for him not a genetic or racial inheritance; it was something to be achieved as part of a concerted, cultural effort.'

[22] On the rivalry between 'Gaelic exclusivism' and 'textual tolerance' in Irish cultural thought of the time see Murphy (2017: 106–29).

'Gael not Greek?'

That classical literature would feature heavily in the writing career of MacDonagh should not surprise, given his grounding in ancient languages and literature. His grandfather, Joseph Parker, was an English printer who moved to Dublin in the mid-nineteenth century to become compositor in Greek for the Dublin University Press. His parents, Joseph MacDonagh and Mary Louise Parker, were the first teachers in the Catholic school in Cloughjordan, Co. Tipperary, where Thomas was born in 1878. The young MacDonagh studied and then taught English and Latin at Rockwell College, where he began training to become a priest. Of the classics and the cloth, only the latter was left behind when Thomas left Cashel in 1902.[23] We see MacDonagh return to teaching the subject at St Enda's School (1908–10) and himself studying Greek and Latin at University College Dublin, where he took his BA degree in French, English, and Irish (graduating in 1910). Of course, given the educational context of the time, it was inevitable that the classics would feature throughout MacDonagh's academic career, even up to the first year of his MA degree in English Literature—and beyond. In the extensive collection of Thomas MacDonagh papers, housed in the National Library of Ireland,[24] one can find a testimonial MacDonagh submitted as part of his application to the Chair of History and English Literature in University College Galway in 1913. In his application, MacDonagh himself highlights his 'five years teaching Classics and Modern Languages' at Rockwell, while referees such as Douglas Hyde and Patrick Pearse also attest to the candidate's knowledge of the classics, modern languages, and history.[25]

Although this close engagement with the classical remained crucial to MacDonagh professionally, he also wrestled with the legacies of Greece and Rome in his writing, where we find many echoes of 'Modernist' frustrations with the ancients, both Celtic and classical. In *Literature in Ireland*, for example, MacDonagh notes the enduring influence of antiquity on the culture of the day, but also points out the limits of that influence:

> The themes of the old sagas have been used by many in our day as the story of the Trojan war has been used by many nations that read Greek... They have not been used as successfully as the Greek models. They are not the inheritance of

---

[23] For details see White (2009b) and Norstedt (1980: 8–51).

[24] The collection, maintained by the Manuscripts Department in the library, has three parts: the 'Thomas MacDonagh Papers, 1898–1916', the 'Thomas MacDonagh Family Papers, 1848–1966', and the 'Thomas MacDonagh Additional Papers, 1870–1967'. All archive material cited in this chapter is from the 'Thomas MacDonagh Papers, 1898–1916', unless otherwise noted.

[25] For the testimonial see MS 44,334/5/6 in the 'Thomas MacDonagh Family Papers, 1848–1966' collection. The archives also include a transcript of the grades MacDonagh obtained in Greek and Latin while at UCD (MS 10,850/14/2).

this alien civilisation. They require different standards…We may admit that we cannot now feel those old emotions at first heart, so to put it. We have not reverence for the same things. We cannot pray to the old gods. We could not blaspheme the old gods. We are of a different day: a different light shines upon us. History is between us and our heroes.[26]

Like much of what we find in *Literature in Ireland*, these thoughts on old sagas and ancient epic are revisions of material previously published by MacDonagh, who presented the same points in his 'Notes for a lecture on ancient Irish literature' in the May 1913 edition of *An Macaomh* (the magazine for St Edna's school, edited by Pearse). Similar arguments can also be found in his article 'Antigone and Lir' (*Irish Review*, March 1914), where MacDonagh praises the 'deep intensity of the splendid eloquence, the passion, the pathos' of Sophocles, but still notes, again, that it is the product of a 'different culture… different ways of thought… different way of religion… different music' (29). For MacDonagh the ancient worlds are of a quite different kind. In *Literature in Ireland*, he insists that the literature of the recent Gaelic renaissance was of real worth and importance, and should be evaluated as such on its own terms:

> It must not be judged as if it were a fragment of a literature of the Hellenic kind. The difference between Greek and Gael is no fiction. In the purely Gaelic-speaking places, the people to the present day have their ways of thought and life different from the ways of Hellenised Europe. The knowledge and the influence of Rome and, through Rome, of Greece has not been unknown, but the matter and the outlook and the manner of the old poems are native.[27]

In these sections of a long chapter on 'Irish Literature', MacDonagh draws from the work of John Eglinton (the pseudonym of William Kirkpatrick Magee), who challenged contemporary literature's preoccupation with visions of archaic heroism— whether inspired by myth or history. For Eglinton, the ancient legends 'obstinately refuse to be taken up out of their old environment and transplanted into the world of modern sympathies. The proper mode of treating them is as a secret lost with the subjects themselves'.[28] MacDonagh, in turn, notes that unless the contemporary author working across these traditions can infuse the ancient material with something of his own 'age or personality', can find some truth in the past and

---

[26] MacDonagh (1916: 111–12). See Gibbons (1991: 564–5).
[27] MacDonagh (1916: 106). Again, these thoughts were published in MacDonagh (1911: 85). On the rivalry between ancient and modern traditions, noted here, see Arkins (2005: 17) and Butler (2016a: 8–9).
[28] See Eglinton (1899: 11). Others, such as Yeats and AE (George Russell), disagreed with the point, as we see in the extended discussion reproduced in *Literary Ideals in Ireland*. On Eglinton's ideas, specifically, see Murphy (2017: 110–11) and Marcus (1970: 80–3).

'resume a broken tradition and make a literature in consonance with our past', the ancient will remain alien.[29]

In MacDonagh's own literary work, we see him give further expression to the difficulty of engaging with the historic and mythic past in 'Of a Greek Poem':

> Crave no more that antique rapture
> Now in alien song to reach:
> Here uncouth you cannot capture
> Gracious truth of Attic speech.
>
> Utterly the flowers perish,
> Grace of Athens, Rome's renown,
> Giving but a dream to cherish
> Tangled in a laurel crown.
>
> I that splendour far pursuing
> Left unlit the lamps of home,
> And upon my quest went ruing
> That I found not Greece or Rome.

'Of a Greek Poem' appeared in the 1913 collection *Lyrical Poems*, but it is a revision of an earlier work—'The Quest'—written nearly a decade before and published in *The Golden Joy* (1906).[30] In his various drafts of the piece, MacDonagh retains those lines that voice the frustration felt when modern speech ('uncouth') fails to do justice to ancient expression.[31] In unpublished comments on the typescript of an early version of the poem, MacDonagh elaborates further and notes:

All the fabric of that Hellenic life, as it was in the day of its beauty and glory, has faded to a vision, a dream that comes with the eternal music of the poets…That vision, that dream, the Poet of the Quest has pursued; for it he has left the real life of his narrow time – though indeed all accidental life is, in the great life, one – for it he has not lighted lamps of more immediate inspiration; nor yet has he attained to the vision he pursues.[32]

Beyond a frustration at being unable to capture and communicate that vision, we also have a sober reflection on the very point of the modern poet's pursuit of these ancient 'splendours'. MacDonagh, as Eglinton had done before, asserts that the exclusive pursuit of the classical past is not the way forward. The poet's work must be of its time, and pursuing the 'antique rapture' on its own represents, ultimately,

---

[29] MacDonagh (1916: 137).   [30] See MacDonagh (1906) and (1913a).
[31] Many thanks to Nicholas Allen for this observation.
[32] Transcribed from MS 10,852/5/6.

something of a distraction from native life ('the lamps of home') and the poet's own 'immediate inspiration'.

That distance between traditions, and the essential differences between 'Gael and Greek', features again in 'Barbara', a poem written by MacDonagh for his daughter, at the other end of his short career, in the spring of 1915. In this long piece, the poet's ardent wish is for his daughter to retain her own native wit as she grows, to remain unacquainted with, and unaffected by, the 'pride of Rome and Greece'. From the second verse we read:

> In other days within this isle,
>> As in a temple, men knew peace;
> And won the world to peace a while
>> Till rose the pride of Rome and Greece,—
>
> The pride of art, the pride of power,
>> The cruel empire of the mind:
> Withered the light like a summer flower,
>> And hearts went cold and souls went blind;
>
> …
>
> I have dreamt of you as the Maid of Quiet
>> Entempled in ecstasy of joy,
> Secure from the madness of blood and the riot
>> Of fame that lures with the glory of Troy—[33]
>
> Barbara, alien to Athens and Rome,
>> Barbara, free from their pride of wit,
> Strange to the country of Exile, at home
>> In Eden, by memory and promise of it.

MacDonagh plays with the etymology of 'Barbara' in this last stanza; as her name suggests, his daughter was born to be 'alien to Athens and Rome'. Instead, MacDonagh presents the infant as the Christian St Barbara, the original 'Maid of Quiet', kept safe in a lonely tower, hidden by her father from the outside world.[34] But beyond the individual child, the poem also sets Ireland's future promise against the faded glories and ruinous legacies of ancient civilizations, contrasting their 'pride of art, the pride of power' with an old, but recently revived, national spirit. Finally, in the closing stanzas of 'Barbara' the poet urges:

---

[33] On Troy and Trojan women and the female political voice in Ireland see further Torrance (Ch. 13).

[34] Thanks to Isabelle Torrance for her thoughts on these points. Of course, the name 'Barbara' derives from the Greek word *barbaros*, meaning 'foreign', 'un-/non-Greek'. St Barbara was a third-century virgin-martyr; according to her *vita*, while Barbara's father was off at war, she was 'imprisoned in a tower to prevent her from enflaming men's hearts'. See further Gnarra (2004: 106).

And, against the Greek, be one with the Gael,
  One knowledge of God against all human,
One sacred gift that shall not fail,
  One with the Gael against the Roman.

So may you go the barbaric way
  That the earth may be Paradise anew,
And Troy from memory pass away,
  And the pride of wit be naught to you.

'Be one with the Gael against the Greek...against the Roman...', MacDonagh calls, in a statement more antagonistic than those we read elsewhere in his writing. But the 'curious doubleness' noted as characteristic of both MacDonagh's general manner and work is evident in his sustained exchanges with these disparate narratives.[35] For MacDonagh himself could not hold to his own advice and 'go the barbaric way'. Instead we see him return repeatedly to the classical: whether reflecting on Platonic themes and the form of Beauty in his early poems,[36] or offering lectures on Xerxes, Thermopylae, and the Persian Wars as part of his Irish Volunteer activities.[37] On stage, too, we find the classical in MacDonagh's work: in *Metempsychosis*, with its satirical presentation of Yeats as the reincarnation of the ancient philosopher-mystic Pythagoras.[38] MacDonagh's *Pagans*, moreover, was produced in a 1915 double bill with Eimar O'Duffy's avant-garde *The Walls of Athens*. Gael and Greek were very much together in that Irish Theatre production, directed as it was by MacDonagh along with Joseph Plunkett, and presenting Willie Pearse (brother of Patrick) and John MacDonagh (brother of Thomas) playing the parts of the Athenian politicians Theramenes and Cleophon on the stage.[39]

MacDonagh and Catullus: Published and Unpublished Translations

MacDonagh's continued interest in—and active engagement with—ancient literature is reflected also elsewhere in *Lyrical Poems*. In addition to 'Of a Greek Poem', that collection also presents a section of translated works with four Irish

---

[35] See X. Z. (1916: 181).

[36] As in *The Golden Joy* (1906), where a long section—'The Praises of Beauty'—presents MacDonagh's search for, and attempts to define, Beauty. Plotinus seems to be the main influence here: see Norstedt (1980: 40–3).

[37] Kenna (2014: 167). On the classes for fellow officers in the Volunteers see the testimony of Liam Tannan in the Military Archives (WS Ref. #242).

[38] See above n. 19. The play was performed by the Irish Theatre. The lead character Earl Winton-Winton de Winton is a barely-disguised caricature of Yeats.

[39] This curious play presented an argument against the Union set in the post-Periclean Athens of 405 BCE. For notes see Flanagan (2015: 54).

poems, including MacDonagh's version of Cathal Buí Mac Giolla Ghunna's paean to alcohol 'The Yellow Bittern'.[40] MacDonagh's later reputation as a poet, such as it is, perhaps rests on the strength of these well-known pieces. But this section also contains two translations of lyrics by the Roman poet Catullus, poems 8 and 76. MacDonagh's translation of Catullus 8 was originally published in the first volume of the *Irish Review* in 1911, and here we have the opening verse of his revised version of 'Catullus to Himself':

> My poor Catullus, what is gone is gone,
>   Take it for gone, and be a fool no more—
> Heaven, what a time it was! Then white suns shone
>   For you, you following where she went before—
> I loved her as none ever shall be loved!

As the original poem moved to its close, Catullus almost abandons all attempts to remain strong and resolute; MacDonagh translates the anxiety of the jilted and jealous lover as follows:

> What life is there for you?—What life is there?
>   Who will come now for love and your delight?
> Whose will they say you are? Who'll think you fair?
>   Whom will you kiss? Whose lips now will you bite?
> But you, Catullus, go your way unmoved.

In addition to Catullus 8, MacDonagh also worked on Catullus 76 in 1911,[41] a piece from the second cycle of Lesbia poems, where the hopeless poet reflects on his loss and prays to be rid of the torment of love. MacDonagh offers this translation of the elegy's opening:

> If there be joy for one who looks back on his youth
>   And knows he has kept faith with God and men,
> Never outraged the sanctity of truth,
>   And never outraged trust—there is joy then
> For you, Catullus, in the long years to be,
> Out of this love, out of this misery.

---

[40] The original, 'An Bonnán Buí', was reworked later by both Thomas Kinsella and Seamus Heaney. Curiously, in his version MacDonagh leaves out the one classical reference in the original; stanza 1, lines 5–6: '*Is measa liom féin ná scrios na Traoi* | *Tú bheith i do luí ar leaca lom*'. Kinsella later rendered these lines as: 'I feel it worse than the ruin of Troy | to see you stretched on the naked stones'; Heaney presented: 'What odds is it now about Troy's destruction | With you on the flagstones upside down'.

[41] For an early draft of the poem, dated to June 18, see MS 10,851/6/4. The earliest draft of Catullus 8 dates to 1 January 1911.

In his final lines the poet again appeals to the gods for release from Lesbia and from the agony caused by an unrequited love that blights all else:

> This lethargy has crawled through all my heart and brain,
>   And driven out joy, like death evil and sure.
> I do not ask that she love me again,
>   Nor—what can not be now—that she be pure.
> Let me be strong, rid of this agony—
> O God, for what I have been grant this to me!

In his early commemoration of MacDonagh's work in *Studies*, George O'Neil considered the Irish translations in *Lyrical Poems* to be 'close and accurate renderings of originals which do not seem to be of great value'; and perhaps we might regard MacDonagh's Latin translations similarly.[42] The poems are well chosen, 8 and 76 operating as an effective pair, both meditating on lost love but in different ways: in the originals, the former is subtle and self-mocking, the latter is styled as a more anguished response to the loss of Lesbia. However, as translations, MacDonagh's revision of Catullus 8 lacks the cutting humour of the original, and, although his version of Catullus 76 does capture its melancholy, it does not shift through a sequence of emotions as the poet struggles to resign himself to rejection.[43] But regardless of how any others might judge these translations, MacDonagh thought enough of them to include them in the only volume of his verse that he wanted to remain in circulation after his death.[44]

One more translation, MacDonagh's version of Catullus 5, was published later in the *Poetical Works of Thomas MacDonagh* compilation.[45] Unlike the other Catullan pieces, poem 5 is a defiant and carefree celebration of the poet's love for Lesbia, building to a climax in a second verse that MacDonagh translates thus:

> Give me a thousand kisses, love,
> Then a hundred,—then rehearse,
> Thousand, hundred, till they mount
> Millions—and then blot the count;
> Lest we know,—or some sore devil
> Over-look and bring us evil,
> Knowing all our kisses' number.

---

[42] X. Z. (1916: 180–1).

[43] For introductory notes on the original versions of each poem see Green (2005: 215, 258). On the irony in the Catullus 8 lament see Simmons (2010: 45–6). The sequence of thought offered in Catullus 76 is the subject of much debate, as explored by J. Powell (1990: 189–202).

[44] See Norstedt (1980: 102–7), who notes: '*Lyrical Poems* . . . is MacDonagh's real poetic testament' (107).

[45] Muriel MacDonagh, aided by Colum and James Stephens prepared this collected edition of poems in 1916, which compiled two previous volumes (*Songs of Myself* and *Lyrical Poems*) and added twenty-two new 'Miscellaneous Poems' selected by Muriel.

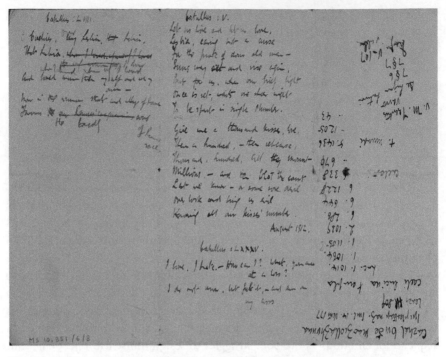

Fig. 4.2. MS 10,851/6/8 from the collection of 'Thomas MacDonagh Papers, 1898–1916', National Library of Ireland. Page presenting Thomas MacDonagh's handwritten translations of Catullus 5 (top centre), Catullus 85 (bottom centre), and Catullus 58 (top left). Image and permission to reproduce provided courtesy of the National Library of Ireland.

Although this translation was published posthumously, the archive in the National Library of Ireland preserves a written draft of 'Catullus 5' that dates to August 1912 (Fig. 4.2), the period when MacDonagh was preparing *Lyric Poems* for publication. In addition, on the same piece of paper from the archives we find two more unpublished translations of Latin poems. Below the draft of Catullus 5, in the centre of the document, we also have MacDonagh's work-in-progress on Catullus 85. One of Catullus' best-known couplets, his declaration of conflicting feeling for Lesbia (*Odi et amo...*), is presented as follows:

> I love. I hate. How can I? What, you are at a loss?
> I do not know, but feel it, and am on my cross.

Above this piece, in the top left-hand corner of the page, we find one more unpublished translation, this time of Catullus 58. The poem is another bitter attack by Catullus on his former love. Here the poet notes that Lesbia—whom 'I loved more than myself and my own'—can be found in dark alleys offering 'favours' to all the 'sons of Remus' race', which is MacDonagh's rough translation of Catullus' infamous final line. Beyond that document, there is another unpublished version of a Catullus epigram, poem 75, among the archived papers, again written in MacDonagh's hand and this time on the reverse of a typescript draft of the Catullus 76 translation noted above. 'My mind is brought to this, Lesbia, by you...' is MacDonagh's first attempt at the opening line of this short epigram, where again the poet is betrayed and bitter but still unable to set aside his love.[46]

The review of the archives in the National Library reveals something of MacDonagh's personal life and private thoughts and offers access to the full scope of his literary career. Crucially, it also highlights the confluence of interests and clash of cultures that occurred in MacDonagh's everyday work. We find scribbled translations of Catullus 8 on the back of part of a letter of business concerning the Irish Self-Government Alliance.[47] A physical embodiment of how classical literature infiltrated the minds of political thinkers, the document preserves Catullus remonstrating with himself about his lack of self-governance on one side of the page while a list of the committee's rules and resolutions fills the other (Fig. 4.3).[48] We also find translations of three further lyrics by Catullus on the same piece of paper as a brief comment on Cathal Buí Mac Giolla Ghunna,[49] and notes on Lucretius' *De Rerum Natura* 1.1014: half of the line is written out (*caeli lucida templa*, 'the shining temples of the heavens'). This is followed by a series of references to further occurrences of *caeli templa* in the *De Rerum Natura*, with a further nod to Varro's discussion of the word 'templum' in *De Lingua Latina* 7.6–7. The combination of Catullus, Lucretius, and Varro on the same page highlights the breadth of MacDonagh's reading here as he worked on his translations and even indulged in a little philological research (Fig. 4.2).[50] The archive reveals the extent of MacDonagh's knowledge of Latin poetry, in particular, and also confirms that classical literature remained a key reference point, a touchstone for his own writing throughout his career. For, all in all, in the MacDonagh papers we have his versions of six Lesbia poems (Catullus 5, 8, 58, 75, 76, and 85), a significant body of work to consider alongside his well-known translations of old Irish verse. MacDonagh, it would seem, aimed at finding his own voice by undertaking all this translation work.

[46] See MS 10,851/6/7; the first page of the typescript is missing.
[47] MS 10,851/6/2, dated to c.1911–12. The Irish Self-Government Alliance maintained committee and reading rooms, open to all, in the O'Connell Buildings. There are a number of snippets scribbled on alliance notepaper in the MacDonagh archives.
[48] Many thanks to Donncha O'Rourke for this observation.
[49] See Fig. 4.2 again. Notes on Cathal Buí are in the bottom right-hand corner of the document.
[50] Once again, thanks to Donncha O'Rourke for his thoughts on these notes in general, and on Varro specifically. He highlights that Varro's discussion of the word 'templum' begins by quoting Ennius—*unus erit quem tu tolles in caerula caeli | templa* ('one there shall be whom you will raise to the sky's azure temples')—which is itself often cited in connection with the *caeli lucida templa* phrase.

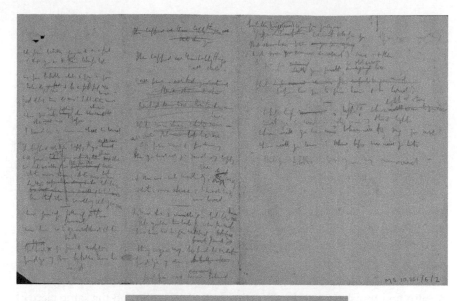

Fig. 4.3. MS 10,851/6/2 from the collection of 'Thomas MacDonagh Papers, 1898–1916', National Library of Ireland. Manuscript draft of Catullus 8, written on the reverse of a partial letter concerning public action on behalf of the Irish Self-Government Alliance (both sides shown). Images and permission to reproduce provided courtesy of the National Library of Ireland.

Earlier in his career, MacDonagh wrote to W. B. Yeats for advice on his poetry prior to the publication of *Through the Ivory Gate* (1903). In his reply, Yeats urged the young poet to

> read the great old masters of English, Spenser, Ben Johnson, Sir Thomas Brown, perhaps Chaucer ....When we study old writers we imitate nothing but their virtues...I will advise you to translate a great deal from the Irish – To translate literally, preserving as much of the idiom as possible – I don't mean that you will stop at this kind of writing, but it will help get rid of the conventionality of language from which we all suffer today.[51]

This is similar to advice previously given to J. M. Synge in the 1890s, with Yeats again prescribing a course of translation to help another poet find his own voice. As Declan Kiberd suggests:

> Whenever MacDonagh wrote subjectively he wrote badly and without the distinction of a personal style. His poems are often a roomful of old echoes. But when he translated from the Irish, he conveyed the urgency of a man speaking with full force...[MacDonagh] was least of all himself when he wrote 'sincere' lyrics, but once given a mask he told a deeply personal truth.[52]

Yeats advised tackling Irish verse, but MacDonagh's translation work in Latin is a variation on the same theme. Whether he managed to find his 'full force' when working on Roman lyrics is perhaps debatable, but nonetheless the general process is significant to note. Imitating the virtues of ancient Roman and old Irish poets alike was a part of MacDonagh's development as a writer, just as he considered translation work to be a necessary stage in the development of a new literary tradition.[53]

But why Catullus, of all the 'old masters' of classical literature available to MacDonagh? Why the fixed focus on his lyrics? Apart from the use of *De Rerum Natura* 5.1190 (*luna dies et nox et noctis signa severa*, 'the moon, day and night, and the night's austere constellations') as the title of another 'Miscellaneous' piece in the *Lyric Poems* volume, no other classical author really features in MacDonagh's poetry.[54] Any who read *The Golden Joy* volume of poetry might expect some

---

[51] The letter dates to 9 November 1902, and Yeats advises the younger writer to postpone publishing the work as 'you have not found yourself as a poet': see Kelly and Schuchard (1994: 246–7).

[52] Kiberd (2005: 32–3).

[53] Kiberd (2005: 33). On MacDonagh and the wider role of translation in Irish literature see Kiberd (1979: 16) and Gibbons (1991: 564–5).

[54] Translation here by Ferguson Smith (2001: 169). There is a draft of 'Luna dies et nox...' in the archives, dated to July 1911 (MS 10,851/5/46), around the time when MacDonagh was working on the Catullus translations in Fig. 4.2. Among the list of lines from Lucretius also noted on that piece of

Horace, given the number of allusions to his work there. Horace is also noted as one of the ever-enduring 'great names' in *Literature in Ireland*, and his work is noted more than any other ancient author in the critical essays.[55] However, Horace, for all his style, lacks spontaneity. MacDonagh goes on to argue that Horace's work has an esteemed reputation in the modern day only because of its great antiquity: some of his *Odes*, for example, 'to a fresh mind, not under the hypnotism, would seem merely fine words well set, and not poetry at all'.[56] The key comparison made here is with Catullus, whose work he judges to be thoroughly superior. MacDonagh offers only one observation on Catullus in *Literature in Ireland*, but it is significant. Presenting notes of clarification on the 'essentials of true poetry', he argues:

> The object of language is to express something. The clearer the expression, the more successful it is. All the great things of literature that live are clear, however obscure to a passing age, even their own, blinded by false knowledge. They are terse and sufficient, yet with great lucid beauty, with the authentic accent of true knowledge, of true feeling, of true interpretation. Perhaps the clarity of some of them seemed in their first day a fault. A critic has written of the 'terrible simplicity' of Catullus. To some of his contemporaries the poetry of Catullus may have seemed bald and obvious, wanting in the graces of art.[57]

The discussion in the essay moves on to consider Matthew Arnold, but the point here about the poetry of Catullus is that it is not at all lacking 'in the graces of art'. This is the same argument MacDonagh offers in earlier work on Thomas Campion; when writing of song-verses in poetry, MacDonagh notes Catullus' lyrics are 'lucid, intense, rapturous, "burning upward to his point of bliss", or else bitter, poignant, in agony, or else impersonal, objective, exquisite, quaint, dainty, singing'.[58] While Catullus' verses

---

paper, we find a reference to 5.1205: both 5.1190 and 1205 come from a section of *De Rerum Natura* that reviews the development of civilization (5.1011–457) and asserts that there was much to envy in the simple lives led by primitive human beings. Although 'Barbara' was composed four years later, the 'primitivism' in that poem echoes Lucretius' *Kulturgeschichte* at the close of book 5. Many thanks to the editors for noting these connections.

[55] MacDonagh (1916: 105) notes of Horace: 'We think of him in terms of his *urbanitas* ['refinement'] and his *curiosa Felicitas* ['careful felicity']; still he may prophesy as of old: *ego postera crescam laude recens* ['I shall grow ever renewed in future praise'], for always we admire his modernness'.

[56] MacDonagh (1916: 121), with the note that 'As a rule posterity soon enough finds out sham in literature'.

[57] MacDonagh (1916: 122–3). The 'critic' noted here is Prof. John William Mackail, who commented: 'It is just this quality, this clear and almost terrible simplicity, that puts Catullus in a place by himself among the Latin poets' (1896: 61).

[58] MacDonagh (1913b: 51). The contrast here is between Catullus' 'clear and terrible simplicity' and Lucretius, whose speech-verse is 'grave, passionate, towering, sublime'.

may be 'terse', they also contain truth and their emotional appeal—crucially—still endures.

It is that emotional appeal that seems to resonate with MacDonagh at a particular point in his life. Reviewing the various drafts of the Lesbia poems in the archives we see that MacDonagh's 'Catullus work' dates to 1911–12, during which time he met, courted, and married Muriel Gifford.[59] But it is also the period in which MacDonagh was recovering from the rejection of an earlier marriage proposal made to Mary Maguire, and it is Mary—rather than Muriel—who is a more likely 'Lesbia' figure in MacDonagh's life. The pair both taught in the Pearse schools in Dublin (St Enda's and St Ita's) and were also involved in founding *The Irish Review* in March 1911. But prior to that, in May 1910, MacDonagh also made an aggressive claim for Maguire's hand in marriage, as Mary recalled later:

> He called at my little flat, armed with an engagement ring, and told me in a very cave-man manner that he had arranged everything, that I was to marry him on a certain date in a certain church, and that I had better accept my destiny. The argument that ensued reduced me to a state of panic such as I had never known, for I was afraid I might be unable to hold out, especially as he said I had encouraged him and ought to have some sense of responsibility about it. But I managed to be strong-minded, and the harassing interview ended with tears on both sides, with his throwing the ring into the fire and leaving in a high state of emotion.[60]

MacDonagh was stung sorely by the rejection, and his pain was not alleviated by the fact that Maguire accepted the proposal of his friend Padraic Colum almost immediately afterwards. In the following month, MacDonagh resigned from St Enda's and left to spend the rest of the summer in Paris. MacDonagh the poet reflects on the sudden loss of love in 'After a Year', published in the autumn of 1910 after his return to Dublin:

> After a year of love
> Death of love in a day;
> And I who ever strove
> To hold love in sure life
> Now let it pass away
> With no grief and no strife.
>
> ...
>
> And there an end of it—

---

[59]   The couple were married on 3 January 1912.

[60]   Colum (1966: 151–2). Maguire does not name MacDonagh in her account of the incident, but contemporaries identify him as the suitor in question. See Norstedt (1980: 71–4) and Ayo (2012: 113–14).

> I who have never brooked
> Such word as all unfit
> For our sure love, brooked this—
> Into her eyes I looked,
> Left her without a kiss.

MacDonagh writes a farewell to love in this poignant poem that hints at personal revelation,[61] composed very much in the Catullan style, and at a time when the young writer was working on a cluster of Latin translations. And, without blurring the lines between the life and the work of the poet too much, one wonders if MacDonagh took Catullus very much to heart as he sought to come to terms with his own recent experiences of love's progress and final end.

Even beyond the personal, however, as a poet MacDonagh should be placed among the ranks of recent writers, from W. B. Yeats to Michael Longley, who have turned to Catullus for poetic inspiration. On the enduring appeal of Catullus' clipped but clear style to other writers, Brian Arkins, quoting John Banville, has noted:

> A number of modern poets have taken Catullus as a model and the novelist John Banville explains why: Catullus is one of those 'artists whom one can use, from whom one can learn one's trade', because 'one can see, or at least glimpse here and there on the surface, the processes by which the work was produced...This generative and transfiguring process is a large part of the greatness of the *Carmina Catulli*.'[62]

Perhaps MacDonagh sought and found something similar from Catullus: for, crucially, here was one ancient author whose 'authentic accent', 'true knowledge...true feeling...true interpretation' could still resonate through the ages and both stimulate and help shape the work of modern poets.[63]

Conclusion

In the opening section of this chapter, it was noted that recent work on MacDonagh's literary career has often highlighted that his was a critical approach subtler than that which came to dominate the Irish cultural landscape in the decades after

---

[61] As noted, first, by Norstedt (1980: 73): the poem 'is almost like a direct statement', very different in style from other poems written in the earlier part of MacDonagh's career.

[62] Arkins (2007: 466). On the unambiguous Catullus often imagined by modern readers see Fitzgerald (1995: 212–35).

[63] Earlier in the same chapter of *Literature in Ireland* (1916: 113), MacDonagh notes: 'We are true to the best of the old literature when we are true to that part of it we inherit now in the twentieth century, when we discover in ourselves something of its good tradition, something that has remained true by the changing standards and measures.'

1916.[64] That classical literature also remained in the wider scope of his vision is a further point that is important to acknowledge, given MacDonagh's standing as a political and cultural figure in Irish history. And we can now consider, in full, how comprehensive the classical allusions in his work were thanks to the recent digitization of the MacDonagh archive material in the National Library of Ireland, which allows easy access to thirteen boxes of literary papers and correspondence donated by the MacDonagh family. This is a crucial body of material for those interested in classical influences in Ireland, and not just because it contains the previously unpublished translations of Latin lyric presented above.

For beyond those individual pieces, a review of the MacDonagh archives allows us to consider something of the man before his 'martyrdom', and to set his public comments on ancient classics in their fullest context. Doing so, it is perhaps surprising to find that MacDonagh's occasional renunciation of the classics was rhetorically at odds with much in his professional life and his personal writing.[65] Indeed, his particular engagement with Catullus only provides the clearest example of what is a general truth: that the texts of antiquity retained a hold on Thomas MacDonagh throughout his short life. In his writing we find, as with Pearse and Yeats, that the contest between the Celtic and the classical remained alive and the resulting tension between self and world is apparent across some key works. MacDonagh's feelings on the Greek and Roman worlds were never quite the extreme of *odi et amo* ('I love and I hate'), in Catullus' famous phrase, as classical texts remained an essential source of inspiration in his mind. With Irish literature at 'an age of beginnings rather than of achievements', these ancient works could be recast to serve a new literature:

> ...eras dovetail and interlace; so the colours shade into one another; so always side by side go reaction and radicalism; so the classic has not died and romance has but revived...These things we should not forget; but these should not at the same time hold us from the perception of change...[66]

Undoubtedly, the 'grace of Athens, Rome's renown' did not always fit even MacDonagh's own 'native wit', but the challenge he set himself and others was to reconcile those ancient and 'alien songs' with new Irish identities.

---

[64] See nn. 20–1 above, especially Goek (2014: 33), who notes MacDonagh's 'forward-looking views of poetry...mark him out from many of his more polemic contemporaries'.

[65] See above n. 15 and Fiona Macintosh's note on this feature of the nationalist self-presentation.

[66] MacDonagh (1916: 9–10).

II
LANGUAGE POLITICS

5

Translating into Irish from Greek and Latin in the Early Years of the Irish State

Síle Ní Mhurchú

The nationwide revival of the Irish language was a key aim of the Irish Free State and the provision of reading material and educational books in Irish was thought to be essential in bringing this about. This chapter discusses Irish-language translations of ancient Greek and classical Latin works, and other works concerning the language and culture of ancient Greece and Rome, that were published during the existence of the Irish Free State (1922–37) and for some years afterwards, with a focus on the work and views of Pádraig de Brún and George Thomson, the two most significant contributors to the endeavour of making the classics accessible in the Irish language. In the following chapter, Pádraic Moran will discuss in more detail Thomson's role in promoting Classics through Irish at University College Galway, specifically. The bibliographical Appendix C to Chapters 5 and 6 which follows Chapter 6, and lists relevant publications in Irish, has been compiled jointly as a further point of reference for our two chapters.

An Gúm's Translation Scheme

The language revival movement that took place in the decades before Irish independence had done much to improve the standing of the Irish language after its catastrophic decline in the early and mid nineteenth century. From the time of its foundation in 1893, the Gaelic League encouraged people from outside Gaeltacht (Irish-speaking) areas to learn to speak and read Irish and it succeeded in inspiring a new generation of writers to produce modern literature in Irish.[1] The League's publication programme was impacted severely by the turbulence of the 1916 Rising and its aftermath, and it was publishing very few books in the early 1920s.[2] The first steps towards establishing a government publication scheme to reverse the decline of Irish-language publishing were taken in the time of the Revolutionary Dáil (Parliament) (1919–22) when money was allocated towards the production

---

[1] Denvir (1978: 257).   [2] Uí Laighléis (2004: 185–6), Uí Laighléis (2007: 199).

Síle Ní Mhurchú, *Translating into Irish from Greek and Latin in the Early Years of the Irish State* In: *Classics and Irish Politics, 1916–2016*. Edited by: Isabelle Torrance and Donncha O'Rourke, Oxford University Press (2020).
© Oxford University Press.
DOI: 10.1093/oso/9780198864486.003.0005

of schoolbooks in Irish, but the project did not come to be known as An Gúm (The Scheme) until 1926.[3] An Gúm's work was a central part of government policy in the 1920s to the point that the Minister for Finance was given regular briefings on its progress.[4] Although An Gúm gave some support to the writing of original fiction and non-fiction in Irish, translation was central during its early years: a translating competition for Irish speakers was run in 1928 and 60 per cent of the first hundred books of fiction published by An Gúm were translations.[5] It was thought that there were not enough writers producing original material in Irish and that translation was the only way to provide a sufficient supply of reading material for those who would learn the language at school.[6]

During the revival period prior to independence, the question of translation into the Irish language had already been a topic of debate: broadly speaking, those who participated in the debate have been characterized as 'nativists' who feared that translation would damage the language and 'progressives' who argued for the benefit of outside influence.[7] Translation was seen by some as a way of restoring contact between Gaelic Ireland and Continental Europe, but the number of translations from European languages other than English in the revival period was rather low.[8] This includes a small number of texts translated from Greek and Latin.[9] The contrasting value placed by An Gúm on translation caused some controversy, therefore, and while some of the debates echo those of the time of the revival, O'Leary detects a new note of seriousness as translation moved from being a pastime to forming a central part of the state's language revival policy.[10] There was much debate about the value of the translation scheme: some critics felt that writers who had the potential to write good original material were putting all their efforts into translation instead and others warned that the Irish language would become corrupted both linguistically and philosophically by translations from English, while An Gúm's defenders argued that translation would aid the evolution of a national literature in Irish after centuries of neglect, supply new styles for writers to emulate, and help develop modern vocabulary and terminology in the language.[11]

After its first meeting in 1927, the members of An Gúm's Publications Committee were asked to compile a list of books that might be suitable for translation into Irish: this list consists of twenty-two books, mostly in the English language, and the only Latin or Greek work listed is Plutarch's *Lives*.[12] Translators were free to translate any text they wished on condition that their choice be approved by An

---

[3] Uí Laighléis (2007: 200–1).   [4] Ó Murchú (2012: 26).
[5] Uí Laighléis (2007: 203 and 205).   [6] O'Leary 2004: 279–80.
[7] O'Leary 1994: 357–69. O'Leary notes (358–9) that people's views 'blurred the usual ideological allegiances': a person who was generally progressive might not be so when it came to the question of translation. Some of those who warned of the dangers of translation during the revival did, in fact, translate works into Irish themselves (O'Leary 2004: 377).
[8] O'Leary (1994: 368 and 370).   [9] O'Leary (1994: 373).   [10] O'Leary (2004: 377).
[11] O'Leary (2004: 377–88).   [12] Uí Laighléis (2004: 190).

Gúm.[13] The scheme did not place any special emphasis on the classical languages: the fact that translations of Latin and Greek were produced reflects the interest of some of the participating translators in those languages and not government policy.[14] Some of the translations of Greek and Latin texts discussed below were labelled as being intended for use in secondary schools but the extent to which they were used for this purpose is difficult to gauge. Instruction through the medium of Irish was seen by the Free State Government as essential in reviving the language and the production of Irish-language textbooks, as mentioned above, was another one of the goals of An Gúm. This led to the production of a good number of editions of Greek and Latin texts with forewords and notes in Irish, Irish-language translations of English-language Greek and Latin textbooks, and a small number of original Irish-language textbooks.

The government's Stationery Office was responsible for sending out tenders for publishing the books: The Stationery Office (Oifig an tSoláthair) is named as publisher for some of the books published under An Gúm's translation scheme while others bear the name of the firms that published them.[15] An Gúm continues to publish Irish-language books and textbooks to this day, but its translation scheme did not last very long. In 1933, it issued a memo stating that original works in the Irish language were to be given preference over translations and the translation scheme was cancelled officially in 1939: the An Gúm file relating to the end of the scheme was lost so we do not have a record of the thoughts of its staff on this matter.[16]

Pádraig de Brún (1889–1960)

Pádraig de Brún was born in Grangemockler, Co. Tipperary and although he was raised through English, he may have been exposed to the Irish language at an early age as it was still spoken by the older generation in that locality during his childhood. However, he stated that it was after a trip to the Gaeltacht in Ballingeary, Co. Cork in 1910 that he began to study the language seriously. His parents had introduced him to Latin, French, and German when he was in primary school and he continued to study both modern and classical languages throughout his secondary schooling and college years. He was to master Italian and ancient Greek as well as the previously mentioned languages. He was also gifted at mathematics: he was awarded an MA in mathematical science by UCD in 1910 and a Doctorat ès sciences by the Sorbonne in 1912 for his thesis on problems in integral equations. He was ordained the following year and held the position of professor of mathematics

---

[13] Uí Laighléis (2004: 197).

[14] For some examples of intellectuals who stressed the importance of translating from the classics see O'Leary (2004: 391 and 637, n. 85).

[15] Uí Laighléis (2007: 204–5).   [16] Uí Laighléis (2007: 208).

and mathematical physics at St Patrick's College, Maynooth from 1914 to 1945. He was president of University College Galway from 1945 to 1959. De Brún was involved in the War of Independence and took the anti-Treaty side in the Civil War. He was deeply upset by the execution of the leaders of the 1916 Rising, and especially that of his friend Seán MacDermott. De Brún's niece, the poet, writer, and scholar Máire Mhac an tSaoi explains that her uncle found solace afterwards in the West-Kerry Gaeltacht of Corca Dhuibhne. He built a house there in the early 1920s and spent time there regularly for the rest of his life.[17]

Pádraig de Brún was one of the Irish-language experts chosen to sit on An Gúm's Publications Committee founded in September 1927: this committee was given the task of increasing the supply of reading material in Irish.[18] De Brún's translations of the following plays were published in book format: *Aintioghoiné/ Dráma le Sofoicléas* [*Antigone*/A play by Sophocles] (1926); *Rí Oidiopús, Dráma le Sofoicléas* [*Oedipus Rex*/A play by Sophocles] (1928); *Oidiopús i gColón/Dráma le Sofoicléas* [*Oedipus at Colonus*/A play by Sophocles] (1929); *Íodhbhairt Ifigéine/ Dráma le Euripides* [*The Sacrifice of Iphigenia*/A play by Euripides (= *Iphigenia in Aulis*)] (1935).[19] De Brún's *Aintioghoiné* was staged for a week in Loreto Hall, St Stephen's Green, Dublin, in the year of its publication. Máire Mhac an tSaoi, then aged only 4, was given a part in the play as the boy who leads Tiresias on- and offstage. She remembers that the play was set to music, which made the stress system of de Brún's verse translation clearer to the actors, and regrets that this music was not published alongside the text. The play ran for a week and appears to have met with success: Mhac an tSaoi describes the performance of the Irish-language scholar Nessa Ní Shéaghdha in the role of Antigone as a memorable one and states that many of those present thought of the staging of the play as the herald of a new golden age in the history of Irish literature.[20] Mhac an tSaoi notes that de Brún continually revised his translations as he directed his plays on the stage but, unfortunately, his annotated scripts are now lost.[21] She discerns an improvement in the style of de Brún's translations as he deepened his knowledge of the Irish of Corca Dhuibhne. Praise came from elsewhere, too: one reviewer contextualized de Brún's achievement stating that he 'created at one stroke an Irish dramatic poetry for which no prototypes existed' and praised the translations as being 'at once idiomatic Irish and a very faithful rendering of the Greek'.[22] Another reviewer declared that de Brún's work was 'excellent', classifying it as 'an undertaking which has justified itself, at least to anyone who has had the good

---

[17] Breathnach and Ní Mhurchú 2018a; White 2009a.   [18] Uí Laighléis 2007: 202.
[19] For more bibliographical infomation see Appendix C to Chapters 5 and 6. The list given there also includes translations of extracts from *Oedipus at Colonus* and *Oedipus Rex* published by de Brún in a newspaper and a journal prior to the publication of the books.
[20] Mhac an tSaoi (1993: 141–6).   [21] Mhac an tSaoi (1993: 148).
[22] T. (1928: 326). 'T.' probably stands for Torna or Tadhg Ó Donnchadha (1874–1949), Professor of Irish in University College Cork at the time the review was published.

fortune to see the translations produced on the stage': this second reviewer also spoke fondly of his experience of playing the lead role in a performance of *Rí Oidiopús* at Maynooth a year earlier.[23]

An elegy that de Brún composed for one his Kerry neighbours, Pádraig Ó Conchúir or Peats Mhíchíl Connor (1881–1944), is interesting in that it shows that de Brún sought the opinions of this man as to the quality of his translations into Irish:

> Léinn duit ó am go ham na haistrithe do rinneas
> Ó dhrámaí stáitse an chlú ón bhFrainc is ón seana-Ghréig;
> Thaitníodh a gcúrsaí leat is chuirtheá feabhas is cruinneas
> Ar mo lag-iarrachtaí le bréithre an bhreithimh réidh.[24]

> I used to read for you from time to time my translations of famous stage plays from France and ancient Greece; you enjoyed their plots and you, with the words of a steady judge, would improve and perfect my weak attempts.

Elsewhere, Mhac an tSaoi describes how de Brún used to read his translations aloud to visiting neighbours in Dún Chaoin and the lively debates on language that ensued.[25] Thus, we see that de Brún's translations of Greek tragedy could appeal both to native Irish speakers of the Gaeltacht and to Irish-speaking Dublin theatre-goers, the latter group being made up primarily of people who had learned Irish as a second language under the influence of the language revival movement. The plays were not staged in any Gaeltacht, however, and they did not become part of the general repertoire of Irish-language stage plays.

De Brún also translated other types of texts: *Beathaí Phlútairc* [Plutarch's *Lives*] was published in 1936. His translation of the *Odyssey* [*An Odaisé*] was to be published by Sáirséal and Dill in the 1950s but was cancelled due to lack of money and fears that it would not appeal to a wide readership; it would not be published until 1990 and de Brún's full translation of the *Iliad* has yet to make its way into print.[26] De Brún's translation of the Irish classical scholar J. B. Bury's *A History of Greece* was published as the three-volume *Stair na Gréige* [History of Greece] in 1954. A short pamphlet by de Brún, *Tús Laidne trí Laidin Eaglasta* [Beginning Latin through Ecclesiastical Latin] appeared around 1957.[27] Here, he argued that then current methods of teaching Latin were ineffective and that Catholic school-children would find it easier to begin learning Latin by studying the Latin Mass

---

[23] M. D. (1929: 531). 'M. D.' is probably the Irish-language scholar Myles Dillon (1900–72) who was lecturing in Dublin at the time the review was published.

[24] Mhac an tSaoi (1993: 148–50).   [25] Mhac an tSaoi (1990: vi).

[26] De Brún and Ó Coigligh (1990: viii–x), Ó hÉigeartaigh and Nic Gearailt (2014: 130).

[27] This was published by Cló Ollscoile Chorcaighe (Cork University Press). No date of publication is given in the book itself.

and biblical stories with which they would already be familiar.[28] He also defended the value of studying classical Latin authors:

> [T]eastaíonn uaim na húdair phágánta Laidne a choinneáil i gcónaí ar chlár meán-scoile is ollscoile. Tá dhá chúis leis sin : An chéad cheann, gurb iad dhá thobar as ar fhás an tsibhialtacht seo againne, teagasc sheana-shaoil lucht cónaithe cois na Meán-mhara, agus teagasc an Bhíobla agus na Críostaíochta; agus an tarna ceann, gurb í an teanga Laidne, go mór-mhór i scríbhinní Chicero, agus i dtánaiste dhósan, i scríbhinní Vergil is Óibhid, gurbh ise a rinne an Droichead a d'fhág ar ár gcumas meabhrú siar go dtí aigne na nGréagach, agus go prinseabálta go dtí aigne a bhfealsún agus a bhfilí.[29]

I wish to keep the pagan Latin authors on the secondary and tertiary curriculum. There are two reasons for this: first, the two sources out of which our civilization grew are the ancient teachings of those who lived by the Mediterranean, and the teachings of the Bible and Christianity; and secondly, it is in the Latin language, especially in the writings of Cicero, and to a lesser extent those of Virgil and Ovid, that we find the bridge that let us reach back to the mind of the Greeks, and principally, to the minds of their philosophers and poets.

A fuller defence of the classics and, in particular, of the value of translating the classics into Irish, is found in two articles published by de Brún in the journal *Humanitas* in 1930. The first of these, entitled 'Ars Scribendi', was published in the first issue of *Humanitas* in March 1930. De Brún, referring to Ernest Renan's notion of the Greek miracle, stressed the exceptionalism of the intellectual achievements of the ancient Greeks, and the extent to which English, German, French, Italian, and Spanish were enriched by the influence of both Latin and Greek from the time of the Renaissance. The Irish language, he argued, was barely touched by the Renaissance and was thus underdeveloped in comparison to other European languages:

> Caithfear a rá go soiléir misniúil nár buaileadh cló na Renaissance riamh i gceart ar an nGaeilge. Agus tá bacaí inniu uirthi dá dheasca sin, bacaí nach mór dúinn a leigheas go luath, más mian linn an Ghaeilge a chur ag obair go líofa láidir i ngort intleachtúil na haoise seo.[30]

It must be said clearly and courageously that the Renaissance was never imprinted properly on the Irish language. Consequently, it is deficient today and

---

[28] De Brún (1957: 7–8).   [29] De Brún (1957: 8).
[30] The excerpts from *Humanitas* articles quoted here are taken from Prút (2005: 26), who has modernized the spelling.

these deficiencies must be remedied soon if we wish to set Irish to work with fluency and strength in the intellectual field of this age.

Translating from the classical languages was thus a prerequisite to developing a modern literature in the Irish language:

> Siad na clasaicí atá uainn: caithfear a n-aistriú go Gaeilge, an chuid is fearr díobh. Do bhí bua acu gur shíolraigh clasaicí eile uathu i litríochtaí na hEorpa, agus oirfidh sé dúinn cuid díobh sin a aistriú ina dteannta...Nuair a bheidh an obair sin déanta—agus tá sí cruaidh go maith—féadfar torthaí an tsaothair d'úsáid in oibreacha liteartha eile.[31]

> The classics are what we need: the best of them must be translated into Irish. Such was their merit that other classics sprang from them in the literatures of Europe and it will be opportune to translate some of those, too...When this work is complete—and it is difficult work—it will become possible to use the fruits of the labour in other literary endeavours.

De Brún's article met with a vehement rebuttal from Daniel Corkery (1878–1964), Professor of English in University College Cork, in the next edition of *Humanitas* which appeared in June 1930.[32] While Corkery was not entirely opposed to translating into Irish, he argued that the language had enough substance and a long enough literary tradition to develop standards of its own and castigated contemporary writers of Irish for ignorance of both of these.[33] The debate continued along these lines in two subsequent issues of *Humanitas* with Corkery's final contribution descending into a mean-spirited attack on de Brún. Corkery had a magnetic personality and his views on translation and other literary matters were taken as gospel by many Irish speakers of his time: Máire Mhac an tSaoi suggests that it is due to his influence that de Brún failed to find a publisher for his translations of the *Odyssey* and *Iliad*, and Liam Prút argues that Corkery's narrow-minded views on what literature in Irish could look like deadened the imagination of writers in the language for decades afterwards.[34] De Brún's masterful command of the Irish of Dún Chaoin and his achievements as a translator have, however, begun to receive renewed acknowledgement in recent decades.[35]

---

[31] Prút (2005: 27).

[32] Corkery was also involved with An Gúm, being a member of its Book Committee which was responsible for accepting or rejecting submitted manuscripts: see Ó Murchú (2012: 25) and Uí Laighléis (2007: 202).

[33] Prút (2005: 29–36).

[34] Mhac an tSaoi (1993: 141), Prút (2005: 11). Ó Buachalla (1979) gives an insightful account of Corkery's personality and discusses the extent to which his literary criticism was shaped by his nationalism. See further Kiberd (Ch. 2).

[35] See, for example, Ua Súilleabháin (1991) and Titley (2005: 315) on de Brún's translation of the *Odyssey*.

A short extract from one of de Brún's translations is included here to give a flavour of his work. Below is an extract from *Oidiopús i gColón*, corresponding to lines 466–75 of Sophocles' tragedy, printed first in Gaelic typeface as it was published followed by my transcription and translation underneath. At this point in the play, the chorus of old men (C.C. = Cóir Sheanóirí Colónach) describe to Oidiopús (Oid.) a ritual act that must be carried out to propitiate the Eumenides after he has trespassed on their sacred ground. Overall, the Irish is at once terse, vivid, and natural: one could imagine some of the lines from the extract below coming from the mouth of a Dún Chaoin farmer.

C. C. Mar sin, déan sásaṁ dos na Déiṫe ban
       Gur leo 'n ball naomṫa do ṡáruiġis ar dtúis.

Oid. Innsiḋ dom caḋ is déanta ḋom, a ċáirḋe.

C. C. Beir leaṫ ar dtúis le láṁa 'tá niġṫe ó smál,
       Uisce as an áiṫ 'na mbriseann sé do ṡíor.

Oid. Is nuair a beiḋ an t-uisce glan agam?

C. C. Tá cuirn le faġáil, a rinne deaġ-ċeárdaiḋe ;
       Cuir fleasca timċeall orṫa, 's ar a gcluasa.

Oid. Éaḋaċ, an eaḋ, nó craoḃ ? Nó caḋ ba ċearṫ ?

C. C. Uan baineann 's í nuaḋ-beárrṫa, a holann soin.

C.C. Mar sin, déan sásamh dos na Déithe ban
      Gur leo 'n ball naomhtha do sháruighis ar dtúis.

Oid. Innsidh dom cad is déanta dhom, a cháirde.

C.C. Beir leat ar dtúis le lámha 'tá nighte ó smál,
      Uisce as an áit 'na mbriseann sé do shíor.

Oid. Is nuair a bheidh an t-uisce glan agam?

C.C. Tá cuirn le fagháil, a rinne deagh-cheárdaidhe ;
      Cuir fleasca timcheall ortha, 's ar a gcluasa.

Oid. Éadach, an eadh, nó craobh? Nó cad ba cheart?

C.C. Uan baineann 's í nuadh-bheárrtha, a holann soin.[36]

C.C. Atone, then, to the female Gods
      Who own this sacred place you infringed upon first.

Oid. Tell me what I must do, friends.

C.C. First take with hands that are washed of taint
      Water from the place where it flows eternally.

Oid. And when I have the pure water?

C.C. There are goblets to be obtained, that were made by an excellent craftsman;
      Put garlands around them and their handles.

Oid. [Of] cloth, is it, or branches? Or what would be proper?

C.C. A female lamb, newborn – her wool.

---

36 De Brún (1929: 16).

Throughout de Brún's text, one finds features typical of Corca Dhuibhne Irish. For example, the past participle 'fachta' (obtained), the variant plural form 'áraistí' (vessels), and the expression 'déanfad rud ort' (I will obey your wishes), all appear on the same page as the extract just quoted. The lines are in iambic pentameter which means that concision is required: one way de Brún achieved this was by showing in his spelling elision, which would be normal in the spoken language but not usually indicated in written texts, marked with an apostrophe as can be seen in the text.

George Thomson (1903–87)

If de Brún's journey to the Irish of Dún Chaoin was remarkable, that of Thomson to the Irish of the Blasket Islands was arguably even more so. Born in West Dulwich, London, Thomson took an interest in Ireland due to the fact that he had a grandfather and mother of Ulster Protestant stock who supported the cause of Irish independence. He began to learn Irish as a teenager, attending classes run by the Gaelic League, and went to read Classics at King's College, Cambridge, in 1922. His interest in Ireland remained strong and he made the first of many visits to the Blasket Islands in 1923. There, he befriended, among others, the islander Muiris Ó Súilleabháin who helped him to improve his Irish and whom he would later encourage to write the now acclaimed autobiography *Fiche Bliain ag Fás* (*Twenty Years A-Growing*).[37]

Thomson thought of the Blasket Islands as having much in common with the Ithaca of the *Odyssey* and believed that the language of the Blaskets shared similarities with the Homeric poems.[38] He was struck by the use of formulas in the speech of the islanders and this led him to be an early proponent of Milman Parry's theory of oral-formulaic composition.[39] Thomson's experience of the speech community of the Blasket Islands was, as the following passage illustrates, a deeply formative one:

Then I went to Ireland. The conversation of those ragged peasants, as soon as I learnt to follow it, electrified me. It was as though Homer had come alive. Its vitality was inexhaustible, yet it was rhythmical, alliterative, formal, artificial, always on the point of bursting into poetry.... One day it was announced that a woman in the village had given birth to a child.... Tá sé tarraingthe aniar aice 'She has brought her load from the west'. I recognised the allusion, because often, when turf was scarce, I had seen the women come down from the hills bent double under packs of heather. What a fine image, I thought,

---

[37] Breathnach and Ní Mhurchú (2018h).   [38] Thomson (1988: 39, 70–1).
[39] Thomson (1988: 39–48), Alexiou (2000: 63).

what eloquence! Before the day was out, I had heard the same expression from three or four different people. It was common property. After many similar experience[s] I realised that these gems falling from the lips of the people, so far from being novelties, were centuries old – they were what the language was made of; and as I became fluent in it they began to trip off my own tongue. Returning to Homer, I read him in a new light.[40]

Thomson's daughter, the Greek scholar Margaret Alexiou, describes the enjoyment and intellectual satisfaction he gained from translating ancient Greek into Irish and English. As target languages, they presented different challenges:

> To his surprise, he found Aristotle and Plato easier to render directly into Irish than English idiom, so he tried more with the same results, recorded painstakingly in his beautiful manuscript hand, in bound trilingual exercise books as yet unpublished.[41]

Thomson was concerned with the status of the Irish language in newly independent Ireland: he held strong opinions on the value of education, including instruction in the classics, as a means of preserving the language and ensuring that its speakers would be treated with dignity. In a letter published in *The Star* newspaper on 20 July 1929, Thomson argued for the importance of providing education in the Irish language from primary school all the way to university level. University teaching through Irish would enhance the status of the language and would enable it to be developed to a higher level:

> Tá dímheas ar an dteangain – ag lucht an iarthair toisc ná fuil sí ag an lucht ceannaíochta ins na bailtí móra; age sna ceannaithe toisc ná fuil sí ag lucht an tsaibhris; ag lucht an tsaibhris toisc ná fuil gá acu léi mar chomhartha dea-oideachais. Ní mar sin a bheadh an scéal aici, dá mbeadh sí in airde ins na hollscoileanna. Rud eile dhe, tá sí rite chun síl ar mhórán slí: is ró-dheacair aon chúrsa casta dá mbíonn dhá dtarrac ag daoine léannta do réiteach tríthi. Ag muintir na n-ollscoileanna atá a leigheas san.[42]

The language is held in contempt – by the people of the west [of Ireland] because it is not spoken by business people in the towns, by business people because it is not spoken by the wealthy, by the wealthy because they do not need it as a sign of good education. This would not be the case if it were promoted in the universities. Another point is that the language has gone to seed in many ways: it is

---

[40] Quoted by Alexiou (2000: 64–5).

[41] Alexiou (2000: 58).

[42] Thomson [Mac Tomáis] and Ó Lúing (1988: 11). This letter was written is response to Michael Tierney who opposed efforts to introduce instruction through the medium of Irish in University College Dublin where he was Professor of Greek. On Tierney's transformation from language revivalist to bête noire of the movement see Briody (2007: 55–6 and 147–8).

very difficult to resolve in Irish any complex matter of the sort that scholars grapple with. Those who work in the universities can remedy this.

In another letter to *The Star*, published on 24 May 1930, Thomson proposed that a 'peripatetic university' be established in Ireland following the approach of James Stuart who succeeded in bringing education to the working classes in cities in the north of England beginning in the 1870s, and he outlined how instruction of this type might be provided in Gaeltacht areas.[43] In a third letter that appeared in *The Star* on 7 June 1930, he argued that education through Irish would be beneficial to all Irish people, not just native speakers of Irish, and expressed his hope that the younger generations would have a less negative attitude towards the idea of instruction in Irish than the older generations of his time.[44]

Thomson had hoped to put his views on education into practice when he was appointed lecturer in Greek through Irish in University College Galway in 1931.[45] Along with teaching, Thomson intended to organize the provision of Irish-language textbooks and studies on classical Greek and other subjects suitable for use at secondary and tertiary level, and to establish extension lectures that would bring modern education to the people of the Connemara Gaeltacht. These endeavours were not successful, however: the parish priests in Connemara refused to let Thomson use school buildings as lecture halls and he was frustrated by the slow pace of his progress with An Gúm. He resigned from his post in Galway in 1934, resuming his fellowship in King's College upon his return to England.[46] He was appointed Professor of Greek in Birmingham in 1936, a position he remained in until 1970. He maintained some contact with Ireland and with Irish speakers in England after leaving Galway and, in 1959, he began a collaboration with the Irish-language academic Pádraig Ó Fiannachta which led to the publication of their joint translation of Augustine's *Confessions, Mise Agaistín*, in 1967.[47] Thomson had started on this translation during his time in Galway.[48]

Some of Thomson's publications appear under the Irish version of his name, Seoirse Mac Tomáis, while for others he used an Irish form of his mother's maiden name, Seoirse Mac Laghmainn. *Breith Báis ar Eagnuidhe: Trí Cómhráidhte d'ár cheap Platón (Apologia, Criton, Phaedón)* [*Sentence of Death on a Sage: Three Dialogues written by Plato (Apology, Crito, Phaedo*] (1929) is the only one of Thomson's Irish translations from Greek that was published in book format during the time of the state's translation scheme: it was deemed by the Department of Education to be suitable for use in secondary schools.[49] The following books of Thomson's contain Greek texts with introduction and notes in Irish: *Alcéstis*

---

[43] Thomson [Mac Tomáis] and Ó Lúing (1988: 15–19).
[44] Thomson [Mac Tomáis] and Ó Lúing (1988: 20–4).
[45] He had done most of his translations before he moved to Galway.
[46] For a more detailed discussion of Thomson's resignation see Moran (Ch. 6).
[47] Ó Fiannachta (1988b: 158), Ó Lúing (2000: 170).   [48] Ó Fiannachta (1988a: 162).
[49] Ó Fiannachta (1988a: 162).

le h-Eurípidés [*Alcestis* by Euripides] (1932) and *Prométheus fé Chuibhreach* le h-Aeschylus [*Prometheus Bound* by Aeschylus] (1933).[50] Thomson's translations of some stories from Herodotus were published in a series of articles in the newspaper *An Phoblacht/The Republic* in 1928 under the title 'An seana-shaol Gréagach: Scéalta ó stair Herodotus' ['Life in ancient Greece: Stories from Herodotus']. The book *Tosnú na Feallsúnachta* [*The Beginning of Philosophy*] (1935) is a history of Greek philosophy from its origins to Plato that is aimed at the general reader. The following translations were published posthumously: 'An lá féile' ['The festival'], a translation of the fifteenth *Idyll* of Theocritus; the first book of Homer's *Iliad*; and 'An Suimpóisiam' or Plato's *Symposium*.[51]

Other works of Thomson's were never to reach the stage of publication: in the flurry of Thomson's move from Galway to England, he lost his translation of the *Odyssey* which he had hoped to work on with Muiris Ó Súilleabháin to ensure that the Irish in it had the authentic flavour of the Blaskets.[52] A book on Greek syntax was refused by An Gúm apparently due to the idiosyncratic spelling style Thomson employed.[53] Another book called *Tosnú na Sibhialtachta* (The Beginning of Civilization) was rejected because An Gúm's readers formed the opinion that certain ideas expressed in it on the subject of evolution were contrary to Christian teaching. Their objections are outlined in a letter to Thomson from An Gúm's publication officer, as follows:

> Maidir le do leabhar, 'Tosnú na Sibhialtachta', iarrtar orm a rádh leat nach bhfuil an Roinn sásta airgead puiblidhe do chaitheamh le tuairimí do chraobhsgaoileadh atá bun-os-cionn leis an gcreideamh Críostaidhe, go sonnradhach an dá thuairim seo:
>
> (1)   gur ó na háinmhidhthe a shíolraigh an duine
>
> (2)   gurb é slighe a chéad-chuir an duine eolas ar Dhia ná gur cheap an duine féin É nuair a bhraith sé go raibh gádh le n-a cheapadh.[54]

> Regarding your book 'Tosnú na Sibhialtachta', I am asked to inform you that the Department is not willing to spend public money on propagating opinions that are contrary to the Christian faith, the two following opinions specifically:
>
> (1)   that humans descended from animals
>
> (2)   that humans first came to know God by inventing Him themselves when they felt a need to invent Him.

---

[50] Thomson's English edition of *Prometheus Bound* was published by Cambridge University Press in 1932.

[51] The first two of these are published in Ó Fiannachta (1988a) and the *Symposium* is published in Ó Fiannachta (1988b; 1989a).

[52] Ó Lúing (2000: 169).

[53] Moran (Ch. 6) further discusses Thomson's interactions with An Gúm.

[54] This letter is now held in An Gúm's archive, file N0394. I am citing here from Uí Laighléis (2017: 51–2).

These objections are followed by suggestions as to how the book might be rewritten but this was never done.

Other Translators and Editors

In spite of the rejections he received, Thomson remains a well-known figure in the dissemination of classical literature through Irish. The work of Thomson's colleague at University College Galway, Margaret Heavey, which has been less studied, is given the attention it deserves by Pádraic Moran in the next chapter. A brief overview of Heavey's output is given here, alongside that of other significant persons who translated texts from Greek and Latin into Irish or who translated or edited textbooks. Others whose work appears in the Appendix C to Chapters 5 and 6 had less of a public profile. Many were teachers or priests who learned Latin or Greek to a high level as part of their education, and most of those who translated from Latin or Greek had learned Irish as teenagers or adults having been inspired by the revival movement, in contrast to many of those who wrote original works in Irish for An Gúm and were native Irish speakers. The work of Patrick Dinneen (Pádraic Ua Duinnín), who was brought up by native Irish-speaking parents, is noted here also but is analysed in detail by Fiachra Mac Góráin (Ch. 7).

Mairghréad Ní Éimhthigh (Margaret Heavey, 1907–80)

Mairghréad Ní Éimhthigh (Margaret Heavey) was a lecturer in Classics in University College Galway where she taught through the medium of Irish. She translated the following textbooks into Irish: *Bun-Chúrsa Ceapadóireachta Gréigise* [*Greek Prose Composition*] (1942) by M. A. North and A. E. Hillard; *Graiméir Gréigise* [*Greek Grammar*] (1942) by E. A. Sonnenschein; *Prós-Cheapadóireacht Laidne* [*Latin Prose Composition*] (1947) by T. K. Arnold and G. G. Bradley. Her Irish-language edition of Book II of Caesar's *De Bello Gallico* was published in 1940.[55] Ó Concheanainn notes that Ní Éimhthigh added extra material to her translation of *Latin Prose Composition* in order to adapt it for Irish speakers.[56]

Cormac Ó Cadhlaigh (1884–1960)

Ó Cadhlaigh was an Irish teacher who was appointed lecturer in Irish in University College Cork in 1930 and Professor of Modern Irish in University

---

[55] Breathnach and Ní Mhurchú (2018b).   [56] Ó Concheanainn (2004: 19–20).

College Dublin in 1932. He translated many texts into Irish from French. His translation of Book II of Caesar's *De Bello Gallico* appeared in 1922.[57]

Maoghnas Ó Domhnaill (*c.*1900–65)

Ó Domhnaill was a member of the Gaelic League and was made editor of the League's newspaper *An Claidheamh Soluis* [*The Sword of Light*] in 1930.[58] He translated texts from Italian and French into Irish and produced the following Latin schoolbooks: *Tosach Laidne* [*Beginning Latin*] (*c.*1930); *Metamorphoses VIII* (1937); *Óráidí Chicero in aghaidh Chaitilína* [*Cicero's Speeches against Catiline*] (1937); *Prós-Cheapadóireacht Laidne do na Meadhon-Rangaibh* [*Latin Prose Composition for Intermediate Classes*] (1937).

Domhnall Ó Mathghamhna (1872–1942)

Ó Mathghamhna was born in Kilrush, Co. Clare. He studied medicine at the Catholic University of Ireland (now University College Dublin) after which he set up a medical practice in Dublin. He learned Irish as an adult, encouraged perhaps by the Irish-language scholar Shán Ó Cuív (1875–1940) who was a patient of his. Ó Mathghamhna was a great admirer of Peadar Ua Laoghaire: he wrote two books on Ua Laoghaire's Irish and prepared a new edition of Ua Laoghaire's book *Séadna* which was published in 1934.[59] Ó Mathghamhna was a prolific translator of Greek and Latin into Irish. The following works of his were published in book format: *Óráid Caointe Phericléis* [*The Funeral Oration of Pericles* by Thucydides] (1930); Lucian's *Vera Historia* (1931);[60] *An Tarna Philippica* [*The Second Phillipic* by Cicero] (1932); *Saoghal-ré na nGracchi* [*The Lives of the Gracchi* by Plutarch] (1933); *Démostenés agus Cicero* [*Demosthenes and Cicero* by Plutarch] (1935); *Inis Atlaint* [*The Island of Atlantis* or *Critias* by Plato] (1935); Cicero's *De Senectute* (1953). He was awarded a prize at the Tailteann Games in 1928 for his translation of the *Vera Historia*.[61] Ó Mathghamhna's *Scéalta a Filí na Rómha* [*Stories from the Poets of Rome*] (1933) is a translation of *Stories from the Latin Poets* by Margaret Pease.

---

[57] Breathnach and Ní Mhurchú (2018c).
[58] Breathnach and Ní Mhurchú (2018d).   [59] Breathnach and Ní Mhurchú (2018f).
[60] This was originally serialized in the *Sunday Independent* in 1925 and 1926. See Appendix C to Chapters 5 and 6.
[61] Breathnach and Ní Mhurchú (2018g).

Pádraig Ua Duinnín (1860–1934)

Ua Duinnín is best known as a lexicographer and editor of Irish poetry.[62] His edition of the first book of Virgil's *Aeneid*, *Aenéis Bhirgil*, was published in 1931, following his 1929 book *Aistí ar Litridheacht Ghréigise is Laidne* [*Essays on Greek and Latin Literature*]. In the introduction to his textual edition, he stated that he was pleased at the growing trend for teaching Latin through Irish and that the book was his contribution to this movement. He argued that it was easier to learn Latin through Irish due to grammatical similarities and stated that Irish was more suited than English to expressing the thoughts and mindset of the time of the *Aeneid* ('[is] oireamhnaighe an Ghaedhealg do smuaintibh is d'aigne na sean-aimsire atá i gceist san Aenéis ná an Béarla'). On the other hand, he acknowledged that some very good books on the Latin language and on Latin poetry had been written in English and urged students not to ignore these.[63]

Peadar Ua Laoghaire (1839–1920)

Ua Laoghaire was a priest and writer who held strong views on the revival of Irish, urging writers to adopt 'caint na ndaoine' (the language of the people) as the basis for their literary efforts in the language.[64] He has been characterized as a 'nativist' by O'Leary due to the fact that he sometimes expressed reservations about translation, but he translated a number of texts into the Irish language.[65] Two of his translations were published posthumously in the 1920s: these are his translation of some of the first book of Euclid which was published in 1922 and *Lúcián* (1924), a compilation of Ua Laoghaire's translations of Lucian's *Dialogues of the Gods* that had previously been published in a series of articles in the *Journal of the Ivernian Society*.[66]

Conclusion

The impact of the textbooks and translations discussed in this chapter needs to be considered separately. Latin and Greek textbooks in Irish were aimed at second-ary schools which were classified as A, B, or C schools, according to how much of the teaching was done through Irish. In 1931, there were thirty-four category A schools where all teaching was delivered through Irish and 113 category B schools

---

[62] Breathnach and Ní Mhurchú (2018e).
[63] Ua Duinnín (1931: [3]–[4]), and see further Mac Góráin (Ch. 7).
[64] Breathnach and Ní Mhurchú (2018f).
[65] O'Leary (1994: 357); for a full list of Ua Laoghaire's translations see Ó Cuív (1954: 28–30 and 33–4).
[66] For details see Ó Cuív (1954: 22).

where some subjects other than Irish were taught through Irish, and the number of schools teaching through Irish continued to increase during the 1930s and 1940s.[67] A and B schools would have provided a market for Latin and Greek textbooks in Irish. Regarding translations, it is clear that An Gúm's scheme encouraged talented individuals to turn their hand to translation from Greek and Latin into Irish, and that it produced books that would otherwise not have come into existence. These vary in quality but the best of them are very good indeed. It is difficult to know how much impact they had at the time of publication: we do not have sales figures for all of them but, in general, An Gúm's translations did not sell particularly well and neither were they borrowed in great numbers from libraries.[68] The translations of Greek and Latin books were not read widely in the Gaeltacht or in other parts of the country and their publication did not lead to an increase in the number of readers of Irish, but on the other hand, they did provide interesting and challenging reading material for existing readers: this is exemplified by the libraries of the poet Seán Ó Ríordáin (1916–77) and of Torna or Tadhg Ó Donnchadha (1874–1949), Professor of Irish in University College Cork from 1916, both of which contain copies of some of the books discussed here.[69]

An Gúm has been praised for preserving dialectical features of the Irish language in many of its early publications: the translations of de Brún and Thomson who, as discussed above, engaged deeply with the south-western Gaeltacht community of Corca Dhuibhne in order to improve their writing style in the language, are a case in point and ought to be given fuller acknowledgement as forming part of the rich literary heritage of that region.[70] The Irish language today is threatened in Gaeltacht areas, and many of the approaches taken by the Irish State, since its foundation, to preserve the language have been less than successful. However, the language still survives against the odds, it is used as a medium for literature, and there exists a small but loyal market for books in the Irish language. Some of the translations commissioned by An Gúm are of books that have now fallen long out of fashion, but the appeal of many of the Greek and Latin translations is relatively timeless. I suggest that many of them would, with modernized spelling, appeal to contemporary readers and are thus well worth republishing; restaging de Brún's translated Greek plays would also be an interesting project.

Irish-language publishers have produced translations from Latin and ancient Greek intermittently since the cessation of An Gúm's translation scheme—a recent example is *Catullus Gaelach* [Gaelic Catullus], which contains translations

---

[67] Adrian Kelly (2002: 61–2).
[68] Uí Laighléis (2007: 210–11). Sales figures for some of An Gúm's publications are included in Appendix C to Chapters 5 and 6.
[69] Ó Ríordáin and Torna's book collections are now held in the Boole Library, University College Cork.
[70] For other evaluations of the translation scheme see Titley (1991: 66–7), Cronin (1996: 159), Adrian Kelly (2002: 96–102), and O'Leary (2004: 406).

of poems by Catullus by a number of Irish-language poets.[71] Many of these poets, however, would not have been able to translate directly from the originals as de Brún, Thomson, and others did some generations before them: in the second half of the twentieth century, the teaching of ancient Greek and Latin in Ireland was on the wane and the vast majority of secondary-level students now study modern European languages instead, reflecting Ireland's increased engagement with other European countries through its membership of the European Union. If the establishment of An Gúm's translation scheme is seen as a sign of faith in the possibility of reviving the Irish language nationwide at the time of the foundation of the Irish State, the obstacles and objections met by both de Brún and Thomson reveal some of the underlying tensions regarding how this aim might be achieved and indeed whether it was possible at all; the eventual scrapping of the translation scheme can be seen as part of a wider and gradual downshift in government language policy from its initial lofty goal of a nationwide regaelicization to its more modest present objective of maintaining Irish as a living minority language.

---

[71] Edited by Pádraig Breandán Ó Laighin and published by Coiscéim in 2010. Catullus also inspired the 1916 revolutionary Thomas MacDonagh, as discussed by Moloney (Ch. 4).

6

Classics through Irish
at University College, Galway, 1931–78

Pádraic Moran

Classics as a modern discipline had a unique expression at University College, Galway (UCG), where Greek and Latin language and literature were taught through the medium of Irish, beginning soon after the foundation of the Irish Free State and continuing uninterrupted down to the 1970s.[1] This initiative is often associated with George Thomson (Seoirse Mac Tomáis), who taught Greek through Irish at UCG from 1931 to 1934. Thomson is best known in Ireland for his connections with the Blasket Islands and his relationship with the islander Muiris Ó Súilleabháin, author of the memoir *Fiche Blian ag Fás (Twenty Years a-Growing)*.[2] Internationally, Thomson's reputation rests primarily on his Marxist treatments of Greek history and literature.[3] But although he was undoubtedly a groundbreaking figure in several ways, his contribution during three years in Galway was small in the context of a project that continued for more than four decades. This chapter follows the story of Irish-language Classics in Galway from its early development down to its eventual suspension in 1978. It draws on new and recent archival work to correct and re-evaluate aspects of the received version of Thomson's Galway career, particularly regarding the circumstances of his appointment and departure.[4] It also tells the story of his colleague Margaret Heavey (Mairghréad Ní Éimhthigh/Mairéad Ní Éimhigh), a figure also groundbreaking in her own way, but whose career has heretofore been almost entirely ignored.

---

[1] Queen's College, Galway, was founded in 1845 and opened its doors to students in 1848. It was reconstituted as University College, Galway, part of the new National University of Ireland (NUI), in 1908. In 1997 it was renamed National University of Ireland, Galway. On the position of Irish in the NUI see Ó Tuathaigh (2008).

[2] Ó Súilleabháin (1933).   [3] See Gathercole (2007); Hall and Stead (2016).

[4] I am very grateful to Séamus Mac Mathúna (former Secretary for Academic Affairs at UCG/NUIG) for sharing his collection of transcripts and copies of archival material relating to George Thomson with me, and for offering detailed comments on this chapter. Mac Conghail (2009) has published some of this material, and more of his own discovery, in Irish translation. I would also like to thank Alderik Blom, Arthur Keaveney, John Madden, Fiachra Mac Góráin, Ann Mohr, and Louis de Paor for their helpful comments and corrections.

Pádraic Moran, *Classics through Irish at University College, Galway, 1931–78* In: *Classics and Irish Politics, 1916–2016*. Edited by: Isabelle Torrance and Donncha O'Rourke, Oxford University Press (2020).
© Oxford University Press.
DOI: 10.1093/oso/9780198864486.003.0006

Early Professors of Classics

The careers of the earliest professors in Classics at Queen's College, Galway, from 1848 down to 1916 have been documented by Arthur Keaveney.[5] The chair of Greek was given pride of place in the rolls of professors printed in university calendars of the time. Its earliest incumbents were William E. Hearn (1849–54), William Nesbitt (1854–64), D'Arcy Wentworth Thompson (1864–1902), and Robert Knox McElderry (1902–16). The Queen's Colleges also provided for professors of Latin, even though the subject did not yet have a dedicated chair in the ancient English universities.[6] Its earliest holders were William Nesbitt (1849–54, who then migrated to the chair of Greek after its vacation by Hearn), Richard Blair Bagley (1854–69), Thomas Maguire (1869–80), John Fletcher Davies (1880–9), Philip Sandford (1890–1903), and Charles Exon (1903–16). After Exon's retirement in 1916, the chairs of Greek and Latin were amalgamated into a new chair of Ancient Classics, which McElderry (until then Professor of Greek) took over until his resignation in 1924.[7]

Most of these men were graduates of Trinity College Dublin.[8] All were of Protestant background with the exception of Maguire, who, though a Catholic, was a staunch Unionist.[9] The twilight of McElderry's tenure, however, coincided with the revolutionary period 1919–23 and the associated demise of the Protestant Ascendancy, and his successors in the Free State era reflected the new social order. The next two holders of the chair of Classics were both Catholic clerics, Thomas Dempsey and Thomas Fahy.

Dempsey was born at Kiltullagh in east Galway, c.1887.[10] He was ordained at Maynooth, where he obtained an MA for a dissertation on the Delphic oracle, afterwards published as a monograph (Dempsey (1918)). Following a period teaching Classics at St Joseph's Diocesan School in Ballinasloe (where he had himself been a pupil), Dempsey was appointed to succeed McElderry in 1924. His career was cut short: he died, after a brief illness, in August 1927.[11] Dempsey was succeeded by a Maynooth contemporary, Thomas Fahy (1887–1973), a native of

---

[5] Keaveney (1999).

[6] Chairs of Latin were established in Oxford and Cambridge only in 1854 and 1869, respectively (Stray 1998: 109, 123). The chair of Latin at Trinity College Dublin was founded in 1870.

[7] Keaveney (1999: 342) puts this down to the decreasing numbers of students taking Greek, though as Greek continued to be taught there was presumably no diminution of teaching hours.

[8] Bagley was an early graduate of Queen's College, Cork. McElderry studied at Queen's College, Belfast, then at St John's College, Cambridge. Thompson is an exceptional figure in many ways: see Keaveney (1999: 331–6). The son of a ship's master contracted to take convicts to Australia, he was born off Van Diemen's Land in 1829. He was educated at Trinity and Pembroke colleges, Cambridge.

[9] Characterized at the time as a 'Castle Catholic': Keaveney (1999: 336–8).

[10] Obituary: *The Irish Times*, 4 August 1927, p. 10.

[11] Dempsey seemed to have been well liked by his students. An editorial in the student *College Annual* for 1926–7 offers warm wishes for his recovery. The following year's issue, after his death, has a very generous appreciation (pp. 62–4) signed 'Discipula' (possibly Margaret Heavey?).

Gloves, near Athenry, in east Galway. Fahy was ordained in 1912, took an MA in Classics and taught at Maynooth before coming to Galway in 1927; he was appointed to the chair the following year, and held the position for three decades, retiring in 1957.[12]

Quite apart from being a Catholic cleric, Fahy reflected the recent social change in his political connections. He was a close friend of the militant republican Liam Mellows and during Easter 1916 was the messenger who brought news to about 600 Galway volunteers serving under Mellows at Limepark, Peterswell (near Gort), that their Dublin counterparts had disbanded, urging them to do the same.[13] He is also said to have written speeches for Mellows during the 1918 election campaign. Fahy was photographed at the wedding party of Pádraig Ó Máille and Eileen Acton on 28 September 1921, the former a founder member of the Gaelic League in Galway and later TD with Cumann na nGaedheal.[14] Fahy (presumably the celebrant) sits near the centre of the group, with the groom on his right and Arthur Griffith on his left; Michael Collins sits in the same row.[15] Within a fortnight, Griffith and Collins had arrived in London to begin negotiations on the Anglo-Irish Treaty.[16]

Margaret Heavey's Background

Dempsey's brief tenure as professor corresponded exactly with Margaret Heavey's undergraduate career. She was born on Old Church Street, Athenry, on 15 September 1907, her father Thomas Heavey a saddler, her mother Alice Kirwan a native of Dublin. She was the eldest of five siblings, all of whom died between the ages of 19 and 35.[17] Heavey enrolled in the Presentation National School, Athenry, in 1911, and left in June 1924 aged 16. She spent the last five years in the 'Secondary Top', during which time she completed Junior, Middle, and Senior grade Intermediate Board exams.[18] In her final exams she obtained honours in

---

[12] His principal publications were Fahy 1919 and Fahy 1963. Obituaries: *Connacht Sentinel*, 19 June 1973, p. 12; *The Irish Times*, 20 June 1973, p. 4.

[13] See Fahy's witness statement (no. 383) made in 1950 to the Bureau of Military History 1913–21, available at http://www.militaryarchives.ie (accessed 5 December 2019).

[14] National Library of Ireland, Dublin: 'Pádraig Ó Máille's Wedding Photographic Print', http://catalogue.nli.ie/Record/vtls000298330 (accessed 5 December 2019).

[15] Ó Máille's brother Tomás (1880–1938) is also present; he was Professor of Modern Irish Language and Literature from 1909 to 1910, then of Irish Language, Philology, and Literature until 1938.

[16] During the ensuing Civil War, Mellows was executed by the Free State in Mountjoy Gaol on 8 December 1922 in reprisal for an attack the previous day on Pádraig Ó Máille and Seán Hales (in which the latter was killed).

[17] Ahern (2009: 243–5). Other biographical sources are Ó Concheanainn (2004); Breathnach and Ní Mhurchú (2018b).

[18] Her academic attainments are detailed in *Application from Margaret M. Heavey for the Professorship of Ancient Classics in University College, Galway, Together with Copies of Testimonials*, dated 12 March 1958 (archived in the James Hardiman Library, Special Collections).

Irish, Greek, and Latin. Her qualification in Greek was highly exceptional. Although the Department of Education's statistical report for the school year 1923–4 provides no information on individual subjects, more detailed figures in the following year's report may be taken as indicative.[19] Out of 745 boys taking the newly instituted Leaving Certificate in 1925, 131 (c.18 per cent) sat the Greek exam.[20] The total number of girls overall sitting the Leaving Certificate was just 250, and of these none at all took Greek.[21] It was uncommon at this time even for girls to take Latin: just 52 (21 per cent) as opposed to 502 boys (67 per cent) sat the exam; more notable still is the fact that just six girls in the whole country took it at honours level.[22] Against this background, then, Heavey's achievements in Latin and particularly Greek are quite remarkable. How she obtained her tuition is unknown. Presumably a teacher spotted her potential and provided or arranged for private classes.[23]

On leaving school, Heavey obtained first place in both Entrance and County Council scholarship exams for UCG, and in her first year at university won the Irish Language Prize and the Peel Prize for English Composition. During the second and third years of her studies, she won first place in the College Scholarships, the Irish Language Prize, and the Blayney Exhibition in Classics and Irish, graduating with a BA degree and a Postgraduate Scholarship in 1927.[24] In the summer of 1928 she was awarded a Higher Diploma in Education and, remarkably, in the autumn of the same year an MA in Classics, by examination as well as for a dissertation titled 'The Galatians', produced under Fahy's supervision.

In the same year Heavey won the prestigious National University of Ireland Travelling Studentship in Classics. This was originally established in 1910 to fund three years' study abroad with an annual stipend of £100. In the near-century between 1910 and 2008, twenty-eight awards were made for postgraduate studies in Classics, Heavey being the only female recipient.[25] She spent two years in Munich, where she studied ancient history with Walter Friedrich Otto; Greek and Latin literature with Rudolf Pfeiffer, Albert Rehm, Johannes Stroux, and Carl Weyman; medieval Latin with Paul Lehmann; and linguistics with Ferdinand

---

[19] Reports are available at https://www.education.ie/en/Publications/Statistics/Statistical-Reports/ (accessed 5 December 2019).

[20] Report of the Department of Education for the School Year 1924–5: 101–2. The proportion taking Greek was roughly on a par with French, with 134 students, while German had only three.

[21] The profile of subjects taken by girls is quite different: French, for example, was taken by 209 girls (84%).

[22] 152 boys (30%) took honours Latin.

[23] It has been suggested to me that Fahy was responsible, though as he was based in Maynooth at the time this seems unlikely.

[24] Her academic ambition was apparently already evident at this point. A skit in the *UCG Annual* for 1925–6 entitled 'Our favourite books' (79) includes 'The Path of Glory, by M. Heavey'.

[25] National University of Ireland (2008: 15). (My thanks to Lisa Nic an Bhreithimh of the NUI for pointing me to this publication.)

Sommer and Hanns Oertel.[26] The value of her German training was emphasized as late as 1958 in references given in support of her application for the chair. Heavey never completed a doctorate, however, for reasons that are unclear.[27] It is possible that only two years of funding were available in that year. Alternatively, she may have decided to return home early, given the prospect of a new teaching position opening in Classics at UCG, a position for which she was ideally qualified.[28]

Irish-Language University Education

In the national economic strain of the 1920s, the very viability of UCG was called into question.[29] From 1924, the college made repeated representations to Ernest Blythe, Cumann na nGaedheal Minister for Finance (1923–33), seeking an increase in its funding. Eventually, Blythe agreed to support the college on the grounds that it had committed to increasing the proportion of its functions delivered through Irish. This resulted in the University College Galway Act, 1929, which increased the annual grant from £12,000 to £28,000 in order to stabilize the college's finances, and allowed for a further annual increase of £2,000 at the discretion of the Minister for Finance, specifically to support new Irish-language initiatives.[30]

The move was not without its critics. In particular, Michael Tierney, Professor of Greek at University College Dublin, was dismissive of the Irish-language project, arguing in the Cumann na nGaedheal newspaper, *The Star*, that instruction through Irish was appropriate for subjects related to Ireland, but that other disciplines would be better served by English.[31] His intervention precipitated a running debate in the pages of the same paper, with counterarguments published (in Irish) by Liam Ó Rinn, Tomás Ó Máille, T. F. O'Rahilly, and a newcomer, George Derwent Thomson, also known as Seoirse Mac Tomáis.[32]

---

[26] These details from Heavey's *Application for the Professorship*.

[27] Compare her older contemporary, Kathleen Mulchrone (afterwards Professor of Old and Middle Irish and Celtic Philology at UCG, 1938–65), who had a Travelling Studentship in Celtic Studies and worked in Bonn under Rudolf Thurneysen from 1921–4, gaining a DPhil.

[28] Heavey maintained contact with her alma mater while away. The *University Annual* for 1929–30 (17–20) carried her humorous review of *Praeco Latinus*, a nineteenth-century periodical written in Latin, which she had found in a Munich bookshop ('A nineteenth century magazine in Latin').

[29] Mac Mathúna (2008: 63–79).

[30] Available in full at http://www.irishstatutebook.ie/eli/1929/act/35/ (accessed 5.12.2019). Compare the annual statutory grants of £20,000 and £32,000 for University Colleges Cork and Dublin, respectively (established in the Irish Universities Act, 1908).

[31] Edition of 29 June 1929. Tierney, another native of east Galway (Ballymacward), had himself received a Travelling Studentship in Classics in 1915, and was later President of UCD, 1947–64.

[32] See editions of 6 July 1929, 20 July 1929, 24 May 1930. Thomson's contributions are collected in Ó Lúing (1988: 10–31).

Thomson's story has been told many times, and so may be summarized here in outline.[33] He was born in London in 1903 and studied Classics at King's College, Cambridge. He first visited the Blasket Islands in August 1923, and befriended Muiris Ó Súilleabháin, whose memoir *Fiche Blian ag Fás* (*Twenty Years a-Growing*) Thomson was later instrumental in publishing. During regular visits to the Blaskets throughout the 1920s he perfected his Irish. After graduating from Cambridge in 1926, Thomson spent a year at Trinity College Dublin, and returned to Dublin again in 1929 while working on his edition of Aeschylus' *Prometheus Bound* (Thomson (1932a)). During this time he also published his own transla-tions into Irish of excerpts from Herodotus and Plato's dialogues *Apology*, *Crito*, and *Phaedo*,[34] and had translations of several other classical works in hand.[35]

It is clear that Thomson was at this time actively pursuing a university teaching post in Ireland. On 14 February 1930, just two months after the 1929 Act was passed (on 17 December), he visited Liam Ó Briain and Thomas Dillon, UCG professors of Romance languages and Chemistry, respectively, on his way to visit Muiris Ó Súilleabháin in Carraroe.[36] The next day, Ó Briain wrote to Ernest Blythe informing him about their conversation, about Thomson's desire to work in Galway, and about his ideas to teach European classics, including Homer, Dante, Shakespeare, as well as the history of artistic movements, making comparison with Irish as far as possible.[37] In the same letter, Ó Briain emphasized Thomson's proven credentials in the Irish language. Three months later, on 30 May 1930, Ó Briain and Dillon put a motion to the Academic Council recommending the establishment of a new lectureship through Irish specifically for him:

[33] Ó Lúing (1980); Mac Conghail (1987: 148–62); Enright (1988); Ó Lúing (1989: 57–99); Ó Lúing (1996); Newman (1998); C. Alexiou (1999a); M. Alexiou (2000) and other articles in Ní Chéilleachair (2000); Mac Conghail (2009); Lysaght (2009); Kanigel (2012); Seaford (2014); Breathnach and Ní Mhurchú (2018h), and Ní Mhurchú (Ch. 5).

[34] The former in editions of *An Phoblacht* between 21 January and 19 May 1928. The dialogues were published as Mac Laghmhainn (1929). For reasons unclear, Thomson published these under an assumed name, a Gaelicized version of his mother's family name, Clements.

[35] Euripides, *Alcestis* (submitted to Oifig Díolta Foillseachán Rialta (ODFR) in September 1929, according to Thomson's report of 22 February 1933 (see Appendix A to Chapter 6), and published in 1932); Aeschylus, *Prométheus fé Chuibhreach* (submitted to ODFR in December 1930, published 1933), an abridged translation of Thomson (1932a). Other translations completed at this time remained in draft until published decades later by Pádraig Ó Fiannachta: Augustine's *Confessions*, books 1–8 (together with books 9–10 translated by Ó Fiannachta in Thomson [Mac Tomáis] and Ó Fiannachta (1967)); parts of Theocritus, *Idyll* 15 and all of *Iliad* 1 (Ó Fiannachta (1988a)); and Plato's *Symposium* (Ó Fiannachta (1988b, 1989a)). A complete translation of the *Odyssey* is now lost: see M. Alexiou (2000: 58). With the exception of the Theocritus poem, all of these translations were listed as complete in his application letter to UCG dated 1 August 1931: see Mac Conghail (2009: 155–6). The letter also mentions a translation of *Iliad* 1–9 (only book 1 was available to Ó Fiannachta) and Plato's *Republic*.

[36] Ó Súilleabháin was posted there as a garda (policeman) in November 1927: see *Fiche Blian* (Ó Súilleabháin 1933), ch. 25. Ó Briain and Dillon had both been active in the War of Independence. They were appointed to UCG in 1917 and 1919, respectively: see Rouse (2009) and Leaney and Lunney (2009).

[37] Mac Conghail (2009: 145–6). University College Dublin Archives Department (UCDAD), P24/342 (52).

That, in the opinion of the Academic Council the Governing Body should make application to the government for funds sufficient to provide for a lecturer in Comparative Literature (or some similar title); a Lecturer who would deal in Irish with the main currents of literary development from classical times, down through the Middle Ages to modern times; also possibly on the principal artistic movements, classic, Romanesque, Gothic, etc.; as we believe that such a course of lectures, especially if given in the evening and open to the public, would be popular and useful and add to the attractiveness of the Irish courses in the College. We advocate the establishment of such a lectureship as in the person of Mr. G. Thompson [sic] (Seoirse Mac Tomáis), fellow of King's College, Cambridge, author of Breith Báis ar Eagnuidhe (a translation of three dialogues of Plato into Irish); of various articles in Irish; of several works of research in Classics in English, and translator of Homer's Odyssey into Irish (as yet unpublished). A man of very distinguished academic attainments and of proved capacity as an Irish writer and speaker would, in all probability, be attracted by such a post and would be a candidate for it.[38]

The Academic Council afterwards amended the motion to invite submissions from all Faculties regarding potential new posts and suitable candidates. It seems that Heavey had also been identified as such. A writer in *The Irish Monthly* in December 1929 commented, also responding to Tierney: 'There are several very competent speakers of Irish well qualified to teach University subjects. Galway College itself already possesses many such—we might instance Miss Heavey in the case of Greek, Professor Tierney's own subject—and will soon possess many more.'[39]

On 27 October 1930, in the following autumn, the Academic Council accepted a recommendation from the Faculty of Arts to create either professorships or lectureships in three subjects: Ancient Irish History and Welsh, Classics, and Education.[40] Suitable potential candidates for each post were identified, respectively, as Michael O'Brien, Margaret Heavey, and Eric Mac Fhinn.[41] The Council further decided that General Literature, for which Thomson had been recommended by Ó Briain and Dillon, was not a priority area. Further decisions were to

---

[38] Transcribed by Mac Mathúna. Ó Briain also forwarded the text of the motion to Blythe (UCDAD P24/342 (36)).

[39] 'Notes on current educational topics' (signed E.H.D.), *The Irish Monthly* 57, no. 678 (Dec. 1929), 617–22: at 621. Posts through Irish had earlier been established in History (1927), Economics, and Mathematics (both 1928).

[40] Also a recommendation from Faculty of Science to establish a lectureship in experimental physics.

[41] The 1929 Act required the minister to give advance approval to new positions. The College presumably wanted to ensure that if the minister approved a position, somebody would be available to fill it.

be postponed until the suitability of all candidates could be confirmed by a board of Irish-language examiners.[42]

Accordingly, following interviews, a panel of eleven assessors reported on 5 February 1931 that Thomson was 'highly competent' to lecture through Irish in either General Literature or Classics, and recommended Heavey and Thomson in first and second order of preference, respectively. A letter by Ó Briain to Blythe two days later brought the minister up to date and noted that the majority of the staff, including Professor Fahy, were entirely in support of the recommendations.[43] Ó Briain expressed the opinion that strengthening Classics by appointing two lecturers would attract students to the university. On 11 February, the Academic Council voted to request two positions in Ancient Classics from the Minister for Finance, recommending Heavey and Thomson. Four days later, the President and Registrar, Alexander Anderson and John Hynes, travelled to meet with the ministers for Finance and Education in Dublin, who approved the establishment of lectureships on a salary of £500 each. Following this, the college drafted Statute XX (passed 2 June 1931) to establish officially the new lectureships; Thomson made a formal application for the post, dated 1 August 1931.[44] The lecturers were then appointed by the Senate of the National University on 16 October 1931, to begin officially from 1 November (even though the lecturers had already been acting in their roles since the beginning of October).

This archival record, uncovered largely through the combined efforts of Séamus Mac Mathúna and Muiris Mac Conghail, and brought to light only in the latter's Irish-language monograph of 2009, is an important corrective to a widely-known narrative that Mac Conghail had previously summarized thus:[45]

There was a story in circulation for many years concerning the appointment of George Thomson to Galway. It is said that the then president and college authorities had decided to give the lectureship to a cleric and when Thomson's application came before them, although well qualified, they felt that a Cambridge graduate could hardly meet the requirement of being able to lecture in Irish. On the appointed day and having satisfied themselves as to Thomson's qualifications they applied the 'failsafe' test by asking Thomson to give a short talk in Irish; a flow of Blasket Irish ushered the young Englishman into UCG.

[42] In the meantime, Thomson visited University College Cork on 20 November 1930, as a respondent to a lecture given by Seamus Dalton on the topic 'fostering our national culture if Ireland is to attain a dignity and be an intellectual force in the future' (notice in Irish Examiner, 20 November 1930, p. 10).

[43] UCDAD P24/342 (32).   [44] Mac Conghail (2009: 154–6).

[45] 'An English scholar of Ireland and Greece', The Irish Times, 11 February 1987, p. 14; similarly recounted in Mac Conghail (1987: 151).

This scenario paints Thomson almost as a classical culture hero, a gifted outsider who cleverly overcomes an ordeal and thereby defeats the forces of corruption; in this case he is assisted not by a magical object, but a flow of 'pure' Irish brought directly out of the otherworldly Blaskets. Though attractive as a narrative, the story distorts the historical reality. The college authorities were considerably better informed and much more open-minded than given credit for.

Thomson himself was not averse to similar romanticization. The story of his first encounter with Muiris Ó Súilleabháin, for example, is told in *Fiche Blian ag Fás* (ch. 19) almost in the manner of a classical divine epiphany. One evening, in the twilight, Muiris was watching sheep when the ground began to shake. Down the hill approaches a strange figure (Thomson) with an otherworldly quality, finely-dressed in a cloak and knee breeches and bearing a mischievous grin. Muiris braces himself to encounter a leprechaun. This was apparently a story of Thomson's own invention. In an interview to Proinsias Mac Aonghusa in 1976,[46] he recalled how Ó Súilleabháin told the story of their first meeting to Peig Sayers. Thomson and Máire White Lane were walking up from the quay as Ó Súilleabháin approached from the opposite direction driving a donkey bearing turf. As they passed, the donkey stopped and Ó Súilleabháin quipped 'féach, ní haon chapall ráis é seo agat, a bhuachaill' ['See—you have no racehorse here, boy'].[47] Evidently the leprechaun was a characterization that Thomson invented for himself. In his own words: 'Nuair a cheap sé [Ó Súilleabháin] an leabhar tháinig smaoineamh eile chugam mar gheall ar an luipreachán. Thaithin sin leis agus chaith sé an leagan eile uaidh.' ['When he [Ó Súilleabháin] wrote the book, another idea came to me about the leprechaun. That appealed to him, and he discarded the other version.']

As the new lecturers through Irish were about to take up their posts,[48] the initiative still faced scepticism from some quarters. An anonymous 'Special Correspondent' in *The Irish Times* for 3 September 1931 discussed the development, attributing the following bizarre remarks to Thomson's own promoter Ó Briain:

We already have one man [i.e. Fahy] lecturing in Classics [...] and this rather overloads that department, as we certainly do not want three. But our policy is to get every suitable person and then create positions, if necessary. For instance, if we knew a man with the necessary qualifications in Irish, whose subject was Chinese pottery, we should establish a department in Chinese pottery, even if there were no students. It might happen that when we advertised the position

---

[46] Mac Aonghusa (1999: 104–5).
[47] This alludes to the proverbial saying that you can't make a racehorse out of an ass.
[48] Mac Fhinn took up the third position, in Education, retiring eventually in 1965.

another man with suitable qualifications might apply as well as the man we had in view. That is unlikely, but if it occurred we would probably appoint both.

The flippant tone of the quotation ascribed to Ó Briain is quite unlike that of his archival correspondence, and suggests that the author of the article was being derisive. If 'Chinese pottery' is to be taken as proverbial for obscure and impractical, then apparently teaching Classics through Irish was equally ridiculous.[49]

Thomson in Galway, 1931–4

In the newly expanded department of Ancient Classics, Fahy continued to teach Latin and Greek through English, as before, leaving instruction through Irish entirely to the new appointees. University calendars at that time indicate a schedule of five teaching hours per week for first-year students (Monday to Saturday) and the same for a combined second- and third-year cohort.[50] In their first year the new lecturers through Irish taught first-year students only. A student of Thomson's at this time, Máirtín Ó Flathartaigh, later recounted how, during the very first term, he attended lectures in Thomson's lodging, sitting on the floor.[51] By the second term, Thomson was allocated a teaching space in the narrow alcoves on the upper level of the Aula Maxima.[52] From May 1932, both Thomson and Heavey taught in the old Arts block (now the Education Building).

The obvious immediate obstacle facing both lecturers was the absence of textbooks in Irish. Thomson was a pioneer in this regard; his translations of Plato's *Apology*, *Crito*, and *Phaedo*, published in 1929, were among the earliest Irish versions of classical texts to appear in print.[53] Not surprisingly, these texts also featured on Thomson's early exam papers. To a large extent, however, both Thomson and Heavey must have relied on their own unpublished notes.[54] Exam papers indicate that Greek authors taught through Irish in the first year of his post were Homer, Euripides, Herodotus, Plato, and Plutarch; later also Aeschines

---

[49] On *The Irish Times'* attitude to the Irish language at this time (particularly in relation to education) see O'Brien (2008: 60–2).

[50] Students could study Latin or Greek at either pass level or honours. The former had three hours of instruction weekly, the latter an additional two.

[51] Máirtín Ó Flathartaigh, 'Cén chúis gur imigh Seoirse?', *Inniu*, 17 April 1981; 'An chúis gur imigh Seoirse?', *Inniu*, 24 April 1981. Corrib Lodge, at 10 Waterside, a short distance from the university, was where Thomson worked on *Fiche Blian*: see his correspondence in Mac Conghail (2009).

[52] Reported by Christopher Townley to Séamus Mac Mathúna. Townley joined the university administration in 1932 and was later Librarian from 1966 until his retirement in 1982.

[53] See Ní Mhurchú and Kelly (2002) and Ní Mhurchú (Ch. 5).

[54] See n. 35 above for Thomson's translations that were still at that point unpublished. Heavey's translation of Caesar's *De Bello Gallico*, book 2, was published in 1940. The James Hardiman Library at NUI Galway holds old photocopies, undated, of translations also appearing to be hers, including parts of Pindar's *Nemean Odes*, Virgil's *Georgics*, and Ovid's *Tristia* (see Appendix B to Chapter 6).

and Aeschylus. Authors on the early Latin exam papers were Cicero, Virgil, Horace, Livy in 1931–2; subsequently also Lucretius, Catullus, Tacitus, Velleius Paterculus, and the anonymous *Bellum Africanum*.

There were no grammatical reference works or textbooks for composition available in Irish for either language at that stage. Although both lecturers could have assumed at least knowledge of the fundamentals of the languages from their students' earlier schooling, the handling of grammatical terminology in Irish must have been a particular challenge for all concerned.[55] Thomson at this time compiled notes on Greek syntax with the intention of publication, though these never appeared (see below, n. 63). As for a lexicon, it is notable that no Irish-language dictionaries of either Greek or Latin to Irish were ever prepared. With the eventual publication of further individual texts, however, students could rely to some extent on their notes and glossaries. It seems that English-language lexica remained fundamental: in his preface to *Prométheus fé Chuibhreach*, Thomson advised advanced students to make full use of Liddell and Scott's Greek lexicon.[56]

Thomson also took the opportunity to pursue his aspirations for public engagement, discussed the previous year with Ó Briain and Dillon. Soon after his arrival, he gave a series of public lectures titled 'Tús na Sibhialtachta san Eoraip' ('The Beginning of Civilization in Europe'). The number of lectures is unclear. The *Connacht Tribune* at the time reported on two only, given on 30 October and 6 November 1931, despite indicating that the series of reports was intended to continue.[57] These articles provided detailed summaries, written in Irish (with English subheadings), reporting that the illustrated lectures were well attended and enthusiastically received.[58] Thomson later wrote in a report to the Academic Council (see Appendix A to Chapter 6):

---

[55] Although Irish-language scholarship on Latin and Greek had a long pedigree going back to the early medieval period, neither Heavey nor Thomson seems to have drawn on the historical tradition (on which, see Ó Cuív (1973); Ahlqvist (1988); Moran (2015a)). Tomás De Bhaldraithe, editor of the *English–Irish Dictionary* (Dublin, 1959), credits Heavey for help with grammatical terminology in his testimonial for her application for professor in 1958 (see n. 18 above).

[56] Thomson (1933: vi).

[57] *Connacht Tribune*, 31 October 1931 (pp. 8, 14) and 7 November 1931 (p. 14). I have not found any further reports.

[58] Given the level of detail, it seems plausible that the articles were based on scripts provided by Thomson or even written by Thomson himself. (The dialect is distinctly Munster.) On the other hand, it is unclear whether the naivety of some of the content should be attributed to the lecturer or the reporter. For example (in English translation): 'It is difficult for people to live in any place where water is too scarce or too abundant. No rain falls on the Sahara Desert and too much falls in Central Africa. This is the reason the peoples of those countries did not manage to found any civilisation.' The first lecture apparently continued to argue the link between rainfall and civilization, while the second discussed the Bronze Age and early Egypt. (The article title 'The Bronze Age in Ireland' is probably inaccurate, as the report makes no reference to Ireland.)

In June 1932 I submitted [to the Department of Education] in book-form the public lectures on ancient history which I delivered here in the autumn of 1931. Last November the MS was returned to me with a note to say that it had been rejected but with no explanation. I then wrote to the Minister and said that unless I received the courtesy of an explanation, I would have to give up my work for his Department. After further delay the Secretary requested me to return the MS for reconsideration. I did so, and the matter is still under discussion.[59]

He later wrote that the publication was blocked 'because I was suspected of believing in the Darwinian theory'.[60]

Thomson later reported that efforts to organize similar public talks in Connemara were thwarted by local clergy: 'I had not proceeded far with my arrangements when it was made plain to me that there was not a priest through-out the length and breadth of Connemara who would dream of permitting his school to be used for anything so subversive as a University extension lecture in Irish or any other medium; nor was any support forthcoming from the National University or the Ministry of Education to induce a change of mind. So that was that.'[61]

Thomson's tenure at Galway was ultimately short-lived. At the end of his third year (1933–4), he tendered his resignation and returned to Cambridge.[62] The Academic Council acknowledged his contribution to Irish in the university in a resolution adopted on 6 October 1934: 'Is cúis aithmhéala dhúinn gur éirigh Seorsa mac Tomáis as a phosta san gColáiste seo. Is eol dúinn an obair mhór ar son na Gaedhilge a rinne sé fhad is bhí sé annseo; agus tá súil againn go n-éireochaidh go geal leis ina phosta nua' ['It is a cause of regret to us that George Thomson has resigned from his post in this College. We are aware of the great work done by him on behalf of Irish while he was here, and we wish him all the best in his new position.'] No reasons for his resignation appear to be recorded in official documents. However, during the previous academic year, he made a lengthy report to the Academic Council (see Appendix A to Chapter 6) detailing his frustration with the government publication office over continuing delays and incompetencies.[63]

---

[59] The minister at the time (since 9 March 1932) was Fianna Fáil TD Thomas Derrig. It is not clear whether Thomson implied by 'giving up my work for his Department' that he would look for another publisher or resign his lectureship altogether.

[60] According to a note in a National Library manuscript of *Fiche Blian*, cited in Ó Fiannachta (1988b: 160, n. 1). This is borne out by An Gúm's archival records: see Ní Mhurchú (Ch. 5).

[61] Thomson (1944: 9).

[62] The Secretary reported his resignation to the Finance and Standing Committee on 27 July 1934.

[63] Some of his criticisms are arguably unfair. The Stationery Office was producing an enormous volume of publications at that time in order to fill the large gap in Irish-language teaching materials, and so delays were unsurprising. *Tosnú na Feallsúnachta* came out in 1935. He complained that his *Notes on Greek Syntax* (giving the title in English) was rejected because of spelling: the creation of a

The reasons for Thomson's departure have been a matter of some discussion.[64] His daughter Margaret Alexiou offered a number of reasons: 'His departure from the University of Galway in 1934 was occasioned not just by the determination of his political opponents to oust him, but also—as he often recalled to me—by his growing sense of unease that his own work was being used by extreme factions in the nationalist cause. He did not wish to get embroiled in either nationalist politics or in factional dispute over which forms of the Irish language should be either prescribed or proscribed.'[65] Taking the last point first, it is certainly clear from his report to the Academic Council (Appendix A to Chapter 6) that Thomson was highly frustrated with official efforts to bring his Irish into line with the emerging standard. Identifying his political opponents or 'extreme factions in the nationalist cause' is more difficult, however. Some discussion has focused on Fahy, a man who has the reputation of being a strong-willed and sometimes difficult character. Ó Briain, however, had noted in his letter of 7 February 1931 that Fahy was fully supportive of Thomson's appointment, and Ó Flathartaigh recounted that it was Fahy himself who persuaded him to take Thomson's classes. The fact that Fahy was a Catholic cleric and Thomson later a committed Marxist (from 1935) does not mean that their personal relationship was necessarily hostile. Later in his life Thomson formed a productive and warm personal relationship with Monsignor Pádraig Ó Fiannachta, who oversaw the publication of several of Thomson's early translations.[66]

Did Fahy use his authority as professor to control (and possibly stifle) Thomson's teaching?[67] Ó Flathartaigh noted that the first-year exam papers for Greek through Irish and English, respectively, were entirely independent. In 1933, however, parts of the pass BA exams, now offered for the first time in Irish, were identical, and similarly the honours BA papers the following year. The Latin papers show the same correspondences. This could be interpreted as Fahy taking an interfering hand in the work of his two junior lecturers. Alternatively (as Ó Flathartaigh suggested), Fahy may have wanted to harmonize parts of the exam papers (most likely unseen translations) in both languages in order to ensure equal standards across both graduating cohorts.[68]

Regardless of his motivation, Fahy, as professor, was the authority in his department (as confirmed in Statute XX). And the situation was unlikely to change. He

---

standard orthography for Irish was a pressing concern for the administration of the time, and Thomson's mixed system, combining historical forms with aspects of the *leitriú shímplí* (simplified spelling) promoted by Shán Ó Cuív and others, was idiosyncratic. See Risteárd Ó Glaisne, 'Seoirse Mac Tomáis: Sasanach a chuir comaoin mhór ar Ghaeilgeoirí', *Inniu*, 16 January 1981, pp. 11–12.

[64] See Ó Glaisne's newspaper article (see n. 63 above) and Ó Flathartaigh's response (see n. 51 above); also Ó Lúing (1989: 91–3).

[65] M. Alexiou (2000: 72).   [66] See n. 35 above.

[67] As suggested by Ó Glaisne (see n. 63 above).

[68] It should also be noted that the final authority on exam papers rested with the external examiners (W. H. Semple for Latin and H. W. Parke for Greek in 1933).

was still a relatively young man, who held on to his position for a further two decades. It would have been obvious to Thomson that there was little prospect of promotion and therefore of autonomy. (Even in the event of Fahy's eventual retirement he would have had to compete with Heavey for the chair.)

Thomson was clearly an idealistic young man with enormous industry and an impatience to get things done. In reflections on his time in Ireland published a decade later, he described an ambition to preserve the culture of Irish-speaking people in terms that were as grand as they were curiously solipsistic. After praising the recent flourishing of regional cultures under the Soviet Union, he concludes: 'Where I had failed with 300,000, they have succeeded with a 100 million.'[69] With such high expectations, failure was inevitable, and Thomson's highly individualistic approach suggests that his failure was felt as personal. It is hardly surprising then that Thomson's early enthusiasm soon gave way to disappointment and frustration. Within the first year of his tenure, his political support must have seemed to evaporate as Ernest Blythe left office after the accession to power of Fianna Fáil on 9 March 1932.[70] His efforts at extramural outreach were unsuccessful. And by all accounts the number of students that he had an opportunity to teach was exceedingly small.[71] There may well have been other, personal factors.[72]

Heavey's Career, 1930s and 1940s

Margaret Heavey's activities during Thomson's time in Galway are almost invisible.[73] Rather than replace him after his departure in 1934, the Academic Council voted to reassign the funding for his post to two assistantships through Irish in Physics and Chemistry, respectively. In the wake, Heavey was given responsibility for teaching both Latin and Greek through Irish. On the face of it, this would have doubled her teaching hours to twenty classes per week (without additional pay), though she would have had help from various teaching assistants.[74]

[69] Thomson (1944: 11); cf. Thomson (1946: 55–6): 'For many years...I was working to save the culture of the Irish-speaking peasantry. In that I was unsuccessful. I failed to see that you cannot raise the cultural standards of a people without raising their economic standards; and in concentrating on the Irish-speaking peasantry, who after all are only three hundred thousand souls, I failed to notice what was going on in the rest of the world.'

[70] Blythe afterwards lost his seat in the election of 24 January the following year.

[71] The annual President's Report for 1934–5 (previous years are unavailable) records only seven students taking Greek across all years; it does not indicate how many were taking Greek through Irish.

[72] It may be significant, for example, that he married Katherine Fraser Stewart immediately after his return to Cambridge, on 4 October 1934.

[73] Ó Lúing (1996: 154) writes that 'she and George Thomson were good friends', confirmed to me by Arthur Keaveney, who recalled that she once expressed to him her fondness for Thomson. In *The Prometheus Bound*, he acknowledged her assistance for part of the introduction: Thomson (1932a: vi).

[74] These are recorded occasionally in the university calendars, though not the extent of their teaching.

These included James Frank Killeen (Prionsias Ó Cillín), who was appointed to the position of Assistant in Ancient Classics in 1944 and eventually succeeded Heavey as Professor of Ancient Classics in 1978.[75]

Heavey was a vocational teacher who published virtually no research during her career of almost five decades.[76] In the 1940s, however, she published a series of textbooks, several of which were foundational for teaching Greek and Latin through Irish. The first to appear was a schools' edition of the second book of Caesar's *De Bello Gallico* (Dublin, 1940).[77] In the following year *Bun-Chúrsa Ceapadóireachta Gréigise* was published, Heavey's translation of M. A. North and A. E. Hillard, *Greek Prose Composition* (London, 1898). And in 1942 there appeared a two-volume translation of E. A. Sonnenschein's *Greek Grammar for Schools* (originally published in two volumes in 1892 and 1894, respectively), entitled *Graiméar Gréigise. Cuid 1: Deilbh-eolaidheacht; Cuid 2: Coimhréir*. Given the delays (already noted) in getting textbooks through the government Stationery Office and the technical challenges in producing such a book with many complex tables in three typefaces—for Greek, Latin, and Irish, respectively—it seems likely that Heavey had begun work on her Greek grammar very soon after Thomson's departure.

The substitution of Irish for the English original of Sonnenschein's *Greek Grammar* presented some interesting opportunities for comparativism. In general, however, Heavey's translation remains very faithful to the original text and avoids digression, whether for practical pedagogical reasons or lack of interest. There are some occasional references to similarities or differences between Irish and Greek: for example, a note that the construction εἷς καὶ εἴκοσι (twenty-one) parallels Irish *aon is fiche* or that Irish prepositional pronouns (*liom, ort, aige*, etc.) need to be separated into preposition and pronoun when translated into Greek.[78] These occur more frequently in the section on syntax, and seem oriented towards practical translation strategies. References to the historical relationship between Greek and Irish are almost entirely absent. One exception occurs at the conjugation of Greek οἶδα 'I know', where Latin *uīdī* is cited as a related form, as well as Irish *feadar*.[79] All three are indeed Indo-European

---

[75] Killeen was lecturer in Ancient Classics 1959–64, associate professor 1964–78, and Professor of Ancient Classics 1978–83. Obituary in *The Irish Times*, 20 August 2001.

[76] The singular exception is Ní Éimhthigh (1955), offering notes on the readings of the Latin part of an inscription to the Wall family in Athenry.

[77] On its intended audience see the remarks by Ní Éimhthigh (1940: 167). Although Heavey did not produce further editions herself, she seemed to have provided generous assistance to her students' efforts: Tomás Ó Cathail, for example, acknowledges her in the foreword to his edition of *Aeneid* V (Ó Cathail (1940: iii)): 'Fhaid is a bhí an obair ar siubhal agam, mheabhruigh sí poinntí sár-mhaithe dhom agus thug sí cead dom leas a bhaint as a leagan maith Gaedhilge féin' ['While I was undertaking the work, she recommended excellent points to me and she gave me permission to use her own good Irish version'].

[78] Ní Éimhthigh (1942: 47–8).   [79] Ní Éimhthigh (1942: 121).

cognates. But in this case Heavey is closely following the text of the original edition, substituting Irish where Sonnenschein cites the archaic English verb *wot*.[80]

Heavey's original contribution is much more evident in *Prós-Cheapadóireacht Laidne* (Dublin, 1947), her translation (with Seán Seártan) of the standard textbook *Latin Prose Composition*, first published by Thomas Kerchever Arnold in 1839, revised by George Bradley in 1884, and updated by James Mountford in 1938. She says in her preface that the work was almost complete when Mountford's edition appeared, again indicating its early inception. In this case, Heavey's work is no mere translation. She thoroughly revised and supplemented her source on every single page, almost doubling Mountford's 443 pages to 852. One of her additions was a 98-page Irish-to-Latin vocabulary, keyed to the individual composition exercises, which partly mitigated the lack of Latin lexicographical resources available in Irish. A review by Piaras de Hindeberg noted: 'But particularly, the nature and usage of the two languages are compared with each other continually in every chapter of the book. That is the area that requires mastery of Irish and of pedagogy. It is my opinion that neither has been neglected at any point.'[81]

Classics through Irish, 1950s to 1970s

Fahy retired in 1957 and was succeeded by Heavey as Professor of Ancient Classics in the following year. Her application for the chair included endorsements from thirteen colleagues in Ireland and the UK, which emphasized repeatedly the special value of her German training; her linguistic skills across Greek, Latin, and Irish;[82] her devotion to teaching; and her personal affability.[83] She served as Dean of Arts from 1970 to 1976, and despite retiring in 1977 continued to teach at the university until very shortly before her death on 15 February 1980.

The duration of Heavey's professorship coincided with a period of rapid change both for the university and for the discipline of Classics. During the 1930s and 1940s the student population was still extremely small. In 1940, for example, the

---

[80] Sonnenschein (1892: 100). Likewise, Sonnenschein rarely drew parallels with English.

[81] De Hindeberg (1948): 'Ach go ró-speisialta, bíonn nádúir agus gnás an dá theangan á gcompráid chun a chéile i gcomhnaí in gach caibidil den leabhar. Sin é an áit a raibh gá le máistreacht Gaeilge agus Paídagóige. Is é mo mheas nár theip in aon phointe ortha ann.'

[82] 'Almost unique', in the words of Michael Tierney, who presumably had softened his position on Irish-language education by this time. (See Tierney (1963) for his later reflections on the Irish-language revival, particularly in relation to primary and secondary education.)

[83] For example, D. E. W. Wormell (Professor of Latin in Trinity College Dublin, and an external examiner at UCG): 'The standard attained by her pupils was high, and they combined accuracy and freshness of approach in a way that suggested thorough preparation by a teacher who was ready to take pains over fundamentals while welcoming originality. Others can testify better than I to her command of Irish: but her mastery of Greek and Latin shows her to be an exceptionally gifted linguist with a feeling for Latin and a sense of style.'

total number of Arts students was 166.[84] Of these, forty-two (25 per cent) were studying Latin, twenty of whom through Irish. The numbers for Greek were much smaller: six undergraduate students (4 per cent) in the same year and one at masters level, of whom two students were studying Greek through Irish. By the 1960s, however, the university was seeing a very rapid expansion. Between 1960 and 1970, the total number of Arts students grew from 421 to 1,321.[85] Not surprisingly, the number of students taking Latin also rose in absolute terms, from eighty-one in 1960 to ninety-nine in 1970, but in relative terms the proportion of students taking Latin fell from 19 per cent to 7 per cent in this period. Meanwhile, even the absolute number of students taking Greek had declined since the 1930s (eight students in 1960, down to two in 1970), despite the student population having grown more than sevenfold.[86]

This trend conforms to a much broader decline of prestige and interest in classical languages both nationally and internationally.[87] During the 1960s Greek was phased out of many Irish secondary schools, including the diocesan schools where it had traditionally been strongest.[88] The Department of Education statistical reports show a huge drop in the number of boys taking Leaving Certificate Higher Level Greek nationally, from 505 in 1960 to 131 in 1970. (As before, no girls took the subject.) Latin remained stronger and its decline was slower in absolute terms, with 4,902 Higher Level students in 1960, falling to 3,544 in 1970.[89] These figures, however, still represent a huge relative decline, from 62 per cent to 19 per cent of the total number of students taking the Leaving Certificate, which more than doubled between 1960 and 1970.[90]

The growth of the student body at UCG necessitated expansion of the campus. President Éamon de Valera laid the foundation stone for the new Library and Arts and Sciences block on 26 February 1971. The text of its inscription, written in both Latin and Irish, was composed by Margaret Heavey, then also Dean of

---

[84] These student numbers are from the annual Presidents' Reports.

[85] The Department of Ancient Classics also expanded around this time. Paulinus (Pól) Ó Súilleabháin, a teaching assistant since 1960, was made lecturer in 1965, retiring in 1987 (died 2000). Colm Luibhéid was assistant from 1961, lecturer from 1965, associate professor from 1980, and Professor of Ancient Classics from 1983 to 2001 (died 2017). In 1970 John Madden and Andrew Smith were hired as junior lecturers. The former was associate professor from 1999 until his retirement in 2007. The latter moved to University College Dublin in 1974 and was replaced by Brian Arkins (associate professor from 1993, retired 2010).

[86] I have been unable to find data for the proportion of students studying through Irish in this period. Already in 1958, however, a report by Tarlach Ó Raifeartaigh, secretary of the Department of Education, to the Dáil Committee of Public Accounts, included Heavey's *Graiméar Gréigise* II and *Prós-Cheapdóireacht Laidne* on a list of books for which 'there is now little or no demand', http://archive.oireachtas.ie/1959/APPENDIX_02071959_XIV.html (accessed 5.12.2019).

[87] For England see Stray (1998), esp. ch. 10.

[88] To take one example from the region, Greek was discontinued in Tuam by 1965: Cunningham (1999: 243).

[89] It is notable that the absolute number of girls taking Latin actually grew very slightly during the same period: the male/female gender breakdown was 3,582/1,322 in 1960 and 2,208/1,336 in 1970.

[90] From 7,966 to 18,975.

Arts. Memoranda from the time record the stages of its composition and reveal something of her attitudes to languages:[91] 'Latin is now beyond space and time and therefore is as Ireland–Galway–1971 as would Irish be itself. Therefore there's no need for an Irish inscription alongside—the Latin subscription subsumes it. [...] Put it this way: Irish would be needed alongside English, but neither is needed alongside Latin.'[92]

Heavey's confidence regarding the timelessness of Latin was misplaced, however. In 1973, the National University of Ireland dropped Latin as a subject required for matriculation, and by 1980 the number of Leaving Certificate students taking Higher Level Latin nationally had fallen to just 3 per cent of the total cohort (from 62 per cent in 1960).[93] In response to this, UCG introduced Classical Civilization (sources studied in translation) as a new subject in 1973–4.[94] With the decline of uptake in ancient languages among new undergraduates and the additional requirements of delivering a new Civilization course, teaching Latin and Greek through Irish was eventually abandoned. Exam papers indicate that Greek through Irish had already been discontinued by 1973. The last bilingual exam paper for Latin was issued in 1978, the year after Heavey's retirement.

Conclusion

The story of the teaching of Latin and Greek through Irish at UCG intersects in several ways with the larger story of the emergence of Ireland as an independent state. The succession of Dempsey and in particular Fahy to the chair of Ancient Classics very soon after the creation of the Free State reflected the new social order, one with Catholic and republican connections, replacing the old Dublin-centred Protestant elite. The new authorities faced considerable challenges: how to advance the aspirations of the cultural nationalist movement that had developed towards the end of the previous century; how to integrate these goals into the institutions of the state; how to represent the new Ireland to itself and to the international community; and how to achieve all of this in a time of severe economic crisis. Ironically, perhaps, the economic situation was a catalyst for the initiative at UCG: providing university education through Irish was a way for the college to justify its continued existence. Nevertheless, it is clear that the advocates of Irish-language education took its aims very seriously. It supported language revival, a cornerstone of cultural nationalism, by embedding Irish for

---

[91] I am very grateful to Séamus Mac Mathúna for making copies available to me.
[92] Dated 27 January 1971. The addressee is not named.
[93] 1,231 students out of 36,539. The total number had again doubled during the previous decade.
[94] The first-year Latin exam paper in the same year (1974) includes the following topical assignment: 'Scríobh paragraf Laidine de do dhéantús féin i dtaobh/Write a Latin paragraph of your own composition on: Women's Lib.'

the first time at all levels in the education system, allowing native speakers to use their language throughout their educational careers and giving new speakers an environment in which they were encouraged to use it.

The teaching of Classics through Irish also made a much broader statement about the cultural standing of the language. Classics is an international discipline, and the promoters of Irish-language Classics at UCG clearly had an international outlook (despite the received narrative), identifying and appointing lecturers trained in Cambridge and Munich. While Michael Tierney had cast doubt on whether Irish was suitable for academic discourse at all, Thomson and Heavey set out to demonstrate that it was equal to the task of handling complex and nuanced discussion of literature, history, philosophy, and linguistics, both in their published work and no doubt especially in their classrooms. Proinnsias mac Giollarnáth, a student of Heavey, described his experience of studying Latin through Irish:[95]

> The honours class was a small one, twelve, I think, all with a very good know-ledge of Irish. The feeling of the lecturer in charge for her subject was matched by her feeling for elegant and accurate use of the Irish language. The atmosphere was that of a seminar rather than a formal lecture, and she insisted on full com-munication in each direction with each student. For the first time we found the challenge of expressing abstract concepts with elegance and conciseness in Irish, and of being constantly tested against the touchstone of the original text. It was a humbling but very stimulating experience, and it made us aware as never before not only of the richness and flexibility of Irish, but also of its lacunae in many areas of expression. It also taught us that these lacunae could be and were being filled.[96]

Although the initiative is most often associated with the early career of George Thomson, his short tenure of three years made a very limited impact, particularly compared with the four decades during which Margaret Heavey and other colleagues continued to provide instruction through Irish. This is regrettable given Thomson's remarkable originality as a scholar and his prodigious early enthusi-asm. His scholarly instincts were highly comparativist and the scope of his ambi-tion to bring classical education to a wider public was vast. It would be fascinating to know, had he stayed in Galway and found ways to advance his agenda, whether his efforts might have contributed to the development of a uniquely Irish approach

---

[95] 'The real reason why', *The Irish Times*, 11 April 1968, p. 12. Mac Giollarnáth was Professor of Romance Languages at UCG, 1959–87.

[96] The same article quotes Heavey in her own words: 'I would like to think that, years hence, our toils of 40 years will have produced somewhat more than a footnote in the history books. [...] Because of our toil in UCG there has been for the first time in the history of Irish education a straight line through the medium of our own language from Gaeltacht cradles into the schools, and then right on to the highest academic degrees of a modern university, with internationally recognised standards, our own NUI.'

to Classics. Under Heavey, the discipline seems to have been more conventional in scope, though by all accounts rigorous nonetheless.

The end of teaching Classics through Irish at UCG in the 1970s must also be understood in terms of two broader contexts. The first is the failure of language revival, despite commitment and best intentions, making continuation of the teaching programme eventually untenable. The second is the radical decline of interest in Classics as a discipline that took place particularly during the 1960s, when access to education was democratized and a new emphasis placed on scientific and vocational subjects. These are issues with which the current generations both of Irish speakers and of Classicists continue to grapple.

Appendix A to Chapter 6: Report
from George Thomson to the Academic Council, 1933

The following is a transcript of a report entered into the minute books of the Academic Council on 22 February 1933, headed 'A report from Mr. Thompson [sic]'. The report is the longest description in his own words of Thomson's activities at UCG, his exasperation with the state publisher, and aspects of the publication process for Irish textbooks. Some text (enclosed here in square brackets) is marked for deletion, presumably intended to be edited out of the version sent to the minister. I have silently incorporated some corrections, handwritten and typed, and presented underlined text in italics.

THE Academic Council begs to draw the attention of the Minister of Education to the delays and difficulties experienced by lecturers of this College in getting textbooks published by the Book Committee of his Department, as shown by the accompanying statement.

IN 1928 I submitted a translation, with introduction and notes, of the *Apology*, *Crito* and *Phaedo* of Plato. When the proofs appeared, I discovered that the Committee's reader was making alterations in the text without my knowledge or consent. The second and subsequent proofs were sent to me without my corrected copy of the previous proof, so that I had the greatest difficulty in correcting them. [After the book had been published,[97] I wrote to the Committee explaining my difficulties and suggesting that in future the author should be allowed greater freedom in correcting proofs, on the understanding that he would pay himself for corrections in excess of a fixed percentage of the total printing costs, according to an arrangement which is general among publishers and is indeed indispensable if technical books are to be accurately produced. My suggestion has never been adopted.]

In September 1929 I submitted an edition of the *Alcestis* of Euripides. It was accepted in the following spring, (and) [Then, at the Committee's request, I withdrew the MS in order to add a vocabulary, and the work] was ready for the press in September 1930. In December 1930 the Committee's reader suggested some verbal alterations, which I accepted, [adding a few others of my own, which he accepted] and I understood that these would be inserted in the MS before it went to the printers. In July 1931, when the first galleys arrived, I found that the reader had inserted none of the alterations which had been agreed on in the previous December, and [accordingly] I had to insert them in the proofs. [When I returned these, I received the MS back from the Secretary, who protested against my excessive alterations and requested me to go through the whole MS again before the printing was proceeded with. I pointed out in reply that I had merely inserted the alterations which his reader had agreed to insert eight months previously.] I was anxious to get the book printed as quickly as possible in order to use it in my lectures here, and in response to enquiries the Secretary had promised me that it would be in page-proof by the end of 1931. When the page-proofs appeared, in May 1932, I had further trouble because the

---

[97] Publication date 1929.

printer persisted in ignoring my explicit and repeated instructions, and in the course of correspondence the Secretary admitted that the Committee's reader was not reading the proofs at all. The book has not yet appeared.[98]

In December 1930 I submitted an edition of the *Prometheus Bound* of Aeschylus, which was accepted early in the following year. It is not yet in page-proof.[99]

In February or March 1931 I submitted a short book, *Tosnú na Feallsúnachta*. In the following September, having heard nothing in the meantime and having no other copy, I asked the Secretary to return the MS, as I required it for my lectures here. He said that he would make enquiries, and several weeks passed. I wrote again and said that I had decided to withdraw the book altogether in order to recover the MS. To this and subsequent letters I received no reply before the official acknowledgement, and I did not recover the MS until February 1932. In the spring of 1932 the Secretary asked me to submit the MS again, and I did so, after making another copy of it. It was then accepted, but at the same time I was informed that the Committee were not satisfied with my spelling and that there were a number of words in the text 'which might well be altered'. I replied that, when I had last discussed the question of spelling with the Secretary, he told me that the Committee were content to allow the author to use his own system, provided that it was consistent, and that mine satisfied this condition; and further that, if they had changed their policy since, surely they should have let the authors (me) know. Still, since my main anxiety was to get the book published, I was prepared to let them spell it as they pleased, but, with regard to the other matter, [I said I presume they would not alter the][100] text without my consent. To this letter I received no reply, and I have heard no more about the book.[101]

In June 1932 I submitted in book-form the public lectures on ancient history which I delivered here in the autumn of 1931. Last November the MS was returned to me with a note to say that it had been rejected but with no explanation. I then wrote to the Minister and said that, unless I received the courtesy of an explanation, I would have to give up my work for his Department. After further delay the Secretary requested me to return the MS for reconsideration. I did so, and the matter is still under discussion.

In June 1932 I submitted my *Notes on Greek Syntax*, a book which is badly needed by my pupils here—in fact, it is impossible for me to do my work properly till I get it. Over seven months have elapsed since then, and I have heard no more about it.[102]

GEORGE THOMSON

NOTE. In recalling dates I have had to rely partly on memory, but I believe they are all at least approximately correct.

---

[98] Publication date 1932. The book must have appeared very late in the year, before Thomson's report was drafted in January 1933 (see n. 102 below).
[99] Publication date 1933.
[100] Revised as 'I pointed out the impropriety' ('of altering' is missing).
[101] Published in 1935.
[102] This suggests that the report was written in January 1933.

Appendix B to Chapter 6: Unpublished Irish Translations of Classical Texts Archived at NUI Galway

In 2017 a collection of old copied documents, once evidently used for teaching, was rediscovered in the department of Classics at NUI Galway. These contain both typescript and handwritten text, the latter identified with the hand of Margaret Heavey by her former student Séamus Mac Mathúna. Though undated, the copies are in foolscap format (13 × 8 in) and seem to have been produced on a Gestetner machine, both factors indicating that they were made in the 1960s or 1970s. The original documents from which the copies were taken could possibly be considerably older; one at least can be dated to before 1940 (see Document 3.II.1 below). The material comprises three separate documents (now archived in the James Hardiman Library, Special Collections). Documents 2 and 3 contain unpublished unique translations of classical texts into Irish.

Document 1: Tacitus, *Agricola*.

Headed 'Tacitus: Agricola (D. O'M.).' Forty-one pages (numbered except for first page), handwritten on one side only. A complete translation (forty-six chapters). D. O'M. is presumably Domhnall Ó Mathghamhna,[103] credited with a translation of *Agricola* dated 1933 in Breathnach and Ní Mhurchú (2018g), though I have not been able to find any further information about this publication. Begins: 'I. Do bě nós de nósaibh ár sinnsear sáir-ghníomhartha agus deigh-bheasa daoine mór-cháile do scao-ildeadh d'á sliocht...'.

Document 2: Extracts from Virgil, *Georgics* and Ovid, *Tristia*.

Typed on one side only. Pages originally unnumbered (pencil marks now added). A translation into Irish of passages from Virgil's *Georgics*. Each page has multiple copies, clearly intended for distribution in a classroom. This is the only Irish translation of the *Georgics* known to me, and is presumably Heavey's own work.

1. 'Georgica I. línte [lines] 1–23', '43–70', '118–46' (13 copies)
2. 'Georgica I. 118–146 ar lean [cont.]', 'I. 287–334' (20 copies)
3. 'Georgica I. 333 ar lean. [cont.]', 'II. 136–66', 'III. 515–30' (17 copies)
4. 'Georgica II. 458–542' (9 copies)
5. 'Georgica II. 530', 'Georgica IV. 453' (7 copies)

---

[103] See Ní Mhurchú (Ch. 5).

6. 'Georgica IV. 505', 'Georgica IV. 149' (17 copies). Breaks off (IV 189): 'Agus ansin nuair bhíonn siad imithe chun suain ina [...]' (*post, ubi iam thalamis se composuere...*).

There is additionally a single folio containing, on one side, an Irish translation (Heavey's own?) of Ovid, *Tristia* III, poem 3, lines 14–88 (end). Begins: '[...] gcéin; agus gach uile ní nach bhfuil agam anseo ag teacht im smaointe agus mé go lagbhríoch.' Ovid's famous self-penned epitaph (III 3.73–6) is translated as follows: 'Mise atá i mo luí anseo, file sultmhar an ghrá mhaoith, Naso file, cailleadh mé de dheasca mo fhéithe féin. Tusa atá ag gabháil thar bráid agus gur thug tú grá, ná bíodh doicheall ort paidir a rá: "Go raibh codhladh sámh ag cnámha Naso"' (*hic ego qui iaceo tenerorum lusor amorum | ingenio perii Naso poeta meo; | at tibi qui transis ne sit graue quisquis amasti | dicere 'Nasonis molliter ossa cubent'*).

Document 3: Pindar, *Nemean Odes* 1–7 and miscellaneous Latin teaching notes.

Twenty-six pages. Two-sided photocopies, hand-stitched together (last leaf now detached). It seems as if the blank sides of various originally discarded copies (passages of the *Aeneid* in Irish, etc.), in jumbled order, were afterwards used to copy an Irish translation of Pindar, now presented as the facing page. There are also additional loose copies of pp. 20–5, identical on both sides to those bound.

I. **Recto side**: handwritten (copy rather blurry) Irish translation of Pindar, *Nemean Odes* 1–7, paginated 1–27 (skipping no. 19, though with no apparent gap in content). Occasional notes and revisions. This is the only Irish translation of Pindar known to me. Presumably Heavey's own work.

II. **Verso side**: miscellaneous copies, all handwritten (clearer reproduction than on the recto), irregularly organized, some consecutive copies, some upside down. There are three distinct parts, catalogued below by reference to the page number on the recto side.

1) Parts of Irish translation of *Aeneid* V–VI (presumably Heavey's own).[104] Page numbers are indicated for the following pages of the original document: p. 10 (containing references to *Aen.* V 244 and 268), p. 16 (*Aen.* V 421), p. 17 (*Aen.* VI 450), p. 20 (*Aen.* V 545), p. 23 (*Aen.* VI 628), p. 26 (*Aen.* VI 703, 714), p. 32 (*Aen.* VI 886, 893). The sequence indicates that each page of the translation covered *c.*25–30 lines of the Latin text, and therefore that the first page in the original document would have corresponded with the beginning of *Aeneid* V.

---

[104] This is the Irish translation cited by Tomás Ó Cathail in the commentary to his edition of 1940 (see n. 77 above). Verbatim correspondences occur, for example, at lines 244–6, 332, 339, 344, 542–3 (cf. 548–9).

- Corresponding to recto pp. 1–3: p. 23 (in the original document); the reference '628', near the bottom of the page, marking the passage beginning at *Aen.* VI 628.
- = recto pp. 4–5: p. 26, '703', '714' (*Aen.* VI)
- = recto pp. 6–8: p. 32 (upside down), '886', '893', 'Tá dhá gheata le dia an chodlata ann' (*Aen.* VI)
- = recto p. 9: p. 17, '450' (*Aen.* VI)
- = recto p. 10: p. 20, '545' (*Aen.* V)
- = recto p. 11: p. 16, '421' (*Aen.* V)
- = recto p. 12: no page number, but probably p. 12 or 13, '340' (*Aen.* V)
- = recto p. 13: p. 10, '244', '268' (*Aen.* V)

2) Latin text of Juvenal, poems 1 and 3. (The pagination indicates that Juvenal's second satire, on sexual perversion, was not in the original document.)

- = recto p. 14: p. 4, Latin text of Juvenal 1, 112–46
- = recto p. 15: p. 8 (upside down), Juv. 3, 73–115
- = recto p. 16: p. 11 (upside down), Juv. 3, 190–225
- = recto p. 17: p. 14, Juv. 3, 297–322 (end of poem)
- = recto p. 18: p. 3, Juv. 1, 77–111

3) Collections of Latin words and phrases for the English-to-Latin composition exercises in Bradley (1884).

- = recto pp. 20–3: Heading 'Bradley's Aids', 'Ex LIII Such was the effect…', 'Ex LXXXI He who died yesterday…', 'Ex CXVII Peace of mind…'
- = recto pp. 24–7 (p. 25 upside down): 'Bradley's Aids', 'Ex XLIV It was a common saying…', 'LXXII But at the very moment…', 'Ex CXXVII There are two maxims…'

Appendix C to Chapters 5 and 6: Irish Translations and Editions of Greek and Latin Texts and Related Works (to 1978)

Síle Ní Mhurchú and Pádraic Moran

This appendix lists ninety-six publications of Irish translations and/or editions of classical Greek and Latin texts, Greek and Latin language textbooks in Irish, and some miscellaneous other Irish-language works concerning ancient Greece and Rome, published in the nineteenth and (mainly) twentieth centuries, down to 1978 (corresponding to the end point of chapter 6).

The list of Greek texts is taken from Ní Mhurchú and Kelly 2002: 89–99.[105] The list of Latin texts was compiled by Síle Ní Mhurchú and Pádraic Moran, with this consolidated appendix produced by Pádraic Moran. Texts are presented alphabetically by name of ancient author and text, and then in order of date of publication. (For discussion on the background to these translations, see Ní Mhurchú (Ch. 5) and Moran (Ch. 6)).

Information on print runs and sales, where available, is taken from two reports to the Dáil Committee of Public Accounts, dated 8 January and 12 July 1958.[106] These reports deal with books for which there was little or no demand by that time, and so other books issued by An Gúm for which no figures are given are likely to have had higher sales.

Abbreviations:
Edco. = The Educational Company of Ireland (Comhlucht Oideachais na hÉireann)
ODFR = Oifig Díolta Foillseacháin Rialtais (Government Publications Sales Office)
OS = Oifig an tSoláthair (Stationery Office)

Greek Authors

Aeschylus

1. *Prométheus fé Chuibhreach* le h-Aeschylus, ar a chur in eagar Gaodhluinne le Seoirse Mac Tomáis. Dublin: ODFR, 1933. vi + 160 pp. [*Prometheus Bound* by Aeschylus, ed. in Irish by George Thomson.]

---

[105] From the Methuen Drama volume *Amid Our Troubles: Irish Versions of Greek Tragedy* (2002), reprinted with permission from authors Síle Ní Mhurchú and Patricia Kelly, from editors Marianne McDonald and J. Michael Walton, and used by permission of Bloomsbury Publishing plc.

[106] Compiled by Tarlach Ó Raifeartaigh, Secretary to the Department of Education. The reports were entered as Appendix XXI and Appendix XIV to the Appropriation Accounts for years 1955–6 [1958] and 1957–8 [1959], respectively, and may be consulted online at http://archive.oireachtas.ie/1958/APPENDIX_19021958_XXI.html and http://archive.oireachtas.ie/1959/APPENDIX_02071959_XIV.html (accessed 5 December 2019).

Aristotle

2. *Leabhar Aristodeil dá nglaetar Béasgna Nichomhach.* Leabh. a I. Tomás Ua Nualláin do chuir Gaedhilg ar Ghréigis Ariostodeil. In *An Claidheamh Soluis* 6, 13, 20, 27 January; 3, 10, 17 February; 2, 9, 16, 23, 30 March; 6, 20 April; 4, 11, 18 May 1912. [The Book of Aristotle entitled *Nicomachean Ethics.* Book I. Aristotle's Greek trans. into Irish by Tomás Ua Nualláin.]

Euripides

Alcestis

3. *Alcéstis* le h-Eurípidés, ar a chur in eagar Gaodhluinne le Seoirse Mac Tomáis. Dublin: ODFR, 1932. 239 pp. [*Alcestis* by Euripides, ed. in Irish by George Thomson.]

Iphigenia in Aulis

4. *Íodhbairt Ifigéine,* dráma le Euripides. Pádraig de Brún d'aistrigh. Dublin: ODFR, 1935. 49 pp. [*The Sacrifice of Iphigenia,* a play by Euripides. Trans. Pádraig de Brún.][107]

Iphigenia in Tauris

5. *Iphigenia in Tauris* le h-Eoirpid, ar n-a chur i n-eagar i nGaedhilg ag an Athair Art C. Mac Giolla Eoin. Téacs Gréigise le brollach, nótaí agus foclóir Gréigis–Gaeilge. Dublin: OS, 1950. xiv + 228 pp. [*Iphigenia in Tauris* by Euripides, ed. in Irish by Rev. Art C. Mac Giolla Eoin. Greek text with foreword, notes, and Greek–Irish vocabulary.]

Trojan Women 799–818

6. 'Traoi ["I Sálamis chumhra na mín-bheach..."]'. Suibhne Geilt d'aistrigh ó'n *Troades,* le Euripides. In *Ireland To-Day* 3 (3) (March 1938): 239–40. ['Troy'. Trans. Suibhne Geilt (pseudonym) from *Troades* by Euripides.]

Herodotus

7. 'An seana-shaol Gréagach: scéalta ó stair Herodotus'. Seoirse Mac Laghmhainn do chuir i nGaoluinn. In *An Phoblacht,* 21, 28 January; 11 February; 10, 17, 31 March; 14, 28 April; 19 May 1928. ['Life in Ancient Greece: stories from Herodotus'. Trans. into Irish by Seoirse Mac Laghmhainn (= George Thomson).]

Homer

Iliad I 225–50

8. 'A mheisgeóir thréith ó fhíon, tá lán dimiadh...', trans. John O'Donovan. In Owen Connellan, *A Dissertation on Irish Grammar.* Dublin, 1834, pp. 38–9. Repr. as 'Dr John

---

[107] 1,000 copies printed, 500 sold by 31 March 1957.

O'Donovan's translation of the speech of Achilles', in *Irisleabhar na Gaedhilge* ii (21) (1885): 287–8.

Iliad I–VIII

9. *An t'Íliad air chogadh na Tróighe ro chan Homear.* Aisdríghthe ó Ghréag-Bhéarla go ran [*sic*] Gaoidhilge le Seághan, Árd-easbog Thúama. Dublin: Goodwin, Son & Nethercott, 1844–71. 478 pp. Published in eight separate parts: i (1844), ii (1846), iii (1851), iv (1857), v and vi (1860), vii (1869), viii (1871). [*The Iliad on the War of Troy which Homer sang.* Trans. from the Greek into Irish verse by John (Mac Hale), Archbishop of Tuam.] Modern edition, in standardized spelling: Seán Mac Héil, *Íliad Hóiméar.* Leabhair I–VIII. Réamhaiste le Breandán Ó Doibhlin. Galway: Officina Typographica, 1981. xvi + 241 pp. [John Mac Hale, Homer's *Iliad.* Books I–VIII. Preface by Breandán Ó Doibhlin.]

Iliad VI 407–502

10. 'Address of Andromache to Hector ["A dhuine dhána faraoir tá air tí…"]. From the original Greek of Homer's *Iliad*, Book 6, by Archbishop McHale.' In *An Gaodhal* (July 1890): 971–3.

Iliad VI 369–502

11. 'Scaradh Hectoir le hÁndromaché. ["Sin mar adubhairt, 's annsoin d'fhág Hector lonnra-chathbhárrach…"].' Pádraig de Brún [d'aistrigh]. In *Irisleabhar Muighe Nuadhad* 22 (1926): 12–15. ['The Parting of Hector and Andromache'. Trans. Pádraig de Brún.]

Iliad I 1–52

12. 'Véarsaí as leabhartha Hómér. I. Tosach na hIléide. An Fiúnach ["Abair, a dhia bhean an bhéil bhinn-bhriathraigh, fiúnach Achilléis…"].' An t-Athair Pádraig de Brún d'aistrigh. In *Humanitas* ii (I) (March 1931): 14–15. ['Verses from Homer. I. The Beginning of the *Iliad*. The Wrath'. Trans. Rev. Pádraig de Brún.]

Iliad VI 390–465

13. 'Véarsaí as leabhartha Hómér. II. Scaradh Hechtóir le hÁndromaché ["Labhair a bhanóglach leis amhalaidh, 's amach ón dteaghlach le Hechtor…"].' An t-Athair Pádraig de Brún d'aistrigh. In *Humanitas* ii (I) (March 1931): 15–16. ['Verses from Homer. II. The parting of Hector and Andromache'. Trans. Rev. Pádraig de Brún.]

Iliad I

14. 'Fuíoll Léinn Sheoirse Mhic Thomáis, II. An tIliad le Hóimear. Leabhar a hAon'. In eagar ag Pádraig Ó Fiannachta. In *Léachtaí Cholm Cille* 18 (1988): 169–82. ['The Scholarly Remains of George Thomson, II. The *Iliad* by Homer. Book One'. Ed. Pádraig Ó Fiannachta.]

Odyssey

15. *An Odaisé.* An Monsignor Pádraig de Brún a d'aistrigh. Ciarán Ó Coigligh a chuir in eagar. Máire Mhac an tSaoi a scríobh an brollach. Dublin: Coiscéim, 1990. xix +

462 pp. [*The Odyssey*. Trans. Monsignor Pádraig de Brún. Ed. Ciaran Ó Coigligh. Foreword by Máire Mhac an tSaoi.]

Lucian of Samosata

Dialogues of the Gods

16. 'Agallamh na ndéithe ó Lúcián'. Peadar Ua Laoghaire d'aistrigh. In *Journal of the Ivernian Society* i (1908–9): 47–51, 119–25; 189–93; 247–52; ii (1909–10): 49–53, 111–17, 161–71, 236–42; iii (1910–11): 49–55, 113–19, 135–41, 207–13; iv (1911): 3–9, 65–72, 129–35, 193–9; v (1912–13): 1–6, 65–70. [*Dialogues of the Gods* by Lucian. Trans. Peadar Ua Laoghaire.] Republished as a single volume: *Lúcián*. An t-Athair Peadar Ua Laoghaire, Canónach, S. P. d'aistrigh. Dublin: Browne & Nolan, 1924. iv + 185 pp. [*Lucian*. Trans. Rev. Peadar Ua Laoghaire, canon and parish priest.]

Vera Historia I–II

17. *Vera Historia*; scéal ainspianta a chéad-cheap Lucian san Ghréigis. Domhnall Ó Mathghamhna a chuir i nGaedhilg. Dublin: ODFR, 1931. vi + 79 pp. [*Vera Historia*, a preposterous tale written originally in Greek by Lucian. Trans. into Irish by Domhnall Ó Mathghamhna.][108]

Plato

Apology

18. 'Socratés ghá chosaint féin'. Uilliam Ó Rinn do thiontuigh i nGaedhilg. In *Irish Freedom* (Oct., Nov., Dec. 1913; Jan., Feb., Mar. 1914). ['The Apology of Socrates', trans. into Irish by Uilliam Ó Rinn.]

19. 'The Apology of Socrates', (trans.) D(omhnall) Ó M(athghamhna). In the *Sunday Independent*, 17 March–1 December 1929.

Apology, Crito, and Phaedo

20. *Breith báis ar Eagnuidhe. Tri cómhráidhte d'ár cheap Platón* (*Apologia, Critón, Phaedón*). Seoirse Mac Laghmhainn do chuir i nGaodhluinn. Dublin, C. S. Fallon Ltd./OS, 1929. 173 pp. [Sentence of Death on a Sage. Three dialogues written by Plato (*Apology, Crito, Phaedo*). Trans. into Irish by Seoirse Mac Laghmhainn (= George Thomson).][109]

Critias

21. *Inis Atlaint*, scéal a chéad-cheap Platón 'san Ghréigis. Domhnall Ó Mathghamhna do chuir i nGaedhilg. Dublin: Browne & Nolan, 1935. 79 pp. [*The Island of Atlantis*, a

---

[108] 750 copies printed, 430 sold by 1955. Originally published in the *Sunday Independent*, 21 June 1925–25 April 1926.
[109] 3,000 copies printed, 800 sold by 1955; remaining stock then reduced to 200.

story written originally in Greek by Plato. Trans. into Irish by Domhnall Ó Mathghamhna. 79 pp.][110]

Crito

22. 'Crito, or the Duty of a Citizen.' (Trans. by) D(omhnall) Ó M(athghamhna). In the *Sunday Independent*, 8 December 1929–30 March 1930.

Symposium

23. 'Fuíoll Léinn Sheoirse Mhic Thomáis, III. An Suimpóisiam'. In eagar ag Pádraig Ó Fiannachta. In *Irisleabhar Mhá Nuad* (1988): 161–89; (1989): 76–102. ['The Scholarly Remains of George Thomson III. The Symposium'. Ed. Pádraig Ó Fiannachta.]

Plutarch, *Lives*

24. *Saoghal-ré na nGracchi*. Plutarchus do chéad-cheap 'san Ghréigis. Domhnall Ó Mathghamhna do chuir i nGaedhilg. Dublin: ODFR, 1933. 64 pp. [*Lives of the Gracchi*. Written originally by Plutarch in Greek. Trans. into Irish by Domhnall Ó Mathghamhna.]

25. *Démostenés agus Cicero: tuairisc a mbeathadh*. Plútarc do chéad-cheap 'san Ghréigis. Domhnall Ó Mathghamhna d'aistrigh go Gaedhilg. Dublin: ODFR, 1935. 116 pp. [Demosthenes and Cicero: an account of their lives. Written originally by Plutarch in Greek. Trans. into Irish by Domhnall Ó Mathghamhna.][111]

26. *Beathaí Phlútairc*. Pádraig de Brún d'aistrigh ón nGréigis. Dublin: ODFR, 1936. 272 pp. [Plutarch's *Lives*. Trans. from Greek by Pádraig de Brún.][112]

Sophocles

Antigone

27. *Aintioghoiné*, dráma le Sofoicléas. Pádraig de Brún d'aistrigh ó'n nGréigis. Dublin: Ponsonby & Gibbs, University Press, 1926. 43 pp. [*Antigone*, a play by Sophocles. Trans. from Greek by Pádraig de Brún.]

Oedipus at Colonus 668–719

28. 'Dán molta na hAittiche ["Fód rí-chapall an tír, a dheoraidhe..."]. As *Oidiopús i gColón*, dráma le Sofoicléas'. Pádraig de Brún [d'aistrigh]. In *The Nation* (2 April 1927): 5. ['Poem in Praise of Attica. From *Oedipus at Colonus*, a play by Sophocles.' Trans. Pádraig de Brún.]

---

[110] Originally published in the *Sunday Independent*, 5 April–2 August 1931.
[111] 1,000 copies printed, 300 sold by 1958; remaining stock then reduced to 100.
[112] 1,000 copies printed, 640 sold by 31 March 1957.

Oedipus at Colonus

29. *Oidiopús i gColón.* Dráma le Sofoicléas. Pádraig de Brún d'aistrigh. Maynooth: Cuallacht Chuilm Cille, 1929. 52 pp. [*Oedipus at Colonus.* A play by Sophocles. Trans. Pádraig de Brún.]

Oedipus Rex 1110–415

30. 'Sliocht as *Rí Oidiopús* ["A shinnsir, muran misde dhom baramhail..."], dráma le Sofoicléas.' Pádraig de Brún d'aistrigh ó'n nGréigis. In *Irisleabhar Muighe Nuadhad* 23 (1927): 6–12. [An excerpt from *King Oedipus*, a play by Sophocles.]

Oedipus Rex

31. *Rí Oidiopús*, dráma le Sofoicléas. Pádraig de Brún d'aistrigh. Maynooth: Cuallacht Chuilm Cille, 1928. 44 pp. [*Oedipus Rex*, a play by Sophocles. Trans. Pádraig de Brún.]

Theocritus, *Idyll* 15

32. 'Fuíoll Léinn Sheoirse Mhic Thomáis, I. An Lá Féile ["An bhfuil Praxinoé istigh?..."].' In eagar ag Pádraig Ó Fiannachta. In *Leachtaí Cholm Cille* 18 (1988): 164–9. ['The Scholarly Remains of George Thomson, I. The Festival'. Ed. Pádraig Ó Fiannachta.]

Thucydides

Peloponnesian War II 34–46

33. *Óráid Caointe Phericléis.* Domhnall Ó Mathghamhna d'aistrigh ó'n mbun-Ghréigis. Dublin: Browne & Nolan, 1930. 23 pp. [*The Funeral Oration of Pericles.* Trans. from the original Greek by Domhnall Ó Mathghamhna.][113]

Peloponnesian War IV 1–49

34. *Tuicid.* Leabhar IV, Caib. 1–49. Pádraig Ó Meachair a chuir in eagar. Dublin: OS, 1964. xxviii + 191 pp. [Thucydides. Book IV, chapters 1–49. Ed. Pádraig Ó Meachair.]

Xenophon

Anabasis II

35. Csenophón, *Anabasis* II. An t-Athair Cathal Mac Giobúin do chuir in eagar. Dublin: OS, 1944. xx + 121 pp. [*Anabasis* II. Ed. Rev. Cathal Mac Giobúin.][114]

Anabasis VII, 4

36. ' "An fhairrge! An fhairrge". Csenofón Aitéanach d'aithris.' Maud Joynt d'aistrigh. In *Celtica* iii (5) (May–June 1903): 86–7. [' "The Sea! The Sea!" by Xenophon the Athenian'. Trans. Maud Joynt.]

---

[113] Originally published in the *Sunday Independent*, April–June 1930.
[114] 1,000 copies printed, 440 sold by 31 March 1957.

Latin Authors

Caesar, *De Bello Gallico*

37. *De Bello Gallico.* Leabhar a dó. Cormac Ó Cadhlaigh, M.A., d'aistrigh. Dublin: Browne & Nolan, 1922. 26 pp. [Book two. Trans. Cormac Ó Cadhlaigh, M.A.]

38. *De Bello Gallico* V. Ar n-a chur i n-eagar fara gluais, nótaí, foclóir & rl. i nGaedhilg don Áthair Tomás Tóibín. Dublin: ODFR, 1934. 127 pp. [Ed. with glossary, notes, vocabulary, etc. in Irish by Rev. Tomás Tóibín.]

39. *De Bello Gallico.* Leabhar V. Ar n-a chur i n-eagar, maille nótaí, foclóir, réamhrádh i nGaedhilg, do Shéamus Ó Ciardha, B.A., H.D.E. agus Domhnall Ó Conalláin, B.A., H.D.E. Dublin: Edco. [1939]. xxxi + 115 pp. [Book V. Ed. with notes, vocabulary, foreword in Irish, by Séamus Ó Ciardha, B.A., H.D.E. & Domhnall Ó Conalláin, B.A., H.D.E.]

40. *De Bello Gallico* II/Caesar. Mairghréad Ní Éimhthigh do chuir i n-eagar. Dublin: Browne & Nolan, 1940. xv + 248 pp. [Ed. Margaret Heavey.]

41. *De Bello Gallico.* Leabhar II. Ar n-a chur i n-eagar maille nótaí, foclóir, réamhrádh i nGaedhilg do Shéamas Ó Ciardha, B.A., H.D.E. agus Domhnall Ó Conalláin, B.A., H.D.E. Dublin: Edco. [1940?]. xxxiv + 83 pp. [Book II. Ed. with notes, vocabulary and foreword in Irish by Séamas Ó Ciardha, B.A., H.D.E. & Domhnall Ó Conalláin, B.A., H.D.E.]

42. *De Bello Gallico.* Leabhar I. Ar n-a chur i n-eagar, maille nótaí do Shéamas Ó Ciardha agus Domhnall Ó Conalláin, léaráidí. Dublin: Edco. [1941]. xxxiv + 114 pp. [Book I. Ed. with notes by Séamas Ó Ciardha & Domhnall Ó Conalláin; illustrations.]

43. *Aistriú i nGaedhilg ar de Bello Gallico Leabhar I (caib. 1–24) agus ar Aenéis Bhirgil Leabhar VI (ll. 1–494).* Domhnall Ó Conalláin, B.A., H.D.E. agus Séamas Ó Ciardha, B.A., H.D.E. do rinne. Dublin: Edco. [1941]. 22 pp + 21 pp. [*A translation into Irish of* De Bello Gallico, *book I (ch. 1–24) and of Virgil's* Aeneid, *book VI (ll. 1–494). By Domhnall Ó Conalláin, B.A., H.D.E. & Séamas Ó Ciardha, B.A., H.D.E.*].

44. *De Bello Gallico.* Leabhar IV. Ar n-a chur i n-eagar, maille nótaí, foclóir, réamhrádh i nGaedhilg do Shéamas Ó Ciardha, B.A., H.D.E. agus Domhnall Ó Conalláin, B.A., H.D.E. Dublin: Edco. [1942]. xxxiii + 81 pp. [Book IV. Ed. with notes, vocabulary, foreword in Irish by Séamas Ó Ciardha, B.A., H.D.E. & Domhnall Ó Conalláin, B.A., H.D.E.]

45. *De Bello Gallico* V (1–30). An tÁthair Pádraic Ó Laoi. Dublin: Sáirséal agus Dill, 1956. 146 pp.

46. *De Bello Gallico* IV. An tÁthair Pádraic Ó Laoi. Dublin: Sáirséal agus Dill, 1957. 148 pp.

47. *De Bello Gallico* I (1–30). An tÁthair Pádraic Ó Laoi. Dublin: Sáirséal agus Dill, 1961. 160 pp.

Cicero

48. *An Tarna Philippica .i. M. Tullii Ciceronis in M. Antonium Philippicarum Liber Secundus.* Domhnall Ó Mathghamhna d'aistrigh go Gaedhilg. Dublin: ODFR, 1932. 83 pp. [*The Second Philippic.* Trans. into Irish by Domhnall Ó Mathghamhna.]

49. *Óráidí Chicero in aghaidh Chaitilína*. Maoghnas Ó Domhnaill do chuir i n-eagar. Dublin: ODFR, 1937. xl + 204 pp. [Cicero's *Speeches against Catiline*. Ed. Maoghnas Ó Domhnaill.][115]

50. *De Amicitia*. Pádraic Ó Meachair do chuir i n-eagar. Dublin: OS, 1945. xxxviii + 196 pp. [Ed. Pádraic Ó Meachair.][116]

51. *De Senectute*. Domhnall Ó Mathghamhna do chuir i nGaedhilg. Dublin: OS, 1953. 60 pp. [*De Senectute*. Trans. into Irish by Domhnall Ó Mathghamhna.]

52. *Cicero Pro Lege Manilia*. Ar na chur in eagar ag an tAthair Seán Mac Cárthaigh. Dublin: Sáirseál agus Dill, 1958. 183 pp. [Ed. Rev. Seán Mac Cárthaigh.]

53. *Pro Archia Poeta*, James J. Carey a chuir in eagar, Pól Ó Súilleabháin a d'aistrigh. Dublin: OS, 1973. V + 91 pp. [Ed. James J. Carey (1967), trans. by Pól Ó Súilleabháin.]

Horace

54. *Ódanna Horáis* maille le réamhrádh, nótaí Gaedhilge agus foclóir iar n-a chur in oireamhaint do Sheán Ó Catháin, S.J., M.A. Dublin: ODFR, 1933. xvii + 119 pp. [The *Odes* of Horace with foreword, notes in Irish, and vocabulary, adapted by Seán Ó Catháin, S.J., M.A.]

55. *Oráid: Ódanna IV*. Tomás Ó Cathail do chuir i n-eagar. Dublin: OS, 1950. cx + 141 pp. [Horace: *Odes* IV. Ed. Tomás Ó Cathail.][117]

56. *Epódanna Oráit. Q. Horati Flacci Epodon Liber*. Flaithrí Ó Rioghardáin do chuir in eagar. Dublin: OS, 1960. xxxi + 130 pp. [Horace, *Epodes*. Ed. Flaithrí Ó Rioghardáin.]

Livy

57. *Libhius XXII*. Curtha in eagar maille le réamhrádh, nótaí, léarscáil agus foclóir ag S. P. Ó Cillín. Dublin: OS, 1954. xxx + 229 pp. [*Livy XXII*. Ed. with foreword, notes, a map, and vocabulary by S. P. Ó Cillín.]

58. *Livias: Leabhar 26*. Dónall Ó Conalláin. Dublin: OS, 1975. xiii + 201 pp. [Livy, book 26. Dónall Ó Conalláin.]

Ovid

59. *Metamorphoses VIII*. Oibhid. Maoghnas Ó Domhnaill do chuir i n-eagar. Dublin: ODFR, 1937. xxiii + 124 pp. [Ed. Maoghnas Ó Domhnaill.][118]

---

[115] 1,000 copies printed, 360 sold by 31 March 1957.
[116] 3,000 copies printed, 100 sold by 31 March 1957.
[117] 1,010 copies printed, 260 sold by 31 March 1957.
[118] 1,000 copies printed, 360 sold by 31 March 1957.

60. Óibhid. *Tristia*. Leabhar I. Brollach, téacs, nótaí agus foclóir. An tAthair Micheál Ó Baoighill do chuir i n-eagar. Dublin: ODFR, 1937. xvi + 142 pp. [Ovid. *Tristia*. Book I. Foreword, text, notes, and vocabulary. Ed. Rev. Micheál Ó Baoighill.][119]

61. *Sleachta as saothar Óivid*. Arna gcur in eagar mar aon le brollach, nótaí agus foclóir ag C. E. Freeman máistir cúnta in Westminster tráth. Micheál Ó hOdhráin, M.A. a d'aistrigh agus a chuir in oiriúint. Dublin: OS, 1972. 152 pp. [*Excerpts from the work of Ovid*. Edited with foreword, notes, and vocabulary by C. E. Freeman, former assistant master at Westminster. Trans. and adapted by Micheál Ó hOdhráin, M.A.][120]

Sallust, *The War with Catiline*

62. *Catilína: Cúntas ar chogadh Chatilína ó Chaius Salustius Crispus*. An t-Athair Peadar Ua Laoghaire d'aistrigh. Dublin: Browne & Nolan [1913?]. 69 pp. [*Catiline: An account of the war of Catiline by Caius Salustius Crispus*. Trans. Rev. Peadar Ua Laoghaire.]

Virgil, *Aeneid*

63. *Aenéis Bhirgil*. Leabhar a h-aon maille le brollach, míniughadh is foclóir. An t-Athair Pádraig Ua Duinnín, M.A., D.Litt. do chuir i n-eagar. Dublin: ODFR, 1931. 226 pp. [Virgil's *Aeneid*. Book one with foreword, commentary, and vocabulary. Ed. Rev. Pádraig Ua Duinnín.][121]

64. *P. Vergili Maronis Aeneidos*. Liber V. Tomás Ó Cathail, B.A. do chuir i n-eagar. Dublin: Browne & Nolan, 1940. xxiv + 125 pp. [Ed. Tomás Ó Cathail, B.A.]

65. *Aenéis Bhirgil*. Leabhar V. Ar n-a chur i n-eagar do Shéamas Ó Ciardha agus Domhnall Ó Conalláin. Dublin: Edco. [1940?]. xi + 90 pp. [Virgil's *Aeneid*. Book V. Ed. Séamas Ó Ciardha & Domhnall Ó Conalláin.]

— *Aenéis Bhirgil*. Leabhar VI (ll. 1–494)—*see above no. 43*.

66. *Aenéis Bhirgil*. Leabhar a dó, maille le brollach, míniughadh agus foclóir. An t-Athair Liam Mac Philibín, B.A., D.D., do chuir i n-eagar. Dublin: OS, 1942. 150 pp. [Virgil's *Aeneid*. Book Two with foreword, commentary, and vocabulary. Ed. Rev. Liam Mac Philibín.]

67. *Aenéis Bhirgil*. Leabhar XII. Ar n-a chur i n-eagar, maille réamhrádh. Séamas Ó Ciardha agus Domhnall Ó Conállain. Dublin: Edco. [1942]. xiii + 105 pp. [Virgil's *Aeneid*. Book XII. Ed. with foreword. Séamas Ó Ciardha & Domhnall Ó Conalláin.]

68. *Aenéis Bhirgil*. Leabhar III. Ar n-a chur i n-eagar, maille réamhrádh do Shéamas Ó Ciardha agus Domhnall Ó Conalláin. Dublin: Edco. [1945]. xi + 164 pp. [Virgil's *Aeneid*. Book III. Ed. with foreword by Séamas Ó Ciardha & Domhnall Ó Conalláin.]

69. *Aenéis Bhirgil*. Leabhar VI. Ar n-a chur i n-eagar, maille le réamhrádh, nótaí, foclóir do Shéamas Ó Ciardha, B.A., H.D.E. agus Domhnall Ó Conalláin B.A.,

[119] 3,000 copies printed, 500 sold by 1955; remaining stock then reduced to 100.
[120] Adapted from C. E. Freeman, *Ovid Selections* (Oxford, 1917).
[121] A reprint of 1935 (or 1939?) issued 6,000 copies, of which 4,000 were sold by 31 March 1957.

H.D.E. Leabhar VI. Dublin: Edco. [n.d.], xi + 135 pp. [Virgil's *Aeneid*. Book VI. Ed. with foreword, notes, and vocabulary by Séamas Ó Ciardha B.A., H.D.E. & Domhnall Ó Conalláin B.A., H.D.E.]

70. *Aenéis Bhirgil*. Leabhar XI. Ar n-a chur i n-eagar, maille réamhrádh, nótaí, foclóir i nGaedhilg do Shéamas Ó Ciardha, B.A., H.D.E. agus Domhnall Ó Conalláin, B.A., H.D.E. Dublin: Edco. [n.d.], xiv + 118 pp. [Virgil's *Aeneid*. Book XI. Ed. with foreword, notes, vocabulary in Irish by Séamas Ó Ciardha, B.A., H.D.E. & Domhnall Ó Conalláin, B.A., H.D.E.]

71. *Aenéis IX*. Tomás Ó Concheanainn do chuir i n-eagar. Dublin: Sáirséal agus Dill, 1956. 216 pp.

[*Aeneid IX*. Ed. by Tomás Ó Concheanainn]

72. *Aistriúchán ar Virgil Aeinéid IX*. Tomás Ó Concheanainn. Dublin: OS [1971] 49 pp. [*Translation of Virgil*, Aeneid *IX*. Tomás Ó Concheanainn.]

73. *Virgil: Aeinéid VI*. Seán Ó Riain. Dublin: OS, 1978. xix + 159 pp. [Virgil, *Aeneid VI*. Seán Ó Riain.]

Miscellaneous Translations

74. *Papers on Irish Idiom together with a Translation into Irish of Part of the First Book of Euclid by the late Canon Peter O'Leary*. Ed. Thomas F. O'Rahilly. Dublin: Browne & Nolan, 1922. iv + 123 pp.

75. *Aesop a tháinig go h-Éirinn*. (*An Chéad Chnuasach agus an Tarna Cnuasach*.) Curtha i n-eagar i n-aon leabhar amháin, le peictiúirí ag an nDochtúir Domhnall Ó Mathghamhna. Dublin: Brún agus Ó Nualláin, 1931. 138 pp. [*Aesop came to Ireland*. (*First and Second Collections*). Edited in one book, with illustrations, by Dr Domhnall Ó Mathghamhna.][122]

76. *Scéalta a Filí na Rómha*. Domhnall Ó Mathghamhna. Dublin: ODFR, 1933. 73 pp. [*Stories from the Poets of Rome*. Domhnall Ó Mathghamhna.][123]

77. *Airgead Beo*: *Cnuasach Gearrscéalta as Seanchas na Gréige*. An Buachaillín Buidhe do scríobh. Dublin: OS, 1944. 82 pp. [*Quicksilver: Short Stories from the Greek Tradition*. Written by The Sallow Boy (= Earnán de Siúnta).]

Language Textbooks

Greek

78. M. A. North & A. E. Hillard, *Bun-chúrsa Ceapadóireachta Gréigise*. Mairghéad Ní Éimhthigh d'aistrigh ón mBéarla. Dublin: OS, 1941. 376 pp. [M. A. North & A. E. Hillard, *Greek Prose Composition*. Trans. Margaret Heavey from English.]

---

[122] Compilation of two collections of Aesop's fables, trans. Peadar Ua Laoghaire. For earlier editions that predate Irish independence see Ó Cuív (1954: 33–4).

[123] 750 copies printed, 460 sold by 31 March 1957. Translation of Margaret Pease, *Stories from the Latin Poets* (London, 1903).

79. *Graiméar Gréigise*, le E. A. Sonnenschein, Mairghéad Ní Éimhthigh M.A. d'aistrigh ó'n mBéarla. Cuid I: Deilbh-eolaidheacht. Cuid II: Cóimhréir. Dublin: OS, 1942. 472 pp. [E. A. Sonnenschein, *Greek Grammar*. Trans. Margaret Heavey from English. Vol. I: Morphology. Vol. II: Syntax.][124]

Latin

80. *Laidean tré Ghaedhilg*. Feargus Ó Nualláin do sgríobh, Riobárd Ó Druaidh do chuir i n-eagar. I: Dlúth-aistriuchán, soluídí agus gluaiseanna. Rathfarnham: Language and Literary Guilds [1924]. 48 pp. [*Latin through Irish*. Written by Feargus Ó Nualláin. Ed. Riobárd Ó Druaidh. I: Close translation, examples, and glossaries.]

81. *Tosach Laidne*. Maoghnus Ó Domhnaill do scríobh. Dublin: Edco. [*c*.1930]. 99 pp. [*Beginning Latin*. Written by Maoghnus Ó Domhnaill.]

82. *Prós-Cheapadóireacht Laidne do na Meadhon-Rangaibh*. Maoghnus Ó Dómhnaill d'aistrigh go Gaedhilg. Dublin: ODFR, 1937 [1938]. xv + 299 pp. [*Latin Prose Composition for Intermediate Classes* (North & Hillard). Trans. into Irish by Maoghnus Ó Domhnaill.]

83. *Bun-chúrsa Laidne*. Mícheál Breathnach, a rinne an leagan Gaedhilge. Dublin: OS, 1939. 307 pp. [*Foundation Course in Latin* (Longman's Latin Course). Irish version by Mícheál Breathnach.]

84. *Gramaduch na Laidne. Cuid I. Deilbheolas*. E. A. Sonnenschein. Mícheál Breathnach, M.A., a rinne an leagan Gaedhilge. Dublin: OS, 1939. 148 pp. [*Latin Grammar. Part I. Morphology*. E. A. Sonnenschein. Irish Version by Mícheál Breathnach.]

85. *Laidean tré Ghaedhilg. Cuimre Gramadaigh*. Feargus Ó Nualláin do sgríobh. Dublin: OS, 1941. 165 pp. [*Latin through Irish. Grammatical Summary*. Written by Feargus Ó Nualláin.][125]

86. *Trialacha Laidne don Mhacléighinn*. Mícheál Ua Briain. Dublin: Edco., 1941. 64 pp. [*Latin Tests for Students*. Mícheál Ua Briain.]

87. *Prós-Cheapadóireacht Laidne .i. Bradley's Arnold aistrighthe go Gaedhilg ag Mairghréad Ní Éimhthigh agus Seán Seártan*. Dublin: ODFR, 1947. viii + 852 pp. [*Latin Prose Composition, i.e. Bradley's Arnold*, trans. into Irish by Margaret Heavey & Seán Seártan.][126]

88. *An Cúrsa Clarendonach Laidne. Cúrsa cheithre mbliadhan le h-aghaidh na sgolta-cha. An chéad bhliadhain agus an dara bliadhain*. T. Ó Raifeartaigh do chuir i nGaedhilg. Dublin: OS [1947]. 303 pp. [*The Clarendon Latin Course. A four-year course for schools. First and second year*. Trans. into Irish by T. Ó Raiftearaigh.]

89. *Nuachúrsa Laidne*. Pól Ó Súilleabháin. Dublin: Sáirséal agus Dill, 1955. 380 pp. [*New Latin Course*. Pól Ó Súilleabháin.]

---

[124]   1,000 copies printed, 160 sold by 31 March 1957.
[125]   1,000 copies printed, 270 sold by 31 March 1957.
[126]   1,000 copies printed, 510 sold by 31 March 1957.

90. *Cúrsa Laidine dár Ré Féin III.* Micheál Ó hOdhráin. Dublin: OS, 1970. ix + 303 pp. [*Latin Course for Our Own Time III.* Micheál Ó hOdhráin.][127]

Other Irish-Language works concerning Greece and Rome

91. An t-Athair Pádraig Ua Duinnín, *Aistí ar Litridheacht Ghréigise is Laidne.* Dublin, C. S. Fallon Ltd./OS, 1929. 162 pp. [Rev. Patrick Dinneen, *Essays on Greek and Latin Literature.*][128]

92. Seoirse Mac Tomáis, *Tosnú na Feallsúnachta.* Dublin: ODFR, 1935. 76 pp. [George Thomson, *The Beginnings of Philosophy.*][129]

93. *Stair na Rómha,* bunaithe ar 'A History of the Roman Republic'. An tAthair Seán Mac Craith. Dublin: OS, 1947. 432 pp. [*History of Rome,* based on 'A History of Roman Republic'.][130] Rev. Seán Mac Craith.][131]

94. *Stair na Gréige.* An Monsignor ró-oirmhidneach Pádraig de Brún do chuir Gaeilge ar *A History of Greece* le J[ohn] B[agnell] Bury. Cuid a hAon: Ón tosach go claoi na bPeirseach. Cuid a Dó: Fás, bláthú agus meath impireacht na nAtaenach. Cuid a Trí: Ó chreachadh na nAtaenach go bás Alastair Mhóir. Dublin: OS, 1954. 914 pp. [John Bagnell Bury's *A History of Greece,*[132] trans. into Irish by the Very Rev. Monsignor Pádraig de Brún. Part One: From the beginning to the defeat of the Persians. Part Two: The growth, rise, and decline of the Athenian Empire. Part Three: From the downfall of Athens to the death of Alexander the Great.]

95. *Foras Feasa ar Stair na Rómha.* H. F. Pelham, M.A., LL.D., F.S.A. do scríobh. Pádraig Ó Moghráin, M.A. d'aistrigh go Gaeilge. Dublin: OS, 1956. 564 pp. [*Foundation of Knowledge on the History of Rome.* H. F. Pelham, M.A., LL.D., F.S.A. Trans. into Irish by Pádraig Ó Moghráin, M.A.][133]

96. *Nótaí ar Stair, Litríocht agus Saíocht na Róimhe.* E. J. Hally. Arna aistriú go Gaeilge ag Fiachra S. Ó Dubhthaigh. Dublin: Edco., 1970. 109 pp. [*Notes on the History, Literature and Civilisation of Rome.* E. J. Hally.[134] Trans. into Irish by Fiachra S. Ó Dubhthaigh.]

---

[127] Translation of Mason D. Gray, Thornton Jenkins, F. Dale, *Latin For Today, Book 3* (London, 1934).
[128] 3,000 copies printed, 1,200 sold by 1955; remaining stock then reduced to 100.
[129] 750 copies printed, 350 sold by 31 March 1957.   [130] Cyril E. Robinson, London, 1932.
[131] 1,000 copies printed, 310 sold by 31 March 1957.   [132] London, 1900.
[133] Translation of H. F. Pelham, *Outlines of Roman History,* 5th ed. (London, 1928).
[134] Dublin: Edco., 1966.

7

Dinneen's Irish Virgil

Fiachra Mac Góráin

Dinneen and the Irish Revival

Brian Friel's play *Translations* is set in 1833 in a hedge school in the fictional village of Ballybeg in rural Donegal.[1] Hedge schools, so called from the erroneous belief that they met behind a hedge or in a ditch, were informal and often ephemeral institutions which in the absence of national schools provided education in reading, writing, and arithmetic, but sometimes also classical languages and literature. They existed from the time that King William's anti-Catholic penal laws forbade the education of Catholics until the setting up of national schools in the mid-nineteenth century, though in many hedge schools the pupils could be Catholics or Protestants.[2] The hedge school in *Translations* meets in a barn, and the pupils, the schoolmaster Hugh, and his son Manus quote and comment on Greek and Latin literature, often noting connections between the point of the classical quotation and their own experience. Already in 1833 many Irish speakers had abandoned Irish for English as the language of social and economic advancement. At the end of *Translations* the hedge school is to be replaced by a more 'practical' national school in which the language of instruction will be English. The play has on its horizons the potato famine of 1845–9, which would deal a further blow to the Irish language through death and emigration. While the playscript is in English, through a dramatic conceit the Irish characters onstage are understood to be speaking Irish, and much of the play's action hinges on the mutual incomprehension between characters, and on the expedients with which they attempt to overcome the language barrier. In more than one interview Friel refers to the 'sad irony' that the play was written in English.[3] The play's themes include language, identity, culture, and education in a colonial context; and, as scholars have recognized, the classical

For their helpful comments I would like to thank Nicholas Allen; Brian Arkins; Aifric Mac Aodha; Máirín Mac Góráin; Philip O'Leary; Diarmuid Ó Mathúna; Donncha O'Rourke; Isabelle Torrance; and the anonymous reviewers for OUP.

[1] Friel (1981), which premiered the previous year at the Guildhall in Derry.
[2] On the hedge schools see Dowling (1968); Stanford (1976: 25–8); McElduff (2006); O'Higgins (2017: 121–39).
[3] Murray (1999: 80, 85).

Fiachra Mac Góráin, *Dinneen's Irish Virgil* In: *Classics and Irish Politics, 1916–2016.* Edited by: Isabelle Torrance and Donncha O'Rourke, Oxford University Press (2020). © Oxford University Press.
DOI: 10.1093/oso/9780198864486.003.0007

references make a significant contribution to the play's discourse about these themes.[4]

Fast-forward a century or so, and after a long struggle Irish is once again being taught in Irish schools and used as a medium of instruction. Already in the 1880s new material was being printed in Irish, but from the mid-1920s onwards Irish-language books and editions aimed specifically at schools and teachers begin to appear.[5] Conradh na Gaeilge (The Gaelic League) was central to the revival of Irish-language education, in particular its members Patrick Pearse, Douglas Hyde, Peadar Ua Laoghaire, and Eoin MacNeill.[6] Among those who contributed Irish-language teaching materials was an t-Athair Pádraig Ua Duinnín, or Father Patrick Dinneen, whose writings on Virgil are the main subject of this paper.

Dinneen, who lived from 1860 to 1934, was a Jesuit priest, scholar, editor, jour-nalist, sometime controversialist, and gargantuan figure in the Irish language revival. He was a contemporary of Synge, Yeats, and Joyce, and even makes a brief offstage appearance in the 'Scylla and Charybdis' chapter of *Ulysses*. Most of his writings were in Irish, and his contribution to the development of Irish cultural identity in the decades after independence was significant.[7] He wrote the first novel in Irish, *Cormac Ua Connaill*, and produced editions of several Munster Irish poets, including Aogán Ó Rathaille and Eoghan Ruadh Ó Súilleabháin. He wrote more than a thousand weekly columns in *The Leader* addressing a wide range of subjects from the Great War to classical literature. He translated Dickens' *A Christmas Carol* into Irish, wrote a visionary *aisling* poem on the 1916 Easter Rising, plays on historical themes including the famine, and books on social life in Ireland, and Kerry before the famine.[8] He is best known for the second edition (1927) of his Irish–English dictionary and thesaurus, which, more than simply a dictionary, has been described as 'an encyclopaedia of the manners and customs, lore and skills, of the pre-industrial society which survived in Dinneen's home place'.[9] Myles na gCopaleen christened Dinneen 'our great comic lexicographer', and mined his dictionary for his *Cruiskeen Lawn* column in *The Irish Times*.[10]

All of Dinneen's writings were part of a conversation about nation-building and the role of culture, language, especially the Irish language, and the arts in the

---

[4] Many scholars have examined the classical references in *Translations*: see in particular Arkins (1991); Cullingford (1996); Saunders (2012); and Passaretti (2014).

[5] For a full list of Irish-language publications of classical texts see Appendix C to Chapters 5 and 6, along with Ní Mhurchú (Ch. 5) and Moran (Ch. 6) for analysis.

[6] See Ó Súilleabháin (1988) and Walsh (2007).

[7] On Dinneen see Ó Conluain and Ó Céileachair (1976); O'Leary (1994) index s.v. Dinneen; Mac Cárthaigh (2009); and the introductions to O'Leary (2013) and Mac Annraoi (2016).

[8] See Ua Duinnín (1901a), (1901b), (1903), (1905), (1919), (1922), (1929), (1931); Ua Duinnín and O'Donoghue (1911); Ua Duinnín (1927); O'Leary (2013); Mac Annraoi (2016). In turn, Dinneen has been fictionalized in detective short stories by Jenkinson (2008) and (2011).

[9] MacLochlainn (2002: 72). On the dictionary see also Riggs (2005); Mac Amhlaigh (2008: 93–103); Titley (2014–15).

[10] On the importance of classical material for Myles na gCopaleen's *Cruiskeen Lawn* columns see O'Hogan (Ch. 8).

new state. Since the beginning of the Irish Literary Revival, commentators had debated what kind of national literature Ireland should have, and what kind of balance it should strike between the different elements that make up the Irish people: Gaelic, Norman, and Saxon, continental and insular, different religious confessions, urban and rural, traditional and modern; and how, if at all, questions of language and culture should inform political aspirations and their execution.[11] In 1893 Douglas Hyde and Eoin MacNeill had founded the Gaelic League to promote the Irish language and culture, but as a strictly non-political association; but in the years leading up to the 1916 Rising it became politicized indirectly through sharing almost all of its membership with the Irish Republican Brotherhood, and directly through the policy changes brought about by Patrick Pearse and Thomas Clarke. Douglas Hyde resigned his presidency of the Gaelic League in July 1915 when it declared a change of policy in favour of armed insurrection. It remains a subject of debate and dispute how much the language and culture movement should be regarded as a springboard for revolution.[12] Almost all of the essays by Dinneen which I shall discuss appeared originally in 1926 issues of *The Leader*. This organ of opinion was founded in 1900 (and directed until his death) by D. P. Moran, whose mission it was to promote a Gaelic, Catholic, Irish-speaking Ireland, which would be unmaterialistic and whose citizens would play only Gaelic games, a view he set out earlier in *The Philosophy of Irish Ireland* (1905).[13] In contrast with the exclusivist Moran, but similar to some other Irish revivalists such as Patrick Pearse and Thomas MacDonagh, Dinneen was intellectually liberal and outward-looking, even though at the same time he was socially conservative, clericalist, and tribal in his thinking. As we shall see, his complex views on Irish culture were interwoven with his understanding of classical antiquity.

Readers of this volume will be interested most in Dinneen's writings on the Classics, in which—like the characters in Friel's *Translations*—he forges strong connections wherever possible between classical antiquity and Irish experience. In fact, Dinneen's entire oeuvre, journalistic and historical as well as scholarly, is generously sprinkled with classical learning, even when classical authors were not his immediate focus. He recognized the classical erudition of Irish poets in his editions.[14] His book on the people of Kerry before the potato famine advances the argument that Kerry people were kinder, more devout, and more welcoming in

---

[11] O'Leary (1994: esp. 1–90); on the Irish Revival see Kiberd and Mathews (2015).

[12] Foster (1988: 446–56) argues that the League was cultural but not political in its nationalism; Hutchinson (1987) and Stewart (2000) for different reasons see cultural nationalism leading to political nationalism. See further McMahon (2008: 2–3), with further references.

[13] On Moran see Hutchinson (1987); Maume (1995) and (1999); Delaney (2003); Murphy (2017: 115–42).

[14] Cf., e.g., Ua Duinnín (1901a: iii, vi, xi); Ó Buachalla (2004: 6) records how the editorial committee of the Irish Texts Society considered Dinneen's first draft of the Ó Rathaille edition 'too much hampered by reminiscences of Classical models'; see Ua Duinnín and O'Donoghue (1911: vii, xxx, xxxvii, and 92) for references to Menalcas (implicit), Archilochus, Homer, and Virgil.

the past, and in line with this thesis, the book is graced with two epigraphs in Latin from the finale of book 2 of Virgil's *Georgics*, describing a bygone golden-age idyll of rustic peace and religious observance.[15] In *The Queen of the Hearth* (posthumously published from the Nachlass) he makes reference to Homer's Nausicaa and Arete to illustrate his argument that women belong in the home.[16] Most arrestingly, he compared the destruction in Dublin after the Easter Rising of 1916 to the burned and wrecked city of Troy.[17]

Conversely, in his works of classical scholarship he introduces topics from antiquity with reference to Irish counterparts. These works comprise an edition with commentary on book 1 of the *Aeneid* and a volume of *aistí* (essays).[18] The edition is typical of school commentaries in that it offers biographical information, linguistic help, and literary background with parallel citations, but it also explains why Virgil should be of interest to an Irish readership. The essays, thirty-seven in number, and all but one about four pages in length, are arranged in chronological order from Homer through to Virgil and then jumping to early Christianity, with two essays appended on the Latin language, and on money and barter. Written when Irish-language literary criticism in any modern sense was still in its infancy,[19] they offer basic critical and historical introductions to Greek and Latin works. Sixteen of these are concerned with Virgil, with particular emphasis on historical and biographical interpretation and on religious matters such as the prophecy of Christ in the fourth *Eclogue* or the eschatology in the sixth book of the *Aeneid*. Before Dinneen gets to Virgil, he compares early Irish saga and the society it depicts with that of Homeric epic, and recognizes both as foundational for European societies and as repositories of moral instruction.[20] He discerns that Homer must have come at the end of a refined poetic tradition, similar in this respect to the Kerry poets Aogán Ó Rathaille and Eoghan Ruadh Ó Súilleabháin, whose works he had also edited.[21] He reports that Geoffrey Keating was often dubbed the Irish Herodotus for the simplicity and excellence of his storytelling.[22] He compares the metrical complexity of Horace's *Odes* to the

---

[15]   Ua Duinnín (1905), quoting *Geo.* 2.467–73 *at secura quies... terris vestigia fecit* and 2.532 *hanc olim veteres vitam coluere Sabini*; in Peter Fallon's translation (2004): 'no, what they have is the quiet life – carefree and no deceit – | and wealth untold – their ease among cornucopiae, | with grottoes, pools of running water and valleys cool even in warm weather, | the sounds of cattle and sweet snoozes in the shade. | There are glades and greenwoods, lairs of game, | young men wed to meagre fare but born and built for work. | Here, too, is reverence for god and holy fathers, and it was | here that Justice left her final footprints as she was taking leave of earth.' ... 'That was the life, and those the ways the Sabines cultivated in the days of old.'

[16]   O'Leary (2013: 73, 88–9).   [17]   Mac Annraoi (2016: 10).

[18]   Ua Duinnín (1931) and (1929), respectively. A 1959 report to the Public Accounts Committee of Dáil Éireann records at Appendix XIV, 'Books in Irish Published by An Gúm', that 6,000 copies of the *Aeneid* 1 commentary had been printed, of which approximately 4,000 had been sold by 1957.

[19]   See Uí Chollatáin (2003), including (2003: 287) a comment from Dinneen on the state of literary criticism in Irish.

[20]   Ua Duinnín (1929: 9); cf. O'Higgins (2017: 187–8) on Thomas Harney's Irish translation of the *Iliad*, which makes links with Irish heroic saga.

[21]   Ua Duinnín (1929: 13).   [22]   Ua Duinnín (1929: 22).

metrical schemes of Irish bardic poetry, while also recognizing differences between the two systems.[23] He endorses the didactic value for the common people of the myths in the early books of Livy, and observes that many other countries including Ireland have mythical elements in their early history.[24]

Virgil in Irish

Perhaps the most significant thing about Dinneen's studies of Virgil and other ancient authors is the language in which they are written. Commending the virtues of a classical education, he notes the recent revival of Irish-language study in the foreword to both commentary and essays, arguing that Irish is a more beneficial avenue than English for classical learning:

> Agus is torthamhla go mór an t-eidirmheadhón an Ghaedhealg 'ná an Béarla don obair sin. Is líomhtha, is ársa, is cruinne de theangain í 'ná an Béarla agus is cómhgaraighe agus is oireamhnaighe do sna teangthaibh ársa í.[25]

> And Irish is a much more fruitful medium for that work. It is a more fluent, more ancient, and more accurate language than English, and closer and more appropriate to the ancient languages.

This said, he adds that teacher and student should of course also take advantage of the knowledge that is to be found in English-language books, and he himself cites English-language scholarship, and occasionally scholarly debates in French and German.[26] In an essay on Virgil and the Roman state, he comments that native Irish speakers should study great world literature in their native tongue.[27] In the commentary he justifies the claim of greater similarity between Irish and the classical languages on the basis that Irish nouns and verbs are highly inflected, and he provides occasional parallels from the Irish for various idioms.[28] In line with this stance, he Gaelicizes Latin and other foreign proper nouns. Thus, *Lavinium* becomes 'Labinium', and Madvig and Servius become 'Madbig agus Serbius';[29] since there was no letter 'v' in the Gaelic alphabet, the 'v' of these names is transliterated with the letter 'b' aspirated with a superscript dot, or in Irish, 'buailte', normally written as 'bh' in roman type. *Alba Longa* becomes 'Alba', which in Irish

---

[23] Ua Duinnín (1929: 71).   [24] Ua Duinnín (1929: 62).
[25] Ua Duinnín (1929: 5), cf. 1931: 3).   [26] Ua Duinnín (1929: 5, 143–4).
[27] Ua Duinnín (1929: 87).
[28] Ua Duinnín (1931: 4 and, e.g., 77, 109, 113, 125); Mac Philibín (1942) was to intensify Dinneen's practice of providing Irish parallels; he gives at least seventeen on *Aeneid* 2, while Dinneen had given only a handful on *Aeneid* 1. Ó Concheanainn (1956: 25) also invoked Irish poetry in a paragraph on Virgil's style, in particular his poetic use of noble historical names.
[29] Ua Duinnín (1931: 102, 132).

strictly means 'Scotland', but Dinneen disambiguates the usage by specifying its location in Latium, and it receives an Irish inflection ('go hAlbain'), while *Albanus* becomes 'Albanač', 'Scotsman'.[30] But Dinneen also asserts that the student will feel that Irish is more suitable than English for the ancient ideas and mentality that are in play in the *Aeneid* ('Mothóthaidh an mac léinn, is dóigh liom…gur oireamhnaighe an Ghaedhalg do smuaintibh is d'aigne na sean-aimsire atá i gceist san Aeinéis, ná an Béarla').[31] Hugh's words in *Translations* spring to mind, where he tells the pupils of his encounter with the English Captain Lancey: 'I went on to propose that our own culture and the classical tongues made a happier conjugation'; or later, to Lieutenant Yolland: 'Wordsworth?…no. I'm afraid we're not familiar with your literature, Lieutenant, we feel closer to the warm Mediterranean. We tend to overlook your island.'[32] Friel's Hugh is harking back to the currents of culture and learning between Ireland and continental Europe which coursed particularly through ecclesiastical channels. Dinneen, of course, would not have overlooked Wordsworth. He had studied at University College Dublin with Gerard Manley Hopkins, and particularly admired Alexander Pope, perhaps partly due to Pope's Catholicism. In his essay on the fourth *Eclogue* he recommends Pope's *Messiah*, and devotes another essay to extolling Pope's translation of the *Iliad*, which he says enriched the English language, and which he considers superior to translations by Tickell, Cowper, and the Earl of Derby.[33] As for English prose, Dinneen cites Macaulay's *History of England*, referring to the author in domesticating terms as 'an Tighearna Mac Amhlaoibh' ('Lord Macaulay'), and to his work as 'Stair Shasana' ('History of England').[34] Dinneen's point, incidentally, in invoking Macaulay's work is to illustrate how oratory in classical historiography has given way to a non-oratorical but still highly rhetorical style among modern historians.[35]

After vigorous debate, the Gaelic League had opted for the Gaelic typography inspired by Irish manuscripts rather than the roman letters with which even most Irish speakers would have been familiar. This choice has its own fascinating and controversial history: on the one hand, the Gaelic font had sometimes been associated with nationalism, even though many in the Gaelic League advocated roman type for practical reasons; on the other hand, the Gaelic font had been cultivated by evangelical Protestants, and went back to a typeface sent over to Ireland by Queen Elizabeth I for the printing of vernacular bibles that would assist in converting the Irish.[36] Readers of Dinneen's Irish Texts Society edition of Aogán Ó Rathaille (1901) will have been struck by the contrast between the

---

[30] Ua Duinnín (1931: 102, 105). 'Albanach' [sing.] is evidently a word of elastic significance for Dinneen, as we see from his dictionary entry (1927: 34): it primarily denotes a Scotsman, and (by extension) 'a Presbyterian or Protestant', but it may also refer to 'a species of puffin (so called possibly from its solemn expression and black drapery)'.

[31] Ua Duinnín (1931: 4).   [32] Friel (1981: 23, 50).

[33] Ua Duinnín (1929: 98 and 15–18, respectively).   [34] Ua Duinnín (1929: 60).

[35] See Ó Conluain and Ó Céileachair (1976: 84–92, 98–100) on Dinneen's love of English literature.

[36] See Ó Cadhain (1971: 141); Ó Ciosáin (2004–6: 90); McGuinne (2010: 163–93).

22

Ḃirgil agus Maecenas

Tugtar Maecenas ar ríġ cuṁaċtaċ nó ar fear saiḋbir, go mórmór má's fear stáit é, a ċuireann suim i litriḋeaċt móir nó i léiġeann, is a ċabruiġeann le scríoḃnóiriḃ móra nó le n-a leiṫéidiḃ is a ġríosuiġeann iad ċum ceapaḋóireaċta nó ċum scrúduġaḋ léiġinn. Fir den tsórt soin do b'eaḋ Cosimo de Medici, an ceaṫramaḋ Laoiseaċ déag, rí na Fraince, an Cardional Richelieu, an Dara Carolus, rí Sasana, do ċuir ar Ḋryden an aoir éaċtaċ soin "Absolam is Achitophel" do ċeapaḋ.

Aċt níor éiriġ le haoinne den ḟuirinn sin ċóṁ mait is d'éiriġ leis an té tug a ainm dóiḃ .i. le Maecenas féin. Is é Maecenas do ċuir ar Ḃirgil an dán aoiḃinn sin "na Georgica" do ċeapaḋ agus do ċuir meisneaċ air is do ġríosuiġ é ċum ceapaḋóireaċta i dtreo gur éiriġ leis fá deireaḋ an Aenéis do ċeapaḋ. Is é do ċuir treo fairsing beataḋ ar Horás i gcuma go raiḃ caoi aige ċum a Óide agus a Eipistile do ċeapaḋ is do ċur os cóṁair an tsluaiġ.

99

Fig. 7.1. Foreign names translated into Irish and printed in Gaelic typeface. Ua Duinnín (1929: 99).

original Irish text printed in Gaelic typeface and the facing English translation and other English-language material printed in roman. But even more striking is the visual effect of Dinneen translating foreign names into inflected Irish and printing them in Gaelic type. Several examples occur on the first page of Dinneen's essay on Virgil and Maecenas (Fig. 7.1).

Again the 'V' of Virgil is transliterated with an aspirated B as Ḃirgil. Other foreign names are rigorously nativized to reflect Gaelic usage and phonetics. 'Cosimo de Medici' is straightforwardly transliterated into the Gaelic typeface, and 'Absalom and Achitophel' is lightly domesticated into 'Absolam is Achitophel'. Louis XIV is translated into 'an ceathramhadh Laoiseach déag' ('the fourteenth Louis'), but 'Laoiseach' is also the adjective derived from 'Laois', or 'Laoighis' in the spelling of Dinneen's day, an Irish county and ancestral kingdom in Leinster, and so like 'Albanach' (above) the translation has indigenous resonances. Charles II of England is given half in Irish and half in Latin as 'an Dara Carolus' ('the second Carolus'). The initial D of Dryden is aspirated, with implications for pronunciation, into an Irish dative. (Incidentally, there is a discreet code-switch in the typesetting which allows Dryden to retain his y, a letter not present in the Irish alphabet.) The practice of translating proper names was to find more fervent expression: in a note on the spelling of Virgil's name—Virgilius or Vergilius?— Liam Mac Philibín, a slightly later commentator, even proposed that the poet should probably be called 'Fearghal' in Irish, since that had been the name of the saint who was named 'Virgilius' in Latin, Virgil of Salzburg, the Irish saint who was threatened with excommunication for believing that the earth was round and positing the existence of the antipodes.[37] Dinneen himself does not go so far, but his spelling and typography still give a strong paratextual signal of native ownership of the material. It is the reverse of the cultural procedure enacted in Friel's *Translations*: there, the translation of place names from Irish into English was an imperial stratagem, assimilation through linguistic erosion; here the appropriation of European culture in Irish is a statement of national resurgence and independence.

There is no full translation of the *Aeneid* in modern Irish, even though the earliest vernacular version of the poem was the twelfth-century *Imtheachta Aeniasa* ('The Wanderings of Aeneas'), which is sometimes mentioned with pride in Irish-language Virgil editions.[38] But there are fragments of Virgil translations scattered through Dinneen's works, which are not the least of his accomplishments, in that they exhibit simple poetic beauty and interpretative acumen. Let us examine for example the translation of the statesman simile from *Aeneid* 1.148–53, and Dinneen's comment on the passage:

> ac veluti magno in populo cum saepe coorta est
> seditio saevitque animis ignobile vulgus

---

[37] Mac Philibín (1942: 1) 'Is dócha gur "Feargal" ba chóir a thabhairt air in nGaedhilg, mar b'in é ainm an naoimh ar ar baisteadh "Birgilius" sa Laidin.' On Virgil of Salzburg see Grosjean (1963) and Ó Fiaich (1985).

[38] On *Imtheachta Aeniasa* see Calder (1907), now Calder and Poppe (1995); Poppe (1995) and (2004); Miles (2011: 57–76); McElduff (2014). It is mentioned by Mac Philibín (1942: 15) and Ó Concheanainn (1956: 20–3; 30). In the early nineteenth century, a schoolteacher Thady O'Conolan declared an intention to translate the *Aeneid* into Irish: see O'Higgins (2017: 128). For partial translations of the *Aeneid* see, e.g., the school editions of Ó Concheanainn (1971) and Carey (1978). Fragments of Margaret Heavey's Irish translation of the *Georgics* survive in her archive at NUIG; I thank Michael Clarke and Pádraic Moran for sending me a copy. On Margaret Heavey's Irish translations and editions of classical material, see Moran (Ch. 6).

iamque faces et saxa volant, furor arma ministrat;
tum, pietate gravem ac meritis si forte virum quem
conspexere, silent arrectisque auribus astant;
ille regit dictis animos et pectora mulcet:

'Agus fé mar, nuair éirigheann go minic coimheascair idir shluaightibh móra daoine agus bíonn an gráscar gan mheas ar buile le mío-iomchar, fá dheoidh bíonn tóirsí is clocha dá raideadh (soláthruigheann buile urchair), má thagann leo a súile do leagadh ar fhear go bhfuil creideamhaint aige de bhárr cráibhtheachta is deigh-ghníomhartha, ciúnuighid agus cuirid cluasa le héisteacht ortha féin; seolann seisean a n-aigne le n-a bhriathraibh agus séimhigheann a gcroidhe.'

San tsamhlaoid sin, an chéad shamhlaoid san Aenéis, cuireann an file i n-umhail dúinn an meas a bhí ag Rómhánachaibh ar an ndlighe, ar chiuineas phuiblidhe agus ar fhearaibh cráibhtheacha creideamhnacha.[39]

'And as a melée often arises between large crowds of people and the unesteemed mob is in a disorderly rage, in the end torches and rocks are being hurled (madness provides weapons), if they chance to set their eyes on a man who has credit due to his religious devotion and good deeds, they fall silent and they prick up their ears to listen; he directs their minds with his words and calms their hearts.'

In that simile, the first simile of the *Aeneid*, the poet conveys to us the Romans' respect for laws, for public quiet, and for men of religious devotion and good repute.

As one might expect from a lexicographer, the language is rich and refined, and he manages to stay very close to the Latin while remaining natural in Irish. The idiom, as so often from the mouths or pens of Kerry people, seems effortlessly poetic, and it is easy to be persuaded of Dinneen's claim as to the superiority of Irish over English for the appreciation of Latin. An Irish readership would be proudly heartened by such a translation, in which Virgil speaks to them in their own language. Beyond style, there are contemporary resonances in 'urchair' ('arma'), a word which suggests gunfire or even artillery. The reference to the unruly mob seems to seethe with the contempt that Dinneen might initially have felt in Easter week 1916 as the plates of the first edition of his dictionary were destroyed in the burning city of Dublin.[40] The translation and comment emphasize the Romans' respect for religious devotion and public order, as against the mob's fury. In one of his essays, 'Curadh ionnraic dílis' ('An upright loyal hero'), Dinneen discusses Aeneas' *pietas* as his main defining characteristic. Responding to the complaint of unnamed German scholars who maintain that Aeneas' *pietas* is overplayed by the poet and by Aeneas himself, Dinneen regards the quality as more important than

[39] Ua Duinnín (1931: 85).
[40] See Riggs (2016) for the destruction of the plates of Dinneen's dictionary in the 1916 Rising.

bravery or deeds of valour or eloquence or wisdom, in that *pietas* is, according to Cicero, what gave Roman rule its durability and commanded respect, and thus an appropriate value for Virgil to privilege in the model of Roman leadership.[41]

Celtic Virgil

A further move in Dinneen's Irish appropriation of Virgil was to foreground his supposed Celtic origins, but he achieved this in a way that was benign rather than divisive:

> Do réir gach cunntais Ceilteach do b'eadh é de bhunadhas, i dtreo gurab ionann cine bunadhasach dó is do Ghaedheal-|aibh. Atá deallramh áirithe ag a shaothar filiota le litridheacht na Sean-Ghaedheal do réir ughdar áirithe; acht, dar liom-sa, is deacair an deallramh soin do dheimhniughadh.[42]

> According to all accounts he was a Celt by origin, such that he and Gaels share the same race of origin. According to certain authors his poetry bears a certain resemblance to ancient Gaelic literature; but in my opinion it is difficult to confirm that resemblance.

There are three interrelated points here: (i) Virgil was a Celt; (ii) this meant that he was of the same basic race as the Gaels of Ireland; and (iii) there may therefore be kinship between Virgil and Gaelic literature on the level of *mentalité*. The somewhat elastic claim was to become a staple of Irish school editions of Virgil and Caesar.[43] As John Gallagher put it in a 1945 introduction to Caesar's *Gallic War*, 'We need mention only Catullus, the Celt, and Virgil, born in Celtic Mantua, son of a Celtic mother, Magia, to realise the extent of the influence which Gaul exercised on the development of Latin literature.'[44] The idea of Virgil's supposed Celticity had in fact been hotly debated since the end of the nineteenth century, at least since Nettleship's observation that the names Andes, Virgil's birthplace, and apparently also Vergilius, were Celtic. The truth is beyond verification for lack of evidence, but that did not stop scholars arguing for or against the Celticity of Virgil, either by reading his family's names against the epigraphic record of Gaul and Italy, or by identifying a Celtic note in the Romantic and tragic sensibility of his poems.[45] One hard-bitten naysayer, Leonora Reilly Furr, concludes that the 'notion' of Virgil's Celticity 'rests on sentiment rather than on logic.'[46]

---

[41]   Ua Duinnín (1929: 143–6).   [42]   Ua Duinnín (1929: 87–8).
[43]   See also Ua Duinnín (1931: 7); Mac Philibín (1942: 5); Gallagher (1945: xlix).
[44]   Gallagher (1945: xliv).
[45]   For: Nettleship in Conington and Nettleship (1881: I, xviii); Garrod (1912); Braunholtz (1915); Conway (1931); Mac Philibín (1942: 13); against: Frank (1922); Furr (1930); overall see Vance (1997: 145–6).
[46]   Furr (1930: 341).

The academic debate about Virgil's Celticity can hardly be separated from a wider racial and political discourse about the place of the Celts in Britain and Ireland, especially as far as Dinneen's claims are concerned. On the positive side, from the mid-nineteenth century onwards, Celtic identity, including language revival movements, was associated with nationalism.[47] On the negative side, social theory and Unionist historiography by the likes of John Anthony Froude were inflected with racial theorizing about the inferiority of the Celtic race.[48] On this view the Celt was disparaged as impulsive, emotional, and incapable of self-government, a gambit familiar in Ireland since Giraldus Cambrensis put cultural belittlement in the service of political disenfranchisement. The connection between culture and politics emerges clearly in Mommsen, for whom the feckless Celt, whether Gaul or Irish, was condemned to be the leaven in the polity of superior nations.[49] Matthew Arnold's re-evaluation of the Celtic note in English literature, ostensibly an olive branch to Ireland, did not extend its sympathies to the Irish nationalist cause, but rather sought to reconcile Ireland and bind her more closely to mother England, in this respect reversing the more nationalistic tendency of his main source, the Breton French anthropologist Ernest Renan's essay on the qualities of Celtic literature.[50] There were, of course, other formulations about the place of the Celt in the Irish nation. Thomas Davis' poem 'Celt and Saxon' had celebrated the hybrid heritage, and the rights of all Irish-born to title in the land, be they Celts, Danes, Normans, Milesians, or Saxons, noting that these peoples were all migrants, irrespective of the circumstances of settlement. Douglas Hyde, in his 1892 lecture 'On the necessity for de-Anglicising Ireland', asserted that Ireland always had been and always would be Celtic to the core, a view which ended up alienating some, including Ulster unionists.[51]

Dinneen himself occupied an ecumenical middle ground between extreme views. He implicitly acknowledged the division of Irish society into 'tribes', including his own Celtic people the Gaels, and 'West-Brits', who ape English manners and customs.[52] But he does not insist on any systematic correlation between culture and ethnicity; indeed, if it came to it, many of the 'West-Brits' would be lapsed Celts. On the other hand, he writes of the Gael's ability to absorb foreign people and influence,[53] and of the importance of working, as Virgil had done, for national unity, and not simply for the good of one particular people or tribe.

[47] See de Barra (2018) and Williams (2001: 9–10).

[48] See Ó Síocháin (2009), especially the contributions by Brady, Bowler, and Watson. See also Kiberd (1995: 29–31, 52–3); on anti-Celtic prejudices during the Irish Literary Revival see Macintosh (1994: 1–18).

[49] Mommsen (1866: IV, 286) concludes as follows a lengthy tirade on the Celts (which is worth reading in its entirety): '[the Celtic people] is, and remains, at all times and all places the same indolent and poetical, irresolute and fervid, inquisitive, credulous, amiable, clever, but – in a political point of view – thoroughly useless nation; and therefore its fate has been always and everywhere the same.'

[50] Arnold (1867); Renan (1970), first published in French in 1854; see also Yeats (1898).

[51] See Stewart (2000) and Delaney (2003).   [52] Ua Duinnín (1929: 142).

[53] Ua Duinnín (1905: introduction).

This view emerges most clearly in a lecture on Virgil which he delivered to the Celtic Society of University College Cork (UCC) in 1923, which is reprinted in the *Aistí*.[54] I quote extensively from this lecture, as it exemplifies the richness of tightly interwoven connections in Dinneen's thought between Virgil and Irish experience:

[I]s é Bhirgil oide scoile is béasmhúinteoir na hEorpa le dhá mhíle bliadhan agus tá gach aon deallramh air go leanfaidh sé dá chuid múinteoireachta go deireadh na scríbe. Is fearrde d'aon mhac léighinn Gaedhealach aithne do chur ar fhilídeacht Bhirgil agus stuidéar do dhéanamh ar chuid dá dhántaibh. Tá brath ag Gaedhealaibh Éireann go mbeidh ar a gcumas litridheacht fheidmeamhail do cheapadh 'na dteangain dúthchais, ceapadóireacht go mbeidh baint aice leis an dtreibh Ghaedhealaigh agus le n-a seanchas, le n-a huirscéaltaibh, le n-a finnscéaltaibh; agus ní miste dhúinn a thabhairt fá ndeara cionnus a chuir file mór de leithéid Bhirgil bunadhas is stair is seanchas is finnscéalaidheacht na Rómha go fuinte daingean i ndán caithréime a mhairfidh go bráth.[55]

Virgil has been Europe's schoolteacher and teacher of manners for two thousand years and it seems that he will continue with his teaching all the way to the end. Any Gaelic student would benefit from acquiring knowledge of Virgil and studying some of his poems. The Gaels of Ireland hope to be able to compose a useful literature in their native tongue, a production which will be connected to the Gaelic tribe, and with their folklore, with their novels, with their legends; and we would do well to observe how a great poet of Virgil's calibre wove together tightly the Roman foundation and history and oral traditions in an epic poem that will live forever.

This was over twenty years before T. S. Eliot dubbed Virgil 'the classic of all Europe'. Although Dinneen does not use any word cognate with 'classic' he admires the durability of the *Aeneid*, a poem that combines many native traditions. In turn he connects Virgil's achievement with the need of the Gaels to produce a national literature from their own traditional materials.

As he concludes the lecture, Dinneen anchors his message in the fortunes of his own family. Before Dinneen was born, they had been evicted from their land in Co. Kerry. Dinneen clearly inherited a dispossession complex, and often refers to the phenomenon in his studies of Munster history and the Munster poets. The landlord's eviction agent (a motif in narratives of landlord–tenant relations, and often satirized)[56] was a distant kinsman of the family, Pádraig Ó Murchú. Dinneen recalls in an unpublished autobiographical manuscript how as a child he raced after this agent, rebuking him for having been instrumental in evicting his own kith and kin.[57] As a result, Dinneen identifies closely with the story of Virgil's

---

[54] Ua Duinnín (1929: 75–86).
[55] Ua Duinnín (1929: 76).   [56] See Ua Duinnín (1905: 32–8).
[57] Ó Conluain and Ó Céileachair (1976: 32–4); NLI MS 8628.

dispossession from his land, which he mentions several times in the *Aistí*.[58] Biographical interpretation had been central to his work on the Munster poets,[59] and not surprisingly it resurfaces in his essays on Virgil. Turning back now to the peroration of the lecture to the UCC Celtic Society, we see that Dinneen makes a veiled reference to his family's dispossession and extracts a rousing protreptic from aligning himself with Virgil:

> Ní miste dúinn sampla Bhirgil do bheith ós ár gcomhair i nÉirinn indiu. Is iomdha mac léighinn éirimeamhail i nÉirinn agus i gCúige Mumhan féin gur ruaigeadh a athair as a chuid talmhan go héagcórach agus go mb'éigean dó féin a cheantar dúthchais do thréigean agus dul i leith a scolaidheachta agus an saoghal go buaidheartha 'na thimcheall mar gheall ar an atharrughadh mór atá ar siubhal ar fuaid na tíre go léir. Má leanann sé lorg Bhirgil, leanfaidh sé dá chuid foghluma i n-aimhdheoin a mbíonn ar siubhal 'na thimcheall agus tumfaidh sé a aigne i dteangain | agus i seanchas a thíre, agus ní bheidh uaidh acht a intleacht agus a cháilidheacht do chur i bhfeidhm ar son na tíre uile agus ní amháin ar son cumainn fé leith ná treibhe fé leith acht chum tír na hÉireann uile do neartughadh agus do mhórughadh agus chum a seanchas, a stair, a húirscéalta, a heachtraí d'fhighe i ndán nó i n-úirscéal a chuirfidh i n-umhail don domhan uile mais is mórdhacht is síbhialtacht na nGaedheal. Ní miste dhúinn go léir ár gcuid féin den obair sin do dhéanamh is í dhéanamh i n-am.[60]

We would do well to keep the example of Virgil before us in Ireland today. Many's the intelligent student in Ireland and even in Munster whose father was unjustly banished from his land, and who himself had to desert his native district and go about his schooling with the world harried around him because of the great upheaval that is in train in the whole land. If he follows in the footsteps of Virgil, he will pursue his learning despite what is happening around him and he will immerse his mind in the languages | and the lore of his country, and his only desire will be to apply his intellect and ability on behalf of the whole country, and not merely for a particular group or for a particular tribe, but to strengthen and exalt the entire country of Ireland, and to weave her traditions, her history, her novels, her adventures into a poem or a novel which will convey to the whole world the gravity and grandeur and civilization of the Gaels. We would all do well to do our share of that work, and to do it in time.

Virgil stands as an example for the Irish people. The analogy which Dinneen implies between himself and Virgil is unmistakable: the scholar whose family lost their land, but who still pursued learning and put his talents to the service of the whole country and national unity. There are shades here, too, of the itinerant

---

[58] Ua Duinnín (1929: 83–4, 88–9).   [59] See Ó Buachalla (2004: 28–30).
[60] Ua Duinnín (1929: 85–6).

scholar-schoolmaster who spreads his learning throughout the community.[61] Like Virgil, Irish people should apply their skills and intellect not only on behalf of their own tribe, but for all the people of Ireland, in order to produce a poem or novel of national significance. One year after the civil war of 1922 which was fought over the Anglo-Irish Treaty, Dinneen urges national unity, regardless of tribal affiliation. He harnesses Virgil's biography (and his own) and the *Aeneid*'s interweaving of traditions in support of this idea. One might invoke Virgil's lines on how the war in Latium was fought between Trojans and Italians, peoples supposedly destined to live in eternal peace (12.503–4: *tanton placuit concurrere motu, | Iuppiter, aeterna gentis in pace futuras?*). Virgil's supposed Celtic origins dissolve into the background amid Dinneen's emphasis on each Irish person following Virgil's example of working for the common good, not just their own tribe.

Virgil and Irish History

An anecdote illustrating Dinneen's legendary secretiveness has it that he once recited to a friend the first line of *Aeneid* book 2, *Conticuere omnes intentique ora tenebant* ('They all fell silent and, rapt, kept their faces turned towards him'), and translated it as, 'Ciarraígh mhaithe a bhí iontu go léir agus d'fhanadar ina dtost.'[62] ('They were all good Kerry people, and so they remained silent.') Virgilian poetry has for Dinneen the quality of a touchstone for Irish affairs. In the remainder of this chapter I shall survey Dinneen's ideas about Virgil as national poet, and some of his views on female heroism, empire, and language, as they emerge in his Virgilian essays.

Dinneen believed that the government of the new Irish state should sponsor the creation of a national literature. He had in mind two models of patronage: the Irish bardic system, which collapsed when Irish chieftains were deprived of their ancestral heritage by foreign violence, and which he hopes will now return in some form, and Maecenas' patronage of Virgil and Horace.[63] He suggested that one native poem composed during his time would be more effective than twenty foreign poems which would be examined in schools. Accordingly, the government should take an interest in literature, and especially in poetry.[64] In the essay on Virgil and Maecenas, he rehearses a conventional narrative about how Maecenas persuaded Virgil to write the *Georgics* to encourage Italian farmers to return to working the land after the ravages of civil war.[65] He emphasizes the beauties of Italy, as praised by Virgil in the *laudes Italiae*, and concludes the essay as follows:

---

[61] See O'Higgins (2017), esp. chs. 4 and 5.
[62] Ó Conluain and Ó Céileachair (1976: 61).   [63] Ua Duinnín (1929: 90 and 85, respectively).
[64] Ua Duinnín (1929: 94).
[65] Ua Duinnín (1929: 100), and see Ua Duinnín (1931: 9) for a similar view.

Ní ar lucht na hIodáile amháin do chuir an file órdha céanna comaoin, acht ar an gcine daonna go léir ó shoin anuas. Mar d'oir a chainnt do gach aon tír is do gach aon treibh daoine; agus oireann an chainnt sin do gach aon tír san Eoraip is ar fuaid an domhain indiu féin; agus ní dóigh liom go n-oireann sí d'aon tír chómh mór is oireann do thír na hÉireann.

Níl tír fá'n spéir níos áilne ná níos saidhbhre 'ná tír na hÉireann. Le déidheann-aighe agus le roinnt mhaith de bhliadhantaibh bhí bruigheanta ar siubhal eadrainn, i dtreo go rabhamar ag déanamh faillighe i saothrughadh an tailimh agus go rabhamar ag éirghe mío-shásta le n-ár dtír dúthchais agus fonn ar ár n-aos óg í thréigean. Is mithid dúinn claoidhe léi agus feidhm do bhaint aiste agus bruighean is coimheascair do shéanadh.[66]

That same golden poet obliged not only the people of Italy, but the entire human race since that time. For what he said was appropriate of every single country and of every single tribe of people; and what he said was appropriate of every country in Europe and even all over the world today; and I do not think it is as appropriate of any country as it is of the country of Ireland.

There is no country under the sky more beautiful or richer than Ireland. Recently and for quite some years there was strife ongoing between us, such that we were neglecting the cultivation of the land, and becoming dissatisfied with our native country, and that the youth was inclined to desert her. We must stand by her and make use of her and say no to struggle and strife.

We see here another version of the 'classic of all Europe' motif, which Dinneen finds particularly relevant to the Irish case because of recent history—the famines and land agitation of the nineteenth century, Irish participation in the Great War,[67] the struggle for independence and the civil war of 1922, all of which have overshadowed the riches and beauty of Ireland. Dinneen draws on the *Georgics* to encourage Irish people to enjoy the land after warfare. One thinks of the French and English translations of the *Georgics* which were done during and after the Second World War. As Wilkinson comments, 'It was surely a yearning to escape from the horror and chaos of a distracted generation into the timeless peace and routine of agriculture that drew these to the *Georgics* in that crisis.'[68]

Virgil himself was an exemplary figure, but so, too, were his characters. As we have seen, Dinneen endorsed Aeneas' *pietas* as more essential than his martial or other heroic values. As a man of the cloth, Dinneen shies away from praising or even commenting on bloodshed in the *Aeneid*.[69] He prefers to focus instead on

[66] Ua Duinnín (1929: 102).
[67] Dinneen's *Leader* articles on the Great War are assembled with introduction and notes by Mac Annraoi (2016).
[68] Wilkinson (1969: 2).
[69] For his views on war and its necessity see O'Leary (2013: xix–xx).

the epic's civic, religious, and family values. In one essay, 'Ban-churadh Ghaelach' ('A Gaelic heroine'), he parallels Aeneas' *pietas* in carrying his father from the burning city of Troy with the exemplary goodness of a poor Irishwoman whom he knew in his youth. To paraphrase, this woman, though evicted from her land, relying only on her husband's daily wage, who had only a tiny abode and many children to feed, still insisted on carrying her aged mother home to her shack, across the hills and the mountains on her own shoulders, with no men to help her, her aged, ailing, and destitute mother, who had become dependent on the neighbour. This woman's noble deed is cited as an example for the Gaels of Ireland.[70] Also in *The Queen of the Hearth* (probably written 1915–18), Dinneen regards a mother's domestic self-sacrifice as a form of heroism; he is prepared to countenance women bearing arms in exceptional circumstances, as Inghinidhe na hÉireann ('Daughters of Ireland'), which merged with Cumann na mBan ('The Women's Association'), had done in the struggle for Irish independence, though he expresses distaste for public female zealotry and women's participation in violence and warfare, drawing as he does so on the classical analogue of the Amazons.[71] 'But,' he says, 'we have an instinctive loathing for a plague of pseudo-Amazonian fury. We detest the race of pygmy martial women that jostle us in the streets, that make night hideous with their brawls, that violate the sacred sanctity of home life, that engage in unequal contests with men.'[72]

Despite his family's experience of land dispossession, Dinneen's view of the Roman Empire appears to be broadly favourable. At one point he explicitly buys into Roman imperial rhetoric, quoting Cicero on the *pietas* of Roman imperialism, and elsewhere he emphasizes how the Empire spread civilization and Christianity.[73] Dinneen's use of Virgil as a figure of Irish national unity *against* empire, which we traced above, conflicts with the endorsement of empire on the basis of its *pietas* and certainly involves a sleight of hand. It is fascinating to observe the parallels in Dinneen's thought between Roman imperialism and the missionary zeal of the Church of Rome, and the inevitable contradiction which arises between Dinneen's nationalism and his approval of the empire which Virgil ostensibly supported. (Similar ironies attend the presence of the *Aeneid* in Friel's *Translations*, where in a game of intertextual substitutions the English play the role of the imperial Romans.[74]) Dinneen addresses the subject of empire and its malcontents, even if he does not quite resolve this contradiction, in an essay on punishments and rewards in the underworld entitled 'Grá tíre agus a mhalairt'

---

[70] Ua Duinnín (1929: 147–50). Compare Brendan Kennelly's assertion that his *Trojan Women* was inspired by the 'Trojan' women of rural mid-twentieth-century Ireland, a reference to their powers of endurance; see further Torrance (Ch. 13) on Irish adaptations of *Trojan Women*.

[71] O'Leary (2013: 92).

[72] For Dinneen's essay on the effects of the Great War on Irish women (*Leader* 13 November 1915) see Mac Annraoi (2016: 72–4).

[73] Ua Duinnín (1929: 144–5, 154).   [74] See n. 4 above, esp. Arkins (1991: 208).

('Love of country and its opposite').[75] Dinneen infers Virgil's great patriotism from the prominent rewards given to those who were wounded for their country, and the punishments given to those who accepted bribes to revoke laws or who sold their country to a foreign ruler. 'But,' he continues, 'even though Virgil's pride in the Roman Republic and Empire was great, he knew precisely that neither the Republic nor the Empire prospered without injustice and without oppression of weaker states, and without evil people belonging to those weak states who sold them for gold and who by their treachery placed the larger state above them; and the poet conveys to us his hatred and contempt towards such people.'[76] In Ireland's case there is a parallel in Patrick Pearse's poem *Mise Éire*: 'mór mo náir – mo chlann féin do dhíol a máthair' ('great my shame – my own family sold their mother'), of Irish collaborationists; another parallel is Owen in Friel's *Translations*, a quisling for most of the play who assists the English with their imperializing cartography, until the violence of the mission becomes manifest. In all three cases the conversion to empire happens from within. Dinneen ascribes Virgil's hatred of these traitors to his own experience of unjust dispossession,[77] and turns next to Anchises' lesson on empire:

Agus dá mhéid molta thugann sé d'impireacht na Rómha san chunntas so, ní miste leis i ndeireadh an chunntais a mholadh don impireacht chumhachtaigh sin gur cheart dí gan bheith dian ar na státaibh do cuireadh fá chois agus dlighe na síoth chána do chur 'na measc, agus nár mhiste dhí stáit an díomais do smachtughadh:

Tu regere imperio populos, Romane, memento,

(Hae tibi erunt artes) pacisque imponere morem,

Parcere subjectis et debellare superbos.

'Cuimhnigh, a Rómhánaigh, gurab é do dhualgas-sa na náisiúin do riaghlughadh fáth smacht (sin iad na healadhanta is dual duit), agus dlighthe na síothchána do chur i bhfeidhm, truagh do bheith agat don druing atá faoi chois agus drong an díomais do mhíniughadh.'[78]

And for all his praise for the Roman Empire in this account, he does not hesitate at the end to recommend to that powerful empire that she should not be harsh on those states which were subjugated and to spread the laws of peace among them and that she should not mind bringing arrogant states to heel:

Tu regere...superbos.

'Remember, Roman, that it is *your* duty to rule the nations under the yoke (those are the arts which come to you), and to put in place the laws of peace, to have pity for the throng that is downtrodden, and to tame those who practise arrogance.'

---

[75] Ua Duinnín (1929: 135–8).   [76] Ua Duinnín (1929: 137).
[77] Ua Duinnín (1929: 137–8).   [78] Ua Duinnín (1929: 138).

The emphasis here is on the duty of empires to be mild to their subject nations. The verb 'míniughadh' ('smooth', 'polish', 'tame', 'subdue', 'soothe' > 'mín', 'smooth')[79] tones down the violence of Virgil's *debellare* several notches. The interpretation shows up the ambivalence of Dinneen's position: on the one hand, the *Aeneid* brings with it a glorification of the empire; on the other hand, Virgil's own experience leads him to see the injustices in play, and this becomes the basis for pleading mildness.

My final example comes from Dinneen's essay on the conversation between Jupiter and Juno in *Aeneid* 12, from an essay entitled 'Béasa is teanga dúthchais' ('Native customs and language').[80] Juno has conceded defeat to the Trojans but extracted a promise from Jupiter that the Latins will not have to renounce their Latin language or customs. Dinneen builds on this passage his most extreme statement in the classical essays on the relationship between national language, culture, and sovereignty, and it seems appropriate to give him the last word:

> Thuig Iuno cúrsaí náisiúin go hálainn. Má leantar den teangain dúthchais is de sna nósaibh is de sna béasaibh dúthchais, abair is go mbeadh rí eachtrannach nó ceannphort eachtrannach i gceannas ar feadh tamail, ní raghaidh an náisiún i mbáthadh; agus ní miste dúinn, ní miste do mhuinntir na hÉireann uile, suim do chur i n-athchuinghe Iuno agus i ngeallamhaint Iupiter.

> Bhí eachtrannaigh 'na righthibh is na gceannphortaibh orainn do dtí le déid-heannaighe; agus cé go bhfuil suathadh maith faghtha aca le tamall, ní'limíd réidh ar fad leo fós. Acht le linn iad do bheith i gceannas, tugadh suathadh mór dár dteangain agus dár nósaibh is dár mbéasaibh dúthchais agus is beag ná gur cuireadh ainm ceart ár dtíre ar gcúl.

> Má éirigheann linn ár dteanga dúthchais do choimeád 'na beathaidh is do shaothrughadh is do chur chum críche agus ár mbéasa is ár nósa dúthchais do shaothrughadh, beidh an lá linn. Imtheochaidh na ríghthe eachtrannacha; beidh deireadh le sna ceannphortaibh iasachta; agus beidh an tír fá ghnáith-riaghail na sean áitightheoirí athuair. Tá na hIar-bhreatnaigh i n-ár measc fós; acht ní dóigh liom go mbuan-bhaistfear an Iar-bhreatain ar Éirinn úrghlais go bráth ná ní dóigh liom go raghaidh ár dteanga dúthchais i mbáthadh go deo.[81]

> Juno had a beautiful understanding of national affairs. If the native language continues, and the native customs and manners, even if a foreign king or a foreign chief is in charge for a time, the nation will not be quenched; and it would be well for us, it would be well for all the people of Ireland, to take an interest in Juno's plea and in Jupiter's promise.

[79] Ua Duinnín (1927: 745).   [80] Ua Duinnín (1929: 139–42).
[81] Ua Duinnín (1929: 141–2).

Foreigners were kings and chiefs over us until recently, and even though they have been given a fair shock recently we are not yet entirely done with them. But while they were in charge, a great shock was visited on our language and our native customs and manners and the rightful name of our country almost went into abeyance.

If we succeed in keeping our native language alive and in cultivating it and in bringing it to perfection, and in cultivating our native customs and manners, we will prosper. The foreign kings will leave; there will be an end to the chiefs from abroad; and the country will be under the ordinary rule of the old inhabitants once again. The West-Brits are still among us; but I do not think that fresh green Ireland will be christened West-Britain in perpetuity, and I do not think that our native language will ever be quenched.

8

Classics, Medievalism, and Cultural Politics in Myles na gCopaleen's *Cruiskeen Lawn* Columns

Cillian O'Hogan

Introduction

Early on in his landmark biography of the Irish author Brian O'Nolan[1], Anthony Cronin paints a vivid picture of the young author in his university days, standing at the entrance to the debating theatre at University College Dublin.[2] The Literary and Historical Society was so popular in the late 1920s that it was not possible for all to enter the theatre, and a 'mob' hung around outside, trying to hear as much of the debates as they could. In Cronin's telling, O'Nolan took up early residence between these two spaces:

> Positioned by the door, so that he was dimly visible from within, but making sure that he was seen to be more a part of the mob than of the assembly proper, he would engage in contests of readiness and repartee with speakers, visiting chairmen and the auditor of the society, sometimes embarking on a flight of oratory himself by way of interjection or intervention in debate. He was the first who proved able to fuse the two parts of the proceedings, those of the unruly mass outside and those of the more orderly gathering within. He began by single quick interjections, to which only his more immediate neighbours in the mob paid attention, and then gradually extended his range. Having scored some successes on his first night, and having experienced the heady delight which a successful interjection in debate can bring, he returned on the following Saturday and soon became a talked-of performer at meetings of the L. & H.[3]

The marginal figure is a fitting image for Brian O'Nolan, who stands on the boundary between modernism and postmodernism, between Irish-language and

---

[1] Extracts from the *Cruiskeen Lawn* columns of Myles na gCopaleen © The Estate of Evelyn O'Nolan are reproduced in this chapter by permission of A. M. Heath and Co. Ltd.
[2] Cronin (1989: 44–7).   [3] Cronin (1989: 45).

Cillian O'Hogan, *Classics, Medievalism, and Cultural Politics in Myles na gCopaleen's* Cruiskeen Lawn *Columns* In: *Classics and Irish Politics, 1916–2016*. Edited by: Isabelle Torrance and Donncha O'Rourke, Oxford University Press (2020). © Oxford University Press.
DOI: 10.1093/oso/9780198864486.003.0008

English-language literature, and (as I argue in this paper) whose allusive practices position him as indebted to both classical and medieval Irish texts.

Born in Strabane, Co. Tyrone, in 1911, O'Nolan produced a range of texts under different pseudonyms over the course of his life.[4] His novels, including his most famous work, *At-Swim-Two-Birds*, were mostly published under the name Flann O'Brien. His Irish-language work, most notably a satire on the early-twentieth-century genre of misery autobiographies entitled *An Béal Bocht* (*The Poor Mouth*), was written under the name Myles na gCopaleen, the name also used by O'Nolan for the medium in which he had the greatest impact in his own lifetime: the *Cruiskeen Lawn* (a transliteration of the Irish phrase *cruiscín lán*, 'full little jug') columns in *The Irish Times* which he wrote several days a week between 1940 and 1966.[5]

While increasing attention has been paid to O'Nolan's imitation of and engagement with medieval Irish literature (the subject of his MA thesis at University College Dublin in the 1930s), the presence of classical literature in his works has not been treated systematically.[6] Catullus features briefly in *At-Swim-Two-Birds*, which opens with an epigraph from Euripides' *Heracles*, and Augustine of Hippo appears as a character living in a hollow rock off the coast of Co. Dublin in *The Dalkey Archive*.[7] Yet it is in the near-daily output of newspaper columns, which deal with a wide range of topics, that we find the greatest preponderance of classical allusions. Quotations from Cicero and Virgil abound, in addition to discussion of Homer, the tragedians, and other Latin authors. Some of the columns are written entirely, or nearly entirely, in Latin, and a number of the punning 'Keats and Chapman' stories require knowledge of Latin phrases or literature to make sense of the punchline.[8]

The columns provide an invaluable window into the changing attitudes towards classical learning and scholarship in Ireland between the early 1940s and 1960s.

---

[4] Numerous book-length studies of O'Nolan exist. Hopper (2009) makes the clearest effort to contextualize O'Nolan within the literary movements of the twentieth century; see also the essays collected in Murphet et al. (2014). A full bibliography is regularly updated by the International Flann O'Brien Society: https://www.univie.ac.at/flannobrien2011/bibliography.html (accessed 18 August 2018). Basic biographical information can be found in any of the major studies of O'Nolan; for sustained biographies, the (now-classic) works are Ó Nualláin (1973) (in Irish) and Cronin (1989) (in English).

[5] Following the convention among Flann O'Brien scholars (Flanneurs), I use O'Nolan to refer to the author *ipse*, and O'Brien and na gCopaleen when referring to the implied author of the novels and newspaper columns, respectively.

[6] For the Irish material see Wäppling (1984); Ó Brolcháin (1994); De Paor (2004, 2017).

[7] Earlier studies dealing with classical aspects of O'Nolan's work are Power (1978); Campbell (2007). The exhaustive recent edition of O'Nolan's letters (Long 2018) reveals the extent of O'Nolan's obsession with Augustine. I hope to explore the wider contexts of O'Nolan's use of the classics in greater detail elsewhere.

[8] Little work has been done on the Latinity of the columns, but see the brief remarks of Coulouma (2011: 172–4).

O'Nolan grew up in a house filled with books and learning.[9] His brother Kevin O'Nolan would later be Professor of Classics at University College Dublin.[10] Brian O'Nolan himself passed honours-level Latin in the Irish Leaving Certificate exam in 1929.[11] On the other hand, it is worth stressing that the persona of Myles na gCopaleen was that of a know-it-all, whose knowledge often was only surface-deep: very many of the quotations of classical literature found within the text may well come from dictionaries, glossaries, and summaries.[12]

The *Cruiskeen Lawn* Columns

Although it is as Flann O'Brien, the author of the novels, that Brian O'Nolan has secured an international literary reputation, within Ireland, the enduring legacy has always been 'Mylesian' (an adjective that has itself entered Irish discourse).[13] *Cruiskeen Lawn*, initially published exclusively in Irish, was placed prominently for many years on the leader page of *The Irish Times*, alongside the editorial and opinion columns. The origin of the columns is now infamous: O'Nolan had engaged in a lengthy letter-writing campaign to the newspaper, arguing with himself under an array of pseudonyms, before eventually being offered a job writing in Irish: this initial offering was intended by the then editor, R. M. Smyllie, to appeal to a young nationalist audience that may otherwise have turned away from the perceived Anglo-Irish leanings of the paper. (*The Irish Times* had the reputation of being the newspaper of the remnants of the Anglo-Irish Protestant ascendancy, in contrast to the more nationalist focus of the *Irish Independent* and *Irish Press*).[14] O'Nolan's job in the civil service meant he was obliged to publish under a pseudonym: the earliest column is signed 'An Broc' (the Badger), but Myles na gCopaleen was adopted relatively early on. Many of the characters and motifs of the columns, such as the Catechism of Cliché, The Plain People of Ireland, and the Brother, have entered the popular imagination in Ireland.[15]

---

[9] Ó Nualláin (1973: 42) on the family 'library': 'Bhí roinnt mhaith leabhar Laidine agus Gréigise ann agus ina measc iomlán litreacha Cicero *Ad Atticum*' ('There were plenty of Latin and Greek books there, among them the complete letters of Cicero *Ad Atticum*').

[10] Kevin O'Nolan published relatively little, and mostly on Homer. There is no discussion of classical matters in the surviving correspondence between him and Brian O'Nolan.

[11] Cronin (1989: 36).

[12] An anecdote records that the Greek epigraph for *At-Swim-Two-Birds* was provided to O'Nolan in the pub by a classical scholar: see Garvin (1973: 55–8).

[13] See, e.g., 'in a Mylesian touch, both managers have the same name', in a report on a Gaelic football game, 'St Vincents hurdle first challenge in Leinster title defence', *The Irish Times*, 9 November 2014.

[14] Cronin (1989: 107–13).

[15] The Catechism of Cliché reworks clichés into the form of question-and-answer on the model of the Catechism of the Catholic Church, e.g. 'What are stocks of fuel doing when they are low? Running.' The Plain People of Ireland ask persistently tedious questions of an increasingly frustrated Myles. The Brother, a character only spoken about, never met, has seen and done all that there is to be seen and done, and is spoken of with great reverence. All three have become so well known beyond the column that they have been rewarded with an entry in *Brewer's Dictionary of Irish Phrase and Fable*.

A large part of the reason why scholarship on the *Cruiskeen Lawn* columns has been relatively sparse until recently is the inherent difficulty of navigating and identifying the columns. A number of anthologies excerpt and reprint selections of the columns, but these rarely (if ever) give details of original dates of publication.[16] The *Irish Times Digital Archive* provides access to all the columns, but this is limited by the present inability to search by the author of a column, and the lack of OCR capabilities for the Irish typeface in which the early columns appeared. In the absence of a full-scale catalogue of the columns, any findings must be partial and incomplete.

The columns themselves are ephemeral, written on whatever topic Myles could think of before a deadline. It is precisely this ephemerality, however, that makes the columns an excellent way to explore the everyday influence of the classical tradition in twentieth-century Ireland: Myles' columns are essentially reactive, playing off other columns, articles, and readers' letters that had appeared in an earlier issue. Consequently we are provided with a sense of what felt important and immediate to Dubliners at any given point between the 1940s and 1960s. Myles is particularly concerned with intellectual matters (the 'corduroys'), and questions of education and learning, rather than wider sociopolitical issues—but in his focus and stance we see a wide range of approaches to contemporary affairs.

Politicization over Time

The columns are written from the perspective of one Myles na gCopaleen. The name itself, which means 'Myles of the Ponies', is taken from the nineteenth-century play *The Colleen Bawn* by Dion Boucicault (1820–90), in which the character is a poacher and poitín maker, and in many ways is a stage Irishman. Myles variously lives up to or punctures the image of this character, occasionally referring to himself instead as a highly educated man of Anglo-Irish stock, whose father was either a major or a colonel. These shifting personae help to make it clear how frequently and rapidly Myles would change tack, arguing for a proposition in one moment and against it the next.[17] In many ways this is a result of the nature of his work, which is inherently responsive, reacting to other sections on the leader page, or to particularly pompous letters to the editor.

Taking a larger view, however, Carol Taaffe has studied the columns in extensive detail and has noted a general development in their focus from primarily literary interests in the early years (i.e. in the 1940s) to more satirical and political

---

[16] See O'Brien (1968, 1976a, 1976b, 1977, 1999).
[17] Long (2015) stresses the contradictory nature of the *Cruiskeen Lawn* columns, while Long (2014) looks at the fragmented nature of O'Nolan's other works.

material in the 1950s and 1960s.[18] This may reflect O'Nolan's career outside the column. Until 1953 he worked for the Irish Civil Service, and it is after his (enforced) departure that the columns become more political.[19] Even earlier, however, the demands of O'Nolan's career brought him into contact with many of the scandals and issues of the Irish twentieth century. In particular, he was tasked with working on the inquiry into the notorious Cavan orphanage fire of 23 February 1943, in which thirty-five children and an adult died at St Joseph's Orphanage in Cavan.[20] There were allegations that the Poor Clares, who ran the orphanage, had prevented men who came to help at the outbreak of the fire from entering the building to rescue the girls lest they see them in their nightdresses.[21] O'Nolan was the secretary to the inquiry, which found fault with lack of proper training and equipment on the part of the volunteer firefighters. O'Nolan objected to these findings and, with Tom O'Higgins, who represented the Electricity Supply Board at the inquiry (and would later become Chief Justice of the Supreme Court), wrote a short poem attacking this finding.[22] Although he rarely spoke of it, several sources reveal how much this experience affected and politicized him.[23]

The Cultural Baggage of the Classics in Ireland

In general, the classical references and allusions in *Cruiskeen Lawn* tend not to be overtly political, instead relating more to matters of cultural, social, and literary significance, although culture itself had become increasingly politicized in mid-twentieth-century Ireland.[24] On occasion, Myles specifically sets out his column as a contrast to the other (more overtly political) sections on the leader pages, especially during the war years. This lack of conspicuous politicization of classical echoes and references may, at first glance, seem to set *Cruiskeen Lawn* at odds with the explicit intent of this volume. However, as we will see, cultural politics were to the forefront in mid-twentieth-century Ireland, as the recently independent nation tried to form an identity distinct from that of Britain.[25] Consequently, the *Cruiskeen Lawn* columns provide an excellent place in which to find evidence of wider Irish attitudes to the classics, classical learning, and the inherent links between a classical education and the appearance of erudition.

---

[18] Taaffe (2008: 11–12). For the political nature of the columns during the World War II years (referred to in Ireland as 'the Emergency') see Asensio Peral (2018).

[19] After several years of tension arising from Myles' criticism of government policy in the columns, things came to a head in February 1953 with the production of a column savagely caricaturing Patrick Smith, Minister for Local Government and thus O'Nolan's boss. Technically, O'Nolan resigned on medical grounds, but there is no doubt that he was forced out. For a full account see Cronin (1989: 179–87).

[20] Cronin (1989: 137–8).   [21] See also Taaffe (2008: 11–12).

[22] Quoted in Cronin (1989: 138).   [23] Cronin (1989: 138); Taaffe (2008).

[24] See Taaffe (2011).   [25] For more on this see Kiberd (1995).

Familiarity with the classics is repeatedly taken in the columns as a shorthand for a sort of pose taken by the educated (frequently Anglo-Irish) elite, a pose itself adopted by Myles on the occasions when he takes on the persona of the distinguished son of a major.[26]

The relative merits of the classical languages in relation to the Irish language provide a common topic of conversation. We find numerous statements in Myles' columns setting Irish on an equal footing to Greek and Latin.[27] To judge from the columns, a frequent concern expressed by the older establishment was about the decline in 'education' (meaning specifically classical learning) due to the promotion of the study of the Irish language. Myles responds to this with predictable indignation, as for instance in this imagined conversation with the editor R. M. Smyllie in 1942:[28]

The Editor: What do you take the readers of this newspaper for?

Myself: I thought they were educated people.

The Editor: Educated, is it? Sure there's no such thing as education in this country, man. God be with the good old days of Mahaffy and Hamilton, before this appalling Gaelic mania started. Do you know what the people of this unfortunate country are at the present time? Illiterate in—

Myself: How dare you try me out in clichés or hoary-whiskered age-caked witticisms? Illiterate in two languages, of course.

The Editor (abashed): Well. yes.

Myself: But surely the readers of the Irish Times—

The Editor: As ignorant as the back of a cab. Not that it would do for me to be heard saying that.

Myself: You mean they have never reached even the first page of a child's Greek grammar?

The Editor: Whole generation stupefied from having Gaelic rammed down their throats. Of course I'm not opposed to Irish...

A year later (16 August 1943) something of the same sort appears in a piece quoting at length from Lady Gregory's *Gods and Fighting Men*, in an attempt to

---

[26] Application of the persona theory used so effectively in Juvenalian criticism, such as Uden (2015) and Geue (2017), could prove fruitful here. Power (1978) is a rare attempt to apply theories of classical satire to another of O'Nolan's works. See also D. Larmour (2016: 306–8 and 313–17) on the Juvenalian aspects of Irish authors Jonathan Swift and Martin McDonagh.

[27] E.g. Myles concludes the column of 25 October 1945 with: 'And, I know of only four languages, viz: Latin, Irish, Greek and Chinese. These are languages because they are the instruments of integral civilisations. English and French are not languages: they are mercantile codes.'

[28] R. M. Smyllie (1893–1954) edited *The Irish Times* from 1934 until 1954, and was responsible for commissioning the *Cruiskeen Lawn* columns. See Brown (2015) for Smyllie's place in the history of the newspaper.

defend Irish literature from the criticism that it is unimaginative and 'low', a
charge levelled at it by Robert Atkinson (1839–1908), who had been the Chair of
Sanskrit and Comparative Philology at Trinity College Dublin.[29] Myles presents
himself as having been friends with J. P. Mahaffy and R. Y. Tyrrell, the two
towering professors of Classics at Trinity College Dublin at the end of the
nineteenth century, notwithstanding Mahaffy's belief that Myles' PhD from
Heidelberg was 'a little joke in bad taste'.[30] Here Myles sets up a subtle opposition
between the new Celtic scholarship, honed by study in Germany, and Classics as
it had traditionally been taught in the English and Irish education systems, which
were themselves only beginning to award PhDs in Classics in the 1930s
and 1940s.[31]

This opposition between classical and Celtic, and Myles' broader engagement
with the past, also needs to be set against the important backdrop of ongoing
conversations in the criticism of early Irish literature. O'Nolan's background in
studying for an MA on Irish Nature Poetry at University College Dublin is
relevant here, since he would have encountered many of the trends I touch on in
this chapter.[32] The 1930s saw the rise of the so-called 'nativism' movement, where
Irish literature was viewed as providing a window into the lost world of
pre-Christian Ireland, untainted by any influence from Graeco-Roman literature.
It was argued that the genius of the great sagas of medieval Ireland should be seen
as equivalent and parallel to, but not influenced by, classical epic, above all the
Homeric poems. This was later challenged by a movement which saw the import-
ation of classical learning, and the Irish classical tales (medieval vernacular
redactions of classical texts) as providing the necessary preconditions for
large-scale composition of sagas.[33] As I show later on in this chapter, Myles
positions himself on the margins of this debate, contributing to it in his own way:
he sets himself up as a twentieth-century equivalent of a medieval reader, adding

[29] Atkinson, initially a scholar of Romance languages, gradually moved to the study of early Irish
literature: see Greene (1966).

[30] The Heidelberg PhD is repeatedly referred to throughout the columns. Ironically, Atkinson's
intervention in the public debate about the value of early Irish came *after* Mahaffy himself had made
similar claims: see Dunleavy and Dunleavy (1991: 209–12).

[31] The earliest record I can find for a doctoral thesis being awarded in Classics by Trinity College
Dublin, for instance, is Hazel Marie Hornsby's 'A commentary on the subject matter of the *Noctes
Atticae* of Aulus Gellius, Bk. I', from 1931. For the wider background to classical learning in the period
see Stray (1998). A comparable study of Classics in the Irish school curriculum over the late nineteenth
and twentieth centuries remains a major *desideratum*, though see O'Higgins (2017) for the eighteenth-
and early-nineteenth-century contexts, and see Ní Mhurchú (Ch. 5) and Moran (Ch. 6) on,
respectively, Irish language publications of classical texts, and on the Classics through Irish curriculum
at University College, Galway.

[32] For O'Nolan's struggles in completing this MA see the account in Cronin (1989: 65–7). For the
contents see de Paor (2004, 2017); Naughton (2011, 2013).

[33] For an early overview of nativism see Carney (1955); for a more recent account see McCone
(1990). The debate continues, though comprehensive arguments in favour of classical influence have
now been set out by Miles (2011) and the essays in O'Connor (2014a).

annotations and glosses to the body of the text (i.e. the main content on the leader pages), and cross-references to classical and other texts, as needed.[34]

Many further examples can be found of Myles' juxtaposition of classical and Irish traditions. He often makes derogatory comments about Greek and Latin literature, on occasion explicitly comparing them (to their detriment) to works written in Irish. Perhaps the best example of this is in a column from October 1953 which begins

> I have been amusing myself reading some of the older writers and being pleased to find they are rather poor....I am impelled to the view – having resisted it for many years – that the study of Greek and Latin is largely a waste of time....I find all ancient writings tend to be solemn and boring.

He proceeds to denounce Plato's *Phaedo* and Socrates' behaviour at his death, before concluding 'Why should the flower of our youth be occupied with deciphering such silly stuff? What's wrong with Canon O'Leary's famous book, *Séadna*?'[35] The recurring claims of the superiority of Irish literature, or at least its equivalence to the classical tradition, are very often explicitly set in opposition to the preferences of the Ascendancy.[36] At the same time, however, Myles also repeatedly expects his readers to be thoroughly familiar with Latin and Greek literature, and is eager to show off his own knowledge of the classical canon.

Mediating Classics through the Medieval Irish Tradition

The representation of Classics that we find in the columns, however, and particularly the representation of Latin, is rarely drawn from direct engagement with classical texts, but rather is almost always mediated through an additional source. In Myles' world view, languages blend into one another, are understood via a third language, and can never be approached directly. Frequently in the columns we find comments suggesting that Latin is only needed to understand what is written in Greek grammars, or the critical apparatus to Greek texts. A good example can be found in a column dated 25 October 1945, in a response to

---

[34] For O'Nolan's awareness of these nascent debates see Taaffe (2008) and de Paor (2017: 190–2).

[35] *Cruiskeen Lawn*, 30 October 1953. *Séadna*, a novel by Peadar Ua Laoghaire serialized in 1898, is a pioneering work of Irish-language fiction. Ua Laoghaire himself translated a number of classical texts into Irish, including parts of Euclid and Lucian. See further Ní Mhurchú (Ch. 5).

[36] The work of McElduff (2006) and O'Higgins (2017) has made it clear that Classics was never solely the domain of the Anglo-Irish elite in Ireland, but nevertheless there was in the mid-twentieth century a *perception* that this was the case, and Myles uses this as a peg on which to hang the contrast between Irish and the Classics. On the complex tensions and contradictions in the literary output of the 1916 rebels Patrick Pearse and Thomas MacDonagh, who both embrace and reject classical models, see McGing (Ch. 3) and Moloney (Ch. 4).

a letter to the editor from Fleming Thompson, the headmaster of Drogheda Grammar School, who complains about a Danish student who is expected under the Irish educational curriculum to study Latin, French, Irish, English, as well as Danish. Myles is aggrieved at the headmaster's claim that language-learning is a 'burden', but his remarks about Latin are particularly intriguing:

> I thought that the sole function of Latin – apart from its occasional inclusion in my discourses – was to enable the educated classes to come to an elucidation of the knottier points in the syntax of the Greek authors, since the footnotes in all proper editions of such work are always in Latin. Yet Greek is nowhere mentioned in Mr. Thompson's correspondence! And whence comes this incompatibility as between Latin and Irish? Irish *is* Latin – surely I explained that before – Latin improved by occidental vernacularity...

This last claim exemplifies the ways in which Myles stresses the blurring of boundaries between classical languages and the medieval vernacular. Myles' own use of Latin in the columns is usually in a distinct form of Latinity that derives from extensive reading of medieval Irish manuscripts, in which code-switching between Latin and Irish is frequent.[37] Numerous references to the Latinity of early medieval Ireland in Myles' columns bear this out, for instance when on St Patrick's Day in 1956 he ruminates on various etymological plays with Patrick's name and also in passing gives what he sees as the clearest proof of Patrick's existence: 'A document attributed to his hand is written in very bad Latin: that is nearly proof that he did live, and became more Irish than the Irish themselves.'[38]

A number of columns, especially in the mid-1940s, were written entirely (or almost entirely) in Latin, and made considerable use of acknowledged or unacknowledged quotation from classical authors. The column of 8 November 1945, for instance, takes the form of a conversation in Latin between an airplane and Air Traffic Control at Rineanna (as Shannon Airport was then known), and quotes liberally from Ovid and Horace, while a piece in May of the following year makes use of Cicero's *Pro Archia* and Propertius in discussing a feud between poet Austin Clarke (1896–1974) and short-story writer Seán O'Faoláin (1900–91).[39] But perhaps the most eloquent use of Latin, and one that speaks indirectly to the dual negotiation of classical and Celtic inheritance, is the long *Dissertatio De Crure Fracto* (Treatise on a Broken Leg), published on 1 March

---

[37] The study of code-switching and bilingualism in early medieval Ireland has taken off in the past twenty years since the publication of Müller (1999); for a recent example of such work see Bisagni (2013).

[38] *Cruiskeen Lawn*, 17 March 1956. In a column published on 24 December 1943, in one of the many instances of the Lives of Keats and Chapman (shaggy-dog stories whose sole purpose is the construction of an elaborate pun), there is explicit discussion of manuscript glossing culture.

[39] *Cruiskeen Lawn*, 15 May 1955. After veering throughout the column between English and Latin, Myles ends: 'I often wonder does everybody *quite* understand my..... my English?'

1947 in a column temporarily rechristened *Crus-Keen Lawn/Amphora Plena* (a literal translation of the Irish 'Cruiscín Lán') and written by 'Melius Equuleus'. This Latin version of the name Myles na gCopaleen, in which *equuleus*, 'young horse', translates *na gCopaleen*, creates an additional pun: the near-honomym *melius* for Myles means 'rather better', alluding to Myles' convalescence.[40] Almost the entire column is written in Latin, and takes the form of an account of how Myles was hit by a bus, broke his leg, and ended up in a Dublin hospital, all of which leads up to the inevitable pun *crus in urbe* 'leg in the city' (for the Latin phrase *rus in urbe*, 'countryside in the city', which references the illusion of rural space created inside a city through a garden, for example).[41] Before that, however, there are numerous quotations taken from across classical literature, including Ennius, Horace, and above all Cicero, whose *De Senectute* (*On Old Age*) is most clearly the model for *De Crure Fracto*.

Particularly notable in this column is the way in which Myles slips between Latin and Irish, including sentences half in Latin and half in Irish, in a manner that is clearly intended to recall Irish texts as they appear in medieval manuscripts, particularly the medieval Irish versions of classical tales.[42] Elsewhere, Myles writes his column as though it were a medieval Irish text, beginning with *Incipit Crusculum Lan* ('the full little leg begins'),[43] moving from the Latin *incipit* gradually into Middle Irish, specifically, rather than modern Irish, thus marking his work as medieval in form.[44] This sort of code-switching is indicative of a culture in which Latinity is not merely classical but also medieval, and in which there is an ever-present awareness of the role played by early medieval scholars in the preservation of classical literature.

Cruiskeen Lawn as Marginalia

The links between classical and medieval become clearest in the repeated ways in which the *Cruiskeen Lawn* columns are set up as being like marginalia in a medieval manuscript. Myles refers to himself on at least one occasion as a medieval author:

[40] I thank Isabelle Torrance for pointing out the pun inherent in *melius* to me.

[41] In a letter of 17 January 1947 to *The Irish Times* (reprinted in Long (2018: 152)), O'Nolan pleads off work on the grounds of having broken his femur in an accident.

[42] On the layout of such Irish classical tales in manuscripts see, e.g., O'Hogan (2014) on the medieval Irish version of Lucan's *De Bello Ciuili*.

[43] *Crusculum*, a rare word meaning 'little leg', appears to have been chosen solely for its phonic similarity to *cruiscín*.

[44] *Cruiskeen Lawn*, 19 July 1943.

Always remember that I am writing, not merely passing trash to stuff a small hole in a businessman's day, but also medieval texts to puzzle those who will attend the Institute of Advanced Studies a thousand years hence.[45]

Myles' foregrounding of the material text is by no means unparalleled in twentieth-century literature: we might think, for instance, of the ways in which Virginia Woolf reflected on how the act of setting type for publications at her Hogarth Press gave her a closer intimacy with the authorial composition process, or the more pragmatic fact of that press' rejection of James Joyce's *Ulysses*, turned down at least in part because it was too big and difficult a text to be published by a relatively small operation.[46] For Myles, however, World War II also had a more immediate impact on questions of printing and text production. The early years of *Cruiskeen Lawn* occurred in the context of the paper shortages of the Second World War, something to which Myles himself refers on occasion. An additional factor brought on by the war may well have been the painful recent memory for O'Nolan of the destruction of the unsold copies of his debut novel, *At-Swim-Two-Birds*, when the London premises of his publisher Longmans, Green & Co. were bombed by the Luftwaffe on 29 December 1940.[47] Only about 250 copies were actually sold, meaning the vast majority of the books in the first print run were lost.

In addition to external pressures that necessitated greater attention to the material, there was the pragmatic question of printing. As the column was originally written in Irish, this necessitated the use of the old Irish typographic script (the *cló Gaelach*) in the early years.[48] This marked *Cruiskeen Lawn* out as typographically distinctive on the leader page of *The Irish Times*, since it contrasted with the rest of the page and indeed with the whole newspaper, written in English and set in roman type. Although the Irish-language dominance of the column only lasted until 1944 (and many columns before then were written in English), its distinct typeface marked it out as something that was to be seen as separate from the remainder of the page.[49]

I argue then that the columns are set out to function as a sort of gloss or commentary on the rest of the paper. Terence Brown, in his history of *The Irish Times*, has called the column 'an anti-newspaper inside the *Irish Times*'.[50] Closer

---

[45] *Cruiskeen Lawn*, 14 January 1942.

[46] For background to Woolf and the Hogarth Press see Battershill (2018).

[47] Cronin (1989: 99); there is no surviving correspondence between O'Nolan and Longmans, Green & Co. on the matter, according to Long (2018: 72 n. 14).

[48] For the complexities of Irish typefaces and the gradual transition to printing Irish in roman type see McGuinne (2010: 167–97), and see also Mac Góráin (Ch. 7).

[49] R. M. Smyllie, the editor, could not read Irish (cf. White (1973: 64), which created a further separation between text and glossator. For more on typographic play in the columns see Day (2011).

[50] Brown (2015: 182), with impressive restraint in avoiding the obvious pun *Myles en abyme*.

to my approach, however, is Carol Taaffe's description, in which the column is 'a kind of critical parasite, with Myles acting the fastidious reader buried under acres of mediocre print'.[51] Indeed, Myles' continual response to items appearing elsewhere in the paper, especially elsewhere on the leader page, makes *Cruiskeen Lawn* into an entity that presents itself as being entirely dependent on external content, and in many ways the column is a reading diary, incorporating what the author has found interesting or (more usually) objectionable. In effect, then, the column provides us with medievalizing marginal notes on the 'main text'. Perhaps nowhere is this clearer than in the use of manicules and arrows pointing to other parts of the page:

The Plain People of Ireland: ☞

Myself: Stop pointing. It's rude.[52]

Although Myles cannot comment directly on what is being said in a given day's editorial or opinion page, he can refer to the location of other parts of the editorial page by pointing and he can talk about the sorts of things individual columns tend to discuss within them. Sometimes he will use deictic speech to identify places elsewhere on the page, such as in his references to '£nunc down to the right' (the £ sign standing in for the slang term 'quid'), referring to 'An Irishman's Diary', written at this time by Patrick Campbell, 3rd Baron Glenavy, under the pseudonym Quidnunc.

Perhaps the clearest example of how this sort of typographic marker is used in a manner reminiscent of medieval scribal practice comes in a column from 1943. After expounding on the horrors being reported from the Russian front in the previous day's editorial, Myles switches tack employing a favourite tactic, quoting from another publication. Under the title 'Do You Want a Husband?', he quotes from *Woman's Life*:

'Resolve in future to peruse the daily papers thoroughly, particularly the editorial which is always full of current interest, and when you have this "course in topical education" completed, there will be at least one subject on which HE will be able to say you can talk intelligently.'

Woman's Life

It astonishes me that anybody should be so anxious to get married as to go over there ← and get a lift on the crossbar in the daily cycle journeys between Kharkov, Bryansk and Orel.[53]

---

[51] Taaffe (2008: 137).
[52] *Cruiskeen Lawn*, 28 November 1941.   [53] *Cruiskeen Lawn*, 16 September 1943.

Using an arrow, Myles points to the editorial column, and suggests that an easier path is to be found in another suggestion from the same issue of *Woman's Life*:

'Again, do not ignore the classics as something which bored you to tears in schooldays. Read them again now, when your mind is more cultured and better able to appreciate them, and you will find that they are "surprisingly" fascinating.'

I know. A little of the *Oracula Sibyllina*, Polyzelus, Lycurgus Orator, a peep into Dioscorides' colourful tracts on physics, Homer, Horace, Virgil, and a very small pinch of Ovid. To describe all this as 'surprisingly fascinating' is to toy with Words. And the young lady will get a drop when she first mentions the classics to her young man and hears him straightway deliver a discourse on the plans of Hartigan, Butters and Jarvis and how the books were a better proposition than the tote at the last Junction meeting.

It's many a man they ruined the same horses.

In many ways this can stand as exemplary for Myles' method of operation. He begins with a quotation from another periodical that allows him to comment on the ongoing preoccupations of another part of *The Irish Times*, then moves to a further quotation that lets him wheel out his classic know-it-all persona. The progression of the list of authors goes from more obscure to less obscure, casually demonstrating his own wide-ranging knowledge of the classical canon (which in reality likely derived from quick perusal of various encyclopedias or the list of authors at the beginning of Liddell and Scott's *Greek–English Lexicon*). But the final, almost incidental author named reveals that this citation has been carefully put together. The mention of a 'pinch of Ovid' in the context of relationship advice brings to mind the *Ars Amatoria* above all, and this combined with advice on how to talk about current affairs, which Myles interprets as military affairs, and on how to talk about the 'classics', which the target will misinterpret as being about the horse races, picks up specifically on two suitable places mentioned by Ovid in the first book of the *Ars Amatoria* as being good places to meet women: at the horse races in the Circus, and at triumphal parades of returning soldiers.[54] At the same time, the reading list Myles prescribes recalls the similar reading list given to women by Ovid in the third book of the same work.[55] This is exactly how the *Cruiskeen Lawn* columns operate: on the surface, we have the posturing of a show-off, who is eager to rattle off a list of names with which he presumes readerly familiarity, while hidden beneath, for those who can find it, is a more sophisticated and sustained allusion.

---

[54] Ov., *Ars Am.* 1.135–228.
[55] Ov., *Ars Am.* 3.311–48. I thank Monica Gale for this reference.

Though the content and structure may be classicizing, the material aspects of this miniature love manual owe a debt to later texts. It is likely that the primary influence for this idea was Sterne's *Tristram Shandy* (itself a major influence on O'Brien's *At Swim-Two-Birds*), which engages in considerable play with the material form of the page, most famously in the insertion of an entirely black page, but also incorporating throughout the book a range of manicules that explicitly allude to the authority of manuscript culture, as Helen Williams has shown.[56] But if Sterne is the primary literary influence, we should look to O'Nolan's abortive academic career for evidence of another key influence, in the form of medieval manuscript culture, and Irish scribal culture in particular. References to early Irish literature abound in the *Cruiskeen Lawn* columns. One of the earliest, in a column of 13 June 1942, contains a quotation from a poem on Alexander written in Irish and preserved in two manuscripts held by the Royal Irish Academy:

An ʋán úʋ aʁ an Impiʁe Alacʁanʋaʁ atá ʁágta aʒainn aʒ an Láiṁ anaitniʋ. Tá an ʁann ʁo ann:

'Oo bi,' aʁʁan tʁeaʁ uʒʋaʁ ʒlic,
'an bit inʋé aʒ mac Philip;
inʋiu aiʒe notan ḟuil
att ʁeatt ʋtʁoiʒte ʋo ṫal ṁain.'[57]

That poem on the emperor Alexander that has been left to us by an unknown hand has the following stanza:

'Philip's son', said the third clever author,
'had the world yesterday;
today he has nothing
except seven feet of earth.'[58]

We are given an excerpt from a short medieval Irish poem about a classical figure. This hybridizing and marginalizing approach to the Classics is in keeping with the wider self-presentation of Myles/Flann/Brian, as seen in the vignette with which I opened this chapter—that of O'Nolan as a figure half-in and half-out of the debating hall of the Literary and Historical Society at University College Dublin, literally on the margins, a position from which he could both participate in a closed elite circle while also mocking it as though from the outside. Similarly, the *Cruiskeen Lawn* columns are located on the leader page of *The Irish Times*, but if Myles is writing in the very heart of the Irish establishment, he positions himself as a scribe on the margins.

---

[56] Williams (2013). See Keymer (2014) for the wider context of typographic play in Sterne's age.
[57] *Cruiskeen Lawn*, 13 June 1942.
[58] The complete poem is edited in O'Rahilly (1927: 191).

Conclusion

The marginal approach to the Classics taken by Myles is effectively an effort at opening the door towards an alternative classical tradition. It is one in which the tradition in English literature is bypassed or at least downplayed, and in which the links between Latin and medieval Irish culture are highlighted. It identifies the tendency in classicizing medieval Irish literature to present material in a scholarly or scholasticizing way, rendering classical tales as digressive entities with scholia and commentary incorporated into the text, and suggests a way forward for this form of writing literature. The novels of Flann O'Brien similarly engage at length with issues of metafiction, literary materiality, textual hybridity, and cannibalization. Brian O'Nolan's output has often been seen as the first serious effort to respond to the burden of coming after Joyce, and I suggest that here, too, we can sense a certain belatedness with regard to the classical tradition.[59] Just as Joyce's *Ulysses* becomes the definitive Irish reimagining of an ancient text, inspired by a medieval source,[60] so, too, do the works of Flann O'Brien and Myles na gCopaleen, following at a distance, react to Joyce in a manner analogous to how medieval Irish authors responded to and reworked classical Latin literature. Moreover, by highlighting the ways in which the classical and medieval are inextricably interlinked, Myles engages with contemporary debates over the cultural politics of Irish language and scholarship: rather than being learned at the expense of Greek and Latin, Irish is shown to be historically connected with classical learning for a mid-twentieth-century Irish audience.

---

[59] On O'Nolan and Joyce see especially Powell (1971), Morash (1997), Dotterer (2004); Hopper (2009); McCourt (2014).
[60] See Hall (Ch. 10).

III
BETWEEN SCHOLARSHIP
AND LITERATURE

9

Abjection and the Irish-Greek Fir Bolg in Aran Island Writing

Arabella Currie

I am not sure why islands possess such a fascination for so many people, but the fact remains that they do. Artists, literary men and even millionaires, take up their abode on isolated islands and find there a retreat...where the primitive virtues and values of mankind are not swamped in a material world which has, to a large extent, lost its soul.

T. H. Mason[1]

For all that the two islands are so near together, *Britain is essentially an island of the North Sea, Ireland of the Atlantic Ocean*; and this difference is fundamental throughout the whole of their mutual relations.

R. A. S. Macalister[2]

Introduction

According to the medieval origin legends of Ireland, the Fir Bolg were among the offspring of Nemed, a descendant of Noah, who sought refuge in Greece after being forced out of Ireland by a great flood. There they were enslaved by the Greeks and forced to transport earth in leather bags to make fertile ground. After many years of servitude, they rose up against their Greek captors, built boats out of the leather bags, and escaped 'in quest of the fatherland from which their ancestors had gone'.[3] When they returned to Ireland, they partitioned the country into five provinces and ruled as kings, before being defeated by the next wave of invaders and driven to the Aran Islands, where they built colossal forts to defend themselves and turned bare rock into fertile land, just as they had done in Greece. Traditionally, the Aran islanders were direct descendants of these early settlers.

---

[1] Mason (1950 [1936]: 1), with the kind permission of Batsford.   [2] Macalister (1928: 52).
[3] Macalister and MacNeill (1916: 119).

Arabella Currie, *Abjection and the Irish-Greek Fir Bolg in Aran Island Writing* In: *Classics and Irish Politics, 1916–2016*. Edited by: Isabelle Torrance and Donncha O'Rourke, Oxford University Press (2020). © Oxford University Press. DOI: 10.1093/oso/9780198864486.003.0009

No matter the belatedness of these stories—Mark Williams describes the composition of the myths as a 'cultural stock-take'—the medieval origin legends have often provided crucial ballast for those concerned, as the monks had been, with linking Ireland to classical and biblical tradition and establishing a coherent, vibrant, and ancient history for the nation.[4] Similarly, while many scholars nowadays see the classical presences in the origin myths as evidence of a sophisticated intertextuality, a display of learning, and an effort to incorporate pagan ideas into a Christian world view, these Greek echoes have often been taken as evidence for historical authenticity (the classical tradition proved the veracity of the Irish, and vice versa) and of extensive relations between the Mediterranean and Ireland.[5] Therefore, despite the apparent 'abstruseness' of the matter at hand, the identity of the Fir Bolg (or 'men of the bags', according to the standard derivation of their name in Irish) has long been a matter of heated debate.[6]

This chapter traces the reception history of the Fir Bolg as figures associated with both Ireland and Greece. It first considers how debates about the Fir Bolg have reflected, and perhaps even contributed to, contested conceptions of Irish national identity, Irish colonial history, and the possibility of Irish independence, from the mid-nineteenth to the early twentieth century. It identifies abjection as one of the primary underpinnings of the Fir Bolg in literary and scholarly discourse, relating it to the characterization within nineteenth-century Anglo-Irish scholarship of the Gaelic Irish as tied to the earth, exotically other, and politically unskilled. However, it also locates a strand of their reception which pushes for a countercultural Fir Bolg, making use of that abjection as a means for emancipation and independence. The first part of the chapter thus establishes the Fir Bolg as crucial players in the postcolonial appropriation of abject identity markers, and aims to shift the focus of twentieth-century Irish reception studies away from the reuse of classical texts, and of classical mythology per se, towards a consideration of how the origin legends, with their Irish-Greek tinge, are filtered through nineteenth-century scholarship and then either absorbed or transfigured in twentieth-century literature.[7]

The chapter then turns to how the Fir Bolg are used in writing about the Aran Islands, in particular, as places both intricately associated with the Fir Bolg and

---

[4] Williams (2016: 129).

[5] Clarke (2009: 238–51; 2014: 101–22), Williams (2016: 63, 70–1). It should also be noted that although 'Greece' in these myths does not necessarily refer to Greece as we understand it, but rather a vague 'east', these nuances are not relevant to their reception, in which Greece, generally, means Greece: see MacNeill (1919: 76), Williams (2016: 302).

[6] Robinson (1986: 75). For the debate on their name from the perspective of a Celtic linguist see Carey (1988: 77–83).

[7] I use postcolonial here in the sense of Said (1994: 220) and Kiberd (1995: 5–6). For an example of this appropriation dynamic see Yeats's 1898 essay, which takes up Arnold's stereotype of the Celt—hapless, feminine, labouring but always failing—and makes it work for his own ends: Yeats (1961a: 173–88). On the stereotype of the Celt see also Mac Góráin (Ch. 7).

crucially important to questions of Irish identity throughout the nineteenth and twentieth centuries. Analysing the presence of the Fir Bolg according to three major features—ruins, rockscape, and race—the chapter suggests that the Fir Bolg as emblems of abjection overwhelmingly win out in Aran writing, shutting down their potential as emancipatory figures and helping to locate the islands in an apolitical, timeless sphere.

In stark contrast to the much better-known phenomenon of Homeric presences on that other western archipelago, the Blaskets, no consideration has yet been made of the persistent classicizing tendency of Aran writing.[8] The story of the Fir Bolg is not only a helpful way into this subject. It is also a microcosm of how classical antiquity is present on Aran, bound up with mythology, antiquarianism, and scholarship far more than with classical texts, and related to Aran discourse rather than Aran life. Additionally, it points to the colonial and primitivist implications of drawing such Aran–Greek parallels. If the story of the Irish-Greek Fir Bolg has tended towards abjection and subjugation in Aran writing, what does that say about the tendency to draw other classical parallels on the islands, particularly on the basis of Homeric Greece and Greek tragedy?[9]

The Abject/Revolutionary Fir Bolg

On that Easter Tuesday morning I knew for the first time that Ireland, my island home, was Mediterranean, but like the magic island of Delos it had escaped from the inland sea and gone wandering, towards the fabled West in the wake of the Hellenic wanderers.

Walter Starkie[10]

In the early part of the twentieth century, one of the key voices in the debate about the Fir Bolg was Eoin MacNeill, the nationalist historian and politician who repeatedly asserted the contingency of historical study on contemporary politics, with a particular focus on the origin myths and their afterlife.[11] In a famous series of lectures in Dublin in 1918, published the following year as *Phases in Irish History*, MacNeill grappled with the mid-seventeenth-century 'genealogical compilation' by

---

[8] For Greece on the Blasket Islands see Luce (1969: 151–68) and R. Martin (2007: 75–91).

[9] I would like to thank the University of Notre Dame's Irish Seminar for the opportunity to visit the Aran Islands. This chapter is also indebted to Allen (2012: 159–71; 2015) and Brannigan (2015: 1–20, 144–206) for the notion of an archipelagic overlap between the islands of the Atlantic and the Mediterranean.

[10] Starkie (1953) *In Sara's Tents*, quoted in Quinn (2005: 178). Quoted here with the kind permission of the Starkie family and with thanks to Jacqueline Hurtley.

[11] MacNeill (1919: 105–6; 1981[1921]:17, 36). According to F. J. Byrne, MacNeill coined the term 'synthetic histories' to describe the origin legends (Byrne 1973: 31).

MacFhirbhisigh, one of the few sources for the nature of the Fir Bolg other than the origin legends themselves. According to MacFhirbhisigh, 'every one'

> who is black-haired, who is a tattler, guileful, tale-telling, noisy, contemptible; every wretched, mean, strolling, unsteady, harsh, and inhospitable person; every slave, every mean thief, every churl, every one who loves not to listen to music and entertainment, the disturbers of every council and every assembly, and the promoters of discord among people; these are the descendants of the Firbolgs.[12]

MacNeill argued that this description of the Fir Bolg was explicitly motivated by a colonial agenda. It disclosed, he argued, 'the contempt of the dominant Gaelic people for the older conquered folk' and was evidence of the 'suppression' of a pre-Gaelic population.[13] 'This is fine old ascendancy talk,' he wrote, 'the sort of language that has served in many ages to justify the oppression of liberty.'[14] The truth of it, according to MacNeill, was that the Fir Bolg had been leather workers or 'skilled artisans', who got their name 'from an industrial connection with leathern bags'.[15] Given that 'the manufacture of bags from hide or leather was no doubt not a highly esteemed occupation', this identity marker was then used by 'the Celtic ascendancy' to cover 'the whole conquered population'.[16]

MacNeill's reading of MacFhirbhisigh is unmistakably glossed by contemporary concerns. Delivered to celebrate his release from prison after his involvement in 1916 and to bring scholarly history into the public sphere, these lectures, Michael Tierney notes, 'constituted a powerful argument for Sinn Féin's claim to full national independence'.[17] On the one hand, MacNeill's reading of the Fir Bolg shines the spotlight firmly on Ireland's colonial past—its treatment, as he puts it, as 'a sort of hotel, in which the important people are always distinguished visitors'.[18] On the other, his focus on the reception of the Fir Bolg—the restriction of the historical sources as 'fine old ascendancy talk'—also brings to mind earlier debates. Although his focus here is MacFhirbhisigh, it is hard not to read this charge as applying equally to nineteenth- and early-twentieth-century Anglo-Irish 'ascendancy' scholars, who had followed MacFhirbhisigh in their presentation of the Fir Bolg as barbaric other.

---

[12] O'Curry (1861: 228, 223–4).   [13] MacNeill (1911–15: 10).   [14] MacNeill (1919: 79).
[15] MacNeill (1919: 78, 76).
[16] In a similar way, R. A. S. Macalister, who coedited a late recension of the *Lebor Gabála* with MacNeill in 1916, linked their name to 'bracati', i.e. 'breeches-wearers', and saw the Fir Bolg as 'plebeians', mocked by the 'patricians' for their habit of wearing trousers ('prehistoric Oxford bags', according to a scathing review): Macalister (1941: 2), de Blacam (1942: 84). For the Fir Bolg as workers in less scholarly interpretations, cf. Henry O'Brien on the Fir Bolg as 'mechanics', and Canon Bourke on 'Bolg' as 'a fossil-term' for 'cow-herd or drover': O'Brien (1834: 428), Bourke (1887: 9).
[17] Tierney (1980: 269). It is worth noting that, as well as a prominent classicist at University College Dublin, Tierney is MacNeill's son-in-law and biographer.
[18] MacNeill (1919: 349).

William Wilde, for example, had compared the Fir Bolg to the Trojans and the Persians (in other words, to the defeated enemies of the Greeks).[19] William Betham, similarly, had designated the Fir Bolg as 'barbarous and ignorant', inevitably subjugated by the more advanced conquering race, 'who reduced them to slavery, made them work in their mines, or exterminated them'.[20] Charles Babington expressed sympathy for contemptuous descriptions of the Fir Bolg, explaining that 'a feeling of enmity towards them is very accountable' as '[t]hey apparently gave much trouble to their victors'.[21] Later, in the immediate run-up to MacNeill's lectures, J. P. Mahaffy could use 'firbolg' as clubby shorthand for unsophisticated and uncouth.[22] MacFhirbhisigh's 'ascendancy talk', in other words, is mirrored in the work of Wilde, Betham, and Mahaffy, with their implicit (and well-studied) characterization of the Gaelic Irish as exotically other, hopelessly inept, and in need of firm-handed guidance or even direct rule.[23] By making visible the motivations behind the prolonged afterlife of the Fir Bolg, MacNeill is therefore pointing both to the politicized nature of the study of the Irish past, and to the continued presence of these downtrodden, colonized 'Fir Bolg' in contemporary Irish life.

In a recent chapter on O'Casey, James Moran has used Georges Bataille's articulation of the term 'abject' to understand the British characterization of Ireland as subordinate territory.[24] As Moran explains, Bataille summons abjection as a conceptual category to cover those 'represented from the outside with disgust as the dregs of the people, populace and gutter'.[25] Occupying one fold of the *misérables/nobles* divide, the abject, according to Bataille, are the working class who literally get their hands dirty through manual labour, particularly dealing with the waste products of the non-abject classes, while the powerful remain pristine.[26] With their slave labour of shovelling dirt for the Greeks and their characterization as 'mean thieves' by MacFhirbhisigh, we can see how the Fir Bolg might become an emblem of abjection in their course through intellectual and literary history. Indeed, we might see this abject status inscribed in their very name, which, in commemorating the bags they used to carry soil for their Greek masters, recalls the tools of their labour. Several writers tried to 'redeem' the Fir Bolg name from this laborious connotation. Losing patience in 1946 with what he saw as 'lame attempts' to explain the Fir Bolg as 'men of the bags', Thomas O'Rahilly,

---

[19] Wilde (1872: 218–20). For Wilde on the Fir Bolg as a 'race' see C. Martin (1935: 32–3). For the Fir Bolg as indexed to a Greek/other binary see also the philologist Alexander MacBain on the Fir Bolg as 'answering to the giants and Titans of kindred Aryan races': MacBain (1885: 65–6).

[20] Betham (1842: i. 15–16). Betham had earlier interpreted 'Fir Bolg' as meaning 'men of the shells', signifying their taste for extravagant decoration: Kane et al. (1836–40: 197).

[21] Babington (1858: 97).   [22] Mahaffy (1912–13: 429).   [23] Leerssen (1996: 66–7).

[24] Moran (2017: 155). Abjection is more usually theorized in an Irish context using Kristeva's terminology, as fruitfully applied to Marina Carr by, e.g., Wallace (2001), O'Reilly (2004) and Trench (2010).

[25] Bataille (1999 [1934]: 9).   [26] Bataille (1999 [1934]: 9).

for example, traced 'bolg' back to an Indo-European word for thunderbolt, imagining the Fir Bolg as Zeus-like figures.[27] He thereby gave them the 'lustre of cosmic origins' and placed them closer to the Tuatha Dé Danann—the conquerors of the Fir Bolg on their return to Ireland—whose name is usually construed as the distinctly unearthly 'peoples of the goddess Danu', and linked by some to the Homeric Danaoi.[28]

Yet it is also possible to trace other forms of reclamation of the Fir Bolg, which make use of this abject status and transform it into a radical potential. To borrow Seamus Heaney's call to celebrate Boeotia as well as Athens (i.e. a space outside the urban, imperial centre), the apparent abjection of the Fir Bolg can in fact be a condition of their future power.[29] A subsidiary line of their reception sees them, for example, as a race of powerful outlaws, whose ransacking of 'Greece and Thrace and the Torrian Sea' is recalled in the origin legends.[30] Similarly, although Joyce used the association of the Fir Bolg with 'the unfree, subjugated, nonnoble populace' to characterize the monocular nationalism of the Citizen in Ulysses, and although Dedalus disparages the 'rude Firbolg mind' of Davin in Portrait, Heaney also noted 'a kind of fir-bolg birthmark' in Joyce's affirmation of ostracized subjects.[31] Given the reorientation of these abject figures, we can also identify the story of the Fir Bolg behind other marginalized figures across twentieth-century Irish literature, including Padraig Fallon's 'Bagman, beggarman going the round' in his play The Bell for Mister Loss, or the disabled child described in Aidan Carl Mathews' 2007 poem as 'an aboriginal Firbolg in a log / Canoe'.[32] The Fir Bolg as 'bagmen' may also foreshadow Frank McGuinness's abused 'baglady', who enters the stage carrying 'on her back…a grey, woollen sack', and dressed in 'the heavy clothes of a farmer'.[33]

The Fir Bolg myth, then, has a kind of dual potential, either as a repressive tool to characterize individuals or groups as abject, or as a more radical pointer towards political change and a way to uncover the repressive strategies of the past. While a 'fir-bolg birthmark' can imply an externally imposed stereotype of abject Irishness, it can also bestow the possibility of rearticulating that characterization and creating new forms of power. Such double, latent potential can be seen in Rosita Sweetman's classic coming-of-age novel set in 1970s Dublin. At the hands of the protagonist's father, an 'Expert on the Fir Bolg', they represent staid scholarship

---

[27] O'Rahilly (1946: 48, 52).

[28] Robinson (1986: 76). For the Tuatha Dé Danann name and their association with the Danaoi see Williams (2016: 186, 302). A recurrent alternative hypothesis of their name is a relation to the Belgae: see, e.g., Pinkerton (1787: 222) and Bryant (1889: 20–1).

[29] Heaney (2002a: 292).   [30] Dalton (1920: 37). Cf. Lynch (1899: 10–11).

[31] Tymoczko (1994: 34); Joyce (1992 [1916]: 195); Heaney (1983: 20). Cf. Gogarty's derision of Joyce for his 'firbolg melancholy'; Ellmann (1982: 118). For Gogarty on the Fir Bolg see also O'Faoláin (1940: 193).

[32] Fallon (1990: 207), Mathews (2007: 64).

[33] McGuinness (1988: 73). Macintosh (2005: 331) has identified this play with Greek tragedy.

and an oppressive tradition.[34] However, the protagonist herself mobilizes their more radical, emancipatory potential, as she flirts with her father's guest across the dinner table: 'One of the distinctive physical characteristics of the Fir Bolg,' she says, 'was their Mediterranean features. Dark, flashing eyes.'[35] In other words, the Greekness of the Fir Bolg is what allows the young protagonist to redirect these figures, using them to pull against the yoke of her repressive, traditional upbringing.

The Fir Bolg on Aran

Can it be that never more
Men will grow on Islands?
Ithaca and Eriskey,
Iceland and Tahiti! ...
Must it be that never more
Men will flower on Islands?
Crete and Corsica, Mitylene,
Aran and Iona!

Padraic Colum[36]

The west of Ireland
Is brute and ghost at once.

Louis MacNeice[37]

Although they washed up on other outlying western islands, including Colonsay and St Kilda in the Hebrides, the Fir Bolg are most often associated with the Aran Islands.[38] Before considering how the debates about the abject/revolutionary Fir Bolg manifest themselves on Aran, I will give a very brief overview of Aran writing as a discourse of great significance to issues of Irish identity, and one with its own identifiable tropes and parameters.[39]

The contemporary Aran chorographer, Tim Robinson, dates the modern scholarly and literary reimagining of Aran to J. T. O'Flaherty's 1825 account in the *Transactions* of the Royal Irish Academy (RIA).[40] Subsequently, Anglo-Irish interest

---

[34] Sweetman (1974: 76).   [35] Sweetman (1974: 78).
[36] Colum (1932: 142), with the kind permission of the Estate of Padraic Colum.
[37] MacNeice (1949: 22), with permission from David Higham Associates.
[38] Grieve (1923: i. 8); M. Martin (1703: 281).
[39] For studies of Aran writing see especially Waddell (1994: 75–135), Robinson (1995: 114–40), Foster (1977: 261–74), Kiberd (2000b: 82–110), Ashley (2000: 175–93; 2001: 5–18) and Fitzpatrick (2012: 121–51).
[40] Robinson (1986: 8). It is worth pointing out that Louise Beaufort, the first woman to be published in that journal, had also written about Aran in 1818: Beaufort (1818: 101–241).

in the islands' archaeology, botany, customs, and language grew with startling momentum, with the result that the islands became, by the end of the century, one of the 'most over-signified, symbolically loaded location[s] in Ireland,' as John Brannigan puts it, 'and perhaps even the British Isles.'[41] In 1857, the British Association embarked on a mass expedition, featuring the likes of William Wilde, George Petrie, John O'Donovan, Eugene Curry, Samuel Ferguson, and other major figures (the prominent continental Celticists Heinrich Zimmer and Kuno Meyer visited in the 1880s).[42] The ethnologists A. C. Haddon and C. R. Browne conducted an 'anthropographical' survey of the islanders in the early 1890s, and by 1895 there were so many studies of the islands that the archaeologist Thomas Westropp warned of the need 'to keep from the temptation of adding another to the many exhaustive accounts of the place.'[43]

From the perspective of revivalists, the Aran Islands were one of the last bastions of true Gaelic, Irish-speaking Ireland, promising the most pristine remnant of the ideal nation. Patrick Pearse, for example, helped establish a branch of the Gaelic League on the islands and named his school in Rathfarnham after Aran's patron saint (St Enda), while Thomas MacDonagh, Eoin MacNeill, W. B. Yeats, J. M. Synge, and Lady Augusta Gregory all spent time there.[44] Miss Ivors (Joyce's parodic revivalist in 'The Dead') condemns Gabriel's reluctance to join the League's excursion to Aran as a mark of his West British proclivities—'It will be splendid out in the Atlantic,' she cajoles.[45] By 1916, the islands had become, as Scott Ashley explains, 'a magnetic place where some of the possibilities of nationalist dreams were played out', and a 'trial run for a future Ireland'.[46] In Yeats's 1919 play about the Rising, The Dreaming of the Bones, the young rebel who has escaped the Post Office waits to be taken to Aran, in hope not only of safety but also of reaffirming the Rising's goals.[47]

Although it is tempting to find a division between pre- and post-1916 Aran writing, in truth there is little to differentiate Aran accounts of either period. Instead, as David Fitzpatrick has pointed out, a 'conventional narrative' of Aran developed as early as the 1890s, with ideas, quotations, stories, and images resurfacing again and again in the later period, instantiating what Ashley calls the 'preformed poetics of Aran writing'.[48] When the ethnologist John Messenger revealed in the 1960s that what were presented as 'facts' about the realities of island life were often simply observations lifted from earlier accounts, he voiced concern about overt governmental resistance to his debunking of Aran myths.[49] Crucially,

---

[41] Brannigan (2015: 37).
[42] For the trip see Haverty (1991 [1859]: 43–6) and Kiberd (2000b: 83).
[43] Westropp (1895: 250).
[44] Foster (1977: 267).   [45] Joyce (1914: 233).   [46] Ashley (2000: 189).
[47] McCormack (2005: 308). For Yeats on the Fir Bolg see Yeats (1997 [1898]: 251; 2000 [1900]: 34) and Gregory (1920: 286).
[48] Fitzpatrick (2012: 125); Ashley (2001: 11).   [49] Messenger (1964: 53).

though, 'Aran began to speak for itself to the world' from around the 1920s and 1930s, as Robinson describes, with the work of Liam and Tom O'Flaherty, Pat Mullen, Máirtín Ó Direáin, and others.[50] Robert Flaherty's notorious 1934 film, *Man of Aran*, painted an anachronistic and immensely popular picture of Aran, which placed the islands firmly on the international tourist map, where they have stayed ever since.[51]

What role, then, do the Fir Bolg play in Aran writing? What work do they do in accounts of these quasi-mythical islands, 'the *Shangri-la*', as Brendan Behan put it in the 1950s, 'of the...intelligentsia'?[52] Before unravelling the nature of their contribution, I will outline three fundamental areas of Aran discourse in which the Fir Bolg make a substantial appearance—ruins, rockscape, and race—focusing on the ramifications of the Greek links bestowed by their legendary exile.

Ruins

'Ruins everywhere meet the eye of the tourist in Aran,' proclaimed Oliver Burke in the first book wholly dedicated to the islands, 'ruined abbeys, ruined monasteries, ruined nunneries, ruined cells, ruined churches, ruined schools, ruined forts, ruined forests, and ruined towers.'[53] 'The islands,' noted Haddon and Browne, 'may not inaptly be described as an unique museum of antiquities.'[54] Among the most celebrated of these abundant ruins was Dún Aonghasa, the fort on Inis Mór which was made a National Monument in 1880 on the back of its 'perceived heroic status'.[55] According to several researchers, the attribution of such 'stupendous barbaric monuments' to the Fir Bolg was secure (occasionally they are also posited as builders of the beehive huts, or clocháins, and even more occasionally, of the churches).[56]

As well as giving an ancient, sublime grandeur to the islands, these 'bewildering' ruins also bestow a substantial classical presence to much Aran writing in the form of a consistent parallelism between Greek and Aran material remains.[57] Louise Beaufort, for example, compared Dún Aonghasa to a temple of Poseidon on Euboea, while several writers pronounce it to be 'the Acropolis of Aran'.[58] In his 1911 study, W. Y. Evans-Wentz alleged Dún Aonghasa was a 'sun-temple', 'with

---

[50] Robinson (1986: 9). Aran writers from a later period include Dara Ó Conaola: see Ó Conaola (1992).

[51] For Flaherty's film see Calder-Marshall (1963: 141–72) and Robinson (1995: 136).

[52] McNeillie (2014: 75).

[53] Burke (1887: 24).   [54] Haddon and Browne (1891–3: 821).   [55] Cotter (1994: 24).

[56] See, e.g., Wilde (1872: 246); Babington (1858: 97); Power (1935 [1926]: 4).

[57] Anon. (1884: 627). For Aran as sublime see Korff (1994: 270) on the artistic licence of George Petrie's dramatic watercolour of Dún Aonghasa. See also Burke (1887: 13, 52) as an example of the frequent quoting of Byron in nineteenth-century Aran writing.

[58] Beaufort (1818: 175–6). For the Acropolis parallel see, e.g., Haverty (1991 [1859]) quoted in Robinson (1986: 73); Wakeman (1862: 469); Power (1935 [1926]: 12).

its tiers of amphitheatre-like seats and the native rock at its centre', in which 'were anciently celebrated pagan mysteries comparable to those of the Greeks'.[59]

Alongside the sheer visual similarities of the forts and other so-called 'cyclopean' ruins strewn across the Atlantic and Mediterranean seaways, the Fir Bolg origin of the forts is consistently harnessed as crucial evidence for a Greek–Aran kinship.[60] The pioneer of modern Irish archaeology, George Petrie, for example, held strongly to a belief in a direct Greek origin of the forts, arguing that the Fir Bolg were 'Greek colonies who had settled in Ireland', as memorialized in 'the historic legends of Ireland'.[61] In a richly illustrated 1897 study, the speleologist Édouard-Alfred Martel expressed surprise at the striking similarity between the forts of the 'Firbolgs' and ruins at Mycenae and Tiryns, an idea later picked up by Ethel Brewer in the 1930s as 'a most interesting point when the traditional return of the Fir Bolg from captivity in Greece is remembered'.[62]

The identity of the Fir Bolg as fort builders clearly works to record Greek–Aran connections at their most tangible, frozen in these 'litanies of stone' as Wilde called them, and made still more palpable given the frequent presentation of the forts as sites of mystical intimacy with the past.[63] Moreover, the contemporary islanders' own limestone building technique is likened to the ancient Fir Bolg ruins, suggesting kinship and continuity across the centuries: 'the style of their walls is even now as cyclopean as that of Dún Aengusa [sic]', wrote the Earl of Dunraven in the late 1860s.[64] The traditional boats of the islanders were also seen as relics of the Fir Bolg past: Mary Banim, for instance, setting out to experience 'a mitigated Robinson Crusoe life' on Aran in 1896, told of how the Fir Bolg had escaped their 'tyrants' in Greece and sailed to Ireland. 'It is supposed,' she wrote, 'that the corrachs [sic] in use to-day scarcely differ in construction from those in which these early colonists came over the waves from the south.'[65]

---

[59] Evans-Wentz (1911: 416). For the fort as an amphitheatre see also Brewer (1937: 353) and Bouvier (1990: 51).

[60] For the importance of 'a belief in Atlantic and Mediterranean contacts' in Irish antiquarianism and archaeology see Waddell (1991–2: 29). For the phenomenon of comparisons between other Irish and Greek material remains in the nineteenth century, particularly the interpretation of cyclopean remains in the context of the Ordnance Survey, see Currie (2017: 54–77).

[61] Stokes (1868: 230–1).

[62] Martel (1897: 145), Brewer (1937: 353). There are also Roman presences on the islands: Bishop Conroy likened the cliffs near Dún Aonghasa to 'one of the arches in the Temple of Peace in the Roman Forum' (Conroy [1870: 24]), and there is much speculation about the mysterious Tomb of the Seven Romans: see, e.g., Ferguson (1853: 495–6); Wakeman (1862: 572); Power (1935 [1926]: 9).

[63] Haverty (1991 [1859]: 45). For the forts as mystical see, e.g., Mullen (1934: 57). It was at Dún Aonghasa that Artaud experienced visions of the future horrors of Europe in 1935: Ó hEithir (1991: 1).

[64] Dunraven (1875: i. 7).

[65] Banim (1991 [1896]: 73, 76). On currachs and the Fir Bolg, cf. Anon. (1895: 246). In the 1920s, Julius Pokorny interpreted the leather bags as skin-boats, equating the Fir Bolg with 'Esquimaux': Lennon (2008: 207).

Rockscape

The second strong association of the Fir Bolg with the islands is through their cultivated environment. The tradition that the Fir Bolg had to transport earth in leather bags to form artificial fields while they were slaves in Greece—to construct, in Samuel Ferguson's version, 'the artificial terrace-gardens of Boeotia'—is regularly likened to Aran agricultural practice, 'where gardens have still to be made and maintained by periodically covering the rocks with sand and clay'.[66] Thus the very earth of Boeotia, and 'the steep sides...of Pindus or Haemus', according to Mary Ferguson, are superimposed onto the fields of Aran.[67] Dealing with an alternative version of the myth, in which the Fir Bolg were forced to put Irish earth into bags and sell it to the Greeks 'to be spread on the ground around their cities as a protection against venomous reptiles', the folklorist Alexander Krappe in the 1940s similarly yoked Aran and Greek earth together.[68] According to Krappe, the myth was 'of Mediterranean origin' and its recycling in the context of the Fir Bolg was a medieval strategy to market the earth of Irish islands as successfully as the Greek soil had been.[69]

A distinctive feature of the characterization of Fir Bolg/Aran agriculture is its hardship. In much Aran writing, the islanders are presented as still drudging on their rocks, like the Fir Bolg on Greek hillsides, 'under the lash of task-masters'.[70] In his 1912 *Rambles in Ireland*, Robert Lynd described 'the children of the Fir Bolg...guarding their little fields of stones with a tenacity of affection', while Jane Barlow, in a series of articles for *Country Life* in 1905, pointed to the slave-like lot of 'these modern Fir-bolgs', describing 'such Bagmen...toiling up the façade of sea-cliffs on rough footpaths...laden with burdens of dripping wrack, or sodden clay, "to form a soil upon those barren places, and make them fruitful and bear corn"'.[71] The islands themselves are consistently characterized as 'devoid of herbage', requiring hard labour to make anything grow: 'Here bleak desolation reigns supreme,' wrote Brewer, '...it is a burnt-out world.' Aran, according to a visitor in 1926, is 'grey, hard, monotonous, solitary', not landscape but 'rockscape'.[72] Other twentieth-century writers note 'a scene of desolation...rock, rock, rock', 'une désolation indicible', a space characterized by 'grey desolation, aridity and treelessness', 'a gaunt height of rock and weather' and, simply, 'three grey slabs of rock'.[73] 'If you were to visit any one of the islands,' wrote Agnes Lehman in 1940, 'your first

---

[66] S. Ferguson (1853: 91); Ua Ceallaigh (1921: xxvii).   [67] M. Ferguson (1868: 5).
[68] MacNeill (1919: 77).
[69] Krappe (1941: 235).   [70] M. Ferguson (1868: 5).
[71] Lynd (1912: 77); Barlow (1905: 862–3), quoting Keating's version of the Fir Bolg story.
[72] Barry (1886: 488); Brewer (1937: 351); Power (1935 [1926]: 4).
[73] Whitty (1911: 12); Bouvier (1990: 40); Brewer (1937: 351); McNeillie (2014: 72); Mould (1972: 11).

impression would be that it was the stoniest place you ever saw, and the greyest... Everybody is poor, but nobody seems to mind.'[74]

Since the islands have a vibrant landscape as well as 'rockscape'—like the Burren in Co. Clare, for example, they are notable for their wild flowers—the idea of Aran as 'no better than a wild rock', as Froude put it in 1868, may be better viewed as a topos of island writing than a reflection of the realities of ecology and agriculture.[75] More specifically, we might link it to a pervasive trope of writing about island territories, which links the barrenness of islands to their ripeness as colonial conquests. As Diane Loxley has shown, islands have frequently functioned as a *tabula rasa* on which colonizing groups can 'erect their own story' and portray islands as in need of conquering. In her study of island ideology in the ancient Aegean, Christy Constantakopoulou has pointed to a 'conceptual link between a scarcity of good agricultural land and insular territories'.[76] Intriguingly, Constantakopoulou points to a particularly prevalent trope within Athenian colonial strategy of islands as places of terraced agriculture (i.e. of artificial fields built into the hillside), despite this technique being a commonplace on mainland Greece.[77]

Race

The 'pristine racial purity' of the islanders is a central conviction through much nineteenth- and twentieth-century thought about Aran.[78] There was an outpouring of controversy and disbelief when a report in the *Irish Journal of Medical Science* in 1958, for example, claimed that the phenotypes and blood groups of the islanders had in fact much in common with the English.[79] The counterclaim continued to be asserted, however, as in Daphne Pochin Mould's 1972 guide, which described the islanders as 'physically rather a race apart'.[80]

Most often, this 'pure and ancient stock' is synonymous with 'Firbolg blood'.[81] As Ashley observes, Haddon and Browne's supposedly quantitative survey of the islanders was framed entirely around an investigation into whether the islanders really were related to the 'Fir-Bolgian...peoples', and Wilde rebuked the contemporary

---

[74] Lehman (1940: 13, 15).
[75] Froude (1868: 373). For the islands' ecology see, e.g., Waddell (1994: 75).
[76] Loxley (1990: 102); Constantakopoulou (2007: 100). For its understanding of island writing as a genre, this chapter is also indebted to Howe (2000), Fischer (2012), and Freitag (2013).
[77] Constantakopoulou (2007: 100). An example of a potentially colonial association of Aran and barrenness is the Reverend Alexander Synge's presentation of Aran as 'a very wretched Island... almost all a barren rock' during his Protestant mission to the islands in 1851: see Ó hEithir (1991: 30). For the wider nineteenth-century tendency to associate the west coast with destitution see Harvey (1991: 237).
[78] Ó Síocháin (1990 [1962]: vii).   [79] Messenger (1964: 48–9).   [80] Mould (1972: 13).
[81] S. Ferguson (1853: 90); M. Ferguson (1868: 7).

islanders for failing to look after the handiwork of their 'forefathers' during the British Association banquet at Dún Aonghasa: 'remember,' he urged, '...that these were the works of your own kindred, long, long dead.'[82] As late as 2014, *The Irish Times* referred to the 'potential Firbolgery' of the islanders.[83]

Not only does this racial categorization set the islands apart from the mainland (and from England), it also sets them nearer to Greece; their 'Firbolg blood' locates them, as a 'dark-haired and dark-skinned race', closer to the peoples of the Mediterranean than the Atlantic.[84] In the 1930s, for example, the artist Charles Higgins used the tradition to affirm his belief that the islanders 'were originally a Mediterranean race'.[85] In 1902, Agnes O'Farrelly, academic and member of the Gaelic League, watched the dancers at a feis ('festival') and mused that 'when the young, strong men step out, it is not surprising that we think now and again of the Olympic games, which were played in Greece long ago.'[86] 'Watching them,' she writes,

> it is not difficult to picture them as the ancient Greeks...We see before us the long neck and bright eye and black hair and fine mouth and almost every part of their bodies like the statue images of heroes of old.[87]

In evoking the first revival of the Olympics a few years earlier—which, as Debbie Challis has explained, was intricately bound up with the late Victorian notion of the Greeks as an ideal 'race'—O'Farrelly is presenting the islanders as a living incarnation of a racial ideal.[88] The bodies of the islanders, in other words, as well as the earth and material remains of the islands, are connected tangibly to Greek antiquity through the connecting medium of the Fir Bolg.

On the basis of these three features of the Aran Fir Bolg—ruins, rockscape, and race—it is hard to resist the conclusion that the power of the Fir Bolg on Aran has tended more towards abjection than revolution. They aid a characterization of the islands as ruined, infertile places of desolate monuments and hard labour, peopled, as a reviewer of Margaret Stokes put it, 'by the dim and shadowy ghosts of unknown warriors, and of fights long ago.'[89] It appears, in other words, that the Fir Bolg as abject are a more useful tool in the 'poetics of Aran writing' than their revolutionary counterparts. Although the racial distinction of the islanders is slightly different (in that it is voiced as a celebratory 'ideal' of purity), not only is it distinctly problematic for that very reason, it is also, fundamentally, a continuation

---

[82] Ashley (2001: 11); Haverty (1991 [1859]: 45). See Robinson (1986: 74) on the 'Firbolgic trumpet-note' of this address. For an argument in support of Haddon and Browne contra Ashley see Fitzpatrick (2012: 127).
[83] Siggins (2014: 4).   [84] M. Ferguson (1868: 7).   [85] Dall (1931: 123).
[86] O'Farrelly (2010 [1902]: 103).
[87] O'Farrelly (2010 [1902]: 103).   [88] Challis (2011: 141–55).   [89] Anon. (1884: 630).

of MacFhirbhisigh, Wilde, Betham, and Mahaffy's insistence on the 'otherness' of the Fir Bolg ancestors, as 'black haired', 'unsteady', 'tale-telling', and 'barbarous'. What is it, then, about Aran's place in the political imaginary of Ireland and Irish identity that requires an abject rather than a revolutionary Fir Bolg?

Enshrinment as Heritage

> The Aran Islands have always lain beyond the main track of Irish history, a refuge of conquered and dispossessed peoples, a burial place of lost causes.
>
> E. W. Lynam[90]

> For the western climate is Lethe
>
> Louis MacNeice[91]

It is important, first of all, to see the abject force of the Fir Bolg as in keeping with the general thrust of Aran writing towards primitivism. The islands are seen as archaic, undeveloped places, and successive waves of Aran writers have voiced concerns about hints of modernity encroaching on the islands, whether as incongruous oddities or more malign omens of degeneration. On seeing a 'bazaar' on Inis Mór in 1897, a member of the Royal Society of Antiquaries, for example, lamented that '"*penitus toto divisa orbe*" is here rapidly losing its significance', while in 1937 Brewer wondered whether it was possible 'for the curious modern to touch Eden without...importing into its tranquillity the dance hall, the petrol pump, and the cocktail bar?'[92]

It could be said, then, that it is simply the pastness of Fir Bolg abjection that lends itself, in a peculiar way, to Aran. It is useful as a means to provide ancient ancestors, an ancient bloodline, and ancient material remains, strengthening Aran's particularly evocative combination of 'past and peasant', to borrow Leerssen's terms.[93] However, we have seen above that the lost-in-the-mists-of-time atmosphere of the myth has actually been used to characterize the Fir Bolg and their ancestors as people of the future—as revolutionaries about to break free from constraints partly on the basis of that long history. It is not so much the antiquity of the myth that matters in Aran writing, but how that antiquity is used.

A more helpful way to think about why the Fir Bolg lend themselves to decay and subjugation on Aran is through Walter Benjamin's model of two ways of using the past (a framework which Kiberd has usefully applied to Ireland in *Irish*

---

[90] Lynam (1914: 13), with the kind permission of *Studies: An Irish Quarterly Review*.
[91] MacNeice (1949: 20), with permission from David Higham Associates.
[92] Anon. (1897: 268), alluding to Virgil's description of the Britons as 'entirely cut off from the whole world' (*Ecl.* 1.66); Brewer (1937: 355).
[93] Leerssen (1996: 221).

Classics). Benjamin conceptualized two chief modes of engagement with tradition, through either enshrinement as heritage or dialectical history. In the dialectical mode, as Kiberd puts it, 'the past can form a constellation with the present, flashing forth as a challenge'.[94] In the enshrinement approach, however, the challenge of the past is deactivated (or, more precisely, never activated in the first place) and the meeting of past and present is something that deadens rather than enlivens the contemporary moment. If the past is enshrined as heritage, Benjamin explains, 'every tradition, even the most recent, becomes the legacy of something that has already run its course in the immemorial night of the ages.'[95]

A crucial result of enshrinement as heritage is that everything about a particular place or culture belongs to the past, and yet, at the same time, nothing about it belongs to history. In what Benjamin describes as 'an extreme foreshortening of the historical perspective', 'everything is placed in some rarefied atmosphere', which exists in the past, but outside of time.[96] Benjamin suggests a possible political drive behind this characterization of somewhere as past but atemporal in a laconic description of his grandmother's house: 'poverty', he writes, 'could have no place in these rooms, where death itself had none.'[97] Part of the usefulness of enshrinement for the 'ruling classes', in other words, is to eliminate death and poverty by creating a space exempt from the needs of security, progress, reform, or practical aid.[98]

Perhaps, then, it is the materiality of the Aran Islands that is disguised or manipulated by the reuse of the Fir Bolg. Belonging solely to the past, the islands cannot be places of need in any urgent sense, because they are, to all intents and purposes, already dead. This can be detected in the late-nineteenth-century debate over a possible telegraph connection between the islands and the mainland. As Harvey has outlined, the County Inspector of the Royal Irish Constabulary resisted the idea on the grounds that the islands could have no need for contemporary intervention. 'Such a scheme', he claimed, 'could never be of real benefit to an island which is almost a desert and which will never have anything but an impoverished population on it.'[99]

There are other ways in which the 'thirst for the past' involved in the reuse of the Fir Bolg myth may feed into the enshrinement of Aran.[100] One is the need for a manageable and packaged Aran identity for the purposes of the tourist market (see Power's oxymoronic description of Aran as 'a living museum').[101] Another may be as a way to underplay Aran's role in the political upheavals of the twentieth century, retaining its ideal status as something to be fought for, not with (i.e. as an

---

[94] Kiberd (2000a: 66).   [95] Benjamin (1999: 116).
[96] Benjamin (1977: 203).   [97] Benjamin (2006: 88).   [98] Benjamin (2007: 255).
[99] Harvey (1991: 240). For a different account of the socio-economic conditions of Aran at the turn of the twentieth century see Fitzpatrick (2012: 142–4).
[100] Benjamin (1999: 407).
[101] Power (1935 [1926]: 7). Cf. O'Sullivan (2007: 180) on Westropp confusing objects he had seen on Aran in the 1880s with artefacts from the RIA Museum.

inspirational ideal rather than political participant).[102] Enshrinement, as Benjamin explains, 'is meant to cover up the revolutionary moments in the occurrence of history,' and it is certainly the case that the presence of contemporary politics is seldom emphasized in Aran writing.[103] When it is, there is a strong sense of incongruence or inconvenience. In 1931, for example, Higgins was disappointed at signs of political engagement on the mainland ('the words "Up de Valera" chalked upon the pig-sty') and so fled to Aran, where he was dismayed to find that the islands, too, were labouring towards 'the dark goal of a free and feminist Ireland'.[104] This apolitical ideal of the islands stands in stark contrast to the political engagement of texts by the islanders themselves. Bridget Dirrane's Aran memoir, for instance, tells of serving tea to Pearse, Ashe, Ceannt, and Joseph Plunkett on Inis Mór, and of her hunger strike in Mountjoy in 1919, while Tom O'Flaherty's 1934 *Aranmen All* shows the protagonist returning from America, noting the Union Jack transformed into 'the tricolour of a Free State of twenty-six of our thirty-two counties', and asserting that it was originally 'a tricolour designed to be the flag of an All-Ireland'.[105]

The ways in which the double-edged potential of the Fir Bolg as abject/revolutionary has shut down on Aran into a one-sided, enshrined heritage remind us that, as Benjamin explained, a great deal hangs in the balance when a tradition is used in the contemporary moment: 'Resolute refusal,' he writes, 'of the concept of "timeless truth" is in order.'[106] If Aran is a place where the use of the past tends so often towards the enshrinement model rather than the dialectical, then the Fir Bolg may have a particular weight on the islands, and the use of the myth as a blueprint for life on contemporary Aran may propagate rather than challenge that tendency.

Conclusions

Abject Classical Presences on Aran

Ireland is...insular but not Isolated

Eoin MacNeill[107]

---

[102] Cf. Kiberd (1995: 286) on how the Blaskets were held up as the ideal of a republic in 1916, an idea totally alien to the islanders themselves.

[103] Benjamin (1999: 474).   [104] Dall (1931: 20, 77).

[105] Dirrane (1997: 27, 39); T. O'Flaherty (1934: 62). Although not from the Aran Islands, Martin McDonagh's *Lieutenant of Inishmore* (2001), which features an Irish National Liberation Army member and Aran islander, Mad Padraic, can similarly be read as an effort to *reassert* the contemporary, political link between the islanders, the island of Ireland, and Britain.

[106] Benjamin (1999: 463).   [107] MacNeill (1935: 57).

This chapter has not meant to deny anything about the antiquity or cultural riches of the Aran Islands. Nor has it intended to suggest that all writing about the Aran Islands can be categorized in one fell swoop. Indeed, it is worth noting an instance where the story of the Fir Bolg *does* come close to galvanizing an Irish–Greek connection into a revolutionary 'constellation': in the unmistakably utopian account of a trip to Aran in 1911 by the woodcarver and member of the United Irishwomen, Sophia St John Whitty. 'It is a fitting spot,' she writes,

> for the last fighting outpost in a nation's long struggle against her conquerors. It is a land as untamed and untamable as the people to whom it belongs. Wild, barren, and poor. Yes! no doubt, yet filled with those reliques that are the true hall-mark of a nation's greatness, and her innate power of life...I lean against unmortared walls built perhaps three thousand years ago by Firbolg chiefs, against their enemies.[108]

While it might be the case that Whitty's use of the Fir Bolg serves to bring the islands' present (or future) alive through 'the fullness of the past', in Benjamin's terms, this chapter has meant to suggest that the story of the Irish-Greek Fir Bolg, by and large, enshrines the islands as heritage.[109] Having highlighted the Fir Bolg as an important instance of the dual potential of tradition, it has been argued here that their abject afterlife trumps their rebelliousness in Aran Island writing.

One question that arises immediately from this chapter's examination of the specific case of the Fir Bolg on Aran has to do with the politics of other classical presences on the islands, particularly the presence of Homer and Greek tragedy. Do these, like the Fir Bolg, bring with them the risk of abjection, and the enshrinement of the contemporary islands into an atemporal, apolitical past? When the islands are characterized as Greek, whether through the Fir Bolg, Homer, or tragedy, does this characterization serve to repress and contain them in useful abjection?

Although less famous than the Homeric parallels on the Blasket Islands, there are frequent comparisons between the Aran Islands and Homeric Greece in the course of Aran writing. In the context of the Revival, Emily Lawless described 'a queer old ragged Ulysses...whose Ithaca was that solitary islet set in the bleak and unhospitable Atlantic', and both Yeats and Arthur Symons mined contemporary scholarship on Celtic–Homeric parallels to detect 'the sensation of Homer' in 1896.[110] Under the influence of George Thomson's Blasket theories, Malcolm

---

[108] Whitty (1911: 13).   [109] Benjamin (2007: 246).

[110] Lawless (1897: 215); Symons (1919: 318). In his unfinished novel *The Speckled Bird* (1896–1902), Yeats noted 'the wisdom of Odysseus' and 'the unclouded eyes of the ancient people who...died gladly for Helen or for Deirdre': Yeats (2003: 86, 87). Cf. McNeillie (2001: 124, 227). More recently, Eamonn Wall has positioned Robinson's Aran chorography as a version of the *Odyssey*, with its exploratory movement around the islands: Wall (2011: 8). Cf. Macintosh (2016: 123–33) on Theresa Kishkan overlaying the islands of Oyster Bay and the islands of the west coast in her 2004 retelling of Homer, *A Man in a Distant Field*.

Kelsall argued in 1975 that writing by Aran islanders was 'the literature of the heroic world', and evidence of the islanders' tendency 'to think Homerically'.[111] 'The islandmen on their windswept Ithaca,' Kelsall described, 'lived still in the world of primitive epic, and their society was heroic, even Homeric'.[112]

One issue with this Homeric approach is that it sidelines the contemporary political engagement of the Aran texts outlined above. Bridget Dirrane's memoir, for example, is an autonomous creation rather than an outpouring from an oral tradition, and the work of Pat Mullen (Kelsall's direct target) is a self-conscious response to the filming of Flaherty's *Man of Aran*, with which he was intricately involved.[113] Having recognized the extent to which classical parallels are part of Aran discourse rather than Aran life (tied to scholarship, antiquarianism, and literature, and bound up with the afterlife of the origin myths), perhaps it is more fruitful to view such echoes as stemming not, or not only, from innate kinship or historic connections, but rather from scholarly, political, and literary discourse. Perhaps, in other words, the islanders of Kelsall's observation may not have been 'thinking Homerically' at all, but rather engaging with the whole trope of Aran islanders thinking Homerically.[114]

Another principal basis on which Aran–Greek parallels are drawn is tragedy. According to Lawless, 'the weather there plays, as it does in my story, the part of Fate in a Greek tragedy,' while Liam O'Flaherty declared that there 'broods' over Inis Meáin 'an overwhelming sense of great, noble tragedy. The Greeks would have liked it'.[115] Does the tragic nature of Aran activate the revolutionary heroism of the Fir Bolg, fighting against the yoke of slavery in Greece? Or, by contrast, does the propulsion of these accounts, when combined with the dominant Aran discourse of ruin and desolation, move towards inactivity rather than uprising, and past suffering rather than future emancipation?[116]

Whatever the answers to these questions might be—and they require further exploration—I would suggest that when these classicizing tropes are set in action on Aran, it is vital at least to bear in mind what has been suggested here about the dual potential of Irish-Greek presences on contemporary islands. By looking at the Fir Bolg, a seemingly obscure people from medieval literature, and at how

---

[111] Kelsall (1975: 267).   [112] Kelsall (1975: 254).   [113] See, e.g., Mullen (1934).

[114] Cf. above on the tendency to view the Irish origin legends' engagement with Classics as instinctive rather than sophisticated, oral rather than textual, a point also evident in the determination of Evans-Wentz to see Aran culture as oral: Williams (2016: 412). Cf. Allen on how Synge's engagement with oral tradition has obscured the importance of texts and, most importantly, intertextuality, in his Aran account: Allen (2012: 160).

[115] Conneely (2011: 13); Tóibín (2007).

[116] Another key way in which classical antiquity is present on Aran is the use of immram narratives to characterize the islands. These early medieval stories of voyages to mythical islands draw extensively on classical mythology, including Plato's Atlantis, the *Odyssey*, and the figure of Neptune: see, e.g., Williams (2016: 62–3), Freitag (2013: 108–10). They are then used, particularly in the Revival, as a way to 'create a new version of island mythology' on Aran: Foster (1977: 265). For Aran as Atlantis itself see, e.g., Bouvier (1990: 49), Ó Síocháin (1990 [1962]: 44).

they shape Aran's role in the conversation about Irish national identity, we can see quite how crucial it is to approach classical parallels on Irish islands with meticulous care as to how that ancient presence contributes to the topos of Irish islands as places of eternal recurrence and apolitical timelessness.

J. M. Synge and the Fir Bolg

Níor éistís scéal na gcloch,
Bhí éacht i scéal an teallaigh.

You didn't listen to the tale of the stones,
Greatness lived in the tale of the hearth.

Máirtín Ó Direáin[117]

Another question for further consideration has to do with the place of J. M. Synge in this narrative. Synge's name is 'inextricably linked' with the islands, as J. W. O'Connell points out, and most Aran writing after 1909 follows in the wake of his 'topographical book', *The Aran Islands*, as Andrew McNeillie explains.[118] He has therefore been conspicuous by his absence from this chapter. However, that absence is part of the point. Where we might expect Synge, as a canonical Aran writer and one whose interest in the Classics has been well established, to engage heavily with the story of the Fir Bolg, we actually find only one reference to the myth in his published work on Aran.[119] His notes and drafts, however, are full of speculation and research about the story, especially its basis in historical fact. He records in detail Petrie's belief in 'the Pelasgic origin of the Firbolg', summarizing his argument for the Greek origin of the Aran forts.[120] He also encountered the legend in Henri d'Arbois de Jubainville's study of Greek–Celtic comparative mythology, in which, as Synge reports in his notebook, d'Arbois argues that 'the fir-bolg were actual people'.[121] On his first visit to the islands in 1898, he wrote about the Aran afterlife of the legend in a letter to Yeats, and makes frequent reference to them in draft passages of what would become *The Aran Islands*, as well as describing Dún Aonghasa as 'a sort of coliseum of fairyland'.[122] However,

---

[117] Ó Direáin (1984: 40–1), with permission of The Goldsmith Press.

[118] O'Connell (1994: 261), TCD MS 4405, f. 8r, McNeillie (2001: 4). For Synge's influence see also, e.g., MacGregor (1972: 79) and Ó Síocháin (1990 [1962]: 159–76). For Synge's own habit of recycling earlier texts on Aran see Kiberd (1993: 129–39).

[119] For Synge's engagement with Irish–Greek parallels see Macintosh (1994: 3–10) and Currie (2017: 157–64, 192–4).

[120] TCD MS 4375, ff. 53v–52v, 50v–50r. All references to the Synge Manuscripts in the Library of Trinity College Dublin follow the itemization and foliation as set out in Grene (1971), and are quoted with the kind permission of Trinity College Library.

[121] TCD MS 4378, f. 64r. See d'Arbois de Jubainville (1884: 134–5).

[122] Yeats (1997: 251); TCD MS 4384, f. 46v. For references to the Fir Bolg see TCD MS 4385, f.53r, TCD MS 4344, f. 348r, TCD MS 4344, f. 243r.

in the final version of the text, the narrator simply describes his habit of going to the cliffs to 'prop my book open with stones touched by the Fir-bolgs, and sleep for hours in the delicious warmth of the sun'.[123] If Synge was so interested in the Fir Bolg, and if they feature so resoundingly in Aran writing as a whole, why do they play so small a role in *The Aran Islands*, the most seminal twentieth-century account of the islands?

Synge was equally silent over Homeric parallels (and equally interested in them, as evident in his engagement with d'Arbois). Richard Martin has noted this silence, and interpreted it as a deliberate tactic designed so that 'the traditions he cites be anonymous, the voice of the folk, coming straight from the soil'.[124] Through this evasion, Synge paints himself as 'a wandering Homer whose Ithaca was Aran', and 'heroizes' the islanders 'through an implicit but constant comparison with the world of Homeric epic'.[125] This chimes with the predominant view in Synge scholarship more generally, according to which Synge's silence on Aran is parallel to the fallacious objectivity of the early anthropologists, thus identifying him as a writer 'intent on pursuing the primitive and rejecting the modern', as Fitzpatrick explains.[126]

However, by returning to Synge's silence in the light of what has been suggested here about classical presences on Aran, we can perhaps recognize a different interpretation. Contextualized within the wider reception history of the Fir Bolg as a mechanism that links the islands and ancient Greece, the reticence of Synge's Aran account may in fact tell us something crucial about the broader politics of Irish–Greek connections. Furthermore, if we look again at the list of those who used the abject status of the Fir Bolg for emancipatory effect, we see that many of them have been greatly influenced by Synge: Joyce, Heaney, and McGuinness most of all. Might, then, Synge's treatment of the myth in some ways have enabled the activation of the abject Fir Bolg into radical, rebellious figures?

These are questions that require further thought.[127] In this chapter I hope to have demonstrated that unearthing the reception history of the Fir Bolg can show us a different way of understanding the narrative of Aran writing, the place of Classics within that narrative, and, potentially, the role of Synge in taking that narrative in new directions.

---

[123] Synge (1966: 69).   [124] R. Martin (2007: 83).   [125] R. Martin (2007: 85, 81).

[126] Fitzpatrick (2012: 124). Fitzpatrick has a different interpretation of Synge's tendency to include things 'sotto voce', seeing it as a 'reticence amounting to deception': Fitzpatrick (2012: 135). For studies of *The Aran Islands* see especially Kiberd (2000b: 82–110), Grene (1975: 19–40), Ashley (2000: 175–93), Garrigan Mattar (2004: 142–8), Fitzpatrick (2012: 121–51), Allen (2012: 159–71) and Brannigan (2015: 37–48).

[127] I have gone into Synge's use of classical presences on Aran in more detail in Currie (2017: 165–83, 189–214).

10

Sinn Féin and *Ulysses*

Between Professor Robert Mitchell Henry and James Joyce

Edith Hall

This is a tale of two classics-related responses to Sinn Féin soon after the 1916 Easter Rising. One is a history of the party, *The Evolution of Sinn Féin*, published in 1920 by Robert Mitchell Henry (1873–1950), Professor of Latin at Queen's University, Belfast, and a Protestant. The other is Episode 12 of the novel *Ulysses*, published by James Joyce in 1922. Henry and Joyce, both Irishmen immersed in classical literature, are linked by their interest in Irish republicanism and by a medieval Irish text telling the story of Odysseus, the *Merugud Uilix Maicc Leirtis* or *Wanderings of Ulysses Son of Laertes*.[1] The classical perspectives on those tumultuous years of Henry and Joyce, however different, reveal complementary dimensions of the drive for Irish independence and the early-twentieth-century Irish reception of ancient literature.

Classicists and Irish Nationalism

Robert Mitchell Henry was hardly the most famous non-Catholic Irish classical scholar to support the goals of the Easter Uprising. That was E. R. (Eric Robertson) Dodds, the politically sensitized son of a County Down Presbyterian. Dodds's career was briefly jeopardized in 1916 when he was still an undergraduate, studying Greats at University College, Oxford, as he explains in his autobiography: he was required, temporarily, to leave the university on account of his public support for

I would like to extend thanks to Isabelle Torrance for inviting me to speak at the important conference which gave rise to this volume, to both editors for their patience during this article's painfully long gestation, to the anonymous reader who made some important bibliographical suggestions, to the AHRC for funding my research trip to Belfast in connection with my project 'Classics and Class in Britain 1789–1939' (http://www.classicsandclass.info/ [accessed 5 December 2019]), and to the extraordinarily helpful archivists in the McClay Library at Queen's University, Belfast.

[1] To which I was introduced through an article by the founding father of Classical Reception in Ireland, Stanford (1951). I have also profited from the earlier work of Ahl (1989) and from O'Nolan (1968), (1969), and (1973).

Edith Hall, *Sinn Féin and* Ulysses: *Between Professor Robert Mitchell Henry and James Joyce* In: *Classics and Irish Politics, 1916–2016*. Edited by: Isabelle Torrance and Donncha O'Rourke, Oxford University Press (2020).
© Oxford University Press.
DOI: 10.1093/oso/9780198864486.003.0010

Irish independence.[2] He remained affectionate towards Ireland, as his friends and protegés—including fellow Irishman Louis MacNeice, who described his 'razor-keen nationalism'—understood.[3] This is expressed in Dodds's own poems in the Irish romantic/lyric tradition, which evoke the strand of Dublin's Merrion and the Vale of St Colum. In 'The Irishman in England' his nostalgia for 'the thrash of hoarser winds across Croagh Patrick's screes' is audible. Its refrain reads,

> For some go north and some go east,
> And some go south to London town:
> But I'd go west to my own country
> To watch the night come down.[4]

Dodds's radical political outlook was amplified in the case of another Irish patriot and classicist, Benjamin Farrington, who was two years older than Dodds. Born in Cork in 1891, the son of the Congregationalist City Engineer, Farrington graduated in Classics from University College, Cork. He then moved to Trinity College Dublin (TCD) to study Middle English. There his political views were shaped by the plight of the Irish working class, which came to a head in the Dublin 'lock-out' of 1913, a traumatic industrial dispute between factory owners and slum-dwelling Dubliners fighting for the right to form trade unions.[5] Farrington was impressed by the speeches of James Connolly, a Scottish Marxist of Irish descent. Connolly saw the need for Home Rule for Ireland as inseparable from the goals of the poor, and in 1912 formed the Irish Labour Party.[6] Farrington later described how Connolly's Marxist analysis of the political situation affected his own understanding of history: 'All through my years as a university student I had been studying the history of thought. Nobody before Connolly had brought home to me that the history of thought does not exist in isolation but is part of the history of the society in which the thought is produced...I am conscious that it is to a workingman that I owe the conviction that learning need not be pedantic or obscurantist but a guide to action in the present.'[7]

As John Atkinson has pointed out, Farrington would have been in Dublin in 1914, when the new Provost of TCD, the renowned historian of ancient Greece, J. P. Mahaffy, banned a meeting of the Trinity College Gaelic Society because one of the speakers, Patrick Pearse, was to be an opponent of recruitment to the

---

[2] Dodds (1977: 45).
[3] See MacNeice's autobiography (2007: 136) and his letter of 31 July 1945 in MacNeice (2010: 458–9).
[4] Dodds (1929: 46–7), reproduced by permission of the executor of E. R. Dodds's estate.
[5] See Yeates (2001).   [6] See Morgan (1988).
[7] Quoted at http://www.communistpartyofireland.ie/s-farrington.html (accessed 5 December 2019). See Cleary (2013: 7).

British army.[8] Mahaffy later wrote that he had loathed Farrington; there was no love lost between the high-handed Provost and his left-leaning undergraduate.[9]

At the height of the 1916 Easter turmoil, Farrington was studying for his Master's degree in English from University College, Cork. He completed it in 1917, writing on the suitably radical poetry of Shelley's translations from the Greek.[10] But the young scholar was busy in these two years, being appointed to a lectureship in Classics at Queen's University, Belfast (QUB), in 1916 and simultaneously taking the LLB course in law there. In 1920, he went to South Africa to assume an appointment as Lecturer in Greek in the Classics Department at Cape Town University. The Easter Rising had traumatized Farrington, as he indicated in four articles he wrote for the Afrikaans newspaper *De Burger* between 15 and 24 September 1920. His hope was to foster Afrikaner support for Sinn Féin and the radical republican wing of the new Dublin-based national government.[11] He therefore stressed the proclamation of the Republic in 1916, the document issued by the Irish Volunteers and the Irish Citizen Army during the Easter Rising in Ireland, rather than the infinitely tamer Declaration of Independence of January 1919. Controversially, the latter did not even mention the hope for independence of the 32-county geographic island, but used the far vaguer terms 'Irish nation' or 'Irish people'.[12]

But Farrington's interest in Marxism and opposition to racism, along with an increasing distrust of both the Boer cause and the de Valera administration in Ireland, soon led him to give up active participation in politics in favour of working, on what Marxists call 'the intellectual plane', to rewrite the world, including the ancient world, from a materialist and labour-focused perspective on history. He was promoted to the chair of Latin in 1929, but left Cape Town in 1935 as the first steps towards institutionalized apartheid were taken. He worked at the University of Bristol for a year, before becoming professor at University College, Swansea, in the heart of the Welsh industrial and mining region, where he remained for twenty-one years.

Farrington achieved a high profile in the UK and Ireland, his major academic contribution being to the history and philosophy of ancient science, expressed in a series of pioneering if controversial books. *The Civilization of Greece and Rome* (1938) was an important attempt to make ancient history available to working people beyond the academy. Farrington's lively, lucid materialist analyses of the

---

[8] Atkinson (2010: 673). On the possible classical influences in Pearse's own rhetoric see McGing (Ch. 3).

[9] Mahaffy's thinking is cited in a letter by W. B. Yeats dated 10 November 1914, as quoted by Foster (2003a: 523).

[10] This led to an article on Shelley's translation of Plato's *Symposium*: Farrington (1919).

[11] Atkinson (2010: 671).

[12] See Atkinson (2010) *passim* with further bibliography, and the study of the impact made by the radical young Irishman's arrival on the Cape Town political scene in Hirson (2001: 122–53). Farrington's Marxism is discussed at greater length in Hall and Stead (2020: 483–4).

relationship between the ancient economy and ideas were often derided by mainstream classical scholars, but they were (and still are) widely read by the more open-minded among them. His commitment to Communist ideals, born in the chaos leading up to the Easter Rising, was lifelong. He taught on socialist summer schools and to working men's educational societies. His pamphlet *The Challenge of Socialism* resulted from a series of lectures he delivered at weekend schools in Dublin in August 1946.[13]

Robert Mitchell Henry's Sinn Féin

Immeasurably more significant in Irish politics than either Dodds or Farrington was the Latin scholar Robert Mitchell Henry (Fig. 10.1), two decades their senior. He knew Farrington, who from the autumn of 1916 briefly worked alongside him at Queen's. Universally known as 'Bob', Henry was an established professor there

Fig. 10.1 Caricature of R. M. Henry, Papers of R. M. Henry, McClay Library, Queen's University, Belfast. Image reproduced courtesy of Special Collections, McClay Library, Queen's University, Belfast.

[13] See Hall and Stead (2016).

and a prominent Ulster public figure, regarded as kind, eccentric, and proud of his Aberdonian ancestry. As a mature, institutionally recognized scholar, he had far more to lose in 1916 than either Farrington or Dodds. He was, nevertheless, involved in the struggle on the ground.

On several dates between January and late March 1916, Henry wrote in his pocket diary that he was attending rifle practice.[14] His diaries lie forgotten among his abundant papers in the archives of the McClay Library of QUB. There are no such rifle practice entries in his other diaries. They cease at the precise moment of the Easter Rising in April 1916. Henry was a lifelong supporter of republicanism and of the cause of the independence of all the people of Ireland from Britain. The rifle practices he was attending were those of the local branch of the Irish Volunteers.

This organization had come into being in Dublin on 25 November 1913, in response to the establishment in January 1913 of the Ulster Volunteers, the militia opposed to the introduction of Home Rule. While its membership overlapped with the constituencies that supported Sinn Féin—the Irish Citizens' Army and the Irish Republican Brotherhood—the Irish Volunteers (I.V.) was a separate initiative.[15] By the outbreak of World War I, there were at least 100,000 Irish Volunteers, which made the British authorities nervous. In July 1914, at Howth, the I.V. unloaded a shipment of 1,500 rifles, with 45,000 rounds of ammunition, purchased from Germany.

There were many Irish Volunteers in the northern counties and in Belfast, although the atmosphere there was threatening to advocates of Irish independence. Henry's involvement is confirmed by his partisan eyewitness account, in *The Evolution of Sinn Féin*, of the training in which both the U.V. and I.V. members engaged:

> ...the sight might have been witnessed in Belfast of Ulster Volunteers and Irish Volunteers using the same drill ground through the good offices of a tolerant Ulsterman...Right through their tragic and tempestuous career the Irish Volunteers in spite of countless difficulties and provocations continued their attitude of punctilious courtesy toward the Ulster force.[16]

His involvement is all the more curious because a born-and-bred Ulsterman and a devout Protestant of Scottish descent was prima facie an unlikely candidate for sympathy with the I.V. cause.

---

[14] See the entries in his diaries, Henry Collection (McClay GB 752 RMHP) for Thursday 13 January and 3, 27, and 29 March. The contents of this collection, when I consulted them in May 2016, had not yet been itemized or numbered.

[15] For an exciting eyewitness account of life inside the I.V. by a Dublin sniper see Shouldice (2015).

[16] R. M. Henry (1920: 139–40).

I first encountered Henry, without knowing he was a classicist, when I read *The Evolution of Sinn Féin* (1920). I became convinced that this historian was in touch with the inner circles of the I.V., because in the course of his argument that the 1916 Rising had little to do with Sinn Féin, he writes as follows (emphasis added):

> The Rising came like a flash of lightning in an evening twilight, illuminating and terrifying. It was not entirely unexpected: those whose duty and those whose pleasure it is to suspect everything had been uneasy for some time. **The few people who were in touch with the inner circles of the Irish Volunteers had long known that something was in progress.** But the authorities had nothing definite to go upon, and the majority of Irishmen knew nothing definite about it.[17]

I read Henry's masterpiece when I was myself a politically active undergraduate in the early 1980s, at the height of the Irish Troubles. I wanted to learn about the history of Ireland and the British Empire in the late nineteenth and early twentieth centuries. *The Evolution of Sinn Féin* was (as it still is) on standard bibliographies circulated by university History departments. It is a brilliant analysis of the fault lines afflicting the Irish independence movement. It is also an exceptional evocation of early-twentieth-century Ireland from the viewpoint of an Irish citizen not blinded by religious, cultural, or sentimental attachments to any narrow strand in, or definition of, Irishness. It built support for Irish independence in Ireland and especially in the USA, where it was published simultaneously with the Dublin edition in 1922 and was widely read and reviewed.[18] It was reprinted in 1970 by Kennikat Press in Port Washington, New York, and will have been consulted by more readers than have ever used Henry's books on classical subjects.[19] Its tone, mordant and tragic by turns, has probably informed our collective picture of the events of 1916.

There is a Tacitean stylistic ring, especially in the use of abstract nouns, often in the plural, when Henry describes the results of human failings: the history of Irish politics after the death of Charles Stewart Parnell 'was a story largely of small intrigue, base personalities, divided counsels and despairing expedients'.[20] There are, however, few explicit classical allusions. Henry sees Ireland as the victim of the familiar colonial model of the British Empire as parallel to the Roman Empire, a model which advocates of British colonialism had used as early as the accession of James I/VI in 1603.[21] But Henry, like Karl Marx, applied it negatively, equating

---

[17]   R. M. Henry (1920: 217).   [18]   See, e.g., Turner (1921); Dixon (1929).
[19]   Which included commentaries on Livy (1905) and (with T. W. Dougan) Cicero (1934), and on a seventeenth-century Irish astronomical work, O'Connell and Henry (1915).
[20]   R. M. Henry (1920: 36); on Tacitus' abstract nouns see, e.g., Damon (2003: 13).
[21]   Hall (forthcoming); Mantena (2010).

the callousness of Roman and British responses towards even minor rebels against their central governments.[22] The book ends with these sentences:

> The means at the disposal of Sinn Féin at present hardly seem adequate to accomplish its object. It may bring about the moral and intellectual independence of Ireland: it may secure a certain measure of economic independence: but to secure political independence, in the face of the forces ranged against it, seems impossible. But what it cannot do for itself may in the future be done for it by the moral forces of which it is a manifestation. It may in the future be recognized by the conscience of mankind that no nation ought to exercise political domination over another nation. But that future may still be as remote as it seemed in the days of the Roman Empire.[23]

But comparing the British and Roman empires was conventional, and the other classical references are no more numerous than would be expected of any university-educated European at the time.

Henry occasionally inserts well-known Latin phrases: Irish nationalism suffered from the *damnosa hereditas* (a legal Latin term) of opposition to Catholicism.[24] The withdrawal of the right of the Irish to an independent legislature was the *fons et origo malorum*, the source and origin of their troubles. The ultimate source of this phrase seems to be Florus' *Epitome of Roman History* 1.51.12, but it was used by nineteenth-century commentators on religious and colonial conflicts.[25] The nineteenth-century revolutionary James Fintan Lalor asked his compatriots to fight for 'a wreath that will be green for ever';[26] Henry translates this into Latin, *perenni fronde corona*, quoting Lucretius' *De Rerum Natura* 1.118, where the perpetual honour crowns the epic poet Ennius.[27] The Catholic authorities colluded in the destruction of Gaelic by attempting, Henry writes, to assuage their Irish-speaking congregations' fear of the English, who were seen as 'the Danai, *dona ferentes*'; Henry thus uses the Virgilian Laocoön's protest against the Trojans' acceptance of the Greek 'gift' of the Trojan Horse (*Aeneid* 2.49) to equate the destruction of Troy and the obliteration of Gaelic. In discussing how quickly the early Anglo-Norman planters adopted Irish identity, he cites the old Latin saying, 'more Irish than the Irish themselves', *ipsis Hibernis Hiberniores*, variously attributed to the priest John Lynch and to Jonathan Swift.[28] A tactic of the officers of the Royal Navy is likened to what Cicero calls Catiline's policy of putting out the fire by demolishing the house, *ruina exstinguere incendium* (*Pro Murena* 51).[29]

---

[22] See further Hall (2010).   [23] R. M. Henry (1920: 284).   [24] R. M. Henry (1920: 14).
[25] R. M. Henry (1920: 14). See, e.g., Didot (1828: 60).   [26] Lalor (1895: 113).
[27] R. M. Henry (1920: 27).
[28] R. M. Henry (1920: 106); see O'Faoláin (1947: 59); Wilson (1804, vol. I: 60).
[29] R. M. Henry (1920: 152).

Greek authors receive only three references, one an unremarkable allusion to the 'Charybdis' of Irish conscription.[30] In the second, Henry invokes Thucydides on 'ancient simplicity' (3.38.1) when describing the naive integrity that marked John Redmond and his proposed terms for the 1914 Home Rule Bill: 'with that simplicity of character, which, as the Greek historian says, "makes up a great part of good breeding", he promised without conditions.'[31] But the only words in ancient Greek in the book are kept for what is, in the arc of Henry's tragic narrative, the most crucial moment. This is when the I.V. became infiltrated by violent advocates of immediate armed rebellion. Henry says they were affected simply by physical contact with weapons:

> The Volunteers were in the opinion of Sinn Féin a useful auxiliary in the task of developing the one quality from which alone ultimate success was to be expected, the self-reliance and moral resolution of the Irish people. But αὐτὸς ἐφέλκεται ἄνδρα σίδηρος—the mere 'sheen of arms' has an attraction superior to all arguments and all policies: and there is little doubt that the superior attractions of the Volunteers proved too strong for many young and ardent Sinn Féiners and induced them to put the means first and the end second.[32]

It was the availability of rifles, suggests Henry, that turned some heads, when what was needed was cool deliberation on the occasions on which the use of armed force might conceivably become legitimate.

The Greek means 'the steel itself draws a man on'. It is a quotation, minus the connective 'for', of a phrase from the *Odyssey*, αὐτὸς γὰρ ἐφέλκεται ἄνδρα σίδηρος, so famous that Juvenal quoted it with an obscene twist (*Sat.* 9.37). In the *Odyssey* it occurs twice (16.294, 19.13), in the mouth of Odysseus when he instructs Telemachus to hide the arms from the suitors. This saying is to be Telemachus' response if they should protest at his removal of access to the weapons. The context may have seemed as appropriate to Henry as the content: Odysseus' instruction is part of his detailed plan, entailing patience, caution, and timeliness, which he says must be implemented before his loyal slaves and impetuous son may begin ridding the household of its unwanted occupants.

The infrequency of Henry's classical references in this book meant that it was years after I had read it that I grasped he was a classicist. When assembling a student bibliography on Livy, I came across his edition of *Ab Urbe Condita* book 26.[33] Its 'Introduction' contains strong words on the heroic loyalty, during the Roman Civil Wars, of Livy's hometown of Patavium to the Republican cause: 'the

---

[30] R. M. Henry (1920: 259). For classicists, the 'Milesians' on p. 2 may at first sight seem connected with ancient Greek history, but they are in fact the 'gairthear Mílidh Easpáinne', Gauls from Spain by medieval tradition, the last continental race of immigrants to settle in Ireland.
[31] R. M. Henry (1920: 163).   [32] R. M. Henry (1920: 142).   [33] R.M. Henry (1905).

very slaves could not be tempted or dragooned into yielding up their masters to Asinius Pollio. Its inhabitants preserved into imperial times the ancient decorum and severity of morals that marked the best days of the old order.'[34] Finally I realized that the author of *The Evolution of Sinn Féin* was a Latinist. Perhaps there was even some thematic connection between the particular book of Livy and the events of 1916.

Livy's twenty-sixth book records a period of the Second Punic War. Hannibal is making progress in southern Italy in 211 BCE. The people of Capua defect to him. The Roman consuls, after a prolonged battle, take Capua. The Capuans are treated brutally by the consul Quintus Fulvius. Some leading Capuans commit suicide by taking poison. The Capuan senators are tied to stakes, to be beheaded; Quintus Fulvius deliberately avoids reading a letter from the Roman Senate ordering him to spare them and the executions take place regardless. Most of the rest of the book portrays the inexorable rise of the Roman Empire during the emergence of the 24-year-old Scipio, who ruthlessly storms New Carthage in southern Spain.

Henry was in his early thirties when he published his commentary on those rampaging Romans. He was senior classics master at the Royal Belfast Academical Institution, and Junior Fellow at what was then Queen's College. In 1907–8 he was finally appointed professor, got married, and moved out of his parents' nearby house. He deserves a biography which does justice to his copious documents in the McClay Library. But a few must be mentioned here, since they paint a portrait of an incorruptible advocate of Irish independence.

Henry became increasingly involved in pan-Irish political affairs. A letter of 20 July 1910 from Joseph Devlin, then Secretary of the United Irish League, shows that Henry had wanted to be elected to its Senate. He collected the hated-filled leaflets circulated by his bête noire Sir Edward Carson, who founded the U.V. One requires 'All True Unionists and Orangemen' to join Carson: 'Don't hesitate!! Advance!! Follow your leaders unhesitatingly for they are fighting your battles against Pope and Popery, and defending your blood-bought heritage of civil and religious liberty!' There are also copies of a petition drafted in an attempt to unite Ulster people of all faiths against Carson's divisive propaganda. It expresses 'abhorrence of the attempt to revive ancient bigotries and dying habits in the province' (Fig. 10.2).

There is a complimentary ticket to a United Irish League event organized by the junior section, Young Ireland, in the Abbey Theatre, Dublin, on 8 April 1913. The ticket was given serial no. 5: Henry was a significant invitee. The lecture, by Protestant United Irishman Professor C. H. Oldham, described 'Ulster's Record in the History of Irish Patriotism'. There is, most importantly, an urgent telegram

[34] R.M. Henry (1905: vii).

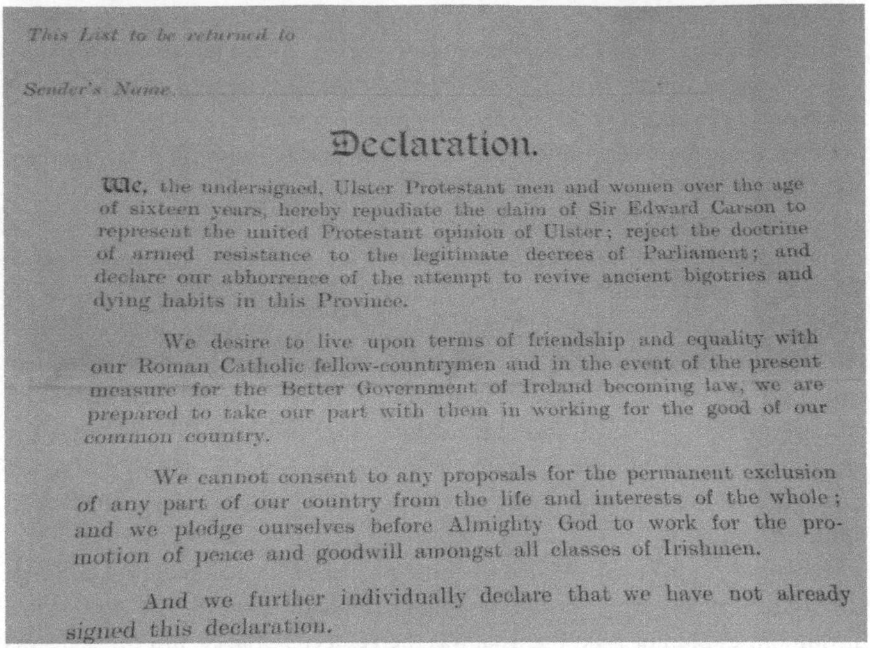

Declaration.

We, the undersigned, Ulster Protestant men and women over the age of sixteen years, hereby repudiate the claim of Sir Edward Carson to represent the united Protestant opinion of Ulster; reject the doctrine of armed resistance to the legitimate decrees of Parliament; and declare our abhorrence of the attempt to revive ancient bigotries and dying habits in this Province.

We desire to live upon terms of friendship and equality with our Roman Catholic fellow-countrymen and in the event of the present measure for the Better Government of Ireland becoming law, we are prepared to take our part with them in working for the good of our common country.

We cannot consent to any proposals for the permanent exclusion of any part of our country from the life and interests of the whole; and we pledge ourselves before Almighty God to work for the promotion of peace and goodwill amongst all classes of Irishmen.

And we further individually declare that we have not already signed this declaration.

Fig. 10.2   Petition against Mission of the Ulster Volunteers, Papers of R. M. Henry, McClay Library, Queen's University, Belfast. Image reproduced courtesy of Special Collections, McClay Library, Queen's University, Belfast.

addressed to Henry in late 1915, at the time of the inauguration of the I.V., urging him to come to TCD: 'holding important conference with Irish leaders Sunday morning inviting one professor from each centre…Deem your presence most necessary can you come.'

The most prominent professor involved in the I.V. was Eoin MacNeill (1867–1945), a working-class Catholic, Queen's graduate, and co-founder of the Gaelic League. In 1908 he was appointed Professor of Early Irish History at University College Dublin (UCD). He chaired the council that formed the I.V. MacNeill, like Henry, was only prepared to resort to military tactics in defence against the U.V. or the British army. But the I.V., as we have noted, were hard to control. They had been infiltrated by members of the Irish Republican Brotherhood in favour of armed revolution. During the very week before the Easter Rising, trust between MacNeill and the Brotherhood broke down. MacNeill and Patrick Pearse had a vitriolic altercation. MacNeill pulled the I.V. out of the uprising. He was arrested, despite having played no part, but released in 1917,[35]

---

[35]   For a searing account of these events in MacNeill's own words see his memoir in the careful edition of Hughes (2016: 65–80).

and became a prominent Sinn Féin politician. He was Minister for Education from 1922 to 1925.

Henry was undoubtedly in danger of being arrested himself. His long-standing commitment to the cause of an independent Ireland had won him few friends professionally. There is evidence in his archived letters that his political views impeded his career; he was routinely passed over in favour of academic rivals who were publicly loyal to the British crown. The letter of 8 July 1907 from a Liverpool University official explaining that he had not been offered the chair of Latin there, despite being invited to apply, was followed by letters from supporters expressing shock, including one from the progressive Edward Sonnenschein, Professor of Classics at Birmingham, addressed 17 July 1907. When Henry did, finally, receive the offer of the Belfast chair, a former pupil of his wrote to congratulate him 'on at last receiving some recognition of your merits'. The correspondent, now a student at Oxford, had feared 'that certain political support given to the present British government in Ireland' by another candidate known to both of them 'was likely to weigh in his favour and therefore against you'.[36]

Henry, an expert in Latin, Greek, and also Hebrew, understood that a shared ancient language and a rich literature were indispensable to any culture's unity. His political views were mirrored in his regret that the majority of his compatriots had been deprived of their ancestral tongue. A searing passage in his history of Sinn Féin records, in his biting Tacitean tone, the impact of the 1800 Acts of Union and the imposition in 1831 of the 'National' Education System:[37]

> Up to the time of the Union the Gaelic language had preserved intact, in spite of the Penal Laws and the instruments of repression, all that was most vital in the national spirit. Tales of warriors and heroes, of the long wars of the Gael with the stranger, the sighs of love and the aspirations of devotion, satire and encomium, all the literature and song of a people were enshrined in the native tongue.... The Irish language was understood all over Ireland, and was the familiar tongue of three-quarters of its inhabitants. It was not a necessary consequence of the Union itself that this should be destroyed, but it was a necessary consequence of the measures which the Act of Union made it possible to take. The English Government decided to embark upon the task of 'civilising' the inhabitants of Ireland.

As Henry mournfully adds, the task of 'educating' the nation out of its traditional language and culture was virtually complete by the end of the nineteenth century.

He supported Sinn Féin's cultural policies. In 1908, his diary includes references to attendance at meetings of the Gaelic Society. He was 'one of the

---

[36] Letter of 3 November 1907 from W. B. Hanna, 'your old pupil', at the Oxford Union Society.
[37] R. M. Henry (1920) 43–4.

staunchest allies' of William MacArthur,[38] another Belfast Protestant (Presbyterian) Gaelic enthusiast, who as a student at Queen's campaigned for the introduction of Gaelic classes from 1903, and founded the College Gaelic Society (Cumann Gaedhealach an Choláiste) in 1906. Henry spoke at its public meeting in the Great Hall in 1908, which resulted in the establishment of a new lectureship in Celtic in 1909.[39] With the man appointed to that post, the Rev. F. W. O'Connell, he co-edited an Early Modern Irish-language astronomical work translated from Latin.[40] Among his papers is a notebook dating from this time with suggested reading for students of Gaelic. He recommends the standard edition of the medieval Irish text telling the story of Odysseus, the *Merugud Uilix Maicc Leirtis* (Fig. 10.3).

We must acknowledge the Latin professor's extraordinary contribution to the historiography of Sinn Féin and the background to the Easter Rising in which he was prepared to risk his life. *The Evolution of Sinn Féin* is a short, intense, and

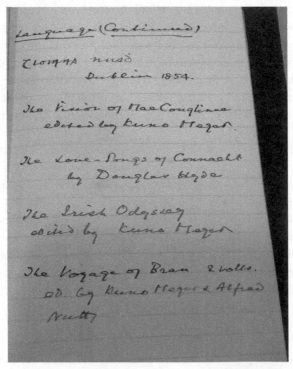

Fig. 10.3 Page from Henry's 'Suggested Gaelic Reading List', Papers of R. M. Henry, McClay Library, Queen's University, Belfast. Image reproduced courtesy of Special Collections, McClay Library, Queen's University, Belfast.

[38] Blaney (1996: 185).   [39] Blaney (1996: 186).   [40] O'Connell and Henry (1915).

exquisitely written tragic history of Ireland culminating in the execution of Patrick Pearse, James Connolly, and their eleven fellow leading rebels. Henry writes, his controlled anger palpable,

> At the same time arrests took place all over the country. Three thousand prisoners who had taken no part in the Rising were collected, many of them as innocent of any complicity in the affair as the Prime Minister. To have been at any time a member of the Irish Volunteers was sufficient cause for arrest and deportation. They were taken through the streets in lorries and in furniture vans at the dead of night and shipped for unknown destinations.[41]

Whether any British official investigated Henry's links with the rebellion is not known; there is no direct trace in his papers. He decided to continue the fight through influencing public opinion by writing rather than fighting. But the tone of his account of the executions in May 1916 suggests that they caused him anguish.

> During the week of the executions an almost unbroken silence reigned in Ireland. The first hint that anything was wrong came on the cables from America....England held Ireland in the hollow of its hand. After four days' cool deliberation it was decided to shoot the leaders. They were not brought to open trial on the charge of high treason or any other charge: the authorities who carried out the sentence were those who passed judgment on their guilt and the only people who ever heard or saw the evidence on which the judgment was based. They were shot in batches: for days the lesson was hammered home in stroke after stroke that these men were entitled neither to open trial and proof of their guilt before execution, nor to the treatment of captured enemies. The conclusion drawn by Nationalist Ireland was that if they had been Englishmen they would have been tried by English courts and sentenced by the judgment of their countrymen: that if they had been Germans or Turks they would have been treated as prisoners of war: but that being Irishmen they were in a class apart, members of a subject race, the mere property of a courtmartial.[42]

After partition, to which he objected, Henry continued to exercise his political muscles in the twin causes of Classics and of the pan-Irish, especially the working class. He supported trade unions and activities such as the Belfast Newsboys' Club. He was key to the foundation of the Belfast Workers' Educational Association (his lectures on ancient women, workers, and slaves are in the

---

[41] R. M. Henry (1920: 219).   [42] R. M. Henry (1920: 220–1).

archive) and the Classical Association of Ireland.[43] He was the force behind the creation at QUB of a new post of lecturer and director of extramural studies in 1928.[44]

He worked for the advancement of Irish historical studies from what would now be called an anti-colonial perspective; in 1929 he donated over 1,000 volumes on Irish civilization to the QUB library, forming the nucleus of the still significant R. M. Henry collection. In 1936 he was elected first President of the Society for Irish Historical Studies. Two years later, with the Irish Historical Society in Dublin, he helped to found the journal *Irish Historical Studies*. In 1933, his political views meant that he was passed over for the appointment of Vice Chancellor after tirelessly working on the Senate (and being publicly acknowledged as unofficial leader of QUB) for more than twenty years. So he retired and was, perhaps surprisingly given his politics, appointed to an honorary chair of classical literature at TCD. Then he took up the Chair of Humanity at St Andrews for eight years, before returning to Dublin, where he continued to lecture until his death on 21 December 1950.

Henry was widowed without children soon after his first marriage and did not remarry again until an advanced age. He was, however, attached to his younger brothers, helping out the impecunious Paul Henry, a painter famous today, whose landscapes of Achill Island and Connemara are associated with the Irish Free State's rural vision.[45] Paul, a Bohemian, spent much of his life in Paris. But he remembered attending marches in 1898 on the Falls Road, marking the centenary of the 1798 uprising. No doubt his older brother had taken him.[46]

Kuno Meyer's Medieval 'Irish *Odyssey*'

The links between this tale's two heroes, Henry and Joyce, are Sinn Féin and the medieval Irish text telling the story of Odysseus which Henry recommended to students of Gaelic. This so-called 'Irish *Odyssey*' was discovered at the precise moment in history when a yearning for a national literature for Ireland—a yearning which produced the 'Celtic Revival'—was gaining ground. Although antiquarian interest in early Irish literary culture began earlier, the Celtic Revival created an urgent need for Celtic literary texts.[47] The archives of ancient monasteries were ransacked with renewed energy. But this was not just an Irish

---

[43] The evidence for Henry's socialist leanings and activities, rather than his support of the Irish independence movement, is discussed in Hall and Stead (2020: 221–4).

[44] All of this information is derived first-hand from his unsorted and unnumbered collection of papers.

[45] See his autobiography, Paul Henry (1951) and Kennedy (1989–90).

[46] See the article 'Paul Henry' on the website *Achill 24.7*, p. 1: http://www.achill247.com/artists/paulhenry.html (accessed 5 December 2019).

[47] See especially O'Halloran (2004).

nationalist matter; not all the enthusiasts were Irish. One was a daring German scholar named Kuno Meyer, a lecturer at Liverpool University (Fig. 10.4). It was his edition of the *Merugud* (1886) that made his reputation and career.[48]

Merugud means something like 'a wandering', and is used as a title in only one other known work, the *Merugud* of another hero Columcille (*Merugud Cléirech Choluim Chille*).[49] The three manuscripts of the Odysseus *Merugud* are all in Dublin: one is the Stowe MS 992, from the early fifteenth century.[50] The Book of Ballymote, also in the Royal Irish Academy, includes several classical tales at the end, one of them the *Merugud*.[51] Kuno Meyer's *editio princeps* did not use the third manuscript, held in a late-fifteenth-century collection of classical material including the Irish *Aeneid* (King's Inns Library No. 12).[52]

The inclusion of the *Merugud* in the King's Inn's Library collection shows that it contributed to the medieval creation of a classical literary culture available in the spoken vernacular of the Irish island. Yet it did not derive from a single source. The stories of classical antiquity were as popular in Ireland as they were

Fig. 10.4 Portrait of Kuno Meyer, 1903. Image courtesy of the National Library of Ireland (ref. NPA POLF211).

[48] K. Meyer (1886).   [49] K. Meyer (1886: vi).
[50] D. iv. 2; fol. 59v, col. 2. 34–fol. 61r, col. 2. 28.   [51] Folios 486a. 29–488b. 27.
[52] See R. Meyer (1952: 73).

elsewhere. We find allusions to Greek and Roman heroes in Old Irish texts. A burst of literary activity and interest in the classics in the twelfth and thirteenth centuries, rather earlier than elsewhere in Europe, resulted in the translation of Statius' *Thebaid*, Lucan's *Pharsalia*, Dares Phrygius' *Historia de excidio Troiae*, and Virgil's *Aeneid*.[53] However, none of these works is a 'translation' in our sense of word-for-word correspondence; they are free adaptations which have been altered structurally, as well as stylistically, to fit native narrative traditions.

Such adaptations, which are important for understanding the relationship between Irish and Latin Christian culture, have received some attention from scholars.[54] Nevertheless, the only translation of the *Merugud* available remains Kuno Meyer's late Victorian version, in the edition recommended to the Gaelic Society by Henry. It is in intrusively archaizing style, as this excerpt from near the beginning reveals. Ulysses' men steal gold (rather than food) from the island of the Cyclops and are then assaulted by him:

> When they had gone on that island, they found a mountain of gold in its midst. 'This is a good find,' said his men to Ulixes. 'How do ye know that?' said he. 'Did ye not get enough treasures out of Troy?' And they began to gather in the gold until they saw the Cyclops coming towards them. And he did not ask tidings of them, but as they were there, so he went among them. Where there was a hero or a battle-soldier he closed his arms around them, and broke and minced their bones and their flesh. Then after having killed a great number of them, he lifted up nine of them between his two arms, together with Ulixes, the son of Laertes. Now when Ulixes, the cunning right clever man, perceived that he was being carried off by force, he escaped between the elbows of his men down to the ground, and his men were carried away from him.
>
> He went up to him, and into the one big eye that was in the front part of his forehead he put the point of his spear, between the two brows, and gave a thrust to the spear in his eye. And he had a difficult task to save himself from the broad and large loch of water that burst from it. However, the mountain shook and the cave resounded with the beating which the huge gigantic man made with his feet and his arms, as he sought for him who had done that outrage on him. And thereupon they went into their ship.[55]

Meyer's translation contains errors. One passage has Odysseus' travelling companions being swallowed by an earthquake:[56] 'And suddenly they beheld the earth

---

[53] Flower (1946: 137).   [54] See, e.g., Poppe (1995); O'Connor (2014b); Poppe (2016).

[55] K. Meyer (1999 [1886]: 3–4), which is the text of his translation cited throughout because it is available free and conveniently online at http://www.yorku.ca/inpar/ulixes_meyer.pdf (accessed 5 December 2019).

[56] R. Meyer (1952) and (1961).

bursting open under the company, so that they saw not one man of them alive.'[57] Yet, as Hillers has shown, there is no earthquake; the Irish text says that the companions are overtaken by a band of marauders.[58]

The prose text is much shorter than the *Odyssey*; it could perhaps be performed orally by a storyteller in three hours. The story is set 'after the capture and destruction of the chief city of the Trojans', when the Greek heroes 'came to their own borders and to their own sweet homeland'.[59] Ulysses, after being lost at sea with his ever-diminishing band of men, escapes from the Cyclops. On their journey home they stay at an inn. Finally, they return home, and find a beautiful young man sitting by Penelope's side. Ulysses determines to avenge himself on his wife for her perceived infidelity. He is about to strike when the queen, waking from a dream, addresses the youth with a male vocative as 'son'.[60] She tells him that she saw her husband in a dream, standing above them about to kill them. Ulysses realizes his mistake and leaves again, using the same secret route by which he came. The next day he reveals himself to Penelope, who is initially as reluctant as her Homeric counterpart to believe him. He offers tokens, but only when Ulysses' dog recognizes him is Penelope convinced. The recognition scene, in Meyer's translation, conveys the liveliness of the dialogue:

'Ye good men,' said the Queen, 'who at all are ye?' 'Ulixes the son of Laertes am I', said he. 'Thou art not the Ulixes that we knew,' said she. 'It is I in sooth,' said he; 'and I shall tell thee my tokens,' said he. And then he went into her sweet secrets and their talks together, and the things she hid in her heart. 'Where is thy form, and where are thy men,' said she, 'if thou art Ulixes?' 'They are gone to ruin', said he. 'What are the last tokens thou leftst with me?' said she. 'A golden brooch,' said he, 'and a head of silver was on it; and thy brooch I took with me when I went into the ship, and it was then thou didst turn away from us,' said Ulixes. 'That is true,' said she, 'and if thou art Ulixes, I will ask thy dog.' 'I did not expect her to be alive,' said he. 'I made her the gruel of long life, for I had seen the great love that thou didst bear her. And what sort of a dog now is she?' said she. 'Two shining white sides has she, and a light purple back and a jet-black belly, and a greenish tail,' said Ulixes. 'That is the description of the dog,' said she; 'and, moreover, no man in the place dared to give her food but myself and thee and the steward.' 'Let the dog be brought in,' said Ulixes. And four men got up for her, and brought the dog into the house. And when she heard the sound of Ulixes' voice, she gave a pull at the chain, so that she sent the four men on their back through the house behind her, and she sprang to the breast of Ulixes and licked his face and his countenance. When the people of Ulixes saw that, they sprang towards him. What man soever could not reach his skin, would kiss

[57] K. Meyer (1999 [1886]: 5).   [58] Hillers (1995). See also Hillers (2003).
[59] K. Meyer (1999 [1886]: 2).   [60] K. Meyer (1999 [1886]: 7).

his garment with many kisses. And his wife did not go to him. 'Thou art Ulixes,' said she. 'I am,' said he.[61]

Elements typical of Irish sagas are richly evidenced. For most of the *Merugud*, Ulysses wanders in the 'borderlands', a convention of the Irish storyteller.[62] He visits a tavern. There are cattle raids rather than Cattle of the Sun. When the Cyclops is blinded, waters burst out from his eye, inundating the world; bursting lakes occur in the *Dinnsenchas* and the *Annals of the Four Masters*.[63] The over-heard pillow-conversation is also paralleled elsewhere in Irish texts.[64] When Penelope thanks the gods for restoring her husband, she swears by the gods in a formula typical of Irish sagas, 'Many are the Mighty Folk'.[65] The *Merugud* also features Irish proverbs and sayings, such as Penelope's claim that she has fed the dog 'the gruel of a long life'.[66] The Irish and their literary artists have long been obsessed with their dogs,[67] which explains the upgrading of the role of the Homeric hound Argos.

The author knows the information given about Odysseus and the Cyclops in the *Aeneid*, and refers to a man who must be Achaemenides. After the Irish Ulysses has blinded the Cyclops and fled with his companions, one of his men is left behind, 'and this,' says the *Merugud*, 'was the man Aeneas son of Anchises met when he was in exile'.[68] Virgil tells us that when Aeneas reaches Sicily, the Cyclopes' home, he is met by a shipwrecked Greek who identifies himself as Achaemenides, son of Adamastus, a follower of Ulysses, and relates the encounter with Polyphemus (*Aen.* 3.588–691).

The awareness of the *Aeneid* in the *Merugud* was the main evidence used in an influential article by Heinrich Zimmer, Professor of Sanskrit and Comparative Linguistics at the University of Greifswald and soon to be founding Professor of Celtic at Friedrich Wilhelm (i.e. Humboldt) University. He urged that many trad-itional Irish tales about the returns of heroes developed only under the influence of Virgil's *Aeneid*, especially books 3–5.[69] The Irish story-type known as the *immram* does indeed depict a hero, accompanied by a few companions, who wanders and meets many 'Otherworld' wonders, before eventually returning to his native land.[70] A good example is *The Voyage of Bran, Son of Febal*, which was also edited by Meyer and published by the ardent English folklorist, Celticist, and publisher Alfred Nutt (1895–7).[71] Yet the Irish writer probably used the Irish version of the *Aeneid*, instead of or in addition to the Latin one; he may also have

---

[61] K. Meyer (1999 [1886]: 9).   [62] R. Meyer (1952: 6).   [63] R. Meyer (1952: 77).
[64] R. Meyer (1952: 77) points out that it is 'reminiscent of the famous pillow-conversation between Ailill and Medb at the opening of the great *Táin Bó Cúailnge*'.
[65] K. Meyer (1999 [1886]: 9).   [66] K. Meyer (1999 [1886]: 9).   [67] McBryde (1998).
[68] K. Meyer (1999 [1886]: 4).   [69] Zimmer (1889: 328–30).   [70] Thrall (1917).
[71] On Nutt see Wood (1999).

known the summary of the *Odyssey* Aristotle offers in his *Poetics* ch. 17, at least through a Latin intermediary.[72]

In the late eighteenth century, the history of the Irish language and literature began to attract at least esoteric interest. Some books of Homer's *Iliad* were published in translation in the 1840s. But getting the Greek classics into Irish has been a long process,[73] encouraged, in part at least, by the Aeschylus scholar George Thomson's interest in the Blasket islanders who, for Thomson, bore strong affinities with Homeric characters.[74] Thomson, whose mother was a Northern Irish Protestant with republican leanings, learned Irish. From the age of 13 in 1916, the year of the Easter Rising, onwards, he took weekly classes held by the Gaelic League while he attended school in London.[75] He was lecturer in Greek at the University of Galway between 1929 and 1934, where he published editions of Greek tragedies in Irish.[76] But the 'discovery' of the *Merugud* in the late nineteenth century corresponds exactly with the birth pangs of the Irish Republic. The *Odyssey* has played a major instrumental role in building national identities across history,[77] and when the Irish needed their own *Odyssey*, Kuno Meyer provided it.

Born in Hamburg, Meyer studied there at the Gelehrtenschule of the Johanneum, and then at the University of Leipzig, where he was taught by Ernst Windisch from 1879. He received his doctorate for his thesis *Eine irische Version der Alexandersage* (*An Irish version of the Alexander Romance*) in 1884. He then took up the post of lecturer in Teutonic languages at the new University College, Liverpool, in England—the precursor of the University of Liverpool. He continued to publish on Old Irish and other Celtic language topics, most notably the *Merugud*.[78] In 1896 he founded, and jointly edited with Ludwig Christian Stern, the prestigious *Zeitschrift für celtische Philologie*.

In 1903 Meyer arrived in Dublin to found the School of Irish Learning, and also delivered six lectures on Gaelic at Glasgow each year between 1903 and 1906.[79] In 1904 he created the journal *Ériu*, and became Todd Professor in the Celtic Languages at the Royal Irish Academy. In October 1911 he followed

---

[72] Hillers (1995).

[73] On the history of Greek tuition in Ireland see O'Higgins (2017).

[74] See Moran (Ch. 6) on Thomson's dedication to teaching Greek through Irish, along with the substantial (and often unacknowledged) efforts of Margaret Heavey; and Ní Mhurchú (Ch. 5) on the Irish translations and editions of classical texts published by Thomson and by other scholars during the early years of the Free State. For the influence of Communism on Thompson's approach to classical texts see Hall and Stead (2016).

[75] Alexiou (2000: 53).   [76] E.g. Thomson (1932a) and (1933).

[77] See Hall (2008: 9, 51) and McConnell and Hall (2016).

[78] His other publications included *The Vision of MacConglinne* (1892), *Selections from Ancient Irish Poetry* (1911), *Sanas Cormaic, an Old Irish Glossary* (1912), *Learning in Ireland in the Fifth Century* (1913), and *Über die älteste irische Dichtung* (1914).

[79] The authoritative biography of Meyer, from which I have drawn much of this information, is now Ó Lúing (1991).

Heinrich Zimmer as Professor of Celtic Philology at Friedrich Wilhelm University in Berlin; in 1912 he received several honours including a volume presented to him by pupils and friends,[80] and the Freedom of the City in both Dublin and Cork. When World War I broke out, Meyer travelled to the USA to lecture at Columbia University in New York City, and at other institutions. But his speech in support of the Germans, which he delivered in December 1914 to Clan na Gael on Long Island, sparked denunciation. He was removed from the roll of freemen in both Dublin and Cork. He was stripped of his Honorary Professorship of Celtic at Liverpool, and he resigned as Director of the School of Irish Learning and editor of *Ériu*. He became an even more controversial figure when he refused to lecture at Harvard after a satirical anti-German poem, 'Gott mit Uns', was published there in an undergraduate magazine. Disgruntled, Meyer returned to Germany in 1917, where he died two years later. Once the war was over, in 1920, he was re-elected to the Freedom of the City of Cork, on 14 May 1920.

James Joyce's Sinn Féin

The reason for including here a summary of Meyer's life is to demonstrate that it is impossible that James Joyce was unaware of him. Let us reprise the rise of Gaelic Studies, of the movement for Irish independence, and Meyer's scholarly activities, but from Joyce's perspective. The novelist was born in 1882, nine years after Robert Mitchell Henry. This was just six years after the foundation of the Society for the Preservation of the Irish Language (*Cumann Buan-Choimeádta na Gaeilge*), and in the same year as the first volume of the *Gaelic Journal* was published. Joyce was 4 years old in 1886, when Meyer published the *Merugud* and the first Irish Home Rule Bill was defeated in the British House of Commons. He was 11 in 1893, which saw the defeat of the second Home Rule Bill in the House of Lords (even though this one had been passed by the Commons) and the foundation of the Gaelic League (*Conradh na Gaeilge*). His Jesuit education took place at Clongowes Wood College in Co. Kildare and Belvedere College in central Dublin, where he read Charles and Mary Lamb's *Adventures of Ulysses* (1808).[81] Joyce studied Modern Languages, Latin, and Logic at UCD, passing his final exams in 1902. But he remained in Dublin, writing and socializing in literary circles, until September 1904;[82] he was therefore active on the Dublin literary scene throughout the entire period of Meyer's arrival. Joyce had already conceived and laid out the plan of *Ulysses* by 1907, and probably earlier;[83] it is inconceivable that he was unaware of the 'original Irish *Odyssey*' on the reading lists recommended

---

[80] Bergin and Marstrander (1912).   [81] B. Bradley (1982: 106).
[82] Stewart (2010: 25–9); Costello (1992: 185–251); Ellmann (1982: 94–179).
[83] See Costello (1992: 218).

by Gaelic Societies across Ireland. He finished writing *Ulysses* between 1914 and 1921, the period during which Meyer's star fell and the Easter Rising occurred. Excerpts of the scandalous novel were published in 1919, and Joyce finally published *Ulysses* complete in 1922, the year that Ireland became independent according to the terms of the Irish Free State Constitution Act. The colourful figure cut by Meyer, and his edition of the *Merugud*, must have informed Joyce's plan and execution of an Irish *Odyssey* at a fundamental—if now unknowable—level.

Joyce's *Ulysses* is the foundational modernist novel and one of the most influential of all time. Through following Joyce, a thousand nations and ethnic groups have produced their own novelistic *Odysseys*, as I suggested in my 2008 book *The Return of Ulysses* and in a 2016 essay collection.[84] The most obvious evidence that the *Merugud* is an important undertext of Joyce's masterpiece lies in Episode 12, 'Cyclops', most of which is set in a pub (had Joyce noticed the detail that Ulysses stays in a tavern in the *Merugud*?). Leopold Bloom, the Jewish Odysseus-figure, confronts the 'Citizen'-Cyclops, with his dog and his racist romantic nationalism, in Barney Kiernan's public house. The Citizen is a thinly disguised Michael Cusack, a historical leader of extreme nationalists, who was attempting to revive Celtic sports and literature. He believed in the need to protect the 'purity' of the superior 'Celtic race'.[85] The Cusack-Cyclops ends up smashing a cash register on Bloom's head because Bloom dares to suggest that he is as much an Irish citizen as Cusack. Joyce describes the Citizen in a string of compound epithets which recall both Homeric and medieval Irish diction, mocking the Celtic Revivalists' penchant for linking their national literature with that of the ancient Hellenes:

> So we turned into Barney Kiernan's and there sure enough there was the citizen up in the corner having a great confab with himself and that bloody mangy mongrel, Garryowen, and he waiting for what the sky would drop in the way of drink. [...]
>
> The figure seated on a large boulder at the foot of a round tower was that of a broadshouldered deepchested stronglimbed frankeyed redhaired freely freckled shaggybearded widemouthed largenosed longheaded deepvoiced barekneed brawnyhanded hairylegged ruddyfaced sinewyarmed hero. From shoulder to shoulder he measured several ells and his rocklike mountainous knees were covered, as was likewise the rest of his body wherever visible, with a strong growth of tawny prickly hair in hue and toughness similar to the mountain gorse (*Ulex Europeus*).[86]

The Citizen is the Cyclops because he is culturally monocular. He has tunnel vision and cannot see the inadequacy of his ideal of racial purity and of an Irish

---

[84] Hall (2008: 9, 51–3, 79–80); McConnell and Hall (2016).
[85] See de Búrca (1989); J. M. Bradley (2002).
[86] Joyce (1992 [1922]: 380–2).

identity based on excluding all the different cultural, linguistic, and ethnic strands of which it really consisted.[87] Joyce ironically points this out by making the Cusack-Cyclops use the metaphor of blindness himself, when lamenting what he sees as the decimation of the 'true' indigenous population of Ireland:

> There's no-one as blind as the fellow that won't see, if you know what that means. Where are our missing twenty millions of Irish should be here today instead of four, our lost tribes?[88]

Joyce sets his story on 16 June 1904, the year after Meyer had come to Dublin to found the School of Irish Learning. Portions of the novel began to appear in *The Little Review* in 1919 during the War of Independence which followed the catastrophic violence of the 1916 Easter Rising. The fighting of that time, and its root causes, are thus projected back more than a decade and filtered through Leopold's encounters that summer day in 1904. Extreme Irish nationalism is identified by Joyce as a threat to the alternative, cosmopolitan Irish identity embodied in Bloom. Yet the British Empire and its smug assumption that it was beneficial to its subject peoples all over the planet are certainly derided as well, as in this description of a bronze tankard in the pub, described in mock-heroic terms like an ekphrasis in Homer:

> Thereon embossed in excellent smithwork was seen the image of a queen of regal port, scion of the house of Brunswick, Victoria her name, Her Most Excellent Majesty, by grace of God of the United Kingdom of Great Britain and Ireland and of the British dominions beyond the sea, queen, defender of the faith, Empress of India, even she, who bore rule, a victress over many peoples, the wellbeloved, for they knew and loved her from the rising of the sun to the going down thereof, the pale, the dark, the ruddy and the ethiop.[89]

The 'Cyclops' episode also describes a meeting of international enthusiasts of Gaelic, a 'viceregal houseparty' organized by Ambassadors to greet 'the picturesque foreign delegation known as the Friends of the Emerald Isle'. The implication is that a new international hobby had been created in celebrating an Irish identity based on a fictional romantic ideal of a great Celtic Ur-race. Joyce makes dazzling sport of foreign nomenclature, concluding with the most ridiculous of all, Kriegfried Ueberallgemein, 'Warpeace Overeverythingingeneral', a German academic and 'special professor' with a ludicrously long title. His name

---

[87] Hall (2008: 92).
[88] Joyce (1992 [1922]: 423). On the Cyclops' monocularity see also Allen (2010: 22–3).
[89] Joyce (1992 [1922]: 387).

shows Joyce projecting back perceptions of Germany that had circulated more recently during World War I:

> The delegation, present in full force, consisted of Commendatore Bacibaci Beninobenone (the semi-paralysed *doyen* of the party who had to be assisted to his seat by the aid of a powerful steam crane), Monsieur Pierrepaul Petitépatant, the Grandjoker Vladinmire Pokethankertscheff, the Archjoker Leopold Rudolph von Schwanzenbad-Hodenthaler, Countess Marha Virága Kisászony Putrápesthi, Hiram Y. Bomboost, Count Athanatos Karamelopulos, Ali Baba Backsheesh Rahat Lokum Effendi, Señor Hidalgo Caballero Don Pecadillo y Palabras y Paternoster de la Malora de la Malaria, Hokopoko Harakiri, Hi Hung Chang, Olaf Kobberkeddelsen, Mynheer Trik van Trumps, Pan Poleaxe Paddyrisky, Goosepond Prhklstr Kratchinabritchisitch, Herr Hurhausdirektorpräsident Hans Chuechli-Steuerli, Nationalgymnasiummuse-umsanatoriumandsuspensoriumsordinaryprivatdocentgeneralhistoryspecial-professordoctor Kriegfried Ueberallgemein.[90]

Kuno Meyer lurks beneath Kriegfried Ueberallgemein. The ancient Irish wolf-hound Garryowen in Episode 12 further supports this. Joyce plays on the aural similarity of Kuno and *kuōn*, the ancient Greek for 'dog'—one that, as it turns out, can speak/bark in medieval Gaelic:

> Then he starts hauling and mauling and talking to him in Irish and the old towser growling, letting on to answer, like a duet in the opera. [...]
> All those who are interested in the spread of human culture among the lower animals (and their name is legion) should make a point of not missing the really marvellous exhibition of cynanthropy given by the famous old Irish red wolfdog setter [...] The exhibition, which is the result of years of training by kindness and a carefully thoughtout dietary system, comprises, among other achieve-ments, the recitation of verse. Our greatest living phonetic expert (wild horses shall not drag it from us!) has left no stone unturned in his efforts to delucidate and compare the verse recited and has found it bears a *striking* resemblance (the italics are ours) to the ranns of ancient Celtic bards. [...] We subjoin a specimen which has been rendered into English by an eminent scholar whose name for the moment we are not at liberty to disclose though we believe that our readers will find the topical allusion rather more than an indication. The metrical sys-tem of the canine original, which recalls the intricate alliterative and isosyllabic rules of the Welsh englyn, is infinitely more complicated but we believe our readers will agree that the spirit has been well caught. Perhaps it should be added

---

[90] Joyce (1992 [1922]: 397–8).

that the effect is greatly increased if Owen's verse be spoken somewhat slowly and indistinctly in a tone suggestive of suppressed rancour.[91]

There could be no noisier reference to the world-famous scholar than Joyce's reassurance that although 'we are not at liberty to disclose' his name, 'we believe that our readers will find the topical allusion rather more than an indication.'

Joyce's views on the Gaelic Revival were conflicted, oscillating between genuine sorrow for the linguistic dispossession of his compatriots and an impatience with the narrow-minded nationalism that so often accompanied attempts to revive the Gaelic language and ancient traditions. In the surviving early sections of *Stephen Hero*, which later became *Portrait of the Artist as a Young Man*, the protagonist Stephen Dedalus (an autobiographical avatar of the young Joyce himself) is ambivalent about Gaelic.[92] He quarrels with a university friend, McCann, who insists that a free Irish nation requires the revitalization of Gaelic. Dedalus does go to study Irish at classes run by the Gaelic League, but only because he is chasing a particular woman. He does not pay the fees; he cracks jokes at the expense of the founder of the League, Michael Cusack, who reappears in *Ulysses*. In *Dubliners* the most cheerful story, 'After the Race', depicts a happy fusion of French, American, English, Italian, and Irish men mingling to drink together. Yet Joyce knew far more Gaelic than he liked to admit,[93] and in later versions of *Stephen Hero* left out some cutting remarks about the nationalists' campaign for the restoration of the Irish language. He even added sad reflections on the 'curious state of linguistic dispossession that marks the Irish experience'.[94] Like Henry, he was an avid reader of the short-lived weekly newspaper *United Irishman*, which combined politics with high-quality cultural and literary discussions, and which he had sent to him every week even after he left for the Continent.[95]

Modern Ireland, when in 1922 it emerged from its distressing history of imperial subjection and cultural-linguistic dislocation, needed its own foundational version of the *Odyssey*, and Joyce's dazzling novel, with its exploration of the thrilling polyphony of Dublin life, was there to fulfil the need. But if it had not been for the *Merugud*, the medieval Irish *Odyssey*, and the celebrated scholar Kuno Meyer, who had brought it to Irish and international consciousness a quarter of a century before, Joyce might never even have chosen the Homeric, Greek *Odyssey* as his *Ur*-text in the first place.

---

[91] Joyce (1992 [1922]: 403–4).
[92] On the crucible of international and national cultures to which Joyce and his avatar Stephen expose themselves as students in this text see Prescott (1954).
[93] Tymoczko (1992).   [94] Sayers (2012).
[95] Tymoczko (1992: 765); on the courage and importance of this newspaper see Henry (1920: 58–78).

Conclusion

The turbulent events in Ireland in 1916 were filtered through minds trained in classical literature in different ways. Among classical scholars, the contribution to the struggle and its analysis made personally and intellectually by Professor Robert Mitchell Henry is unparalleled. But his conviction that Ireland belonged to all its residents, regardless of ethnic origin, was shared by James Joyce and informs *Ulysses* at every level. Some will prefer the Protestant Latin professor's serious, Tacitean, historiographic annals of British imperial misconduct against the ideals of Sinn Féin, written from the perspective of an eyewitness and member of the I.V. Others may begin with the Catholic Joyce's use of Greek myth, refracted from the safety of Continental Europe through a medieval Irish prism, to satirize Sinn Féin. But a fuller understanding of those tumultuous years can be gained from reading both together.

11

Yeats and Oedipus

The Dark Road

Chris Morash

Forbidden in London

Speaking ahead of a BBC Radio Belfast broadcast of his translation of Sophocles' *Oedipus the King* on 8 September 1931, W. B. Yeats told his listeners:

> Nearly thirty years ago I was at the Catholic University of Notre Dame in Illinois. I had come there to give a lecture about Irish literature and stayed for a couple of days. A certain monk, specially appointed I think to look after the guests, was the best of companions and told me a great many exciting things about his monastery, about the Irish in America, and about his own thoughts. The thing that stayed longest in my memory was that 'Oedipus the King' had just been performed under the auspices of the university.[1]

As ever with Yeats, this recollection of his visit to the US in January 1904 is both gloriously unreliable and richly suggestive. Notre Dame is not actually in Illinois (it is in Indiana), nor is it a monastery; and the 'monk' who was his host was the Rev. John W. Cavanaugh CSC, who would become President of the University the following year. However, his memory of a Notre Dame production of *Oedipus Tyrannus* was accurate, for the play had been staged on campus five years earlier, on 15 May 1899. This means that (in a coincidence of which Yeats seems unaware), it took place within a week of the first production of the Irish Literary Theatre in Dublin, Yeats's *The Countess Cathleen*. Yeats's play resulted in a minor theatre riot. By contrast, the college newspaper, the *Scholastic*, heralded the production of *Oedipus* as 'the greatest dramatic event that occurred at Notre Dame in many years'. Its director, the Rev. Nicholas J. Stoffel, had previously directed a production of *Antigone* in 1883, and an earlier *Oedipus* in 1882 (both, like the 1899 production, in the original Greek), and had only been thwarted from producing what would have been the first Greek tragedy performed in the original language

---

[1] Yeats (1931a: 1).

Chris Morash, *Yeats and Oedipus: The Dark Road* In: *Classics and Irish Politics, 1916–2016*. Edited by: Isabelle Torrance and Donncha O'Rourke, Oxford University Press (2020). © Oxford University Press.
DOI: 10.1093/oso/9780198864486.003.0011

in North America in 1879 when the Notre Dame university hall burned down, allowing Harvard to claim that particular distinction in 1881.[2] Far from provoking clerical ire or protests, then, the 1899 *Oedipus* in Notre Dame was attended by one of the most senior figures in the Catholic Church in America at the time, the Apostolic Delegate, the Most Rev. Sebastian Martinelli, who was welcomed with an address in Latin. *The Scholastic* devoted a half page to the names of distinguished guests in the audience, from senior clergy to academics, politicians, and journalists, who joined him to enjoy Sophocles' tale of incest and parricide. In short, it would be difficult to imagine an event in which the inherent respectability of classical culture trumped its potentially disturbing content more resoundingly.

'Yeats was an inexhaustible source of delight,' his host, John Cavanaugh, later recalled, finding great amusement in the fact that the famous poet kept forgetting things, such as his hat, notes for a lecture, and, when finally driving off from the campus, his false teeth.[3] Yeats did not forget Cavanaugh's account of *Oedipus*, however; and for Yeats, the details were always going to be less important than the ways in which people, events, and places could be simultaneously specific and symbolic. This would be true not only of the major people, events, and places in his life—Synge, the 1916 Rising, or Thoor Ballylee—all of which acquired densely woven symbolic values, while remaining concrete and specific; it was equally true of people and places he met along the way, who were almost inevitably woven into the fabric of his personal mythology, while at the same time retaining their specificity. And so, for Yeats, Notre Dame would become the locus for a vortex of ideas that were already forming for him in 1904 around Greek theatre, Sophocles, and Oedipus; and which over the next thirty years would spin out to include some of his most challenging and foundational political, aesthetic, and philosophical ideas.

When Yeats visited America in late 1903 and early 1904, the outlines of those ideas were already coalescing. The *Notre Dame Scholastic* reports that in the course of his three-day visit, he gave versions of what were his stump speeches for the tour. In his first talk, he told his listeners (according to the *Scholastic*) that 'in earlier centuries the rich and poor, noble and humble, shared a culture not born of books but of stories and traditions. In those days culture was the priceless treasure of the many. It was like a pyramid, having its foundations in the minds of the people. Now all this was changed; the pyramid was turned upside down.'[4] This idea was, of course, already a recurrent thread in Yeats's writing by 1904, and it would persist throughout his life. Indeed, in the 1931 BBC broadcast, he would claim that 'Greek literature came like old Irish literature out of the belief of the

---

[2] 'Editorial' and 'The Greek Play', both in *Notre Dame Scholastic* 32 (1899: 558 and 559–64, respectively).
[3] Schmuhl (2011–12: 2).   [4] MacDonough (1904: 276).

common people'.[5] In his final lecture in Notre Dame in 1904, speaking on 'The Modern Stage', Yeats returned to this idealized notion of an 'equality of culture' that had existed in the time of Sophocles. 'He said that the theatre of to-day had deteriorated,' reported the *Scholastic*. 'It had tied itself to the mob.'[6] Again, this was not new territory for him. In the Irish Literary Theatre's first journal, *Beltaine*, in 1899, Yeats had contrasted modern theatre with that of classical Greece, which, he claimed, by valuing language over scenery, 'needed some imagination, some gift for day-dreams, to see the horses and the fields and flowers of Colonus as one listened to the elders gathered around Œdipus'.[7] Again, this understanding of the audience as the key to the theatrical event would become a fixed cornerstone in Yeats's understanding of theatre, so much so that in *On the Boiler* (1938), written in his final year, he would once again ask, 'Why has the audience deteriorated?', again contrasting the theatre culture of classical Greece with modern theatre, to the latter's detriment.[8]

From the time Yeats arrived back in Ireland later in 1904, through to his final visit to the US in 1933 (when he would once again regale a *New York Times* reporter with an account of the Notre Dame *Oedipus*),[9] he would make use in his own political battles of that disjunction between the inherent respectability of classical culture, and the raw strangeness of the Oedipus story. Put in its simplest terms, Yeats was engaged in a delicate balancing act that, on the one hand, involved laying claim to a collective national (and hence politicized) tradition that channelled the traditions of 'the people'; and, at the same time, insisted on the uncompromising moral autonomy of the aesthetic, strenuously resisting any calls for an art bound by politics or religion. It would be a war of many skirmishes, fought on multiple fronts. Indeed, shortly before he left for the American tour that brought him to Notre Dame in 1904, Yeats had locked horns with Maud Gonne and James Connolly in the pages of Arthur Griffith's *United Irishman* in a debate occasioned by the premiere of Synge's *In the Shadow of the Glen* on 17 October 1903, which had been denounced in the nationalist press for the immorality of an Ibsenesque situation in which a wife decides to leave her husband. 'If Ireland were self-governed, self-centred in speech and thought,' declared Connolly, '*then* our dramatists might choose their field of action from China to Peru, and our national dramatic literature would be none the poorer.'[10] Yeats responded with what would be a foundational statement for him not just on the definition of a national theatre, but on the autonomy of the aesthetic: 'That theatre where the capricious spirit that bloweth as it listeth has for a moment found a dwelling-place, has a good right to call itself a National Theatre.'[11]

[5] Yeats (1931a: 1).   [6] MacDonough (1904: 276–7).   [7] Yeats (1899: 150–1).
[8] Yeats (1938: 254).   [9] Yeats (1933: 244–5).
[10] Connolly (1903: 2).   [11] Yeats (1903: 35).

One strategic way in which Yeats could resist pressure to produce art in the service of the national cause (particularly art that pandered to the growing influence of Catholic social teaching in the nationalist movement) was to denounce the one form of censorship that no Irish nationalist could support: English censorship. 'In England there is a censor,' he informed readers of *Samhain* in 1904, 'who forbids you to take a subject from the Bible, or from politics, or to picture public characters, or certain moral situations which are the foundations of the greatest plays in the world.' In contrast to what he calls 'British puritanism', Yeats told his readers: 'When I was in the great American Catholic University of Notre Dame I heard that the students had given a performance of *Oedipus the King*, and *Oedipus the King* is forbidden in London.'[12] At a stroke, the Notre Dame *Oedipus* allowed Yeats to stake his claim to artistic freedom and to fend off his Irish nationalist critics. He accomplished the former by attacking censorship as being British (and hence, in the crude political mathematics of the day, fundamentally anti-Irish). And, in the same gesture, he was able to take a not-so-subtle swipe at Irish Catholic attitudes by making censorship—in one of those audacious historical reversals at which Yeats was so adept—appear to be at odds with the more sophisticated understanding of Catholic dogma to be found in 'the great American Catholic University'.

The next logical step in this campaign was to perform *Oedipus* in Dublin, taking advantage of a legal loophole in theatre legislation extending back to the eighteenth century, which meant that the Lord Chamberlain's writ did not extend to Ireland. So, not long after he returned from Notre Dame, Yeats approached both Oliver St John Gogarty and Gilbert Murray to write translations, with a view to staging the play at the Abbey. 'Will you translate Edipus [*sic*] Rex for us?' he asked Murray. 'Our company are excited at the idea. [...] When we have performed Edipus the King, and everybody is proud of having done something which is forbidden in England, even the newspapers will give [up] pretending to be timid.'[13] Murray and Gogarty both dropped out of the project (Gogarty declaring that he had 'lost interest in the Yeats Theatre. The Art is bad, real bad').[14] Undeterred, Yeats announced a forthcoming Abbey production of *Oedipus* in the 1906 issue of *The Arrow*, the Abbey's in-house journal; but nothing came of it. His interest in the project only really reignited in 1909 when the Lord Chamberlain's Office fell into Bernard Shaw's carefully baited trap by banning his 'sermon in the form of crude melodrama', *The Shewing Up of Blanco Posnet*. Set on a stage version of the Wild West, Shaw's play is a studiously moral tale about a reformed drunkard risking his life to save a sick child, in which the protagonist just happens to curse God—'He's a sly one,' Blanco says at one point. 'He's a mean one.'[15] The Lord Chamberlain could not possibly condone a play that called God 'a sly

---

[12] Yeats (1904a: 45).   [13] Cited in Clark and Maguire (1989: 8).
[14] Clark and Maguire (1989: 11).   [15] Shaw (1970–4: v3, 774).

one', no matter how morally uplifting its narrative, and banned it from the British stage on grounds of blasphemy.

Yeats and Lady Gregory immediately announced a production of Shaw's play for the busiest week of the theatre year—Dublin Horse Show Week, in August— provoking a showdown with the Lord Lieutenant. 'If our patent is in danger,' Yeats and Lady Gregory declared in a public statement on 22 August 1909, 'it is because the decisions of the English Censor are being brought into Ireland.' This forcibly recruited to the Abbey's cause Catholic nationalists who had opposed Synge's *Playboy*. 'Whatever our opinions as to the general policy of the Abbey Theatre,' admitted an outmanoeuvred Patrick Pearse in *An Claidheamh Soluis*, 'we are bound to stand by the Theatre in its fight against the imposition of a British Censorship.'[16] 'We had an exciting week in Dublin with *Blanco Posnet* and our fight with the Castle,' Yeats wrote to Herbert Grierson in Scotland, showing his usual enthusiasm for a fight. 'It has ended our quarrel with the extreme party over *Playboy*.'[17] Meanwhile, in heated behind-the-scenes negotiations with a Lord Lieutenant, the Earl of Aberdeen, who did not want this particular battle, Yeats was upping the ante. 'Yeats said that we intended to do *Oedipus*,' Lady Gregory noted in her journal for 13 August 1909, 'that this is also a censored play [in England], although so unobjectionable to religious minds that it had been performed in the Catholic University of Nôtre Dame.'

The threat of a Shaw/Sophocles double bill convinced Aberdeen to back down, and *Blanco Posnet* was performed in November of 1909; but not before Yeats resolved to do his own translation of *Oedipus* (or, more precisely, his own version, since he had no Greek). To this end, he ordered for himself a copy of R. C. Jebb's translation of the play, which had been used in a private performance in Cambridge in November of 1887. It also helped that, although Jebb himself was born in Dundee, his family had Irish roots as tangled as those of the Yeats family. So, although Yeats would later claim that he worked with multiple translations, the copy of Jebb's *Oedipus* in Yeats's library is the only one for which there is any substantial evidence of use. At the same time, he wanted something quite differ- ent from Jebb's version. From the outset, Yeats was clear that what was needed was an acting script, with lines meant to be spoken, even if that meant sacrificing accuracy of translation. 'Something had to be done,' he wrote to A. H. Bullen, 'for the existing translations won't speak.'[18] To this end, he made a conscious decision to work primarily with theatre people, not Greek scholars. In the summer of 1911, he began workshopping the play with the director Nugent Monck (who was associated with the Abbey) and a small team of actors. He later described this process: 'I spoke out every sentence, very often from the stage, with one sole object, that the words should sound natural and fall in their natural order [...].'[19]

---

[16]   Pearse (1909: 9–10).   [17]   Wade (1954: 536–7).
[18]   Clark and Maguire (1989: 22).   [19]   Yeats (1933: 245).

At the same time, he was also talking to Edward Gordon Craig about the possibility of using Craig's moveable scenery for the Abbey production, writing to Lady Gregory in December of 1911 that they had 'had in a man with a magic lantern & made all sorts of experiments'.[20] By early 1912, armed with his marked-up Jebb and the fruits of his experiments, Yeats finally set to work on his own acting edition of *Oedipus the King*.

However, at that point the Lord Chamberlain's Office lifted its ban on the play in England, which allowed Max Reinhardt to bring a version of his acclaimed 1910 production from the Zirkus Schumann in Berlin to Covent Garden. Yeats saw Reinhardt's production late in January 1912—'the most imaginative production of a play I have ever seen,' he wrote to Lady Gregory, not without some despondency[21]—and promptly lost interest in doing his own *Oedipus*. With the play no longer banned in England, its strategic value in Ireland was gone; and it was also highly unlikely that the Abbey's relatively meagre scenographic resources were going to match Reinhardt's oceans of moving bodies. In addition, Yeats's attention was being drawn elsewhere in those years. He would spend the winter of 1913–14 in Stone Cottage with Ezra Pound, where he became fascinated with a classical theatre of a different kind entirely, the Japanese Noh, which would result in one of his most productive periods as a playwright, during which he wrote the works that became *Plays for Dancers*.[22] The period from 1912 until 1925 would also be the period in which increasingly his energy would be drawn into the exhausting creative maelstrom that produced *A Vision*. It was only after *A Vision* was published in 1925 that Yeats returned to Sophocles, later telling *The Irish Weekly and Ulster Examiner* at the time of the Belfast broadcast that he had placed earlier drafts of his *Oedipus* translation 'into the file with my letters and forgot it, and then four or five years ago my wife found it and persuaded me to finish it and put it on the Abbey stage'.[23]

Battling the Obscurantists

As with his account of the Notre Dame production, there was more to the story than this charming domestic scene might suggest. As early as the spring of 1924, elements within the Catholic Church in the newly independent Ireland were advancing an agenda of Catholic social teaching by taking aim at 'offenders against our standard of public decency',[24] to use the words of a Lenten Pastoral read simultaneously that year by the Bishops of Dublin, Galway, Tuam, and Clogher.

---

[20] Clark and Maguire (1989: 21).   [21] Clark and Maguire (1989: 33).
[22] On Yeats, Pound, and the Classics see also O'Rourke (Ch. 15).
[23] Clark and Maguire (1989: 34).
[24] O'Reilly (1926: 20), entitled *The Problem of Undesirable Printed Matter*.

'Indecency is indecency,' thundered one of the most prominent campaigners for literary censorship, Fr Richard Devane, SJ, 'even though the cunning hand of some degenerate artist pretends to hide its nakedness under the transparencies of a seductive style.'[25] As Lauren Arrington has shown in her book on Yeats and censorship, Yeats's public skirmishes in the years before and after the Censorship of Publications Act in 1929 would pick up where his battles over Synge's *Playboy* and the Hugh Lane bequest left off.[26] By the mid-1920s, however, Yeats had refined his understanding of the value of classical culture in these struggles. In August of 1924 he published 'Leda and the Swan' (like *Oedipus*, a work that combines an impeccably respectable classical source with content guaranteed to run afoul of the censor) in the inaugural issue of *To-morrow*, a journal started by Francis Stuart and Cecil Salkeld. Yeats also wrote an anonymous editorial for that same issue, which gives us a flavour of his provocation: 'we can forgive the sinner, but abhor the atheist, and that we count among atheists bad writers and Bishops of all denominations.'[27] To that first issue of *To-morrow* Yeats's friend and fellow Abbey director, Lennox Robinson, also contributed a story entitled 'The Madonna of Slieve Dun'; and while Yeats escaped relatively unscathed, Robinson's story was deemed blasphemous, and he was ultimately forced to resign from his work with the Carnegie Libraries. 'It's a complete victory for the obscurantists,' Robinson wrote ruefully to Lady Gregory, 'but only a temporary one I think.'[28]

Yeats had no intention of allowing 'the obscurantists' even a temporary victory. Over the course of 1924 and 1925, the campaign to introduce print censorship picked up pace, the term 'evil literature' began to gain currency, and by the end of the year the Cumann na nGaedheal government was promising action. On 12 February 1926, the Minister for Justice, Kevin O'Higgins, announced in the Dáil the creation of a 'Committee on Evil Literature', a body whose very name already decided the question as to whether literature could, in fact, be evil. The Committee was charged with reporting to the Dáil 'whether it was necessary or advisable, in the interests of public morality, to extend the existing powers of the State to prohibit or restrict the sale and circulation of printed matter.'[29] The night before the announcement, O'Higgins' republican adversaries from the Civil War had rioted in the Abbey in protest against Sean O'Casey's *The Plough and the Stars*, famously prompting Yeats's speech from the stage in which he told the audience: 'You have disgraced yourselves again.'[30] For the rest of the week, attacks on O'Casey's play were mingled with calls for literary censorship, and Yeats waded into the controversy with the same brio that he had shown nineteen years earlier at the time of the *Playboy of the Western World* riots. A little over a week later, on

---

[25] Devane (1925:16).   [26] Arrington (2010).
[27] Yeats (1924: 1).   [28] Robinson (1924: n.p.).
[29] *The Irish Times* (13 Feb. 1926: 7): 'Evil Literature: Committee of Inquiry Set Up'.
[30] Hunt (1979: 128–9).

21 February 1926, Yeats wrote to Herbert Grierson that he had started 'writing the material [presumably "metrical"] version of a chorus for a version of *Oedipus* intended for the stage'.[31]

In other words, Yeats's decision to complete what became *Sophocles' King Oedipus*, and to stage it at the Abbey Theatre in 1926, was made during a crucial week in the battle over Irish literary censorship. Lest there be any doubt about the matter, when Yeats's Sophocles translation finally made it to the Abbey stage in December 1926, the curtain raiser was Shaw's *The Shewing Up of Blanco Posnet*, which has nothing in common with Sophocles' *Oedipus* other than the fact that both had once been banned in England, and Yeats had previously threatened the Earl of Aberdeen that he would put them on the same bill back in 1909. Likewise, while the decision to have Lennox Robinson direct is not itself remarkable—he was responsible for more than fifty productions in the decade 1920–30 alone—no one would have had to explain to Robinson that successful productions of the two plays could be an effective blow against 'the obscurantists'. 'My version of *Oedipus* comes on to-night,' Yeats wrote to Olivia Shakespear before the curtain went up on the opening, 7 December 1926, '[...] but how will the Catholics take it?'[32]

Reading Yeats's *Oedipus* in this context helps explain why Yeats wrote the sort of play he did. If Yeats's censor-baiting were to work, the play had to first provoke an outcry from the 'obscurantists' (because everyone knew it dealt with incest and parricide); and then it had to sweep aside that outcry in the applause of the audience (because it worked as theatre). Yeats knew from the outset that the play must be 'simple enough and resonant enough to be instantaneously felt and understood [...] something that everybody in the house, scholar or potboy, would understand as easily as he understood a political speech or an article in a newspaper'.[33] One of the first things Yeats did to achieve this, as Robert Tracy has pointed out, was strategic, but counter-intuitive;[34] he toned down some of the passages that seemed to visualize most clearly Oedipus in the same bed with his mother, such as a line that refers to 'the monstrous marriage wherein begetter and begotten have long been one',[35] which is heavily scored out in Yeats's copy of the R. C. Jebb translation from which he worked. That copy of Jebb's translation in Yeats's library also shows Yeats vigorously crossing out some of Jebb's bloodier passages from an early phase of his work on the script before 1912:

[...] ~~not once alone, but oft struck he his eyes with lifted hand, and at each blow the ensanguined eye-balls bedewed his beard, nor sent forth sluggish drops of gore, but all at once a dark shower of blood came down like hail.~~[36]

[31] Wade (1954: 710).   [32] Wade (1954: 720).   [33] Yeats (1931a: 219).
[34] Tracy (1993: 116–28).   [35] Jebb (1887b: 98).   [36] Jebb (1887b: 104).

Not that Yeats was shy about sex and violence, particularly by the mid-1920s; in this case, however, thwarting some of the audience's expectations of gratuitous gore would seem to have been part of a plan to make literary censorship seem ridiculous.

More importantly, however, going back to his workshops with Nugent Monck in 1911, Yeats wanted to write words that actors could speak. So, where Jebb's translation of *Oedipus Tyrannus* has the kind of Latinate syntax and King James diction that seemed obligatory in Victorian translations of classical Greek tragedy, Yeats rejected this out of hand. 'I think that those great scholars of the last century who translated Sophocles into an English full of Latinised constructions and Latinised habits of thought, were all wrong,' he told his radio audience in 1931. Instead, Yeats's version of *Oedipus* has the kind of clear, forceful syntax that we might expect of 'A version for the modern stage'. 'I think my shaping of the speech will prove powerful on the stage,' he wrote in that same opening night letter to Olivia Shakespear, 'for I have made it bare, hard and natural like a saga.'[37] The result is, as Fiona Macintosh has argued, 'lithe and supple like a well-tuned athlete; capable of flexibility as well as taut muscular contraction'.[38] Macintosh points to technical features of the writing that make Yeats's such an effective acting script, above and beyond getting rid of the 'thees' and 'thous'. For instance, in contrast to Jebb's translation, Yeats favours short sentences, active verbs, and, on occasion, the precise, metaphorical word that replaces a whole clause: so, where Jebb writes: 'the city, as thou thyself seest, is now too sorely vexed,' Yeats turns this to: 'the city stumbles towards death.'[39]

'The one thing I kept in mind was that a word unfitted for living speech, out of its natural order, or unnecessary to our modern technique, would check emotion and tire attention,' Yeats wrote in his brief introduction to the published text in 1928.[40] He also made sure, in more subtle ways, that the play would resonate for an Irish audience, *albeit* the Irish audience that Yeats had been imagining for three decades. 'Before the modern movement,' he wrote in *Samhain* in 1904, 'the ordinary man, whether he could read and write or not, was ready to welcome great literature.'[41] In the 1930s, Yeats still clung to this idea of an audience of 'zealous bricklayers and clerks and the odd corner boy or two'[42] (as he had described Abbey audiences to Gordon Craig in 1902) who instinctively understood great art. So, with his translation of *Oedipus*, as he later told *The New York Times*, 'I went through it all, altering every sentence that might not be intelligible on the Blasket Islands.'[43] For instance, his early experience with *The Countess Cathleen* in 1899 would have taught him that even a passing evocation of the Irish Famine produced a strong response from Irish audiences. Accordingly, in Yeats's 1926

---

[37] Wade (1954: 720).   [38] Macintosh (2008: 524–47).   [39] Macintosh (2008: 534–5).
[40] Yeats (1928: v).   [41] Yeats (1904b: 59).   [42] Kelly and Schuchard (1994: 258).
[43] Yeats (1933: 537).

manuscripts we find him searching for ways in the first chorus to condense an image that will evoke a memory of Irish famine:

> ~~The season brings no good thing round~~
> ~~The crops all rot~~ away
> ~~We die of Famine & of Death* the crops rot and fall~~
> ~~And~~
> ~~We die of plague plague~~
> ~~If plag~~
> Those that plague spares the famine takes for all
> the crops are lost.
> ~~No new life wakes~~
> ~~Old life dies out~~
> No new life comes to take the place of old
> ghost after ghost
> ~~Flit~~ to the god-trodden western shore ~~even as d~~
> even as flit the birds[44]

In the published text, this becomes:

> Famine takes what the plague spares, and all the crops are lost;
> No new life fills the empty place – ghost flits after ghost
> To that god-trodden western shore, as flit the benighted birds.[45]

Here we see Yeats going beyond simply reshaping Jebb's earlier translation, trusting to an imagined Irish audience's collective memories of the Famine (even if, by 1926, those memories were heavily mediated) to produce something like that communal experience he believed had been lost in contemporary theatre. Here, he is less concerned with being true to the Greek original than he is with creating a contemporary Irish version of the bond between performers and audience that he imagined in the Athens of the fifth century BCE. The text condenses a set of images—rotting crops, empty cottages, the abandoned landscape of the 'western shore'—into the kind of terse poetic diction that Yeats had mastered by the mid-1920s. We recognize this idiom from the poems in *The Tower*, for instance, so that dextrous repetition, alliteration, assonance, and hard final consonants make the lines seem like something from a half-remembered song: 'ghost'/'ghost'/'god'; 'fill'/'flit'/'flit'; or in the sparse, unexpected adjectives: 'god-trodden'; 'benighted' (what makes a shore 'god-trodden'? does a 'benighted' bird fly at night, or is it

---

[44] Yeats (1926a: 3).   [45] Yeats (1928: 5–6).

cursed?); and, finally, we have the whole structure held together with tight, simple, syntax. This is, in short, instantly recognizable late Yeats.

On the envelope of his opening night letter to Olivia Shakespear, Yeats scribbled the lines: 'Oedipus great success. Critics and audience enthusiastic.'[46] The Irish Times called Oedipus 'the most powerful thing that the Abbey Theatre ever staged'.[47] Even the Irish Independent (not a paper notably sympathetic to Yeats or to the Abbey at the time) headed its review 'Enthusiasm at Abbey', itself enthusing about the 'spell that last night held us in thrall'.[48] Interest was not confined to Ireland. The New York Times, in a review reprinted on the cover of the 1928 Macmillan edition, was equally effusive: 'One does not expect to see an audience, drawn from all ranks of life, crowding a Theatre beyond its capacity and becoming awed into spellbound, breathless attention by a tragedy of Sophocles.'[49] Already at work on his translation of Oedipus at Colonus while these glowing notices flowed in, and simultaneously starting work on what would be an abandoned translation of Antigone, Yeats wrote to Lady Gregory on 18 December 1926: 'I feel that these three closely united plays put into simple speakable prose may be my contribution to the Abbey Repertory.'[50] This was prescient, for Yeats's Oedipus was to have a durable stage afterlife. For instance, as Fiona Macintosh reminds us, Laurence Olivier chose Yeats's version of Oedipus for his acclaimed 1945 Old Vic production, as did Tyrone Guthrie for his 1956 film. In the early 2000s, there were rumours that Al Pacino was working on a production in New York; it never came to pass, but the text he used in rehearsals was Yeats's.[51] In each case, the theatrical attraction was not Yeats, but the actor/director—Olivier, Guthrie, Pacino; Yeats had simply provided the most effective stage version for their respective purposes.

The Dark Road

By the 1920s, however, the association of Oedipus with a particular version of Christianity (which he seems to have associated with the 1899 production in Notre Dame) was taking on a new significance for Yeats, one that went far beyond local battles over censorship. In one of his sallies against Catholic arguments for literary censorship, in an article in The Irish Statesman in 1928, Yeats maintained that the views circulating in Ireland at the time ran counter to the thought of St Thomas Aquinas, for whom, Yeats claimed, 'the soul is wholly present within the body', and thus the body was to be celebrated. There was, for Yeats, a Catholicism other than that he saw around him in the Ireland of the 1920s, a Church of the

[46]   Wade (1954: 720).
[47]   The Irish Times (8 December 1926: 6): 'Oedipus the King: Sophocles at the Abbey Theatre'.
[48]   Irish Independent (8 December 1926: 6): 'Enthusiasm at Abbey'.
[49]   Yeats (1928: front jacket).   [50]   Yeats (1926b: n.p.).   [51]   Macintosh (2008: 524–5).

high Medieval and Renaissance period that could accommodate the body, and which had given rise to 'an art of the body', capable of producing images of the Virgin Mary 'so natural that nobody complained when Andrea del Sarto chose for his model his wife, or Raphael his mistress'.[52] At the same, Yeats had begun to believe that it was precisely this western world of embodied belief that was dying in 1928; and, for Yeats, this was a matter on an entirely different scale than the impending Irish censorship legislation.

In some respects, the Yeats who used his production of *Oedipus* as a weapon in the struggle against Irish literary censorship was Yeats the senator, the 'sixty-year-old smiling [or sometimes not-so-smiling] public man', as he imagines himself in 'Among School Children'. It is worth recalling here that 'Among School Children' first appears in Yeats's notebooks in March of 1926, and the first full draft is dated 14 June 1926, which means that he was writing the poem at the same time as he was translating *Oedipus the King*.[53] It is possible, then, to read 'Among School Children' at least partly as a reflection of Yeats's immersion in Sophocles and classical culture, particularly when the poem abruptly shifts register in its second stanza, turning inward, away from the public face of the poet towards what Yeats calls 'the dream': 'I dream of a Ledean body, bent | Above a sinking fire [...].'[54] Here and elsewhere in his writing, the 'dream' for Yeats is the thing that only poetry can approach, that which escapes the public languages of politics and strategy. To put it simply, running contrary to, but necessarily bound up with, the public uses of Sophocles for Yeats, there is a very different Yeatsian Sophocles, far removed from the politics of the day. This is the Sophocles that we glimpse in that opening night letter to Olivia Shakespear of 1926, in which he tells her that when watching rehearsals of *Oedipus*, he experienced 'but one overwhelming emotion, a sense as of the actual presence in a terrible sacrament of the god. But I have got that always, though never before so strongly, from Greek Drama.'[55]

This sense of the ritual power of Greek tragedy—and of Sophocles in particular—was a part of Yeats' conceptual world from very early in his development as a theatre artist. In the first issue of *Beltaine*, from 1899, he writes that 'the audiences of Sophocles and of Shakespeare and of Calderon were not unlike the audiences I have heard listening in Irish cabins to songs in Gaelic about "an old poet telling his sins"'.[56] The idea that Sophocles existed in a moment that was historically analogous to his own in Ireland in the early twentieth century appears repeatedly in Yeats' writings over the ensuing decades, so that it was more reflex than reflection to tell his BBC listeners in 1931 that 'when Oedipus takes refuge in a wood beside the road [in *Oedipus at Colonus*] it is just such a wood as blind Raftery might have found, for it is sacred to certain spirits called Eumenides which means

[52] Yeats (1928: 47–8).   [53] Finneran et al. (2007: 360/1, 372/3).   [54] Yeats (1957: 441).
[55] Wade (1954: 720).   [56] Yeats (1899: 148).

Good People'. He goes on to take the analogy further: 'Greek literature, like old Irish literature, was founded upon belief.'[57] As he put it a few years earlier when speaking to *The New York Times* in 1931: 'Men have trembled on dark roads in Ireland and in Greece.'[58]

By 1931, Yeats's 'dark road' had taken some very strange and dark turnings indeed. 'The other day Lady Gregory said to me,' he wrote in 1928: ' "You are a much better educated man than you were ten years ago." '[59] Yeats was not only an autodidact, but an idiosyncratic autodidact, with an uncanny ability to absorb and to selectively make his own whatever he read; regardless of what he read, it all came out Yeats-shaped. This was never more true at any point in his life than during the period when he first put aside his attempt at a version of *Oedipus* in 1912, and when he picked it up again in 1926—the years during which he was working on *A Vision*. Although *A Vision* was substantially based on the automatic writings that his wife George Hyde-Lees started after their honeymoon in 1917, Yeats's highly selective readings in classical literature are everywhere in the completed text, and his personal library contains, for instance, a heavily annotated edition of Herodotus, several editions of Plotinus, and standard works on classical culture.[60] Among the most heavily marked of any book on his shelves was John Burnet's *Early Greek Philosophy* from 1892. Yeats bought his copy in May 1923, and George Mills Harper has shown just how extensively Yeats drew upon it for *A Vision*, scribbling cones and gyres in the margins, underlining large sections, and borrowing extensively from it, particularly for the central 'Dove or Swan' section that opens with 'Leda and the Swan'. Most vigorously underscored are Burnet's fragments from Heraclitus of Ephesus, notably the following, underlined: 'Mortals are immortals and immortals are mortals, the one living the other's death and dying the other's life.'[61]

This, of course, is a phrase that Yeats would use many times over the coming years to explain the basic principle of his own system of interpenetrating gyres in *A Vision*; indeed, it is almost a catchphrase by the time he comes to write *On the Boiler* in 1938, and the casual reader might be forgiven for thinking that Yeats had coined it himself. It is also the concluding line of *The Resurrection*, the play that effectively forms the companion piece to *Oedipus the King* and *Oedipus at Colonus*. An early version of *The Resurrection* appeared in *The Adelphi* in June 1927, but Yeats wrote his first treatment of the idea in 1925; the first recognizable draft of the play dates from 1926, and he worked on it extensively over 1926 and 1927, which makes it, like 'Among School Children', directly contemporary with his translations of Sophocles.[62] At the play's conclusion, having just come face to

---

[57] Yeats (1933: 245).   [58] Yeats (1931b: 5).   [59] Yeats (1937: 8).
[60] Kenny (2004–5); see also Arkins (1990).   [61] Burnet (1892b: 139).
[62] Curtis and Guinness (2011: xxiii–xxx).

face with the bodily resurrected Christ, the character simply called 'The Greek'
cries out in horror and recognition:

> *The Greek*: O Athens, Alexandria, Rome, something has come to destroy you.
> The heart of the phantom is beating. Man has begun to die. Your words are clear
> at last, O Heraclitus. God and man die each other's life, live each other's death.[63]

There then follows a song, which Yeats would later include as a separate poem in
The Tower in 1928:

> In pity for man's darkening thought
> He walked that room and issued thence
> In Galilean turbulence;
> The Babylonian starlight brought
> A fabulous, formless darkness in;
> Odour of blood when Christ was slain
> Made all Platonic tolerance vain
> And vain all Doric discipline. [64]

Earlier drafts have 'Spartan discipline' for 'Doric' in the final line; however, the
verse seems to have taken shape in relatively few drafts. In part, this was because
by the time he came to write his Oedipus plays, and the poems in *The Tower*,
Yeats had constructed for himself in *A Vision* a model of history that involved
cyclical transformations that constituted 'a great year', and any understanding of
his work from that period needs to take account of the extent to which this system
increasingly shapes his poetry, his theatre, and, indeed, his thought.

A very particular understanding of the classical world was at the heart of the
system of gyres, which not only enabled much of Yeats's writing in the years
during which he worked on *A Vision* (effectively, from 1912 until 1937), but
which also shaped the way he understood a world that had torn itself apart in
one world war, and was slouching towards another barbarism. To put something
dazzlingly complex relatively simply, for Yeats, the early twentieth century was
witnessing the final implosion of an historical cycle that had begun 'when Christ
was slain | Made all Platonic tolerance vain | And vain all Doric discipline'. If the
historical cycle coming to an end began with the death of Christ, however, the
previous cycle began with the death of Oedipus. In the 1937 version of *A Vision*,
Yeats makes it clear that the Oedipus who 'sank down body and soul into the
earth' at the end of *Oedipus at Colonus* is the counterpart to the 'Christ, who was

---

[63] Yeats (1966b: 931). He also uses the phrase, for instance, in *On the Boiler*: see Yeats (1938: 15).
[64] Yeats (1957: 438); also Yeats (1966b: 931).

crucified standing up, went into the abstract sky, soul and body'.[65] 'What if,' he goes on to ask, 'Christ and Oedipus [...] are the two scales of a balance, the two butt-ends of a seesaw? What if every two thousand and odd years something happens in the world to make one sacred, the other secular?'[66] In other words, the figure of Oedipus was important to Yeats because his death stands as a symbol of the coming of the classical era of 'Platonic tolerance' and 'Doric discipline', in the same way that the crucifixion and resurrection of Christ opened the door to the two millennia that followed. And, just as Christ arises out of the era that he brings to an end, so, too, does Oedipus. In the case of Oedipus, he also looks back to a time of 'Babylonian starlight', or, to use the phrase from the end of *The Resurrection*: 'a fabulous formless darkness'.[67]

This image of a 'formless darkness'—and it is a terrifying image for Yeats—runs like a black thread through the sequence of poems in *The Tower* that includes both the final song from *The Resurrection* and a choral ode from his version of *Oedipus at Colonus*. It is there in 'The dark night where lay | The crowns of Ninevah' in 'Two Fragments'; in 'the mad abstract dark [...] | Where seven Ephesian topers lay' in the disturbing 'Picture of the Black Centaur by Edmund Dulac', again referencing Heraclitus of Ephesus; and it is there again in 'the starry towers of Babylon' in 'Wisdom'.[68] In the midst of this sequence is one of the choral odes from *Oedipus at Colonus*, in which the blinded Oedipus praises 'The wine-dark of the wood's intricacies', a place 'unvisited by tempest or by sun'.[69] However, it is in a draft of 'Among School Children', from June 1926, that we most clearly see Yeats formulating the relationship between the classical 'Platonic' period and the 'Babylonian' cycle which preceded it. The sixth stanza of the final version begins: 'Plato thought nature but a spume that plays | Upon a ghostly paradigm of things,' and ends by dismissing Plato, Aristotle, and Pythagoras as all 'Old clothes upon old sticks to scare a bird'.[70] However, in the earlier draft, this stanza is much more clearly about classical thought giving shape to what Yeats imagined to have been the madly whirling heavens of a time before rational abstraction:

> Ceasar Augustus that made all the laws
> And ~~org~~ ordering of every thing
> Plato that learned geometry & was
> The foremost man at the souls meaning
> ~~That golden thighed far famed~~ Pythagoras
> Who taught the stars of heaven what to sing
> And the musicians how to measure cords
> Old clothes upon old sticks to scare the birds.[71]

[65] Yeats (1937: 28).   [66] Yeats (1937: 18–19).   [67] Yeats (1925: 151).
[68] Yeats (1957: 442, 440).   [69] Yeats (1957: 446); also Yeats (1966b: 872).
[70] Yeats (1957: 244).   [71] Finneran *et al.* (2007: 372/3).

In the conclusion to the 1937 *Vision*, Yeats wrote that he saw Oedipus as 'altogether separated from Plato's Athens, from all that talk of the Good and the One, from all that cabinet of perfection.'[72] Instead, for Yeats Oedipus belongs to 'the mad abstract dark' that was tamed by figures such as Creon, Caesar Augustus, Plato, and Pythagoras, who 'made all the laws | And ordering of every thing'.

We can trace the origins of this uniquely Yeatsian Oedipus in his readings on classical culture, and their traces in his library. There we find among his more heavily annotated books (along with Burnet's *Early Greek Philosophy*) a copy of Franz Cumont's *Astrology and Religion among the Greeks and Romans* (1912)—a title certain to attract Yeats the practising astrologer. Yeats's marginal notes show that he was clearly most excited by the earliest sections of the book, beginning with a paragraph that is heavily underscored: 'Now here is one first discovery pregnant with consequences,' writes Cumont, 'before the eighth century [BCE] no scientific astronomy was possible owing to the absence of one indispensable condition, namely, the possession of an exact system of chronology.' 'Farther back,' Cumont claims, 'there was no certainty in regard to the calculation of time.' Cumont goes on to note that 'a valuable tablet, dated 523 [BCE], shows [...] for the first time [...] the relative positions of the sun and the moon calculated in advance'. In the margin Yeats has written: 'Sophocles dies 406, Plato dies 348.'[73]

Yeats appears to have taken as fact Cumont's claim that what he calls 'the Babylonians'—the Asiatic culture that precedes Greece and Rome—lacked 'an exact system of chronology'. He seems to imagine those cultures as living, effectively, outside of time; or, at least, outside of measurable time, in a world in which the stars spin randomly and unpredictably in the heavens, uncharted by the shaping maps of astronomy or astrology, in a 'mad abstract dark', 'a fabulous formless darkness'. 'When in my ignorance I try to imagine that older civilisation,' Yeats writes at the beginning of the 'Dove or Swan' section of *A Vision*, '[...] I can but see bird and woman [Leda and the Swan] blotting out some corner of the Babylonian mathematical starlight.'[74] Memories of that 'abstract dark', in Yeats's imagining, lasted up until 523 BCE. Sophocles (who died in 406) was born in 497 BCE, just after the end of the 'Babylonian' dispensation, and thus had the same relationship to it that Yeats considered himself to have with Irish folk culture, the two worlds intersecting, 'one living the other's death and dying the other's life'. Yeats also located Oedipus on the cusp of that transition, born into the 'formless dark' of prophecy, but defeated by a new era of law. Comparing Greek to Irish culture in *On the Boiler*, Yeats writes: 'The old Irish poets lay in a formless matrix; the Greek poets kept the richness of those dreams, but were completely awake.'[75] *On the Boiler* also contained the first printing of what we might now read as Yeats's anti-Oedipus play—*Purgatory* (1938), in which an old man kills his son, while his

---

[72] Yeats (1937: 18–19).   [73] Cumont (1912b: 8, 11).
[74] Yeats (1925: 151).   [75] Yeats (1938: 28).

ghostly mother and father enact his conception. All of the elements of Sophocles' *Oedipus Rex* are present, but in a different configuration, and yet the outcome dramatized in *Oedipus at Colonus* is the same: a haunted old man is left wandering the roads.

What Oedipus confronts in Yeats's *Oedipus the King*, then, and which leaves him as the blind beggar of *Oedipus at Colonus*, is not for Yeats a Freudian version of repressed desire: it is the 'mad abstract dark', a world where systems, including systems for measuring time and space, had not yet come into being. Yeats's Sophocles writes from a perspective that can still glimpse the mad starlight; and this is precisely how Yeats imagines himself in relation to Irish folklore. Understood in this way, we can read one of Yeats's best-known poems, 'The Second Coming' (first drafted in 1919), as if the speaker in the great second stanza were both a contemporary of Yeats at the beginning of the twentieth century and Oedipus returned to Thebes, seeing the Babylonian sphinx once again arising up out of the desert:

> [...] somewhere in sands of the desert
> A shape with lion body and the head of a man,
> A gaze blank and pitiless as the sun,
> Is moving its slow thighs, while all about it
> Reel shadows of the indignant desert birds.
> The darkness drops again;[76]

The key word if we understand history as cyclical is not 'darkness', but 'again'. 'Men have trembled on dark roads in Ireland and in Greece', Yeats told his BBC listeners in 1931. Yeats is partly looking back here, making an association between the half-remembered folk culture of Sophocles' Greece and the increasingly residual Irish folk culture of his own time. However, he is only partly looking back. For Yeats, writing in the first decades of the twentieth century, 'the mad abstract dark', the dark road, lay not only behind, but ahead: 'the darkness drops again'. The Oedipus who had walked the dark road, and glimpsed the 'fabulous, formless darkness', was not just a figure from the distant classical past; he was also Yeats's contemporary, staring with him into a new dark that was gathering in the 1930s throughout the European continent.

[76] Yeats (1957: 402).

IV

GENDER, SEXUALITY, AND CLASS

12

Wilde, Classicism, and Homosexuality in Modern Ireland

Eibhear Walshe

This essay will consider how Hellenism has been used in the past by Irish writers to locate strategies of concealment or justification when public exposure of their homosexuality threatened. The central figure here is Oscar Wilde, a poet trained in the Classics, who drew on classical imagery in much of his writing.[1] Wilde was also the most public Irish figure to be 'outed' when he was tried for gross indecency in 1895 and sentenced to two years' hard labour in Reading Gaol. During his trial, Wilde came under pressure to explain his close relationship with the young aristocrat Lord Alfred Douglas and, at one moment, was pressed on the meaning of the phrase, 'The Love that Dare not Speak its Name,' a line from a poem by Douglas that referred directly to love between men. Aware that he might be sent to jail, Wilde made a speech in which he sought to neutralize his sexual relationship with Douglas by locating it in the canonical discourse of Hellenism. Wilde was in a great deal of danger at this moment and so Socrates became one of his defence witnesses, so to speak. He sought a justification for his criminalized sexuality by appealing to a higher cultural genealogy, thus denying the physical and elevating his homosexuality into a safer aestheticized discourse. Citing Wilde's speech, which was a plea for the purity and the Hellenic idealism of his same-sex relationship, subsequent Irish writers viewed Wilde as an Irish patriot at bay in the dock of an English court. Some of these writers, especially those who were gay themselves, also saw him as a prophet of liberating sexual dissidence, empowered by Hellenism. His defiance in the face of British legal scrutiny was seen as a counter-attack on British imperialism and the institutions of colonial patriarchy. As I have suggested elsewhere, in Irish culture Wilde came to be perceived as a dissident Irishman, and is a crucial figure for linking Irishness and 'queerness' in relation to homosexuality in modern Ireland.[2]

Here I will draw on these earlier receptions of Wilde to examine the precise links between classicism and homosexuality in moments when Wilde was invoked (or

---

[1] On Oscar Wilde's debts to ancient Greece, in particular, see Ross (2013).
[2] See Walshe (2011: 1–2).

Eibhear Walshe, *Wilde, Classicism, and Homosexuality in Modern Ireland* In: *Classics and Irish Politics, 1916–2016*. Edited by: Isabelle Torrance and Donncha O'Rourke, Oxford University Press (2020).
© Oxford University Press.
DOI: 10.1093/oso/9780198864486.003.0012

evoked) as an emblematic figure by Irish writers dealing with taboo subjects. I will consider how classical Greek models have informed the politics and the literary representations of homosexuality in Ireland from Wilde to the present. Wilde became a model for dissidence in Irish writers of the early twentieth century, notably James Joyce, and was an unacknowledged presence in the thorny question of Patrick Pearse's sexuality and his enthusiasm for classical Greece. Wilde and the Greeks also gave an enabling discourse to mid-century nationalist (and gay) Irish writers like Brendan Behan, whose work will be discussed below, along with contemporary novelist Jamie O'Neill. Finally, I will consider the ways in which classical referents persisted in the debate surrounding the 2007 documentary about Irish-language poet Cathal Ó Searcaigh, and the 2011 presidential campaign of philhellene and gay rights activist Senator David Norris. In both debates, Wilde and Hellenism were invoked in the backlash against these two public and openly gay figures where a new taboo was located: now Hellenism found itself linked not so much with homosexuality as with paedophilia. It is significant that both figures referenced Wilde for their defence. Although contemporary Irish legal and cultural attitudes towards homosexuality have become radically enlightened, as evidenced by the overwhelming support for marriage equality in the 2015 referendum, Irish gay public figures could still be seen as suspect by drawing a connection between the classical phenomenon of pederasty and the crime of paedophilia.

The Aesthetics of Dissent from Oscar Wilde to James Joyce

For Ireland, Wilde has always been an ambiguous figure, particularly in terms of his perceived 'foreignness', arising from his links to the Decadent Movement in France. Matthew Sturgis in his study *Passionate Attitudes* argues that 'although decadence in England during the 1890s never quite managed to refine itself into a movement, it did create a pungent and distinctive flavour'. Sturgis identifies as hallmarks of this movement a 'distrust of Victorian confidence in society's common aims and standards – both artistic and moral; belief in the essential loneliness of the individual consciousness and the consolation of aesthetic impressions; belief too in art's superiority to nature – and to life'.[3] I want to suggest that Wilde's interest in the classical was just as vital a part of his 'foreignness' as his decadence, part of his threat and also his allure. Michael Foldy points out that Wilde 'represented a frightening constellation of threats which conflated all these disparate elements and associations: he represented foreign vice, foreign art and, indirectly, the legacy of foreign rulers'.[4] To the extent that the 'foreignness' that the British public distrusted in Wilde was French decadence, it could be argued that his

---

[3] Sturgis (1995: 299).   [4] Foldy (1997: 149).

classical Greek education, his Hellenism, was potentially both respectable and acceptable in a society largely run by those who had had a public school (and therefore classical) education. Wilde's assessment of the Greek gods in *De Profundis* might equally well have described his own situation: 'For the Greek gods, in spite of the white and red of their fair fleet limbs, were not really what they appeared to be.'[5]

Finding himself in grave danger in the Old Bailey, Wilde was forced to define 'The Love that Dare not Speak its Name', and he did so in a celebrated speech that both named homosexuality and, at the same time, desexualized it. In this speech, Wilde set up an acceptable yet evasive discourse where a dissident sexuality could be made 'respectable' via the claims of high cultural validation:

> The 'Love that dare not speak its name' in this century is such a great affection of an elder for a younger man as there was between David and Jonathan, such as Plato made the very basis of his philosophy...It is that deep, spiritual affection that is as pure as it is perfect...There is nothing unnatural about it. It is intellectual, and it repeatedly exists between an elder and a younger man, when the elder man has intellect, and the younger man has all the joy, hope and glamour of life before him.[6]

All through his writing career, Greek literature, like French decadent poetry, provided Wilde with a literary means of rebelling against Victorian heteronormativity and with a language to hint at the unmentionable nature of his own sexuality. As Linda Dowling comments, 'Saturated in the language and literature of ancient Greece, Wilde would repeatedly grasp his own life in the terms supplied by such ancient Greek forms as the life of Socrates or the plays of Aeschylus – which were ever to him a reality more compelling than the lurid implausibilities published in the daily newspapers.'[7] Greek literature was key to Wilde's development as a writer and he called his professor in Trinity College Dublin, John Pentland Mahaffy, 'my first and best teacher' and 'the scholar who showed me how to love Greek things'.[8] Significantly, Mahaffy had written sympathetically on Greek homosexuality in the preface to his 1874 study *Social Life in Greece from Homer to Menander*. However, having applauded the potential benefits of a relationship between a younger and an older man in the first edition, he found that he had to withdraw it in the second edition the next year. Later, after Wilde's downfall, Mahaffy called him 'the one blot on my tutorship' and refused to support him in his disgrace.[9] His influence on Wilde had nevertheless been significant, particularly for opening up an avenue of acceptance for homosexuality through classical Greek models. In a

---

[5] Wilde (1986 [1905]: 171).   [6] Ellmann (1988: 435).   [7] Dowling (1994: 123).
[8] Ellmann (1988: 27).
[9] Ellmann (1988: 28); on the relationship between Wilde and Mahaffy see Blanshard (2018).

lecture in the US in 1882, for example, Wilde had discussed the gay American poet Walt Whitman, suggesting that there was something very Greek and sane about his poetry, and implicitly connecting Whitman's sexuality with the rational thought of classical Greece.[10]

Arrested for gross indecency in 1895, and under great pressure, Wilde's speech from the dock forced him into open ground and yet failed to save him from a prison sentence. While in Reading Gaol, Wilde composed his prison letter *De Profundis*, where he single-handedly rebuilt his ruined reputation and shaped his posthumous reputation by Hellenizing both Christ and, by implication, himself. In this letter, written over three months to Lord Alfred Douglas, reproaching him with his part in Wilde's disgrace, Wilde sought to ensure control of his posthumous reputation. To rehabilitate himself, Wilde recast Christ as a poet who spoke Greek and who was, by implication, an outcast like Wilde himself, thus subverting the very Christianity that had put him in prison. 'I had said of Christ that he ranks with the poets. That is true. Shelley and Sophocles are of his company,' writes Wilde in *De Profundis*, further arguing that Christ must have spoken and conversed in Greek such that Socrates might have reasoned with him and Plato understood him, and concluding that Christ 'has fascinated and dominated art as no Greek god ever succeeded in doing'.[11]

Wilde was himself keenly aware of his blighted reputation and that of his parents, writing of his mother, 'She and my father had bequeathed me a name they had made noble and honoured, not merely in literature, art, archaeology, and science, but in the public history of my own country, in its evolution as a nation.'[12] He rebuilt that lost reputation with *De Profundis* and enabled his downfall to be interpreted in Ireland in the light of the literary and political career of his mother, the nationalist poet Speranza. This aligned him with the rhetorical traditions of nineteenth-century Protestant Irish Republicanism and, indirectly, with the many impassioned speeches made by Irish activists in English courtrooms during the nineteenth century. Since all subsequent biographical accounts of Wilde take their cue from *De Profundis*, with its strongly philhellenic underpinnings, classical Hellenism has been implicit in the understanding of Wilde's own beliefs. His use of Hellenism to make respectable his criminalized sexuality meant, however, that in later controversies where homosexuality was linked to other taboo sexualities, Wilde could be invoked by Irish writers as an emblematic figure of martyrdom and persecution.

In the immediate aftermath of the trials, during the early revolutionary years of the twentieth century in Ireland, Wilde was 'nationalised' (a phrase from Margot

---

[10]   Ellmann (1988: 159).   [11]   Wilde (1986 [1905]: 166).   [12]   Wilde (1986 [1905]: 141).

Norris)[13]—that is, claimed as a figure of transgressive aesthetic empowerment—by Yeats, Joyce, Shaw, and other Anglo-Irish writers. This mitigated his aberrant sexuality for those writers and indeed for their society. For a brief period, Wilde became popular with Irish cultural nationalists of a certain radical persuasion and his Hellenism was celebrated because of this.[14] To take one key example, Wilde became a figure of profound emblematic and aesthetic empowerment for James Joyce, a Catholic by upbringing and education. Joyce's appropriation of Wilde as a symbolic figure of sin and dissidence was vital in mediating Wilde's presence in twentieth-century Ireland. Joyce was 13 years old when Wilde's trials took place and 18 years old when Wilde died, and so his view of Wilde is constructed very much at a distance, both temporally and spatially. In March 1909, Joyce published an article called 'Oscar Wilde: The Poet of Salome' in a newspaper in Trieste to mark a performance of Richard Strauss' opera *Salome*. In this article, the question of Wilde's homosexuality is tackled directly and with Joyce's characteristic forthrightness, though this was possible only because he was writing outside Ireland. Joyce goes on to make the much more radical point that Wilde destabilized the widespread homosocial structures underpinning Victorian British male culture by bringing his sexuality into the open, however unwittingly. Joyce identifies precisely the homophobic panic that Wilde's 'outing' unleashed in the male social structures of his time: 'Anyone who follows closely the life and language of men, whether in soldiers' barracks or in the great commercial houses, will hesitate to believe that all those who threw stones at Wilde were themselves spotless.'[15] The consequent rage against Wilde in Britain was the rage of a society recognizing itself. 'What Dorian Gray's sin was no one says and no one knows. Anyone who recognizes it has committed it.'[16] At this very early point, Joyce was making the enlightened observation that homophobia is generated as a counter-discourse against which heterosexuality can define itself and thus become assured of its own naturalness and centrality.

The imaginative need of the exiled Joyce was to see Wilde as an artist who challenged the political and moral hegemony of the British Empire; Joyce begets him, as it were, as a precursor in his own aesthetics of exile, disgrace, and defiance. He writes, 'Here we touch the pulse of Wilde's art – sin. He deceived himself into believing that he was the bearer of good news of neo-paganism to an enslaved people.'[17] Thus Joyce saw Wilde as an exemplar, refashioned in his own likeness as a subversive and a rebel, affording him both a counter-tradition of Irish dissent and also an attack against Ireland and Britain. Paganism was Hellenism, Greek

---

[13] M. Norris (1998: 19–33).   [14] See Walshe (2011: 17–31).
[15] Joyce (1959 [1909]: 204).   [16] Joyce (1959 [1909]: 204).
[17] Joyce (1959 [1909]: 204).

love. It can be argued, then, that Hellenism was a key element in Joyce's reconstruction of Wilde. As Joseph Valente writes:

> Mediated by his compatriot Wilde, Oxford Hellenism afforded Joyce a script to be performed or mimicked in his youth and a narrative code to be implemented and manipulated in his fictive representations of that youth. It lent the lived and the written story a shared ideological basis: a discourse of individual freedom and self-development that could address and resist, in concerted fashion, the main intellectual, sexual and aesthetic constraints of Irish Catholic life and the political inequalities of British colonial rule.[18]

Wilde's sexuality, then, created for Joyce a platform for constructing his own aesthetics of dissent as an Irishman, where the politics of sexuality were less important than the politics of pluralism and defiance.

Patrick Pearse: Unacknowledged Wildean Influences

Joyce was just one Irish nationalist writer who remade Wildean Hellenism as dissent. In terms of the influence of Wilde and Hellenism on subsequent Irish figures, the case of the young Irish revolutionary and intellectual Patrick Pearse, who was executed for his role in the 1916 Rising, is intriguing. Pearse never directly mentions or alludes to Wilde's influence, substantial though this clearly was.[19] In many ways, Wilde was a shadow figure for Pearse, and is all the more significant for his absence. Pearse must have been influenced by Wilde's poems and stories, in particular 'The Selfish Giant' and 'The Happy Prince', in some of his writings for children.[20] However, Pearse never directly acknowledged Wildean influence in any form, an issue which is relevant to Pearse's much-discussed sexuality. Elaine Sisson comments as follows in her study *Pearse's Patriots*:

> Lack of documentary evidence and the limitations of research methodologies make it impossible to determine whether Pearse practised or thought about same-sex relationships. Given his orthodox Catholic background, his highly principled, highly disciplined life and the sheltered conservative social circles in which he moved, it seems highly unlikely that Pearse envisaged the possibility of sexual relations between men. The trial and death of Oscar Wilde happened within Pearse's adult lifetime, yet there is no mention of Wilde in any of Pearse's papers, although it seems unlikely that he could have been unaware of Wilde's fate.[21]

---

[18] Valente (1998: 11).

[19] Similarly, Pearse eschews any mention of classical oratory that evidently influenced his public rhetoric: see McGing (Ch. 3).

[20] See Sisson (2004) for more detail on this influence.

[21] Sisson (2004: 140).

Pearse, moreover, never directly acknowledged his own sexuality, whatever that was, but his writings reflect a connection around the configuration of the homo-erotic. In her study *Gender and Modern Irish Drama*, Susan Harris analyses Pearse's representations of the homoerotic in a chapter called 'Excess of Love: Padraig Pearse and the Erotics of Sacrifice'.[22] She identifies the connections between Irish republican ideology and the aesthetics of male sacrifice in Pearse's plays, making the point that, in the years after the Wilde trials and leading up to the 1916 Easter Rising, the nineteenth-century concept of a female Ireland in flight from a male aggressor, Britain, was becoming less viable. Harris argues that this paradigm shift was due to male Irish republican anxieties about perceived female weakness and passivity. Instead, in nationalist newspapers, ballads, and dramas, like those written by Pearse for the education of young Irish boys at his school St Enda's, the battle between British imperialism and Irish nationalism was being regendered as a masculine one, the struggle between two equal males. In this way, the Hellenized aesthetic of homoerotic conflict and sacrifice could find its counterpart in Pearse's republican writings and educational system. Harris suggests, 'Like Pearse's political speeches, his sacrificial plays show how and why the story of the male martyr's self-sacrifice became so important to him'.[23] Wilde's own writings are filled with images of male sacrifice and suicide, of beautiful St Sebastian figures, but Pearse never made any such link or influence explicit. Wilde attempted to make his own homosexuality acceptable by claiming that it was Platonic, Hellenic, and asexual. Pearse never made such a claim but, like Wilde, he saw himself as a sacrificial victim and looked to Greek culture for the inspir-ation for his young male pupils.

As Elaine Sisson has shown, Pearse's writings make frequent reference to the similarity between the physicality of the ancient cultures of Greece and Ireland, as for example in his lecture 'In First Century Ireland' (first delivered in 1906 and published in 1907), which 'recasts the desired Hellenic body of late Victorian cul-ture into the naturalized form of the Irish boy'.[24] These connections included, in Pearse's account, a culture of heroic nudity from boyhood: 'a cultured Gael' in early Ireland, he wrote, 'would no more have been shocked at the sight of…a nude young lad' or of 'a nude athlete or warrior than would a cultured Greek of the days of Socrates,' and the warriors of the Red Branch 'often went nude into battle' like Homeric heroes.[25]

Overall, then, Pearse's Hellenism and his idealization of male youth have argu-ably clear, if unacknowledged, similarities to Wilde. In a parallel context, Jeff Dudgeon, a recent biographer of Roger Casement, has compared Casement with Wilde as 'another Irish Protestant whose life patterns and national sympathies

---

[22] Harris (2002: 123–66).   [23] Harris (2002: 144).
[24] Sisson (2004: 133).   [25] Quoted from Sisson (2004: 136).

were remarkably similar'.[26] Susan Harris, on the other hand, links Casement with
Pearse by suggesting that

> in 1916 homosexuality was thoroughly pathologized; to have suggested then
> that Pearse felt the same desires that Casement's diaries recorded could only
> have had the effect of discrediting both him and the republican cause. But that
> climate of homophobia did not arise spontaneously out of some essential and
> unchanging 'natural' human disgust for homosexuality; it was produced and
> maintained by cultural forces that were more powerful then than now, and one
> of them, certainly, was the public-health discourse that supported Britain's
> attempt to keep its grip on Ireland. Eighty-five years later the power of that dis-
> course has weakened enough to allow us to discuss Pearse's sexuality without
> maligning his character.[27]

Pearse cannot have been unaware of Wilde's writings, nor of the controversy surrounding his sexuality. The fact that Pearse nowhere alludes to either, along with
his silence on the issue of his own sexuality, is symptomatic of the cultural context
in which he operated and of the Catholic faith to which he adhered. This does not
mean, however, that Wilde's Hellenism does not colour Pearse's own thought and
writings.

Oscar Wilde, Brendan Behan, and the
Legalization of Homosexuality in Ireland

With independence and the development of the Irish Free State, Wilde remained
a semi-submerged cultural presence in Ireland. In spite of criminal prohibitions
surrounding homosexuality, Wilde's plays were nevertheless staged all through
the 1930s and Irish biographers writing in the 1940s acknowledged Wilde's sexuality, albeit through the homophobic language of mainstream culture. Wilde's
influence thus continued even within the highly conservative landscape of de
Valera's Ireland, although in a restrained manner.[28] By the 1960s, Micheál Mac
Liammóir's popular one-man show *The Importance of Being Oscar*, based on
Wilde's writings and biography, had further secured the importance of Wilde,
both as an author and as an individual, within Irish cultural consciousness more
generally.[29] The mid-twentieth-century influence of Wilde, moreover, can be

---

[26] Dudgeon (2002: xix). Casement's diaries, circulated in the context of his trial and conviction for
high treason, contained details of homosexual encounters, but the authenticity of these diaries has
been the subject of much debate. See also MacDiarmid (2005) for an excellent discussion of
Casement's life and legacy.

[27] Harris (2002: 145).   [28] Cf. Walshe (2011: 57).

[29] See further Walshe (1997a).

traced along similar lines in the works of Brendan Behan. Born in 1923 into a republican family in a working-class tenement in Dublin's north inner city, Behan joined the IRA as a teenager and, as a result, was sentenced to time in a borstal reformatory in England between 1939 and 1941. In works by Wilde such as *De Profundis* and *The Ballad of Reading Gaol*, Behan found a mixture of the homo-erotic, of a higher intellectual tradition, of Irish defiance of British justice, of let-ters written in English gaols, and of powerful courtroom speeches, and his own work reflects these influences. Behan's biographer Michael O'Sullivan records the first encounter between the teenage Irish republican, confined in the borstal, and the emblematic and decadent name of his fellow Irishman:

> In the library, he met a fey young man of about nineteen, who wore a rose-coloured silk tie and smoked through a cigarette holder. This young man was reading a copy of Frank Harris's *Oscar Wilde, His Life and Confessions*. He explained to Brendan exactly why Wilde had been jailed. This revelation was meant to be disturbing but Brendan responded sharply: 'Every tinker has his own way of dancing, and I think that if that shocks you, it's just as well ordinary people didn't hear about it. Because, bejasus, if it shocked you, it'd turn thousands grey.'[30]

Although Behan later married, O'Sullivan's biography notes: 'When among friends, he often used to boast drunkenly of his "Herod Complex", or preference for young boys.'[31] Behan's 1954 prison play *The Quare Fella*, which centred on the imminent execution of a wife-murderer, is a work which pays direct homage to the influence of Wilde. As O'Sullivan notes: 'It was inevitable that reviewers in Ireland would make a comparison with Wilde's *The Ballad of Reading Gaol*. In the *Evening Press*, Gabriel Fallon found it more profoundly moving and deeply reli-gious than Wilde's great prison letter.'[32] Wilde was a key figure for Behan, particu-larly during his time in Paris in the late 1940s, when he was writing homoerotic prose and poetry. One example was his 1949 poem, originally written in Irish, 'Do Sheán Ó Súilleabháin' ('To Seán O'Sullivan'), which celebrates Wilde on his deathbed in Paris. The poem casts Wilde as 'ógrí na háilleacht | ina Narcissus briste' ('The young king of Beauty | A ravished Narcissus') as it juxtaposes classical imagery with the Catholic language of 'sin'.[33]

The Narcissus image here is a significant moment within Behan's writings, both as a nod to Wilde, whose poem *The Disciple* has Narcissus as its subject, and as an indication of Behan's awareness of and interest in the Hellenic as homoerotic. The influence of Wilde's Hellenism is again felt in Behan's 'After the Wake', a short story written during his time in Paris. As the young narrator gradually seduces his married friend, he uses much of the same cultural justification that was used

---

[30] O'Sullivan (1997: 63).   [31] O'Sullivan (1997: 139).
[32] O'Sullivan (1997: 181).
[33] Behan (1949), with English translation by Valentin Iremonger quoted in O'Sullivan (1997: 150–1).

by Wilde in his speech defending the 'Love that dare not speak its name', and references Wilde specifically:

> The first step – to make him think it manly – ordinary to manly men – ... that Lord Alfred Douglas was son to the Marquess of Queensberry and a good man to use his dukes himself. Oscar Wilde throwing old 'Q' down the stairs and after him his bully boy attendant.
>
>   On the other front, appealing to that hope of culture – Socrates, Shakespeare, Marlowe – lies, truth and half-truth.[34]

As in Wilde, Socrates appears in Behan as a coding for an acceptable homosexual tradition, a means by which heterosexuality can be seduced and somehow subverted using the 'respectable' justification of a higher cultural literary and philosophical identity.

With the gradual liberalizing of homosexuality laws in Ireland, cultural perceptions changed. Literary representations of non-heterosexual relationships became more acceptable, often via the discourse of a valid Hellenic genealogy of same-sex desire. As Matt Cook writes, 'Following Michel Foucault and Jeffrey Weeks's pioneering work in the 1970s, literary and lesbian and gay scholars have variously examined the significance of the law, newspapers, sexology, aestheticism and decadence and Hellenism to shifting ideas of homosexuality.'[35] Nevertheless, the battle to legalize homosexuality in Ireland was a fraught one. Tom Garvin's assessment of two other bitter social battles in Ireland, the legalization of divorce (finalized in 1996) and of abortion (voted through in 2018), could equally well describe the fight to legalize homosexuality (which was decriminalized in 1993): 'In the 1980s, Catholic forces in the form of the priests, bishops and Knights fought aggressive, successful and often unscrupulous battles on the issues of divorce and abortion. These were Pyrrhic victories which possibly merely rendered the emergent liberal consensus far more angry and even implacably anti-Catholic than it ever need have been.'[36]

A central figure in the battle to decriminalize homosexuality in Ireland was the academic, and later senator, David Norris, who took a case in the Irish courts against the Irish government in 1980, arguing that the criminalization of homosexuality in Ireland was an infringement of his civil rights as an Irish citizen. The High Court in Dublin found that the anti-gay laws were not unconstitutional. Diarmuid Ferriter writes:

> As Norris recalled, the difficulty was not just a legal one, but also 'a barrier in terms of popular and political prejudice'. When his High Court case was dismissed in 1980, he appealed to the Supreme Court, which also rejected his case,

---

[34] Behan (1981: 48).   [35] Cook (2003: 3).   [36] Garvin (2004: 209).

the Chief Justice, Tom O'Higgins, asserting that 'the deliberate practice of homosexuality is morally wrong, that it is damaging both to the health of individuals and the public and finally, that it is potentially harmful to the institution of marriage. I can find no inconsistency with the Constitution in the laws that make such conduct criminal.'[37]

Despite the concerted efforts of right-wing activists, however, decriminalization eventually took place after lobbying led the European Court of Human Rights to rule that Ireland's anti-gay laws contravened the European Convention on Human Rights of 1988. In response to this ruling, on 24 June 1993 Dáil Éireann passed a bill decriminalizing homosexuality. Within this process of liberalization, Wilde could be constructed as gay and Irish as part of the general process of social secularization in Ireland during the 1990s, particularly after the decriminalization of male homosexuality in 1993, the Civil Partnership Act in 2010, and the referendum on marriage equality in 2015. One of the results of these legal actions was a sense of empowerment for the Irish gay community. Oscar Wilde could be modernized, made contemporary with 'Celtic Tiger' Ireland as the citizen of a queer Irish nation, and reappropriated as a new symbol of modernity and post-imperialism within Irish writing.[38]

Jamie O'Neill, Wilde, and 1916 Irish Patriotism

Such is the case, for example, in Jamie O'Neill's 2001 novel At Swim, Two Boys, a narrative of homoerotic love and romance set around the Easter Rising of 1916, in which the figure of Oscar Wilde functions as both iconic queer and a symbol of patriotic rebellion. Notably, the title alludes to the well-known 1939 metafiction At Swim-Two-Birds by Irish author Brian O'Nolan, who frequently alludes to classical material in his writings.[39] The particular texture of Irish gay Hellenism is the focus for much of O'Neill's novel, and the text draws knowingly on Wilde, Pearse, and Casement. One of the central characters, Anthony MacMurrough, is directly figured as a Wildean transgressor, as he has also been imprisoned for gross indecency and has served the full sentence of two years' hard labour. MacMurrough constantly invokes the shade of the now dead, queer Wilde in this time of nationalist agitation.

At one point, MacMurrough and his aunt are on a tour of Dublin given by a nationalist Irish priest. They arrive in Merrion Square, where the priest remarks

---

[37] Ferriter (2009: 117).   [38] Cf. Walshe (2011: 202).
[39] O'Nolan's At Swim-Two-Birds, published under the pseudonym Flann O'Brien, opens with an epigraph from Euripides' Heracles, and his Cruiskeen Lawn columns, written for The Irish Times under the pseudonym Myles na gCopaleen, engage extensively with Greek and Latin material: see O'Hogan (Ch. 8).

that he does not know of any patriot associated with that location.[40] MacMurrough, to annoy his aunt, intervenes, telling the priest that there was, in fact, one Irishman associated with Merrion Square whom the English had put on trial no less than three times. The narrative progresses with great humour as MacMurrough lures the priest in with his account of this Irish patriot's persecution by the British and his moral victory in the face of their underhanded manipulation of public opinion. As it becomes ever clearer to the reader that the patriot in question is none other than Oscar Wilde, the priest remains oblivious, effusing about the speech from the dock as a quintessentially Irish type of drama.[41] The priest never discovers the name of this great Irish patriot, MacMurrough's aunt intervening before Wilde's unmentionable name can be spoken. The whole Irish patriot reincarnation of Wilde is here teased and undermined by O'Neill, while the Catholic priest's rejection of Wilde's sexuality is implicitly mocked. MacMurrough's horrified aunt reproves her nephew for having been about to mention Wilde to the parish priest, and when he protests that he has merely told the truth, she remains outraged, retorting that the name of the so-called 'love that dare not speak its name' is 'buggery'.[42]

In this tale of love between Irish men in time of war, the image of Wilde presides, even to a point of parody and farce. At one point, for example, MacMurrough rescues a swimmer in difficulty from Dublin Bay. Upon discovering that he has actually rescued Edward Carson, the prosecuting barrister at Oscar Wilde's trial for gross indecency, MacMurrough insists on giving him a full-on kiss, just to revenge himself for Wilde's sake. At another moment, the Irish patriot Tom Kettle, here presented as an old schoolfriend of MacMurrough, is appalled when confronted with MacMurrough's homosexuality. When Kettle asks MacMurrough if he is of Oscar Wilde's unspeakable ilk, MacMurrough exposes the discriminatory tone with his response that he is, indeed, Irish.[43]

In terms of education, too, O'Neill's novel makes the link between Wilde, Hellenism, and homosexuality through reference to Patrick Pearse and his system of education at St Enda's. In one scene, MacMurrough attends a school band concert playing 'A Nation Once Again' by Thomas Davis, and muses on the lyrics and the use of Hellenic reference for young Irish nationalists. Alluding to the opening phrases of the song, 'When boyhood's fire was in my blood | I read of ancient freemen | For Greece and Rome who bravely stood | Three hundred men and three men', he comments that although the lyrics are rousing, some three hundred and three objectified warriors may be taking it a bit far.[44] Directly after this

---

[40] O'Neill (2001: 436).   [41] O'Neill (2001: 436–7).   [42] O'Neill (2001: 438).
[43] O'Neill (2001: 309).
[44] O'Neill (2001: 258); for further discussion of Thomas Davis' 'A Nation Once Again' and its classical references see McGing (Ch. 3).

performance, when the boys change into the heroes of Celtic Ireland, they are duly feminized in the eyes of the onlooking MacMurrough.

At another point in the novel, in the school attended by the young protagonists, a priest turns a lesson on Virgil's *Aeneid* into a sermon on the subject of same-sex desire.[45] Having asked the boys under his charge to decline the phrase 'fidus Achates' ('faithful Achates'), the priest exploits Virgil's presentation of Aeneas and Achates as an opportunity to extol the paradigm of intimate but Platonic male friendship, before going on in more vociferous tones to rail against alternative forms of male friendship that he deems deceitful and sordid.

These examples will suffice to illustrate the extent to which O'Neill engages directly with a cluster of sociopolitical issues surrounding the connections between classical literature and sexuality in Ireland. His novel retrospectively liberates Irish patriotism from homophobia in the context of 1916, and does so by alluding extensively to Wilde, again as a rehabilitated Irishman and patriot. At the same time, the novel demonstrates how the Catholic educational system in Ireland valued classical texts for accessing the traditional languages of the Church (particularly Latin for Roman Catholicism) while at the same time sublimating any intimations of same-sex desire that appear in such texts.

New Taboos: Cathal Ó Searcaigh, David Norris, and the Classical Greek Phenomenon of Paederasty

The several literary prizes won by O'Neill's novel evidence a cultural acceptance for homosexuality in twenty-first-century Ireland. Against this background, a new sociopolitical controversy emerged which linked the classical Greek phenomenon of pederasty (normally characterized as an intellectual and erotic relationship between an older and a younger man) with the crime of paedophilia. The media storm engulfed two openly gay Irish public figures, celebrated Irish-language poet Cathal Ó Searcaigh and the aforementioned gay rights campaigner and senator David Norris. The two controversies were quite different and were separated by several years, but were linked by a rhetoric which drew upon the legacy of Hellenism and of Wilde.

Ó Searcaigh began publishing poetry in the Irish language from 1975, when being gay was still illegal, and thus his poetry was both radical and instantly popular. He was acclaimed for working in the Irish language and for bringing his homosexuality directly into visibility, deploying famous gay writers such as Wilde, Whitman, and others in his work. Key, however, to Ó Searcaigh's poetics is the

---

[45] O'Neill (2001: 258 and 152).

figure of the gay Hellenist poet, Constantine Cavafy (1863–1933), whose own work is thoroughly infused with classical material. In an interview, Ó Searcaigh made this link clear and spelled out his own attempts in his writing to merge the Hellenic, the sexually 'other', and contemporary Irish poetry: '[Cavafy's] favourite age being the pan-Hellenic world of the diasporic Greeks in Europe in Asia Minor after the collapse of the Alexandrian Empire.... It's my attempt to Hellenize my surroundings.'[46] Ó Searcaigh's poetry has been widely translated and critically engaged with. Reading Cavafy's sexual sensibility and poetic practice in the work of Cathal Ó Searcaigh, Christopher Robinson looks at a progression of influences within Ó Searcaigh's poetry, starting with Wilde and then suggesting both Jean Genet and Cavafy as part of a tradition of poetic homoeroticism. Interestingly, Robinson anticipates the controversy that later erupted around Ó Searcaigh by arguing that 'invoking the Greek anthology suggests a pederastic orientation which simply isn't there in the Irish poet, any more than it is in Cavafy'.[47] He goes on to argue that 'Cavafy is fundamentally different from the contemporaries he has so often been "classified" with... Doty and Ó Searcaigh are not out to "queer" Cavafy by recalling him in their writings, only to show how he has already done so himself.'[48]

The idea of the Hellenic within Ó Searcaigh's poetics came to be tested with the making and screening of a 2007 documentary, *Fairytale of Katmandu,* by Neasa Ní Chianáin. With Ó Searcaigh's cooperation, the film-maker accompanied the poet on a trip to Nepal, where she interviewed a number of young men, some of them just 16 years old. In its final edit, the documentary presented the trip as a moment of disillusion, with Ní Chianáin's discovery of the poet's 'true' relationship with these young men. In her view, the relationships were inappropriate and exploitative, and she subsequently reported Ó Searcaigh to the police on her return to Ireland. The film-maker confronted the poet on camera and raised the issues of exploitation and economic advantage, Ó Searcaigh having raised money in Ireland to help young men in Nepal with various business ventures. Ó Searcaigh defended himself, protesting that these were loving relationships and that the documentary misrepresented him and the Nepalese themselves. In an interview with *The Irish Times* published on 12 February 2009, Ó Searcaigh admitted to being 'incensed' at the suggestion that his generosity towards families in Nepal was a ruse for him to have sex more often: 'No, no, no, that is ridiculous,' he protested. 'It was never shown in the film that I spend so much time with families, older people, conduct workshops with women in Nepal, the literati of Nepal are up in my room, elderly men talking about poetry, translating poetry, none of that comes across in the film.'

---

[46] Ó Searcaigh and McGrath (2002: 224).   [47] Robinson (2005: 227).
[48] Robinson (2005: 270).

When the film was shown on RTÉ television on 11 March 2008, a heated public debate ensued. As with Wilde before him, the perceived imbalance of the relationship between older and younger men became the focus for discussion. Ó Searcaigh defended himself stoutly, denying any inequality in his relationships with the Nepalese youths, seeing them as consensual, and citing Wilde as a precursor. In an *Irish Times* interview, published on 27 March 2008, in the immediate aftermath of the erupting controversy, Ó Searcaigh made his kinship with Wilde and Wilde's perceived martyrdom explicit. Remarking that the events of recent weeks would continue to affect his life in the future, Ó Searcaigh said: 'It upsets me greatly. But when you're in an abyss, there is always hope. I think a lot these days of Oscar Wilde, who went through this kind of hardship as well in his day and who said "we are all in the gutter but some of us are looking up at the stars". This gives me encouragement, to look from the abyss to the stars.' Ó Searcaigh found that many attacked him.[49] But many also came to his defence. Fellow Irish poet Paddy Bushe, for example, produced his own documentary, *The Truth about Kathmandu*, in 2009, where he alleged that the real views of the Nepalese youths had been ignored by the documentary. This led to legal action being taken by the original film-makers.

Under discussion at the time was the possibility that Ó Searcaigh be made to leave Aosdána, the official body for writers and artists, which provided him with financial security. It was also suggested that his poems should be removed from the school curriculum. Likewise offence was taken with his radio interview on Radió na Gaeltachta in March 2008, where he once again called upon the example of Wilde as parallel to his own fate. The *Irish Independent* (13 March 2008) reports that he was defended by artist Robert Ballagh: 'Mr Ballagh... did not feel the poet should be asked to leave Aosdána, and described Deputy Brian Hayes' suggestion to drop his work from the school syllabus as "idiotic".... He said history did not suggest a "happy outcome" for the poet. "Oscar Wilde did not write very many great works after his court case, apart from *De Profundis*. But if you start removing works by artists with dubious moral backgrounds, you would have very few works and paintings left." ' David Norris also defended Ó Searcaigh in a statement that was quoted during the controversy over Norris' own sexuality that erupted some years later: 'He [Norris] stood up and declared that the film's broadcast, scheduled for that night, should be cancelled until its veracity could be ascertained by "experts". "Gloriously," he went on, "the artists of Ireland have supported Cathal Ó Searcaigh as they previously did in the case of Oscar Wilde. This is

[49] A news feature about Ó Searcaigh published in *The Irish Times* by Kathy Sheridan on 2 February 2008 quoted Ní Chianáin as saying 'The rumour is that I've "stitched up a vulnerable gay man." ' Rather ironically, the article appeared alongside an advertisement for Dublin port with a cartoon of Wilde saying 'I have nothing to declare but my genius.'

because they have a unique insight into the processes of works of creation and destruction." '50

Ó Searcaigh's career was, to an extent, derailed temporarily by the controversy. When his memoir *Light on Distant Hills* was published in 2009, however, there was nothing about Wilde or about the controversy; rather it was all about Cavafy: 'His random pickings allowed me to read about life in the city states of ancient Greece.'51 Developing this connection, Ó Searcaigh goes on to describe how

> I couldn't get 'Ithaca', a poem by Cavafy, out of my mind...In the poem, Cavafy commends the voyage. Arriving at one's destination is nothing, it is the journey itself that is important, the adventures and the intoxications of it, the knowledge gleaned along the way; and finally, when one arrives in Ithaca, it may be disappointing but nevertheless, you have been strengthened and made wise by the voyage. Ithaca is not to be faulted, however dreary, tame and commonplace it is, it provided you with that voyage – your passage to maturity.52

Having come to Ó Searcaigh's defence, it would later be David Norris' turn to face public ire and career derailment for similar reasons, though in entirely different circumstances. In 2011, Norris had launched what seemed to be a successful campaign to succeed Mary McAleese as President of Ireland. Front runner in the opinion polls, his chances for success came to an abrupt end when a 2002 interview with *Magill* magazine resurfaced and was widely condemned for its report of Norris' views on the classical Greek practice of pederasty. In the interview, which took place over dinner and was recorded, the journalist Helen Lucy Burke reported the following statements made by Norris:

> I cannot understand how anybody could find children of either sex the slightest bit attractive sexually....But in terms of classic paedophilia, as practised by the Greeks, for example, where it is an older man introducing a younger man or boy to adult life, I think there can be something said for it. Now, again, this is not something that appeals to me, although when I was younger...I would have greatly relished the prospect of an older, attractive, mature man taking me under his wing, lovingly introducing me to sexual realities and treating me with affection and teaching me about life.53

The interview was very badly received. Norris was furious with Burke's account of their discussion and disputed it, but he was attacked in public debates and his

---

50 Victoria White writing in the *Irish Examiner*, 29 November 2012.
51 Ó Searcaigh (2009: 185).   52 Ó Searcaigh (2009: 268).
53 Originally published as 'David Norris: the free radical' in *Magill* (January, 2002: 34–6), and later cited in, e.g., *The Guardian* (31 May 2011).

ratings fell. In his subsequent memoir, Norris wrote that Burke had 'blurred the distinction I had made between paedophilia and classic Greek pederasty',[54] leading to headlines such as 'Senator backs sex with children'.[55] In a statement released at the time Norris explained: 'During the course of a comprehensive conversation, Miss Burke and I engaged in an academic discussion about classical Greece and sexual activity in a historical context; it was a hypothetical, intellectual conversation which should not have been seen as a considered representation of my views on some of the issues discussed over dinner'.[56] All of Norris' attempts to open this discussion, however, failed to help his disintegrating presidential campaign, and when he tried to explain his position on RTÉ radio, the interviewer, Áine Lawlor, interrupted him to say 'But Senator Norris, you are not running for President in Ancient Greece'.[57] Inevitably, Norris failed to win the presidency but defended himself in his subsequent memoir, where he disputed Burke's account of what happened.

Conclusion

Oscar Wilde's attempt to justify his relations with younger men via classicism and a Greek model of intellectualized same-sex relationships have a significant reception history in the sexual politics of twentieth- and twenty-first-century Ireland. Wilde became an implicit model for Irish dissidence against British tyranny, crystallized through the nationalist lens of James Joyce, and was a covert influence on Patrick Pearse, who was never open about his sexuality, whatever that actually was. Political nationalism and homosexuality converge also, through the inspiration of Wilde's dissident Hellenism, in the literary works of Brendan Behan and Jamie O'Neill. In the public sphere, Irish poet Cathal Ó Searcaigh would cast himself as a Wildean figure of tragic loss when accused of having inappropriate relationships with young men, while his own writings have been deeply mediated by the further Hellenizing influence of nineteenth-century gay Greek poet Constantine Cavafy, whose work is saturated with classical allusions and musings on same-sex love. Finally, discussion of the Greek phenomenon of paederasty would derail the 2011 presidential campaign of gay rights activist and senator David Norris. Hellenism, homosexuality, and Irish politics have thus been inextricably linked in the long twentieth century. Even as homosexuality became decriminalized (1993), civil partnerships and same-sex marriage eventually legalized (2010 and 2015), and the first openly gay Taoiseach (prime minister) elected (2017), the cases of Norris and Ó Searcaigh illustrate how the classical Greek phenomenon of paederasty can lead to controversy in sociopolitical contexts.

[54] D. Norris (2012: 302).   [55] D. Norris (2012: 302).   [56] D. Norris (2012: 303).
[57] D. Norris (2012: 304).

13

Trojan Women and Irish Sexual Politics, 1920–2015

Isabelle Torrance

Dublin as Troy

A leading scholar in both Irish and classical languages during the first decades of the twentieth century, Fr Patrick Dinneen, saw fit to compare the destruction in Dublin after the Easter Rising of 1916 to the burning, sacked city of Troy.[1] As Suzanne O'Neill discusses (Ch. 19), the neoclassical facade of the General Post Office, which was the iconic focal point of the Easter Rising from which the proclamation of independence was declared, came to be an emblem of national pride divested of its imperial symbolism. W. B. Yeats, too, applies the metaphor of Troy to Dublin in his famous poem 'No Second Troy', first published in 1916, in which he casts the Irish revolutionary Maud Gonne as a new Helen wreaking in her wake the destruction not of Troy, since it no longer exists, but of contemporary figures including Yeats himself. In a 1920 production of Euripides' *Trojan Women*, however, Maud Gonne casts off the mantle of the Greek Helen by starring as the devastated Trojan queen Hecuba, who represents the defeated city of Troy.

The original play was first performed in 415 BCE in the context of the Peloponnesian War between Athens and Sparta and is set in front of the smouldering ruins of Troy as the Greeks prepare to set sail and the captive women of Troy await formal enslavement to their Greek captors. It is arguably the most relentless of Greek tragedies. The structure is uncomfortably linear and without the kind of plot development usually found in Euripidean drama.[2] It is the only Euripidean tragedy to conclude in sung lyrics (expressing a heightened emotional state) without any moralizing message or predictions for the future.[3] The main

This chapter has benefited, at various stages in its development, from the feedback of Fiona Macintosh, Laurie O'Higgins, and Donncha O'Rourke, and I am indebted to each for their insights and encouragement.

[1] Mac Annraoi (2016: 10), referenced by Mac Góráin (Ch. 7).

[2] For example, there is no messenger speech, and no use is made of the stage machinery available in classical Athenian theatre, leading Goff (2009: 23) to comment that the 'poverty of device is like the destitution of the women themselves'.

[3] Noted by Dunn (1996: 102), and cf. Barrett (1964 *ad* 1423–30).

Isabelle Torrance, *Trojan Women and Irish Sexual Politics, 1920–2015* In: *Classics and Irish Politics, 1916–2016*. Edited by: Isabelle Torrance and Donncha O'Rourke, Oxford University Press (2020). © Oxford University Press.
DOI: 10.1093/oso/9780198864486.003.0013

character, Hecuba, is assailed by grief upon grief, and the play powerfully exploits expressions of novelty to meditate on violent events of the past and to suggest that tragic events are being repeated anew.[4] The drama privileges didactic potential over plot structure and, in the immediate context of the violent sack of the island of Melos by Athenian military forces in the winter before *Trojan Women* was performed, this war tragedy questions imperialist agendas through the lens of the Trojan War.[5]

All of the expected outcomes that we know from Greek mythology come to pass. Hector's wife Andromache is carted off to become the slave of the son of her husband's killer. Her son, the last remaining male survivor of the Trojan line, is thrown to his death from what is left of the Trojan walls. Polyxena, Hecuba's teenage daughter, is killed as a human sacrifice at Achilles' tomb to appease his ghost. Cassandra, another of Hecuba's teenage daughters, has gone mad and performs a bizarre parody of a marriage ritual in celebration of her enslavement to Agamemnon, king of the Greeks. And the Greek Helen wins over her former husband Menelaus, in spite of Hecuba's powerful rhetoric, which assigns blame to Helen for causing the Trojan War.[6] In contrast to Euripides' earlier *Hecuba* where the title character, together with other Trojan women, takes bloody revenge on the man who murdered her youngest son, this Hecuba has no recourse to action against her predicament. Nevertheless, her strength to withstand the onslaught of debilitating blows has been understood as giving her character its power. She physically represents Troy, defeated but remembered through song and poetry, of which the play is itself one example.

If we pose an adapted version of Hamlet's famous question, 'What is Hecuba to Ireland or Ireland to Hecuba?' (*Hamlet* Act 2, Scene 2), an obvious answer is that Ireland, like Hecuba, understands the impact of colonial aggression. The potential identification of Dublin as Troy, in the context of the imperial suppression of the 1916 Rebellion, is evoked arrestingly in the cover image of the playbill for the 1920 Dublin production of *Trojan Women*, with smoke billowing forth from the three flaming castles which form Dublin's traditional crest (Fig. 13.1). Although the Dublin Drama League apparently used the same image on its programme cover from its inception in 1919 until 1925, it seems remarkably appropriate to *Trojan Women* where Dublin implicitly becomes the city of Troy over which a larger-than-life heroic male figure reclines, veiled in grief, reminiscent of the god Poseidon who opens *Trojan Women* and laments the destruction of his city.[7] It is

---

[4] For a detailed discussion of this phenomenon see Torrance (2013: 218–45).

[5] See esp. Croally (1994) and also Gregory (1991: 155–83) and (2002), Dué (2006: 148–50), Rosenbloom (2006).

[6] Easterling (1997a: 175) argues that familiar scenes from *Odyssey* 4 'of Menelaus and Helen happily settled back home' will have surfaced in the minds of a fifth-century BCE Greek audience.

[7] The Holloway Book Collection at the National Library of Ireland includes a significant number of the Dublin Drama League's theatre programmes from the years 1919–36, although the programme for 1920 is not among them (reference no. 15A171).

Fig. 13.1. Programme cover for the 1920 production of *Trojan Women* by the Dublin Drama League. Artist not credited. Held by the Bodleian Library, Papers of Gilbert Murray 507, fol. 92r. Permission to reproduce comes courtesy of the Keeper of Special Collections, Bodleian Libraries, supported by an Orphan Works Licence.

not difficult to map the *Trojan Women* story onto a colonial conflict. Gilbert Murray's 1904 translation, which kindled enthusiasm for performances of this previously neglected play, implicitly condemned British actions in the Boer War.[8] Meanwhile, one of the most famous twentieth-century adaptations of the play, Jean-Paul Sartre's 1965 *Les Troyennes*, casts the Greeks as thinly veiled French colonists and the Trojans as suffering Algerians during the Algerian War.[9]

Perhaps surprisingly, however, that is not the primary thematic trajectory that links the Irish plays addressed in this chapter. Spanning almost the entire century from the 1916 Rising to its centenary anniversary, I will discuss the aforementioned 1920 production by the Dublin Drama League, along with Brendan Kennelly's 1993 *Trojan Women* and Marina Carr's 2015 *Hecuba*. These plays, it will be argued, rather than becoming anti-imperial manifestos, as might reasonably have been expected, in fact serve to expose the objectification of women in a way that highlights their perceived or actual lack of political agency.

Maud Gonne as Hecuba (1920): Female Objectification Exposed

In 1920, the Dublin Drama League produced Euripides' *Trojan Women*, which was performed at the Abbey Theatre in the rhyming translation of Gilbert Murray, starring Maud Gonne (MacBride), the Irish revolutionary, in the role of Hecuba. The Dublin Drama League had been founded the previous year in 1919 with the aim of producing a broad and experimental repertoire of plays, to escape from the Irish peasant play that dominated the Abbey Theatre's main stage. The Abbey allowed the League to avail of its theatre on Sundays and Mondays when it was not otherwise in use.[10] The League's dramatic premiere on 9 February 1919 was an obscure contemporary Balkan play called *The Liberators*, written in 1912 in the aftermath of the First Balkan War by a Croat who had been director of the National Theatre in Sofia. This play about war and national territories clearly announces 'a measure of intentionality within the League to stage dramas which would resonate with Irish audiences'.[11] In 1920, then, just four years after the Easter Rising, the execution of its leaders, and the ensuing turmoil, the choice of performing *Trojan Women* seems topical, given its focus on the fates of defeated (female) subjects.

This was also Maud Gonne's first return to the stage since she starred in Lady Gregory and W. B. Yeats's nationalist *Cathleen ni Houlihan* of 1902 as a symbol of Ireland requesting blood sacrifice during the 1798 rebellion.[12] An analogy

---

[8] Goff (2009: 35, 79).
[9] Goff (2009: 81–3).   [10] Clarke and Ferrar (1979: 13).   [11] Sisson (2010: 135).
[12] The language of blood sacrifice in Patrick Pearse's nationalist rhetoric and in Irish nationalist drama focuses on male bloodshed for an allegorical fertile female figure. This is very different from the female virgin war-time sacrificial victims which dominate Greek tragedy, such as Iphigenia and

between Maud Gonne as Hecuba and Irish nationalist suffering at the hands of imperialist forces (here the Greeks) seems like a fairly natural one. However, any political significance to the performance was lost in the review of the play for the *Irish Independent*.

Trojan Women was produced along with Chekov's *A Tragedian In Spite of Himself*, but most of the review focuses on *Trojan Women*. Published on Monday 8 March 1920, following the Sunday performance, it is worth quoting in its entirety:

Two Plays at the Abbey
Old Greek and Modern Russian

About two hundred people came to the Abbey Theatre yesterday afternoon to witness the efforts of the Dublin Drama League in two plays, one by Anton Tchekov and the other by – Euripides.

In the Petrograd play Mr. J. A. West successed [*sic*] in making "A Tragedian in Spite of Himself" a thing of grotesque farce. His mission is to tell the woes of a civil servant. Mr. Peter Nolan stood by and listened to him.

Next came "The Trojan Women", an English verse translation of Euripides' "Troiade" [*sic*] by Gilbert Murray. With commendable prudence the producers did not attempt any ornate setting. They opened with cavernous darkness and progressed in grey light.

This tragedy of the Trojan women, which is the tragedy of all women of all time, is not exactly the kind of entertainment one would voluntarily choose to merrily pass the time on a bright and bracing Sunday afternoon. The fate of the war-stricken women of Troy left to work out their miserable destiny is the fate of millions of women in Europe to-day. We would like to have been able to enter into the spirit of the work from this view-point, but really the interpretation given the work rather hurt us than helped us. We wanted a tragic narrative pouring in red-hot sentences from the lips of soul-seared women. We got instead for the most part dreary, dirgey, sing-song rhyming. It was all unrelieved gloom, devoid of those sensations that come from action in drama, from crescendos in music.

Without apportioning blame or praise, I give the names of those who took part. These were: - F. J. McCormick, Christine Hayden, Maud Gonne Macbride [*sic*], Elizabeth Young, Maire [*sic*] Nic Shiubhlaigh, Cathleen Murphy, Arthur Shields, Anne Page, Nell Byrne, Dympna Daly, Una Hannigan, M. McShane, Columba O'Carroll.

Polyxena in the Trojan War, and Macaria in the Athenian tradition. On the gendered nature of blood sacrifice in Irish nationalist drama see Harris (2002: esp. 3–11). On sacrificial virgins in Greek tragedy see Wilkins (1990).

The finest moments were reached in Andromache's renunciation of her infant son, Hector [sic], and in Helen's subtle defence of her lapses from rectitude. These moments were welcome.

Jacques [pseudonym for John Rice][13]

The review is extraordinary on multiple levels. Acknowledging on the one hand that the suffering represented in Trojan Women is not only timeless but reflective of the fate of millions of women in the Europe of his day, the contemplation of that fate is deemed an unpleasant and unwelcome imposition. The language used to describe the desired type of performance is evocative of sexual passion— 'red-hot sentences [pouring] from the lips of soul-seared women'—and suggests that the Trojan women in the performance did not display souls seared to a sufficiently appropriate degree. At the same time the play is paradoxically condemned for its 'unrelieved gloom', which would be precisely the anticipated effect of a successful production of Euripides' Trojan Women. The reviewer's unconscious desire for a more sexualized performance, implied by the expressions he uses, is confirmed in his approval of Helen's role as one of the performance's only saving graces, since she epitomizes in this play (and elsewhere) the power of seductive female rhetoric as a sexually desirable woman. Rice was presumably not properly cognizant of the suggestive nature of his language since he was generally ultra-conservative in his opinions on dramatic taste. According to Patrick Maume's brief biography, he often criticized Abbey Theatre plays for 'morbidity', considered Synge's In the Shadow of the Glen to be 'a farcical libel on the character of the average decently-reared Irish peasant woman', and supported the riots that followed Synge's The Playboy of the Western World as 'a tribute to the good taste and common sense of the audience'. He also 'denounced Charlie Chaplin as vulgar, and regularly demanded that plays he disliked be censored by a 'sanitary inspector'.'[14]

Rice sees Helen's arguments in Trojan Woman as a 'subtle defence of her lapses from rectitude', but a Greek audience would have been unsettled by her rhetorical ability and the questions her arguments raise regarding the causes of the Trojan War. Helen's logic is both ruthless and self-serving.[15] Rice seems to have fallen prey to Helen's persuasion along with her estranged husband Menelaus, who is always negatively portrayed in Euripidean drama as blustery and ineffectual.[16] In fact, the language of Rice's review eerily mirrors that of Menelaus in the play, since both incongruously reflect on the brightness of the day while the women of Troy are suffering. In the translation of Gilbert Murray that Rice would have heard performed, Menelaus' opening words are as follows: 'How bright the face of heaven,

---

[13] Jacques (1920).   [14] Maume (2009).   [15] Mossman (2005: 362).

[16] In addition to Trojan Women, he features as a character in Andromache, Helen, Orestes, and Iphigenia in Aulis. In his Poetics (52a29) Aristotle considers Menelaus in Euripides' Orestes to be an example of an unnecessarily nasty character.

and how sweet | The air this day...'[17] (*Tro.* 860–2 which read more literally 'O gloriously bright and sunny day, on which I will lay hands on my wife Helen!'). The other performance to receive praise from Rice, that of Andromache's 'renunciation of her infant son' (who is not Hector, but Astyanax; Hector was her husband) is also a scene in which Helen's character is a focal point, since Andromache blames her for all of her griefs during her speech of lamentation (*Tro.* 766–73).

Rice is moved by Helen and the question of her guilt, which always comes down, in essence, to sexual guilt since her relationship with the Trojan prince Paris is ostensibly the cause of the Trojan War, whether she eloped willingly or was forced to leave. He is apparently not moved by Maud Gonne MacBride as Hecuba, whose demanding role has her onstage for the entire play, whose husband was executed by the British in 1916, and who was a formidable supporter of Irish independence. Although Maud Gonne and John MacBride were estranged, she nevertheless refers to him as her husband in her correspondence to W. B. Yeats after his execution and considers that he has 'entered Eternity through the great door of sacrifice'.[18] Two other performers in this production were notably active supporters of Irish independence—Arthur Shields and Máire Nic Shiubhlaigh. The latter was a feminist and nationalist activist who had joined the Irish nationalist women's movement Inghinidhe na hÉireann (Daughters of Ireland) at its foundation in 1900 and who had been drawn to the egalitarian spirit of the early days of the Irish National Theatre Society. She had participated in the 1916 Easter Rising and remained politically active thereafter through her work at Cumann na mBan (the Irish Women's Council) but only in the reduced capacity available to women who were subordinated to an auxiliary role supporting the all-male Irish Volunteers.[19] Indeed the whole enterprise of the Dublin Drama League was, as we have seen, political as well as artistic.

And yet, the political resonances of the performance within an Irish context go completely unnoticed in Rice's review. The Proclamation of the Irish Republic in 1916 had explicitly stressed equality among the men and women of Ireland, but this aspirational ideal was never fulfilled and the government which took control of the Irish Free State in 1922 was far more conservative than the rebels of 1916. In 1920, then, Rice's reception of this Irish Hecuba story is a stark confirmation of the contemporary mainstream suppression of women's voices from Irish politics in the struggle for independence, voices which current scholars are seeking to retrieve.[20] The pairing of *Trojan Women* with Chekov's farce also seems pointed. The real griefs and desperate suffering of war widows are further highlighted by

---

[17]   Murray (2006: 45), translating E. *Tro.* 860.

[18]   On 8 November 1916; see White and Jeffares (1993: 384). On Yeats's perception of Gonne and MacBride see O'Rourke (Ch. 15).

[19]   On Máire Nic Shiubhlaigh's career and political activism see McGarry (2016: 13–42, 237–46); on Arthur Shields, see McGarry (2016: 109–16, 265–320).

[20]   See, e.g., Kiberd and Mathews (2015), McGarry (2010) and (2016), Pašeta (2016).

contrast with the farcical 'woes of a civil servant'; but nevertheless the plight of the Trojan women is found to be a bore.

Kennelly's *Trojan Women* (1993): Demonizing Female Sexuality

What Rice would have made of Brendan Kennelly's 1993 *Trojan Women*, we can never know for certain, but he would undoubtedly have been appalled by the typical vulgarity of some of Kennelly's language. What we know from Kennelly about his *Trojan Women* is that he was inspired to write the play by the Irish women he had met in rural villages in the 1940s and 1950s; women who had 'tremendous powers of endurance and survival', hard-working 'women whose husbands had gone to England to find work, to send money back home. Hecuba was Maggie, Mollie and Liz.'[21] In fact, Kennelly effectively explains what is, as Lisa Fitzpatrick points out, an 'Irish colloquial use of the word "Trojan" to describe a woman who endures through every adversity'.[22] Moreover, as he often does with his characters, Kennelly presents us with a 'complex reality' in his representation of Hecuba.[23] She remains the long-suffering queen, buffeted by the waves of misfortune. She maintains our sympathy as each new woe afflicts her. And yet, there is an ugliness of character in Kennelly's treatment of Hecuba that goes far beyond the original. This development reaches its climax in the Helen scene, which John Rice had found so compelling in the 1920 production. In Kennelly's version, Hecuba's behaviour degenerates into shocking verbal abuse against Helen which is entirely absent in Euripides. Kennelly's Hecuba repeatedly calls Helen a 'bitch' and a 'cunt';[24] she blames Helen for all male crimes of murder and rape, saying 'Helen, you are whatever | turns a man into a murderer, | you created the thought of rape, | you are the cause of all our torture.'[25] The other women, together with Hecuba, exhort Menelaus to kill Helen, encircle her, hurl vicious abuse at her, and chant death wishes and curses. Meanwhile Helen remains calm, as the stage directions indicate,[26] casting the visceral rage of Hecuba and the other Trojan women into sharp relief, and, true to form, Menelaus falls under Helen's spell.

In the original, Hecuba's anger may shine through her rhetoric, as Mossman puts it,[27] but there are no obscenities or aggression of the kind we witness in Kennelly. Helen incites such ugly rage in Kennelly's Hecuba because Helen, a married woman, had allegedly seduced Hecuba's son. Hecuba becomes, all of a sudden, a purist matriarch, whose son can do no wrong, while all the blame for his misguided actions falls on the degraded woman who had allegedly seduced him. The fact that this woman

---

[21] Kennelly (2006: 138).   [22] Fitzpatrick (2018: 140).   [23] Kennelly (2006: 139).
[24] Kennelly (2006: 190, 192, 194).   [25] Kennelly (2006: 191–2).
[26] Kennelly (2006: 194).   [27] Mossman (2005: 362).

is an outsider, a Greek and not a Trojan, solidifies the blame. And now, she is getting away scot-free and going back to her first husband.

Kennelly's slut-shaming scene must make for uncomfortable viewing. It is remarkable that Desmond Rushe drew no attention to this challenge to the audience's sympathy for Kennelly's Hecuba when he wrote in his review of the 1993 production that 'Catherine White is largely blameless as an admirably resolute Hecuba: she epitomizes powerfully the great feminine strength that Mr Kennelly salutes.'[28] The qualified 'largely blameless' may be telling here. Another surprising review was Emer O'Kelly in the *Sunday Independent*, who strangely focuses on the issue of Hecuba's rape, presumably metaphorical or anticipated rather than literal, saying 'Kennelly gives us a Hecuba determined to preserve her essence even as she is raped, to go away into her own being', and following up with the criticism that '[t]he real horror of rape is that it does defeat women's essential core'.[29] O'Kelly's focus is strange because the issue of Hecuba's rape is far less immediate in the play than the rape of Cassandra and the rape of Andromache, both of whom are carted off to their assigned male captors during the course of the drama.[30] A further generally negative review by Patsy McGarry for the *Irish Press* complained that 'characterisation hardly exists' and the women are 'symbols of WOMAN in various manifestations'.[31] For McGarry there was not enough conflict in the play, nor sufficient clashes between the symbolic women. Arguably the most sensitive of the reviewers was Kay Hingerty for the *Cork Examiner*. She noted that Kennelly's Helen is 'programmed for depths of humiliation' and that in this play '[e]motions whirl, searching for a base'. Hingerty asks of Kennelly, 'is this poet waging his own war for the vengeance of women? And why? In his manacling accounts of us, women become spiteful, that's often a violence [*sic*]. Their assailed-by-men-strength is resilient, thereby leaving men guilt-free. "They'll survive."'[32]

What Kennelly exposes, I suggest, through his Hecuba figure, is the destructive nature of female collusion in sexist discourse. The women's attempt to shame Helen's sexuality leads only to their own debasement. What his representation also confirms, however, as Hingerty observes, is that men continue to escape blame. In 1993 when Kennelly's *Trojan Women* was produced, women's rights were still creeping out of the dark ages in the Irish Republic, and the control of sexuality was very much a political issue. One of the front page stories in the edition of the *Irish Independent* that published Desmond Rushe's review of Kennelly's *Trojan Women* proclaimed 'Bishops condemn condoms move by Cabinet', referring to the Catholic Church's condemnation of government attempts to make condoms more widely available in the fight against AIDS; the story was also

---

[28] Rushe (1993).   [29] O'Kelly (1993).
[30] Roche (2005a: 162–4) makes insightful remarks on Kennelly's presentation of Cassandra's and Andromache's perspectives on rape.
[31] McGarry (1993).   [32] Hingerty (1993).

covered in the *Irish Press*. In addition, we may observe that it was not until 1990 that marital rape was defined as a crime in Ireland and it has proven extremely difficult to prosecute.[33] The last of the infamous Magdalene laundries were still operational (until 1996), where young women who were deemed sinful for whatever reason were sent to wash away their sins as effective prisoners working the laundries. In 1993 divorce was still illegal in Ireland after the 1986 divorce referendum had overwhelmingly upheld the constitutional ban on divorce. In the bitter campaign of 1995 which finally overturned the ban by a tiny margin of 50.3 per cent against 49.7 per cent, the anti-divorce campaigners, as noted by James Clarity in *The New York Times* 'largely ignored statistics showing that most separations in Ireland are...sought by women', and often by wives who had been the victims of repeated abuse by their husbands or whose children had been abused by their fathers.[34]

There is no doubt, however, that many women voted against divorce in the 1995 referendum, particularly in rural areas where women's rights were most seriously repressed by social structures and lack of opportunities for independence. But in Dublin also, I personally knew young well-educated women, admittedly unmarried themselves, who were voting against the legalization of divorce because of their religious beliefs in a country where church and state continued to be inseparable.[35] In this context of the fragility of women's rights in Ireland, Kennelly's Hecuba serves as a warning on how women can undermine the rights of their own gender by turning on each other and demonizing female sexuality.

Carr's *Hecuba* (2015): Embracing Sexuality as Political Agency?

If Kennelly's Hecuba demonizes female sexuality, Marina Carr's Hecuba embraces it, allowing herself to find some momentary comfort from her grief in Agamemnon's bed. But does this give her any political agency? Carr's 2015 play, entitled *Hecuba,* adapts elements from Euripides' *Hecuba* and *Trojan Women* as well as from Homer's *Iliad*. In this drama, Hecuba and her daughters have become sexually liberated. In one of Carr's many innovations, we hear that it is perfectly acceptable in Troy for a wife to have an extra-marital lover if things cool down within her marriage, as long as discretion is practised.[36] Cassandra flirts

---

[33] For a brief overview of Irish law on marital rape see Gráinséir (2018). At the time of going to press, there had been only two successful convictions since 1990, as discussed by Holland (2016).

[34] Clarity (1995).

[35] On the interconnection of church and state in the Irish Republic, it is worth noting that 90 per cent of the state's primary schools are Catholic and that these had regularly given priority to baptized pupils against local but unbaptized children. In 2018, legislation was finally passed to remove the so-called 'baptism barrier' faced by parents who did not wish to baptize their children. See, e.g., Donnelly (2018).

[36] Carr (2015a: 253).

openly with Agamemnon, and although this meets with Hecuba's disapproval (she calls her a 'little trollop')[37], Cassandra is unfazed. She later boasts that she's 'going to have a mad passionate affair with the barbarian king', i.e. Agamemnon, and recounts matter-of-factly that she was raped by Ajax on a ship.[38] Fourteen-year old Polyxena has been involved in a serious and intimate relationship with Achilles while the war was ongoing, and is entirely unrepentant. She claims Achilles had asked her to marry him and she had agreed.[39] But it is Hecuba's relationship with Agamemnon that is arguably the most complex in the play.

From the opening scene Hecuba is sexually objectified by Agamemnon. He observes that 'there's bedding in her yet' and wonders if she still bleeds. He posits that the '[o]nly way to sort a woman like that out is in bed'[40] and muses that she must be '[m]agnificent in the sack'.[41] During the course of the play, Hecuba's proud spirit is crushed as she must watch the gruesome sacrifice of her daughter Polyxena over the tomb of Achilles, slaughtered by Agamemnon to appease the troops in a remake of the sacrifice of his own daughter Iphigenia at the start of the war. Alone, Hecuba ends up leaning on her captor Agamemnon as he offers her support. Bizarrely yet plausibly Agamemnon and Hecuba are brought close by the shared experience of witnessing the human sacrifice of their daughters. Agamemnon takes Hecuba to bed and she does not resist.

In Euripides' *Hecuba*, Hecuba discovers that the former Trojan ally, Thracian king Polymestor, had killed her last remaining son Polydorus who had been sent to him for safe-keeping with a large sum of gold to guarantee his safety and survival. She plots and executes a horrific revenge, murdering Polymestor's two sons and blinding the king. This is a personal act but also a political one against the king who betrayed her son. The blinded Polymestor then predicts Hecuba's fall to her death from the ship's mast into the sea, her metamorphosis into a dog, and the fact that the marker of where she perished, given the name 'Hound's Grave', will denote a place for sailors to avoid. Carr rewrites these events substantially, and draws attention to her metaliterary treatment by having the prophetic Cassandra say, 'They will lie about what happened this day.'[42] All murderous impulses are transferred to the Greeks. Polymestor has not betrayed Hecuba in this version. Her boy is safe until he ends up in the hands of the Greeks. They are the ones who kill Polymestor's sons also and blind him as punishment for a skirmish early in the war. There is no prophecy of metamorphosis for Hecuba. Rather she awaits her death on the shore.

This Hecuba is compelling if flawed. The way she tries to shame Cassandra for flirting with Agamemnon, for example, calling her a 'trollop' as we noted above, is spiteful and may even imply a jealous streak. Hecuba finds her way into

---

[37] Carr (2015a: 213).
[38] Carr (2015a: 224–5).   [39] Carr (2015a: 228).   [40] Carr (2015a: 213).
[41] Carr (2015a: 215).   [42] Carr (2015a: 257).

Agamemnon's bed, but the young and beautiful Cassandra is his chosen war prize. As is typical of Carr's characters, Hecuba is humanized by her lack of revenge.[43] That transformation, however, also deprives this Hecuba of the agency granted to her in the original. In fact, we see this pattern in all four of Carr's adaptations of central female characters from Greek tragedy. In *By the Bog of Cats...*, Carr's Medea figure (Hester) is not motivated by revenge but by grief and loss. She does not concoct any plot to kill the Jason figure's new wife Caroline or her father Xavier (the Creon character), who is a thoroughly odious man, and far more unpleasant than his original counterpart in Euripides; nor does Carr's Medea figure have any plan to kill her child. Rather she plans to commit suicide and, when her daughter begs to be taken with her on the journey, it is clear that she kills her child in order to spare her the lifetime of longing for a mother's return to which she had herself been subjected. In *Ariel*, Carr's Clytemnestra figure similarly lacks any premeditation in her actions (unlike her counterpart in Aeschylus). She does kill the Agamemnon character when she discovers he has killed their daughter, but she does so in a moment of psychotic rage after ten years of torment wondering how she had disappeared. Finally, in *Phaedra Backwards*, Phaedra is not an agent in her own right, as in Euripides, but is compelled to act against Theseus by the ghosts of her family members.

It is striking that in each of Carr's adaptations from Greek tragedy, the agency of the female characters is severely reduced in contrast to the originals that inspired them. Regarding her *Hecuba*, Marina Carr has stated that she does not consider it an Irish play at all,[44] and it is true that it is not Irish in the way some of her other plays are. It is not set in Ireland; the characters do not speak in Irish dialect. And yet there is a distinctive and inevitable Irish quality to the language, and the woman cast to play Hecuba for the Royal Shakespeare Company premiere was Derbhle Crotty, a well-known Irish actor, who used a natural Irish accent in the performance. No doubt there is a global message in Carr's play, which resonated strongly in the context of the Syrian refugee crisis.[45] Carr's Trojan women are the women who are left behind in warfare of any kind, who find themselves at the mercy of enemy troops. It can be argued that in taking ownership of their sexuality, and of its potential to influence their captors, the women empower themselves. If survival is the goal in a situation of captivity, then Stockholm syndrome is a likely human response. This kind of empowerment, however, is to a large extent illusory. Rather like Iphigenia in Euripides' *Iphigenia at Aulis*, who 'chooses' to die willingly even as the Greeks threaten to drag her to the sacrificial altar by the hair,[46] the captive women of Carr's play can only choose the manner

---

[43] Cf. Wilmer (2017: 281): 'Carr transforms these female figures from monstrous murderers into precarious beings.'
    [44] Carr (2015b: 11).   [45] Wilmer (2017: 279–80).
    [46] On the illusory nature of Iphigenia's choice see Rabinowitz (1993: 47).

in which they accept their inevitable fate. Hecuba is not shamed or degraded by her sexual encounter with Agamemnon, but she is deprived of any personal revenge and left to wait for death on the beach. The relationship that Carr invents between Hecuba and Agamemnon might have provided the perfect stage for Hecuba to effect her revenge on the Greeks, by finding a way to murder their leader while unarmed and unsuspecting. This would also have been a more justifiable form of revenge than Hecuba's murder of two boys in Euripides' original (to which Carr objected). As it is, Carr's Hecuba has no political agency, and neither do any of the other Trojan women. Hecuba may well be humanized by her lack of vengeance but both she and the audience are left without its consolatory power. Women in war have few options is the message communicated through an Irish voice on an international stage.

In September 2019, Carr's *Hecuba* received its Irish premiere at the Dublin Theatre Festival in a production by Rough Magic, and was positively reviewed, but we might pause to consider the timing of this production, which overlaps with new work by Irish scholars shedding light on the sexual violence suffered by Irish women during periods of Irish warfare in the twentieth century. A 'dark secret' of the Irish war of independence and the Irish civil war, not to mention the Northern Irish 'Troubles', sexual violence against women is part and parcel of the machine of war.[47] Greek tragedy never lets us forget the suffering of women in war, and while Ireland has been slow to acknowledge the painful realities of its own history in this regard, Carr's *Hecuba* is a timely vehicle for reflecting on women's limited options during periods of warfare.

Trojan Women and Irish Sexual Politics: Conclusions

The fact that Hecuba's sexuality is a focal point in Carr's adaptation is remarkable, not only because it is not at all a concern in Euripides where the younger Trojan women are more obviously sexualized, but also because female sexuality connected with political disempowerment, in different manifestations, has been the thread that links all three plays discussed in this chapter. John Rice focused on Helen's seductive power and ignored the obvious political analogies of Maud Gonne as Hecuba in 1920. Kennelly, in 1993, created a one-ring circus of Trojan women hurling sexually charged verbal abuse at the Greek Helen, drawing

---

[47] On 10 January 2019, for instance, *The Irish Times* published a piece by Prof. Linda Connolly discussing the importance of acknowledging sexual violence against women in the context of Ireland's Decade of Commemorations. This was followed by Connolly's 'Sexual Violence in the Irish Revolution' in *History Ireland* (27.6, 2019) published in conjunction with a public event and panel discussion on the subject at the National Photographic Archive in Dublin (26 November 2019). Stacey Gregg's *Ismene*, discussed in Ch. 17 of this volume, engages with the issue of gang rape in the context of the Northern Irish conflict.

attention to the ugly shaming and blaming of women by other women. And while Carr can, in 2015, present sexually liberated Trojan women, the way in which the women take possession of their sexual powers essentially represents a defiant acceptance of the inevitable rather than a truly free choice. In former times of peace Carr's Troy seems egalitarian. Women as well as men are allowed to have extra-marital affairs. But if we look more closely at how this is expressed we see that the terms are still unequal. It is assumed that a Trojan woman may only look for another man *if her husband cools*, and that she must be discreet.[48] The woman's freedom to seek relations elsewhere thus depends on a husband's waning interest; her discretion presumably assists in safeguarding the man's reputation. Meanwhile there are apparently no such restrictions placed on Trojan men.

Irish sexual politics have come a very long way for women in recent decades. Divorce was legalized in 1996, and it has been possible (if difficult), since 1990, to bring criminal charges for marital rape. There have been two female presidents deeply committed to human rights advocation, Mary Robinson (1990–7) and Mary McAlesse (1997–2011), and 2018, the centenary anniversary of women's suffrage in Ireland, saw a landmark referendum overturning the absolute ban on abortion. Nevertheless, there remain social structures, hierarchies, and assumptions that mean complete equality of the sexes continues to be difficult to achieve. In fact, one need only look to the world of Irish theatre to see that this is the case. When the Abbey Theatre announced its 'Waking the Nation' 2016 commemoration programme, in a completely unconscious display of gender imbalance, only one of the ten plays for the programme was written by a woman, thus perpetuating the male domination of an industry in which Marina Carr is often singled out as a lone successful female playwright. The programme provoked many theatre professionals to challenge the Abbey Theatre on its failure to interrogate its own gender bias, generating the #WakingtheFeminists (or #WTF) movement which galvanized huge support on social media. The movement was awarded funding from The Arts Council/ An Chomhairle Ealaíon to produce a detailed research report into gender imbalance in Irish theatre, which has had an impact on policymaking in the industry.[49] What connects gender inequality in the workplace to gendered oppression of a sexual nature is the invisibility of the disempowered and of their suffering, which is masked by the status quo and by the narrative dictated by those in power. Over the past one hundred years, however, Euripides' *Trojan Women* has afforded Irish voices the opportunity of lifting the veil and of highlighting and interrogating issues of painful sociopolitical subjugation.

---

[48] Carr (2015a: 253).

[49] The report can be downloaded at http://www.wakingthefeminists.org/research-report/ (accessed 5 December 2019). One may also compare, in terms of scandal and impact, the Field Day Anthology of Irish Literature originally published in three volumes in 1991, which was heavily criticized for the dearth of female authors in the collection, leading ultimately to the publication, in 2002, of an enormous two-volume collection of Irish women's writing to accompany the first three volumes.

14

Irish Didos

Empire, Gender, and Class in the Irish Popular Tradition to Frank McGuinness's *Carthaginians*

Siobhán McElduff

> Here in this province the whole principle of Empire is at stake: we, the people of Ulster, are the children of the Empire.
>
> Hugh Pollack, Empire Day 1922[1]

The British Empire evoked by Hugh Pollack when presenting his inaugural budget as finance minister of the first Parliament of Northern Ireland, was already fading in 1922, and always had mixed feelings about its Irish 'children', irrespective of their loyalties. In Frank McGuinness's *Carthaginians* (1988),[2] the central character, an openly gay nationalist male called Dido, reduces the representatives of empire into one 'faceless, nameless... working class boy sent here to oppress the working class'.[3] Derry may be 'a harbour. An empire. Part of a great empire',[4] but the greatness of empire was in very small supply in Northern Ireland of the 1970s and 1980s, and in *Carthaginians*:

> DIDO: They've got me. I join the dying. What's a Brit under the clay? What's a Protestant in the ground? What's a Catholic in the grave? All the same. Dead. All dead. We're all dead. I'm dying. They've got me. It's over. It's over. It's over. (*dies*) That's it. What do you think?[5]

Many thanks are owed to the editors of this volume for their suggestions and help, and to their work in organizing the conference where this was first presented, as to the audience there, and to Nadine Knight for her many helpful suggestions.

[1] Parliamentary speech, cited in Hume (1996: 159).

[2] I use here the considerably revised 1992 version of *Carthaginians* as reprinted in McGuinness (1996); the play's first performance took place in Dublin at the Peacock Theatre in 1988. On the nature and significance of the revisions especially in the area of gender see Harris (2009).

[3] McGuinness (1996 [1992]: 334).   [4] McGuinness (1996 [1992]: 310).

[5] McGuinness (1996 [1992]: 344).

Siobhán McElduff, *Irish Didos: Empire, Gender, and Class in the Irish Popular Tradition to Frank McGuinness's Carthaginians* In: *Classics and Irish Politics, 1916–2016*. Edited by: Isabelle Torrance and Donncha O'Rourke, Oxford University Press (2020). © Oxford University Press.
DOI: 10.1093/oso/9780198864486.003.0014

McGuinness's Dido does not want to be remembered for his travails in navigating various British Army roadblocks throughout Derry to reach the other characters as they sit in the graveyard where the play is set. Nor does he aspire to a traditional patriotic memorial commemorating his work corrupting 'every member of Her Majesty's forces serving in Northern Ireland'.[6] Instead, he yearns to be commemorated by a nude statue with a blue plaque before his genitals describing him as 'patriot and poof', openly embracing both his gay sexuality (and sexuality in general) in ways that were neither normative nor accepted in either nationalist or loyalist culture in Northern Ireland of the time.[7]

In this chapter, I will re-examine the ways in which *Carthaginians* interrogates what empire means, the role ordinary people play in empires, and the legacies of these historically (and epically) unimportant subjects who do not, unlike Virgil's Dido, immolate themselves on grand pyres when their Roman lover has sailed away.[8] I will do so by placing McGuinness's version of Dido within the context of the complicated ways in which Rome, Dido, and Carthage have functioned in Irish popular and peasant culture from the 1700s onwards. In doing so I will complicate the view that *Carthaginians* 'draws subversive power from an identification between Ireland and Carthage that since the eighteenth century has focused Irish resistance to British colonial rule'.[9] In advancing that argument, Elizabeth Butler Cullingford investigates what is indeed an important strand of Irish historical and cultural understanding, one based around erudite manuscripts and lengthy printed volumes, perhaps most famously represented by Geoffrey Keating's *Foras Feasa ar Éirinn/ History of Ireland* (1630s).[10] It is, however, not the only tradition in play.

Classical Mythology in Irish Ballads

No discussion of the use and abuse of classical mythology and history in Ireland can be complete without taking into account their wide circulation in popular,

---

[6] McGuinness (1996 [1992]: 302).

[7] Abdo (2007: 219) points out that Dido's proposed statue mocks both the traditional notion of masculine sacrifice and the nationalist 'myth of Ireland as beautiful maiden, Ireland as the woman with the harp, Ireland as mother'. Dido consistently refuses to be a martyr of the traditional Irish variety, popular as that role might be in Irish historical understanding; on this theme in the play see Ford (2001).

[8] Dido does just that, but not before cursing Aeneas and asking an avenger to 'rise from her bones' (4.625). Dido would have many afterlives, but the avenger to whom she alludes here is Hannibal, Carthage's greatest general, and the losing general in the Second Punic War that ultimately led to the final destruction of Carthage in 146 BCE at the end of the Third Punic War.

[9] Cullingford (1996: 222).

[10] On this see Cullingford (1996) and (2002: 99–110), Leerssen (1986: 41–71), and O'Higgins (2017: 28–33). On the social and intellectual circles in which Irish scribes and their manuscripts moved in Dublin see Ní Shéaghdha (1989).

cheap, and ephemeral forms of print. Of particular importance is the high volume of popular ballads inexpensively printed and sold in Ireland from the 1700s until the middle of the twentieth century.[11] These were mainly 'slip' ballads, cheaply printed on sheets of coarse paper, cut into slips, and costing a fraction of a penny.[12] Ballad singers were omnipresent in Irish towns and at Irish fairs, sometimes to the annoyance of the authorities, especially when they ventured into political territory.[13] Some, like the blind Dublin ballad singer Zozimus Moran (c.1794–1846), might fall back on classical examples to defend themselves: when arrested he claimed that he was doing nothing that had not been done before by Homer and Horace.[14] Ballads were omnipresent, both textually and orally, and were consumed eagerly by a range of individuals from the very poor, who could at least listen to and learn ballads even if they could not read or afford to buy them, to collectors like Sir Frederick Madden, one-time keeper of the manuscripts in the British Library, and whose massive collection is now held by Cambridge University. It is important to understand the massive reach, both regionally and temporally, of this popular material (some ballads, such as 'Glendalough', are still in circulation), especially compared to less accessible manuscript histories of Ireland and the more expensive printed and manuscript scholarly texts that Cullingford discusses. Where those texts traced connections between Ireland and the East, and rejected Roman models and origins for the Irish people, the ballads presented a different picture. They circulated in both oral and printed forms: printed material was of particular importance in the north and east of Ireland, which were highly literate regions for a country where literacy rates were generally lower than in England.[15] Belfast was a very important centre of regional printing, and the province contained a large number of regional distributors; their ballads helped spread an anarchic and sometimes confusing alternative version of the ancient world throughout the Ulster region in particular.

The Trojan War, Dido, and the Erasure of Aeneas

Heroes of the Trojan War were popular in Ireland. This is especially true of Hector, who is compared with Saint Patrick in 'The Irish Maniac' (Belfast); with two

---

[11] John Moulden's 2006 thesis is an excellent, if sometimes overwhelming, place to start with ballads; for popular printed material in general see Adams (1987).

[12] There are considerable difficulties in referring to or citing ballads in any consistent fashion; unfortunately they are poorly catalogued, and printers, place of printing, and dates can be difficult or impossible to recover. Additionally, they can change considerably even within the same town. In the above, where possible, I cite from ballads I have physically seen, even if that sometimes results in quoting from some less ably printed, spelt, and punctuated specimens.

[13] Neilands (1991).   [14] McCall (1894: 28–9).

[15] Literacy rates for men were above 50 per cent for Ulster and Leinster, compared to 30 per cent in Connaught (Higgins 2010: 30).

mythical Irish heroes in 'The Rigs of the Times';[16] and with Julius Caesar and Milesius in 'A New Song on the Times'.[17] On the non-professional stage, the prologue of Robert Ashton's massively popular tragedy *The Battle of Aughrim* refers to the doomed, but noble and brave, Irish losers of the battle as 'Hectors'. The ribald ballad 'The Cuckoo's Nest' by John Shiel[s] (*c.*1800–*c.*1860) reels off 'Hector Paris Achilos [*sic*] Patriclos [*sic*] and Hercules'. It is typical of these texts, however, that they display no comparable interest in Aeneas. Given this absence, we can see that in McGuinness's *Carthaginians* the lack of interest in Aeneas (who has no clearly identifiable counterpart in the play: see below) has parallels in earlier Irish popular tradition—which, in contrast to its silence about Aeneas, also shows a great deal of interest in Dido.

Dido frequently appears in one of the most idiosyncratic features of these ballads, the 'goddess routine', a feature borrowed from a Gaelic poetic form known as the *aisling* or 'vision' poem. In a traditional *aisling* the poet falls asleep, meets a beautiful woman with whom he instantly falls in love, and addresses her by comparing her to a range of classical women. The woman turns out to be Ireland, mourning, and usually closes the poem by giving a rousing prophecy of Irish success in the coming years and expressing support for the Jacobite cause. 'The Distressed Maid of Erin' from Cork (*c.*1790s; Madden Vol. 24)[18] is a good English-language example of the older goddess routine in which the 'distressed maid' is Ireland. In the second stanza the narrator compares her to the 'mother of Cupid' (i.e. Venus); in the third he says that if he had 'Homer's eloquence' then he would speak of her 'to each distant settlement', so much that she would attract Hector, Jason, Achilles, and Hercules—no mean haul of classical heroes. Two stanzas later he asks her,

> ...are you the lightsome Dido or Proserpine
> Or the Queen who voluntarily did accompany,
> And was decoyed by Paris to Troy [i.e. Helen],
> And left many a list to muster her energy,
> Deranged by jealousy in pausing soliloquy [*sic*],
> Trying once more his sights to enjoy?[19]

The maid, however, refusing to be compared with any classical woman, declares herself Erin (Ireland personified), and the ballad ends.

---

[16] Ó Muirithe (1980: 59).   [17] Ó Muirithe (1980: 134).

[18] See Moulden (2006: 580). The Madden Ballads are held at Cambridge University Library.

[19] The author also throws in Venus again at the end, describing her as 'a sporting roving frolicker, | From Paphos' grove, for the use of foreignors' [*sic*]: it is not clear if she or the grove is thought to be for the use of foreigners.

Ballads of this type, so-called 'hedge schoolmaster songs',[20] whether by schoolmasters or not, show knowledge of an enormous array of classical goddesses and heroines. The most popular were Aurora, Flora, and Pandora, because their names enabled the internal rhyming of which Irish ballads were especially fond. Also to be found, however, are Ceres, Cleopatra, Diana, Dido, Europa, Eurydice, Hebe, Helen, Juno, Medea, Minerva, Pallas (Athena), Polyxena, Procris, and Venus, along with many other far more obscure classical females. The range testifies to the force that these allusions had on their audiences, especially when employed en masse; we should not forget that ballads were written and sung to be *sold*, as well as enjoyed, and relied on wide popular appeal as texts worth carrying and committing to memory. Classical allusions and names were frequently tossed together in a heady mix, with little regard for different traditions, context or, often, spelling—a respect in which (aside from erroneous spelling) they resemble the quizzes that occupy the characters in *Carthaginians*, where all information is levelled to the same value, as I discuss further below.

As songs that were disseminated through performance and printing, without much idea of the precise storyline they were referencing, or much concern about it either, ballads changed across their various iterations even within a single town. For example, in 'The Tin Ware Lass', one edition by the Cork printer Haly[21] refers to 'Paris, Priam's darling son | by his beloved Hecuba'; this was printed as 'Paris prim a Darling son | by his beloved Ecobagh' by a different printing firm in Cork (J&H Baird), strongly suggesting that Hecuba/Egobagh is in a relationship with Paris that is very definitely not maternal. From such misprintings it is easy to see that the material travelled orally, and that it was extremely fluid and unstable. In 'The Flowers of Edinburgh', a macaronic Irish and English ballad,[22] the author differs from the tradition regarding who was at fault in Dido's departure from Tyre:

> I freely asked with submission whether she was Helen or Juno,
> Whom that great deity received as a host,
> Or Diana who delights in fields, or Venus who such
>   beauty yields,
> Or Palace [=Pallas Athena] who destroyed the Greeks and
>   dispersed thro' the shore,
> Or Dido who Pegmalion [=Pygmalion] discharged for being a
>   tyrant queen,
> Or the charmer that caused all our harbours to groan.

---

[20] Henigan (2016: 111–50), and see further Mac Góráin (Ch. 7) on hedge schools.
[21] Joseph Haly, who seems to have pioneered ballad printing in Cork and whose firm lasted until the 1870s: Moulden (2006: 198, 204); Madden Vol. 24.
[22] Madden Vol. 24; on macaronic ballads see Ó Muirithe (1980).

Aside from the creative spelling, what is startling about this ballad is that it reverses the traditional story of how and why Dido left Tyre to found Carthage. Rather than leaving the city at the behest of her dead husband's ghost, who tells her he was murdered for his wealth by her brother Pygmalion (as reported by Venus in *Aeneid* 1), she is dispatched for being a 'tyrant'. In 'King Billy's Downfall' (1836), whose subject was the destruction of the statue of William III in College Green, Dublin, on 8 April 1836, Zozimus Moran relocates the scene of Dido's death back to her place of origin, Tyre, as he invokes the names of various legendary figures to swear that he played no part in destroying the statue:

> by our champion Fingal, who invaders beat all,
> by hebrew king saul, and Drumcondra big tree,
> by zozymus moran, and catholics shorn [?],
> by dido forlorn, at Tyre who did fall;
> by tighe's dirty breeches, that both stinks and itches,
> i ne'er had a hand in king billy's downfall.[23]

What is noticeable about these references is not just how they rewrite the story of Dido to suit the circumstances and to make a good line, but also how they completely exclude any reference to Aeneas—and even Carthage.[24] Dido as a classical female is a familiar figure in Irish ballads, even receiving the honour of having her name spelled correctly by printers such as Baird and Peter Brereton (active 1872–c.1879 in Dublin),[25] whose orthography was otherwise highly unreliable. One reason for Dido's popularity might be a fondness for invoking the names of classical wanderers, such as Ulysses, Jason, Medea, and Hercules, a development perhaps to be linked to the turmoil of the eighteenth and nineteenth centuries in Ireland.[26] That said, we can also see that popular impressions of Dido were sometimes rather ambiguous ('lightsome' is not exactly a compliment, nor is 'tyrant').

However, while the tradition had space for Dido, it did not for the equally peripatetic Aeneas. No one who researches ballads can claim completeness, but so far I have encountered only a single Irish ballad in which he is mentioned, 'The Dear Belfast Maid'. Even there his appearance is fleeting. One printing claims that the dear Belfast maid is more gorgeous than Dido: 'Dido sure that virgin pure that for Anias [*sic*] sake had died' (Harding B 25 (165)); no printer); another, however,

---

[23] All spelling and orthography as printed; 'Billy's Downfall' (Madden Vol. 25).

[24] It is possible that the presence of Tyre, rather than Carthage, as the home of Dido is an influence from the more literary and historical traditions that were focused on Irish origins in the Lebanon: see Cullingford (1996: 225–8); the popular tradition is also fond of referring to the Irish as 'Milesians'. This suggests some interaction between the popular and more literary traditions, but charting those interactions is very difficult.

[25] See Moulden (2006: 968).

[26] In England the instability of the period for many members of the labouring classes was reflected in popular ballads in their use of transient and unsettled figures such as sailors: see Fumerton (2006).

replaces Aeneas with 'his', and prints the line as 'Dido sure that virgin pure that for *his* sake had died' (my italics). While errors in transferring names are common (e.g. Acteon becomes Action/action and Ulysses becomes Uclopeous in Roud V3060; and Dido is even misspelled as Deido, though as a one-time occurrence this is unusual in its rarity), the printer or copyist of the song nearly always recognizes a name as a name, and tries to replicate it as best they can; whoever cut Aeneas from the second printing seems not to have known either of his existence or his connection with Dido.

In eighteenth- and nineteenth-century popular Irish culture, then, as in McGuiness' *Carthaginians,* Dido was of far more significance and interest than Aeneas, who is essentially erased. Indeed, if we take into account that some of the ballads mentioned above were still being collected from ballad singers in the 1950s, we could extend this lack of interest well into the twentieth century. This is despite the fact that Aeneas was an important figure in Jacobite literature,[27] and at least one major eighteenth-century Irish-language poem, Donncha Rua McNamara's *Eachtra Giolla an Amaráin* (c.1745), used Aeneas as a parodic model for its author's travels and misfortunes.[28] It is also surprising because classical couples usually appear in the ballads as couples; it is common to hear of Jason *and* Medea or Orpheus *and* Eurydice, for example. The only other comparable omission is Andromache, who is also erased entirely, perhaps so that Hector can be a paragon of unattached manly beauty (it also did not help that her name does not lend itself to rhyme in English or Irish). Aeneas' erasure might be prompted in popular ballad-making by a desire to have Dido equally unattached, and by a belief that he was the least interesting thing about her and her story. Whatever the case, his absence gives a surprisingly high profile to Dido, comparable to that of Hector, in Irish ballads.

Popular tradition in Ireland treats Dido and her narrative as extremely malleable, then, and happily inserts her into an array of local contexts and comparisons. This is paralleled by Dido in *Carthaginians,* where McGuinness remakes her into a male, gay, working-class Derry nationalist, who controls no empire, but who embraces his sexuality and refuses to hide his desires. For both this drama and the earlier popular tradition, Dido is not the 'defeated queen' of the *Aeneid,*[29] but an independent character with her own story.

---

[27] Pittock (1994: 38–42, 66–8). See, for example, *The Young Ascanius* (1746), a popular account of Bonnie Prince Charlie's struggles on behalf of his deposed father after Culloden, and available widely in cheap chapbook format.

[28] His name is also transliterated as Donnchadh/Donough/Denis Ruadh McConmara. For a complete text see Hayes (1853), Ó Flannghaile (1897), Ó Foghludha (1908). For fuller discussion of the poem's interaction with the *Aeneid* see O'Higgins (2017: 95–8) and McElduff (2011).

[29] Quotation from Cullingford (1996: 223).

Virgil as a Love Poet

Parallel to these developments, Irish ballads were turning to the Virgil of the *Eclogues* and the *Georgics*, discarding his epic reputation and seeing him as a poet of love or of rural praise. 'O'Sullivan's praise of his Lovely Dame' (Haly, Cork) sees Virgil—as well as Ovid and Julius Caesar[30]—as a love poet, exclaiming:

> If Ovid and Caesar strenuously,
> Or Virgil whose fame increased indeed,
> In chorus praised their fairest queen,
> Were unlike my dame whoe'er she be.

In 'A new song called Margaret Allen' the singer calls upon 'Virgil or great Homer' to assist him in his praise of the lovely Margaret (Cicero is also cited later in the ballad). Elsewhere the ballad tradition paired Homer and Virgil to praise hurling games,[31] landscapes ('Glendalough'), and oratory ('Famed O'Connell the Shamrock shall Wear'). In contrast to Virgil, however, it was Homer who played an exemplary role in patriotic ballads.[32] As we have seen above, when Zozimus Moran was defending himself in court, he called on Homer and Horace as patriotic praise singers, *not* Virgil. In the words of an 1805 ballad from Laggan (a region in the north-east of Donegal close to McGuinness's birthplace in Buncrana), Virgil wrote 'Sylvanian lays',[33] not heroic stories. Just as Dido's story was being shaped to the needs of the ballad tradition, so, too, did Virgil undergo a transformation, and that transformation frequently erased his connections with epic, Dido, Aeneas, and even Roman imperialism.

Popular Culture and Rome as a Model

None of this means, however, that Roman imperialism and Rome are absent from popular and peasant culture. Given a chance, Irish peasants, both Catholics and Protestants, could enthusiastically embrace Rome as a potential historical model, and celebrate her imperial victories. A phenomenally successful folk drama, *The Battle of Aughrim, or the fall of Monsieur St. Ruth* (1728) by Robert Ashton, shows considerable interest in connecting its Irish characters with Rome, both in its

---

[30] Julius Caesar is not exactly known as a love poet, though Caesar did write poetry and Pliny *Ep.* 5.3.5 cites him as a precedent in lighter/scurrilous poetry. Caesar was known, however, for his intense and public relationship with Cleopatra, which may have been a consideration, although it is more likely that the audience had no knowledge of such details and simply enjoyed the lyrics at face value.

[31] Crofton Croker (1839: 153).

[32] E.g. 'The Brave Defenders'; 'Irelands (*sic*) Lamentation for her beloved Canning'.

[33] Adams (1988: 68).

classical form *and* as the seat of the pope.[34] According to the writer and one-time hedge-school student William Carleton (1798–1869), this work was 'acted in barns and waste houses night after night' throughout Ulster,[35] although it never got a single official production on an Irish stage.

The play is a dramatic rendering of the bloodiest battle ever fought on Irish soil, the decisive clash at Aughrim between the troops of William of Orange and those of King James on 12 July 1691 in the old calendar (22 July in the new). The French and Irish are led by the villainous Charles Chalmont, Marquis de St Ruth (who was decapitated by a cannonball during the battle), but it is the Irish and English officers who are the heroes of the piece. The English get saddled with an unlikely and tragic romantic subplot, while the Irish spend nearly all their stage time talking of or engaging in war, or, in the case of Patrick Sarsfield, occasionally accusing St Ruth of treachery towards the Irish. The Irish are also constantly and positively compared to Roman heroes. In the very first scene St Ruth enthusiastically describes Colonel Talbot as an 'Irish Scipio',[36] and, later in the same act, describes Sarsfield returning to the camp 'like Great Emilius, when he enter'd Rome | In Pomp, bedew'd with Macedonian Tears'.[37] 'Great Emilius', i.e. Scipio the Younger, not only defeated the Macedonians and the Greeks, but was responsible for the complete and utter destruction of Carthage in 146 BCE; that fact clearly gave the participants no pause when they spoke these lines. Significantly, no one in the play—English, Irish, or French—is very keen on being identified as a Carthaginian or even compared to Hannibal, its greatest general. After the inevitable Irish defeat, right as the play reaches its final moments, Sarsfield rants that he will not

> …beg for Charity and seek Relief
> Like *Hannibal* the *Carthaginian* Chief
> Who when by *Scipio* he was overthrown,
> He fled to *Africk* like a Vagabond,
> Cloath'd as a Slave, dejected and obscure,
> He wander'd all alone from Door to Door:
> Then shall an Irish Soul submit like him,
> To forfeit Honour, and renounce a King?[38]

[34] On the play see Adams (1987: 69); Wheatley (1999: 63–84). The *Battle of Aughrim* was deeply unusual in that it featured performances by members of both religious communities, bringing them together to perform Ireland's past, even if sometimes those performances ended in pitched battle between the two sides (Carleton 1896: 28). The play saw a huge number of printings, including many in Ulster: still extant are editions from Belfast (1767 and 1800), Newry (1781) and Strabane (1785); and we have most likely lost a number of other local editions (Adams 1987: 70).

[35] Carleton (1896: 26); Carleton was involved in productions, helping the illiterate to learn their lines. We know the play was performed elsewhere: for example, Thackeray mentions a production in Galway, and found it easy to obtain a copy of the drama while in that city (1843: 173).

[36] Ashton (1777: 19).   [37] Ashton (1777: 27).   [38] Ashton (1777: 50).

When General Dorrington asks Sarsfield to leave the field shortly thereafter he is careful to use examples of others who fled to fight another day, including Darius, the Persian king defeated by Alexander the Great, as well as Regulus, Paulus, and Scipio, all Roman heroes of the First or Second Carthaginian Wars. Given a choice, Irish peasant audiences did not necessarily side with Hannibal and doomed Carthage over the more militarily glorious Romans. In contrast to works aimed at other audiences, such as Lady Morgan's 1806 novel *The Wild Irish Girl*, which 'bristles with antiquarian allusions to the Phoenicians' and sees them as a positive model,[39] popular culture gives us a very different understanding of the roles that Carthage, Rome, Dido, and Aeneas played in Ireland.

Carthaginians and a Boy Named Dido

Dido; a girl who makes herself ridiculous with fantastic finery. (Carlow)
Didoes (singular *dido*); tricks, antics: 'quit your didoes.' (Ulster)[40]

The malleable legacy of Dido lived on well into the twentieth century and in some-times rather startling ways. Uniquely among all classical figures, her name was used, at least in Co. Carlow until the early twentieth century, to refer to women who wore flashy clothing to the point of ridicule—queening it up a bit too much, one might say. Even gender fluidity makes it into the mix: a boy who attended school alongside McGuinness in Buncrana was called Dido, leading him to assume it was a man's name until he read the *Aeneid*.[41] McGuinness's Dido thus continues in a long tradition when he shrugs off social norms, dresses in miniskirts, embraces his sexual-ity, and plays continuous games with the other characters of *Carthaginians*. Irish popular culture of the nineteenth century would have had little trouble incorporating a male Dido who is erotic and unconstrained by the suffocating legacy of a Virgilian namesake who kills herself for love, whereas in late-twentieth-century Derry, prior to McGuinness's play being performed, the portrayal of these elements in a nationalist male caused considerable public anxiety.[42] Dido's cross-dressing and open homosexuality might have given the tradition some pause—but even then it was in

---

[39] Cullingford (1996: 226).   [40] Joyce (1910: 247).   [41] Lojek (2004: 180).
[42] The production that McGuinness directed for Druid in 1992 was scheduled to coincide with the twentieth anniversary of Bloody Sunday, and toured to Derry only after considerable controversy about the character of Dido and the play's bad language: see Foley (1992); Lojek (2004: 127). On the slow road to the legalization of homosexuality in Ireland, which occurred only in 1993, and the appeals of gay rights activists to models from classical Greece, see Walshe (Ch. 12).

the nature of popular tradition to reshape characters, even eminent ones, to the needs of the moment.

But if McGuinness's Dido manages to escape the tragic role that a Dido is traditionally expected to play, he is surrounded by characters who have all in some way failed to properly play the social roles expected of them, and bear the scars from their attempts: Maela, a loving mother, lost her child to cancer on the day of Bloody Sunday and cannot accept that death; Greta mourns a brother that never existed and as a result of an early hysterectomy feels less than a full woman; Sarah left Ireland for greater things but became a drug addict and prostitute in Amsterdam. The men fare no better: Seph refuses to speak after informing on an IRA operation; Paul is building a pyramid of rubbish to bring back the dead as the only way to deal with the pain he sees around him; Hark acts the hard man, but did not volunteer to go on hunger strike with other IRA prisoners. No one in this play can comfortably fit into the roles they were handed by tradition and society, but Dido seems untroubled with that, even as the other characters struggle with their pasts.

The Rejection of Epic and High Tradition

Carthaginians opens as if it were firmly within high tradition, as the strains of the aria 'When I am Dead and Laid in Earth' from Purcell's seventeenth-century opera *Dido and Aeneas* echo across the stage while three women in a graveyard worry about the fate of a dying bird. The stage directions for the first production directed that the graves resemble the burial chambers at the Irish Neolithic site of Knowth,[43] evoking the more elevated world of Punic round towers from Carthage and the noble Irish past that Cullingford discusses.[44] The most monumental feature that Carthage and Derry share, great defensive city walls, is not mentioned at all, however. What we get instead is Paul's pyramid of rubbish under construction—an example of how in this play great imperial and military symbols are replaced by ones that might hold great hopes, but are nonetheless built out of waste material discarded by the city. After the opening strains from Purcell, we hear a few lines of David Bowie's 'Amsterdam' sung by Sarah, followed by a dirty joke. Shortly thereafter, Dido appears, he, too, singing, with slight changes, the second verse of 'Danny Boy' as he wheels a pram filled with deliveries for the women (perhaps poking fun at the expense of the abandoned Dido in the *Aeneid*,

---

[43]   Gleitman (1994: 65).
[44]   In the production for Derry these ancient grave markers were replaced by 'huge, set flats of layered headstones coloured in psychedelic strokes of orange, red and blue' (Foley (1992: 37)).

who wails that Aeneas hasn't even left her a 'little Aeneas' to comfort her (4.328)). In this way, we are separated from high tradition as quickly as it was invoked, a move that will be replayed throughout the drama.

At the moment of Dido's arrival the women's discussion moves from death to survival:

MAELA: Hello, Dido. How are you, son?
DIDO: Surviving, Maela. How are yous?
MAELA: Grand. Surviving.[45]

The audience knows that Maela is barely surviving. Before Dido arrived she was singing happy birthday to her dead daughter and refusing to acknowledge her death. Dido's arrival brings back basic and physical concerns: food, coffee, cigarettes—and the payment for them. From the start Dido is openly concerned with money and its acquisition, telling Greta, who complains about his late arrival, 'Listen, wagon. I'm not running a charity service. Business, baby. I've other commitments.'[46] This Dido, a 'queen of Derry', neither wants nor can afford to be hosting guests night after night, even if he might stretch to a few cigarettes and some other treats for Hark (who gives Dido his regal title, and not as a compliment).[47]

Dido's unepic nature is further highlighted by the story of how he got his name. He claims he was named by a beautiful, drunk Lebanese man, whom he stumbled across on the docks:

DIDO: When he gave me the flowers I was sure I'd scored and then he put his hand on my face and I thought, Yippee, but he just knelt down on the ground like this. (*kneels*) He said, 'Listen, listen to the earth. The earth can speak. It says, Cease your violent hand. I who gave birth to you will bring death to you. Cease your violent hand. That is my dream. I pray my dream comes true.' I said, 'I pray your dream comes true as well, but failing that I'll settle for Derry City winning the European Cup.' He smiled and called me Dido. I'd never met him or any like him before. It was like as if he knew me. I turned on my heel and ran like hell. (*He rises.*)
HARK: Derry City will never win the European Cup.
DIDO: Where's your loyalty? We need to build up a good team. Local, loyal.[48]

We are far from any epic model here. McGuinness's Dido wanders along the docks while looking for paid sex and comes upon this Lebanese man, a potential 'john' pointedly named John. In contrast, Virgil's Dido meets a princely Aeneas, enhanced

[45] McGuinness (1996 [1992]: 301).
[46] McGuinness (1996 [1992]: 301).
[47] McGuinness (1996 [1992]: 364).
[48] McGuinness (1996 [1992]: 326).

in beauty by his mother Venus, in the middle of her people as her city rises around her (*Aen.* 1.494–508). The fact that Dido's encounter in McGuinness is with a man from Lebanon, the region from which Dido set out for Carthage, complicates matters even further: is it Dido or John who is playing Aeneas here? Between this and Dido's words about building a 'loyal' team, which hints at loyalism (i.e. political allegiance to the British crown), or at least echoes it,[49] one begins to wonder exactly what sort of figure he is: is he supposed to be a victim or an oppressor? Or, like Dido, can he simultaneously be both?

At least this Dido's decision to flee is sensible: to anyone who has read the *Aeneid* and knows that Dido's affair with Aeneas ends with her suicide, McGuinness's Dido turning on his heel and fleeing was the most sensible option. Noticeably, whatever lasting effects this scene had on him, Dido finishes by being more interested in Derry City's unlikely hopes for football glory than anything else. 'Local, loyal', indeed. *Carthaginians* delights in shrugging off moments (first encounters, naming scenes) that would occupy an epic text for lines and lines; whether Derry City wins or loses is also of great importance and will receive as much attention.[50] Dido's naming is important, and presented in language that suggests how significant the encounter with John was. When he describes his first meeting with Maela in the graveyard while looking for suicide sponsors he uses far less elevated language.[51] Dido's name is also one that can be reshaped. Before the *Aeneid*, Virgil's Dido is a sailor, a wanderer, but she is also a settler looking for land to occupy; in the *Aeneid* and other texts she is fixed in Carthage and its environs, to the point of tragedy.[52] McGuinness's Dido is also a settler, with all that implies: he moves into Maela's house without her permission, telling her, 'I've moved into it for safety. Don't thank me. You're doing me a favour as well.'[53] The implication that the property has been occupied because its owner is not managing it appropriately echoes the land-politics and settlement issues in Northern Ireland, adding a further layer of complexity to the play's engagement with Virgil.

At the same time, Dido is also the most mobile character in *Carthaginians*. He may bear the name of a Punic queen, but he gets to move around like Aeneas, and even flees awkward situations like him. When he is not running away from Lebanese men, he is being carried out of the cinema, having been overcome by the

---

[49] Thanks to the editors for this suggestion.

[50] We might parallel here the ballads' fondness for evoking great classical heroines and heroes to talk about local beauties, events, and even in one case a garden.

[51] McGuinness (1996 [1992]: 304).

[52] According to Timaeus, a Greek historian of the third century BCE, Dido did not meet and fall in love with Aeneas, but instead killed herself to avoid marriage to Iarbas, an African king, and to stay true to her first husband (a similar story is told in Macrobius, *Saturnalia* 5.17.5–6). Dido thus saves her city and her chastity in one move. This was the version picked up and made perhaps most popular through Justin's *Epitome of Roman History*, a text which was popular and quite cheaply available in England and Ireland in the nineteenth century (it is attested in Irish hedge schools, and appears frequently in catalogues of cheaper printed material).

[53] McGuinness (1996 [1992]: 306).

gore of *Poltergeist* for the fifth time,[54] or wandering in graveyards, or flirting his way through checkpoints. When Hark viciously spurns and expresses his disgust for him,[55] rather than mope and mourn, Dido retaliates by smushing a pile of sausages into his chest.[56] Moments later he exclaims, 'Jesus, I wish I could meet somebody. Somebody really rich and wonderful. I need money.'[57] It is clear that this Dido, unlike his Virgilian counterpart, is never destroyed by his love affairs and will be able to move on from Hark. McGuinness rejects the epic Dido's noble but despairing death, and substitutes resilience, albeit a mercenary kind of resilience, for the original despair. Throughout *Carthaginians*, then, as we have seen, motifs and indicators of high culture and traditional epic are evoked only to be drawn down to popular and human levels, whether it is drama, love affairs, music, naming scenes, or colonization. It is not only Dido who is reshaped; rather, the whole structure and content of the play demand to be read as reclaiming and reshaping key indicators of culture for a world of ordinary, working-class imperial subjects.

Dido as Storyteller

In the *Aeneid* Dido falls in love with Aeneas at a banquet, where he tells the story of the destruction of Troy, a story she ends up making him tell over and over, night after night (4.77–9). In doing so, she forces her guest to become a storyteller of what is the worst night of his existence, the night he saw his city destroyed. It is a powerful story and through it Dido falls in love with Aeneas. But it is also a story that cannot but make intolerable demands on him: each night he must describe the disappearance, murder, rape, and enslavement of his friends and family. McGuinness's Dido is not so cruel; rather than force others to tell him their sufferings, like Virgil's Aeneas he creates stories (as Maela says, 'Dido always had a way with words').[58] In *Carthaginians* his literary achievement is represented by *The Burning Balaclava*, a play that is justly described by the other characters as 'shite'.[59] It was written by Dido in the persona of Fionnuala McGonigle, a French woman who has changed her name in empathy with the sufferings and changed name of ~~London~~Derry.[60] Names in *The Burning Balaclava* are meaningless except by the very precise criteria of Northern Ireland: every character is named some variant of Doherty, but the differences in spelling, e.g. Dogherty and Docherty, indicate—to those in the know—different religious backgrounds.[61]

---

[54] McGuinness (1996 [1992]: 374).   [55] McGuinness (1996 [1992]: 313–15).
[56] McGuinness (1996 [1992]: 324).   [57] McGuinness (1996 [1992]: 325).
[58] McGuinness (1996 [1992]: 330).   [59] McGuinness (1996 [1992]: 344).
[60] On self-dramatization by characters in McGuinness's drama see Dean (1999).
[61] McGuinness (1996 [1992]: 331).

In this play within the play, Dido alone takes on two roles, perhaps mirroring the way his own character incorporates elements of both Dido *and* Aeneas.[62] He plays Doreen O'Doherty (most of the characters play a role of the opposite sex), a suffering Derry woman with a cocker spaniel named Boomer, *and* a 'faceless, nameless' working-class English soldier who is in deep torment because 'he is a working class boy sent here to oppress the working class'.[63] The soldier's torment, however, does not stop him from shooting Doreen's dog as a representative of the bourgeoisie. The highest rank anyone gets to play is that of a savage Royal Ulster Constabulary Sergeant (Dogherty), who beats Catholic suspects over the head with a crucifix and strangles them with rosary beads.[64] It is remarkable that although all the cast later call the play 'shite', they nevertheless participate enthusi-astically, whether they are called on to re-enact their own oppression, albeit in ridiculous forms, *or* to perform the actions of their oppressors. In the play they lay down their lives, but through the power of drama they rise again—as they hope the dead in the graveyard will. All this Dido achieves through his storytelling.

Class and Gender in *Carthaginians*

The Burning Balaclava, the play produced by the characters in *Carthaginians*, hor-rifically distorts some iconic moments of the tragedy that unfolded on 30 January 1972, known as Bloody Sunday, when the British Army shot dead thirteen protes-tors on a march for civil rights (a fourteenth later died of his injuries) and falsely claimed the victims were rioting or carrying weapons. Seph plays a priest, Father O'Doherty, who has lost his voice and communicates via semaphore, evoking a famous photograph of Father Edward Daly waving a blood-stained handkerchief as a white flag in front of others carrying a body. Father O'Doherty uses his sheet to communicate more mundane matters, such as saying hello and the like,[65] and occasionally less mundane ones, such as going on missions of peace to Protestant areas.[66] In Dido's version of these events there is no one in charge—no officers giving commands, no British authorities, no leaders of the various nationalist and loyalist factions. Nor does the play feature any of those brought in after Bloody Sunday, such as Lord Chief Justice John Passmore Widgery, to whitewash the deaths.

Instead, *The Burning Balaclava* presents a plebeian British Empire violently tormenting working-class Irish nationalists, and a degraded version of empire in which two sets of plebeian groups struggle in an endlessly replicating series of atrocities. In *The Burning Balaclava*, the cast swap their gender and religious

---

[62] I owe this suggestion to the editors of the volume.
[63] McGuinness (1996 [1992]: 334, and see also 344).   [64] McGuinness (1996 [1992]: 333).
[65] McGuinness (1996 [1992]: 336).   [66] McGuinness (1996 [1992]: 341).

identities, but not their class. This is not unique to this part of *Carthaginians*, however. Elsewhere in the play it is suggested that changing gender is easier and more natural to imagine than altering one's class. Greta reports that when she got her first period her mother told her it came from the tooth fairy,[67] an unconvincing explanation that resulted in Greta's belief that she was turning into a man. When Sarah exclaims at the weirdness of her reasoning, Greta replies, 'Don't knock it if you haven't tried it. Whenever I was feeling lonely, it was some con solation to think I'd grow into my own brother. And I grew out of it.'[68] *Carthaginians*, then, repeatedly insists that gender fluidity is more attainable than class mobility.

Quizzes, Ballads, and the Value of Knowledge

Carthaginians also uses the quiz format to further drag Carthage, Rome, Virgil, and other elements of high culture into direct contact with popular culture. The play's quizzes do not distinguish between so-called 'high' and 'low' categories of knowledge: sometimes the quizmasters ask about composers and history, while other questions are based on the trivia of captains of sports teams and TV shows. Since the players get two points for knowing who won an Oscar as well as for knowing who wrote the *Aeneid*, the quiz levels the value accorded to certain types of information. In this respect the quizzes of the play resemble the ballad tradition: everything goes in, and everything has equal value, whether it is Dido, Venus, or a particularly good-looking woman or garden. In *Carthaginians*, quizzes also bring the characters together in the brief flourishing of the 'Derry Renaissance', whose sole product is quiz night, and which ends its brief and glorious reign in a single pub due to an unfortunate incident involving mustard, a cat's posterior, and animal protection.[69] Throughout the play quizzes continue to bind the characters in rituals of question and answer, and help them to restore each other in moments of crisis. When Maela finally accepts the death of her daughter and breaks down at the horror of it, and of Bloody Sunday, and cries out to Dido to take her to mass, the other characters respond by improvising a quiz to bring her back to them:

DIDO: Who wrote *The Firebird*, Maela?
Silence
        Who, Maela?
MAELA: No.

---

[67] McGuinness (1996 [1992]: 349.

[68] McGuinness (1996 [1992]): 349). The first production of the play was more interested in issues of gender and gender fluidity than subsequent versions; many of the changes between the versions involved cuts in this area: see Harris (2009).

[69] McGuinness (1996 [1992]: 355–8).

PAUL: *The Firebird,* who wrote it, Maela?
MAELA: Stravinsky.
PAUL: What nationality?
MAELA: Russian.[70]

On the other hand, quizzes also move on relentlessly from question to question. The minimal time they allow for reflection troubles some of the characters:

> PAUL: I was at a quiz tonight, but I said nothing. I used to run it. Questions and answers. What's the capital –? Who won an Oscar for –? Who captained Arsenal –? Fuck sports questions. Selling out. Who wrote *The Aeneid?* Virgil. Who did Virgil guide through the city of hell? That's a tough one, boys. Who will guide me through this city of hell?[71]

Paul is silenced because this quiz, which takes place outside a graveyard, does not allow for further reflection on the correct answers. Once back in graveyard space, however, he finds himself able to break out of the structure of quizzes and turn the conversation where he wants it to go:

> PAUL: Roman. This city is not Rome, but it has been destroyed by Rome. What city did Rome destroy?
> GRETA: Carthage.
> PAUL: Correct. Two points. Carthage.
> GRETA: How are we in Carthage?
> PAUL: Tell them you saw me sitting in the ruins, in the graveyard. I live in Carthage among the Carthaginians, saying Carthage must be destroyed, or else – or else –
> GRETA: What?
> PAUL: I will be destroyed. I would like to go to Carthage.
> GRETA: I would like to go to Rome.
> PAUL: I would like to see the pyramids. I'm building a pyramid. But I'm no slave. I am Carthaginian. This earth is mine, not Britain's nor Rome's. Am I right?[72]

The character who turns out to be obsessed with Carthage and the *Aeneid* is Paul rather than Dido.[73] He repeatedly brings us back to them, but in deeply unstable ways, as the passage above shows. The most famous person to sit in the ruins of Carthage was not a Carthaginian (there were few of them still alive when it fell), but Gaius Marius, a general of the late Roman Republic, who sat there and wept when he was on the losing side of a bloody civil war, making him an appropriate analogue, in some ways, for a man despairing in the middle of another. It was

---

[70] McGuinness (1996 [1992]: 352).   [71] McGuinness (1996 [1992]: 309).
[72] McGuinness (1996 [1992]: 309–10).   [73] McGuinness (1996 [1992]: 365; cf. 368–9).

Cato the Elder who pushed his fellow Romans to raze Carthage by repeatedly stating that 'it must be destroyed'. These allusions suggest that Paul wants to visit Carthage as a *Roman* destroyer or as a tourist, not a mourner. We might even call him an Irish Scipio (another Roman who wept outside Carthage as he was destroying it), as Talbot and Sarsfield were termed in *The Battle of Aughrim*. Such shifts and connections easily destabilize the identification of those in the graveyard with those Carthaginians who sat in their city waiting for the Romans to come over the wall and end their city's existence, and suggest that even those who reject imperialism are not free from its seductions.

History and Memory

The repetition of historical knowledge or trivia in quizzes is a key way in which characters in *Carthaginians* defuse situations or speak of their desires, as if only in repeating fragments of history can they find their footing once more amid the horrors of Derry, and face the truth. But this approach to history has a levelling effect: the fate of empires and great cities has the same value as remembering that Frank McClintock and his lovely legs captained Arsenal in 1971[74]—and missing the latter point prompts as much self-reflection among the characters as questions about Carthage or the *Aeneid* do, highlighting how trivial information is placed alongside great historical questions and tragedies. Gleitman notes that in this respect *Carthagianians* resembles the pyramid that Paul is building: 'this play – with its allusive title and its wealth of allusions to other texts is constructed from a long swath of cultural material leveled to a common factor, like the trash of the pyramid, and piled into a structure.'[75] This aspect of the play is troubling within the larger context of the role of memory in Ireland: memory, representation of the past, and performing the past, whether through parades or other means, has particular resonance in Ireland, where 'perhaps more than in other cultures, collective groups have...expressed their values and assumptions through their representation of the past'.[76]

But to what memories do the characters in *Carthaginians* give cultural weight? What great loss do they enact on the stage for us, comparable to the great loss of Aeneas suffered by Dido in Virgil? The answer is the enactment of Bloody Sunday, and the recognition of the names and identities of the slain, and of the streets in which they lived. Historical figures have cried over Dido from St Augustine to William Carleton; in contrast, McGuinness's characters take as their concern the mourning of ordinary imperial subjects for other ordinary subjects. These dead

---

[74] McGuinness (1996 [1992]: 363).   [75] Gleitman (1994: 65).   [76] McBride (2001b: 3).

were not just residents of Derry, of an ancient town with famous walls; they lived along small streets, in particular neighbourhoods with their own meanings and histories. This is how Paul remembers the dead of that terrible day in the last scene of the play:

> Bernard McGuigan, forty-one years, Inishcairn Gardens, Derry. Patrick Doherty, thirty-two years, Hamilton Street, Derry. Michael Kelly, seventeen, from Dunmore Gardens, Derry. William McKinney, twenty-seven, from Westway, Derry. James Wray, twenty-three, Drumcliffe Avenue, Derry. Hugh Gilmore, seventeen years old, Garvan Place, Derry. Jack Duddy who was seventeen, Central Drive, Derry. William Nash, nineteen, Dunree Gardens, Derry. Michael McDaid, twenty-one, Tyrconnell Street, Derry. Gerald Donaghy, seventeen, Meenan Square, Derry. John Young, seventeen, Westway, Derry. Kevin McElinney, Knockdara House, Waterside, Derry.[77]

In contrast, when Maela earlier described Bloody Sunday and its body count,[78] she mentioned no names: just streets and the rising number of the dead as she moves through the city. Catalogues of troops, their leaders, and their origins have been a feature of epic since Homer's 'Catalogue of Ships' in book 2 of the *Iliad*. However, in *Carthaginians* no admirals or generals are named; instead, we hear the names of ordinary people living ordinary lives until the day of their deaths, and, as the drumbeat of repetition emphasizes, all from one city, Derry, not all Ulster, Ireland, England, Greece, or Italy, as in the *Aeneid*'s catalogues (7.647–817; 10.163–214). These people came from 'little streets', to borrow from W. B. Yeats's 'No Second Troy', first published in 1916; and when little streets get 'hurled upon the great' in Ireland, things do not go well for the little streets. The epic catalogue is transformed and humbled by Paul, just as he reduces the colossal architecture of pyramids to a construction of insubstantial rubbish.

Conclusion

Empire is an engine whose fuel is the labouring classes and the poor. Rome's late Republican army was increasingly drawn from its landless urban poor after an expanding Roman state imposed impossible demands on, and chewed its way through, the smallholders who were supposed to make up its backbone. The British Army in Northern Ireland was made up of working-class boys and men from economically deprived areas of England, sent to Northern Ireland under the

---

[77] On the records of those who died during the Troubles in Northern Ireland, see also Alden (Ch. 16).

[78] McGuinness (1996 [1992]: 351–2).

command of officers who came from a different class. Those who died on Bloody Sunday at the hands of the army were also working-class young men, whose lives in those moments did not matter particularly to anyone in charge. *Carthaginians* brings to the fore that the costs of empire are not generally paid for on the floors of senates or in the houses of the wealthy; they are paid for by the poor, the working classes. Even the prophecies of fated, proper, and eternal rule in which empires invest are punctured:[79] *Carthaginians* has no time for prophets. At the end of the first scene Paul attacks St Malachy, an Ulster saint and author of dire (and surprisingly popular) prophecies:

> He saw the end of the world. He prophesied it. He saw the waters rise over Derry. He saw the Foyle and the Swilly meet, and that will be Derry gone. He saw it, but will he stop it? No. He sees the state of this town, but so do I see it. And I will search every dump in this town for rubbish. I'm building a pyramid. When the dead rise, I'll walk into the pyramid again and walk away from this town and the state it's in. And if I find St Malachy hiding in this city, I'll kill him, I'll kill him, I'll knock his teeth down his throat.[80]

St Malachy might have written apocalyptic and biblical fantasies of a great cataclysm swallowing Derry, but the pyramid of *Carthaginians* is decidedly non-epic.

The only way to escape from the demands of empire is to reject historical models and refuse to accept them as destiny, to see instability as a form of possible escape, to reject that Dido, for example, must mean only one thing: suicide and the loss of empire. In doing so, in refusing to die for a non-existent Aeneas or even for Hark, McGuinness's Dido 'survives rejected love, does not die, does leave Carthage.'[81] As the other characters sleep in the graveyard, waiting for the dead to rise, he creeps away from them and out of the city, in a final scene where he has all the words: 'If I meet one who knows you and they ask, 'How's Dido? Surviving. How's Derry? Surviving. Carthage has not been destroyed. Watch yourself.'[82] With these words he leaves, reversing not only the fate of Dido, but that of the working-class soldier whose part he plays in the lines quoted at the start of this chapter. But even as Dido escapes Derry and his own fate, he carries with him an ambiguity that would have been familiar, at least in part, to earlier audiences who listened to ballads and performed their history in the *Battle of Aughrim*.

---

[79] See, for example, Jupiter's words to Venus in the *Aeneid* that Aeneas' heirs will be given 'empire without end' (1.279, where 'without end' is both spatial and temporal) and are destined to be 'lords of all' (1.282).

[80] McGuinness (1996 [1992]: 308).   [81] Lojek (2004: 125).

[82] McGuinness (1996 [1992]: 379).

V

CLASSICAL POETRY AND NORTHERN IRELAND

15

Elegies for Ireland

W. B. Yeats, Michael Longley, and the Roman Elegists

Donncha O'Rourke

The poetic genre of elegy was popularized in antiquity by the Latin love poets Propertius (*c.*56–*c.*16 BCE), Tibullus (*c.*55–19 BCE), and Ovid (43 BCE–CE 17) during Rome's troubled passage from the internecine wars of the late Republic to the uncertain peace of the early Empire. This long tradition surfaces in the work of a number of Irish poets, particularly in the context of their own country's *impia bella*—or, in the words of one, 'the sticky intimate violence of our tawdry little civil war'.[1] The genre of tears as well as of love, 'elegy' was derived by some ancient etymologists from the Greek '*e-legein*' ('to cry *ah!*'), though in origin its interests ranged well beyond love and lament to embrace political and ethical themes that have remained embedded in its genetic make-up throughout its multifaceted history.[2] In antiquity the genre's identifying and unifying quality was first and foremost formal, but the elegiac couplet's alternation of hexameter and pentameter lines was also what mobilized its introspective pullback from purely hexametric monologism. The elegiac voice, then, defines itself in contradistinction to that of epic, which one Virgilian critic has characterized as '"objective", credible, univocal...unshocking in tone and substance, indeed (and more particularly) patriotic and inspiriting', even if it was also that critic's purpose to amplify epic's 'further voices'.[3] Elegy might thus be considered as a 'further voice' for private, sentimental, and, very often, critical reflection.

If elegy can be heard as epic's 'further voice', it speaks in Ireland through the work of W. B. Yeats and Michael Longley in a way that pulls back from the violent narratives their times were telling. This is also true, ostensibly at any rate,[4] of the Roman elegists, and perhaps especially of Propertius, not least as championed by Ezra Pound, whose 1917 'Homage to Sextus Propertius', the modernist poet's first

For discussion of this paper in various stages of its gestation I warmly thank Maureen Alden, Stephen Harrison, Aifric Mac Aodh, Fiachra Mac Góráin, Cillian Ó Hogan, Isabelle Torrance, Mark Usher, and the anonymous reviewers appointed by OUP.

[1] Longley (2009: 101).
[2] See Nagy (2010) in the first chapter of Weisman (2010).
[3] Lyne (1987: 2).
[4] For a discussion of elegy's identification with the violence of its time see O'Rourke (2018).

Donncha O'Rourke, *Elegies for Ireland: W. B. Yeats, Michael Longley, and the Roman Elegists* In: *Classics and Irish Politics, 1916–2016*. Edited by: Isabelle Torrance and Donncha O'Rourke, Oxford University Press (2020).
© Oxford University Press.
DOI: 10.1093/oso/9780198864486.003.0015

large-scale work, mediates subsequent reception of the elegist.[5] Defending his version of Propertius from the derision it attracted for its apparent misconstruals of the elegist's difficult Latin (itself nowadays regarded by some as proto-modernist),[6] Pound explained that his poem was not a translation but, precisely, an homage inspired by his affinity, in the context of the First World War, with Propertius' anti-imperialist posture:[7]

> I may perhaps avoid charges of further mystification and wilful obscurity by saying that it presents certain emotions as vital to me in 1917, faced with the infinite and ineffable imbecility of the British Empire, as they were to Propertius some centuries earlier, when presented with the infinite and ineffable imbecility of the Roman Empire.[8]

This reading of Propertius also informs the work of another Belfast-born poet, Derek Mahon, whose own Propertian set includes a version of Propertius 3.4 and 3.5 ('Love Not War') in which Augustus' campaigns in India are made to foreshadow the imperial interests of the Raj:[9]

> Augustus aims to raid the wealth of India,
>   Our oars will strike her pearl-providing sea.
> Great victories there, rich pickings in the East!
>   Indus will flow at the imperial whim.
> One of these mornings I expect to see
>   our wagons groaning with the spoils of war
> and read the stickers – 'Patna', 'Kandahar' –
>   while I recline upon my Cynthia's breast.

Pound, for his part, seems to have considered the First World War as a consequence of capitalist overproduction, to which he saw an antidote in the economic-stimulus theory of Social Credit proposed by Major C. H. Douglas, whose model Pound actively promoted in his *Cantos* and later distorted in his antisemitic broadcasts on the airwaves of his hero Benito Mussolini.[10] Pound's espousal of Italian fascism

---

[5] On Pound's Propertius and its critical reception see Sullivan (1965); Comber (1998); Hooley (1988: 28–54); Rudd (1994: 117–50); Davidson (1995); Usher (1996); Willett (2005); Liebregts (2010).

[6] See, e.g., Benediktson (1989). Longley (2009: 105; 2015: 35) describes Propertius as 'neurotic and strangely à la mode'.

[7] Thomas (1977: 39–58) suggests that it was, rather, a mid-career poetic crisis that prompted Pound to identify with the middle and transitional books of Propertius.

[8] Ezra Pound, *Collected Letters* 246 (to the Editor of the *English Journal*, 1931) (= Paige [1971: 230–1]).

[9] Mahon (2009: n.p.) = Mahon (2011: 18). From *Raw Material* (2011), by kind permission of the author and The Gallery Press (Loughcrew, Oldcastle, County Meath, Ireland).

[10] On Pound's politics and economics see Redman (2010); on the radio broadcasts see van Ert (1994); Friedlander (2010).

squares rather oddly with his liberal (in all senses) reading of Propertius, and attracted about as much criticism. Indeed, the two motives for vitriol were wont to be combined each in justification of the other: after Pound was convicted of treason and committed to a psychiatric facility in 1945, one critic took the opportunity to revisit the 'Homage' and concluded, with bitter irony, as follows:

> But how profoundly mournful is the present spectacle of the sage of Rapallo, driven mad by his much learning and incarcerated in a madhouse instead of being shot for treason. Classical scholars, grateful for Pound's homage to Sextus Propertius, will unanimously lament this sorry miscarriage of justice.[11]

Propertius thus enters Irish poetry already heavily politicized, especially in relation to the British Empire. Of the surviving Roman elegists he is also the one with the most conspicuous Irish legacy, making at least one cameo appearance in Yeats and providing a recurrent source of inspiration for Longley, whether in direct or indirect connection with Ireland's troubled history. Yeats's learning in Greek and Latin was rather more desultory and idiosyncratic than that of Longley, who read Classics formally at Trinity College Dublin from 1958 to 1963.[12] Given the former's greater sympathy for the Hellenic than for the Roman imagination, there seems little reason to doubt Pound's insistence (in the letter quoted above) that it was Yeats, with whom he enjoyed close professional and personal ties at the time, who borrowed from the 'Homage' rather than the other way around.[13]

Longley, for his part, describes Propertius as 'my soul mate, love's polysyllabic | Pyrotechnical laureate reciting reams by heart' in his retrospective poem 'Remembering the Poets' (from *The Weather in Japan* [2000] = *CP* 280).[14] In this roll call of Latin authors idolized by the teenage Longley, Propertius takes his place alongside Macer, Ponticus, Bassus, Horace, Virgil, and Tibullus. Several of these poets Longley cannot, however, actually have read, since they are no longer extant. That oddity, and the curious omission of Ovid (elsewhere very evident on Longley's reading list), are explained by the fact that 'Remembering the Poets' is itself a version of Ovid's autobiographical retrospective at *Tristia* 4.10.41–54. Notwithstanding this Ovidian source, it is true that Longley's youthful

---

[11] Forbes (1946: 179).

[12] On Yeats's classical learning see Stanford (1976: 94–102) and Arkins (1990: 1–23). Recalling his university days, Longley (1994: 51) writes 'my already half-hearted hold on Latin and Greek was further enfeebled by a now all-consuming desire to write poetry', and he later (2009, 2015: 26–7) describes himself diffidently as a 'lapsed classicist'.

[13] On the association of Yeats and Pound see Paul (2010).

[14] Citations of Longley's poems are given from Michael Longley, *Collected Poems* (= *CP*), published by Jonathan Cape (reprinted by permission of The Random House Group Limited, © 2006) and Wake Forest University Press (reprinted by permission of WFU Press, © 2007).

enthusiasm for Propertius was ignited by the lively recitations of Professor Donald Wormell at Trinity College Dublin, and his earliest published poems in the 1960s were versions of Propertian elegy.[15] Little could Longley have known at the time, however, that Latin love elegy would later prove a suitable medium through which to approach the Northern Irish Troubles, as it had previously done for Yeats writing about Ireland after 1916.

Longley's 'Remembering the Poets' is also a poem that indirectly and playfully describes the political clout of classical reception in Ireland. Both Ovidian and autobiographical, it has suggested to its readers, and to Longley himself as his own reader, a contemporary *sodalicium* of poets gathered behind the ancient celebrities: 'The personalities of my own brilliant contemporaries kept crowding in from the back of my mind. The poem expresses brotherly love for them and for the poets I converse with across the millennia.'[16] In the first of the poem's more conspicuous departures from its Ovidian source, one of these alter egos, 'Virgil, our homespun internationalist', is said to be sighted at 'government receptions'. Irrespective of the identity of this latter-day Virgil (the posthumous publication of Heaney's *Aeneid VI* all but confirms the identification suspected by most), Longley's supplement to Ovid points to the powerful encounter of classical reception and Irish politics. Similarly pointed is Longley's elaboration on his *amicitia* with Tibullus, which implicitly records 'Peace' (a version of Tibullus' elegy 1.10) as the most extended political reception of a classical text in his own oeuvre: more than twenty years since that appearance in Longley's 1979 collection *The Echo Gate*, Tibullus is now 'An echo from the past' who gets pride of place at the end of this intensely personal translation of Ovid's elegiac catalogue. Such listing of canonical poets is a feature of elegy at least since Hermesianax in the early third century BCE (fr. 7 Powell; cf. Prop. 2.34; Ov., *Am.* 1.15);[17] assuming Ovid's voice, Longley confidently locates himself in this tradition as 'the last of the singing line'—a punning in-joke in view of Longley's description elsewhere of his contemporary (and later Propertian) Derek Mahon as 'our bravest and most stylish wielder of the singing line'.[18] It is a confidence that also locates Longley's work alongside that of Yeats in a pan-Irish and highly political tradition of classical reception.

---

[15] For a sensitive appreciation of Propertius by the young Longley see his 1962 address to the Classical Society of Trinity College Dublin, now reprinted in Longley (2017: 121–31).

[16] Longley (2009: 112; cf. 2015: 40). For this reading see also Nice (2005: 239); Harrison (forthcoming). For a Hellenic counterpart see Longley's 'The Group' from his 2004 collection *Snow Water* (*CP* 321–2), discussed at Longley (2009: 111–12; cf. 2015: 38–9).

[17] See Farrell (2012).

[18] So Longley on the dust jacket of Mahon (1999); see also E. Longley (1986: 170–84): 'The Singing Line: Form in Derek Mahon's Poetry'. For the pun see Nice (2005: 239), but the Ovidian model indicates that the phrase now applies to Longley himself.

Yeats and Propertius

Yeats's encounter with Propertius comes, first and foremost, in the form of a short poem entitled 'A Thought from Propertius', included in both the first (1917) and expanded (1919) editions of *The Wild Swans at Coole*:

> She might, so noble from head
> To great shapely knees
> The long flowing line,
> Have walked to the altar
> Through the holy images
> At Pallas Athena's side,
> Or been fit spoil for a centaur
> Drunk with the unmixed wine.

The poem reworks Propertius 2.2.5–10, prose and verse translations of which Yeats most likely consulted in W. K. Kelly's collection of *Erotica* (London, 1854), this being the only edition in his library that contained the poem.[19] In *The Wild Swans at Coole*, the poem features within a sequence that centres on Maud Gonne, whom critics identify also with the 'She' of this poem.[20] As Brian Arkins has shown, in both Propertius and Yeats the lover concludes that his girl is the fairest of them all, and Cynthia's further comparison to Helen suggests that other poems by Yeats, such as 'No Second Troy', might owe something to Propertius, too.[21] Certainly it is apt, given the turbulent nature of their relationship, that Gonne should play Cynthia to Yeats's Propertius, and in this configuration the elegiac conceit of *militia amoris* ('the warfare of love') takes on a suggestively literal dimension in the *domina* who 'hurled the little streets upon the great'.

That context may seem remote from Yeats's 'A Thought from Propertius' and its surrounding collection, but for a number of reasons it would be more accurate to say that England's difficulty and Ireland's opportunity are thematically present under erasure. First, Yeats had originally mapped out the earlier (1917) edition of *The Wild Swans at Coole* to begin and end with the poems now entitled 'Easter 1916' and 'On Being Asked for a War Poem', thereby framing the collection with poems on the wars in Ireland and Europe.[22] In the event, 'Easter 1916' was

[19] Kelly (1854: 30 and 167). The library of W. B. and George Yeats is catalogued at Chapman (2006). Yeats might of course have consulted the Latin, but he preferred Greek—and was in any case an unsuccessful student of both: see n. 12 above.

[20] See Albright (1990: 574–9, esp. at 576). On Yeats and Gonne see, e.g., Cullingford (1993); Toomey (1997a); Steele (2010).

[21] See Arkins (1990: 146). See also Sullivan (1965: 178–80) and Arkins (1985).

[22] See Chapman (2010: 78–96).

withheld and replaced with the volume's titular poem 'The Wild Swans at Coole', an elegiac meditation on how 'All's changed'; but 'On Being Asked for a War Poem' made the final cut, and in publically demurring the invitation to write a war poem—what Latin scholars would call a *recusatio* or poem of refusal—it registers how the poet's antipathy to the British Empire's involvement in Ireland had left him indifferent to its involvement in the First World War. Such thoughts were also much in the poet's mind when organizing the definitive 1919 edition of the collection, which includes elegies that lament the death of Lady Gregory's son and decry the war in which the airman was killed.

A second context that politicizes 'A Thought from Propertius' is Yeats's close collaboration at the time with Ezra Pound, whose 'Homage to Sextus Propertius' was completed in the same year (the title page dates the poem to 1917). Through association with a text already enlisted against the 'imbecility of the British Empire', Yeats's inclusion of Propertian love lyric takes the stance adopted by other poems in the collection against Britain's wars—this despite Pound's earlier opinion piece on 'The Non-existence of Ireland', a bilious response apparently to the debacle over the Hugh Lane bequest, in which he writes: 'There is no State, no recently promoted territory in the Union, which has not more claim to being a nation in itself than has this "John Bull's Other Island," this stronghold of ignorance and obstruction.'[23]

Thirdly and finally, its connection with Maud Gonne imbricates 'A Thought from Propertius' with the Irish political situation at the most intimate level. Yeats had proposed to Gonne for one last time in 1916 following the execution of her husband, the rebel fighter Major John MacBride,[24] a man whose violent ways were alleged by Gonne to have spilled into the domestic sphere.[25] He was, as Yeats puts it in the poem that almost stood at the head of this collection, 'A drunken, vainglorious lout. | He had done most bitter wrong | To some who are near my heart'. Gonne declined Yeats's hand (as subsequently did her daughter Iseult) but in 1917 Yeats married Georg(i)e Hyde-Lees with Ezra Pound as his best man. Read with this heady mixture of politics and gender in view, 'A Thought from Propertius' seems to look back at Gonne at a fateful crossroads: that 'she might...have walked to the altar' beside the patron goddess of the arts makes a Yeatsian nuptial of the Propertian source (where Athena alone *spatiatur ad aras*); her alternative destiny (fulfilled, to Yeats's chagrin, by MacBride) sees the marriage gatecrashed by 'a centaur | Drunk with unmixed wine'. That Yeats's Hippodamia is 'fit spoil' gives a rather darker focalization of Propertius' *grata rapina* than either of the translations he may have consulted in Kelly's edition ('delightful booty' in Grantillon's prose version, 'her charms' in Elton's verse

---

[23] Pound (1915: 453).
[24] Foster (2003b: 54–5) argues that Yeats's proposal was motivated by duty more than love.
[25] The point remains controversial: Jordan (2000) argues that MacBride was maligned.

translation): depending on whether 'fit' is taken to represent the centaur's perspective or the poet's, Gonne is seen as a victim either of her nobility or, alternatively, of the violence her violent choice deserves.

Yeats's ambivalent handling of Cynthia/Gonne in this poem speaks in interesting ways to his handling of the classical tradition. In her book *Gender and History in Yeats's Love Poetry*, Elizabeth Butler Cullingford has argued that '[a]s a white, male, middle-class, Protestant citizen of the British Empire, with an acknowledged debt to canonical English writers, Yeats belonged to the dominant tradition', but that '[a]s a colonized Irishman…he was acutely conscious of repression and exclusion.[26] Yeats's classical learning might likewise have been centrifugal to the revival of Irish culture that he championed, but he deploys the classics in a way that seeks to resist empire, with the result that even in his love poetry woman is not just a Muse or 'The long flowing line', but also, as M. Wyke has argued in the case of Propertius, a space in which discourses of power are thrashed out.[27]

Longley and Propertius

In its incorporation of Propertius into the Irish lyric tradition, Yeats's 'A Thought from Propertius' invites comparison with Longley's similarly titled 'An Image from Propertius', the final poem of his second collection *An Exploded View*, published in 1973 in the wake of the outbreak of the Troubles (= *CP* 80):[28]

> My head is melting,
> Its cinder burnt for this:
>
> Ankle-bone, knuckle
> In the ship of death,
>
> A load five fingers gather
> Pondered by the earth.

The brevity of this poem should not deceive. The Propertian 'image' in question takes its cue from Propertius 4.11, an elegy of some 102 lines in which the noble Cornelia speaks from beyond the grave in defence of her conformist life. This Cornelia was stepdaughter of the emperor Augustus, and the morality she is made to champion is entirely the opposite of that for which Propertius and his mistress Cynthia stand in the earlier books. Here Propertius finally seems to make good

---

[26] Cullingford (1993: i, cf. 6).
[27] See Wyke (2002: 11–114) on Propertius.
[28] The connection with Yeats (and Mahon: see below n. 32) is also noted by Harrison (forthcoming), with corroboration *per litteras* from the poet. For other remarks see Arkins (2009: 154–5).

on the abandoned promises of his earlier *recusationes* and addresses contemporary political themes—much to the approval of his critics.[29] It was on this poem, the 'regina elegiarum' as Scaliger called it, that Longley had cut his teeth as a translator in the 1960s with a full version ('Cornelia') in eleven freely-rhymed stanzas of ten lines apiece.[30] Since then, however, Longley had not returned to the Latin poets; now, as the finale of *An Exploded View*, he revisits the poem and his earlier translation in just twenty-six words, fragmenting the grandeur of the originals into a few relics gathered apparently at random, like Cornelia's remains, but in fact carefully arranged at the end of the collection to mirror the position of its counterpart at the end of Propertius' oeuvre. As the comparative table below shows, the final couplet of 'An Image from Propertius' preserves the most intact of these fragments, each plucked from disparate points in the longer versions:

'An Image from Propertius'	'Cornelia'	Propertius 4.11
My head is melting	The funeral trumpets meant this when my head | Was put above the blaze, and was melted (9–10)	sic maestae cecinere tubae, cum subdita nostrum | detraheret lecto fax inimica caput. (9–10)
Its cinder burnt for this:[31]	Our marriage, Paullus, my family name, | All the assurances of motherhood– | What help were they to me? (11–13)	quid mihi coniugium Paulli, quid currus avorum | profuit aut famae pignora tanta meae? (11–12)
Ankle-bone, knuckle[32]	cf. 'Skara Brae' 11: 'Knuckles'	cf. 4.7.12: pollicibus fragiles increpuere manus
In the ship of death,	My bones conveyed there in the ship of death (110)	cuius honoratis ossa vehantur aquis (102)
A load five fingers gather	and reduced me to a load | Five fingers gather (14–15)	et sum, quod digitis quinque legatur, onus (14)
Pondered by the earth.	While my reward is pondered by the earth (108)	dum pretium vitae grata rependit humus (100)

[29] For a representative appraisal of Prop. 4.11 see Highet (1957: 106–11).

[30] The version, entitled 'Cornelia', was published in *Poetry Ireland* 5 (Spring 1965: 19–22), in which Seamus Heaney's 'End of a Naturalist' and 'Valedicton' also first appeared. It is quoted here by kind permission of *Poetry Ireland*. Longley (2009: 106) comments that formally 'Cornelia' was a 'breakthrough' in his evolution: ' "Cornelia" helped me to discover the sort of noise I was looking for in a line of verse.'

[31] Comparison with 'Cornelia' and Prop. 4.11 reveals the speaker's 'this' as a more subtly plaintive assessment of the pathetic outcome of her life: see discussion below.

[32] This line finds no correspondence in 'Cornelia' or Prop. 4.11, but does resonate with neighbouring poems in both collections, as indicated; it also resonates with the phrase 'Our knuckle bones' in the later version of Derek Mahon's thematically and titularly similar 'An Image from Beckett' (Mahon 1999: 40–1), the earliest versions of which (published in *Ecclesiastes* [1970] and *Lives* [1972: 8–10]) themselves show a possible debt to Longley's original 'Cornelia' (e.g. 'And my one marriage \| Was over as soon as it started'). For further discussion see Haughton (2007: 64–6).

This Propertian image of decay is profoundly effective at the close of a collection that bleeds with the violence of the Troubles from the moment of its title (*An Exploded View*), at least at first blush. Even if the phrase 'exploded view' turns out to be a technical term in the poem 'Skara Brae', the volume's epigraph suggests that this is a red herring we are supposed to catch:[33]

> We are trying to make ourselves heard
> Like the lover who mouths obscenities
> In his passion, like the condemned man
> Who makes a last-minute confession,
> Like the child who cries out in the dark.

As the last word in such a collection, then, 'An Image from Propertius' resonates with preceding glimpses of sectarian atrocity (e.g. 'Kindertotenlieder' [*CP* 61]: 'fingerprints | Everywhere, teethmarks on this and that') and foreshadows later poems in which Longley witnesses the horror of terrorism in unflinching autopsy (e.g. 'Wreaths' [*CP* 118–19]: 'When they massacred the ten linen workers | There fell on the road beside them spectacles, | Wallets, small change, and a set of dentures: | Blood, food particles, the bread, the wine.').

The vast differences between Longley's 1965 and 1973 versions of Propertius 4.11 are instructive in respect of classical reception pre- and post-Troubles. In whittling down the great scale of Propertius 4.11 to a few fragments in this brief compass, 'An Image from Propertius' occludes the patriarchal certainties articulated by 'Cornelia' in a way that many Latin scholars would say is entirely in keeping with the resurgent feminine and elegiac agenda that deconstructs Propertius' poem as a final indictment of Roman culture.[34] For example, despite her conformism, Longely's earlier Cornelia wonders, 'Our marriage, Paullus, my family name, | All the assurances of motherhood– | What help were they to me? (11–13, *quid mihi... profuit* in Propertius). This sense of disquiet is preserved in the couplet that sets up 'An Image from Propertius': '*My head is melting, | Its cinder burnt <u>for this</u>:*', where 'this' turns out to be her own remains—'a load five fingers gather'. Longley's elegiac retuning of the poem leaves the confidence of orthodox society in smithereens, and explodes the 'polysyllabic pyrotechnics' of his own youthful tour de force. Comparing Longley's 1965 and 1973 versions of Cornelia's death-poem reveals a far more troubled Propertius.

'An Image from Propertius' is preceded in *An Exploded View* by Longley's reworking of Propertius 2.10 (*CP* 76), a programmatic *recusatio* or 'refusal' poem in which the elegist announces—only to decline—a change of inspiration from love and elegy to war and epic, the 'different lyre' (10 *aliam citharam*) that Longley's

---

[33] See the discussion in Brearton (2006).
[34] For this reading of Propertius 4.11 see, e.g., Janan (2001: 146–63).

title, 'Altera Cithera', conspicuously misquotes. Longley's equally programmatic and rather quirky poem identifies itself in its second stanza (quite literally printed as an aside) as a self-consciously modern ('ballpoint') version of Propertius:[35]

> A change of tune, then,
> On another zither,
> A new aesthetic, or
> The same old songs
> That are out of key,
> Unwashed by epic oceans
> And dipped by love
> In lyric waters only?

> Given under our hand
> (With a ballpoint pen)
> After the Latin of Gaius
> Sextus Propertius,
> An old friend, the shadow
> Of his former self
> Who – and this I append
> Without his permission –

> Loaded the dice before
> He put them in his sling
> And aimed at history,
> Bringing to the ground
> Like lovers Caesar,
> Soldiers, politicians
> And all the dreary
> Epics of the muscle-bound.

When the comparatists have done Longley's bidding they will find that the first stanza synopsizes all twenty-six lines of the Propertian original. In recasting the Latin *recusatio* in the form of this question, Longley's version formulates one of the central issues of Propertian scholarship: to what extent *does* Propertius engage with the politics of his day? This is a question of some pertinence also to Longley, whose readers (including, once again, the poet himself) have likewise grappled with the largely unspoken relation between, for example, Longley's botanical poems, or indeed his many versions of Greek and Roman authors, and the

---

[35] For discussion see Arkins (2009: 153–4); Impens (2018: 89); Harrison (forthcoming).

Northern Irish Troubles.[36] Identifying himself as Propertius' 'old friend', the poet of 'Altera Cithera' justifies the liberty taken in the third stanza (added, as we are told, without the Roman elegist's permission) to answer the question posed in the first. Unlike some of the Propertian scholarship which Longley might have read as an undergraduate classicist, this response refuses the false dichotomy of the *recusatio* by recognizing the political power already inherent in Propertian love elegy.[37] In a letter in *The Irish Times* of 8 June 1974, Longley wrote that the artist 'would be inhuman if he didn't respond to tragic events in his own community, and an irresponsible artist if he didn't seek to endorse that response imaginatively. This will probably involve a deflection or zigzag in his proper quest for imaginative autonomy...'. It may be a critical commonplace in today's scholarship that Propertius configured the civil war of his lifetime within the framework of erotic elegy,[38] but this view was not especially prominent when 'Altera Cithera' was published in 1973. In the context of the Troubles in Northern Ireland, Longley discovered a new dimension to his affinity with the poet he had studied during his undergraduate days in Dublin.

In meditating through Propertius on the relationship between poetry and politics, Longley invites comparison with Ezra Pound, who also included a version of Propertius 2.10 in the 'Homage to Sextus Propertius'.[39] Longley's modernist and imagist poetics owes much to Pound, such that 'Altera Cithera' is something of an homage to the 'Homage':[40] the title's apparent misquotation of Propertius' Latin replicates the kind of schoolboy error of which Pound was accused, but without actually making an error of Latinity (the alteration of Propertius' *alius* to Longley's *alter* points not so much to a 'different' mode of expression as to an 'alternative' one); similarly, 'Gaius Sextus' gives Propertius two *praenomina*, of which 'Gaius' sounds like a dubious confusion with Gaius Catullus;[41] also in the indented verse (which reads and looks like the kind of paratextual gloss familiar in Pound), Longley's 'ballpoint pen' confidently trumps the pencil used by Pound's Propertius (and the pumice used by Propertius himself) in contrast to less discerning

---

[36] Brearton (2006: 135–43); Arkins (2009, esp. 152); Cieniuch (2010: 114–15). See also Longley (1969: 11): 'Anything I may write in the future is bound to be influenced by the recent turmoil. Whether the influence will be obvious or even recognisable, I couldn't say'; Longley (1971b: 8): 'Too many critics seem to expect a harvest of paintings, poems, plays, and novels to drop from the twisted branches of civil discord. They fail to realise that the artist needs time in which to allow the raw material of experience to settle to an imaginative depth where he can transform it and possibly even suggest solutions to current and very urgent problems by reframing them according to the dictates of his particular discipline. He is not some sort of super-journalist commenting with unfaltering spontaneity on events immediately after they have happened.'

[37] Contrast, for example, the readings of Highet (1957: 111) or Hubbard (1974: 100–3) with Keith (2008: 131–3) or Roman (2014: 169–201, esp. 172–4).

[38] For a reading along these lines see, e.g., O'Rourke (2016).

[39] 'Homage' Part V.1 gives Prop. 2.10.1–20, i.e. up to the lacuna indicated in Müller's Teubner edition from which Pound worked: see the collation in Willett (2005: 216–17).

[40] On 'Altera Cithera' and Pound see Peacock (1988: 66–7).

[41] See Cairns (2006) 15 n. 77. *CIL* IV 1501 mentions a Gaius Propertius Postumus who may have been our Propertius' cousin: see Cairns (2006: 16–18); Keith (2008: 5).

poetasters: 'Out-weariers of Apollo will, as we know, continue their | Martian generalities, | We have kept our erasers in order' (*Homage to Sextus Propertius* I.10–12, cf. Prop. 3.1.7–8 *a valeat, Phoebum quicumque moratur in armis!* | *exactus tenui pumice versus eat*). Such wit aside, Longley seems to acknowledge that Pound before him had recognized Propertius as a poet of Callimachean refinement, 'unwashed by epic oceans', no lover of the 'dreary | Epics of the muscle-bound'.

As a modernist take on the Propertian *recusatio* of overtly political poetry, then, 'Altera Cithera' is instructive in respect of the way in which Longley does engage with Homeric epic.[42] As Longley has later written in essays on his classical allusions, 'in my Homeric poems I pushed against the narrative momentum and "freeze-framed" passages to release their lyric potential.'[43] What 'Altera Cithara' adds to this analysis is the potential of this technique to make incisive comment on the political domain inhabited by epic, a poetry that aims at history 'Bringing to the ground | Like lovers Caesar | Soldiers, politicians'. Just as the stop-start runs of Propertian elegy fragment epic and reframe it from the perspective of the poet-lover, so, too, does a poem like 'Ceasefire' (to pick the most famous example) distil from *Iliad* 24 a lyrical vignette in which, rather elegiacally, Achilles is 'moved to tears' and Priam 'Wept with him until their sadness filled the building', and in which 'it pleased them both | To stare at each other's beauty as lovers might'.[44] Elegy is, after all, the genre of tears as well as the genre of love par excellence. It is its elegiac 'further voices', then, that appear to draw Longley and Propertius to Homeric epic.

For all its affinities to Pound's 'Homage', Longley's version of Propertius 2.10 offers a programmatic reading of the politics of classical reception that is rather less partisan than either Pound's fulmination against British imperial 'imbecility' or Yeats's identification with the Republican Propertius. Longley's Propertius is no less political, but his vision is more objective (which is not to say detached), refusing to enter into any war of words and instead bringing into the compass of his poetic oeuvre different systems of violence that resonate with one another in different times and places.

Longley and Tibullus

A key example of Longley's non-partisan and global perspective, and an early inkling of the reconciliatory potential of classical allusion that would find its fullest expression in 'Ceasefire', comes in his poem 'Peace' (*CP* 134–6), a version of Tibullus 1.10 on the same scale as the earlier 'Cornelia' and regarded by some as

---

[42] See also Volsik (2009: 676) on the negotiation between elegy and epic in Longley.
[43] Longley (2009: 99).
[44] On Longley's 'Ceasefire' see further Alden (Ch. 16).

the culmination of Longley's engagement with Roman elegy.[45] Originally composed at the behest of Belfast's Peace People, it later took its place in *The Echo Gate* (1979), where it resonates with the most urgent concerns of the collection.[46] Tibullus' poem decries the warfare of the present and longs for the simple life of yore; in Longley's version the linguistic register vacillates suggestively between ancient Rome and modern Ireland: 'Who was responsible for the very first arms deal— | The man of iron who thought of marketing the sword?' (1–2 *Quis fuit, horrendos primus qui protulit enses? | quam ferus et vere ferreus ille fuit!*); 'I've been press-ganged into service, and for all I know | Someone's polishing a spear with my number on it' (13–14 *nunc ad bella trahor, et iam quis forsitan hostis | haesura in nostro tela gerit latere*); 'And don't be embarrassed by this handmade statue | Carved out of bog oak by my great-great-grandfather | Before the mass-production of religious art' (17–20 *neu pudeat prisco vos esse e stipite factos: | sic veteris sedes incoluistis avi. | tum melius tenuere fidem, cum paupere cultu | stabat in exigua ligneus aede deus*); 'If the good Lord keeps me out of the firing line | I'll pick a porker from the steamy sty and dress | In my Sunday best, a country cousin's sacrifice' (25–8 *at nobis aerata, Lares, depellite tela, | hostiaque e plena rustica porcus hara. | hanc pura cum veste sequar myrtoque canistra | vincta geram, myrto vinctus et ipse caput*); 'You keeping track of the sheep, your son of the lambs, | While the woman of the house puts on the kettle' (41–2 *ipse suas sectatur oves, at filius agnos, | et calidam fesso conparat uxor aquam*). As these samples show, Longley's version slips in just enough contemporary idiom (e.g. 'arms deal', 'bog oak') to update Tibullus' poem, orienting but not confining it to an Irish audience. In reply to Tibullus' opening question about the origin of violence, he writes 'Blame the affluent society: no killings when | The cup on the table was made of beechwood, | And no barricades or ghettos when the shepherd snoozed', taking us from Tibullus' *non arces, non vallus erat* (Tib. 1.10.9) to the Falls Road of the 1970s and to Warsaw of the 1940s. As A. J. Peacock has noted, 'The avoidance of strict determinacy is part of a broad, non-parochial conspectus on conflict and violence offered by the poem.'[47]

Tibullus and Longley end by petitioning Peace herself to bestow a Golden Age in which warfare occurs only as *militia amoris*, joined when the *rusticus* (Longley's 'labourer') comes home *male sobrius* ('a trifle sozzled'). In both poems, however, the speaker's naive idealism is difficult to share (cf. Tib. 1.10.53–66):

> Then, if there are skirmishes, guerilla tactics,
> It's only lovers quarrelling, the bedroom door
> Wrenched off its hinges, a woman in hysterics,

---

[45] Reprinted at Longley (2006: 134–6). For discussion see Peacock (1988); Kennedy-Andrews (2000: 88–9); McDonald (2000: 36–8); Potts (2011: 85–7); Impens (2018: 90–1); Harrison (forthcoming).

[46] The genesis of the poem is described at Longley (2009: 106–7; 2015: 35–6).

[47] Peacock (1988: 60).

Hair torn out, cheeks swollen with bruises and tears—
Until the bully-boy starts snivelling as well
In a pang of conscience for his battered wife:
Then sexual neurosis works them up again
And the row escalates into a war of words.
He's hard as nails, made of sticks and stones, the chap
Who beats his girlfriend up. A crime against nature.

Enough, surely, to rip from her skin the flimsiest
Of negligees, ruffle that elaborate hair-do,
Enough to be the involuntary cause of tears—
Though upsetting a sensitive girl when you sulk
Is a peculiar satisfaction. But punch-ups,
Physical violence, are out: you might as well
Pack your kit-bag, goose-step a thousand miles away
From the female sex.

sed Veneris tum bella calent, scissosque capillos
     femina perfractas conqueriturque fores.
flet teneras subtusa genas, sed victor et ipse   55
     flet sibi dementes tam valuisse manus.
at lascivus Amor rixae mala verba ministrat,
     inter et iratum lentus utrumque sedet.
a, lapis est ferrumque, suam quicumque puellam
     verberat: e caelo deripit ille deos.   60
sit satis e membris tenuem rescindere vestem,
     sit satis ornatus dissoluisse comae,
sit lacrimas movisse satis: quater ille beatus,
     quo tenera irato flere puella potest.
sed manibus qui saevus erit, scutumque sudemque   65
     is gerat et miti sit procul a Venere.

In both texts the pacifist speaker attempts to distance himself from wife-beating in favour of purely metaphorical *militia*, but the argument will hardly wash with readers, especially when they are the Peace People of Belfast (formerly Women for Peace). Tibullus' and Longley's panoptic view here presents political and domestic violence as coordinate systems—a point that Maud Gonne, at least as presented by Yeats, may have appreciated all too well. Longley's poem offers through Tibullus an early exposé of the toxic alliance of paramilitary, domestic and sexual violence that is still slowly coming into public focus.[48]

---

[48] See, e.g., McKay (2016). I thank M. Alden for drawing this article to my attention. On Roman elegy's coordination with what, in the Northern Irish context, academic and activist Eileen Evason has termed an 'armed patriarchy' (see McKay [2016: 38]) see O'Rourke (2018, esp. 126–7 on Tib. 1.10).

Longley's version does not, therefore, shy away from the darker implications of Tibullus' meditation on the fragility (if not impossibility) of 'peace born from war', thus anticipating the more disquieting implications of 'Ceasefire', especially when it appeared in *The Ghost Orchid* (1995) alongside other Iliadic poems ('The Campfires', 'The Helmet', 'The Parting') suggestive of continuity rather than decommissioning.[49] As Longley himself wrote in 1971, citing Wilfred Owen, 'it is the artist's first duty to warn, to be tuned in before anyone else to the implications of a situation'.[50] At the same time, however, the final lines of Longley's poem work towards resolving the impasse of Tibullus' 'cycle of violence'. Whereas the Latin speaker merely repeats his invocation of Peace (67–8 *at nobis, Pax alma, veni spicamque teneto, | perfluat et pomis candidus ante sinus*), Longley's Tibullus goes one further in making her his lover:

> As for me, I want a woman
> To come and fondle my ears of wheat and let apples
> Overflow between her breasts. I shall call her Peace.

These last lines pull away from the Latin original in seeking more harmonious consummation in contrast to Tibullus, and Roman elegy generally, where woman is enmeshed in the very systems of war that the poetry ostensibly resists. Here in Longley the elegiac mistress continues to play a role as a space for political discourse, but figured as Irish Peace she pacifies earlier revolutionary muses such as Cathleen Ní Houlihan and Maud Gonne.[51]

A similar move is witnessed a little further on in the same collection, following two war poems ('The War Poets' and 'Bog Cotton'), in 'Sulpicia' (*CP* 137). This sonnet takes its title from the name of the only extant female Roman elegist, to whom are ascribed at least six poems preserved in the third book of the Corpus Tibullianum ([Tib.] 3.13–18), though several others (3.8–12) are about her if not also by her. Longley's 'Sulpicia' is in part a collage of lines from these poems (chiefly: lines 1–2, cf. 3.8.1; line 3, cf. 3.8.9–10; lines 9–14, cf. 3.9.5–18), but the speaker's rustic charm ('When I let my hair down I am a sheaf of wheat | And I bring in the harvest without cutting it') also seems to have an affinity with that of Tibullus'/Longley's personified Peace just across the page, or perhaps with the speaker of that poem ('As for me I want a woman | To come and fondle my ears of wheat...'). The blending of Sulpicia's voice with that of Longley is sensitive to the gender politics that have centred on the identity of this female elegist,[52] and also to the ambivalent subject position of a female who attempts to assert her

---

[49] See Cieniuch (2010: 117–19).   [50] Longley (1971b: 8).
[51] So Kennedy-Andrews (2000: 88–9).   [52] See Skoie (2002).

subjectivity in the masculinist commerce of elegy:[53] in that predatory world
Sulpicia runs the risk of the passions of war ('Round this particular date I have
drawn a circle | For Mars, dressed myself up for him, dressed to kill', cf. 3.8.1
Sulpicia est tibi culta tuis, Mars magne, kalendis) and of objectifying identification
with the land ('Were he to hover above me like a bird of prey | I would lay my
body out, his little country'), but like Longley's Peace she also turns the chase on
its head, achieving in the sestet a greater degree of autonomy than in the Latin
source at [Tib.] 3.9.9–18:

> I will stumble behind him through the undergrowth
> Tracking his white legs, drawing about us both
> The hunters' circle: among twisted nets and snares
>
> I will seduce him, tangle his hairs with my hairs
> While the stag dashes off on one of its tangents
> And boars root safely along our circumference.

> quidve iuvat furtim latebras intrare ferarum
>   candidaque hamatis crura notare rubis?   10
> sed tamen, ut tecum liceat, Cerinthe, vagari,
>   ipsa ego per montes retia torta feram,
> ipsa ego velocis quaeram vestigia cervi
>   et demam celeri ferrea vincla cani.
> tunc mihi, tunc placeant silvae, si, lux mea, tecum   15
>   arguar ante ipsas concubuisse plagas:
> tunc veniat licet ad casses, inlaesus abibit,
>   ne Veneris cupidae gaudia turbet, aper.[54]

These two poems from the Tibullan corpus furnish Longley with a rich supply of
the erotic and rustic themes that are characteristic of his own poetry. Longley,
however, reorients the optic away from the masculinist and martial ethos of the
Roman source and reconfigures love as a source of tenderness and optimism,
capable of offering, like the landscape of his beloved Co. Mayo, a sanctuary from a
sometimes violent world,[55] even if necessarily one from which that world is also
more painfully understood.

---

[53] See, briefly but insightfully, Arkins (2009: 156). See also Impens (2018: 89) and Harrison
(forthcoming).

[54] 'Or what pleasure is there in entering the hideouts of beasts and scratching your white legs on
thorny briars? And yet to have the chance to wander with you, Cerinthus, I myself will carry the
pleated nets over the mountains, I myself will track the swift stag's trail and remove the iron chains
from the fast hound. Then, yes, then would the woods please me if, my light, I were alleged to have
lain with you before those very nets: though a boar may then come to the toils, it will depart
unharmed, lest it disturb the joys of passionate love.'

[55] So Brown (2003: 146–7). To the extent that *No Continuing City* (1969 [= *CP* 1–38]) seems to
echo 'No Second Troy', the epithalamial quality of its poems reminds us that for Longley love is about
harmony. On Longley's environmental elegies see Potts (2011: 75–97).

Conclusions: the Elegiac Continuum in Ireland

In a concinnity that would have appealed to ancient biographers, the year of Yeats's death (1939) was also that in which Longley was born. Their respective oeuvres might be said thus to conjoin to form a continuum of classical reception in Ireland across the twentieth century and beyond. The differences between their responses, as well as the similarities, sharpen our sense of how both poets stand at different points in that continuum, and of how classical reception has changed, but also remained a constant presence, in a shifting political landscape. For both Yeats and Longley, writing more than half a century apart, Latin elegy has provided a suitable medium through which to approach the present, perhaps because the genre's brief flowering at Rome itself coincided with and reflects, in its collision of love and war, the trauma of civil conflict and the pain of reconciliation. As for Yeats, classical allusion locates Longley in canonical English-language poetic traditions.[56] Like Yeats, too, Longley brings together the First World War, in which his father fought, and the Irish Troubles, sometimes within the compass of a single poem, as for example in 'Wounds' from *An Exploded View* (1972) or 'Wreaths' from *The Echo Gate* (1979). Unlike Yeats, however, Longley's poetry declines to take sides. This is true not only of the poems most immediately relevant to this chapter. 'Wreaths', for instance, is a triptych on the tit-for-tat IRA/UVF murders of the 1970s ("The Civil Servant', 'The Greengrocer', 'The Linen Workers'), the third panel of which widens its compass to take in the deaths of Christ and of Longley's father. In the same way, as if to consider a remote aetiology (or perhaps just an analogue) for the sectarianism of the present, the preceding poem 'Oliver Plunkett' gives a macabre ekphrasis of the relics of the Catholic archbishop martyred in 1681 on trumped up charges in the so-called Popish Plot. Later classicizing poems such as 'Ceasefire', discussed in the next chapter by Maureen Alden, and 'The Butchers' are similarly unconcerned to press their allusions to the service of any ideology. Rather, in Longley classical allusion ecumenically exposes ideology itself, looks unflinchingly at its violent consequences, and offers a common ground for dialogue between opposing traditions.[57]

---

[56] In an interview with Brearton (1997: 37), Longley remarks: 'The stepping stones for me would be Hughes and Larkin, to a lesser extent Hill, then back to the 'thirties – Auden and MacNiece – then back to the trenches – Owen, Rosenberg, Edward Thomas. And then the great resumption – Hardy, Tennyson, Keats, Clare, Herbert, Donne, back to Propertius, Catullus…'

[57] See Rankin Russell (2003).

16

Michael Longley's 'Ceasefire'
and the *Iliad*

Maureen Alden

On 10 August 1973 Joseph Murphy heard his wife scream. His daughter had to tell him that his son, Joe, had been shot dead by loyalist terrorists. She described her father's reaction to the news: He got down on his knees and beat the path and cried, 'My son, my son, I loved my son.' He suffered a massive heart attack and died. He and his son were buried together.[1] Heart attack, cancer, and suicide were frequent in the families of victims of the Troubles. You can die of a broken heart.

The Troubles

In this chapter, I shall consider the Northern Irish Troubles as seen through Michael Longley's poem, 'Ceasefire', modelled on Priam's supplication of Achilles in *Iliad* 24.[2] Longley's poem represents the meeting of a grieving father with the killer of his son, a situation reflected in the Troubles, in which the decorum displayed by those bereaved is very close to that displayed by Priam and Achilles in the *Iliad* and in Longley's 'Ceasefire'. Both poems address the problem of what to do in the face of unfathomable loss: this, too, has had to be confronted all too often by those who have suffered in the Troubles. Longley said of the state of affairs:

> We [Longley and his fellow poets] learned from each other how complex the situation was, and how inadequate the political certainties – Green Ireland, Orange Ulster.[3]

---

[1] McKittrick et al. (2007) nos. 913 and 914; McKay (2008: 206). The young man was 22 years old, a roofer. He was returning with his pregnant wife and his mother-in-law from Musgrave Park Hospital. On Kennedy Way a youth leaped out of a taxi and shot him. Joe Murphy's father had come out of hospital two weeks before. He had angina, but had been told that he would live another fifty years if he had no severe shocks.

[2] All translations from Greek are my own. I am grateful to Michael Longley for lending me his manuscript of 'Ceasefire' and his diaries, and for discussing 'Ceasefire' and related matters with me. I also wish to thank Kate and James Arnott, Linda Ballard, Margalit Finkelberg, Sophia Hillan, George Huxley, Geraldine Ó'Néill, Anne Tannahill, and the editors for reading drafts of the manuscript, and for their suggestions and advice.

[3] Longley (2017: 410).

Maureen Alden, *Michael Longley's 'Ceasefire' and the* Iliad In: *Classics and Irish Politics, 1916–2016.* Edited by: Isabelle Torrance and Donncha O'Rourke, Oxford University Press (2020). © Oxford University Press.
DOI: 10.1093/oso/9780198864486.003.0016

The violence which became the Troubles began in earnest with three murders in 1966.[4] When David McKittrick's *Lost Lives* was first published in 1999, it listed 3,637 deaths: by the time of the 2007 edition, the death toll had risen to 3,720. Until the violence stops completely, all statistics concerning the Troubles must be incomplete. McKittrick's figures include those who died of heart attacks, or suicide, or accidents directly related to the Troubles. Time and again the 'wrong' person was killed: William Gordon Gallagher (aged 9) was killed when he upset a tripwire in the corner of the garden where he was playing cowboys with his brother. The bomb appeared to have been intended for soldiers lured into the area by an anonymous telephone call.[5] The savagery was unbelievable: 'I set myself up as judge, jury and executioner. I beat him to death with a breeze block in an alleyway,' said the killer of Alexander Reid.[6] There is no collective record of the injuries which did not kill, but left many people in wheelchairs, or brain-damaged. James Seymour, a married man with two children, lay in hospital for twenty-two years with a bullet in his head, conscious, but unable to move or speak. His wife May visited him every day from May 1973 when he was shot, until his death at the age of 55 on 2 March 1995.[7] Bomb injuries are horrific. They inflict a life sentence. A bomb which exploded at the Abercorn Bar restaurant in Belfast at 4.30 p.m. on a Saturday afternoon (4 March 1972) killed two young women[8] and injured around seventy people. Of the casualties, it was reported:

> Two sisters have both been seriously maimed. One, who planned to marry a Co. Donegal man, has lost both legs, an arm, and an eye. Her sister has lost both legs…A male victim lost two legs, and a female lost one leg and one arm. Another female lost one limb, and three of the injured have lost eyes.[9]

There is no complete record of the mental and emotional suffering caused by the Troubles.

'Ceasefire' and its Reception

Michael Longley's 'Ceasefire' made what the poet Nuala Ní Dhomhnaill described as 'its first electrifying appearance' in *The Irish Times* on Saturday 3 September

---

[4] John Patrick Scullion, 28, shot near his home in Oranmore Street, Belfast on 27 May 1966 by Ulster Volunteer Force (UVF) members: he died in hospital on 11 June 1966; Paul Ward, 18, shot by UVF members in Malvern Street, Belfast on 26 June 1966; Matilda Gould, 77, burned in a fire started by UVF members by mistake at her home in Upper Charleville Street, Belfast on 7 May 1966: she died of her injuries on 27 June 1966: McKittrick et al. (2007) nos. 1, 2, and 3.

[5] McKittrick et al. (2007) no. 779.   [6] McKittrick et al. (2007) no. 2200.

[7] McKittrick et al. (2007) no. 3522.

[8] Ann Frances Owens, 22, comptometer operator, and her friend, Janet Bereen, 21, radiographer: McKittrick et al. (2007) nos. 293 and 294.

[9] As n. 8 above.

1994, after the Irish Republican Army (IRA) announced a ceasefire from midnight on 31 August 1994. She wrote that the poem 'was dynamic and rippled right through the community, both North and South, having a galvanising effect'[10] as people struggled with the difficulty of overcoming the past, of trying to break a cycle of violence.[11] 'Ceasefire' connects the Trojan War with the worst atrocities of the Northern Irish Troubles. It reflects on the courage of the old king, Priam, who begs Achilles to return the body of his son Hector for burial. Priam does not hesitate to go alone at night to the enemy camp, and kneel and abase himself to his son's killer in person, and Achilles, astounded by the old man's courage, respects and admires him, and treats him with humanity:

I

Put in mind of his own father and moved to tears
Achilles took him by the hand and pushed the old king
Gently away, but Priam curled up at his feet and
Wept with him until their sadness filled the building.

II

Taking Hector's corpse into his own hands Achilles
Made sure it was washed and, for the old king's sake,
Laid out in uniform, ready for Priam to carry
Wrapped like a present home to Troy at daybreak.

III

When they had eaten together, it pleased them both
To stare at each other's beauty as lovers might,
Achilles built like a god, Priam good-looking still
And full of conversation, who earlier had sighed:

IV

'I get down on my knees and do what must be done
And kiss Achilles' hand, the killer of my son.'[12]

This is what Longley says about the poem:

In August 1994 there were strong rumours that the IRA were about to declare a ceasefire. I had been reading in Book XXIV the account of King Priam's visit to Achilles' tent to beg for the body of his son Hector. Power shifts from the mighty

---

[10] Ní Dhomhnaill (1999: 222–3, 1st pub. *The Irish Times*, 27 November 1999).

[11] Reception of the poem was actually more complicated than Ní Dhomhnaill implies. *The Irish Times* is a middle-class newspaper of Anglo-Irish origins and is not read by all sections of the community, although consistent efforts have been made since Irish independence at appealing to a broader readership. For an example, see O'Hogan (Ch. 8) on Myles na gCopaleen's *Cruiskeen Lawn* columns.

[12] Longley (1995b: 39), cited from *Collected Poems* by Michael Longley, published by Jonathan Cape (reprinted by permission of The Random House Group Limited, © 2006) and Wake Forest University Press (reprinted by permission of WFU Press, © 2007).

general to the old king who reminds Achilles of his own father and awakens in him suppressed emotions of tenderness. Psychologically it feels pretty modern. I wanted to compress this scene's two hundred lines into a short lyric, publish it and make my minuscule contribution to the peace process. I got started by tinkering with the sequence of events. Priam kisses Achilles' hand at the *beginning* of their encounter. I put this at the *end* of my poem and inadvertently created a rhyming couplet. Three quatrains followed. I sent my sonnet to the then literary editor of *The Irish Times*, John Banville,[13] who called 'Stop Press' and published it on the Saturday immediately following the IRA's declaration of a ceasefire from midnight on 31 August 1994.[14]

Also:

The sort of lyric I write almost always makes its occasion in private. 'Ceasefire' was an exception. But it seems important to keep at a distance whatever political parallels the story may suggest. It was Homer who spoke to us across the millennia. I was only his mouthpiece.[15]

The poem enabled Homer to speak across the millennia in other troubled contexts, too. The Hebrew translation of 'Ceasefire' was published in the Israeli newspaper *Ha'aretz* in summer 2006 in the week of the UN-brokered ceasefire that put an end to the Second Lebanese War (12 July–14 August 2006).[16] Writing to the Shakespeare Association of America two months after the events of 11 September 2001, its president, Tony Dawson, suggested that the complexity of the time might be addressed by reading 'Ceasefire' in conjunction with Troilus and Cressida: Longley took us

back to Homer and that somber, magnificent ending. The extended discussion between Priam and Achilles, which Longley brilliantly compresses into a few lines, is tense with danger, the fury of Achilles only just contained in sympathy, raising fear in the steady persistent old king.... We read, clearly, out of where we are. I am reading out of a mixed sense of mourning, ironic dismay, and pained hopefulness. Embattled cities are lined up in my mind: Troy, Ypres, Sarajevo,

---

[13] The *Ghost Orchid*, the collection in which 'Ceasefire' was later published, is dedicated to John Banville, who held 'Ceasefire' poised for the right moment: see Allen (2000: 129). (Longley was away on holiday from 29 August until 11 September.)

[14] Longley (2009: 104–5); (2017: 328–9).

[15] Michael Longley, 'One Wide Expanse': lecture as Ireland Professor of Poetry to Queen's University Belfast: see now Longley (2017: 329).

[16] The war left 1,191 Lebanese dead (Amnesty International and Lebanese government estimate) or 1,109 (Human Rights Watch estimate), among them 500 Hezbollah fighters (Lebanese and UN officials estimate) and thirty-one belonging to other militias. Forty-four Israeli citizens and 121 Israeli defence forces died. 1,500,000 people were displaced: Wikipedia, Second Lebanon War, https://en.wikipedia.org/wiki/2006_Lebanon_War (accessed 5 December 2019).

Belfast, New York, Kabul, attended by the bitter poetry of war, which, remembering the cost, always elegiac, finds both skepticism and hope in the form and sound of words...even Shakespeare doesn't cover everything—which is why I was led to bring him into relation with Homer and Longley. Reading *Troilus and Cressida* beside 'Ceasefire' beside the *Iliad* yields a complex picture of the waste and shattered hopes of war, where loss and yearning go briefly hand in hand, and the hope of reconciliation sits down beside the most outrageous cynicism.[17]

The hope of reconciliation is a difficult matter. In *The Ghost Orchid*, the page arrangement of 'The Helmet' and 'The Parting' together on one verso page facing 'Ceasefire' on the opposite recto, is immediately repeated on the next two pages, where 'Poppies' and 'Partisans' face 'Buchenwald Museum', thereby insinuating the enduring power of the cycle of violence.[18] But although the ceasefire from 31 August 1994 did not hold,[19] after it things were no longer quite the same. The following week Seamus Heaney wrote:

> The cessation of violence is an opportunity to open a space – and not just in the political arena, but in the first level of each person's consciousness – a space where hope can be developed and can grow. And I mean hope in the sense that Václav Havel has defined it,[20] because it seems to me that his definition has the kind of stoical clarity that should appeal to every realist in the north, Planter or Gael, Protestant or Catholic, optimist or pessimist.[21]

The poem's emergence was more complicated than Longley lets on. He began composing it in an exercise book on 25 August 1994, on his way home from Dublin on the train. (The previous week he had composed 'The Oar' amid a general feeling that the Troubles might be coming to an end. 'The Oar' is based on *Odyssey* 11.121–37, Tiresias' instruction to Odysseus to make a final journey with the oar which a fellow traveller will mistake for a winnowing fan. Then he can go home, where a gentle death will come to him 'from the sea'—ἐξ ἁλός—an

---

[17] Tony Dawson, January 2002. Letter from the President of the Shakespeare Association of America: www.shakespeareassociation.org/wp-content/uploads/2013/06/jan2002.pdf (accessed 6 January 2020). On the hope of reconciliation, see n. 20 below.

[18] Allen (2000: 122–5).

[19] It ended after seventeen months with the Canary Wharf bomb of 9 February 1996 in London, which killed Inam Bashir (29) and John Jeffries (31), and injured more than a hundred. Wikipedia: 1996 Docklands bombing, https://en.wikipedia.org/wiki/1996_Docklands_bombing (accessed 5 December 2019).

[20] 'Hope is not prognostication. It is an orientation of the spirit, an orientation of the heart; it transcends the world that is immediately experienced, and is anchored somewhere beyond its horizons...[It is] an ability to work for something because it is good, not just because it stands a chance to succeed...the certainty that something makes sense, regardless of how it turns out.' (Havel 1990: 180–6 at 181).

[21] Heaney, 'Light Finally Enters the Black Hole', *The Sunday Tribune*, 4 September 1994, reprinted in Hillan-King and McMahon (1996: 219–21).

exhalation. In 'The Oar' Longley adopts the voice of Odysseus, which is well suited to a poet of the Troubles who senses that that part of his work may be done.) He finished the poem that became 'Ceasefire' at home at 4.30 a.m. on 26 August, and gave it this title because everyone was praying for a ceasefire.[22]

When the poem appeared, Longley received a letter from the father of Paul Maxwell,[23] the 15-year-old boy who had been blown up at Mullaghmore, Co. Sligo on 27 August 1979 with Louis Mountbatten in the boat, Shadow V.[24] Much earlier, after reading on the radio his elegy for 'The Ice-Cream Man', Constable John Larmour,[25] shot dead by the IRA on 11 October 1988 as he served in his brother's ice-cream parlour in the Lisburn Road, Longley had received a letter from a lady who wrote:

> I do appreciate that someone outside our family circle remembered my son John. May God bless you.

And she signed herself 'The Ice-Cream Man's mother'. Longley said:

> Those letters matter more to me than any amount of criticism I might receive in literary journals or attention in the public world.[26]

Some time later, he was in a bookshop when a man took his elbow. He told him that he was the Ice-Cream Man's brother, and that their father had died of a broken heart on the anniversary of his son's murder.[27] Like 'The Ice-Cream Man', 'Ceasefire' spoke directly to those bereaved in the Troubles, as well as to its wider audience. It is time now to look at the poem's humane and authoritative model in the *Iliad*, to see what Longley managed to distil into his fourteen lines, and what had deliberately to be left out.

---

[22] Longley, private conversation, 2 April 2014; see also Longley (1997); McDonald (2000: 46).

[23] McDonald (1998/9); Longley (2017: 395–6). Mr Maxwell said that 'Ceasefire' helped him to come to terms with his loss: Longley, private communication (email) 2 October 2016.

[24] Louis Mountbatten was 79. His 14-year-old grandson Nicholas Knatchbull was also killed, as was Paul Maxwell, who was Mountbatten's boatman for the summer. Doreen Brabourne, who was 83, died of her injuries the next day in Sligo hospital. See McKittrick et al. (2007) nos. 2133, 2134, 2135, 2155. Nicholas' mother and father and identical twin brother, Timothy, survived, but were badly injured. Timothy was left blind in one eye and deaf in one ear. In 1989 Timothy was involved in setting up a register of lone twins at a London hospital. He said that for many twins the emotional impact of bereavement was 'savage and almost impossible for others to understand'. In an interview with *The Times* on 1 May 1989, Timothy said his older sister had told him of his twin's death when he was in Sligo hospital. He said: 'I knew in the first minute that this was so calamitous for me that I must either get over it in that minute, or I was never going to get over it. We had not spent more than five days apart in fifteen years.'

[25] Longley (1991: 49); McKittrick et al. (2007) no. 2992. John Larmour, 42, married, with a son, was looking after the shop for a week while his brother was on holiday. See now G. Larmour (2016).

[26] McDonald (1998/9); Longley (2017: 395–6).

[27] John Larmour's father, also John, was buried a year later to the day, on 11 October 1989. His mother, Rosetta, died on the first day of the ceasefire, 1 September 1994: G. Larmour (2016: 41, 46, 79).

Dealing With the Death-Dealer

Priam's first reaction to Hector's death is to go to the Greek camp and entreat Achilles (22.416–21):

σχέσθε, φίλοι, καί μ᾽ οἶον ἐάσατε κηδόμενοί περ
ἐξελθόντα πόληος ἱκέσθ᾽ ἐπὶ νῆας Ἀχαιῶν,
λίσσωμ᾽ ἀνέρα τοῦτον ἀτάσθαλον ὀβριμοεργόν,
ἤν πως ἡλικίην αἰδέσσεται ἠδ᾽ ἐλεήσῃ
γῆρας· καὶ δέ νυ τῷ γε πατὴρ τοιόσδε τέτυκται,
Πηλεύς ...

Stop, friends, and although you are concerned, let me
go out of the city alone and arrive as a suppliant at the ships of
  the Greeks,
let me entreat this reckless man, this doer of violence,
to see if somehow he will feel shame before his equals or pity
my years: for his father Peleus, too,
is such as I ...

Priam does not say here what is the object of his entreaty of Achilles, but John Maxwell felt the same imperative to negotiate with the killers of his son, Paul, murdered in 1979 (see n.24 above). It took Mr Maxwell eighteen years to realize that he needed to speak about his grief. Francis McGirl, one of the men arrested for the crime, was acquitted: he died in a tractor accident some years after the bombing.[28] The other, Thomas McMahon, served eighteen years. On his release, Mr Maxwell tried to contact him through various channels, including a priest. He wanted to ask him to justify the murder, to show some sort of humanity or remorse. But there was never any response.[29] Another bereaved father, Gordon Wilson, whose daughter was murdered in 1987, went to meet the IRA in Co. Donegal in 1993. They wore masks. Referring to the Enniskillen bomb which killed his daughter and to the Warrington bomb of 20 March 1993, which killed Jonathan Bell, aged 3, and Timothy Parry, aged 12,[30] he pleaded with them to end their campaign of violence. They apologized for Enniskillen and for Warrington. They said it was not their intention to kill innocent civilians or children. They were doing what they were doing in response to the British presence in Ireland.[31] People said Mr Wilson was naive to have tried to reason with them. In *Iliad* 22,

---

[28] Knatchbull (2009: 337–8).   [29] McKay (2008: 205, 236–7).
[30] Jonathan Bell: McKittrick et al. (2007) no. 3383; Timothy Parry: McKittrick et al. (2007) no. 3390. Jonathan was with his father, shopping for a Mother's Day present. Timothy was shopping for football shorts.
[31] McKittrick et al. (2007) no. 2893; McKay (2008: 231–2).

Priam is forcibly prevented from going to Achilles (22.412–13), but in book 24 he tells Hecuba again that he wants to go to the ships to ransom the corpse (24.194–9). She tries to hold him back (24.201–9),[32] but he will have none of it (24. 218–19).[33] He is prepared to die to recover his son's body (24.224–7):

> ... εἰ δέ μοι αἶσα
> τεθνάμεναι παρὰ νηυσὶν Ἀχαιῶν χαλκοχιτώνων
> βούλομαι· αὐτίκα γάρ με κατακτείνειεν Ἀχιλλεὺς
> ἀγκὰς ἑλόντ' ἐμὸν υἱόν, ἐπὴν γόου ἐξ ἔρον εἵην.

> ... and if it is my fate
> to die by the ships of the bronze-shirted Greeks,
> I prefer it. Achilles is welcome to kill me straightway when
> once I have taken my son in my arms, when I have satisfied my
> desire to weep.

He embraces his own death like a warrior: ransoming Hector is his ἀριστεῖα, his 'daring', in going alone to the Greek camp, and his abasement of himself to Achilles is one of the supreme feats of courage and endurance in the poem. This is what the *Iliad* has been leading up to. Endurance and necessity are the key to *Iliad* 24. When Apollo is arguing that Achilles should learn to endure, and leave off his mistreatment of Hector's corpse now that Patroclus has been mourned and buried (24.46–54), he tells the gods (24.49):[34]

> τλητὸν γὰρ Μοῖραι θυμὸν θέσαν ἀνθρώποισιν.

> the Fates put an **enduring** heart into mankind.

There is something of this endurance in John Maxwell's account of his emotions as he held his son's body in his arms in Gus Mulligan's boat:

> I feel an uncontrollable rage...I call the IRA cowards. I yell that Paul is as good an Irishman as anyone else...I want those who did it to hear me...maybe to kill them. The anger suddenly leaves me...I feel utter desolation...Now I become conscious that my reaction to Paul's death could lead to others suffering as I am,

---

[32] Cf. Andromache (6.431–9).

[33] Cf. Hector (6.441–9), and see Kakridis (1949: 43–60); Schein (1984: 173–4); Alden (2000: 265–9, 311–18).

[34] Cf. above all 24.527–33, but also καί που σοὶ τάδ' ἔδωκε, σὲ δὲ χρὴ τετλάμεν ἔμπης (*Od.* 6. 190 'and I suppose he [Zeus] has given you these [troubles], and you must endure them at all events'); *Od.* 12.208; *Od.* 20.18; Archil. fr. 13. 507 (*IEG* i. 6)...ἀλλά θεοὶ γὰρ ἀνηκέστοισι κακοῖσιν| ὦ φίλ', ἐπὶ κρατερὴν τλημοσύνην ἔθεσαν| φάρμακον ('but the gods, my friend, made stalwart endurance the remedy for incurable troubles').

if I react in any way which invites retribution and I determine that I will try not to contribute in any way to this kind of action.[35]

In Seamus Heaney's posthumously published translation of *Aeneid* book 6, Deiphobus' ghost asks Aeneas in the underworld why he came to 'this land | Of troubles' (721–2). Those caught up in the Troubles are forced to descend into Hades. The Greek term for 'descent into Hades' is *katabasis*.

The Father's *Katabasis*

What Priam must endure is unprecedented (24.505–6):

> ἔτλην δ᾽ οἷ᾽ οὔ πώ τις ἐπιχθόνιος βροτὸς ἄλλος,
> ἀνδρὸς παιδοφόνοιο ποτὶ στόμα χεῖρ᾽ ὀρέγεσθαι.

> **I have endured** what no other man on earth has endured,
> to reach to my mouth the hands[36] of the man who killed my son.

His courage and endurance are the true marks of his nobility. Achilles, who recognizes the real thing immediately, asks (24.519–21):

> πῶς ἔτλης ἐπὶ νῆας Ἀχαιῶν ἐλθέμεν οἶος,
> ἀνδρὸς ἐς ὀφθαλμοὺς ὅς τοι πολέας τε καὶ ἐσθλοὺς
> υἱέας ἐξενάριξα; σιδήρειόν νύ τοι ἦτορ.

> **how did you prevail on yourself to come** alone to the ships of
>   the Achaeans,
> to appear before my eyes, the man who killed
> your many noble sons? Your heart must be of iron.[37]

Achilles' question is echoed by the question Odysseus is asked in Hades by Heracles' ghost (*Od.* 11.475–6):

> πῶς ἔτλης Ἀϊδόσδε κατελθέμεν, ἔνθα τε νεκροὶ
> ἀφραδέες ναίουσι, βροτῶν εἴδωλα καμόντων;

> **how did you prevail on yourself to come down** to Hades,
>   where dwell
> the senseless dead, the ghosts of men who have died?

---

[35] Maxwell (2000).
[36] Understanding the dual 'χεῖρε' with Sch. T on 24.506. If we understand 'χειρί' with Leaf (ed.) (1900–2: ii. 572) *ad loc.*, translate 'to reach with my hand to the mouth of the man who killed my son' (i.e. the gesture is one of supplication).
[37] Cf. 22.357 (Hector to Achilles).

Sending Heracles to Hades was the most dangerous labour Eurystheus could impose on him (*Od.* 11.623–4):

> καί ποτέ μ' ἐνθάδ' ἔπεμψε κύν' ἄξοντ'· οὐ γὰρ ἔτ' ἄλλον
> φράζετο τοῦδέ τί μοι χαλεπώτερον εἶναι ἄεθλον.

> and once he sent me here to fetch the dog: for he did not think
> that any other labour would be worse for me than this one.

Priam says that his grief for Hector will carry him to Hades (22.424–6):

> τῶν πάντων οὐ τόσσον ὀδύρομαι ἀχνύμενός περ
> ὡς ἑνός, οὗ μ' ἄχος ὀξὺ κατοίσεται Ἄϊδος εἴσω,
> Ἕκτορος·...

> over all of them I do not grieve so much
> as over one, for whom piercing grief will carry me to the house
>   of Hades,
> over Hector...

In a sense it does, and it is Hermes, the escort of the dead, who becomes Priam's driver (24.182–3, 440–2) on the way to Achilles' tent. In other respects, too, his journey to the Greek camp is like a journey to Hades to bring someone back from the dead. Priam drives through the city in his chariot (24.327–8):

> ...φίλοι δ' ἅμα πάντες ἕποντο
> πόλλ' ὀλοφυρόμενοι ὡς εἰ θάνατόνδε κιόντα.

> ... and all his family were following
> lamenting much, as if he was going to his death.

The family turn back when the procession reaches the plain (24.330–1), and Priam continues on his way. At the tomb of the hero Ilos, the mules and horses drink from the river as darkness comes down.[38]

The Father as Suppliant

The *Iliad* began as it ends,[39] with a father bringing ransom to the Greek camp for a casualty of the war. Chryses was a priest of Apollo (one of Troy's divine defenders): he accompanied his offer of a ransom for his daughter with a prayer for the Greeks to sack Troy and get home safe. Agamemnon was mad to refuse, and his rejection of the old man's appeal led to his quarrel with Achilles and to the Wrath which is the subject of the poem. When Achilles is reconciled with Agamemnon,

---

[38] On the katabatic aspects of Priam's journey see Herrero de Jáuregui (2011).
[39] For the verbal echoes see Macleod (1982: 34).

his wrath is not ended but transferred to Hector, the killer of Patroclus. Priam hopes that his predicament as a bereaved father will remind Achilles of his own father, and awaken his pity, as we saw earlier (22.416–22). He receives some encouragement when, on the way to the Greek camp, Hermes, posing as one of the Myrmidons, speaks of his father, Polyktor, and says that Priam is like him (24.370–1):

> ... καὶ δέ κεν ἄλλον
> σεῦ ἀπαλεξήσαιμι· φίλῳ δέ σε πατρὶ ἐΐσκω.

> ...and I would also ward off
> anyone else from you: I think you are like my own father.

The first words Priam speaks to Achilles are an instruction to remember his own father (24.486–9):

> μνῆσαι πατρὸς σοῖο, θεοῖς ἐπιείκελ' Ἀχιλλεῦ,
> τηλίκου ὥς περ ἐγών, ὀλοῷ ἐπὶ γήραος οὐδῷ·
> καὶ μέν που κεῖνον περιναιέται ἀμφὶς ἐόντες
> τείρουσ', οὐδέ τίς ἐστιν ἀρὴν καὶ λοιγὸν ἀμῦναι.

> Be mindful of your father, godlike Achilles,
> of such an age as I am, on the deadly threshold of old age:
> and really, it seems to me, the neighbours who live round about
> oppress him, and there is no one to ward off war and destruction.

Achilles knows he has neglected Peleus (19.323–5), and he has been thinking about his father's grief at not seeing his son return home (18.329–32; 19.334–7; 23.144–50). He has been indulged (disastrously) by his mother throughout the *Iliad*, and neither is much pleased with the result: when Iris goes to summon Thetis to Olympus to receive Zeus' instructions, she finds her lamenting the prospect of Achilles' death (24.84–6), which is to follow soon after Hector's (18.95–6; 24.131–2). Perhaps we should think of Periander's daughter in Herodotus, who warns her brother that 'many people who seek out their mother's side throw away their patrimony' (Herod. 3.53.4 πολλοὶ δὲ ἤδη τὰ μητρώια διζήμενοι τὰ πατρώια ἀπέβαλον).[40] Achilles *has* thrown away the marriage his father would have arranged for him, and the inheritance he would have given him (9.394–400). He has thrown away his life, too, since his own death will follow soon after Hector's. He has angered the gods by his treatment of Hector's corpse, and he has already witnessed the divine anger consequent on Agamemnon's rejection of Chryses' ransom and entreaties for the return of his daughter. The best he can achieve in the time which remains to him will be the κῦδος ('renown') that Zeus is prepared

---

[40] The reference is to inheritance suits. The heir who tries too hard to obtain his mother's inheritance can risk being disinherited by his father, or contesting the case against a claimant with a stronger right: Asheri et al. (2007: 449) *ad loc.*

to allow him (24.110) if he behaves honourably towards Priam, and respects the divine command (24.113–16, 137) to accept ransom for Hector's corpse.[41]

Priam addresses Achilles λισσόμενος (entreating) (24.485), the same verb used of Chryses' appeal (1.15). He offers ransom (24.502) like Chryses (1.20), he embraces Achilles' knees, kisses his hands,[42] reminds him of his father (24.478, 486),[43] and describes his own wretchedness (24.493–501). When Achilles pushes him away (24.508), Priam weeps, curled up at his feet.[44] The gestures of supplication are intended to disarm aggression in the person supplicated, and the reminders of mortal wretchedness to invite his pity. The loss of Patroclus has given Achilles some insight into Priam's grief: at Patroclus' funeral pyre, he mourned 'as a father mourns as he burns the bones of his son, the (new) bridegroom...' (23.222–4 ὡς δὲ πατὴρ οὗ παιδὸς ὀδύρεται ὀστέα καίων, | νυμφίου...).[45] When they have wept together, Achilles raises Priam up: raising a suppliant amounts to saying 'yes' to his request, and makes the person supplicated into his guardian (or κύριος).[46] When Achilles invites Priam to sit down, he shows him the deference and care he has not shown to Peleus (24.522–3):[47]

> ἀλλ' ἄγε δὴ κατ' ἄρ' ἕζευ ἐπὶ θρόνου, ἄλγεα δ' ἔμπης
> ἐν θυμῷ κατακεῖσθαι ἐάσομεν ἀχνύμενοί περ.

> but just sit down on my chair,[48] and at all events
> we will allow our griefs to lie in our hearts, although we are
>   troubled.

In Priam's dream, Iris promised that Achilles would behave with courtesy (24.185–7):

> οὔτ' αὐτὸς κτενέει ἀπό τ' ἄλλους πάντας ἐρύξει·
> οὔτε γάρ ἐστ' ἄφρων οὔτ' ἄσκοπος οὔτ' ἀλιτήμων,
> ἀλλὰ μάλ' ἐνδυκέως ἱκέτεω πεφιδήσεται ἀνδρός.

---

[41] Until his quarrel with Agamemnon, it was not unusual for Achilles to accept ransom. He did so for Andromache's mother (6.425–7); Priam's sons, Isus and Antiphus (11.104–6); and Lycaon (21.37–48, 75–82). He also offered to protect Calchas when he was afraid to speak in the assembly (1.85–91).

[42] On Priam's gestures see Boegehold (1999: 19) and Naiden (2006: 46–8 with figs. 2.2 and 2.3). On supplication see Gould (1973); Burkert (1979: 44–5 with 164 n. 42, and 46–7, figs. 3 and 4); Crotty (1994: 3–104); Alden (2000: 185–91). Naiden (2006: 3–167, esp. 4, 15) argues that it is a discourse, a quasi-legal process with four steps: approach, gesture, request, response.

[43] Parents are sacrosanct: see Naiden (2006: 98–9); Crotty (1994: 97–8).

[44] On throwing oneself at the feet of the person supplicated see Naiden (2006: 50).

[45] For a modern Cretan parallel see Alexiou (2002: 186 and 239 n. 7, 1st pub. 1974). On the similarities between wedding and funeral see Alexiou (2002: 120–2).

[46] Naiden (2006: 108–9, 295), and personal communication (email), 26 April 2016.

[47] Falkner (1995: 11–14).

[48] Cf. 11.645–6, where Nestor rises from his θρόνος (chair) and invites Patroclus to sit, and see Frazer (1971).

> and he will not kill you himself, and he will hold back all others
>> from you:
>> for he is not stupid, or thoughtless, or malicious,
>> but very kindly will he spare a man who is a suppliant.

Although Achilles shows sympathy to Priam, there is no question of reconciliation or equality, and Achilles even threatens him (24.560–70) when he refuses to sit down, and tries to give the ransom and leave immediately with the body (24.553–6).[49] He makes clear that the interview with Priam would not be happening if the gods had not commanded it, and Priam would never have driven his vehicles into his compound if a god had not brought him there. He knows that a god will take Priam back to Troy, and he is not expecting to see him in the morning.[50] Achilles is in control, as indicated by the way he leads Priam to a bed in the πρόδομος (porch) at 24.671–2:

> ... ἐπὶ καρπῷ χεῖρα γέροντος
> ἔλλαβε δεξιτερήν ...

he took the old man by the right arm, on the wrist.

This is how the bridegroom leads the bride:[51] if the gesture is kindly and reassuring,[52] it is because it signifies ownership and control.[53] Achilles' mastery of the situation is also indicated by the mild sarcasm with which he greets Priam's demand to go to bed (24.649–55):

> τὸν δ' **ἐπικερτομέων**[54] προσέφη πόδας ὠκὺς Ἀχιλλεύς·
> ἐκτὸς μὲν δὴ λέξο, γέρον φίλε, μή τις Ἀχαιῶν
> ἐνθάδ' ἐπέλθῃσιν βουληφόρος, οἵ τέ μοι αἰεὶ
> βουλὰς βουλεύουσι παρήμενοι, ἧ θέμις ἐστί.
> τῶν εἴ τίς σε ἴδοιτο θοὴν διὰ νύκτα μέλαιναν,
> αὐτίκ' ἂν ἐξείποι Ἀγαμέμνονι ποιμένι λαῶν,
> καί κεν ἀνάβλησις λύσιος νεκροῖο γένοιτο.

---

[49] Achilles' hostility again threatens to break out as Hector's body is lifted onto the cart (24.582–6).

[50] He has already corrected Priam's description of himself as πανάποτμος ('most ill-fated'), pointing out that the gods have given good and bad to both Priam and Peleus (24.525–49): Lohmann (1970: 121–4).

[51] Illustrated on British Museum 1894, 0719.1, a white-figure pyxis of 470–450 BCE from Eretria by the Splanchnopt painter: see Jenkins (1983).

[52] Leaf (1900–2: ii. 585); Macleod (1982: 144); Richardson (1993: 346) all ad loc.; Taplin (1992: 278).

[53] Boegehold (1999: 17–18). Brides and slaves are introduced into the household as suppliants: they go to a hearth, rise, and are given a place (an inferior place) in the household: see Naiden (2006: 117–18).

[54] See Clarke (2001); Lloyd (2004); Brugger (2017: 239–40) on 24.649–58.

> Swift-footed Achilles addressed him, **undermining** him:
> Go to bed outside, dear old man, lest some counsellor of
>   the Greeks
> may come here, who are always
> coming here and making plans, as is proper.
> If some one of them were to see you in the swift black night
> he would report straightway to Agamemnon, shepherd of
>   the people,
> and there would be a delay in ransoming the corpse.

Priam is used to giving orders (as 24.553, 555), and cannot get out of a habit which is inappropriate in a suppliant.[55]

Decorum

Achilles undertakes part of Hector's funeral ritual, arranging for the body to be washed and laying it out (24.580–90). He also comforts Priam (24.524–51) and persuades him to eat for the first time since his son's death (24.601–27). It is Achilles who negotiates the terms of the truce with Priam (24.656–67): Agamemnon, the leader of the Greek army, is sidelined. Priam, who has clearly picked up on Achilles' sarcasm at his imperatives, is formally polite in proposing terms (24.661):

> ὧδέ κέ μοι ῥέζων, Ἀχιλεῦ, κεχαρισμένα θείης.
>
> you would do me a kindness, Achilles, if you did as I shall say.

And now that his suppliant has got the register right, Achilles is gracious in return (24.669):

> ἔσταί τοι καὶ ταῦτα, γέρον Πρίαμ', ὡς σὺ κελεύεις.
>
> this, too, shall be as you command, revered Priam.

This decorum is important. In an interview with Margaret Mills Harper (28 July 2003), Longley said:

> I'm interested in decorum and manners...It's how we interact with one another, civilisation. On the one hand, I'm interested in how we avoid tearing one another to pieces. Peace is not that, peace is the absence of that, peace is the absence of war. Civilisation is custom and manners and ceremony, the things that Yeats

---

[55] On Priam's multiple faux pas see Martin (1989: 144–5); Taplin (1992: 269, 273); Redfield (1994: 218, 1st pub. 1975); Rabel (1997: 202).

says in 'A Prayer for my Daughter'. We have a vocabulary of behaviour, as well as things to say to one another... and out of that come laws and agreed ways of doing things... that in daily life are a bit like form in poetry.[56]

Longley told me that in his mind, as he composed 'Ceasefire', Priam had the face of Gordon Wilson, the draper from Enniskillen whose 20-year-old daughter Marie, a student nurse, was the youngest of eleven people killed by the IRA at the Enniskillen cenotaph on 8 November 1987.[57] Sixty-three were wounded, including Mr Wilson, who told the BBC the next day that he bore 'no ill will to anybody. Dirty kind of talk isn't going to bring her back. She was a great wee lassie.'[58]

Longley was proud of 'Ceasefire' but had reservations about it. He said:

There is perhaps something a bit middle-class and presumptuous about the poem. It went down well with politicians and priests. But who am I to say that people should forgive? A man came up to me in the street shortly after it was in the paper and he said, 'I admired your "Ceasefire" poem but I'm not ready for it.'[59]

And again:

I certainly did have misgivings. In my poem, as in my political attitude, was I pressurising those who had been bereaved or maimed to forgive before they were ready to forgive? Was I in my presumption suggesting that widows, widowers, orphans might kiss the hands (as it were) of self-appointed murderers and torturers?[60]

The poet cannot be held responsible for the way the poem has been construed by those who want to preach Christian forgiveness.[61] Patrick McGurk, whose wife

---

[56] Longley (2004).
[57] William Mullan, 74 (2883); Nessie Mullan, 73 (2884); Kitchener Johnston, 71 (2885); Nessie Johnston, 62 (2886); Wesley Armstrong, 62 (2887); Bertha Armstrong, 55 (2888); Edward Armstrong, 52 (2889); John Megaw, 67 (2890); Alberta Quinton, 72 (2891); Samuel Gault, 49 (2892); Marie Wilson, 20 (2893). Adam Lambert, 19 (2894), a Protestant student from the University of Ulster, was killed the next day, 9 November 1987, by the Ulster Defence Association (UDA) in Belfast in a revenge attack while he was doing his work experience on a building site. His killers believed he was a Catholic. Numbers in brackets refer to McKittrick et al. (2007).
[58] www.bbc.co.uk/news/2057328 (accessed 15 April 2016).
[59] McKay (2008: 350).
[60] Speech made at the American Ireland Fund Literary Awards, 19 June 1996. Text held in Emory University, Robert W. Woodruff Library, Stuart A. Rose Manuscript, Archives and Rare Book Library, Michael Longley Papers 1960–2000, Series 2, Subseries 2. 2 Prose, box 35, folder 1, Longley papers, collection 744: see Brearton (2006: 271 n. 27).
[61] See for example www.irishnews.com/lifestyle/faithmatters/2019/03/07/news/-peace-and-for-giveness-needs-to-flow-up-the-hill-to-stormont-1564913/ or https://www.irishexaminer.com/break-ingnews/lifestyle/features/forgiveness-allows-you-to-break-free-from-bad-baggage-922810.html (both accessed 6 January 2020).

and daughter were murdered with many others in the bombing of McGurk's Bar on 4 December 1971,[62] forgave those who planted the bomb and prayed for them. Gordon Wilson (who never actually said that he forgave them)[63] prayed for his daughter's killers. Of the bombing in 1979 which injured him and killed his twin brother (see n.24 above), Timothy Knatchbull wrote: 'My return to Ireland [in 2003] equipped me with a far greater understanding of the situation...I gained a firm basis for...forgiveness...Perhaps the most difficult question was how I felt about Thomas McMahon [who planted the bomb]. At the end of the year I accepted at least this: that if I had been born into a republican stronghold, lived my life as dictated by conditions in Northern Ireland, and been educated through the events of the 1960s and 1970s, my life might well have turned out the way Thomas McMahon's did.'[64] But neither *Iliad* 24 nor 'Ceasefire' says anything about forgiveness:[65] rather, both insist on decorum and necessity. Longley's Priam says he must '...do what must be done'.

Doing What Must be Done: Conclusions

In his mistreatment of Hector's body, Achilles has been indulging passionate private grief, but ultimately he must accept (like Priam) that sorrow is part of his lot. Priam asks him to act in accordance with shame and pity (24.503) and accept the gifts that are the public currency of his society. Longley tried to make this clear:

> I was...sickened by the so-called punishment beatings. (The 400th took place in Belfast 2 weeks ago.) [This was in 1996.] So last December I wrote a lopsided eleven-line poem to accompany my sonnet 'Ceasefire' – an amplification; a qualification.[66]

---

[62] Fifteen people were killed by the bomb: Elizabeth Philomena McGurk, 46, married, four children (192); Maria McGurk, 14 (193); James Francis Cromie, 13 (194); Edward Keenan, 69, married (195); Sarah Keenan, 58, married (196); John Colton, 49 (197); Thomas McLoughlin, 55 (198); David Milligan, 52 (199); James Patrick Smyth, 55 (200); Francis Bradley, 61 (201); Thomas Kane, 45 (202); Phillip Garry, 73 (203); Kathleen Irvine, 45, married (204); Edward Laurence Kane, 25, married, with family (205); Robert Spotswood, 38 (206). Major Jeremy Snow, 36, married, two children (209), died on 8 December 1971 from injuries received in a gun attack in the rioting which followed immediately after the bombing. What is believed to have been the revenge attack came at lunchtime on Saturday 11 December 1971 when a car drew up at the Balmoral Furniture Store on the Shankill Road and a box was set in the doorway of the premises. There was no warning. The bomb killed Harold King, 20, a Catholic salesman at the shop (213); Hugh Bruce, 50, the shop's commissionaire (216); Tracey Munn, 2, who was in her pram when the whole front of the building collapsed on it as her mother was pushing it past the shop (214); and Colin Nicholl, 17 months, who was in the pram with Tracey, whose mother was looking after him (215). Mrs Munn suffered a fractured skull and pelvis. Eighteen other people were injured. These two attacks hardened attitudes on both sides, and many joined paramilitary organizations as a result. Numbers in brackets refer to McKittrick et al. (2007).

[63] See Wilson and McCreary (1990: 89, 91–4).

[64] Knatchbull (2009: 367).   [65] Crotty (1994: 80).

[66] Brearton (2006: 212). See n. 60 above for details.

The poem is called 'All of These People':

> Who was it who suggested that the opposite of war
> Is not so much peace as civilisation? He knew
> Our assassinated Catholic greengrocer[67] who died
> At Christmas in the arms of our Methodist minister,
> And our ice-cream man[68] whose continuing requiem
> Is the twenty-one flavours children have by heart.
> Our cobbler mends shoes for everybody; our butcher
> Blends into his best sausages leeks, garlic, honey;
> Our cornershop sells everything from bread to kindling.
> Who can bring peace to people who are not civilised?
> All of these people, alive or dead, are civilised.[69]

The question at the start of the poem is rhetorical: the person who knew the Catholic greengrocer and the ice-cream man is Longley. He explained to Fran Brearton:

> amnesty isn't amnesia...When I would be asked, especially in North America, to read...'Ceasefire', I used to point out – I'm ashamed to say I didn't point it out often enough – that after the ceasefire, which was to collect the body and have a funeral, twelve days, the Trojan War resumes and Achilles gets killed. It was my way of saying 'watch out'. If the problems which cause any conflagration are still there...So I wrote a poem which roughly says something along the lines of 'who was it who suggested that the opposite of war is not so much peace as civilisation?' Peace is just the absence of war, civilisation is the impossibility of war. We really do have to imagine the nightmare backwards, imagine every last bit of it, and try to make sure it won't happen again.[70]

The point surely is that, although there is more grief to come in the narrative of the Trojan War, the *Iliad* does *not* resume that narrative, and does not relate the terrible events of the city's fall. It ends with the ceremony of Achilles' reception of Priam, and the formal mourning for Hector, one of war's casualties. Priam ransoms Hector to give him decent burial, something denied to a number of victims of the Troubles.[71] In the context of the recent centenary of the 1916 Easter Rising, I would like to turn again to Longley:

---

[67] Jim Gibson, 42, a married man with five children. He was shot on 8 December 1973 in his shop on Stranmillis Road: McKittrick et al. (2007) no. 975. He is commemorated in 'Wreaths': Longley (1979: 12–13).

[68] See n. 25 and n. 27 above.   [69] Longley (2000: 16).

[70] Brearton (1997: 36).

[71] Joe Lynskey; Columba McVeigh, 17 (1511); Captain Robert Nairac, GC, 29 (1932); Seamus Ruddy, 33 (killed in France by the Irish National Liberation Army [INLA]) (2699). The remains of

We Irish are good at claiming a monopoly on human suffering. We are good at resurrecting and distorting the past in order to evade the present. In Ireland we must break the mythic cycles and resist unexamined, ritualistic forms of commemoration. If we don't it will all happen again.[72]

He is right, of course, and 'it' has not stopped happening. Two weeks before the 100th anniversary of the Easter Rising, Mr Michael McGibbon (33, married, four children) bled to death in an alley in Ardoyne on 15 April 2016 after being shot three times in the leg by dissident republicans, who claimed that their intention was to carry out a 'punishment shooting'.[73] As Longley says:

> To write carelessly and self-indulgently in a place like Northern Ireland could have terrible consequences...In its language the Good Friday Agreement depended on an almost poetic precision and suggestiveness to get its complicated message across.[74]

Priam and Achilles have irreconcilable grievances against each other, but in the end they are forced to cooperate. Priam must accept that his son's killer is not ἄφρων οὔτ' ἄσκοπος οὔτ' ἀλιτήμων (24.157 'stupid, or thoughtless, or malicious'). He manages φίλον ἐλθεῖν ἠδ' ἐλεεινόν (24.309 'to come as a friend and an object of pity') to Achilles,[75] who must see, not an enemy, but his own father in the grief-stricken old man. 'Ceasefire' and its model, the *Iliad*, end on notes, not of incitement or forgiveness, but of endurance, pity, and doing what must be done:...ἄλγεα δ' ἔμπης| ἐν θυμῷ κατακεῖσθαι ἐάσομεν ἀχνύμενοί περ (24.522-3 'we will allow our griefs to lie in our hearts, although we are troubled').

---

many others 'disappeared' were missing for decades. Father Denis Faul said: 'It is a very serious religious, cultural and anti-Irish action to deny these people a burial. Of all the most savage and barbarous acts the Provos [Provisional IRA] have committed over the years, this is the worst' (http://www.theguardian.com/uk-news/2014/may/10/disappeared-ira-troubles-northern-ireland [accessed 28 April 2016]). Numbers in brackets refer to McKittrick et al. (2007) in which see also Jean McConville, 37, widow, ten children (699).

[72] Longley (1995a: 158); (2017: 200).
[73] *Irish News* 20 June 2016.   [74] Longley (2017: 396).
[75] As Odysseus comes to the Phaeacians (*Od.* 6.327).

17

Post-Ceasefire Antigones and Northern Ireland

Isabelle Torrance

It is well known that Antigone has been a contested allegorical figure in Northern Irish discourse. Evoked in 1968 by Conor Cruise O'Brien as an analogue for the growing civil unrest, and categorically condemned by him in 1972, Antigone is rehabilitated in 1984 by Northern Irish playwright Tom Paulin. Some twenty years later, during the first decade of the Peace Process, Antigone is represented again first by Seamus Heaney, then by Stacey Gregg, and thirdly by Owen McCafferty. This chapter will begin by reviewing the context in which Antigone came to be a relevant political figure in Northern Irish narratives before addressing why the Antigone myth has continued to prove popular with twenty-first-century Northern Irish playwrights. Developing the proposition of Fiona Macintosh, that Irish writers have returned to Sophocles' *Antigone* so frequently because burials and funerals continue to hold such an important and public place in Irish culture, it will be argued here that there are further determining factors that continue to make the Antigone story relevant for Northern Ireland specifically.

Background: Tom Paulin and Conor Cruise O'Brien

Tom Paulin's *The Riot Act*, first staged in 1984 and published the following year, makes a powerful political statement. His Antigone represents nationalist Ireland and evokes the figure of Bernadette Devlin, a civil rights activist who had won a seat in the British parliament for the Mid-Ulster constituency in 1969 at just 21 years of age, and who had, in December that same year, been incarcerated for 'incitement to riot' before being successfully re-elected to her position as MP in 1970. The title of Paulin's play, which is not referenced within the drama itself, alludes to that context, aligning Antigone with Devlin, while the expression the title evokes, 'to read someone the riot act', implying, as it does, an overly harsh reaction, suggests that the punishment suffered by Antigone exceeded her crime. Subsequent to the events of Bloody Sunday (30 January 1972), when British

I am most grateful to Donncha O'Rourke for constructive feedback on an earlier draft of this chapter.

Isabelle Torrance, *Post-Ceasefire Antigones and Northern Ireland* In: *Classics and Irish Politics, 1916–2016.*
Edited by: Isabelle Torrance and Donncha O'Rourke, Oxford University Press (2020). © Oxford University Press.
DOI: 10.1093/oso/9780198864486.003.0017

soldiers shot twenty-eight unarmed protesters in Derry killing fourteen, Devlin, who had witnessed the shootings, was repeatedly denied the floor in the House of Commons by the Speaker Selwyn Lloyd. In a gesture of defiance and frustration, she famously slapped the Home Secretary Reginald Maudling across the face when he claimed that the British troops had fired in self-defence, a claim only finally laid to rest by the Saville Report in 2010 which found that the actions of the British troops had been unjustifiable. It was Devlin, it seems, who also inspired an analogy with Antigone in the 1972 book *States of Ireland*, published by Irish politician Conor Cruise O'Brien shortly after the events of Bloody Sunday. O'Brien's views had a direct impact on Paulin's presentation of Antigone, so we will consider, in outline at least, what Paulin was reacting against.

O'Brien became infamous in Irish politics for switching from a nationalist position to a unionist one. It was 1996 when he joined the United Kingdom Unionist Party, but O'Brien had first aired his revised views on Irish nationalism much earlier in *States of Ireland*. There he quoted an extended passage from an essay on civil disobedience which he had published in *The Listener* (24 October 1968). In that essay, the exemplum of Antigone's non-violent action of performing a symbolic burial for her brother Polyneices, undertaken in direct defiance of Creon's edict (issued by him as leader of the state), is identified by O'Brien as generating and precipitating all the subsequent death and violence in the tragedy. Many scholars, including Paulin himself, have noted O'Brien's position and its influence on *The Riot Act*;[1] but there remain sinister details of O'Brien's arguments which have not received enough attention. O'Brien had blamed Antigone for the conflict in spite of the fact that, aside from Creon, all the other characters sympathize with her—her sister Ismene, Creon's son Haemon, the Chorus of elders, the people of Thebes, and the prophet Tiresias, who reveals that Polyneices must indeed be buried in order to avert pollution on the land. Furthermore, O'Brien makes a number of startling statements. 'Creon's authority, after all, was legitimate,' we are told, '*even if he had abused it*, and the life of the city would become intolerable if citizens should disobey any law that irked their conscience.'[2] The abuse of power, so long as that power is legitimate, is thus defended here, while the deep human suffering experienced by being prevented from burying a loved one is reduced to a bothersome vexation. We read further that 'Creon's responsibility was the more remote one of having placed this tragic power in the hands of a headstrong child of Oedipus.'[3] The logic of this sentence is opaque.

---

[1] E.g. Roche (1988: 222–4), Murray (1991: 122–4), Jones (1997: 233–4), Paulin (2002: 166–7), Macintosh (2011: 93–4), Pelletier (2012: 87), Wallace (2015: 65–8, 71–6), Impens (2018: 170–2). See also Paulin's essay 'The making of a loyalist' in Paulin (1996: 1–17), first published in 1980, which criticizes O'Brien's application of the Antigone myth to the situation in Northern Ireland along with O'Brien's political views in general.

[2] C. O'Brien (1972: 157, emphasis added). The passage is cited only by Roche (1988: 222) among critics referenced in n. 1 above.

[3] C. O'Brien (1972: 157).

O'Brien seems to imply that Creon, as a tragic character, somehow placed power into the hands of Antigone who was headstrong because she was the child of the troubled Oedipus. Suffice it to say that this makes no sense on multiple levels.[4] O'Brien had then continued by commenting on the civil rights march in Derry, which had taken place on 5 October 1968, just weeks before his essay was published. The police, we are told, used force 'to disperse a non-violent *but illegal* civil rights march',[5] as if the fact that the march might have contravened some law made it responsible for the unnecessary use of violence by the police against peacefully demonstrating civilians. Some brief closing concessions are nevertheless made to Antigone towards the end of O'Brien's 1968 essay, where 'the spirit of Antigone' is held to '[animate] the bravest of the war-resisters', and is found to symbolize human dignity.[6] In losing that dignity, mused O'Brien, 'man might gain peace at the price of his soul', the final phrase eerily anticipating the title of Bernadette Devlin's 1969 autobiography *The Price of My Soul* as O'Brien later noted.[7] By 1972, however, O'Brien has rejected his former identification between Antigone and human dignity 'after four years of Antigone and her under-studies and all those funerals'.[8] In one fell swoop, the young oppressed female figure, Antigone/Devlin, is found responsible for over 460 murders that had occurred during the Troubles at the time O'Brien's book went to press.

In response to O'Brien's crude and inflammatory rhetoric, Paulin's intransigent but humane Antigone is pitted against an entirely odious Creon. Far less sympathetic than his Sophoclean counterpart, Paulin's Creon is a sinister politician and a brutal individual. His opening speech, which announces 'that public confidence and order are now fully restored',[9] smacks of insincerity and self-righteousness. His first words, 'Mr. Chairman, loyal citizens of Thebes',[10] evoke a formal government framework and the charged language of loyalism, which in a Northern Irish context denotes a staunch loyalty to the British monarchy or to an independent Ulster and may be related to paramilitary activities. He uses the well-worn cliché of Secretaries of State to Northern Ireland expressing their intention to do 'a very great deal of listening', while offering just one minute for questions at the end of his speech followed by a '*stonewall smile*'.[11] Paulin's Creon code-switches between

---

[4] Creon has no clue that Antigone is the one who has performed the symbolic burial, and there is much irony developed in the play around the fact that all assume the perpetrator of the act to be male. It is not possible to interpret Antigone's act as a consequence of Creon granting her tragic powers by some oversight. Similarly, Ismene who is too afraid of acting against the state is just as much a child of Oedipus as is Antigone. The identification, then, of Antigone as problematic because she is a child of Oedipus is fatuous in this regard.

[5] C. O'Brien (1972: 157, emphasis added).   [6] C. O'Brien (1972: 158).

[7] C. O'Brien (1972: 158, with n.3).   [8] C. O'Brien (1972: 159).   [9] Paulin (1985: 15).

[10] Paulin (1985: 15).

[11] Quotations from Paulin (1985: 16–17). On the parodic echo of a Northern Ireland secretary see Roche (1988: 224) and Paulin (2002: 167).

an upper-class English public school affect, reminiscent of the Secretaries of State to Northern Ireland, and 'a deep menacing Ulster growl'.[12] He thus also evokes Ulsterman Ian Paisley, the notoriously conservative loyalist founder and long-serving member of the Democratic Unionist Party (DUP).[13] With this remarkable melding, Paulin's Creon represents a confluence of forces oppressing disenfranchised Northern Irish Catholics. Antigone, meanwhile, is refashioned as a political prisoner. When the Guard delivers the news to Creon that the perpetrator has been apprehended and found to be Antigone, he tells Creon 'you can lock her up now and knock a statement out of her',[14] an allusion to police brutality against political prisoners during the Troubles in Northern Ireland. Antigone suggests that Creon will torture her when she says to him: 'You'd do more than murder. | I can tell it by your eyes,' and her suspicion seems corroborated when Creon threatens to make his son 'hear | her every scream'.[15]

To Creon, Antigone is a creature who can easily be broken, a beetle, a 'hard bitch' and a 'dirty bitch'.[16] For her crime, she is to be walled into one of the caves on 'the far ridge ... with sheep-dirt in them', left there with some bread, olives, and drinking water.[17] Called a 'dirt-watcher' by Creon earlier in the play,[18] Antigone is cast as an abject figure in a system of imagery that functions on two levels. Antigone's association with the earth, through her act of covering her brother's body, along with her confinement to a rural landscape, speak to prejudices against a rural ethnic Irish identity.[19] At the same time, the demeaning way in which Creon uses the language of dirt to degrade Antigone evokes the 1980 'dirty protests' of female political prisoners in Armagh Women's Prison, who alleged mistreatment by male prison officers.[20] Antigone is to be imprisoned in a dirty cave and left to die of starvation once the food she has been given runs out. Death by starvation once again echoes contemporary Northern Irish experiences not long after ten political prisoners had died on hunger strike in 1981.[21] Although Creon eventually goes to free Antigone, on the advice of the prophet Tiresias, it is too late. She has already hanged herself.

---

[12] Paulin (2002: 167).

[13] Roche (1988: 224) discusses some of the language that evokes Paisley specifically.

[14] Paulin (1985: 25).   [15] Quotations from Paulin (1985: 28 and 42).

[16] References are taken from Paulin (1985: 27, 30, 34, 42, respectively).

[17] Paulin (1985: 43). The description may evoke Cave Hill on the outskirts of Belfast, as Donncha O'Rourke points out to me.

[18] Paulin (1985: 26).

[19] Paulin (2002: 167–8) reveals that the original set was 'three whitewashed walls splashed with red paint', though this 'ethnic Irish' configuration, which was rather crude, was abandoned for a more neoclassical look.

[20] On the dirty protests in the Armagh women's prison see, e.g., Weinstein (2006). Male political prisoners in the Maze (Long Kesh) prison also staged dirty protests from the late 1970s to the early 1980s.

[21] Those who died were Bobby Sands, Francis Hughes, Raymond McCreesh, Patsy O'Hara, Joe McDonnell, Martin Hurson, Kevin Lynch, Kieran Doherty, Thomas McElwee, and Michael Devine.

Seamus Heaney: *The Burial at Thebes* (2004)

As the Peace Process in Northern Ireland became more stable, however, it is striking that three Northern Irish authors returned to the Antigone myth within the
first ten years following the Good Friday Agreement. This is remarkable because,
as we have seen, the tragedy of Antigone had been the original classical model for
mapping the political crisis of the Troubles during some of the worst periods of
violence. It was just a few months shy of twenty years since Paulin's *The Riot Act*
was first produced in Derry (opening 19 September 1984) that Heaney's *The
Burial at Thebes* premiered at the Abbey Theatre in Dublin (4 April 2004). A version of *Antigone* had been commissioned from Heaney to mark the centenary
anniversary of the Abbey Theatre, an institution founded in 1904 by Lady Augusta
Gregory and W. B. Yeats specifically as a platform for nationalist artistic expression, all while the movements to armed insurrection against the British Empire,
which were eventually successful, gathered momentum. The commission thus
bore a subtle but nevertheless significant political load.

Heaney had previously turned to Greek tragedy to express hope, as well as
frustration and anger, in relation to the Northern Irish Troubles. His 1990 adaptation of Sophocles' *Philoctetes, The Cure at Troy*, had advocated reconciliation
between the bitterest of enemies, and while his 'Mycenae Lookout' poems in the
1996 collection *The Spirit Level*, inspired by Aeschylus' *Oresteia*, also concluded
on a note of hope, they were unusually graphic within Heaney's oeuvre for their
representation of wartime violence.[22] In composing his version of *Antigone*,
Heaney discussed several influences. The voice of his Antigone was inspired by
the eighteenth-century 'Caoineadh Airt Uí Laoghaire' (The Lament for Art
O'Leary),[23] a famous Irish keen composed for her husband by Eibhlín Dubh ní
Chonaill (aunt of Daniel O'Connell, who campaigned for Catholic emancipation). O'Leary had been shot dead by a Protestant landlord after a dispute over
O'Leary's horse, which had been instigated through the Penal Laws against
Catholics. In Heaney's play, Creon's veto on keening has entirely negative consequences.[24] The voice of Heaney's Chorus, meanwhile, was inspired by Anglo-
Saxon poetry.[25] This makes for a historical, if barely perceptible, colonial
undertone to the play, which is reinforced through expressions that momentarily
evoke Ireland's colonial history. The concluding lines of the Chorus' second ode,
for example, consider the man who would trample and overstep the laws of the
city, saying: 'He'll have put himself beyond the pale. | When he comes begging we

---

[22] For discussion of the political implications of these works in relation to Northern Ireland, particularly insightful are Denard (2000) on *The Cure at Troy* and Vendler (2002) as well as Hardwick
(2016: 292–302) on 'Mycenae Lookout'.
[23] Heaney (2004: 75–8).   [24] Heaney (2004: 17, 53).   [25] Heaney (2004: 78–9).

will turn our backs.'[26] Reference to 'the pale', the name for the seat of British rule in Ireland, and the attendant expression 'beyond the pale' used to describe 'uncivilized' people, and later repeated to describe Antigone,[27] is coupled here with imagery that evokes the Great Hunger of the 1840s. During this famine, which decimated the rural population of Ireland, wealthy landlords often ignored or exacerbated the sufferings of the local tenant farmers by burning them out of their cottages when they were unable to pay the rent (thus turning their backs as they begged for clemency).[28]

At the same time, the first point of reference Heaney mentions in his process of inspiration is the retrieval and burial of the body of Francis Hughes, who had died in custody on 12 May 1981 after fifty-nine days on hunger strike. Heaney had not known Hughes personally, but he 'knew and liked other members of his family'.[29] Before the body could be released for burial, it was escorted 'as state property' by the police along some thirty or forty miles from the Maze prison to Toome, generating a rage in the awaiting crowd 'that something inviolate had been assailed by the state'.[30] The confrontation at Toomebridge, for Heaney, formed a clear parallel for the clash between Antigone, whose instinct prioritizes the sacred ritual of burial, and Creon, whose view of criminality is entirely inflexible. In this sense, Heaney's approach echoes that of Paulin, with Antigone representing Irish nationalism, though a different focus is clear from the title. *The Burial at Thebes* highlights the issue of proper burial above all else, the act of allowing a departed loved one to rest in peace. As such, it differs markedly from Paulin's *The Riot Act* whose title evokes political violence. Nevertheless, the issue is not simply about burial in Heaney, but also about ownership of the body. Does it belong to the family or does it belong to the state? As Eugene O'Brien observes, bodies act as signifiers of patriotism or betrayal in Northern Ireland: 'The honouring of one's own glorious dead and the dishonouring of those who broke the code of the tribe is a vital signifier in nationalist and unionist rhetorical structures.'[31]

For most audience members, the focal point of reference in *The Burial at Thebes* may well have appeared to be the Iraq War, with Heaney's Creon evoking a Bush-style position, as has been discussed elsewhere.[32] However, it is clear that the primary cargo of inspiration for Heaney came from deep within Irish historical and political conflicts, aware, as he had been since 1968, of Antigone's political symbolism in relation to Northern Ireland.[33] If Heaney felt that, by 2003, the

---

[26] Heaney (2004: 25).   [27] Heaney (2004: 31, 53).

[28] It was at the height of the Great Hunger, in 1847, that The Vagrancy (Ireland) Act was introduced, which made begging a public offence.

[29] Heaney (2009: 123).   [30] Heaney (2009: 122, 124).   [31] E. O'Brien (2009: 41).

[32] The global 'war on terror' was the most obvious and contemporary point of reference, while historical Irish conflicts are not so overtly evoked. See Wilmer (2007), Heaney (2009: 133–4), Arkins (2010a: 41), Impens (2018: 63–7), Parker (2019: 102–3, 111), Pitman-Wallace (2019: 75–6, 81).

[33] Heaney (2009: 127–32). Younger (2006: 159) is entirely mistaken in claiming that there is 'no ... hint at an Irish subtext' in Heaney's play.

Antigone allegory was a relic in Northern Irish politics, which had become 'thankfully more like a squabble in the *agora* than a confrontation at the barricades',[34] he did not foresee either Stacey Gregg's 2006 *Ismene* nor Owen McCafferty's 2008 *Antigone*. Still, he was correct in intuiting a paradigm shift in the relevance of this myth for Northern Ireland, since both Gregg and McCafferty transfer the play's focus to a significant degree onto the experiences of Ismene and Creon, respectively.

Stacey Gregg: *Ismene* (2006)

Written while she was an undergraduate at Cambridge, *Ismene* was Stacey Gregg's first play. It was produced by the Drama Society of King's College, Cambridge in 2006, and was subsequently shortlisted for the Royal Court Young Writers' Festival. In 2010 it was performed in staged readings through the Onassis Programme for the Performance of Greek Drama at Oxford University. The script for Gregg's *Ismene* contains the epigraph, 'Written in response to the McCartney case, and a tradition of Greek Tragedy appropriated by Irish writers'.[35] The case that inspired Gregg to turn to the Antigone story involved not only the murder of Robert McCartney outside a central Belfast bar in January 2005, but also, important-ly, the efforts of his sisters in going public to discover what had happened.[36] As we shall see, the difficulty of ascertaining what actually happened in murder cases in a community where witnesses refuse to give evidence for fear of retribution is a significant theme addressed by Gregg through her rewriting of Sophocles' tra-gedy. Following the list of characters, a brief 'Note' concludes: 'Post Agreement Northern Ireland faces issues such as the residual structures of gang rule, poverty, poor men's health and suicide, to name a few.' The gendered suffering of women, moreover, is a further social issue that Gregg illuminates in this work.

The play is set in a non-specific (i.e. neither Protestant nor Catholic) working-class community in Northern Ireland, and Gregg is much bolder in her departure from the structure of the original *Antigone* than other Irish playwrights. Gregg's *Ismene* does, of course, follow in the tradition to which she alludes. The Ismene figure is not entirely absent from earlier Northern Irish analogies. O'Brien had applauded Ismene's 'commonsense and feeling' in a black-and-white analysis,

---

[34] Heaney (2009: 132).

[35] I am indebted to colleagues at the Archive for the Performance of Greek and Roman Drama at Oxford University, especially Helen Eastman and Fiona Macintosh, for assistance in accessing a copy of the script, which is dated to 2007, and to Douglas Cairns for alerting me to the existence of Gregg's play. Quotations from the unpublished script are reproduced here with kind permission of Stacey Gregg.

[36] E. O'Brien (2009: 42–3) independently notes the resonances of the Antigone myth with the mur-der of Robert McCartney.

which meant, Paulin suggested, that O'Brien, like Ismene, sided with Creon.[37] Heaney is more generous to Ismene, calling her the 'prudent sister...who refused to help [Antigone] in her transgression, [and] survives'.[38] If Antigone is a martyr to her cause, Ismene is the one who must live with the consequences and grief as the sole surviving member of her nuclear family. This is precisely Ismene's defining quality in Gregg's play. Ismene is a survivor.[39]

Gregg is unflinching in her portrayal of the grinding poverty and terrible violence that affect working-class Northern Irish communities. The living room of the family house is 'in a poor state; stained, bare floor, peeling paint'.[40] Ismene and her siblings Paul (Polyneices), Ian (Eteocles), and Tigs (Antigone) had grown up in the house of their uncle Creon after their parents' deaths, crowded together in one bed. The place was cold and the bed soiled with urine; when it was too cold to go outside, the boys would urinate in a pot in the hallway but would often miss and hit the carpet.[41] The house remains bleak and there is a dismal pathos evoked by the corned beef and brown sauce sandwiches that Tigs prepares for a funeral. When Ismene reminisces about 'that pissy bed' and Tigs protests that they 'don't live like that anymore', Ismene takes a dirty knife and wipes it on her sleeve to demonstrate that 'Nothin's changed.'[42]

In the opening scene, Paul and Ian, both now 18 years old, play a computer game 'expressionless'. Ian then pulls out a gun and asks 'Ya ready?' He shoots Paul dead before turning the gun on himself. Like the other characters in the play, the brothers had become completely desensitized to violence. Life seems no more valuable in this community than in a video game. The Chorus describe the bodies of Paul and Ian as a 'scene out of Tomb Raider'.[43] Paul's corpse, reanimated as a ghost, will later explain: 'Once you [sic] pulled the trigger into flesh before it's just like a game. Like a spud gun.'[44] The potato/game imagery returns when Ismene scolds Antigone for removing Paul's limbs and keeping them in a sports bag: 'He's not a Mr. Potato Head you know.'[45] Life comes to an end as in a fiction 'all because two boys | didn't want to play anymore'.[46] Ismene, as much as all the other characters, is used to death. As Scene 2 progresses, and each new character discovers the murder scene, no one is shocked and there is little expression of grief. The man who is first on the scene moves swiftly on from banal articulations of sorrow to thinking about his lunch and a cup of tea. Tigs surveys the carnage with the detachment of a detective. She takes pictures of the corpses, marks the outline of the bodies with chalk, prods around in their eyeball sockets, and removes Paul's arm, placing it in a plastic bag before putting on her headphones and dancing to

---

[37] C. O'Brien (1972: 159), cf. Paulin (2002: 166).   [38] Heaney (2009: 125).
[39] Gregg (2007: 12, 40).   [40] Stage direction in Gregg (2007: 2).
[41] Gregg (2007: 14, 18, and Scene 8 passim). This was not 'a carefree childhood', pace Remoundou-Howley (2011: 62).
[42] Gregg (2007: 21).   [43] Gregg (2007: 5).   [44] Gregg (2007: 26).
[45] Gregg (2007: 41).   [46] Gregg (2007: 53).

herself. Only much later, at the end of Scene 7, does she cry briefly into Paul's body. Creon's first concern is finding out whether or not the man who discovered the bodies knew who they were. Ismene warns that they need to watch out and suggests making tea when she arrives at the crime scene, commenting on the cold. This lack of expressed grief echoes the experience of McCartney's sisters in seeking justice, with one sister Paula acknowledging that a month after the murder she had not yet cried because the campaign for justice was more important than the sentiment of grieving.[47]

In Gregg's *Ismene*, no one knows what happened. 'No one's claimed responsibility,' say the Chorus, with the most urgent concerns being to avoid the 'peelers' (i.e. police) and to '[c]lose the ranks'.[48] Creon's 'Cleaners' turn up to remove Ian's body and forensically clear any trace of it, but Paul's body is left where it is. The brothers were 'in different organisations'.[49] Ian was one of Creon's 'boys', but Paul was not. We hear that Paul was 'freelancin'', making independent drug deals to pay the rent.[50] The audience will discover from Paul's ghost that Creon had ordered Ian to kneecap his brother as punishment. Ian and Paul had discussed doing it 'properly' instead; 'Men go for the gun or hanging,' observes Paul's corpse.[51] Essentially, it was a suicide pact. Tigs is desperate to find out *why* her brothers died but the Chorus of witnesses, confronted by the police, refuse to cooperate:

> We weren't there. We didn't see. We were in the toilet. He had it coming. You don't squeal on your own. We don't talk to you. We stare at the wall and hide in silence. I have a family. I kiss my wee boy on the head every night when I tuck him into bed. We didn't hear anything.

> We don't speak / We won't spill / We can't squeal / We can't see.[52]

This premise is radically different from Sophocles' original, and speaks directly to the McCartney case. Although his sisters had learned the grim details of what happened to their brother from the many witnesses who saw what happened, these witnesses (over seventy) all claimed officially to have been in the toilet during the time of the attack, terrified of brutal reprisals for speaking to the police.[53]

Similarly, Antigone's act of defiance in Gregg's *Ismene*, an instigation of reciprocal violence, is decidedly un-Sophoclean. It is not so much through her attempt

---

[47] Chrisafis (2005). Cf. Santino (2001: 78) on the normality of violence for children growing up in certain Northern Irish communities.

[48] Gregg (2007: 9). The colloquialism 'peeler' referencing the police comes from the name of Robert Peel (as does the term 'bobby'); Peel's legislation introduced the first organized police forces in Ireland in 1814.

[49] Gregg (2007: 28).   [50] Gregg (2007: 20, 29).   [51] Gregg (2007: 25, 26).

[52] Gregg (2007: 32).

[53] The horrifying reconstruction of events is summarized in Chrisafis (2005); the fatal beating was followed by a forensic clean-up of the scene. Remoundou-Howley (2011: 54–5, 66) notes the connections between *Ismene* and certain details of the McCartney case.

to bury Paul that she asserts her rebellion. Rather she plots to murder Creon with the assistance of unspecified assassins. This becomes apparent in Scene 9 when Haemon turns up unexpectedly just as she is leaving the house and unwittingly sets off the trap meant for Creon. Tigs is gunned down in the mix-up and Haemon, wounded, elects to commit suicide over her body with his own gun. It is clear that Tigs did not plan this alone. The implication is that she has been used as a pawn by Creon's enemies, becoming another instance of collateral damage. Once again, it seems that no one will find out what really happened since the guns disappear and the note attached to a brick hurled through the window is secretly pocketed by one of the policemen.[54]

Although Creon is described as *'benign looking'* when we first meet him, his congenial exterior is exposed as sinister and utterly deceptive as the play progresses and there can be no sympathy left for him at the tragedy's conclusion. Apart from ordering the maiming of his own nephew, it transpires that he had executed the son of his neighbour Annie and had forced her to take the blame for the murder. The devastated mother, now a mentally unstable alcoholic nicknamed 'CrazyAnnie', still claims responsibility for the death of her son Jack but the truth has finally begun seeping out through her drunken ramblings. Creon has threatened her with eviction, and in the final scene he mimes shooting Annie in both knees.[55] Annie's son had been the friend of Creon's own son Haemon, and Paul's corpse suggests that it was Haemon's knowledge of these events that caused him to join the police force in defiance of his father.[56] When Haemon's ghost confronts Creon about the murder, he accuses Creon of shooting Jack in the face when the 'romper room would've been enough'.[57] Creon is now the victim of the same kind of loss, caused by murder instead of maiming.

We also discover that Creon forced his mistress (May) to have multiple abortions against her wishes and has now cast her aside.[58] May suffers from severe alcoholism and ends up committing suicide by leaping out of an upstairs window. Ismene has also had an abortion after she was brutally gang-raped years earlier, a crime for which no one was ever punished, and there is no indication that Creon or anyone else came to Ismene's assistance: 'A rapes [sic] not a rape if its [sic] one of the boys...and no one believes the girl like.'[59] In fact, it seems that Creon may have been complicit in the attack.[60] Meanwhile Creon's own wife, referred to only as 'Aunty', has long lived with the humiliation of her husband's affair and has attempted suicide on multiple occasions.[61] Gregg thus highlights the different

---

[54] Gregg (2007: 52).   [55] Gregg (2007: 56, 59).   [56] Gregg (2007: 50).

[57] Gregg (2007: 58); a 'romper room' refers to a space used by paramilitaries for torture and violent intimidation.

[58] Gregg (2007: 37–8, 57).   [59] Gregg (2007: 22, 27).

[60] Remoundou-Howley (2011: 61) argues that the gang intimidating the *polis*, those responsible for removing Ian's body and abandoning Paul's, and the gang who raped Ismene are all one and the same, acting 'as accomplices of Creon's orders'.

[61] Gregg (2007: 26).

ways in which women, specifically, are victimized through gang violence and a deeply patriarchal society. Moreover, the abortions forced upon May and on Ismene (through her rape) turn the women into criminals since abortion had long been illegal in Northern Ireland unless the life of the mother was in danger.[62]

The criminal violence instigated by Tigs, followed as it is by Haemon's subsequent suicide, is not presented as productive. The Chorus plead with Haemon not to take his own life:

> This is senseless. You will not be a martyr.
> If you die who will reconcile?
> Don't waste your power, Haemon.[63]

Gregg presents life and survival as the only ways forward, and this is why it is Ismene's play. Ismene remains stoical in the face of vicious gossip, and maintains her dignity and independence with her own flat, her job, and a pride in her professional attire. She is repeatedly reported to have done well for herself, but this is ultimately because she refuses to get involved in cycles of violence.[64] Where Tigs complains about people forgetting and having selective memories, Ismene responds: 'life's too short to spend dwelling on – ...you just get through things, manage to – '.[65] Ismene may be blind to Creon's crimes until the final scene, but she is not blind to the destructive impact of retribution.

Patterns of imagery related to sight and vision in Gregg's play are reminiscent of Sophocles' *Oedipus*, where the metaphorically blind Oedipus hunts relentlessly for the murderer of the former king without realizing that he is looking for himself, rejecting the physically blind seer who tells him the awful truth. Heaney had applied analogous imagery to his Creon, who asks to be blindfolded at the end of *The Burial at Thebes*, but Gregg's exploitation of the metaphor is far more extensive.[66] In the opening scene of *Ismene*, Ian shoots himself through the eye, and Paul, too, is missing an eye from his fatal bullet wound.[67] Tigs later prods around in Paul's eye socket, removes Ian's remaining eye, and puts it into Paul's empty socket. With dead eyes, Paul's ghost will reveal the terrible truth that no one can figure out. Meanwhile, those who can still see, the witnesses quoted above, claim they cannot. Others, such as one of Creon's heavies, James, who is reluctant to

---

[62] At the time of writing, a landmark ruling by Belfast's high court in October 2019 had asserted that Northern Ireland's ban on abortion constituted a breach of human rights thus finally ushering in the decriminalization of abortion in line with the rest of the United Kingdom and with the Republic of Ireland.

[63] Gregg (2007: 52).   [64] For Ismene's stoicism and dignity see Gregg (2007: 9, 12, 27).

[65] Gregg (2007: 24).

[66] On Creon's request to be blindfolded in the final scene of Heaney's play see Heaney (2004: 74) and Parker (2019: 119).

[67] Robert McCartney, whose murder inspired Gregg, also lost an eye during his fatal beating, as observed in Chrisafis (2005).

remove his sunglasses at the crime scene, do not want to see.[68] Tigs, on the other hand, is accused by Creon of having 'selective hearing', like her mother or, if we follow Sophocles' *Oedipus*, like her father whom Tiresias calls 'blind in his ears as in his eyes and mind'; she claims, moreover, to be 'deaf' to Ismene's warnings.[69] Imagery of the senses is further deployed when CrazyAnnie and May separately sing the same version of the opening lines of Dean Martin's 'That's Amore': 'When the moon hits yer eye like a big apple pie.' In both cases, however, the love song intrudes in an ungainly manner on grotesque situations. Annie drifts into the song after remembering her son's death and how she 'held his bloody head in [her] bloody hands'.[70] May sings the lines, and inserts 'you're well fucked!' where the concluding refrain 'that's amore' should have been, in a scene where the ghosts of Paul and Haemon, along with Ismene, repeatedly taunt Creon with the fact that they can now *see* him (and his crimes).[71] Replacing the original lyric 'pizza pie' with 'apple pie' creates a play on the phrase 'apple of his eye' used to describe Creon's affection for Ian.[72] Meanwhile, the 'amore' that is conspicuously omitted both times from the song, manifests itself perversely as gruesome violence where a bullet rather than the moon is what is likely to hit your eye. By the end of the play, Ismene, who had earlier defended Creon as doing 'his best', can see him for who he truly is and makes him scrub the floor to clean the house before the wake.[73]

Ismene has the final word of the play, completing the sentence of Paul's ghost:

Paul: ... I can see the sea from here.
Ismene: and the sea sees me.[74]

The nursery-rhyme quality of the concluding lines give them a comforting if somewhat detached tone, while the image of the sea implies a cautious hope for escape from cyclical and nonsensical murders and brutality. The funeral procession of dead and living bodies has just been '*tidied away*' in the closet. Ismene is urged by the Chorus to 'survive', to 'mother again', to 'bear the strain' and to 'tidy'. They will 'close the door' after her and '[b]ring an end to revenge, if no solution'.[75] There is a hope for Ismene's future happiness at the end of the tragedy, and a more optimistic conclusion than Paulin's 'There is no happiness but there can be wisdom.'[76]

The gory content of Gregg's play is offset by the kind of black humour often employed in Northern Irish theatre, such as the physical tidying away of the corpses and funeral procession in the closet, and there are many potentially funny moments in the drama.[77] Nevertheless, by mapping Northern Irish problems

---

[68] Gregg (2007: 5).   [69] Gregg (2007: 6, 25), cf. Soph. *OT* 370–1.   [70] Gregg (2007: 35).
[71] Gregg (2007: 58). The word *see* is repeatedly italicized in the text of the script.
[72] Gregg (2007: 50).   [73] Gregg (2007: 19, 58–60).   [74] Gregg (2007: 62).
[75] Gregg (2007: 61–2).   [76] Paulin (1985: 63).
[77] Remoundou-Howley (2011: 56) notes the humorous remark of the man who discovers the bodies of Ian and Paul in the Scene 2: 'I'm sure someone'll be along to sort these boyos out soon. Not like

onto the Antigone story, the tragedy insists on the inbred nature of the conflict. The myth is repackaged as intrinsically Irish when the young Ismene tells a child's version as a bedtime story to her younger siblings and concludes by saying that the (unnamed) boy (ostensibly Haemon) decided he would be better off with his dead beloved (again unnamed but ostensibly Antigone) 'in the land of the dead, Tír na nOg [sic]'.[78] Grafting Tír na nÓg, the mythical land of eternal youth in Irish mythology, onto the Greek tragic tale is a stark and unexpected move. The famous story of the human hero Oisín, whose divine consort Niamh conspires to bring him to Tír na nÓg, has nothing substantive in common with that of Haemon and Antigone.[79] It is implied, then, that the Antigone myth has become as native and relevant to Irish culture as the myth of Tír na nÓg.

This scene, moreover, goes further still in revising mythology. When Ian objects that being dead together does not sound very happy, a brief discussion ensues:

> **Ismene:**   It is so. They were together. And she hadn't to do the dishes or any of the housework or tell shites like you stories ever again.
> **Ian:**   What, the princess?
> **Paul:**   She wasn't a princess.[80]

The girl is recast as working class. This is not just an Irish story, then, it is an Irish (specifically Northern Irish) working-class girl's story. Gregg's *Ismene* asks its audience to consider how such girls and women are affected by the male-dominated gang mentalities that continue to exert a tenacious grip on local communities, a world now commonly obscured from view because of the internationally acclaimed success of the Peace Process. As May says of the carnage in *Ismene*, 'it wouldn't be on the English news.'[81] For all the achievements of the Peace Process, punishment beatings, maimings, and executions continue with dead bodies often dumped or left in the open.[82] The CAIN web service on conflict and politics in Northern Ireland gathers information on 108 identifiably conflict-related murders during the period 1999–2018, with many more deaths suspected of being conflict-related.[83] In these communities, Ismene's strength to endure and survive with dignity, along with her hope that happiness might yet be found through motherhood, seem to be the only options for breaking the cycle.

---

they'll be going anywhere fast, like?' (Gregg 2007: 3). On the use of comedy in Northern Irish theatre as a means of neutralizing trauma see, e.g., Fitzpatrick (2009a: 177–9).

[78] Gregg (2007: 16).
[79] Remoundou-Howley (2011: 62) misinterprets this passage as 'the Irish myth of *Tír na nÓg*'.
[80] Gregg (2007: 16).   [81] Gregg (2007: 55).
[82] McGarry et al. (2017) give some statistics with information on the burden of costs for health services.
[83] See https://cain.ulster.ac.uk/issues/violence/deaths.htm (accessed 5 December 2019). See also Alden (Ch. 16).

Owen McCafferty: *Antigone* (2008)

An insistence on the physicality of dead bodies is something that Gregg's *Ismene* shares with Owen McCafferty's 2008 *Antigone*, which was produced at Waterfront Hall, Belfast, for the Ulster Bank Festival at Queen's University, by Prime Cut Productions. Where one or more dead bodies of significant characters are present onstage for the entirety of Gregg's play, McCafferty rather confronts his audience with '*A stack of dead soldiers in body bags*' in part of the ruined palace hall which is being used as a mortuary.[84] The Old Man, who functions as the Chorus, methodically trails body bags across the stage to add to the pile, unzipping each bag to look at the dead soldier's face until the climactic final moment of the play when he opens a bag and finds his own son. Alone onstage in the closing scene, the Old Man briefly holds his son's body close before zipping up the body bag, stacking it with the rest, and moving on to the next body bag. The pile of bodies thus generates a constant visual reminder of the cost of the war throughout the entirety of the drama, while the tragedy is framed by the Old Man and his experiences. He is the 'survivor' character in McCafferty's play rather than Ismene. As in the original and most adaptations, Ismene's character is present only in the first half of the play. She is a foil for Antigone in refusing to act against the state, while also functioning to expose Creon's extremism when he threatens to punish her for her sister's illegal actions. The Old Man has 'served and cleared up after many kings', and he has survived by knowing that the only 'right answer' when dealing with a king is to agree with their statements, express support for their rule, and obey their commands. This alone will keep him 'away from death's door'.[85]

The substance of McCafferty's *Antigone*, then, is in many ways quite far removed from the original Sophocles even though his play follows the structure of the original rather closely. Unlike the Chorus in Sophocles, the Old Man articulates the extent to which his own life, and the lives of others, depends on obedience to the commanding king. Antigone is also aware of this. She defies the king with her 'eyes...wide open' on the grounds that whatever pain Creon puts her way is nothing compared to the pain she has already suffered.[86] It is clear that Creon has the power and capacity to torture and maim as well as to kill. The Guard who brings him the news that someone has 'tampered with' Polyneices' body against his commands is terrified of reprisals either through reporting the deed or in case of failing to do so, and Creon's responses show his fear to be justified: 'i decide blame or punishment', 'speak and speak now or i'll cut your damn tongue out'.[87] As for Antigone, Creon says to her: 'i will do with you what i want – when i

---

[84] McCafferty (2008: 2).   [85] McCafferty (2008: 10–11).   [86] McCafferty (2008: 6, 18).

[87] The Guard repeatedly describes his predicament as being 'in shit street', but also fears that he might end up dead if he fails to report the crime ('will it be curtains for me if the king hears this from another punter'); all quotations from McCafferty (2008: 12–13; cf. 15 where the phrase 'shit street' is repeated twice more and the Guard observes 'that could've been curtains for me – he's the type of man

want' and later threatens to 'gut her from head to toe'.[88] The punishments, moreover, must be public. The Guard will be 'strung up for all to see' if he fails to find the culprit and 'thebes will know the penalty', while 'thebes must see [Antigone] punished'.[89] Creon will change his mind about Antigone, ultimately electing for her to die 'alone .... in a deserted place... with just enough food for her to slowly starve to death'.[90] All the punishments proposed echo different aspects of the Northern Irish conflict: public humiliations, bodies dumped in the open, bodies disappeared, hunger-strikers' deaths.

By implicitly casting Polyneices' body as a piece of evidence through the insistent repetition that it has been 'tampered with', a phrase very commonly associated with criminal evidence, McCafferty's play suggests that a crime has been committed in relation to Polyneices.[91] In fact, McCafferty inserts a justification for Polyneices' attack on Thebes that is entirely absent in Sophocles: 'polyneices – him and his younger brother eteocles – the sons of oedipus lest we forget – were to share their inheritance – the royal seat – the running of this great city – ...each of these noble brothers should govern turn about – eteocles backed out of the deal and refused to let go of the reins – abuse was hurled and then he turfed his brother out'.[92] So McCafferty's Polyneices gathered an army and returned. This explanation for the war at Thebes exists in other classical sources, notably Euripides' *Phoenician Women*, but it is conspicuously absent in Sophocles, and serves in McCafferty's play (as in Euripides) to generate additional sympathy for Polyneices. McCafferty's language, however, brings the audience beyond the mythological and into the contemporary. For the five years immediately preceding McCafferty's play (2002–7), the Northern Ireland Executive instigated by the Belfast Agreement of 1998 had been suspended because the Ulster Unionist Party refused to share power with the republican party Sinn Féin. This situation is clearly echoed by McCafferty's Eteocles who 'backed out of the deal' and refused to share his inheritance. Moreover, the phrase 'lest we forget', frequently evoked in commemorating the World War I dead, subtly alludes to unionist sectarianism which prizes the sacrifice of Ulster at the battle of the Somme as a heroic indication of loyalty to Britain.[93]

By May 2007, the impasse to the power-sharing executive in Northern Ireland had finally been resolved through the joint leadership of the Democratic Unionist Party and Sinn Féin, with Ian Paisley and Martin McGuinness nominated as First Minister and Deputy First Minister, respectively. McGuinness, a former leading

– i know that – i dodged one there'). Note that the text of all McCafferty's plays are written entirely in lower case with phrases and sentences separated by dashes and no other punctuation. Quotations from McCafferty's *Antigone* are given as printed.

[88] McCafferty (2008: 6, 18, 29).   [89] McCafferty (2008: 14, 19).
[90] McCafferty (2008: 31).
[91] The phrase is used four times in quick succession at McCafferty (2008: 13).
[92] McCafferty (2008: 7–8).
[93] On the significance of the Somme for Ulster unionists see Jarman (1997: 71–2).

member of the IRA, who had later turned to politics, would hold the position of Deputy First Minister until he resigned in January 2017, not long before his death in March that same year. He had been chief negotiator for Sinn Féin in the Peace Process and had overseen the IRA's decommissioning of weapons. Against this political landscape, McCafferty's Creon is cast as 'our new ruler – a military man – a political man – a man with plans – a man with worries', at a time that requires 'strong leadership' and 'good leadership'.[94] Creon reflects: 'i have always thought like a soldier, now i must think like a politician'.[95] Such a distinction is entirely absent in Sophocles, and highlights a Northern Irish experience of former paramilitary commanders moving into positions of political leadership, reflecting also how such figures continue to be feared and retain powers of intimidation in spite of their non-violent political achievements.

There remains a sense of clan mentality in Northern Ireland that McCafferty refracts through the Antigone story. We are repeatedly told that what has happened is 'family business' echoing a phrase used by paramilitary groups (e.g. 'this is IRA business'), issued as a warning and a threat indicating that they are operating independently, outside the law, and that those who interfere will be severely punished.[96] It is important to point out, however, that for all McCafferty's evocations of Northern Irish experiences, which are typical of his oeuvre more broadly, his *Antigone* cannot be mapped onto Northern Irish politics in a straightforwardly analogous way.[97] We are far removed from Paulin's clearly nationalist Antigone and unionist Creon. Rather McCafferty's 'royal family' has a generically paramilitary hierarchy, and Antigone actively chooses to become a dissident within that structure when she disagrees with the policies of the leadership. Nobility is a metaphor for a cause, so that Antigone can accuse the king, her uncle, of having 'not one single drop of royal blood running through [his] cowardly veins', whereas she and Ismene are 'the last two drops of royal blood'.[98] In a further departure from Sophocles, Creon acknowledges that Antigone's actions are worthy of her cause when he says: 'as a soldier i admire your conviction – your courage'.[99] Creon understands commitment to a cause, though Antigone's actions must be punished because he 'will not tolerate dissent from any quarter'.[100] McCafferty thus turns our attention to the transition Creon must undergo in order to become an effective political leader. During the course of the play, Creon fails in his duty as political leader because he refuses to listen to the will of his people and continues to enforce the kind of absolute and inflexible rule typical of (para)military

---

[94] McCafferty (2008: 8, 1, 11).   [95] McCafferty (2008: 11).
[96] McCafferty (2008: 3, 21; cf. 25, 30, 37); compare the report of the McCartney case in Chrisafis (2005) where witnesses to the crime were instructed: 'Nobody saw anything; this is IRA business.'
[97] On McCafferty's evocation of Northern Irish experiences in his previous dramas see Grant (2005).
[98] McCafferty (2008: 3–4).
[99] McCafferty (2008: 18).   [100] McCafferty (2008: 9).

commanders. He claims his punishment of Antigone is 'deserved', and that he is doing 'what needs to be done', while Antigone charges that he is ultimately sentencing her to secret and undeserved torture; Creon continues, claiming in his own words to be doing 'what any good soldier would do – unite against your enemy in order to gain strength', but, as the Old Man points out, 'the fighting has stopped – maybe other thinking is required now'.[101]

In McCafferty's final reckoning, Creon is recast as perverse conflation of a military beserker and a bereaved father through an intertextual allusion to Michael Longley's famous 1994 poem 'Ceasefire'. When we hear that Creon's wife Eurydice cursed him before taking her own life, blaming him as 'the killer of her son', this concluding line of the Messenger's speech quotes the memorable final words from the closing couplet of Longley's poem, in which the Trojan king Priam says, 'I get down on my knees and do what must be done | And kiss Achilles' hand, the killer of my son'.[102] A warrior known for his intransigence as well as his for formidable military skill, Achilles is moved when the elderly king comes under cover of night to his tent to beg for the return of his dead son's body. Creon, too, has finally been moved from his intransigence, but in this case it has been too late and he has already precipitated the death of his own son for whom he will now grieve. The war fought between Eteocles and Polyneices had been cast by McCafferty's Old Man as 'a battle worth fighting'; 'battles need to be worth dying for', he continues, 'or else they are just bloodbaths for angry young men to drown in'.[103] This assessment, once again a proposition completely absent in Sophocles, speaks directly to Northern Irish politics. The decades of violence, maiming, and deaths which eventually led to the Peace Process did engender political reform. What happens subsequently, however, is presented as needless and wasteful disregard for human life.

In his final words, McCafferty's Creon continues to defend his actions: 'i did it for thebes and its citizens – but the gods were lying in wait – as they always are – a smile on their faces'.[104] It is true that Creon has been concerned for the welfare of the city and its citizens. He has important practical considerations on his mind, 'food – water – housing – sanitation', echoing Ismene's opening observation that 'his head's full of burst pipes and dead bodies on the street'.[105] But his identity and experiences as a soldier are so ingrained that he concludes with the invocation of a cause (he acted for Thebes), imagery of military ambush ('the gods were lying in wait' for him), and appeals to the arbitrary nature of divine interference in human

---

[101] McCafferty (2008: 33, 37).

[102] McCafferty (2008: 43). Parker (2019: 117 n. 68) identifies 'a nod from Heaney' to this same Longley couplet in the representation of Creon's decision to free Antigone where he says, 'I know what must be done' (Heaney (2004: 63)). On the significance and impact of Longley's poem see Alden (Ch. 16).

[103] McCafferty (2008: 8).

[104] McCafferty (2008: 43).   [105] McCafferty (2008: 11, 3).

affairs (gods smiling) as a means of exculpating himself even after seemingly accepting the blame for the deaths of his son and his wife. What McCafferty's play represents, then, is the challenge facing leaders who hold deeply entrenched views, and who have been involved in bitter military conflicts, at the very time when two such figures in Northern Ireland (Ian Paisley and Martin McGuinness) were pledging to set aside their differences and work together in a power-sharing executive.

Dead Bodies and Funerals: Conclusions

Fiona Macintosh has argued persuasively, in an insightful analysis, that Sophocles' *Antigone* speaks to Irish authors because 'death and dying in Ireland are not hidden as they are in other Western countries'.[106] Some distinction, however, remains to be made between Northern Ireland and the Republic. Burials and funerals in Northern Ireland can be, and have been, deeply political and public moments in a way that does not apply to the Republic.[107] There is a marked lack of scholarship, moreover, on the politics of the treatment of corpses in Northern Ireland. Existing discussions of conflict-related deaths focus almost exclusively on the forensic processes of enumerating the dead, mapping their deaths, and retrieving 'disappeared' bodies.[108] The politics of funeral rituals are rarely addressed, although other sociopolitical markers of identity, such as flags, parades, and murals have been well researched.[109] Jack Santino has discussed the spontaneous erection of commemorative shrines at the locations of murders, but his scope does not include funerals.[110] A new study of the Catholic Church during the Northern Irish Troubles by Maggie Scull contains a rare and welcome discussion of the tensions between the Church and the community that developed over the issue of paramilitary-style republican funerals, and some valuable observations were made by Neil Jarman on funeral parades in both unionist and republican contexts in his landmark study of visual displays in Northern Ireland.[111] Jarman identifies an overlap between funeral parades and commemorative parades in general, since commemorative parades essentially serve to remember the dead.[112] On the unionist side, parades are a historic feature of the masonic culture of Ulster Orangeism, and are marked by the triumphalist remembrance of military victories from which women are largely excluded. Republican commemoration parades, on the other hand, 'draw more heavily on the tradition of the funeral procession',

---

[106] Macintosh (2011: 91).   [107] Cf. Jarman (1997: 153).
[108] E.g. Ruffell (2005), McKittrick et al. (2007), Mesev et al. (2008) and (2009).
[109] E.g. Rolston (1991), Jarman (1997), Jarman and Bryan (1998), Bryan (2000), Santino (2001), Bryan (2018).
[110] Santino (2001: 75–97).
[111] Scull (2019: 147–55); Jarman (1997).   [112] Jarman (1997: 52).

include women and children in the crowd, and tend to honour fallen heroes.[113] Parades, of course, are often occasions around which sectarian violence erupts.[114]

The differences observed by Jarman between unionist and republican funeral parades can be seen reflected particularly in Paulin's *The Riot Act*, discussed above, where Eteocles, the favoured nephew of the unionist-sounding Creon, is to be given 'a full state funeral – reversed arms, carriage and so on'.[115] This military procession for Eteocles, a male-dominated affair, is countered by Antigone's spiritually-inspired symbolic act of burial in covering her brother with earth. Her action in Sophocles, and in Paulin, is gendered and personal. Antigone's behaviour thus speaks clearly to the nationalist tradition of religiously charged mourning characteristic of republican funeral parades. Violence ensues when the opposing sides become deadlocked, a familiar pattern in Northern Ireland. These kinds of parallels do not apply so specifically to the more recent Northern Irish Antigones, which are not as overtly allegorical in their treatment of the brothers. Nevertheless, the Antigone myth seems to provide a valuable vehicle for Northern Irish writers to confront a sensitive and painful reality of life in Northern Ireland that is rarely addressed directly. If Heaney originally struggled with his commission to produce a version of *Antigone*, his first point of inspiration came from the funeral procession of the dead hunger-striker Francis Hughes. Gregg, similarly, responded to a specific conflict-related death where a body was viciously attacked and left out in the open to die, in order to raise broader issues regarding the carnage generated by cycles of vengeance and their contingent waste of life. McCafferty, meanwhile, may well reduce our focus on the issue of Polyneices' burial as Macintosh observes,[116] but the question of a single burial is superseded by the ever-increasing pile of bodies displayed onstage during the course of the play in what might be described as a theatrical analogue to the forensic practice of counting individual deaths. For each body there is a family and a community that want and need to perform a burial.[117]

The manner of burial, moreover, and its impact on the family remain sensitive issues in relation to Northern Ireland, as articulated through yet another Irish rewriting of the Antigone myth in Gerard Humphreys' play *Norah*, which toured Ireland (north and south) in 2018.[118] Set during the 1981 hunger strikes, *Norah* dramatizes the experience of a fictional hunger-striker's family during the Troubles. The influence of Sophocles' *Antigone* on the plot is revealed in the final scene when Norah is shot dead by the IRA as she carries her brother's corpse because she has defied their orders for a paramilitary funeral. Instead of

---

[113] Jarman (1997: 152–3, quotation at 152).   [114] Cf. Jarman (1997: 52).

[115] Paulin (1985: 17).   [116] Macintosh (2011: 102).

[117] In considering burials and funerals in Northern Ireland, I am indebted to Ian McBride, Laura McAtackney, and Dominic Bryan for their advice.

[118] I am indebted to Fiona Macintosh for access to a copy of the script, through Oxford's Archive of Performances of Greek and Roman Drama.

interment in a coffin draped in the flag of the Irish Republic and escorted by masked and armed members of the IRA, Norah had insisted on burying Kyran without a paramilitary presence and in his prison blanket as he had requested. With the blanket representing a shroud of sorts, the dead brother is cast as a Christ-like figure in a common pattern of imagery connected with deceased hunger-strikers.[119] Norah simply becomes collateral damage. She dies because, like Antigone, she refuses to comply with orders on the issue of her brother's burial.

A playwright and former Irish soldier with extensive experience serving on international peace-keeping missions, Humphreys returned to the issue of the hunger strikes and their consequences because he believes that Ireland has never properly dealt with this trauma; the inspiration of Greek tragedy came from a long association in Humphreys' mind between the hunger strikes and this classical art form.[120] The potential for classical poetry, then, to act as a vehicle for reflection on Northern Ireland remains very much alive, and we might recall that Seamus Heaney, in his posthumously published translation of *Aeneid* 6, gives a pointed rendering of the personification of Hunger encountered by Aeneas in the underworld. The Latin *malesuada Fames*, meaning 'ill-counselling Hunger', is presented and extended by Heaney as follows: 'Hunger that drives men to crime, agonies of the mind'.[121] Heaney's expansion on and reframing of the original, which is printed on the facing page in the bilingual edition, is suggestive in the context of the legacy of the hunger strikes, related criminal activities, and the anguish they caused. Similarly, the request made in Heaney's translation by the shade of Palinurus to 'scatter the handful of earth | On my corpse' in order to effect a proper burial significantly amplifies the Virgilian *mihi terram | inice*, literally 'throw earth over me'.[122] The act of burial, which defines Antigone, resurfaces eloquently here through Heaney's Virgil. Arguably, however, it is the corpse and the impact of its presence that have been most significant in *Antigone*'s dialogue with Northern Ireland. A site for conflict, left exposed, buried, multiplied, tidied away in a closet, the corpses of the Antigone plays discussed here speak to Northern Irish experiences.

---

[119] As observed by Kearney (1985: 67): 'Just as Pearse identified his death with the sacrifice of Christ in the poem *A Mother Speaks*, written on the eve of his execution, so too the death of the hunger-strikers in Long Kesh was frequently presented in sacrificial terms. Posters showed battered, tortured or starved prisoners in Christ-like posture, the wire of Long Kesh transformed into a crown of thorns, the H-Block blanket into a crucifixion cloth.'

[120] Sweeney (2018).

[121] Heaney (2016: 30–1), the original *Aeneid* 6.276 corresponding to Heaney's line 367.

[122] Heaney (2016: 38–9), with *Aeneid* 6.365–6 corresponding to lines 485–7.

VI
MATERIAL CULTURE AND
(DE)COLONIALISM

18

Classicism and the Making of Commemorative Monuments in Newly Independent Ireland

Judith Hill

Five prominent civic memorials were commissioned in Dublin shortly after independence in 1922 during the early years of the Irish State. They were completed
between 1923 and 1971. Two of these honoured the assassinated Irish revolutionary and political leader, Michael Collins, along with the recently deceased politician and founder of Sinn Féin, Arthur Griffith, first through a temporary
cenotaph and later through a permanent structure. The temporary cenotaph was
commissioned by the Cumann na nGaedheal government in 1922; it was designed
by George Atkinson for the lawn of Leinster House in Dublin city centre and
unveiled in 1923. The permanent structure for the same location, commissioned
by the Fianna Fáil government in 1947, was designed by Raymond McGrath for
the succeeding coalition government in 1948, and finished in 1950. Some eight
years after independence, in 1930, the Irish National War Memorial, designed by
Sir Edwin Lutyens as a memorial to the Irish who died in the First World War,
was commissioned by the Irish National War Memorial Committee. With support from Cumann na nGaedheal and Fianna Fáil, the memorial was erected at
Islandbridge and completed in 1938. Two further memorials commemorated the
1916 Rising in particular. The 1916 Garden of Remembrance in the Rotunda
Gardens, Parnell Square, was commissioned by Fianna Fáil in 1935, designed by
Daithi Hanly, and completed in 1971, while Oliver Sheppard's 1912 sculpture *The
Death of Cúchulainn* was erected by the Fianna Fáil government in 1935 as a

I would like to acknowledge the invaluable financial and intellectual support of the Moore Institute
for the Humanities and Social Studies at NUI Galway, which awarded me a fellowship for 2017–18.
I wish to thank Dr Nessa Cronin of NUI Galway for her advice and enthusiasm, Dr Pádraic Moran of
NUI Galway for his comments on classicism, Dr Fidelma Mullane for her insights into the vernacular
in monuments, Mr Mitch Pope for discussions of Lutyens' classicism, the assistance of the staff at the
National Archives of Ireland and the Irish Architectural Archive, and the helpful comments and
insights of the editors of this volume.

Judith Hill, *Classicism and the Making of Commemorative Monuments in Newly Independent Ireland* In: *Classics and
Irish Politics, 1916–2016.* Edited by: Isabelle Torrance and Donncha O'Rourke, Oxford University Press (2020).
© Oxford University Press.
DOI: 10.1093/oso/9780198864486.003.0018

memorial to those who died in 1916 in the General Post Office (GPO), itself a central battleground of the 1916 Rising.[1]

Celtic Revival imagery defined three of these memorials: the Garden of Remembrance in Parnell Square and the Cúchulainn sculpture in the GPO referred to Irish mythology, while the temporary 1923 cenotaph referenced the early medieval Irish high cross. Two of the memorials were statements made through the medium of classicism: Lutyens' First World War memorial employed a version of the classicism he had used for the Imperial War Graves Commission cemeteries and English war memorials. Raymond McGrath's permanent cenotaph for Collins and Griffith was designed in a stripped modernist classical idiom. This chapter will focus on the two memorials that use the language of classicism to interpret the role played by classicism as an expressive medium for national memorial projects which grew out of the uncertainties generated by political polarizations, counterbalanced by the need for reconciliation, that characterized the newly established state. Can it be shown that classicism was employed to establish a rhetorical relationship with the former British Empire? Or does the evidence suggest that the rhetoric generated by classicism referred to an Irish past, present, and future? In order to answer these questions, I will investigate the values and intentions of those commissioning the memorials to unpick the commissioning process and to discover their influence and agency, and I will describe and analyse the form, composition, materials, and iconography of the memorials within their social, political, historical, and cultural contexts. It is hoped that this micro-study and its conclusions will contribute to an understanding of the complexity inherent in the application of classicism as an expressive visual medium in a postcolonial context.

The cultural significance of the political monuments mentioned here, and others erected in Dublin in the nineteenth and twentieth centuries, has received attention from cultural geographers, historians, and art historians.[2] One conclusion implicit in these studies and articulated by the cultural geographer Yvonne Whelan, is that monuments embody collective memory, and thus a sense of political and cultural identity, while giving meaning to specific places within the city.[3] Where a country has undergone political transformation, that change is inscribed in the history of its public buildings and monuments; for example, a regime change may inspire the destruction of memorials associated with the previous polity, or change may be tracked in new memorials celebrating a different past and projecting a variant identity.

---

[1] On the significance of the GPO as a neoclassical building divested of its colonial symbolism, see O'Neill (Ch. 19). Other memorials were erected in Dublin in the period which either did not have active government involvement (Custom House memorial, 1953) or were located in cemeteries (1916 memorial in Arbour Hill military cemetery, 1949–64).

[2] Bhreathnach-Lynch (1999), Bhreathnach-Lynch (2007: 203–15), Fitzpatrick (2001), Hill (1998), Jeffery (2000: 107–43), Murphy (2010), Turpin (2000), Whelan (2002), Winter (1995).

[3] Whelan (2002: 508–10).

Partisan Contexts and Monuments to Reconciliation

Dublin is the capital of a country that underwent significant political transformation after independence from Britain and the establishment of the Irish Free State in 1922. Because the new state was born out of violent and multifaceted conflict, a number of concurrently existing and conflicting definitions of national identity were conferred on independent Ireland.[4] The five memorials listed above reflect these tensions. The Irish National War Memorial at Islandbridge, completed in 1938, represented the interests of those who had fought in the British Army during the First World War. Among these were Protestant unionists, as well as a significant contingent of constitutional nationalists, mostly Catholics. When the surviving soldiers returned to Ireland in 1918 they found that, for the majority of their compatriots, service in the British Army was incompatible with the current form of Irish nationalism, which was marked by the violent separatist tradition in Irish politics that had prevailed when the leaders of the 1916 Rising were executed. With the Anglo-Irish war of 1919–22, which culminated in the Treaty, nationalist Ireland was split. 'Treatyites' accepted a compromise agreement with the British, including partition, which left a 26-county Irish Free State; 'Republicans' held out for independence for the whole of Ireland. This conflict hardened with the civil war fought between June 1922 and May 1923. The Cumann na nGaedheal government, which came to power in 1922 under W. T. Cosgrave, accepted the Treaty and partition. Within a year of taking office it had erected a temporary cenotaph on Leinster Lawn to two of its leaders. When the first Free State elections were held in 1932, it was Fianna Fáil, the republican party under Éamon de Valera, that came to power. This government inscribed its nationalist identity on the city by erecting memorials that celebrated 1916: the Cúchulainn statue in the GPO was erected in 1935, the same year that plans were approved for the Garden of Remembrance for those who had died in the 1916 Rising.

All these projects were partisan in spirit, but the politicians of these Free State governments were also capable of making reconciliatory gestures.[5] After initial opposition to proposals advanced by the Irish National War Memorial Committee, Cosgrave's government offered a site and found money to support the realization of a memorial to the First World War dead, a project that was continued by de Valera in 1932. Further, in 1939, after initial reluctance, de Valera's government decided to replace the temporary cenotaph erected by Cumann na nGaedheal in 1923 with a permanent structure. However, pressure to make partisan gestures was maintained from party members and some elected TDs (Teachtaí Dála, members of the Irish Assembly). An example of pressure exerted within government is evident in a 1950 Dáil (Irish Assembly) debate.

---

[4] Discussed in Fitzpatrick (2001).
[5] For discussion of government motivation see Jeffery (2000: 107–43), Fitzpatrick (2001: 184–203).

Although de Valera's government had made the decision to erect a permanent cenotaph, it was the subsequent coalition government led by Fine Gael, the effective successor to Cumann na nGaedheal, which oversaw its construction in 1949–50.[6] Because the cenotaph project—which honoured those who had supported the Treaty—was in Fine Gael's political interest, and because the Fine Gael-led government had deferred the 1916 Garden of Remembrance project in 1948, members of the Fianna Fáil opposition accused the government of being partisan.

On 14 July 1950, the Fianna Fáil politician Seán MacEntee, needling the government from the opposition benches about its inaction with regard to the 1916 memorial, quoted the memorable phrase, 'keep the past for pride': 'we,' he said, 'in relation to these [1916] men "keep the past for pride".'[7] However, in his speech he also paid lip service to the idea that all shades of opinion could be accommodated: 'We do not want to deny any honour to men to whom the cenotaph is raised ... we will stand for their memory and venerate it and we expect any Government that purports to speak for the Irish people to give them the veneration that is their due.'[8] To underline his point, MacEntee noted that the phrase he had used about keeping the past for pride had been coined by 'another Irishman who died in a cause we did not believe in but in which he thought he was fighting Ireland's battle', making an oblique reference to a soldier who had died fighting in the British Army. These allusions epitomize the ambivalence, nearly always masked by trenchant statements, that successive governments demonstrated towards setting markers of nationalist identity in this early period of the state. Unspoken questions haunted the debate: whose past were—whose past should—we be memorializing? Is it possible to honour the memory of all groups and encompass conflicting views in the one city?

Classicism and Politics

The relationship between classicism and politics in the early twentieth century is complex. Classicism was manifestly the style of the British Empire. However, within architectural circles there was debate about the nature of imperial classicism and whether it should accommodate the vernacular. In a paper on the architecture of empire, Sir Herbert Baker (1862–1946), architect of some of the most prominent imperial buildings of the early twentieth century, argued

---

[6] Fine Gael was founded in September 1933 as a result of a merger of Cumann na nGaedheal and two other parties.

[7] Extract from Dáil debate, 14 July 1950, cutting in S 5734C, Department of the Taoiseach Papers, National Archives, Dublin (NA).

[8] Extract from Dáil debate, 14 July 1950, cutting in S 5734C, NA.

that the most suitable architecture for the Empire was classicism.[9] He did not advocate the pedantic rule-bound classicism that had characterized nineteenth-century imperial architecture, but one that honoured the tradition of accumulated knowledge derived from a variety of architects and periods—the ancient world and Renaissance Europe—and that made room for the changes generated by modern science and the aesthetic contributions of indigenous cultures of the component nations of the Empire. Classicism was also the style that was chosen for memorial projects in a number of postcolonial contexts. For example, the Voortrekker Monument erected south of Pretoria in 1938–49 by descendants of Afrikaans pioneers who had emigrated from the Cape to settle in the Transvaal, referenced classical architecture—the Mausoleum at Halicarnassus and the Pantheon in Rome—while also gesturing to the local in the use of materials and the subject of the sculpture.[10] Richard Evans has argued that those commissioning the memorial used classicism to signify that they were the descendants of Graeco-Roman culture, while the indigenous details denoted their present abode in sub-Saharan Africa.[11]

The Irish Free State inherited a capital city whose core was defined by classicism; Dublin's streets were lined with red-brick Georgian town houses and punctuated by the grand classical gestures of its public buildings.[12] Significant parts of these public structures were devastated in the sporadic fighting of 1916–23. Public debate about whether to restore these buildings, as well as discussion about where to locate the Dáil permanently—by 1922 it was temporarily situated in Leinster House—provide evidence that these buildings were read in symbolic terms.[13] There was, of course, no consensus on interpretation. The government devoted a considerable proportion of its scarce resources to restoring classical buildings such as the Custom House, Four Courts, and GPO from 1922 to 1932, in part responding to pressure from the Irish and British architectural press to recognize their architectural quality.[14] The restorations also signal an acknowledgment that these distinctive and exemplary public buildings were intrinsic to the identity of Dublin, a view expressed by the *Irish Builder* in October

---

[9] Sir Herbert Baker, 'Paper for the "Round Table" architecture of empire', n. d., BaH/64/2, articles and lectures by Sir Herbert Baker, 1902–33, British Architectural Library, London. The paper, which has marginalia by Lutyens, was written in response to the controversy over the style of architecture to be employed in the new Indian capital at Delhi, a project in which both Baker and Lutyens were involved.

[10] Evans (2007).   [11] Evans (2007).

[12] Prominent public buildings in the classical style include: Bank of Ireland (formerly Parliament House), College Green, Edward Lovett Pearce, 1729, completed Arthur Dobbs, 1739, additions 1785 by James Gandon and 1787 by Edward Parke; Four Courts, Inns Quay, Thomas Cooley and James Gandon, 1776–1802; Custom House, Customs House Quay, James Gandon, 1780–91; General Post Office, Francis Johnston, 1814–18.

[13] For discussion see Whelan (2003: 118–90). Leinster House was the grandest eighteenth-century Dublin town house. It was built by the Duke of Leinster in 1745–7 and, from 1815, was in the ownership of the Royal Dublin Society.

[14] O'Dwyer (1987: 32).

1922: 'Dublin without its Custom House! It would be better to hammer blocks upon the cupola of St Peter's.'[15] The extreme republican position, on the other hand, which equated eighteenth- and early-nineteenth-century architecture of Dublin with British rule, and rejected both, was expressed in the Dáil by the Fianna Fáil TD Seán McBride: 'Dublin is really a foreign town. The streets as you pass along speak of the foreigner and of the foreigner's power.'[16] Meanwhile, for nationalists who interpreted the partially independent late-eighteenth-century Irish parliament as a nationalist assembly, its former home—the magnificent building on the corner of College Green—was championed as a location for the Dáil; this was regarded as an opportunity to reclaim the building symbolically.[17] Although the final decision to locate the Dáil permanently in Leinster House was couched in terms of practicalities, such as cost and its central location, it is clear that the classicism of its architecture was no impediment.[18] It is evident from this discussion that although classicism was linked by republicans to the former colonial status of Ireland, the consensus among journalists and the Free State government was that classicism was bound to notions of architectural quality and the identity of Dublin as a capital city.

Concerns that were central to the discussion about the new Dáil, such as location and style, would also have a strong bearing on post-independence memorial projects. The significance of location, and locale—the context in which a building or memorial is placed—has been identified as important by cultural geographers who argue that public buildings and memorials give meaning to specific places within cities.[19] Dublin had been engaging in debates about the location of public monuments since at least 1861, when the proposal to erect a statue to Prince Albert in front of the former Parliament House on College Green was successfully contested by nationalists in Dublin Corporation who wanted to reserve the location for a statue of Henry Grattan, one of the so-called 'patriots' in the late-eighteenth-century Irish House of Commons.[20] Albert's memorial was erected not far away on Leinster Lawn, overlooked by the Royal Dublin Society and the newly established National Gallery and Natural History Museum. These institutions, concerned with the arts and sciences, were regarded as being connected with a man who had done so much to promote culture in Britain and Ireland. There were two issues at stake in this debate. One was association: both the memorials had found locations that had appropriate associations for the figures commemorated. The other theme that emerges is the relationship to the centre of the city; the memorial to Grattan, the nationalist figure, was more centrally placed than the monument to Albert. These issues are further evidenced in the placing of

---

[15] *Irish Builder*, 7 October (1922: 670).
[16] Extract from Dáil debate, 6:37, p. 18, 4 April 1924.   [17] Whelan (2003: 126).
[18] Whelan (2003: 129–30).   [19] Whelan (2003: 118–90), McCarthy (2004).
[20] Hill (1998: 100–1). Henry Grattan was seen by some nationalists in the late nineteenth century as a proto-nationalist.

monuments erected for other figures in the later nineteenth century. Memorials to men connected with the British Army and the viceregal establishment, such as Viscount Gough, a field marshal in the British Army, and the Earl of Carlisle, a mid-nineteenth-century viceroy, were placed to the west of the city centre in Phoenix Park. There were associational reasons: the battery and the viceregal lodge were located there. But it was also distant from the political focus of a city whose corporation was dominated by nationalists. Monuments to nationalist figures, like Daniel O'Connell, John Grey, William Smith O'Brien, and Charles Stewart Parnell, were erected on the primary route through the city in a bid to claim the centre—interpreted as the symbolic heart of the city, and by extension of the polity—for nationalist Ireland.[21]

First World War Memorial (1919–39): Postcolonial Complexities and Reconciliation Through Classicism

The surviving archives recording the vicissitudes of the project to erect a memorial to the Irish who died in the First World War reveal that location was the first concern of both the committee and the government.[22] The Irish National War Memorial Committee was established at a meeting hosted by the viceroy, Viscount French of Ypres and High Lake, on 17 July 1919 in the viceregal lodge in Dublin.[23] The meeting included unionists such as the judge and politician, Sir Dunbar Plunket Barton, and nationalists such as the writer and politician, Captain Stephen Gwynn, many of whom, like Gwynn, were ex-servicemen. One of the most active members of the standing committee appointed to realize the project was Andrew Jameson, a whiskey distiller and director of the Bank of Ireland, who became a senator when the Free State was established in 1922. Having raised over £40,000 through subscriptions by August 1920, the committee decided to erect an impressive memorial of undefined form—'a statue, obelisk or cenotaph of exceptional beauty and grandeur'—in a central part of Dublin.[24] By March 1924 the

---

[21] Hill (1998: 101–8).

[22] The location of the Irish National War Memorial and its political significance has been the focus of much writing on the memorial: see Jeffery (2000: 107–43), Fitzpatrick (2001: 184–203), Bhreathnach-Lynch (2007: 203–15).

[23] 'History of the War Memorial' (1937), RDFA/020/056, Irish National War Memorial Committee Archive: Correspondence, Dublin City Archives (INWMCA).

[24] 'History of the War Memorial' (1937), RDFA/020/056, INWMCA. The initial proposal was to build a 'Great War Memorial Home' to provide board, lodging, and recreation for soldiers and sailors passing through Dublin: 'The Irish national war memorial; its meaning and purpose' (1941), British Legion Annual, Irish National War Memorial Special Number, p. 19. When this idea was replaced by the aspiration to erect a memorial, a significant contingent within the committee and among the subscribers was not convinced that a symbolic statement was preferable to a utilitarian project that could relieve the hardship that was manifestly experienced by many ex-servicemen, something that emerged in public debates in 1926 and 1927: Extract from Senate debate, 7 April 1927, cutting in S 4156A, NA.

committee proposed that their fund be used to acquire Merrion Square, a large private garden opposite the Dáil in Leinster House, lay it out as a park, and erect a cenotaph at the centre.[25] The committee looked for government investment to create a public park and pay for the maintenance of the memorial.

The government's response was ambiguous. The Minister of Finance initially acquiesced, but by early December 1924 the government claimed that it had insufficient funds for the maintenance of any new Dublin park.[26] A letter from Cosgrave to the Irish ambassador in London written in April 1926 reveals that this refusal was inspired by the government's awareness of republican resentment against a memorial to the dead of the 1914–18 war.[27] Cosgrave also articulated the feeling that it would be undesirable to have 'a memorial distasteful to a large body of citizens directly facing the seat of Government'. This idea that the proposed location for the memorial had the wrong political associations was persuasively presented by Kevin O'Higgins in the Dáil debate of 1927 on the Merrion Square (Dublin) Bill when he proclaimed, 'I believe that to devote Merrion Square to [a memorial to those who died fighting with the British Army] would be to give a wrong twist ... to the origins of this State.'[28] He continued, 'No one denies the sacrifice, and ... patriotic motives which induced the vast majority of those men to join the British Army to take part in the Great War, and yet it is not on their sacrifice that this State is based.'[29]

The government, however, was under pressure to support the memorial. In a letter to Jameson, Cosgrave revealed that he could not ignore a project that, despite its controversial nature, concerned 'a big section of the citizens'.[30] As David Fitzpatrick has observed, not only were the numbers sizable—about 200,000 Irish veterans—but the survivors and the dead 'touched every parish and most families'.[31] In 1929, the government offered the committee a site in the Long Meadows estate at Islandbridge.[32] Situated between the Inchicore Road and the River Liffey to the south of Phoenix Park, it was marginal land, steeply sloping

[25] 'History of the War Memorial' (1937), RDFA/020/056, INWMCA.

[26] 'History of the War Memorial' (1937), RDFA/020/056, INWMCA. Copy of memo from Minister of Finance, 1 December 1924, S 4156A, NA. The war memorial trustees obtained the agreement of Dublin City Commissioners to maintain Merrion Square as a park in 1925: correspondence in S 4156A, NA.

[27] Cosgrave wrote: 'A large section of nationalist opinion regards the scheme as part of a political movement of an imperialist nature and view it with the same resentment as they view the exploitation of Poppy Day in Dublin by the most hostile elements of the Old Unionist Class': letter from W. T. Cosgrave to James McNeill, 8 April 1926, S 4156A, NA.

[28] Extract from Dáil debate, 19:5, p. 10, 29 March 1927.

[29] The government was not in principle opposed to a Great War memorial in central Dublin; in his 1927 Dáil speech O'Higgins had entertained the possibility of other central Dublin squares for the memorial: Extract from Dáil debate, 19:5, p. 10, 29 March 1927.

[30] Copy of letter from W. T. Cosgrave to A. Jameson, 2 December 1929, S 4156B, NA. The letter was published in The Irish Times on 15 December 1931.

[31] Fitzpatrick (2001: 191).

[32] Copy of letter from the Office of Public Works (OPW) to W. T. Cosgrave, 23 October 1929, S 4156A, NA.

towards the river, pitted, scarred, and almost inaccessible.[33] The committee, which had requested a place within Phoenix Park, the location of the remembrance ceremony in 1926 and identified as a highly visible and accessible site, was disappointed but acquiescent.[34] For the government it was a politically expedient choice, as *The Irish Times* pointed out in 1930 when it observed that Islandbridge was a location 'the protection of which can be reasonably assured'.[35]

The story of the acquisition of a site for the war memorial reveals that the government was pulled in opposite directions, by, on the one hand, its political rhetoric (and beliefs), and on the other, the interests of a significant proportion of its citizenry. Meanwhile, the memorial committee demonstrated ambition tempered by pragmatism. With the commissioning of the architect Sir Edwin Lutyens, the committee identified a designer who would give them an outstanding memorial, turn a miserable site into a distinctive part of the city, and, through the classical language he employed, symbolically point to a resolution of the conflicts inherent in the enterprise.

In statements made by the memorial committee prior to 1929, Celtic Revival and classical designs were evoked interchangeably; style was not a subject of debate. In 1924, as recorded above, the trustees proposed a cenotaph for the centrepiece of the Merrion Square scheme, while those who championed a free-standing memorial in Phoenix Park threw out several alternatives: 'a Celtic cross, cairn, a triumphal arch or anything else', as long as it was impressive and durable.[36] Prior to the appointment of an architect for the Islandbridge site, T. J. Byrne (1876–1939), the principal architect of the Office of Public Works (OPW), produced a sketch plan, which designated a square memorial garden of about nine acres accessed from the Inchicore Road (a bridge was proposed over the intervening railway), with a perimeter path, and other paths connecting the garden to the wider public park.[37] No physical link with Phoenix Park was proposed. The suggested monumental element was a wall punctuated by square columns accessed by steps at the high south end of the garden. In a statement written a month later, Byrne proposed either a 'mural decoration or a Celtic Cross' as a focus for the garden.[38] This modest scheme was approved by the government.

---

[33] The site had been acquired by the state in 1907 to protect the environs of Phoenix Park from unwanted development: Memo, 16 February 1934, S 4156B, NA. By 1929 the land was used for market gardening, as a source for gravel, and for dumping waste.

[34] Letter from A. Jameson to W. T. Cosgrave, 29 July 1929, S 4156A, NA. Sir Bryan Mahon's speech in the 1927 senate debate on the Merrion Square Bill quoted in Jeffery (2000: 112).

[35] *The Irish Times*, 31 August 1930, cutting in S 4156B, NA.

[36] Copy of letter to Irish National War Memorial Executive Council from Minister of Finance, 24 November 1924, S 4156A, NA. Extract from senate debate, 9 March 1927, cutting in S 4156A, NA.

[37] The plan is inscribed, 'Plan submitted to and approved by Cabinet 29 Oct. 1929', in S 4156B, NA. The park was to be financed by the government.

[38] 'Notes in connection with proposed war memorial park, Islandbridge',19 November 1929, 4156B, NA. The government approved the proposal on the grounds that it was to be a public park. The government undertook to augment the funds held by the memorial trustees to lay out the park and undertake the maintenance of the park and memorial.

Sir Edwin Lutyens (1869–1944) was approached by Jameson on behalf of the Trustees after Jameson had obtained the agreement of Cosgrave and Byrne in December 1929.[39] The following July, Lutyens visited the site and met Cosgrave, producing plans and cost estimates three months later, on 1 October 1930.[40] Responding to the brief, Lutyens sketched a sophisticated design for a memorial garden within a larger park, to be linked to Phoenix Park by a bridge. The scheme was immediately recommended to the government by Byrne, though it took over a year for the government and the memorial committee to commit to the design.[41] Luytens was a well-established British architect, highly regarded as a designer of country houses in an Arts and Crafts idiom as well as grand classical public buildings, the most prestigious being the imperial government buildings in New Dehli. As one of the principal architects of the Imperial War Graves Commission, Lutyens designed the Great War Stone that appeared in the larger battlefield cemeteries built by the commission. He also had a decisive influence in establishing a pared-down classicism as the architectural style of the battlefield cemeteries, a style that he also used for urban war memorials across the Empire.[42] T. J. Byrne recognized Lutyens' ability, describing him in an internal memo 'as among the greatest architects of today'.[43] Appreciation of the potentially expressive power of Lutyens' architecture was only recently apparent in Dublin. When, in September 1919, it was proposed that a replica of Lutyens' temporary London cenotaph (work on the permanent structure began in October 1919) be the model for the Great War memorial in Dublin, the *Irish Builder* had found it too plain, and had called for 'something more ornate and imposing, and enriched with appropriate sculpture'.[44]

Lutyens' involvement in the Imperial War Graves Commission connected his work to the imperial nature of British involvement in the Great War. The Commission's brief covered cemeteries for soldiers from all parts of the Empire, and the design approach, although sensitive to individual places, imposed a readily identifiable style. There is, however, no evidence in surviving correspondence between the Dublin committee and the Irish government that the Irish National War Memorial Committee intended to convey allegiance to British imperialism with a Lutyens design. No connection was made publicly either, by those directly

---

[39] Copy of letter from W. T. Cosgrave to T. J. Byrne, 12 December 1929, S 4156B, NA.

[40] Letter from Edwin Lutyens to Emily Lutyens, 24 July 1930, LuE/19/15/5, Papers of Sir Edwin Lutyens, British Architectural Library, London. *The Irish Times*, 31 August 1930 cutting in S 4156B, NA. T. J. Byrne, Report on Lutyens' design for Irish National War Memorial, 23 October 1930, S 4156B, NA.

[41] T. J. Byrne, Report on Lutyens' design for Irish National War Memorial, 23 October 1930, S 4156B, NA. *The Irish Times* 15 December 1931. Memo for Executive Council, 15 February 1933, T. J. Byrne, Report on Lutyens' design for Irish National War Memorial, 23 October 1930, S 4156B, NA.

[42] For assessments of Lutyens' architecture see Butler (1950), Hussey (1950), Skelton and Gliddon (2008), Geurst (2010).

[43] T. J. Byrne, Report to accompany Lutyens' drawings and model, 14 December 1931, S 4156B, NA.

[44] Quoted in Jeffery (2000: 110–12).

or indirectly involved. In fact, rather than expressing the hope that the memorial would embody ideological or political meaning, it was regarded as a focus for personal and communal mourning.[45] For example, Lord Glenavy, a former unionist politician and former chairman of the senate, speaking at a reunion of ex-servicemen under the auspices of the British Legion in April 1930, stated categorically that, regardless of political allegiance, those supporting the erection of a Great War memorial did not want 'to signalize any political triumph, not to signalize any political party, but solely and only [to] honour ... their brave dead'.[46]

It is also clear that the committee's choice of an Imperial War Graves Commission architect did not deter the government, sensitive though it was to hostility from sections of the nationalist community. In his letter to Jameson in December 1929, Cosgrave had emphasized the function of the memorial as a focus for mourning: 'It is in the main a big question of remembrance and honour to the dead. Fair and generous emotions should be stirred by the adoption of a scheme to effect that purpose.'[47] Mourning was an existential need for the ex-servicemen and the bereaved. However, a monument whose primary purpose was to be a vehicle for personal grief was politically expedient for the government. Did the government also entertain the hope that a powerful statement by an architect of Lutyens' calibre might promote reconciliation?

Lutyens himself conceived his war memorial designs for the Imperial War Graves Commission in a visionary frame. From the start, he championed abstract monumental design for the cemeteries to encompass the magnitude of loss and its vast geographical spread. He began with an elemental object, which he first conceived in May 1917: 'On platforms made of not less than 3 steps[,] the upper and the lower steps of a width twice that of the centre step, to give due dignity, place one great stone of fine proportion 12 feet long set fair or finely wrot, without undue ornament and trickery and elaborate carvings, and inscribe thereon one thought in clear letters so that all men for all time may read and know the reason why these stones are so placed throughout France, facing West and facing the men who lie looking eastward towards the enemy.'[48] This was to be the Great War

---

[45] Jay Winter (1995: 78–9) has argued that historians, primarily interested in war memorials as conveyors of political messages, have undervalued the need for a focus for mourning that underlay the erection of memorials.

[46] *The Irish Times* 7 April 1930, p. 7, cutting in S 4156B, NA.

[47] Copy of letter from W. T. Cosgrave to Jameson, 2 December 1929, S 4156B, NA.

[48] Quoted in Geurst (2010: 20). The Great War Stone was interpreted by Lutyens' contemporaries as an altar, and criticized as such: Geurst (2010: 22, 26, 35). Lutyens accepted its connotations as an altar. His Imperial War Graves Commission working drawings for the stone were captioned 'Great War Stone', but on one drawing he labelled the stone 'Altar Stone': Section, dated October 1918, PA1460/AHP[275] (5), Collection of Drawings, Sir Edwin Lutyens, Working Drawings for the Great War Stone, British Architectural Library, London. A letter reveals that Lutyens imagined that the War Stone at Islandbridge would function as an altar for Catholic and Protestant clerics in a future dedication ceremony: Letter from Lutyens to Jameson, 6 February 1935, RDFA/020/026, INWMCA. The 'one clear thought' that was inscribed on the War Stones (including the War Stone at Islandbridge) was a quotation from Kipling, 'Their Name Liveth For Evermore'.

Stone. Another early vision was of an open-air cathedral in which trees represented columns and the sky a dome.[49] Lutyens brought the two ideas together in August 1917 when he advocated a design with a numinous resonance, in which the individual cemeteries could be imagined as chapels within a cathedral structure: 'But I most earnestly advise that there shall be one kind of main monument throughout, whether in Europe, Asia or Africa … They should be known in all places and for all times as the Great War Stones, and should stand, though in three continents, as equal monuments of devotion, suggesting the thought of memorial chapels in one vast cathedral whose vault is the sky.'[50]

Lutyens had a profound understanding of the geometric considerations that underpinned classical architecture, and relished the complexity of meaning that classicism could convey in the hands of the great architects of the past. Classicism was well established as a signifier of the universal, derived from its traditional associations with timelessness and permanence. Lutyens worked hard to deepen this resonance for the twentieth century by reducing and eliminating elements of the orders, and incorporating subtleties to produce what Christopher Hussey has termed his 'elementalism'.[51] One example of a geometric-based subtlety was his use of entasis, a device borrowed from Greek architecture and understood by Vitruvius as being 'soft and appropriate' (De arch. 3.3.13 mollis et conveniens), in which the diameter at the middle of a column is increased to produce a subtly convex swelling. Lutyens applied this principle to the Great War Stone working with an imaginary sphere of precisely 1,801 feet and 8 inches.[52]

The monolithic Great War Stone is the centerpiece of the memorial Lutyens designed at Islandbridge (Figs. 18.1 and 18.2).[53] The Stone stands above the River Liffey on a vast oval lawn enclosed by dark rubble limestone walls, which are punctuated by pale ashlar granite piers and gateways and terminate in ashlar screens. The War Stone is backed by a great cross, raised on semi-circular steps, behind which further steps lead up towards the Inchicore Road. Within the walled enclosure on either side of the War Stone are two wide circular basins out of each of which an obelisk rises and a fountain plays. To the east and west of the basins are pairs of granite pavilions (designed to house books of the dead) linked by granite colonnades supporting timber pergolas.[54] Beyond these colonnades

---

[49]   Geurst (2010: 8).

[50]   Quoted in Geurst (2010: 33). Lutyens' championing of abstract monumental design can be compared with the ideas of his friend and rival, the architect Herbert Baker, who took his inspiration from English churchyards: see Geurst (2010: 26).

[51]   Hussey (1950: 462). Hussey regarded the most 'complete and extant monument in this key [to be the] Thiepval arch'.

[52]   Skelton and Gliddon (2008: 32).

[53]   In the war cemeteries the War Stone was more often placed on the east side: Skelton and Gliddon (2008:118). The majority of Great War memorials in the Irish Free State were crosses: Jeffery (1993: 147).

[54]   The eight-volume Ireland's Memorial Records recording the names of the fallen was published in the early 1920s decorated with intricate borders designed by the artist Harry Clarke: see Jeffery (2000: 111).

Fig. 18.1. Irish National War Memorial, 1929–38, view of Great War Stone and cross. Photograph and copyright Judith Hill, 2018.

are circular terraced rose gardens that sink beneath the level of the great lawn. The original idea was to approach the gardens from across the River Liffey, stopping first at a temple. The bridge was never built, but the temple was constructed when the site was restored in 1988 after a period of neglect.[55] From this temple only the cross is visible, the Great War Stone becoming apparent as one climbs the steps from the riverside towards the lawn. Other paths, lined with trees, radiate from the two fountains, the sunken gardens, and the temple, providing oblique views that counterbalance the central axis and the formal symmetry of the design. A semi-circular path defines the outer perimeter of the gardens. Because of the absence of a bridge there is no physical link to Phoenix Park. However, Robert Smirke's Wellington Testimonial, an austere and formidable granite obelisk erected in 1820, and no doubt inspected by Lutyens, can be seen in the distance: a vertical object set in trees, it joins the collection of granite verticals—columns, obelisks, great cross—within the memorial gardens (Fig. 18.2).

[55] The river bridge was designed in 1936 but was unrealized: listed in bibliography of OPW drawings of Irish National War Memorial, Islandbridge. Until the late 1980s the approach was from the Inchicore Road to the south. The intended northern approach was realized with the construction of the temple in 1988. This circular temple is different from the design proposed by Lutyens in 1930 which was based on a heptagram: Working drawings of a temple, DR 24/5 (3), Collection of Drawings, Sir Edwin Lutyens, Dublin Irish National War Memorial, 1930, British Architectural Library, London (INWM drawings).

Fig. 18.2. Irish National War Memorial, 1929–38, view of sunken garden to the west, looking past the pavilions to the enclosed lawn with the Wellington Testimonial in the background. Photograph and copyright Judith Hill, 2018.

It is a monumental landscape.[56] The layout, inspired by baroque urban planning, was extensive and formal, the views within, across, and out orchestrated by distinctive architectural features. The piers, gateways, screens, and pavilions, originally conceived in the Doric order, were realized in the simpler Tuscan, associated with military fortifications.[57] Even from this austere order Lutyens omitted details, such as the curving cyma recta and separating fillet, to simplify the profiles and enhance the massive character of the architecture. Discreet baseless engaged columns and the rhythm of ball finials characterize the structures that punctuate the surrounding wall, while the pavilions stand authoritatively with four pedimented faces, above which rise stone pyramidal roofs. It is expressive architecture, projecting strength and conviction, entirely in keeping with the monumentalism of the landscape. The same theme is evident in Lutyens' cross, which, with its short arms, approaches the blunt form of an obelisk.[58] The austere grandeur is counterbalanced by the intimacy of the terraced rose gardens,

---

[56] Hussey (1950: 476) has argued that Dublin was the fullest expression of the monumental landscape which Lutyens initially worked out at Tyringham Hall, Buckinghamshire.

[57] For the earlier scheme see 'Working drawings for the pergola and book rooms', DR 20/7(2), INWM drawings.

[58] Crosses were intrinsic to the battlefield cemeteries, but it was Reginald Blomfield's 'Cross of Sacrifice', which incorporated a sword on one face, that was used in preference to Lutyens' proposal: see Ward and Gibson (1995: 52).

punctuated by many flights of steps and centred on round pools, which reference Lutyens' work at Heywood, Co. Laois, and drew on his long association with the British garden designer, Gertrude Jeykell. The effect was summed up by Sir Dunbar Plunket Barton, chair of the executive council of the memorial committee, when he described the whole memorial as having 'simple dignity'.[59]

Not only did the government readily acquiesce to the trustees' suggestion that Lutyens be commissioned, but when Lutyens' scheme was costed in October 1930 and it came to the very substantial sum of £167,000, the government put up no resistance to the large outlay it would have to provide for the public park.[60] The surviving documents that chart the progress of the project suggest that Lutyens worked harmoniously with all involved in Ireland. A contract was drawn up in which the OPW would supervise the works designed and directed by Lutyens. Lutyens' correspondence reveals that he was sensitive in his dealings with T. J. Byrne and the garden designers, making suggestions and accommodating others' views. When Lutyens met President Cosgrave at the start of the design process in July 1930, they may have come to an understanding about the purpose of the memorial, for the resulting design was discussed in a number of documents in terms that coincided with Cosgrave's hopes for a non-divisive memorial. In the description of the design that Lutyens sent to Byrne he drew attention to the variety of elements and multiple directions of the axes; particularly striking— because it is not the most obvious axis—was his emphasis on the diagonal vistas to the cross punctuated by the fountains.[61] His description evoked a well-ordered memorial without a single perspective. Byrne picked up on this aspect of the scheme in a report which played down the architectural impact: '[The design] will rely in execution much more upon gardening and arboriculture than upon building work; it will derive its effect not from the presence of an overpowering monumental structure but from the beauties of a "Garden of Remembrance" set amid the simple and appropriate surroundings which will be provided by the extension of Phoenix Park into the Estates.'[62] With these words he drew attention to the absence of an element that could be interpreted as triumphalist and consequently draw nationalist opposition.

Although the project was underpinned by political caution, aspects of the way in which it was handled spoke of active attempts at reconciliation. The labourers

---

[59] *The Irish Times*, 16 April 1937, cutting in S 4156B, NA.

[60] T. J. Byrne, Report on Lutyens' design for Irish National War Memorial, 23 October 1930, S 4156B, NA. The government had agreed in principle to contribute a substantial sum for the laying out of a public park in December 1929: 'Notes' by T. J. Byrne, 19 November 1929, S 4156B, NA. The government contributed £50,000: Memo for Executive Council, 15 February 1933. The memorial itself was estimated to cost £50,000, considerably more than Lutyens' memorials erected in English cities in the 1920s: a cenotaph, figures, obelisk, and war stone in Manchester had cost £6,490, for example: see Skelton and Gliddon (2008: Appendix 1).

[61] Lutyens' description is included in T. J. Byrne's report, 14 December 1931, S 4156B, NA.

[62] T. J. Byrne, Report on Lutyens' design, 23 October 1930, S 4156B, NA.

who prepared the ground and constructed the roads were composed of ex-servicemen paid from the allocation provided by the Unemployment Relief Act 1931, half from the Irish Army and half from the British Army.[63] The concept of reconciliation was articulated by Lutyens when he proposed that the inscription for the walls flanking the cross—'A.D. 1914' on the east, 'A.D. 1918' on the west—be in both Irish and English on each side. 'There would then be no question of precedence, and the Altar and the Cross would become a bond between our two peoples,' he wrote to Jameson in 1935.[64] In the end a longer inscription was agreed—'To the memory of 49,000 Irishmen who gave their lives in the Great War, 1914-1918'—picked out in gold on the granite band capping the flanking walls. The principle of including both languages was retained, though with Irish to the east and English to west the question of precedence was not entirely eliminated. Nevertheless, the inclusion of the vernacular on a monument defined by classicism was in itself a significant gesture of integration.

When de Valera's government was elected in February 1932 there was a hiatus in the government's commitment to the project, and Lutyens was told to 'mark time'.[65] But work was resumed the following September, The Irish Times commenting that activity continued 'in the same spirit of toleration, co-operation and mutual goodwill in which it had been inaugurated'.[66] The memorial was handed over to the Board of Works in spring 1938.[67] De Valera, too, hoped that the memorial would draw people together, for on 25 April 1939 he conveyed to members of the British Legion that he had hoped the ceremonial opening, planned for 30 July, 'would have a good effect by signifying that Irishmen who took different views in regard to the war of 1914-18 appreciated and respected each other's views'.[68] But by then the unveiling plan had been postponed indefinitely in the face of what would become the Second World War, with possible conscription in the six counties belonging to the United Kingdom. When the war was over, formal recognition was slow to come. The gardens, neglected, were vulnerable to vandalism, especially in the 1960s and 1970s. It was not until 1987 that the gardens were restored by the OPW and Irish National War Memorial Management

---

[63] OPW memo, 8 January 1932, S 4156B, NA. Photograph, Irish Press, 31 December 1931, p. 5, cutting in S 4156B, NA. The work on the park began in December 1931 and was completed two years later: Memo, 16 February 1934, S 4156B, NA. The architectural elements were constructed from December 1933 to March 1936, while the planting was designed and realized between March 1935 and spring 1938. See Irish Press, 19 December 1933, S 4156B NA; Letter from Edwin Lutyens to Emily Lutyens, 25 March 1936 in Percy and Ridley (1988: 438); Copy of letter from T. J. Byrne to Lutyens, 2 October 1935, RDFA/020/056, INWMCA; Memo, 10 October 1938, S 4156B, NA.

[64] Letter from Lutyens to Jameson, 6 February 1935, p. 2, RDFA/020/026, INWMCA.

[65] Letter from Edwin Lutyens to Emily Lutyens, 24 March 1932, in Percy and Ridley (1988).

[66] Cabinet minutes 22 September 1933, S 4156B, NA. Quotation in Jeffery (2000: 122). In 1941 the British Legion emphasized the impartiality of the two governments, commenting in the British Legion Annual (1941: 17): 'they showed that there are solemn and sacred occasions when men can lift themselves above the sometimes rigid and petty limitations of politics and when all can unite to do honour to the imperishable grandeur of great and noble sacrifice'.

[67] Memo, 10 October 1938, S 4156B, NA.   [68] Quoted in Jeffery (2000: 123).

Committee.[69] The memorial was reopened and blessed by church leaders on 10 September 1988. Formal government recognition did not occur until April 1995 when John Bruton as Taoiseach presided over a ceremony at Islandbridge that recognized Irishmen who had died in the Second World War.[70]

A Place for Classicism in the Permanent Cenotaph for Collins, Griffith, and O'Higgins (1939–50)

There was no debate about the location of the temporary cenotaph erected in August 1923. Intended to mark the memory of two leaders of the pro-treaty faction who had died suddenly during the civil war in August 1922, the cenotaph was placed in front of Leinster House where the Dáil had found provisional accommodation. Arthur Griffith, the president of the second Dáil, who had been at the forefront of the treaty negotiations in 1921 and vigorously defended it in the Dáil, had died from a cerebral haemorrhage on 12 August. Michael Collins, commander-in-chief of the National Army and chairman of the provisional government, had died in an ambush at Béal na Bláth in Co. Cork on 22 August. The cenotaph was one of several projects by the pro-treaty party to honour the two men.[71] The projects were conceived after September 1922, once the new government of the Free State, inaugurated by the treaty signed in December 1921, had been established. By that September, the civil war had been going on for over two months, so that the commissions for death masks, busts, and plaques of the two leaders, and the cenotaph itself, were attempts to cement the authority of the government in a politically and militarily volatile atmosphere. By August 1923, when the cenotaph was unveiled, the pro-treaty party had become Cumann na nGaedheal (launched in April 1923), led by W. T. Cosgrave, so that the cenotaph was associated with that party. This connection was carefully underlined in an unveiling ceremony made memorable by Cosgrave's oration, in which he described Griffith as the architect and Collins as the master builder 'of our nation'.[72]

The cenotaph, commissioned from George Atkinson, a designer and the headmaster of the Metropolitan School of Art, focused on a stylized ringed cross, forty feet high, placed in the centre of a wall about twelve feet high, on which were attached two circular plaster medallions decorated with the busts of Collins and Griffith (Fig. 18.3).[73] A medallion of pro-treaty politician Kevin O'Higgins was

---

[69] Office of Public Works, 'Irish National War Memorial Park Restoration Report' [1988]. For location of the proposed temple see Lutyens' plan in Butler (1950, vol. 2: fig. 103). For Lutyens' design see n. 55 above.

[70] *The Irish Times*, 28 April 1995.

[71] For discussion of these projects see Bhreathnach-Lynch (1999).

[72] *The Irish Times*, 14 August 1923, p. 7.

[73] Photographs of different views of the cenotaph are published in Bhreathnach-Lynch (1999: 151) and Jeffery (2000: 124). The medallions were modelled by Albert Power.

Fig. 18.3. The temporary cenotaph, Leinster Lawn, 1922–3. Fergus O'Connor Collection, OCO 227. Image and permission to reproduce provided courtesy of the National Library of Ireland.

added in August 1928, following his assassination in 1927. The cenotaph was constructed using a timber frame covered with expanded metal laths (strips) coated in cement.[74] It was placed close to Merrion Square, in front of the Albert Memorial, which stood in the centre of Leinster Lawn. Surviving photographs reveal that it was crude, lacking in surface detail, but large enough to hold its own in the spacious square addressed by monumental civic buildings.[75] The ringed cross referred to early Christian Irish crosses, a staple of the late-nineteenth-century Gaelic Revival. The allusion to Irish culture anticipated Cumann na nGaedheal's policy of projecting Irish cultural identity through the encouragement of the Gaelic Revival in the fields of education, publishing, and the theatre. As Roy Foster has observed, the inculcating of national pride through distinctive cultural signifiers was typical of many postcolonial societies, keen to play down the influence of the former ruler.[76] Catholicism was another way in which the young State could distinguish itself from its Protestant neighbour. This strategy is evident in

[74] Letter OPW to W. T. Cosgrave, 18 September 1928, S 5734A, NA. The cenotaph cost a modest £995.
[75] Jeffery (2000: 124, fig. 4.4).   [76] Foster (1988: 518).

the press release issued for the unveiling, which stressed the religious nature of the memorial: 'The conception of the monument is spiritual. In the centre towers a celtic cross of early form, symbolic of the faith of the men commemorated.'[77]

Underlying such Irish signifiers, however, was classical decorum. The wall, with its projecting base, recessed top, and two projecting 'pylons' (a Greek-derived word for a doorway flanked by masonry towers), and the clear symmetry of the memorial have classical resonance.[78] The 1923 press release stated that the 'strength of character' of Collins and Griffith was 'symbolized in the simple pylons'. This made oblique reference to the personification attributed to classical columns, an idea initiated by Roman writers and popularized by Renaissance architect-writers in the sixteenth and seventeenth centuries.[79] The classical references were more than likely inspired by the context. Leinster Lawn, a well-proportioned space which flows into Merrion Square, is defined by three fine classical buildings; the mid-eighteenth-century Leinster House flanked by the identical facades of the mid-nineteenth-century Natural History Museum and National Museum which, with their rusticated bases, pedimented *piano nobile* niches, and generous entablatures, were modelled on the Roman palazzo.[80] Cumann na nGaedheal's commitment to the reconstruction of prominent classical buildings in Dublin, mentioned above, makes it likely that the memorial was designed to respond to the architectural setting of Leinster Lawn, even though the budget was not available to respond to its quality. Cosgrave revealed his understanding that the new government should rise to the standards set by the existing architecture when he rejected the idea of accommodating the Dáil in a new building on Leinster Lawn, arguing that 'it would destroy the beauty of Merrion Square and of this building [Leinster House]'. 'I do not believe,' he continued' '[that] you would put up a building there which you could point out with any degree of pride or satisfaction to a visitor as the place where the Parliament of a nation meets.'[81] The Gaelic Revival might have been asserted as a distinctive Irish gesture, but the Free State also accepted its architectural inheritance from the eighteenth and nineteenth centuries and aimed to rise to the standards set by Ireland's former rulers.

A proposal for a permanent cenotaph was presented by Harold Leask to de Valera's government in August 1939.[82] De Valera had delayed attending to the problem of replacing the cenotaph dedicated to the leaders of his political rivals.

---

[77] *The Irish Times*, 14 August 1923, p. 7. The press release also referred to a crucifix, which was to surmount the cross.

[78] The treatment of the cross, in which the ring appears as a disk with four holes bored in it, makes a play of abstract shapes which owes something to modernism.

[79] Summerson (1980: 14–15).   [80] Casey (2005: 560–1).

[81] Extract from Dáil debate, 6:37, p. 18, 4 April 1924.

[82] H. G. Leask, Report, 19 August 1939, S 5734A, NA.

The structure was expected to last until 1932, the year Fianna Fáil came to power, but it was not taken down until summer 1939 when it was ready to collapse.[83] Apart from being forced to make a decision by the condition of the memorial, de Valera's government was, by 1939, in a stronger position to make the statesman-like gesture of honouring the memory of its political opponents. Not only had it transformed itself into a constitutional party, but it had asserted its political values by redefining Ireland's relationship with Britain through a number of measures including the abolition of the oath of allegiance and the introduction of a new constitution in 1937.[84]

Harold Leask, who had trained as an architect and worked as an assistant surveyor for the OPW, was, by 1939, Inspector of National Monuments, and he brought a sophisticated understanding of Irish architecture to the project. He rejected a government request for a cross, arguing that the Latin cross was essentially a timber form, unsatisfactory at a large scale, while the tenth-century Celtic cross, with its biblically-inspired figurative sculpture, was not viable in the twentieth century. He proposed a stepped wall construction of broadly classical character, its central element displaying a cross and three medallions portraying Collins, Griffith, and O'Higgins (Fig. 18.4).[85] In the report that accompanied his proposal, Leask explained that this classical structure was intended to harmonize with the buildings surrounding Leinster Lawn.[86] He had also chosen a classical style because he viewed it as congruous with Irish design and, by implication, as a relevant style for an Irish memorial. 'I have,' he wrote, 'chosen a form ... embodying the tapered or battered wall face which is both Greek and Irish,' a statement which drew together the battered walls of twelfth-century Irish churches and the entasis of Greek architecture.

The idea that these two cultural traditions were compatible was not novel in the context of architecture; since the mid-1830s writers had drawn comparisons between the simplicity of early medieval Irish Gothic architecture and the fine proportions of Greek architecture.[87] The perceived parallel was no doubt appealing to those in government who admired Dublin's classical architecture, and may have persuaded them that a more confident classically derived statement was desirable. When, after an eight-year delay, the project was resumed in September 1947, there was a request for 'a monument in the form of a column or obelisk,' with subsidiary provision for a cross and the portrait plaques.[88] The delay was due to the Second World War. This no doubt also played its part in the brief for a grander and more orthodox classical monument, for Ireland had successfully

---

[83] Memo, 15 August 1939, S 5734A, NA.
[84] Brown (2004: 130).   [85] Drawing in S 5734B, NA.
[86] H. G. Leask, Report, 19 August 1939, S 5734A, NA.
[87] See Niamh NicGhabhann (2015: 26, 125). In her introduction to *Notes on Irish Architecture* published in 1875 Margaret Stokes compared Irish early Christian architecture with Greek classicism, observing that 'a classic character marked by a certain simplicity and repose, as well as a delicate perception of fitness in ornament, with a noble reserve in its use, has been attained by both' (ibid, 125).
[88] Memo, 16 September 1947, S 5734B, NA. Copies of Harold Leask's original and revised designs were sent to the Minister of Finance in May 1947, note dated 29 May 1947 in S 5734A, NA.

Fig. 18.4. Drawing of the proposed permanent cenotaph for Leinster Lawn, Harold Leask, 1939. National Archives of Ireland, S 5734B. Image and permission to reproduce provided courtesy of the National Archives of Ireland.

executed a policy of neutrality during the conflict, confirming its independent status with regard to Britain, and increasing Fianna Fáil's confidence as a party that represented a significant section of the Irish population. This assurance was articulated by Seán MacEntee in the Dáil debate of 14 July 1950 when he asserted (from the opposition benches) '... we will stand for [the] memory [of those to whom the cenotaph is raised] and venerate it and we expect any Government that purports to speak for the Irish people to give them the veneration that is their due.'[89]

Raymond McGrath, having recently become principal architect with the OPW, designed a memorial for the new brief in spring 1948. By that date he was working for the coalition government, led by the Fine Gael politician John Costello, which came to power in February 1948.[90] Born in Australia, McGrath had moved to England in 1926, establishing himself as a modernist architect at a time when the modern movement was slowly finding a place in Britain and Ireland.[91] Apart from commissions for a BBC studio, showrooms, exhibitions, and private houses,

---

[89] Extract from Dáil debate, 14 July 1950, cutting in S 5734C, NA.

[90] Memo, 15 July 1948, S 5734C, NA. McGrath had taken up a position as architect with the OPW in 1940 and was promoted to principal architect in spring 1948.

[91] For an assessment of McGrath see O'Donovan (1995), and cuttings of obituaries, Raymond McGrath Collection, 78/30 Box 15, Irish Architectural Archive (IAA).

he had published the well-received *Twentieth-Century Houses* in 1934.[92] In an article for *Architectural Design and Construction* he presented one of the core credos of the modern movement when he wrote that the 'subtlety and grace of clear-cut form must make lavish ornament unnecessary'.[93] But he was not without an awareness of historic architecture: he had a long-term interest in Italian Renaissance architecture, appreciated eighteenth-century town houses, and was alert to urban context.[94] This was expressed in exquisite ink and watercolour sketches of London, and, soon after he arrived in Dublin in 1940, of that city.

Although Ireland was culturally conservative, the Fianna Fáil government promoted modernism in state-sponsored building programmes to improve the country's provision of hospitals and schools. It also championed modernism for buildings with an international profile: most notably Dublin airport built between 1936 and 1940, and the New York World Fair pavilion in 1939.[95] But in 1935, faced with a site on Kildare Street in the centre of Georgian Dublin for a new Department of Industry and Commerce building, the government awarded the commission to an architect who proposed a stripped classical design.[96] This stylistic flexibility was echoed in McGrath's design for the cenotaph which marries modernism to classicism in a tall, slender, limestone obelisk, sixty feet high, emerging from a sloping granite base on which are fixed four wreathed medallions executed by the sculptor, Lawrence Campbell (Fig. 18.5).[97] Three of these medallions are inscribed with bronze relief profiles of Collins, Griffiths, and O'Higgins, one bears an inscription in Irish.[98] The obelisk supports a gilt flame, while a simple cross, picked out in gold, is incised near the base of the obelisk facing Merrion Square.

The obelisk supplanted the nineteenth-century Albert Memorial, which was relocated to the south side of Leinster Lawn. The retention of the Albert Memorial was surprising given that, since independence, monuments in Dublin connected with the British monarchy had been removed. In 1928 the monuments to King William III and George I were blown up, while the one to George II was destroyed in 1930 and Queen Victoria's was removed in 1948.[99] There was also the fact that the statue of Queen Victoria had been located in front of the Molesworth Street

---

[92] In 1984 the *Architects Journal* considered that McGrath's design for a house in Chertsey, Surrey epitomized 1930s modernism: *Architect's Journal*, 26 September 1984, pp. 28–32 in Raymond McGrath Collection, 78/30 Box 15, IAA.

[93] Raymond McGrath, 'Progress or period', *Architectural Design and Construction* (December 1930), 3, in Raymond McGrath Collection, 78/30 Box 15, IAA.

[94] Sheaff (1984: 37).   [95] Rothery (1991: 144–229).

[96] Construction began in January 1939 and was completed by October 1942. For assessment see Rolfe and Ryan (1992). R. Ryan (1992: 45) has suggested that the government was attracted by the straightforward and comprehensible nature of the architect's scheme.

[97] McGrath chose Campbell for his sense of portraiture, feeling for lettering, and practical experience of bronze casting.

[98] Memo from OWP, 20 July 1949, S 5734C, NA. The scheme had been costed at £20,000.

[99] Whelan (2002: 522–8).

Fig. 18.5. Permanent cenotaph, Leinster Lawn, 1948–50. Photograph and copyright Judith Hill, 2018.

side of Leinster House, and that its removal had been the subject of countrywide discussion since 1929.[100] There was demonstrably no political will to destroy the Albert Memorial in 1948. Instead, the OPW report discussed the memorial in aesthetic terms, describing it as 'a happy example of the work of John Foley, the Irish Sculptor.'[101] McGrath proposed its relocation in order to create a single focus for the lawn, which he envisaged as a three-dimensional space rather than as a backdrop to Merrion Square; '[I]t would be incongruous,' the report observed, 'to have two disparate monuments in visual competition for the Lawn, one in front of the other.'[102] The report recorded that the obelisk had been chosen for its suitability—its classicism matched the surrounding buildings of Leinster Lawn—and that it had been designed to relate to the context.

---

[100] None of these monuments were formally replaced as would be the case elsewhere in Ireland: the statue of an army officer, Viscount Fitzgibbon on Sarsfield Bridge in Limerick, destroyed in 1930, was replaced with a 1916 memorial in 1959; in Westport the figure of the philanthropist George Glendining situated on top of a large column was removed in 1943 and replaced in 1990 with a figure of St Patrick. See Hill (1998: 113, 174, 231).

[101] 'Observations of Commissioners of Public Works', n. d., S 5734C, NA.

[102] 'Observations of Commissioners of Public Works', n. d., S 5734C, NA.

Its proportions were scaled to fit the space, and its slenderness intended to minimize any obstruction of the view of Leinster House.[103] The lawn was redesigned to concentrate attention on the obelisk. McGrath, inspired by the remodelling of Grosvenor Gardens in London to accommodate the Roosevelt Memorial, removed the dense evergreens and introduced sparser, more controlled, planting.[104] McGrath's eloquent watercolour of the scheme reveals a picturesque element derived from silver birch and beds of flowers.[105]

Although the OPW report failed to hint at a political message, the design is expressive of the political confidence inherent in the brief. The obelisk, even more than the column, is a symbol of civic and political pride. This is in part related to the gargantuan effort expended by various imperial powers over 2,000 years—the Roman emperor Augustus, Pope Sixtus V, Napoleon Bonaparte, English archaeologists and civil servants of the British Empire—to transport monolithic Egyptian obelisks to European capitals. The Wellington Testimonial in Dublin's Phoenix Park, the second largest obelisk in the world, had been explicitly chosen because of its grandeur.[106] By refining and elongating the obelisk for Leinster Lawn, McGrath made it site-specific and contemporary, appropriating the form for that time and place. The monument incorporates specifically Irish elements. Apart from the bronze medallions with their finely drawn profiles of the three men, the granite blocks that form the shaft, base, and radiating pavement are from Co. Dublin quarries, and the inscription, derived from the temporary memorial, is in Gaelic script.[107] By the 1950s the inclusion of the vernacular language on public monuments was common, but there was still no consensus about the form of the letters and their spacing. Taoiseach Costello's original suggestion (perhaps indicative of his limited acquaintance with Irish) that Campbell follow the printed precedents of the University College Dublin 1928 examination papers and the text of the constitution was rejected by Campbell as of insufficient artistic quality.[108] Campbell proposed the Book of Kells as an exemplar. Costello consulted the Gaelic scholar and printer Colm Ó Lochlain, who proposed extensive revisions, which Costello accepted as authoritative and instructed Campbell to follow.[109] The carefully considered Irish vernacular stands as an equal partner with the classicism of the obelisk in a scheme that reworked tradition and gestured towards the future.

---

[103] 'Observations of Commissioners of Public Works', n. d., S 5734C, NA.

[104] 'Observations of Commissioners of Public Works', n. d., S 5734C, NA.

[105] The watercolour is illustrated in Griffin and Pegum (2000: 101). Memo, 15 July 1948, S 5734C, NA.

[106] Hill (1998: 69).

[107] The inscription is a dedication which reads: 'Do chum glóire Dé agus onóra na hÉireann' ('Composed for the glory of God and honour of Ireland'). A version of Gaelic script was used on the temporary memorial.

[108] Letter from Costello to OPW 16 March 1949, S 5734C, NA; letter from Campbell to McGrath, 21 February 1950, S 5734C, NA.

[109] Minute from Costello to OPW, 27 February 1950; minute from OPW to Costello enclosing Ó Lochlain's comments, 11 March 1950; minute from Costello to OPW, 13 March 1950, S 5734C, NA.

Classicism and Political Idealism

Classicism, it is argued here, was employed in Irish memorials as a language of idealism. In the case of the Irish National War Memorial, the collaboration of both major parties of government with the memorial committee meant that the monument reflected aspirations that were common to these disparate groups. Rather than deliberately referencing British imperial values, the classicism of the Irish National War Memorial expressed aspirations associated with the present: to create a place where everyone could honour the dead, and to acknowledge the need for reconciliation in the aftermath of the violence that surrounded the gaining of independence. In the case of the permanent cenotaph for dead political leaders, all governments gave allegiance to a project which, in its original, temporary, form had been a partisan statement. The classicism of the obelisk encompassed all political parties, with all their 'pasts', in a single integrated symbol for the polity that had survived the divisions of the civil war.

Classicism was not employed in either case as an appropriation of the language of the former ruler. Rather, it is argued here that successive Irish governments accepted classicism as intrinsic to the identity of Dublin. The obelisk, located at the centre of a square surrounded by fine public buildings designed in the classicism of the eighteenth and nineteenth centuries, paid handsome tribute to its setting, while simultaneously securing its place in history with an original gesture that made Leinster Lawn the symbolic heart of the new dispensation. At Islandbridge, the architecture of the memorial linked Ireland to the wider world through the creation of an internationally significant monumental landscape. It is a place, once peripheral in Dublin, where the inclusivist ideals, implicit in the 1930s when the memorial was erected, could finally be publically articulated in 1995. Together, these classical memorials play their part in defining and enhancing Dublin, a city where the classicism of the past was given currency in two significant memorials engendered in post-independence Ireland.

19

The Politics of Neoclassicism in Belfast and Dublin

A Tale of Two Buildings

Suzanne O'Neill

Introduction

This chapter examines the architecture and symbolism of two buildings: the Northern Ireland Parliament Buildings (Fig. 19.1), better known as Stormont from the site of its location on the Stormont estate east of Belfast, and the General Post Office (GPO) in Dublin (Fig. 19.3). The chapter will reveal how the neoclassical forms of Stormont's design represent the political oratory of early- to mid-twentieth-century mainstream Ulster unionism realized in stone. It will also demonstrate that this imposing building, which exudes Olympian calm and imposing confidence, was constructed to symbolize the division of 'Planter' and 'Gael' and to represent visible and physical proof of unionist self-determination to remain within the British Empire at a time when the rest of Ireland had gained independence from Britain. While in Belfast the newly formed Northern Ireland was constructing the colossal parliament building that would become a unionist bastion of British imperialism, in Dublin the new Irish Free State government was repairing the neoclassical General Post Office building. The GPO had been reduced to a burnt-out shell after it was bombarded by the British Army during the 1916 Rising and was destined to become the principal commemorative site for those who fought for Irish independence from Britain. The recent life of Stormont, on the other hand, as the seat of the Northern Ireland Assembly since 2007, reveals how Stormont's British and unionist identity is still actively promoted and relevant, and presents a contrast with the GPO building in Dublin, which since 1916 has had its British colonial memory erased and replaced by new Irish nationalist narratives.

Suzanne O'Neill, *The Politics of Neoclassicism in Belfast and Dublin: A Tale of Two Buildings* In: *Classics and Irish Politics, 1916–2016*. Edited by: Isabelle Torrance and Donncha O'Rourke, Oxford University Press (2020).
© Oxford University Press.
DOI: 10.1093/oso/9780198864486.003.0019

Fig. 19.1. The Northern Ireland Parliament Building (Stormont) designed by Sir
Arnold Thornely and opened in 1932. Photograph and copyright Suzanne
O'Neill, 2019.

Stormont: A Temple to Unionism and Empire

Stormont was built to house the new Parliament of Northern Ireland, which came
into being in May 1921, following the 1920 Government of Ireland Act and the
partition of Ireland. The Ulster unionists, led by Sir James Craig (Lord Craigavon),
dominated the new government securing forty parliamentary seats in the opening elections, compared to the Sinn Féin and Irish Nationalist parties who secured
only six seats apiece.[1] Craig became the first Prime Minister of Northern Ireland,
and with his unionist cabinet ensured that Stormont was built in a style and scale
befitting their image of a colonial house of parliament.

The Northern Ireland Parliament Buildings are neoclassical in design and fuse
austere Greek architectural features with Italian Palladian elements. The structures dominate the surrounding landscape. Architectural historian Paul Larmour,
writing in a neutral style and employing the detached language of aesthetics, has
described Stormont as having 'a very dignified exterior'[2] and of being 'one of the

---

[1] Officer (1996: 132).   [2] Larmour (1987:110).

most outstanding architectural sites in Ireland'.[3] Such descriptions overlook the building's political implications. Since its construction in 1932, Stormont has stood at the apex of contested representational space in Northern Ireland.[4] Stormont was viewed by all political sides in Ireland as a tangible representation in stone of unionist and British power. This political narrative was further accentuated in 1940 when, in an unprecedented act, Craig was laid to rest in Stormont's grounds. Regarded by unionists as one of the key founding fathers of Northern Ireland and a resolute defender of the democratic right to remain part of the United Kingdom, Craig had famously proclaimed: 'we are a Protestant Parliament and a Protestant State.'[5] The decision to inter this champion of unionism in such a significant site was a determined political act which symbolized unionist territorial ownership of Northern Ireland.

Stormont was officially opened by the Prince of Wales on 16 November 1932. Approval to construct the Parliament Buildings had been secured a decade earlier in 1922 and the British Imperial Exchequer was legally obliged to fund the cost. Stormont was formally constructed under the supervision of the Office of Works in London's Whitehall, but there is clear evidence that Craig and his party had direct contact with, and exercised considerable influence on, this government body.[6] The Office of Works was responsible to the Imperial Treasury for expenditure and had also appointed Arnold Thornely (FRIBA) as chief architect.[7] Thornely had by this stage come to prominence though his imposing buildings in Liverpool; in similar taste, his initial neoclassical design for Stormont included a huge dome, but this plan was abandoned in 1925 due to its prohibitive cost.[8] A scaled down (but equally impressive) neoclassical building was eventually completed at a cost of £1.2 million.[9]

The commanding and monumental character of Stormont and its location cannot be overstated. A publication by The Ulster Architectural Heritage Society describes the building and its situation as follows:

> It is generally accepted that Thornely succeeded in both siting and design, taking full advantage of the elevated location and creating a well-proportioned, dignified and impressive building of Portland lime-stone resting on a plinth of unpolished Mourne granite. The hill-top background of dark trees both absorbs and sets off the substantial dimensions – 365 feet long, 164 feet deep and 70 feet high rising to 92 feet at the centre of the main façade.[10]

---

[3] Larmour (1987:110).   [4] Neill (1998: 4).
[5] See, e.g., the discussion of this quotation in the Northern Ireland Assembly by Democratic Unionist Party MLA Mervyn Storey on the seventieth anniversary of Craig's death: Storey (2010).
[6] Greer (1999: 375–6).   [7] Kennedy and Wheeler (1999: 16).
[8] Kennedy and Wheeler (1999: 18).   [9] Kennedy and Wheeler (1999: 16).
[10] Kennedy and Wheeler (1999: 19).

This art-historical description of Stormont is, for the most part, accurate. However, the driving force behind the choice of site for Stormont was not the architect Thornely, but Craig and his government. Craig was so determined that the new Northern Ireland Parliament Buildings should be built on the site of the Stormont estate that in 1921 he secured a personal bank loan of £3,000 to place a deposit for its purchase.[11]

There were objections to the Stormont site from sections of the business, legal, and farming communities in the Belfast area, as well as from nationalist politicians. Many of those who opposed Craig's plans felt that the new building should be in Belfast City. This was especially true of Northern Ireland nationalist MP Joe Devlin, who complained that the parliament buildings were 'not in a convenient place' and 'too far away'.[12] Despite such opposition, Craig was easily able to secure parliamentary approval through the ruling Unionist Party, and his choice of site was endorsed by a resolution of the Northern Ireland Parliament on 20 September 1921.[13] The site was symbolically loaded from the outset. Dominating the surrounding countryside from its elevated position, the terrain also demanded that the buildings should face south towards the Irish Free State. While this orientation may have been an accident of the topography, it nevertheless embodied an articulation of superiority and separation in relation to the independent Irish south. Craig, moreover, remained very much personally invested in the development of the building designs.[14]

At Stormont, as in other political contexts, the new buildings reflect the power of the dominant political group and its leader.[15] In newly formed Northern Ireland, the government was keen to advertise its national and international legitimacy. As such, neoclassicism is exploited to reflect British imperial ideology and unionist values. In *Belfast: An Illustrated Architectural Guide*, Larmour describes Stormont's architectural design and sculptural decoration as follows:

> It is designed in a Neo-classical style which is fairly plain in treatment except around the three entrance bays. Elaborate central feature to the main façade with a wealth of Greek detail and a grand Ionic temple front. Pediment carved with a

---

[11] Greer (1999: 377). Significantly, this was before the location was approved by either the Imperial Treasury in London, the architect Thornely, or most importantly the new parliament in Northern Ireland. The latter's approval was legally required by section 8 (7) of the Government of Ireland Act for any location of the new parliament building outside of Belfast City boundary.

[12] Stormont Papers (1931–2: 13, 1501–2).

[13] Regarding the purchase of the site, Craig justified his unilateral actions to the Imperial Treasury by citing the need to act quickly to procure such a 'suitable location' at a bargain price. His gamble paid off and the Imperial Office of Works and Thornely both acquiesced.

[14] Craig's longest letter as Prime Minister (to the cabinet secretariat) was about the design of the fence posts around Stormont's grounds: see Buckland (1980: 98).

[15] Architectural theorists observe that the designs of parliament buildings are strongly influenced by personal predilections, both those of the architect and those of the sponsoring politicians and regimes: see Vale (1992: 316).

group showing 'Ulster bearing the Golden Flame of Loyalty to the Crown', carved by Malcolm Miller and Rendal Bond of Earp, Hobbs and Miller of Manchester. [16]

Stormont's principal neoclassical architectural feature is its grand 'hexastyle' Ionic temple front, featuring a triangular pediment placed on top of an entablature supported by six columns in the Greek Ionic order. Set within the tympanum (the space inside the pediment) is a sculpted female personification of Ulster bearing the golden flame of loyalty to the British crown—an overtly political gesture that symbolizes Ulster's union with Britain (Fig. 19.2). Larmour does not mention the huge stone statue of Britannia, flanked by two lions, which sits on a prominent attic block at the very top of Stormont high above the pediment. Nor does he reference the presence of the British Crown's coat of arms over the main entrance to the building. When Stormont opened in 1932, this potent image of Britannia, combined with such explicitly loyalist sculptural arrangements inside the pediment, received countless endorsements from Ulster unionists, but at the same time alienated many in the minority Irish nationalist community.

A further voice in the building's rhetoric that will have estranged the nationalist community from Stormont was the very choice of a monumental neoclassical design. In 1932 *The Builder* was warm in its praise of what it called the 'Greek Classical design' of the building, claiming that it was 'an excellent example of the modern use of ancient art' and a style that provided 'the dignity associated with Parliament'.[17] For many commentators in both the nationalist and unionist communities, the style, with its then perceived ideals of law, order, and supremacy, represented the architecture of empire at the beginning of the twentieth century. As such, many in Northern Ireland found themselves encouraged in the view that, by building Stormont in such a titanic style, the British were effectively staking a permanent claim to the six counties of Antrim, Fermanagh, Down, Armagh, Derry, and Tyrone. This narrative finds expression in the six giant Greek Ionic columns which form part of Stormont's elaborate central facade and serve as symbolic representations of the six counties.[18]

Unionist Party MPs and other loyalist commentators openly supported and encouraged these readings of the building. With reference to the laying of Stormont's foundation stone in May 1928, the *Belfast News Letter* claimed:

> It would be a great waste of money and of effort to erect a magnificent building as the home of a merely temporary institution. The laying of the foundation stone is a formal and public declaration that the state of Northern Ireland is firmly established and that it will never surrender its parliament.[19]

---

[16] Larmour (1987: 110–11).   [17] Anon. (1932: 806–12).
[18] See Parliament Building Facts at http://www.niassembly.gov.uk/assembly-business/office-of-the-speaker/80th-anniversary-open-day/parliament-buildings-facts/ (accessed 12 January 2019).
[19] *Belfast News Letter*, 21 May 1928.

Fig. 19.2.   Statue group in the tympanum of Stormont's pediment depicting Ulster presenting a flame of loyalty to Britain and the Commonwealth. Photograph and copyright Suzanne O'Neill, 2019.

In 1926, the Independent Unionist MP Thomas Henderson gave a speech in the Northern Ireland Parliament (convening at this time in the Presbyterian Assembly's College) in which he declared:

> The citizens of Ulster have been the backbone of the Empire, and in return for the great services they have rendered they shall be provided with proper buildings at Stormont.[20]

Echoing these sentiments, the *Northern Whig* published a speech by the Rev. Brett Dean of Belfast proclaiming:

> The dominant characteristic of Ulstermen…was a passion for liberty.…[T]he building to be erected thereon, was regarded as a symbol of a dearly cherished possession, of an attitude of mind as well as a trait of blood. And Ulster

[20]   Stormont Papers (1926: 6, 1929).

identified with the ideal it represented. But the Imperial idea was, after all, the idea of Ulster.[21]

Such imperial and unionist orotundity further isolated the Irish nationalist minority in Ulster. It became increasingly clear to many nationalists that Stormont was an embodiment of the unionist regime, both politically and iconographically. The Greek classical forms of Stormont were seen as representing liberty and democracy but only under British imperialism.

Stormont's Portland Stone: Imperial Symoblism

Nationalist and Sinn Féin politicians in Northern Ireland had objected to the building of Stormont for several major reasons. Apart from seeing it as a structure which confirmed the partition of Ireland, they felt it was far too big for its purpose and a grotesque waste of money at a time when Ulster was experiencing an economic depression.[22] In some ways this echoes Henry Grattan's objections in the eighteenth century to the amount of money that was spent on neoclassical public buildings in Dublin, as discussed below.

Nationalists also objected to the use of English Portland stone to build a Northern Irish Parliament building. During the construction of Stormont, Portland stone was required at a rate never before demanded in Ireland. At the height of the contract 1,600 cubic feet were laid in a week and a remarkable 135,000 cubic feet of Portland stone was used in total.[23] Objections rested on a complex mix of patriotic, aesthetic, and socio-economic considerations. Having accepted that they could not prevent Stormont from being constructed, nationalists felt it was their patriotic and moral duty to try and ensure that local Irish industries and Irish working-class people benefited from this enormous construction project. The use of local stone would also give the building a stronger native Irish visual dimension and increase its nationalist symbolic load. So constructed, there might be some counterbalance to the intensive unionist and imperial elements in Stormont's design and imagery.

An undeniably strong influence on nationalist sentiment and policy was the Irish Free State government's commitment to using Irish resources. From 1926 strict legal specifications in the Irish Free State stipulated the procurement of Irish materials. Thus the Portland stone dome of the eighteenth-century Dublin

---

[21] Dean (1928).
[22] In the context of these misgivings, nationalist MP Joe Devlin commented: 'The number of members in the house is too small for a parliament building of that size. No doubt you will say that when the British government gave a million or million and a quarter, it was not your business to prevent the building being so colossal.' See Stormont Papers (1931–2: 13, 1501–2).
[23] Kennedy and Wheeler (1999: 23).

Custom House (which had been destroyed in 1921 during the Anglo-Irish War) was rebuilt using Irish Ardbraccan stone. This gave the Custom House a greater native Irish content both physically (within the very fabric of the building) and conceptually. Within this political and cultural context nationalist politicians in Northern Ireland persistently argued that native Ulster stone be used to build Stormont. Their case rested on the principle that the edifice was, in theory, meant to represent all of the people and communities of Ulster.[24]

Craig and his ministers, however, maintained that the decision as to which stone was to be used to build Stormont, and the cost of doing so, were the full responsibility of the Office of Works in London. This was a disingenuous response, since Craig in particular was examining and making recommendations for almost every aspect of the building's design. Moreover, when the Imperial Treasury refused to pay for Portland stone to be used for the new Royal Courts of Justice in Belfast, Craig and his government protested relentlessly. The British government was legally obliged to pay for the new Law Courts in Belfast (as well as Stormont) and the Imperial Treasury informed the Northern Ireland government that this building would have to be constructed in brick to keep costs under control. Craig and his ministers responded by claiming that brick was wholly inappropriate for such an important state building and that they would meet half the cost of using English Portland stone. In response, nationalists protested that English Portland stone was being used for a second major government building in Northern Ireland and demanded that Newry granite be used for both buildings.[25] Nationalists were also supported in this argument by a few businessmen in the unionist community, such as W. Campbell, who had interests in the Newry granite quarries. To the abhorrence of many nationalists, it was also reported that 'the only thing in the shape of Ulster granite that is going into the building is for the steps'.[26]

It is clear that Craig and his government wanted English Portland stone to be used for both Stormont and the Law Courts, as befitted their imperial vision for the new regime's government buildings. Portland stone had been used to build many government buildings in London and around the British Empire. The

[24] For example, the nationalist MP Cahir Healy questioned Craig openly in parliament: 'He is building a new Parliament house at Stormont and he could have had for it the most beautiful, the most artistic and most durable stone in the Kingdom from the granite quarries at Newry. Instead of that he goes to Portland for stone.... The money that ought to be giving employment to people in the vicinity of Newry is going to employ people in Portland.' See Stormont Papers (1929: 10, 110).
[25] A nationalist MP, John Henry Collins, stated in reference to Craig that 'for both of the buildings he is importing Portland stone. I think I have never heard anything more unpatriotic or disgraceful': see Stormont Papers (1929–30: 11, 57–8).
[26] Stormont Papers (1929: 10, 145–6). Nationalist MP Joe Devlin further argued against the cost of Portland stone and emphasized that local Newry granite was as aesthetically pleasing as Portland stone, if not more so: 'For the law courts they consent to pay the margin between the cost of brick and the cost of stone and allow the money to be spent on Portland stone instead of granite. It could not be said that granite was inferior, because anybody who has seen buildings built of Newry granite will admit that from the point of view of beauty as well as enduring qualities, they are incomparable in any country of the world.' See Stormont Papers (1929–30: 11, 1013–30).

official home of the British monarch at Buckingham Palace is a neoclassical building built of Portland stone. Portland stone was also used to construct the Cenotaph war memorial at Whitehall in honour of the British and Commonwealth soldiers who died in the First World War. The Cenotaph was designed by Sir Edwin Lutyens in 1920 and incorporates a simple neoclassical pylon with a sarcophagus on top.[27] For the majority of Ulster unionist war veterans, many of whom were present at the ceremony for the laying of Stormont's Portland foundation stone, an emblematic connection to their deceased 'brothers in arms' in the other dominions of the British Empire was very important. A concluding statement was delivered in 1930 by minister Pollock of the Unionist Party, again justifying the use of Portland stone in Ulster and also underlining the new Northern Irish state's architectural aspirations and connections to the capital of the British Empire: 'the whole of London is being largely rebuilt at the present time of Portland stone.'[28] Within two years of this remark, Craig and his Unionist Party had finally succeeded in realizing their architectural vision for the new parliament building and Stormont was completed in their imperial and political image.

The GPO: From Empire to Iconic Rebellion

In Dublin, over a century earlier, the General Post Office had been constructed as a monumental physical manifestation of British power in Ireland, and part of a rich tradition of neoclassical architecture which first makes an appearance in Ireland in the seventeenth century. An early example is the Royal Hospital at Kilmainham (begun in 1680), a complex described by art historian Christine Casey as 'grand in scale, robust in execution, superlative in craftsmanship and gauche in classical articulation.'[29] However, it is in the eighteenth-century public architecture of Dublin that the most spectacular legacy of British government patronage is witnessed, as successive viceroys of Ireland were steered by Westminster's need to win parliamentary support for the administration and were encouraged to build impressive public buildings to achieve this. Distinguished examples of such buildings are the Four Courts and the Custom House in Dublin, both designed by James Gandon and built in the 1780s. For Henry Grattan and his Irish Patriot Party these buildings were simply instances of government spending to ensure support. He infamously referred to the Custom House as 'six-rank in architecture but of first-rate in extravagance.'[30]

In fact, it is generally agreed that neoclassical buildings come no finer than Dublin's Custom House. It has been widely acknowledged among architectural

---

[27]   For Luytens' design of the World War I memorial at Islandbridge in Dublin see Hill (Ch. 18).
[28]   Stormont Papers (1929–30: 11, 1013–30).   [29]   Casey (2005: 25).
[30]   Casey (2005: 47).

historians that Grattan was wrong aesthetically, but he was certainly correct with regards to the expense of such buildings and the political motivations behind their construction. Moreover, these grand colonial buildings in Ireland feature Irish and British motifs set within an architectural frame of reference that is unmistakably classical. For example, the pavilions of the Custom House are adorned with the coat of arms of Ireland and Britain (a unicorn and lion with a harp in the centre and a crown on top) and the pediment features a personification of Hibernia being embraced by Britannia. Similar integration of native motifs and features in British neoclassical colonial buildings in India have been discussed by Phiroze Vasunia.[31]

It was within this context that the GPO was designed by the architect Francis Johnston of Armagh, completed in 1818 at a cost of £50,000 (Fig. 19.3). Although constructed after the 1800 Act of Union between the British and Irish parliaments, the GPO bears similarities to the earlier Irish neoclassical civic buildings, in that they all served as important public amenities, while also transmitting British imperial symbolism and political messages. While Ireland was legally united with Great Britain in January 1801 as the Kingdom of Great Britain and Ireland, in many ways it was still treated as a colony, especially in terms of law-making and policing.[32] The tympanum of Johnston's GPO originally contained the British Crown's coat of arms, but no other figural sculpture. Additionally, there were three stone statues of Hibernia, Fidelity, and Mercury placed on top of the GPO's pediment, with Hibernia (a female personification of Ireland) occupying the central position on the apex of the triangular pediment. The presence of the royal coat of arms, placed unambiguously alone and visually prominent in the GPO's tympanum, communicated the message that Ireland was a subject of the British Crown. The three statues have appropriately been described as conveying the postal system in Ireland, with Mercury (on Hibernia's left) overseeing the post office as messenger of the gods, and Fidelity (on Hibernia's right) suggesting the nation's confidence in their postal system.[33] While this reading is reliable, sculptural arrangements will convey more than one message; it is also possible that in early-nineteenth-century colonial Ireland the sculptural ensemble alluded to the idea that prosperity (also represented by Mercury as god of commerce, travel, and economic prosperity) would attend an Ireland (Hibernia) who stayed loyal (Fidelity) within the British Empire. The figure of Mercury thus plays a dual role in the pedimental symbolism: standing on the GPO by a ship's prow he could symbolize both the straightforward delivery of mail and the benefits to be accrued from being part of the global British Empire and the imperial postal system.

---

[31] Vasunia (2013: 34).   [32] Colls (2002: 93).

[33] So Irish schoolchildren may inform themselves via the An Post education outreach website at https://www.anpost.ie/anpost/schoolbag/secondary/history/the±gpo+and±the+1916±rising/ (accessed 16 May 2019).

Fig. 19.3. The Dublin General Post Office (GPO) designed by Francis Johnston and opened in 1818. Photograph and copyright Suzanne O'Neill, 2019.

The GPO was constructed just twenty years after the failed 1798 Irish Rebellion against British rule. The political ideology of the 1798 rebels was coloured by the same classically inspired enlightenment ideas of freedom and liberty that had driven the American and French Revolutions of the late eighteenth century. These enduring ideas later manifested themselves in the Proclamation of the Irish Republic written by the rebels who participated in the 1916 Rising. Following that rebellion, all that remained of Johnston's original building were the damaged Georgian neoclassical facades. In the early twentieth century, while unionists in Northern Ireland were exalting Craig as a great democratic statesman and proclaiming their loyalty to the British crown through the building of Stormont in an imperial neoclassical style, the Irish Free State government was asserting its independence through its own rebuilding of the neoclassical GPO in Dublin. Repaired between 1924 and 1929, the GPO's neoclassical facade was retained, but the building had become vested with a completely new nationalist political narrative. Formerly a symbol of British rule in Ireland, the facade was now a visual reminder of the 1916 Easter Rising *against* that power. The GPO had been the headquarters of the 1916 Rebellion, and it was in front of this building that Patrick Pearse stood and read the Proclamation of the Irish Republic. From this point forward, the GPO's neoclassical facade became an iconic site for commemorating one of the most important events in Ireland's fight for independence.

During the reconstruction, the British royal coat of arms was removed from the building's pediment,[34] a significant step in erasing the visual record of the

---

[34] The coat of arms was removed with chisels and has since been lost. The only trace left of its presence is discernible in the faint hue of slightly lighter coloured stone in the area at the centre of the pediment where it was once placed.

GPO's British and colonial past. On the other hand, the three statues of Hibernia, Fidelity, and Mercury (although damaged) have remained on top of the GPO's pediment. In 1929, when W. T. Cosgrave as president of the executive council of the Irish Free State government officially reopened the GPO, a small number of troops marched past the building and the Irish tricolour was hoisted on the roof where, prior to independence, the British union flag once flew. In an eloquent speech, Cosgrave spoke of 'the radically altered political landscape',[35] and it is clear that the symbolic visual political message transmitted by the statues on the GPO had altered, too. These statues, now located under the tricolour, told a new political narrative: Hibernia was no longer a subject of the British crown, and Fidelity to the new Irish Free State would result in prosperity.

Two commemorative panels inside the GPO record the building's construction and reconstruction. Both are written in English and Irish. The first panel states: 'The General Post Office, built 1814–1818 to designs by Francis Johnston RA 1761–1829. Altered and enlarged 1904–1916. Reopened March 1916. Destroyed during Easter Rising April 1916. Rebuilt and reopened 1929.' This panel on the architectural history of the building has the English text on top with an Irish translation underneath. The second accompanying panel reverses this arrangement so that the Irish text is on top with the English translation underneath. This second panel thus begins: 'Ar an láthair seo, Luan Cásca 1916, léigh Pádraic Mac Piarais forógra Phoblacht na hÉireann. Ón áras seo threoraigh sé na fórsaí a dhearbhaigh faoi airm ceart na hÉireann chun a saoirse.' This is translated as 'Here on Easter Monday 1916 Patrick Pearse read the proclamation of the Irish Republic. From this building he commanded the forces that asserted in arms Ireland's right to freedom.' A final line of text in Irish rounds off the panel. It reads 'Is iad a d'adhain an tine bheo', and is untranslated. The sentence means 'It was they who kindled the embers to flame';[36] it thus explicitly associates the actions of Patrick Pearse and the other rebel leaders at the GPO with kindling the subsequent fight for independence. The arrangement of text in the second panel, then, clearly asserts its message about Ireland's right to freedom from Britain.

Craig's Legacy: A 'Hero Cult' at Stormont

As we have seen, the creation of Stormont was largely the individual vision of Sir James Craig, as a material unionist representation of the enduring legitimacy of Northern Ireland. Craig's death in 1940 further augmented that agenda, when, in

---

[35] See Martin (2016: 42).
[36] Fiachra Mac Góráin points out that this is the last line of the historical lament 'Maidin Luan Chincíse' by Mícheál Óg Ó Longáin. As a song about the 1798 rebellion, the allusion is especially apt in the context of the rekindled uprising of 1916.

an unprecedented move, the Unionist Party rushed the Craigavon Burial Bill through the Northern Ireland Parliament on 26 November 1940 to authorize the interment of Craig within the grounds of Stormont.[37] Craig was given a state funeral two days later on 28 November, his body (draped in the Union flag) carried on a gun carriage drawn by an armoured vehicle through Belfast streets lined by the Ulster Special Constabulary and thousands of onlookers. Craig's body was entombed in a plot next to the neoclassical parliament building which he had worked so hard to fashion. The *Irish Press* reported that as Craig's coffin was lowered into the tomb, soil from each of the six Irish counties which constituted the Northern Irish State was sprinkled on the coffin, while the last post was sounded from a military bugler.[38] This represented Craig's continued commitment to the Northern Ireland State in death, just as had been the case during his life. Craig became nothing less than the physical and eternal embodiment of loyalist Ulster and Northern Ireland.[39]

Craig's austere and simple 'stripped classical'[40] sarcophagus was designed by R. Ingelby Smith and was fashioned in the same Portland stone from which Stormont was built (Fig. 19.4). The sarcophagus is reminiscent of the design of the sarcophagus which forms the top part of the Cenotaph war memorial at Whitehall in London. Both sarcophagi are made out of Portland stone and both are executed in a simple unadorned neoclassical style, with its universal and enduring potential to evoke memories of all those who have died heroically in war from classical times to the present. As with the Cenotaph in London, Craig's tomb is also a focal point of commemoration on Armistice Day. Red poppy wreaths are placed at the tomb by unionist and military groups which honour Craig's service in the British Army during the imperial Boer Wars and his steadfast loyalty to Britain in the First and Second World Wars.

The positioning of Craig's remains and his funerary monument so close to the Stormont building, in all its Hellenizing symbolic power, is reminiscent of the location of the tomb of the Athenian hero Theseus, which similarly was placed in the vicinity of the buildings that administered the classical Athenian democracy. The arrangements made for Craig's tomb, then, might be interpreted as alluding to a modern form of classical Greek 'hero cult'.

The connection could have some significance for a political elite in Europe in the first half of the twentieth century, schooled as they were in classical culture and likely to have known about the legendary Athenian hero Theseus who was credited with the formation (synoecism) of the Athenian *polis* and hailed as a steadfast defender of Athens and her democracy. Plutarch tells us that Theseus

---

[37] *Irish Press*, 27 November 1940: 7.   [38] *Irish Press*, 29 November 1940: 7.

[39] On the politically charged symbolisms of burial in Northern Irish culture see also Torrance (Ch. 17).

[40] Stripped classicism or 'Grecian Moderne' is an architectural style that is austere, simplified, and devoid of traditional classical decorative detailing.

Fig. 19.4. The tomb of Sir James Craig at Stormont. The sarcophagus is decorated with the Craigavon coat of arms supported by a constable of the Ulster Special Constabulary and a soldier of the Royal Ulster Rifles. Photograph and copyright Suzanne O'Neill, 2019.

demarcated the territorial boundary between the communities of Dorian and Ionic Greeks. Athenians were Ionic Greeks and their great rivals were the Spartans, Dorian Greeks who resided in the Peloponnese in the south-west of Greece. Theseus was said to have erected a pillar on the isthmus of the Peloponnese peninsula with an inscription facing east that declared: 'Here is not Peloponnesus but Ionia,' and a second inscription facing south-west stating: 'Here is not Ionia but Peloponnesus' (Plut. *Thes.* 24–35).

Theseus' remains were said to have been placed with great pomp and ceremony in a tomb in the Athenian agora (Plut. *Thes.* 36.). The sacred tomb was called the Theseion and was close to all the buildings which housed the functioning arms of the ancient Athenian democracy, including the Bouleuterion (council chamber); the Athenian assembly also met on the nearby Pnyx Hill at the north-west end of the agora. According to Pausanias, the Theseion was covered with paintings depicting Theseus fighting and repelling various mythological barbarians such as centaurs and Amazons (Paus. 1.15). Such images were used by the ancient Greeks as an analogy for the Persian invasions of Greece in the fifth century BCE which had threatened the autonomy of the Athenian state and the nascent democracy. Athens had gained a reputation for its courage and had famously repelled the first

Persian invasion at the battle of Marathon in 490 BCE despite being massively outnumbered. It was this courage, combined with a civilized and learned culture, democracy, and willingness to confer these 'benefits' on others, which made Athens a worthy recipient of an empire in the eyes of many Athenians.[41] By the fifth century BCE Theseus was the embodiment of these ideas. Plutarch tells us that many Athenians who fought at Marathon 'thought they saw the spirit of Theseus in arms rushing on in front of them against the barbarians' (Plut. *Thes.* 35). It is evident that at the height of Athenian power in the mid-fifth century BCE Theseus was a hero whose tomb and image could galvanize Athenian defiance against their enemies, barbarian or otherwise.

Placing Craig's classical tomb at Stormont in the deeply divided State of Northern Ireland served to galvanize the unionist associations with Stormont in an arguably analogous fashion. The Craigavon coat of arms is carved on one side of the sarcophagus and states (in English) that 'charity provokes charity'. This laconic motto is reminiscent of the declaration made by Athenian statesman Pericles in his famous funeral oration, as related by Thucydides. Pericles reportedly stated: 'we do the opposite of what most people do; not by receiving benefits, but by giving them do we make friends.'[42] To excel in benefiting others is an utterly traditional definition of classical Greek and Athenian male virtue,[43] and this was also a widely accepted and revered ideal among the Victorian educated classes of the British Empire. Additionally, the moral justification of empire rested on the ideology (real or imagined) that imperial expansion brought benefits of law, order, and civilization to the subjugated.

Craig's coat of arms is also supported by two armed male military figures. On the left there is a constable of the Ulster Special Constabulary and on the right there is a soldier of Royal Ulster Rifles with whom he served. For several decades Craig had been the undisputed leader of unionism and was perceived by many to excel in courage and virtue. His character and leadership had managed to forge a unionist alliance across all classes, whose differences had been subsumed in the interests of the survival of Northern Ireland against its opponents, internal or external, real or imaginary. In the manner of Theseus in Athens, Craig was celebrated as a unionist democratic hero who had the ability to unite his community. His consecrated resting place symbolized the permanent territorial possession of Northern Ireland against the claims of the nationalist Catholic 'other', and the unionist resolve to raise arms against those who threatened their dominion and political system of government.

On the day after Craig's death on Sunday 24 November 1940, the then acting Prime Minister of Northern Ireland, J. M. Andrews, stated in a radio broadcast that Craig had 'erected the structure [of Northern Ireland] and made it

---

[41] See Mills (1997: 43–4). [42] Thuc. 2.40.4, trans. cited from Mills (1997: 73).
[43] Mills (1997: 74).

impregnable'.[44] The following day he further eulogized Craig as 'a great Ulsterman, a great Irishman and a great Imperialist...and by instinct and training a democrat'.[45] In death, Craig interred in his simple Portland stone sarcophagus, with its focal location on the east flank of Stormont, would forever remain an emblem of unionist ideology and defiance.

Neoclassical Political Icons

The architecture at Stormont, in a similar way to that of Irish public buildings from the eighteenth and nineteenth centuries, combines Irish (Ulster) and British motifs in a neoclassical building, constructed, as it was, to represent the values of the ruling Unionist Party who formed the government of the newly created Northern Ireland within the British Empire. The main building material for Stormont was finely dressed English Portland stone which was set on a plinth of unpolished native Northern Irish granite. This architectural arrangement was the choice of the architect Thornely in consultation with Sir James Craig and his unionist government. It is clear that this use of English and Irish stone symbolically represented the union of Ulster with England within the British Empire. Not insignificantly, the Portland stone (which was used to build so many British imperial buildings) was placed on top in an arrangement that stood as a metaphor for the dominant forces of empire and 'Planter' over 'Gael' and native. The unionist concept that the British Empire had been a 'civilizing' force in Gaelic Ireland is also suggested in the contrast between the carefully dressed Portland stone and the unpolished rustic native Irish stone. Equally pointed is the fact that Stormont's most symbolic piece of masonry, the foundation stone, was in Portland stone and not Ulster granite. At its very symbolic core, then, the building had a British and imperial identity rather than a native Irish one.

Portland stone has been used to a lesser extent in the building of Francis Johnston's 1818 GPO in Dublin. The design of the frontal facade of the GPO is similar in some ways to that of Stormont in that both are a fusion of Palladian and Greek revivalist architecture. Casey describes the GPO as 'a large and sober three-storey granite-faced building, monumental by virtue of its size and the Greek Ionic hexastyle portico of Portland stone on its principal east frontage'.[46] Both the GPO and Stormont, then, have monumental Greek Ionic hexastyle porticos made of Portland stone, but a key difference is that the main body of the GPO is faced entirely with Irish granite from the Wicklow mountains. A further difference is that the GPO's hexastyle portico rises from the pavement at street level

---

[44] *Irish Examiner*, 26 November 1940: 5.   [45] *Irish Press*, 27 November 1940: 7.
[46] Casey (2005: 147).

(formerly Sackville Street but since independence O'Connell Street), whereas Stormont's portico is situated above a rusticated ground floor. The GPO and Stormont are both embellished with many classical architectural details such as the dentils (small rectangular blocks resembling teeth) used extensively on both buildings, and the anthemia (palmette leaves) used as akroteria (pedimental ornaments) at Stormont and present also on the frieze of the GPO with its richly carved tendrils. The Hellenizing key-shaped design is used as decorative detail on the ceiling of the GPO's portico and this motif is also present inside both buildings. It is clear that the British crown's coat of arms on the GPO (and, in a more subtle way, the pedimental sculptures) were a nineteenth-century visual message executed in stone to communicate that Ireland was a colony of Britain. This figurative political statement is arguably less triumphalist and hierarchical in nature than the sculptural arrangements on Stormont, since the GPO's symbolism hinted at a level of participation and inclusion for all the people of Ireland in the prosperity of the country under the British crown, even if this was not an economic or social reality. At Stormont, by contrast, the image of Britannia and her fierce lions staring down from the building's rooftop, together with the sculptures which depicted Ulster offering the flame of loyalty to the British crown, were an unshakeable communication in stone of the permanent partition of Ireland, and also of the hegemony of those who favoured union with Britain over the minority Northern Irish population who objected to that union.

The rebuilt GPO has become the central site in the commemoration of the struggle for Irish independence. Irish historian Mary E. Daly has argued that in the early years of the Irish Free State it was far from certain that this would happen. On one occasion, for example, W. T. Cosgrave proposed that the ruined GPO be given over to the Archbishop of Dublin as the site for a Catholic cathedral.[47] It was in 1935 that the GPO's position as the principal commemorative site of the Irish rebellion was fully confirmed when Éamon de Valera unveiled Oliver Sheppard's bronze statue, 'The Death of Cúchulainn', as a memorial of the Easter Rising located in the central opening of the GPO's glazed portico arcade. During this carefully choreographed 1935 commemoration, the Republic was once again declared as 2,500 veterans of the 1916 Rebellion lined up outside the building's now 'iconic' classical Greek portico.[48] As Clair Wills put it, the GPO was now totally transformed 'into a place of para-religious worship of the spirit of the nation' and 'the classical pillars' did nothing to discourage this identification.[49]

Since then, the GPO's portico has become a globally recognizable symbol of Irish independence and nationalism. In 2016 it featured on a €2 coin issued by the Republic of Ireland to commemorate the centenary of the 1916 Rising. The design included the figure of Hibernia on the apex of the GPO's pediment with

[47] Daly (2009).   [48] Martin (2016: n. p.).
[49] Wills (2009: 14).

sunbeams behind as if to symbolize the new dawn of Irish independence. The GPO's facade is also present on many nationalist murals on the streets of Belfast and Derry. In Long Kesh prison there is a well-known image of the GPO (dating from 2000) on the walls of the 'H Blocks' formerly occupied by members of the Irish National Liberation Army (INLA).[50] The image depicts an Irish tricolour alongside the burning GPO of 1916. The GPO's Ionic portico and the statues of Hibernia, Mercury, and Fidelity on the pediment are clearly visible. Instead of the royal coat of arms that was still located in the tympanum in 1916, however, portraits of the seven signatories of the Proclamation of the Irish Republic are painted in its space. Situated at the apex in the most elevated position of the tympanum is socialist James Connolly, leader of the Irish Citizen Army and the last of the 1916 rebels to be executed by the British at Kilmainham Gaol in Dublin. In a sense, the mural creates Irish nationalist sculptures for the interior of the GPO's pediment, thereby representing the GPO as a sacred temple to the martyrs who died for independence.

Stormont, with its easily distinguishable facade is also featured in many of Northern Ireland's street murals. As a bastion of unionism, it is naturally represented most often in loyalist murals with the British union flag flying above the building. Since 2007 (and following on from the 1998 Good Friday Agreement) Stormont has been home to the power-sharing administration of the devolved Northern Ireland Assembly. Despite the increased nationalist presence in the twenty-first-century Northern Ireland Assembly, Stormont, with all its imposing and British imperial imagery, has remained an iconic building for the broad spectrum of unionists and their traditions. For example, the centenary marches to commemorate the thousands of unionists who signed the 1912 Ulster Solemn League and Covenant against Irish Home Rule were focused on Stormont, with a huge rally culminating in the building's grounds. As a part of the United Kingdom, only the British union flag is flown at Stormont. In 2015 an Irish nationalist movement known as the 1916 Societies hoisted the Irish tricolour and a green and gold Irish nationalist flag above Stormont on either side of the statue of Britannia. Although the flags flew for only ten minutes before being removed, unionist politicians were united in their condemnation of this act and demanded a police investigation.[51] For many unionist politicians and the communities they represent, Stormont is still a building whose neoclassical forms unequivocally symbolize the sovereignty of Britain in Northern Ireland. As such, it continues to act as a powerful emblem of unionist traditions, imperial history, and a resolve always to remain part of the United Kingdom of Great Britain and Northern Ireland and the British Commonwealth.

---

[50] Rolston (2003:28).   [51] Breen (2015).

Conclusion

Since its construction, Stormont has stood at the apex of contested representational space in the six counties which constitute Northern Ireland. The building occupies a highly visible and commanding location on a hill to the east of Belfast City, and faces south towards the Irish Republic. Both the choice of materials used in the construction, and the positioning of the building, were consciously conceived by the dominant Unionist Party led by Sir James Craig to demarcate Protestant loyalism as physically and psychologically different from the Catholic nationalist 'other'. This colossal building of white, finely dressed Portland stone sits on a plinth of unpolished Ulster granite and loudly proclaims the union of Ulster with the British Empire, and the dominant forces of 'Planter' over 'Gael'. Crucially, the most symbolic piece of masonry in the entire building, the foundation stone, is Portland stone. The symbolic core of the building is not native Irish, but British and imperial. Stone suggests permanence, and for unionists, Stormont symbolically represents the permanent partition of Ireland and the legitimacy of the Northern Ireland State. Conversely, since March 2016 the GPO has housed a permanent exhibition entitled 'GPO Witness History' which commemorates the 1916 Rising. The Taoiseach at the time, Enda Kenny, made a speech at the opening of the exhibition in which he stated that 'we owe much credit to the early nation-builders who built up our public institutions as unassailable pillars of democracy'.[52] Kenny's political rhetoric references the 1916 rebels as heroes who fought for democracy as well as Irish independence. Although the GPO was originally built as a physical manifestation of British colonial power in Dublin, it was reconstructed to strip the building of its colonial past while at the same time preserving and repurposing its neoclassical architecture. In the ensuing century since the 1916 Rising, the neoclassical GPO has been symbolically transformed from a building which represented British imperial power and dominion over Ireland into a political and cultural space which signifies Irish independence and nationalist martyrdom. What is clear from this analysis of the construction and history of both Stormont and the GPO is that these two buildings continue to project in stone the contrasting and evolving political narratives of Ireland.

---

[52] For a report on the occasion see Kelly (2016).

20

The Classical Themes of Irish Coinage, 1928–2002

Images from a Usable Past

Christine Morris

In 2002, Seamus Heaney crafted this touching lament on the demise of the animal images that had graced Irish coins since 1928 ('A Keen for the Coins'):[1]

> O henny penny! O horsed half-crown!
> O florin salmon! O sixpence hound!
> O woodcock! Piglets! Hare and bull!
> O mint of field and flood, farewell!
> Be Ireland's lost ark, gone to ground,
> And where the rainbow ends, be found.

In collaboration with Heaney, Irish sculptor Carolyn Mulholland created a bronze version of the text of his poem together with images of the set of coins (also 2002); thus the demise of the coins was commemorated through both poetry and physical imagery. Mulholland's engagement with this theme has continued, with a new, larger version of her bronze sculpture produced in 2018 (Fig. 20.1).

The context of the coins' final demise was, of course, Ireland's entry into the Eurozone in 2002, together with the decision to retain only a single national symbol, the harp, on the obverse or national side of the new coinage. By strong contrast, Heaney's animal ark, or the 'barnyard set' as it was also often known, had been commissioned, following the Coinage Act of 1926, by a Coinage Committee established under the Chairmanship of Senator W. B. Yeats, as a unified set of designs intended to assert and express Irish independence and Ireland's distinctive identity. As Heaney's poem indicates, the animal coins had become much loved in Ireland and were also globally admired as among the most beautiful examples of modern coinage. It seems fitting, therefore, in the context of the theme of Classics

---

[1] Heaney (2002b; 2002c). Reproduced here with the kind permission of *Irish Pages*.

Christine Morris, *The Classical Themes of Irish Coinage, 1928–2002: Images from a Usable Past* In: *Classics and Irish Politics, 1916–2016*. Edited by: Isabelle Torrance and Donncha O'Rourke, Oxford University Press (2020).
© Oxford University Press.
DOI: 10.1093/oso/9780198864486.003.0020

Fig. 20.1. Carolyn Mulholland's bronze sculpture for 'Keen for the Coins', new version cast in 2018, 33 × 20 cm. Image and permission to reproduce provided courtesy of the artist.

and Irish politics, to revisit the classical inspiration that lies behind their designs and to explore the wider impact of the coins and their imagery.

It will be useful to begin by reminding ourselves of the animal themes on the original eight coins. The animals chosen were the horse, salmon, bull, hare, wolf-hound, hen and chicks, pig with her litter of piglets, and woodcock. The assignment to a denomination was purposeful with the higher-value coins reserved for the more 'noble' animals and the copper coins for the more humble (Fig. 20.2).[2] Only four of the animals survived the transition to the decimal system in 1971— the horse, salmon, bull, and woodcock, to which was added a new animal for the punt (Irish pound) coin, the stag. The direct influence of classical models on the content and style of the Irish coins is widely known among classicists in Ireland. W. B. Stanford, for example, discusses it in *Ireland and the Classical Tradition*, as does Brian Arkins in *Builders of My Soul: Greek and Roman themes in Yeats* and, more briefly, in *The Thought of W. B. Yeats*.[3]

[2] See McKenna (2015/16) for an interesting discussion of the complex layers of significance of the animals within their specifically Irish context.

[3] Stanford (1976: 125–7); Arkins (1990: 170–1), (2010b: 77–8).

Fig. 20.2. The eight animals of the new Irish coinage (1928, designed by Percy Metcalfe): horse (half-crown); salmon (florin); bull (shilling); hound (sixpence); hare (threepence); hen and chicks (penny); pig and piglets (halfpenny); woodcock (farthing). Image personally held by Christine Morris.

My paper offers a social biographical perspective on the 1928 Irish coins and their imagery; this approach encourages us to think of both objects and imagery as having complex, and sometimes contradictory, 'life histories' or 'biographies' that develop and transform over time and in different contexts. The biographical approach, widely used within anthropology, archaeology, and material culture studies, also foregrounds the idea that objects and images have agency and can be affective, rather than simply being a passive 'reflection' of social and political trends.[4] Coins, as small objects embedded in everyday lives, can communicate complex messages of public identity, nationhood, and imperialism, a point not lost on those empowered to design and make coins.[5] Yeats's much-quoted phrase that the coins were 'silent ambassadors of taste' captures a similar point about the symbolic dimension of coinage, making it worthwhile to cite a fuller quotation:

I wish to take this opportunity to thank the Minister for Finance for the speech which he made in the Dáil promising to get together a competent, artistic

---

[4] Kopytoff (1986); Gosden and Marshall (1999); Hoskins (2006); Joy (2009); Burström (2014).
[5] Van Wie (1999: v); in a similar vein Millar (1993: 230) writes of Roman coins and inscriptions as being 'the most deliberate of all symbols of public identity'.

committee to advise on the designs of our coinage. The official designs of the Government, especially its designs in connection with postage stamps and coinage, may be described, I think, as the silent ambassadors of national taste. The Government has now taken the right step. They may not get a beautiful coinage, it is difficult to get beauty of any kind. At any rate, the Government has the right ambition. Two days ago I had a letter from an exceedingly famous decorative artist, in which he described the postage stamps of this country as at once the humblest and ugliest in the world. At any rate our coinage design will, I hope, be such that even the humblest citizen will be proud of it.[6]

The dialogue between the ancient coins and the modern ones they inspired is explored here through the lens of production to consumption. In other words, I begin with the initial stages of the commissioning and production of the coins, and then move to their reception and influence, both locally and globally. Finally, I will more briefly consider the rich 'afterlife' of the coins and their imagery, following their demise as legal currency.

Commissioning the New Coinage

The background to the commissioning of the coins is well documented.[7] As noted earlier, the committee was set up in May 1926, under the Chairmanship of W. B. Yeats, with the remit of recommending themes for the coins and of inviting selected artists to submit designs and compete for the commission. Certain features had already been agreed upon: the harp would feature on all the coins; the inscriptions would only be in Irish; no portraits would be used.[8] This meant that earlier suggested images such as St Patrick or Michael Collins were excluded from consideration.[9] Importantly, it was also made clear from the outset that Ireland, unlike other self-governing parts of the British Empire, would have coins that did *not* carry the head of the reigning British monarch, whose image had long been an integral part of imperial power and pageantry.[10]

It is worth pausing at this point to reflect on the appearance of the coinage that the new Irish Free State coins were designed to replace. Following the 1800 Act of

---

[6] Yeats, Seanad Speech: 3 March 1926, Coinage Bill 1926 Second Stage.

[7] Caffrey (2011); Cleeve (1972); Colgan (2003: 178–9); Fordonski (2004); Foster (2003b: 332–5); Morris (2004), (2005); Doggett (2011); Mohr (2015); McKenna (2015/16).

[8] McCauley (1972 [1928]: 26–7).

[9] Portraits of significant individuals have, in more recent times, appeared on Irish commemorative coin issues; included among them is a 2015 silver €15 collector's coin depicting Yeats himself: https://www.collectorcoins.ie/en/w-b-yeats-15-silver-proof-coin-2015.html (accessed 5 May 2018).

[10] Van Wie (1999: 55); Cannadine (2002: 103); Mohr (2015: 454–5). From 1922 the Irish Free State was a dominion of the British Commonwealth of Nations, until the Republic of Ireland came into being in December 1937.

Union which brought Ireland into full political union with Britain, the Coinage Act of 1826 marked the withdrawal from use of coinage with any distinctive Irish features. This earlier coinage combined the standard arrangement of an obverse or 'heads' depicting the ruling British monarch with a reverse or 'tails' which might bear local Irish elements such as the personification of Hibernia, or the Irish harp (albeit often surmounted by a British crown). Once this Irish regal coinage disappeared from use, there followed one hundred years of British imperial coinage; this depicted the monarch with titles in Latin (strongly evoking, of course, Roman imperial coinage), and reverses bearing an array of regal and imperial imagery, such as crowns and a heraldic lion passant guardant astride the crown. Another important image, and one with a venerable classical origin, was a seated Britannia attired with helmet and shield, and holding out her trident. The goddess Britannia had her origins in Roman art, including coinage; her appearance owed much to the armed goddess Athena (Minerva), but Britannia's trident had 'belonged' to Athena's Olympian uncle, Poseidon (Neptune), who was represented by the Victorian period as having ceded his trident, and thus control of the seas, to Britannia.[11] It is clear, then, that the contrasts that emerged—Irish inscriptions, not Latin or English; the full removal of regal imagery; and the return of the harp, minus any controlling crown—constituted a bold announcement of Ireland's new independent identity.

It was the Committee's decision, strongly influenced by Yeats, that the new coins should show 'the produce of the nation'. In Yeats's words, 'what better symbols could we find for this horse riding, salmon fishing, cattle raising country.'[12] The significance of each animal was carefully thought out in terms of its importance to farming, hunting and sport, trade, and in some cases to Irish mythology, as well as with a view to how appealing they might be to the wider public. There were some considerable misgivings about the pig, due to its well-known negative use in British caricatures of the Irish, so the artists were also invited to submit a ram as an alternative.

The seven invited artists—of whom more shortly—were provided with detailed guidelines and visual inspiration for their designs. These included photographs and drawings of animals, as well as photographs of classical coinage depicting animals.[13] There were two coins for the horse—from Larissa in Thessaly and from Carthage—while the western Greek states were represented by a bull from Thurii in southern Italy and a hare from Sicilian Messana (Fig. 20.3). The artists were specifically asked 'as far as possible, to take them as a model' for their coinage.[14]

[11] Warner (1985: 46).   [12] Yeats (1960: 162).
[13] Yeats (1972 [1928]: 9–10); McCauley (1972 [1928]: 30–2).   [14] Yeats (1972 [1928]: 9).

Fig. 20.3. Greek coins from southern Italy. Left: coin depicting a bull from Thurii, *c.*400–350 BCE. Right: coin depicting a hare from Sicilian Messana, fifth century BCE. Images personally held by Christine Morris.

Why classical coins? The obvious answer lies in Yeats's presence on the committee, since his own writings were so deeply influenced by the classical world. And, as Arkins has noted, the visual arts as well as literature were an important source of inspiration for Yeats.[15] Yeats states that the commission included coins from western Greece as models because they have produced the 'most famous and beautiful coins',[16] giving a special mention to Sicily. This specific reference to Sicily offers an additional insight into the context which placed Greek coins foremost in Yeats's mind as an ideal model. It can be no coincidence that Yeats and his wife had been travelling in Sicily and southern Italy only the previous year in the company of his old friend Ezra Pound. As recounted in Pound's letters, they had met up in Sicily early in 1925 and together visited a number of ancient sites, including Taormina, Palermo, Syracuse, and Agrigento.[17] Archived among Yeats's photographs and postcards acquired on the Sicily trip are postcards of western Greek coins from various European museums.[18]

As well as offering an aesthetic model for the coin designs, the ancient Greek coins also provided an important model for Ireland in other ways. It cannot have escaped Yeats that individual Greek city states produced distinctive coinage, which could be seen as marking their identity and autonomy in stark contrast to the coinage of imperial powers, ancient and modern, such as Rome or Britain. As noted earlier, British coins, with their traditional imagery of monarchy and imperial insignia together with Latin titles, had been the official coinage in Ireland since 1826, erasing any Irish dimension of earlier coinage which had included harps and

---

[15]   Arkins (1990: 156–74).   [16]   Yeats (1972 [1928]: 9).   [17]   Foster (2003b: 279).
[18]   Finn (2004: 70); Murphy (1996: 89–90).

the personification of Hibernia alongside the ubiquitous British ruler iconography. Thus, prior to 1928, every economic transaction acted as a reminder of British rule, and hence Patrick Pearse's comment, made in 1913 in the context of a discussion on the power of symbols, that 'a good Irishman should blush every time he sees a penny'.[19] The Greek model was also more appropriate in terms of subject matter since animals regularly appear on Greek coinage, both as symbols of economic wealth and in relation to deities and myths. Thus, both the ancient Greek and the modern Irish coins share a range of ideological, mythic, and economic referents, together with other layers of symbolic meaning. Importantly too, while it seems unsurprising to see animals and other national products and symbols on coins today, this was, in the 1920s, a radical move away from the usual run of royal portraits and heraldic symbols.

Of the seven artists invited to submit designs, three were Irish: Oliver Sheppard, Albert Power, and Jerome Connor.[20] The remaining four were Carl Milles (Swedish), Publio Morbiducci (Italian), Paul Manship (American), and Percy Metcalfe (British).[21] The designs, as was the custom, were mostly submitted as plaster models, though some of the artists also produced pattern designs in metal.[22] The committee had intended to represent the work of several of the artists in the final coin set, arrived at through the process of anonymous review.[23] However, they were so impressed with the style and quality of Metcalfe's work that they decided to give him the commission for the whole set. Four of his original plaster designs show the horse for the florin, the shilling based on the Thurii bull, and the two options for the halfpenny—the pig and her litter, and the ram (Fig. 20.4). For comparison of style, use of the circular space, and the specific instruction to use the classical coins as models, it is interesting to look at some of the other shillings alongside Metcalfe's design (Fig. 20.5). Manship's bull bears the least resemblance to the Thurii model, choosing instead an unusual protome view (the animal's head only).[24] Yeats expressed appreciation for the energy of Milles's 'strange bull', poetically imagining his high relief designs as having 'been dug out of

[19] Pearse (1916e: 151).

[20] Oliver Sheppard (1865–1941), Albert Power (1883–1945), Jerome Connor (1876–1943).

[21] Carl Milles (1875–1955), Publio Morbiducci (1889–1963), Paul Manship (1885–1955), Percy Metcalfe (1895–1970).

[22] Morbiducci produced patterns in a series of different metals, including silver and bronze. See http://www.irishcoinage.com/MODCOIN.HTM (J. Stafford-Langan) for the bronze threepence and the silver shilling (accessed 5 May 2018). Manship also produced a set of nine coins in bronze: see Gardner (1965, 154: cat. 29.38.1–9).

[23] McCauley (1972 [1928]: 36–7).

[24] Bronze model for the Irish shilling: Smithsonian American Art Museum, 1965.16.68 https://americanart.si.edu/artwork/irish-free-state-coinage-design-scillint-15900 (accessed 5 May 2018). Manship's travels in Italy and Greece (1909–11) are known to have greatly influenced his art, with powerful images of bulls appearing in his compositions of Herakles and the Cretan bull, and of Europa and the Bull. It is tempting to speculate that his protome bull drew inspiration from Minoan art, such as the famous bull rhyton from Knossos.

Fig. 20.4. Plaster models of Percy Metcalfe's original designs. Left to right: halfpenny pig and ram (two alternate designs); bull; horse. Images and permission to reproduce provided courtesy of the National Museum of Ireland.

the Sicilian earth' after two thousand years in the ground.[25] Metcalfe's and Morbiducci's designs stand out aesthetically; both are quite faithful to the Greek coin from Thurii, and also make effective use of the space. However, the Italian's design seems about to burst energetically out of the space,[26] whereas Metcalfe's bull and the curving lettering of the 'scilling' sit more pleasingly within the circular frame.

Metcalfe was asked to make modifications to several of his designs as a result of discussions with the Ministry of Agriculture experts who were preoccupied with physical accuracy and breeding standards in contrast with the Committee's prioritizing of an aesthetically pleasing design. Thus, Yeats writes that 'the first bull had to go, though one of the finest of the designs, because it might have upset, considered as an ideal, the eugenics of the farmyard, but the new bull is fine, in a different way.'[27] It is this new, somewhat less vigorous bull that finally appeared on the shilling and then later on the five-pence coin.[28]

---

[25] Yeats (1972 [1928]: 16, with images); D. Tyler (1963) recounts Milles's severe disappointment and shock at not receiving the commission to produce the coins.

[26] Bruce and Michael (2007: 1153), illustrating the full set of Morbiducci's pattern designs.

[27] Yeats (1972 [1928]: 19).

[28] Yeats (1972 [1928]: 14, for the designs as submitted, including the extra ram as an alternative to the halfpenny pig); (1972: 20, for the final minted designs).

Fig. 20.5. Bull designs submitted by other invited artists. Left to right: Paul Manship; Carl Milles; Publio Morbiducci. Images and permission to reproduce provided courtesy of the National Museum of Ireland.

Reception of the Coinage: From Local to Global

I turn now to the next stage in the 'biography' of the coins, that of their consumption, starting with the initial receptions at home and abroad. From the beginning, there was international praise for their beauty. The British classical archaeologist Stanley Casson, for example, described them as 'one of the most beautiful and appropriate series of coins in modern times',[29] while the London correspondent for *The Manchester Guardian* told readers that 'the Irish coinage will be acknowledged as the most beautiful in the world ... and I doubt if any country but Ireland would have had the imagination and freedom to lay down the conditions that would have made such designs possible.'[30] The response at home was much more mixed, as might be expected in the divisive political atmosphere of 1920s Ireland. It may be useful here to recall the famous saying of Levi-Strauss that 'animals are good to think with',[31] meaning that in their complex and culturally constructed relationships with humans they can carry complex, contradictory, and highly varied values and messages. In this case, the animal imagery garnered mixed responses, pleasing some but offending others. The coins were considered by some to be too 'pagan' (by which they meant too secular) because they bore no religious symbols as was deemed appropriate to a Christian people.[32] Others bemoaned the absence of more obvious national symbols, reinforcing the point that—for the time—the animals were a bold and unusual iconographic choice. The pig, as noted earlier, drew particular criticism as evoking negative connotations because British cartoons such as *Punch* had represented the Irish as pigs, characterizing them as rustic, indifferent to dirt, and disorderly.[33] Given the pig's

---

[29] Dyer and Gaspar (1992: 570, n. 290, citing Casson in *The Listener*, 10 February 1932).
[30] *The Manchester Guardian*, 1 December 1928: 12, 'A Great Achievement'.
[31] Levi-Strauss (1963: 89).   [32] Morris (2005: 94–6); Foster (2003b: 334).
[33] De Nie (2005); Townsend (2016).

unfavourable profile, it is perhaps surprising that it was finally chosen over the less controversial ram, though its economic value seems to have been a decisive factor.[34] Negative comments on the choice of animals are also recorded from the British Parliament. Lord Danesfort (a unionist peer) complained about the absence of the head of the king, but he was also vocal about the appearance of 'ignoble animals such as pigs and barn door fowls'.[35]

The cutting criticism that the coins were somehow too 'British' came from republican Maud Gonne, who described them as 'designed by an Englishman, minted in England, representative of English values, paid for by the Irish people', while the Catholic Bulletin scathingly described the designs as the 'beast coinage from Yorkshire'.[36] Given that the coins were to be a public manifestation of Ireland freeing itself from the British 'imperial family', it is remarkable that Metcalfe's nationality did not preclude his being given the commission. As to the question of the coins being minted in Britain, it seems that the Royal Mint offered the best price at tender. Consumption and reception are by no means only a local phenomenon. As mentioned earlier, the Irish coins made a considerable impact internationally and were appreciated for their artistic beauty as well as for their modernity and breaking with more traditional imagery. Beyond that, it can be argued that the Irish animal ark designs, with their classical aesthetic and their association with Metcalfe, exerted an international influence, creating global ripples in the world of coin design.

While the idea for the animal theme on the Irish coins came from Yeats and his committee, Metcalfe had been working on an animal theme shortly before focusing on the Irish coins, albeit of a very different type. He had been commissioned to sculpt a lion for the Palace of Industry at the British Empire Exhibition of 1924 (Fig. 20.6), where lions—symbolic of British imperial power—were to be found everywhere, from the more traditional couchant beasts outside the Government Pavilion[37] to lions on commemorative guides, stamps, metalware, and china.[38] Metcalfe's strikingly modern stone sculpture so impressed that he was also asked to design commemorative medals bearing a lion. One such bronze medallion shows the lion's head in profile and bears the text 'struck at the British Empire Exhibition 1924' on the beast's shoulder, while a second medal features the exhibition's iconic roaring lion with the towers of Wembley in the background, and depicts the head of George V on the obverse.[39] The same fierce, angular features of the art deco lion were also reproduced in ceramic form at the Ashtead pottery in Surrey.[40] Another work by Metcalfe for the exhibition offers a further glimpse

---

[34] Yeats (1972 [1928]: 32)   [35] Mohr (2015: 465) citing Hansard.
[36] Foster (2003b: 334–5).   [37] Knight and Sabey (1984: 19, with image).
[38] Knight and Sabey (1984: 155–250).   [39] Brown (1995: 127, cat. no. 4193)
[40] Attwood (2003); Forrester (2006); see also http://www.ashteadpottery.com/metcalfe.html for the Palace of Industry lion and http://www.ashteadpottery.com/wembley.html for ceramic version (both accessed 10 May 2018).

Fig. 20.6. Percy Metcalfe with his lion sculpture for the Palace of Industry at the British Empire Exhibition of 1924. Image and permission to reproduce provided courtesy of the Brent Museum and Archives.

into the power of animal imagery; commissioned by the Mond Nickel Company, the art deco-style medal, appropriately made from nickel, depicts a helmeted Britannia holding a trident. The arc of her shield bears low relief animals, cleverly depicted as a porthole scene with the tiger appearing to be padding into the scene. It seems to be intended to represent global imperial reach in the context of the exhibition: springbok (South Africa); beaver (Canada); kangaroo (Australia); tiger (India).[41]

Metcalfe continued to have a highly successful career designing both coinage and commemorative medals. It is interesting, given the classical connections of the Irish coins, that he was shortly afterwards commissioned to design the obverses for two coins for the newly independent Greek state in 1930. Unsurprisingly, they are close copies of images on ancient Greek coins with Greek deities chosen for the 'heads' or obverses, in association with appropriate products or objects. Thus, the ten-drachma coin has Demeter with her sheaf of grain: the goddess is modelled on the obverse of a silver stater of the Delphic Amphictyony, while the sheaf on the reverse, designed by Michael Axelos, is an exact copy of a coin from Metapontum, a Greek colony in southern Italy. The twenty-drachma coin bears Metcalfe's Poseidon (with his distinctive initials 'PM' nestled in the god's hair locks) and a

---

[41] Trusted (2007: 90 with pl. 156).

ship at sea on the reverse, both faces drawing upon the imagery of a Macedonian tetradrachm issued by King Antigonos Doson.[42]

Other areas that had become self-governing dominions within the British Empire were also actively drawing upon coinage as a means of expressing a discrete, national identity, though unlike Ireland their coinage continued to carry the monarch's head. Metcalfe went on to work on coins in many parts of the Empire such as Australia, Canada, New Zealand, Fiji, and Mauritius.[43] He had a hand in many more animal designs, such as the beautiful turtle on the shilling coin of Fiji first minted in 1934. He also submitted a design for the coins for New Zealand in 1933. The set referenced local identity through images of Maori culture and local animals such as the kiwi. On this occasion, Metcalfe went for a very modern angular style, reminiscent of his earlier art deco lion sculpture. It was, however, passed over in favour of a more traditional design by Kruger Grey, although the head of the monarch on the obverse was Metcalfe's work.[44] Animals, national produce, and cultural heritage have all become familiar staples on coinage in modern times. But traces of the legacy of the specific style and content of the Irish 'barnyard' coins can also be seen nearly half a century after their creation in the coins of Tonga from 1975, which bear a pig and a hen and her chicks (a Tongan 'henny penny').[45]

The Irish animal designs have been displaced by the euro with its new demands for expressing both national and European identities within a single coin. However, special commemorative issues of non-circulating collectors' coins contribute another layer to the numismatic picture, providing the opportunity to celebrate or mark important themes as well as being economically profitable for the state. In this context, Ireland has briefly renewed its affectionate engagement with the animal coins, issuing three €15 coins between 2010 and 2012 in tribute to the 1928 animals. Each is close in style to the original horse, salmon, and wolfhound, but shows the animal with its young—an obvious nod back to some of the other Metcalfe designs.

Object Biographies

In the world of object biographies, objects and images more often have 'second lives' or 'afterlives' than suffer death or demise.[46] Coins, ancient and modern, may maintain and even gain in value as they move through the hands of collectors. It is interesting to note, too, that one stated reason for avoiding religious imagery on the 1928 designs was a fear that this would lead to them being (illegally) modified,

---

[42] Tzamalis (1980: 162, 164)   [43] Dyer and Gaspar (1992: 570).   [44] Stocker (2015).
[45] Michael and Judkins (2016: 2124: pig; 2015: hen and chicks).   [46] Kopytoff (1986).

usually through piercing, for talismanic use as religious amulets.[47] The modification of coins for ritual use has a long and widespread history from antiquity onwards, indicating that this was a very reasonable cause for concern.[48] Coins can also be transformed into other 'usable' artefacts such as cufflinks, earrings, and pendants. The sales pitch for such commodities tends to draw on ideas of nostalgia, authenticity, and rarity, and is, in this case, a particular reminder of Irish identity.[49] Finally, one of the original Metcalfe coins—the shilling bull—has acquired a different kind of robust afterlife, not as a physical commodity but as a symbolic image. It now forms part of the logo of the Irish Institute of Hellenic Studies at Athens, which celebrated twenty years of work in 2016. The Institute, a collaboration of the Irish universities that teach Classics and archaeology, supports and promotes Irish-based scholars and students in their research and study of Greek culture in all periods. The version of the bull used on the logo comes from Metcalfe's original design, closest to the Thurii bull. It is joined by a spiral design that is intended to evoke similar images in both Celtic and Greek art, while the overlapping circles symbolize the links between the two countries and their cultures. This particular 'afterlife' reasserts for the viewer the classical roots of the Irish coin designs through this particular member of the barnyard set.[50]

Coinage and National Identity: Conclusions

This paper has explored some of the ways in which the 1928 Irish coinage with its distinctive classical influences in both themes and style can be usefully discussed in terms of its social biography. The links between the Irish Free State coinage and the classical world are firmly Greek not Roman: the Greek world offered an attractive model of independent city states with coinage that signalled their distinctive identities, whereas Roman imagery, including its coinage, was mirrored by its modern counterpart of imperial Britain. Coins, ancient and modern, are economic and affective, practical and symbolic. Human relationships with the 1928 coins have shifted over time as social and political circumstances have also changed. The designs that held the deep responsibility of expressing Irish identity and independence are no longer embedded in our daily lives, jangling in our pockets or purses. The issues that caused offence—such as their perceived 'paganism'—are largely irrelevant in 2016, and the religious images, portraits, and personifications

---

[47] Bodkin (1972 [1928]: 43).   [48] Burström and Ingvardson 2017; Houlbrook 2018.
[49] For example, http://www.irishcoincufflinks.com (accessed 5 December 2019) makes cufflinks and pendants from Irish coins, stressing their age (some as old as 1928) and authenticity.
[50] http://www.iihsa.ie/logo.html (accessed 5 December 2019): the Institute's website features a coloured version of the design, and a page explaining the provenance and symbolism of the imagery. A line drawing of the design also appears on the cover of an Institute publication: Luce, Morris, and Souyoudzoglou-Haywood (2007).

that were so poorly thought of by Yeats and his committee have more recently found their way onto special issue coinage. Yet the coins and their animal imagery retain a physical and symbolic presence, and they remain awash with meaning: transformed from everyday transactional objects into artefacts of personal adornment, recreated as collectors' coins which pay homage to Metcalfe's artistry, or immortalized in Heaney's 'lost ark'.

21

Epilogue

Richard P. Martin

'Everybody who writes is interested in living inside themselves in order to tell what is inside themselves. That is why writers have to have two countries, the one where they belong and the one in which they live really.' For Gertrude Stein, born in Allegheny, Pennsylvania in 1874, it was France, her acquired homeland from 1903 until her death forty-three years later.[1] For another transplant, 1,500 years earlier, 'a simple country person, a refugee, and unlearned' (*rusticus profuga indoctus*), Ireland was the dream country—literally. Patrick, who became patron saint of Ireland, came there from Britain first as a captive, but his second sojourn began when he was seized and pulled back by the power of imagination—a letter read and summoning voices heard in a night-time vision.[2] And for the Irish? The continuing dream—always available, infinitely malleable—was of ancient Greece and Rome, yes, but as these essays brilliantly demonstrate, that arrived in a manner both more intricate and with greater consequence, wielding more social and political heft, than the way the classical tradition captivated other nations.

One convenience about ancient Greece and Rome is that they can never now be visited except in spirit, making the vision more powerful than reality, and impermeable to facts on the ground. But 'in dreams begin responsibilities', as the poet had it. Ancient visions carve out a contemporary space of lived reality. One of the great virtues of this volume is that it forces us to look hard at the ancient worlds that the Irish of the last few centuries have reimagined and reused, reacted to and revived—or at least dreamt that they had. This can usefully dislocate our assumptions about the ancient world itself, its practices and personalities, as well as sharpen our understanding of the modern. Most importantly, this pioneering book raises a key question which should be (but often isn't) at the heart of the now ubiquitous study of classical 'reception'—*cui bono*? Which segments of Irish society benefited from deploying antiquity, under what conditions? It is more than a question of historical curiosity. In the era of 'Identity Evropa' (or 'American Identity Movement') and the alt-right, when the 'Red Pill' community has hijacked everything from ancient statuary to Marcus Aurelius in the service of their misogyny and white supremacy, learning to trace the dynamics of politicized

---

[1] Quoted from Stein (2013 [1940]: 4).   [2] *Confessio* para. 12 and 23.

Richard P. Martin, *Epilogue* In: *Classics and Irish Politics, 1916–2016*. Edited by: Isabelle Torrance and Donncha O'Rourke, Oxford University Press (2020). © Oxford University Press.
DOI: 10.1093/oso/9780198864486.003.0021

classical reception can be a security measure; scholarship on the issue is a public service, helping prevent reckless culture-hacking.[3]

Of course, the vastly varied Irish engineering of the past has been generally more benign. It is also, as the editors point out, a good deal more complicated. Unlike Greeks and Italians, whose modern nation states were forged (and sometimes deformed) with the aid of a persistent discourse of classical rebirth, the Irish, never a part of those ancient Mediterranean empires, could not rally to visions of repossession and revived unity. Greeks were (aspirational) ancient Greeks, Italians ancient Romans; French self-presentation still plays it both ways, creating a backstory blend of warlike other-worldly Gaul and sober bureaucratic Roman, Asterix meets Ausonius. By contrast, the Irish, with no plausible genealogical ties to classical peoples, made do in the medieval period with tenuous connections (the Fir Bolg were slaves of the Greeks; other primeval settlers were identified in the *Lebor Gabála* as wandering Scythians). In modern times, the connection was strengthened by its transformation into the assertion of a spiritual and intellectual affinity, pointedly transcending the mere missing fact of bloodlines. The further complication posed by the gradual rediscovery, from the eighteenth century onwards, of a deep Celtic past, meant that, on the one hand, the Irish could claim their place in a broader European community not predicated on some shared classical heritage, but on linguistic and cultural bonds with Wales, Brittany, even ancient Gaul and Galicia. On the other hand, it meant a gnawing sense that Irish indigenous literature and culture might not come up to the acclaimed standards set by Greece and Rome, a fear that vexed the Irish revivalists. Assertions of equality, if not superiority, broke out in different modes. Within Celtic Studies there was the long-running dispute between 'nativists' and 'Classicists' as to whether the medieval heroic tradition was the purest expression of an isolated but glorious Iron Age past, or a hybrid product of Late Antique learning. Like George Thomson, who caught glimpses of Homeric society on the Great Blasket, Yeats, too, could resort to the trope of shared origins, as in the claim (cited by Morash) that 'Greek literature came like old Irish literature out of the belief of the common people'. Pearse pushed beyond such separate-but-equal rhetoric in the claim that early Irish writers '...saw certain gracious things more clearly and felt certain mystic things more acutely and heard certain deep music more perfectly than did men in ancient Greece'. Brian McGing and Eoghan Moloney make us aware of the 'dual dialogue' these figures carried on with the combined Gaelic and classical traditions. While the pangs of Romantic nationalism gave new urgency to the conundrum (*which* antiquity is really Ireland's?) it may be worth remembering that the urge to recruit ancient culture for Irish ends appears in the earliest surviving piece of Irish literature, the sixth-century *Amra*

---

[3] On which see Zuckerberg (2018).

Choluim Chille, in which the late saint Columba is eulogized for having conversed with an angel and learned Greek grammar (*fri angel n-acallastar, atgaill grammataig greic*)—high praise that offers optimistic Hellenists hopes of canonization.[4]

This book's meticulous account of the encounters between the classical and the Irish, focused on the politics involved, reveals a vast range of strategies and ideologies, bold moves and clashes. Rather than adduce new material in this brief afterword, I wish instead to sketch a meta-analysis, trying to detect in these beautifully detailed essays a few unifying modes and recurrent themes. Three features emerge in my bird's-eye view: contiguity; affinity; and chance. Let me explain.

Contiguity takes several forms. First, there is the purely physical—the interwoven cultural and natural spaces occupied by statues and monuments, buildings and objects, ruins and find-spots, even coins. One can reach out and touch these today in a way that eludes us when it comes to ideas and texts. A number of the chapters here turn towards the material world, in a welcome trend that is finally reuniting classical philologists, archaeologists, and historians. Applied to Irish objects, this point of view can single out the literal contiguity of 'carefully dressed Portland stone and the unpolished rustic native Irish stone' that Suzanne O'Neill notices in the Parliament Buildings at Stormont, with its suggestion of British neoclassical civilization built over Gaelic Ireland. The contiguity of Sir James Craig's final resting place, on Stormont's grounds, to the monumental building he helped plan echoes the ancient Theseion, as O'Neill astutely observes (itself an early Athenian manipulation of the semiotics of space). The General Post Office in Dublin, on her showing, offers another significantly shifting contiguity: the statues of Hibernia, Fidelity, and Mercury atop its pediment, which have seen both Union Jack and Irish tricolour flap above them.

On the Aran Islands, it is contiguity that energizes the memory of the Fir Bolg, the mythistorical 'bag men' responsible for lugging earth onto the bare rocks and building the surviving prehistoric fort on Inis Mór. Temporally distant but bound to the present by the selfsame soil, the Fir Bolg in Arabella Currie's exciting interpretation shift from being the essence of 'abjection' in nineteenth-century accounts of Irish primitivism, to 'radical, rebellious figures' in treatments by Joyce, Heaney, and McGuinness, with the ubiquitous J. M. Synge the moving spirit in the transformation. One personal contiguity to mention here: I am happy to accept Currie's new interpretation that analogizes Synge's lack of attention to the widespread Fir Bolg connection (something he demonstrably knew) with his notable silence concerning classical parallels. Currie's is a more wide-reaching explanation than my own earlier suggestion, to which she generously refers.

Judith Hill's essay can be read as a study in comparative contiguities. Of the Dublin civic memorials she studies, the permanent cenotaph for Collins and

[4] Stokes (1899).

Griffith combines modernist and classical idioms, while dominating Leinster Lawn, the nation's political epicentre, with an architectural form evoking the erstwhile power of the emperor Augustus. The Irish National War Memorial, by contrast, a potentially radioactive political space, lies an hour's walk to the west, across the Liffey from (therefore not literally contiguous to) Phoenix Park, a landscape containing its own fraught set of political monuments and memories. The combination of memory, symbol, and the material environment characterizes, as well, the story of pre-euro Irish coinage, as told by Christine Morris. What is remembered, in this case, is double: an agrarian and heroic past (proud bulls and horses; piglets; hens), but also the ancient Greek coin models for these images. With these fondly recalled pieces of nickel or silver, you held in your hand an echo of two landscapes in one, an assertion by itself of contiguity over time and space. Wonderfully, these small machines for memory are now themselves memorialized by Carolyn Mulholland's bronze version of Seamus Heaney's 'A Keen for the Coins', complete with replicas.

There is another sort of contiguity, beyond the material, that reminds me of Aristotle's formula for intellectual pleasure—the realization, often through mimesis, of *touto ekeino*, finding 'this is that' (*Poetics* 1448b17; cf. *Rhetoric* 1410b19). We might see in this phrase the ruling principle behind much classical reception, Irish or other, political or not. Think of another island, the St Lucia of Derek Walcott's *Omeros*, envisaged as the realm of Homeric struggles and returns (but also colonialized decay). At its best, but also most dangerous, finding homologous realms, ancient and modern, produces a fresh view about the particularities of the present, sometimes with uncomfortable clarity. Fr Dineen used the force of such analogy when comparing Dublin after the 1916 Rising to the burnt remains of Troy—a brief comparison that carries worlds of context, and flips on its head any smug regard for victorious Greeks. As Fiachra Mac Góráin skilfully demonstrates, Dineen's reading of Virgil's *Eclogues* involves an entire structure of parallels between Augustan Rome and his own Irish era, from famine and land agitation to the experience of civil wars, both international and civil. Through another sort of contiguity (commentary on text), the politically attuned reader makes old poems burn with new relevance. Along the spectrum of such comparative exercises, we have at one end the analogizing of historical situation, expressed in action as well as words.

Emulation of ancient heroes, whether Hector or Cúchulainn, runs through the life and death of Pearse. The Iliadic packaging of the heroic ideal (a doer of deeds and speaker of words: *Il.* 9.443) would accommodate his oration over the grave of O'Donovan Rossa, which McGing shows to be 'stylistically so full of the figures and tropes of Greek and Roman rhetoric that it could almost have been written by Gorgias, Demosthenes, or Cicero'. Yet another productive contiguity conjured by McGing: Pearse stalks through the Green at Trinity College among statues of Edmund Burke ('Cicero's reincarnation if ever there was one') and Henry Grattan ('the Irish Demosthenes'). Pearse's fellow poet and comrade in the Rising, Thomas

MacDonagh, admirer of both the Gracchi and the rebel Owen Roe O'Neill, was all too aware of the risks of investing rashly in historical nostalgia, as Eoghan Moloney reconstructs his life from a meticulous reading of the archives. The complex thinker who wrote 'History is between us and our heroes' could nevertheless lecture fellow officers in the Irish Volunteers about Thermopylae, and find inspiration in the equally complex figure of Catullus. His 'scribbled translations of Catullus 8 on the back of part of a letter of business concerning the Irish Self-Government Alliance' capture exactly the paradoxes of contiguity. Moloney suggests these are two sides of the same coin.

A respect for differences, the treasuring of nuance—fruits (so we wish to think) of humanistic education—are what characterize another subset of this 'mimetic' contiguity, comprising poetic or dramatic reproduction of the classical, and the practice of translation. Isabelle Torrance's twin analyses of the reception of two Greek tragedies trace with fine precision the pressures—social, political, religious—that shaped the staged works. Euripides' *Trojan Women*, a radical interrogation of Athenian imperialism through the lens of the 'other' (enemy, female), becomes, in Torrance's view, a means of dramatizing, over the course of eighty-five years, the political disempowerment of Irish women. From the 1920 staging of Gilbert Murray's version, starring Maud Gonne as Hecuba, to Brendan Kennelly's 1993 *Trojan Women*, and Marina Carr's 2015 *Hecuba*, the trajectory curves downwards until the essential problem women's lack of agency seems more ineradicable than the ravages of war. Maud Gonne's heroic stance and personal tragedy might have sustained an overtly political reception (though the contemporary reviewer did not stress it), but more recent versions just as overtly proclaim their difference from the Euripidean configuration of forces. Similarly, the post-Ceasefire Antigones studied in Torrance's second contribution move steadily away from the Sophoclean model, even as they dwell on the primal crisis of politicized burial, all too real in the tortured province of Northern Ireland. Who is most blameworthy—Creon, Ismene, Antigone herself? The problematic examined in this kaleidoscopic rotation of dramatic reproductions—though it is, as Torrance makes clear, inextricable from the province's specific troubles—strikes me as metonymic for larger issues looming over the whole island: who owns this land? Whose heritage counts? Which past is ours?

As Torrance notes, Owen McCafferty's 2008 *Antigone* alludes to Michael Longley's 1994 poem 'Ceasefire', the subject of Maureen Alden's chapter. Another 'this is that' it would seem, but one with telling differences, given its context. Although modelled on the denouement of the epic (Priam supplicates Achilles in *Iliad* 24—like *Antigone*, another story of corpse retrieval), Longley's is a lyric evocation of paternal grief that cries out to (and for) the entire community. Its remarkable 'Stop Press' publication, right after the IRA declared a ceasefire, was equalled only by its amazing immediate effect on the public. Uncannily, like Homeric poetry, Longley's sonnet became a poem for everyone (imagine the *Iliad* recited while families went about claiming their dead).

Fourth in this series of 'reproductions'—(more dynamic than 'receptions', more capacious than 'reperformances') we might read Frank McGuinness' *Carthaginians* (1988) as an emphatic 'this-is-(*not*)-that' configuring of contiguities and difference. As Siobhán McElduff carefully unpacks the drama, 'Dido', its gay nationalist hero, displays an unsuspected relationship to the Carthaginian queen as represented, not in learned classicizing literature, but in earlier Irish popular culture, where she put Aeneas totally in the shade. (Recall the anecdote that Ezra Pound claimed was Yeats's favourite: 'A plain sailor man took a notion to study Latin, and his teacher tried him with Virgil; after many lessons he asked him something about the hero. Said the sailor: "What hero?" Said the teacher: "What hero! Why Aeneas, the hero!" Said the sailor: "Ach, a hero, him a hero? Bigob, I t'ought he waz a priest." ')[5] The arresting contiguity outlined by McElduff lies in the dramatic form (the recurrent staged 'quizzes') blending into that omnivorous equalizer, the ballad tradition, to produce hard wisdom ('gender fluidity is more attainable than class mobility').

A final form of contiguity—translation—brings together two tongues in the same mouth. The 'same' ideas (we innocently think) take the form of different words, with the putative equivalent bringing its own burden of connotation and tradition. Síle Ní Mhurchú and Pádraic Moran demonstrate the highly politicized parameters in which texts of the Classics were reproduced or learned in the medium of Irish. One immediate gain is the rediscovery of the long and productive career of Margaret Heavey, usually overshadowed (outside of Galway) by the story of George Thomson's years at UCG from 1931 to 1934 (a story a bit de-mythicized here). It is good to see, as well, another figure given due recognition, Pádraig de Brún, tireless translator of tragedy and Homeric epic. His *Odaisé* offers many an example of the weight of associations involved in translating from ancient Greek to modern Irish. Take, for instance, the words of Aiguptios (*Od.* 2.26: οὔτε ποθ' ἡμετέρη ἀγορὴ γένετ' οὔτε θόωκος, 'Never has our gathering taken place nor any session') rendered as *Dáil mhór dhaoine againn riamh níor tharlaigh san áit seo ná seisiún.*[6] On reading the first word, does a native speaker fail to hear *Dáil* (as in the national parliamentary assembly)? What of the third-language-learner, who sees the Greek ἀγορὴ—with all *its* connotations—transmuted this way? There is plenty of opportunity in this sort of close-reading experiment for good work by future philologists and translation theorists. (Ní Mhurchú's analysis of de Brún's *Oedipus at Colonus* provides a fine start.) What advantage might Irish dialect variants, for instance, play in translating the polyphonic *Kunstsprache* of Greek epic? A challenging further experiment: how would this compare with the infamous modern Greek *Iliad* of Nikos Kazantzakis and Ioannis Kakridis (1955), composed in an often baffling dialect patchwork?

[5]   E. Pound, *ABC of Reading* (London 1934) cited in Hardie (2014: 79).
[6]   De Brún and Ó Coigligh (1990: 17).

Affinity covers those examples of reception that reflect idiosyncratic and personalized choice, often in addition to an underlying realization of sameness and difference, ancient and modern (the 'contiguity' sketched above), but sometimes outweighing it. Politics, after all, is about private persons in social roles: reception can be a vivid means for the discovery of the self, bringing a particular view of the agent onto (sometimes literally) the public stage. As Declan Kiberd writes here in parsing Daniel Corkery's 'very interesting poppycock' from *The Hidden Ireland*: 'The task was not so much to become like the Greeks as to reproduce the ways in which the Greeks once had the courage to become and assume their own deepest, destined selves.' Yeats would top any list of self-mythologizers, and it is not amiss to read his 'translation' (or version) of *Oedipus the King* in these terms. Chris Morash makes the case that highly conscious political considerations—baiting the censors and 'obscurantists'—led Yeats to stage the Sophoclean drama when and how he did (after having kept it on the boiler more than two decades). The personal Yeatsian imprint is legible in his search for plain speech (interestingly, Blasket Islands talk is once more the litmus test) and his sacramental understanding of the tragedy; less visible, but one of the many remarkable connections found by Morash, is Yeats' fascination in the run-up to the production with John Burnet's *Early Greek Philosophy*. It is difficult to imagine a more idiosyncratic mix.

Donncha O'Rourke's essay on Yeats, Longley, and the Roman elegists presents further fascinating personal affinities powering the processes of reproduction. With Pound's version of Propertius providing a model for this sort of deeply individualized reach back to Rome, the working out of an anti-epic (read: imperial) viewpoint might have led to oversimplified receptions by Irish poets. But as O'Rourke shows, the result was more complicated, involving reflection on the very process, so that 'Longley's version of Propertius 2.10 offers a programmatic reading of the politics of classical reception'. We are led to appreciate the multilayered nature of poetic art, with elegists (ancient or modern) never mere blank slates: Longley's Propertius and Catullus, by the time he writes them, have traversed his soul's other affinities from Keats, Donne, and Herbert to Larkin, Auden, and MacNiece.

Eibhear Walshe examines an intricate tapestry where the intersection of the personal and the political generates the greatest visibility and conflict. 'Affinity' in a discussion of homoerotic relations works on a number of levels. As with the elegists, it can denote discovery of companionability in a distant culture with different norms and values, countering the contemporary. Wilde's deployment of the Hellenic precedent for his own sexuality becomes itself a model to inheritors as different as Joyce and Brendan Behan, and template, as well, for more recent political eruptions—the cases of David Norris and Cathal Ó Searcaigh, the latter looping back to yet another creative reshaper of the Hellenic past, Constantine Cavafy, the former showing that under outside pressures a gap can open between personal and political: elective affinities can lose elections.

Joyce's affinities, like those of Yeats, were catholic (small 'c'). If we tend to forget his youthful appreciation of Wilde (Walshe points to his 1909 newspaper article), we are even less likely, given his ambivalence about the Gaelic Revival, to think he absorbed medieval Irish texts. No smoking gun here, yet Edith Hall's diptych convincingly argues that it is impossible to imagine Joyce did *not* know the middle Irish prose *Odyssey* (*Merugud Uilix Maicc Leirtis*) published by Kuno Meyer in 1886. A close reading of the 'Cyclops' episode in *Ulysses* cements the case. Hall's hinge to the other panel of her essay is the same *Merugud*, which crops up on a recommended Gaelic reading list compiled by Robert Mitchell Henry, Professor of Latin at Queen's University, Belfast and unlikely member of the Irish Volunteers, with whom he practised riflery in the months before the Rising. His professional reading of ancient history may have influenced his affinity for the Volunteers and Sinn Féin—another twist on the political reception of Classics in early-twentieth-century Ireland.

As for Kuno Meyer, Celticists, for whom his work remains essential, may be fewer than the general educated readers (still a small number) familiar with his name from the rousing ballad, 'Binchy and Bergin and Best' by one Brian O'Nolan aka Flann O'Brien aka Myles na gCopaleen:[7]

> They worked out that riddle
> Old Irish and Middle,
> Binchy and Bergin and Best.
> They studied far higher
> Than ould Kuno Meyer
> And fanned up the glimmer
> Bequeathéd by Zimmer,
> Binchy and Bergin and Best.

The triune author who sang of this triad had affinities all over the shop. Walshe's essay has already mentioned the influence of O'Nolan's 1939 parodic novel *At Swim-Two-Birds* on Jamie O'Neill's 2001 fiction (*At Swim, Two Boys*). Even within the narrower comic columns of *Cruiskeen Lawn*, as Cillian O'Hogan demonstrates, 'Myles' could brilliantly juggle allusions to all sorts of classical and medieval Irish works, when not writing entire pieces largely in Latin. Comedy is the hardest thing to write about seriously, but O'Hogan is entirely persuasive regarding O'Nolan's highly sophisticated, classically-inflected send-ups of paratexts as well as texts, not to mention of those people promoting insular stultification in any tongue.

---

[7] From the *Cruiskeen Lawn* column of *The Irish Times*, 18 March 1942, reprinted in O'Brien (1968: 265–7). 'Binchy and Bergin and Best' (copyright © Flann O'Brien, 1942), reproduced by permission of A. M. Heath & Co. Ltd.

Affinity might seem less compact a category than contiguity, and indeed none of the three leitmotifs of Irish political reception is meant to be exclusive. Metaphors from fluid dynamics (vorticity, viscocity, turbulent flow) would perhaps have been more appropriate for the ever-morphing systems analysed by these essays. **Chance** comes closest to that. More a motif to muse on than an organizing principle, it is still not lightly dismissed in a study of cultural transmission. Coincidence and ser-endipity can lead to a life's occupation. Afforded the rich details in this book, one wonders, for instance, how Longley's poetic career might have gone, had he not heard Donald Wormell recite at Trinity College Dublin, or what would be Dineen's sensitivity to language, had he not studied at University College Dublin with Gerard Manley Hopkins. Would today's generation of brilliant women poets writing in Irish have emerged without the example of Máire Mhac an tSaoi, and would she have become a writer and scholar absent the influence of her mother's brother, Monsignor de Brún? Could some chance acquaintance with the slightly older Queen's man, Eóin MacNéill (BA 1888) have drawn Robert Henry (BA 1893) into Irish Studies and the politics of revolution? Had not an incidental clas-sical connection led to Thomas MacDonagh being born in Ireland (his maternal grandfather obtaining a job as compositor in Greek for the Dublin University Press)? And did not Yeats's 1925 spring vacation in Magna Graecia result in the beauty of Irish coin designs? Such quotidian cultural flows are not totally chaotic: in them, affinity and contiguity combine with pure chance.

Which brings me (taking the liberty) to an autobiographical flashback in con-clusion. Among the Irish of the diaspora, chance relics of the past survive, some-times with more power and meaning than in the homeland—call it the archaism of the periphery. One floor below our apartment in a 'three-decker' house in the Dorchester section of Boston, where my maternal grandparents lived (a Cusack grand-aunt and her Daly husband dwelt one floor below *them*), a copy of the dec-laration of the Irish Republic was reverently displayed on the living room wall, its thrilling central text framed by cameo headshots of the martyrs of 1916. I remem-ber trying, from the time I could read, to figure out why, against every spelling rule the nuns were teaching us, some of these words had a small 'h' clinging to the front of a capital letter—*Poblacht na hÉireann*, for example. Family acquaintances who had been on the run—the mysterious 'Silver Fox' was one—were darkly alluded to in hushed tones. The occasional Irish phrase punctuated conversations, but no one ever spoke a full sentence of the language in my hearing, other than in prayers. (Only much later did I learn from the 1901 census that both grandpar-ents, Clare natives, had been listed as bilingual when children—something I believe may have been true, as at that period, pre-Free State, no one was winning points for it.) A tattered but cherished Irish songbook from the 1930s, binding ripped off, was in the piano bench; nearby in the bookcase, at child's-eye level, the two fattest volumes were *The Story of the Irish Race* and *1000 Years of Irish Poetry*. The latter was a gift from my grandfather's sister, Mary Daly Slattery, who as a young woman had been despatched around 1907 from their bare hilltop farm near Corofin (in a manner still mystifying) to Manhattan, to staff the Irish Industries Depot run by the Gaelic League. It was she, an elderly great-aunt by then, who initiated my 10-year-old self, on a family journey to the New York World's Fair, into modern poetry, promising to give me a coveted new Irish postage stamp commemorating Yeats, only on the condition that I memorize and perform the 'Lake Isle of Innisfree'. I still have the stamp.

Of course, a heritage-culture (Irish in America) lives and dies by biology, petering out after generations unless given enhancements and injections; otherwise diffusing and metamorphosing amid the distractions of the new land. A lot is left to chance. In my own case, Greek, Latin, and Irish all lined up as available 'others', the exotic lattermost forming the entrée for the first two, all three nurtured by home and religion, inherited habit, and Jesuit education (Latin having not yet been replaced in my early altar-boy years). Normally, the Old Country takes more effort to retain. Contrast the classical: a culture that no one claims (modern Greeks and Italians perhaps excepted) can be claimed by *anyone*, and almost everyone respects the claim; not requiring bloodlines, by the same token it does not run dry. Desiccation might set in (usually through misdirected compulsory schooling), but then (and probably because of it) reaction erupts, to fire up and reorient the past in a new direction. In this uniquely triangular cultural formation, you can reject your immediate ancestors' past in order to lay hold of another without insulting or letting wither your direct inheritance. A win-win: like learning a second language in which to dream, tell secrets, or get around the police.

This is to say, at last, that culture—as the desired, and obscure, useful or alluring 'other'—seeps in diurnally, like weather, comes slowly to occupy the same space, like randomly acquired furniture. How did Greece and Rome penetrate an Irish household, day by day, in each of those 1,000, 2,000, or more years when they could have been a presence, materially or ghostly, on the island? It would be good for someone to attempt a time-travel account of a small synchronic slice— or several, juxtaposed (fifth century, fifteenth, twenty-first)—imagining what one would have encountered, in terms of texts, translations, ideas, constructions, even actual Byzantine Greek or Late Antique Roman bodies, over those years. Perhaps a *History of Ireland in 100 Classical Moments* would work, but it would take real novelistic skill to weave together the contemporary connections—a Burke quoting Demosthenes to a Dublin debate society at the same moment, for instance, that a displaced poet in Kerry enthralled a hut full of illiterate neighbours with a tale first created about events in Troy.

The disparity of levels, the dips and hillocks in the landscape of reception, would be good to capture in this sort of topographic study: what social, political, educational, and religious forces brought it about that, on one smallish island in one year, 'Greece' could, to one set of people, signal high intellectual ideals—artistic, philosophical, democratic—to another, a suspect strain of Christianity that was not Roman, and to yet another a misty world in the far East, home of folk-tale queens and princes? Or maybe another angle would work: parallel lives, not of the Plutarchan variety but tracing how people in the landscape—a Maria Edgeworth, a Piaras Feiritéar—took possession of Greece and Rome within their own limited lifespans. The 'social biographical perspective', proposed in Christine Morris's essay, offers another way forward, best combined with a counterbalance articulated by Declan Kiberd. What he writes about bardic verse here might be expanded to appreciating the dynamics of reception as a whole: one wants to retain that elusive 'tension between the language of poetry and of everyday life. If they grow too close, there is a loss of that imaginative challenge and redemptive strangeness.'

Bibliography

Abdo, D. M. (2007) 'Redefining the warring self in Hanan Al-Shakyh's *The Story of Zahra* and Frank McGuinness' *Carthaginians*', *Pacific Coast Philology* 42: 217–37.

Adams, J. R. R. (1987) *The Printed Word and the Common Man: Popular Culture in Ulster 1700–1900*. Belfast.

Adams, J. R. R. (1988) 'The Poets Laureate of Donegal: rural rhymers of the Laggan in the first decade of the nineteenth century', *Ulster Folklife* 34: 68–75.

Adorno, T. (2005) *Minima Moralia: Reflections from a Damaged Life*, trans. E. F. N. Jephcott. London.

Adorno, T. and Horkheimer, M. (2002) *Dialectic of Enlightenment*, trans. E. F. N. Jephcott. Stanford.

Ahern, G. (2009) *The Story of the Presentation Sisters, Scoil Chroí Naofa and Presentation College, Athenry 1908–2000*. Athenry, republished at http://athenryparishheritage.com/an–tollamh–mairead–ni–eimhigh–professor–margaret–heavey/ (accessed 5 December 2019).

Ahl, F. (1989) 'Uilix mac Leirtis: the classical hero in Irish metamorphosis', in Warren 1989: 173–98.

Ahlqvist, A. (1988) 'Notes on the Greek materials in the St Gall Priscian (Codex 904)', in Herren 1988: 195–214.

Akenson, D. H. (1976) *A Mirror to Kathleen's Face: Education in Independent Ireland*. Montreal.

Albright, D. (ed.) (1990) *The Poems of W. B. Yeats*. London.

Alden, M. (2000) *Homer Beside Himself: Para-Narratives in the Iliad*. Oxford.

Alexiou, C. (1999a) 'Εισαγωγή', in C. Alexiou 1999: 7–55.

Alexiou, C. (ed.) (1999b) *George Thomson, Τό αειθαλές δέντρο. Διαλέξεις και άρθρα για τον ελληνικό πολιτισμό*, 2nd edn. Athens.

Alexiou, M. (2000) 'George Thomson: the Greek dimension', in Ní Chéilleachair 2000: 52–74.

Alexiou, M. (2002) *The Ritual Lament in Greek Tradition*, 2nd edn., rev. D. Yatromanolakis and P. Roilos. Lanham. 1st edn. 1974.

Allen, M. L. (2000) 'Longley's Long Line: looking back from *The Ghost Orchid*', in Peacock and Devine 2000: 121–41.

Allen, N. (2010) 'Out of eure sanscreed into oure eryan: Ireland, the Classics, and independence', in Stephens and Vasunia 2010: 16–33.

Allen, N. (2012) 'Synge, reading and archipelago', in Cliff and Grene 2012: 159–71.

Allen, N. (2015) 'Misplaced islands: Ireland and the archipelago', paper delivered at the Atlantic Archipelago Research Consortium's 'Unencompassing the Archipelago' conference, 14 November, Oxford.

Allen, N. (2016) 'Imagining the Rising', in Grene and Morash 2016: 155–68.

Al Sayyad, N. (ed.) (1992) *Forms of Dominance: on the Architecture and Urbanism of the Colonial Enterprise*. Aldershot.

An Crann/*The Tree*. [collective group] (ed.) (2000) *Bear in Mind: Stories of the Troubles*. Belfast.

Anon. (1884) 'Miss Stokes on early Irish ecclesiastical architecture', *Irish Monthly* 12.138: 624–36.

Anon. (1895) 'Excursion to Aran Islands, Galway, &c. July, 1895', *Journal of the Royal Society of Antiquaries* 5.3: 239–79.

Anon. (1897) 'Account of summer excursion', *Journal of the Royal Society of Antiquaries* 7.3: 265–72.

Anon. (1932) 'Parliament Building in Northern Ireland', *The Builder*, 11 and 18 November: 806–7 and 812.

Appadurai, A. (ed.) (1986) *The Social Life of Things: Commodities in Cultural Perspective.* Cambridge.

Arkins, B. (1985) 'Yeats and Propertius', *Liverpool Classical Monthly* 10: 72–3.

Arkins, B. (1990) *Builders of My Soul: Greek and Roman Themes in Yeats.* Irish Literary Studies 32. Gerrards Cross.

Arkins, B. (1991) 'The role of Greek and Latin in Friel's *Translations*', *Colby Quarterly* 27: 202–9.

Arkins, B. (1999) *Greek and Roman Themes in Joyce.* Lewiston.

Arkins, B. (2005) *Hellenising Ireland: Greek and Roman Themes in Modern Irish Literature.* Newbridge.

Arkins, B. (2007) 'The modern reception of Catullus', in Skinner 2007: 461–78.

Arkins, B. (2009) 'Michael Longley appropriates Latin poetry', in Harrison 2009: 152–62.

Arkins, B. (2010a) *Irish Appropriation of Greek Tragedy.* Dublin.

Arkins, B. (2010b) *The Thought of W. B. Yeats.* Bern.

Arnold, M. (1853) *Poems.* London.

Arnold, M. (1867) *On the Study of Celtic Literature.* London.

Arrington, L. (2010) *W. B. Yeats, the Abbey Theatre, Censorship, and the Irish State: Adding the Half-Pence to the Pence.* Oxford.

Asensio Peral, G. (2018) ' "One does not take sides in these neutral latitudes": Myles na gCopaleen and the Emergency', *International Journal of English Studies* 18: 1–16.

Asheri, D., Lloyd, A., and Corcella, A. (2007) *A Commentary on Herodotus Books I–IV.* Oxford.

Ashley, S. (2000) 'Primitivism, Celticism and morbidity in the Atlantic fin de siècle', in McGuinness 2000: 175–93.

Ashley, S. (2001) 'The poetics of race in 1890s Ireland: an ethnography of the Aran Islands', *Patterns of Prejudice* 35.2: 5–18.

Ashton, R. (1777) *The Battle of Aughrim: or, the Fall of Saint Ruth. A Tragedy.* Dublin.

Atkinson, J. (2010) 'Benjamin Farrington: Cape Town and the shaping of a public intellectual', *South African Historical Journal*, 62.4: 671–92.

Attwood, P. (2003) Percy Metcalfe, *Grove Art Online*: https://www.oxfordartonline.com/groveart/view/10.1093/gao/9781884446054.001.0001/oao-9781884446054-e-7000057457 (accessed 9 December 2019).

Augusteijn, J. (2009) 'The Road to Rebellion: the development of Patrick Pearse's political thought 1879–1914', in Higgins and Uí Chollatáin 2009: 3–18.

Ayo, D. A. (2012) 'Mary Colum, modernism, and mass media: an Irish-inflected transatlantic print culture', *Journal of Modern Literature* 35.4: 107–29.

Babington, C. C. (1858) 'On the Firbolgic forts in the south isles of Aran', *Archaeologia Cambrensis* 4.13: 96–103.

Baines, J. (ed.) (2011) *'Is it about a Bicycle?': Flann O'Brien in the Twenty-First Century.* Dublin.

Banim, M. (1991) 'Here and there through Ireland', in B. and R. Ó hEithir 1991: 73–83. 1st publ. 1896.

Barlow, J. (1905) 'Irish peasant life', *Country Life* 18.467: 862–5.

Barrett, W. (ed.) (1964) *Euripides: Hippolytus*. Oxford.

Barry, J. G. (1886) 'Aran of the saints', *Royal Historical and Archaeological Association of Ireland* 7.67: 488–94.

Bataille, G. (1999) 'Abjection and miserable forms', in Lotringer 1999: 8–13. Written 1934; 1st publ. 1970.

Battershill, C. (2018) *Modernist Lives: Biography and Autobiography at Leonard and Virgina Woolf's Hogarth Press*. London.

Beaufort, L. C. (1818) 'An essay upon the state of architecture and antiquities, previous to the landing of the Anglo-Normans in Ireland', *Transactions of the Royal Irish Academy* 15: 101–241.

Behan, B. (1949) 'Do Sheán Ó Súilleabháin', *Comhar* 8.8: 14.

Behan, B. (1981) *After the Wake*. Dublin.

Benediktson, D. (1989) *Propertius: Modernist Poet of Antiquity*. Carbondale.

Benjamin, W. (1977) *The Origin of German Tragic Drama*, trans. J. Osborne. London.

Benjamin, W. (1999) *The Arcades Project*, trans. H. Eiland and K. McLaughlin. Cambridge MA.

Benjamin, W. (2006) *Berlin Childhood Around 1900*, trans. H. Eiland. Cambridge MA.

Benjamin, W. (2007) *Illuminations*, trans. H. Zohn, ed. H. Arendt. New York.

Bergin, O. and Marstrander C. (1912) *Miscellany Presented to Kuno Meyer... on the occasion of his appointment to the chair of Celtic philology in the University of Berlin*. Halle.

Bery, A. and Murray, P. (eds.) (2000) *Comparing Postcolonial Literatures. Dislocations*. London and New York.

Betham, W. (1842) *Etruria-Celtica: Etruscan Literature and Antiquities Investigated*. 2 vols. Dublin.

Bhreathnach-Lynch, S. (1999) 'Commemorating the hero in newly independent Ireland: expressions of nationhood in bronze and stone', in McBride 1999: 148–65.

Bhreathnach-Lynch, S. (2007) *Ireland's Art, Ireland's History: Representing Ireland, 1845 to Present*. Omaha.

Bisagni, J. (2013) 'Prolegomena to the study of code-switching in the Old Irish glosses', *Peritia*, 24–5: 1–58.

Blair, H. (1783) *Lectures on Rhetoric and Belles-Lettres*. Edinburgh.

Blaney, R. (1996) *Presbyterians and the Irish Language*. Belfast.

Blanshard, A. J. L. (2018) 'Mahaffy and Wilde', in Riley, Blanshard, and Manny 2018: 19–36.

Bodkin, T. (1972) 'The Irish coinage designs, a lecture delivered by Thomas Bodkin, D.Litt. at the Metropolitan School of Art, Dublin, 30th November 1928', repr. in Cleeve 1972: 40–54.

Boegehold, A. L. (1999) *When a Gesture Was Expected*. Princeton.

Boltwood, S. (ed.) (2009) *Renegotiating and Resisting Nationalism in 20th-Century Irish Drama*. Gerrards Cross.

Borg, R., McCourt, J., and Fagan, P. (eds.) (2017) *Flann O'Brien: Problems with Authority*. Cork.

Bourke, A. (2002) *The Field Day Anthology of Irish Writing. Vol. 5: Irish Women's Writing and Traditions*. New York.

Bourke, U. J. (1887) *Pre-Christian Ireland*. Dublin.

Bouvier, N. (1990) *Journal d'Aran et d'autres lieux*. Paris.

Bradley, B. (1982) *James Joyce's Schooldays*. Dublin.

Bradley, G. G. (1884) *Aids to Writing Latin Prose*, ed. T. L. Papillon. London.

Bradley, J. M. (2002) 'Unrecognized middle–class revolutionary? Michael Cusack, sport and cultural change in nineteenth–century Ireland', *European Sports History Review* 4: 58–72.

Bradley, M. (ed.) (2010) *Classics and Imperialism in the British Empire*. Oxford.

Brannigan, J. (2015) *Archipelagic Modernism: Literature in the Irish and British Isles, 1890–1970*. Edinburgh.

Braund, S. and Torlone, Z. M. (eds.) (2018) *Virgil and his Translators*. Oxford.

Braunholtz, G. E. K. (1915) 'The nationality of Vergil', *Classical Review* 29: 104–10.

Brearton, F. (1997) 'Walking forwards into the past: an interview with Michael Longley', *Irish Studies Review* 5.18: 35–9.

Brearton, F. (2006) *Reading Michael Longley*. Tarset.

Breathnach, D. and Ní Mhurchú, M. (2018a) 'De Brún, Pádraig (1889–1960)', https://www.ainm.ie/Bio.aspx?ID=420 (accessed 5 December 2019).

Breathnach, D. and Ní Mhurchú, M. (2018b) 'Ní Éimhigh, Maighréad (1907–1980)', https://www.ainm.ie/Bio.aspx?ID=2156 (accessed 5 December 2019).

Breathnach, D. and Ní Mhurchú, M. (2018c) 'Ó Cadhlaigh, Cormac (1884–1960)', https://www.ainm.ie/Bio.aspx?ID=182 (accessed 5 December 2019).

Breathnach, D. and Ní Mhurchú, M. (2018d) 'Ó Domhnaill, Maoghnas (c.1900–1965)', https://www.ainm.ie/Bio.aspx?ID=722 (accessed 5 December 2019).

Breathnach, D. and Ní Mhurchú, M. (2018e) 'Ó Duinnín, Pádraig (1860–1934)', https://www.ainm.ie/Bio.aspx?ID=330 (accessed 5 December 2019).

Breathnach, D. and Ní Mhurchú, M. (2018f) 'Ó Laoghaire, Peadar (1839–1920)', https://www.ainm.ie/Bio.aspx?ID=210 (accessed 5 December 2019).

Breathnach, D. and Ní Mhurchú, M. (2018g) 'Ó Mathghamhna, Domhnall (1872–1942)' https://www.ainm.ie/Bio.aspx?ID=763 (accessed 5 December 2019).

Breathnach, D. and Ní Mhurchú, M. (2018h) 'Thomson, George Derwent (1903–1987)' https://www.ainm.ie/Bio.aspx?ID=1607 (accessed 5 December 2019).

Breen, S. (2015) 'Republican 1916 group claims Stormont Irish flag stunt', *Belfast Telegraph* 10 June: https://www.belfasttelegraph.co.uk/news/northern-ireland/republican-1916-group-claims-stormont-irish-flag-stunt-31291492.html (accessed 10 May 2019).

Brenton, H. (1980) *The Romans in Britain*. London.

Brewer, E. (1937) 'The other side of Aran', *Contemporary Review* 152: 349–55.

Briody, M. (2007) *The Irish Folklore Commission 1935–1970: History, Ideology, Methodology*. Helsinki.

Brown, L. (1995) *British Historical Medals 1760–1960. Volume III, The Accession of Edward VII to 1960*. London.

Brown, T. (2003) 'Mahon and Longley: place and placelessness', in Campbell 2003: 133–48.

Brown, T. (2004) *Ireland: A Social and Cultural History 1922–2002*. London.

Brown, T. (2015) *The Irish Times: 150 Years of Influence*. London.

Bruce, C. R. and T. Michael (2007) *2008 Standard Catalogue of World Coins, 1901–2000*. Iola.

Bruce, S. (2006) *The Harp and the Eagle. Irish-American Volunteers and the Union Army 1861–1865*. New York.

Brugger, C. (2017) *Homer's* Iliad. *The Basel Commentary*, eds. A. Bierl and J. Latacz, trans. B. W. Millis and S. Strack, ed. D. Olson. Berlin.

Bryan, D. (2000) *Orange Parades: The Politics of Ritual Tradition and Control*. London.

Bryan, D. (2018) 'The material value of flags: politics and space in Northern Ireland', *Review of Irish Studies Journal in Europe* 2.1: 76–91.

Bryant, S. (1889) *Celtic Ireland*. London.

Buckland, P. (1980) *James Craig: Lord Craigavon*. Dublin.

Bull, J. (ed.) (2005) *British and Irish Dramatists Since World War II Fourth Series*. New York.

Bullard, P. (2011) *Edmund Burke and the Art of Rhetoric*. Cambridge.

Bullock, K. (2014) 'From revival to revolution: Thomas MacDonagh and the *Irish Review*', in Steele and de Nie 2014: 181–204.

Burke, O. J. (1887) *The South Isles of Aran (County Galway)*. London.

Burkert, W. (1979) *Structure and History in Greek Mythology and Ritual*. Berkeley.

Burnet, J. (1892a) *Early Greek Philosophy*. London and Edinburgh.

Burnet, J. (1892b) *Early Greek Philosophy*, with annotations by W. B. Yeats. National Library of Ireland MS 40,568/36.

Burrow, C. (2016) 'You've listened long enough', *London Review of Books* 38.8: 13–14.

Burström, N. M. (2014) 'Things in the eye of the beholder: a humanistic perspective on archaeological object biographies', *Norwegian Archaeological Review* 47: 65–82.

Burström, N. M. and G. T. Ingvardson (eds.) (2017) *Divina Moneta. Coins in Religion and Ritual*. London.

Butler, A. S. G. (1950) *The Architecture of Sir Edwin Lutyens*. 2 vols. London.

Butler, S. (2016a) 'On the origin of "Deep Classics"', in Butler 2016b: 1–19.

Butler, S. (ed.) (2016b) *Deep Classics. Rethinking Classical Reception*. London and New York.

Byrne, F. J. (1973) 'MacNeill the historian', in Martin and Byrne 1973: 17–36.

Caffrey, P. (2011) 'Nationality and representation: the Coinage Design Committee (1926–8) and the formation of a design identity in the Irish Free State', in King and Sisson 2011: 75–89.

Cairns, F. (2006) *Sextus Propertius: The Augustan Elegist*. Cambridge.

Calder, G. (1907) *Imtheachta Aeniasa: The Irish Aeneid: being a translation made before A.D. 1400 of the XII books of Vergil's Aeneid into Gaelic*. London.

Calder, G. and Poppe, E. (1995) *A New Introduction to Imtheachta Aeniasa: The Irish Aeneid. The Classical Epic from an Irish Perspective*. London.

Calder Marshall, A. (1963) *The Innocent Eye: The Life of Robert J. Flaherty*. London.

Callaghan, D. M. (2006) *Thomas Francis Meagher and the Irish Brigade in the Civil War*. Jefferson.

Campbell, G. (2007) 'Bicycles, centaurs and man-faced ox-creatures: ontological instability in Lucretius', in Heyworth, Fowler, and Harrison 2007: 39–62.

Campbell, M. (ed.) (2003) *The Cambridge Companion Contemporary Irish Poetry*. Cambridge.

Cannadine, D. (2002) *Ornamentalism: How the British Saw Their Empire*. Oxford.

Canter, H. V. (1914) 'The impeachment of Verres and Hastings: Cicero and Burke', *Classical Journal* 9: 199–211.

Carey, C. (2010) 'Epideictic Oratory', *A Companion to Greek Rhetoric*, ed. I. Worthington. Malden and Oxford: 236–52.

Carey, James J. (ed.) (1961) *C. Iuli Caesaris De Bello Gallico Commentariorum Libri I–II*. 2 vols. Dublin. 1st edn. 1945.

Carey, James J. (ed.)(1978) *P. Vergili Maronis Aeneidos Liber VI*. Seán Ó Riain a d'aistrigh. Dublin.

Carey, John (1988) 'Fir Bolg: a native etymology reconsidered', *Cambridge Medieval Celtic Studies* 16: 77–83.

Carey, John, Herbert, M., and Murray, K. (eds.) (2004) *Cín Chille Cúile: Texts, Saints, and Places: Essays in Honour of Pádraig Ó Riain*. Aberystwyth.

Carleton, W. (1896) *The Life of William Carleton, his Autobiography and Letters, and an account of his life and writings by D. J. O'Donoghue*. Vol. I. London.

Carnall, G. (1989) 'Burke as modern Cicero', in Carnall and Nicholson 1989: 76–90.

Carnall, G. and Nicholson, C. (eds.) (1989) *The Impeachment of Warren Hastings*. Edinburgh.

Carney, J. (1955) *Studies in Irish Literature and History*. Dublin.

Carr, M. (2015a) *Plays 3*. London.

Carr, M. (2015b) 'Beautiful lofty things', in Programme for *Hecuba* at the Royal Shakespeare Company, 7–12.

Casey, C. (2005) *Dublin: The City within the Grand and Royal Canals and the Circular Road with the Phoenix Park*. New Haven and London.

Challis, C. E. (ed.) (1992) *A New History of the Royal Mint*. Cambridge.

Challis, D. (2011) 'The race for a healthy body: the ancient Greek physical ideal in Victorian London', in Goff and Simpson 2011: 141–55.

Chapman, W. K. (2006) *The W. B. and George Yeats Library: A Short-Title Catalog*. Clemson. https://cup.sites.clemson.edu/pubs/yeatsstc/ (accessed 24 October 2016).

Chapman, W. K. (2010) *Yeats's Poetry in the Making: Sing Whatever Is Well Made*. Basingstoke.

Chrisafis, A. (2005) 'How pub brawl turned into republican crisis', *The Guardian*, 28 February: https://www.theguardian.com/uk/2005/feb/28/northernireland.northernireland (accessed 5 December 2019).

Cieniuch, M. (2010) 'To will one myth out, to will a different one into history – contemporary Irish history written through the classics in the poetry of Michael Longley and Seamus Heaney', in Sikorska 2010: 113–25.

Clarity, J. (1995) 'Irish vote to end divorce ban by a tiny margin', *The New York Times*, 26 November: http://www.nytimes.com/1995/11/26/world/irish-vote-to-end-the-divorce-ban-by-a-tiny-margin.html (accessed 5 December 2019).

Clark, D. B. and Maguire, J. B. (1989) *W. B. Yeats: The Writing of Sophocles' King Oedipus*. Philadelphia.

Clarke, B. K. and Ferrar, H. (1979) *The Dublin Drama League*. Dublin.

Clarke, M. (2001) 'Heart-cutting talk: Homeric κερτομέω and related words', *Classical Quarterly* 51.2: 329–38.

Clarke, M. (2009) 'An Irish Achilles and a Greek Cú Chulainn', in Ó hUiginn and Ó Catháin 2009: 238–51.

Clarke, M. (2014) 'Demonology, allegory and translation: the Furies and the Morrígan', in O'Connor 2014: 101–22.

Cleary, J. (2013) 'Marxism, capitalist crisis and Irish Literary Studies', *Irish Review* 46: 4–13.

Cleeve, B. (ed.) (1972) *W. B. Yeats and the Designing of Ireland's Coinage*. Dublin.

Cliff, B. and Grene, N. (eds.) (2012) *Synge and Edwardian Ireland*. Oxford.

Clune, A. and Hurson, T. (eds.) (1997) *Conjuring Complexities: Essays on Flann O'Brien*. Belfast.

Cohn, R. (ed.) (1984) *Samuel Beckett. Disjecta: Miscelllaneous Writings and a Dramatic Fragment*. New York.

Colgan, E. (2003) *For Want of Good Money: The Story of Ireland's Coinage*. Dublin.

Colls, R. (2002) *Identity of England*. Oxford.

Colum, M. (1966) *Life and the Dream*, rev. edn. Dublin.

Colum, P. (1916) 'Padraic Colum on Sir Roger Casement', *Gaelic American* 13.19: 4–5.

Colum, P. (1932) *Poems*. London.

Colum, P. and O'Brien, E. J. (eds.) (1916) *Poems of the Irish Revolutionary Brotherhood. Thomas MacDonagh P. H. Pearse, Joseph Mary Plunkett, Sir Roger Casement*. Boston.

Comber, M. (1998) 'A book made new: reading Propertius reading Pound. A Study in Reception', *Journal of Roman Studies* 88: 37–55.

Conington, J. and Nettleship, H. (1881) *P. Vergili Maronis opera. The Works of Virgil*. 4th edn. London.

Conneely, M. (2011) *Between Two Shores/Idir Dhá Chladach: Writing the Aran Islands, 1890–1980*. Oxford and New York.

Connolly, J. (1903) 'National drama', *United Irishman* 10, 244: 2.

Conroy, G. (1870) 'A visit to the Aran-more of St. Enda', *Irish Ecclesiastical Record* 7: 19–31, 105–23.

Constantakopoulou, C. (2007) *The Dance of the Islands: Insularity, Networks, the Athenian Empire, and the Aegean World*. Oxford.

Constantinidis, S. (ed.) (2016) *The Reception of Aeschylus' Plays Through Shifting Models and Frontiers*. Leiden.

Conway, R. S. (1931) 'Further considerations on the site of Vergil's farm', *Classical Quarterly* 25: 65–76.

Cook, M. (2003) *London and the Culture of Homosexuality, 1885–1914*. Cambridge.

Cooke, P. (2009) 'Patrick Pearse: the Victorian Gael', in Higgins and Uí Chollatáin 2009: 45–62.

Coolahan, J. (1981) *Irish Education: History and Structure*. Dublin.

Corkery, D. (1924) *The Hidden Ireland: A Study of Gaelic Munster in the Eighteenth Century*. Dublin.

Costello, P. (1992) *James Joyce: The Years of Growth, 1882–1915*. London.

Cotter, C. (1994) 'Atlantic fortifications: the Duns of the Aran Islands', *Archaeology Ireland* 8.1: 24–28.

Coulouma, F. (2011) 'Tall tales and short stories: *Cruiskeen Lawn* and the dialogic imagination', *Review of Contemporary Fiction* 31: 162–77.

Croally, N. (1994) *Euripidean Polemic: The Trojan Women and the Function of Greek Tragedy*. Cambridge.

Crofton Croker, T. (1839) *Popular Songs of Ireland*. London.

Cronin, A. (1989) *No Laughing Matter: The Life and Times of Flann O'Brien*. London.

Cronin, M. (1996) *Translating Ireland: Translation, Languages, Culture*. Cork.

Cronin, M. and Ó Cuilleanáin, C. (eds.) (2003) *The Languages of Ireland*. Dublin.

Crotty, K. (1994) *The Poetics of Supplication: Homer's* Iliad *and* Odyssey. Ithaca NY and London.

Cullingford, E. Butler (1993) *Gender and History in Yeats's Love Poetry*. Cambridge.

Cullingford, E. Butler (1996) 'British Romans and Irish Carthaginians: anticolonial metaphor in Heaney, Friel, and McGuinness', *Proceedings of the Modern Language Association* 111: 222–39.

Cullingford, E. Butler (2002) *Ireland's Others: Gender and Ethnicity in Irish Literature and Popular Culture*. Cork.

Cumont, F. (1912a) *Astrology and Religion among the Greeks and Romans*. New York.

Cumont, F. (1912b) *Astrology and Religion among the Greeks and Romans*, with annotations by W. B. Yeats. National Library of Ireland MS 40,568/62.

Cunningham, J. (1999) *St Jarlath's College, Tuam: 1800–2000*. Tuam.

Currie, A. (2017) *Those Swans, Remember: Graeco-Celtic Relations in the Work of J. M. Synge*. Diss. Oxford.

Curtis, J. and S. Guiness (eds.) (2011) *W. B. Yeats: The Resurrection: Manuscript Materials*. Ithaca NY.

Dall, I. [= C. S. Higgins] (1931) *Here are Stones: An Account of a Journey in the Aran Islands*. London.

Dalton, J. (1920) 'Loch Garman', *The Past: The Organ of the Uí Cinsealaigh Historical Society* 1: 15–61.

Daly, M. E. (2009) 'The GPO and the Rising revisited', *The Irish Times*, 4 April: https://www.irishtimes.com/news/the–gpo–and–the–rising–revisited–1.738243 (accessed 10 May 2019).

Damon, C. (ed.) (2003) *Tacitus,* Histories *I*. Cambridge.

d'Arbois de Jubainville, H. (1884) *Le cycle mythologique irlandais et la mythologie celtique*. Paris.

Davidson, J., Muecke, F., and Wilson, P. (eds.) (2006) *Greek Drama III: Essays in Honour of Kevin Lee*. London.

Davidson, P. (1995) *Ezra Pound and Roman Poetry: A Preliminary Survey*. Amsterdam.

Day, J. (2011) 'Cuttings from *Cruiskeen Lawn*: bibliographical issues in the republication of Myles na gCopaleen's journalism', in Baines 2011: 32–48.

Dean, B. (1928) 'Passion for liberty', *Northern Whig*, 21 May: 9.

Dean, J. Fitzpatrick (1999) 'Self-dramatization in the plays of Frank McGuinness', *New Hibernia Review* 3: 97–110.

Deane, S. (ed.) (1991) *The Field Day Anthology of Irish Writing*. Vol. 3. Derry and London.

Deane, S., Heaney, S., Kearney, R., Kiberd, D., Paulin, T., and Donoghue, D. (1985) *Ireland's Field Day*. Field Day Theatre Company. London.

de Barra, C. (2018) *The Coming of the Celts, AD 1860. Celtic Nationalism in Ireland and Wales*. Notre Dame.

de Blacam, A. (1942) Review of Macalister (1941), *Irish Monthly*, 70.824: 83–5.

de Brún, P. (1929) *Oidiopús i gColón: Dráma le Sofoicléas*. Maynooth.

de Brún, P. (1957) *Tús Laidne trí Laidin Eaglasta*. Cork.

de Brún, P. (trans.) and Ó Coigligh, C. (ed.) (1990) *An Odaisé*. Dublin.

de Búrca, M. (1989) *Michael Cusack and the GAA*. Dublin.

de Hindeberg, P. (1948) Review of Ní Éimhthigh and Seán Seártan (1947), *Irish Monthly* 76.901: 335–6.

Delaney, P. (2003) 'D. P. Moran and *The Leader*: writing an Irish Ireland through partition', *Éire-Ireland* 38: 189–212.

Dempsey, T. (1918) *The Delphic Oracle: Its Early History, Influence and Fall*. Oxford.

Denard, H. (2000) 'Seamus Heaney, Colonialism, and the Cure: Sophoclean re-visions', *Journal of Performance and Art* 22.3: 1–28.

de Nie, M. (2005) 'Pigs, Paddies, prams and petticoats: Irish Home Rule and the British comic press, 1886–93', *History Ireland* 13: 42–7.

Denvir, G. (1978) *Aistí Phádraic Uí Chonaire*. Indreabhán.

de Paor, L. (2004) 'An tsídheoig is an scian dochtúra: Flann O'Brien agus seanlitríocht na Gaeilge', in Carey, Herbert, and Murray 2004: 64–76.

de Paor, L. (2017) 'Brian Ó Nualláin and early Irish literature', in Borg, McCourt, and Fagan 2017: 189–203.

Devane, R. S. (1925) *Indecent Literature: Some Legal Remedies*. Dublin.

Didot, J. (1828) *The Catholic Question Considered in its Various Relations Religious and Political*. Paris.

Dillon, J. and Wilmer, S. (eds.) (2005) *Rebel Women: Staging Ancient Greek Drama Today*. London.

Dinneen, P. *See* Ua Duinnín, P.

Dirrane, B. (1997) *A Woman of Aran: The Life and Times of Bridget Dirrane. As told to Rose O'Connor and Jack Mahon*. Dublin.

Dixon, H. (1929) Review of R. M. Henry (1920), *Catholic Bulletin* 19: 57–62.

Dodds, E. R. (1929) *Thirty-Two Poems*. London.

Dodds, E. R. (1977) *Missing Persons: An Autobiography*. Oxford.

Doggett, R. (2011) ' "Emblems or Symbols, Not Pictures": W. B. Yeats and Free State coinage design', *Éire-Ireland* 46: 87–105.

Donnelly, K. (2018) ' "Baptism barrier" lifted as schools can't choose children based on religion', *Irish Independent*, 3 October: https://www.independent.ie/irish-news/education/baptism-barrier-lifted-as-schools-cant-choose-pupils-based-on-religion-37379362.html (accessed 5 December 2019).

Dooley, C. (2015) *Redmond. A Life Undone*. Dublin.

Dotterer, R. L. (2004) 'Flann O'Brien, James Joyce, and "The Dalkey Archive"', *New Hibernia Review/Iris Éireannach Nua* 8: 54–63.

Dougherty, C. (2001) *The Raft of Odysseus: The Ethnographic Imagination of Homer's Odyssey*. Oxford.

Dowling, L. (1994) *Hellenism and Homosexuality in Victorian Oxford*. Ithaca NY.

Dowling, P. J. (1968) *The Hedge Schools of Ireland*. Dublin.

Dubost, T. (ed.) (2012) *Drama Reinvented: Theatre Adaptation in Ireland (1970–2007)*. Brussels.

Dudgeon, J. (2002) *Roger Casement: The Black Diaries*. Belfast.

Dudley-Edwards, R. (1977) *Patrick Pearse. The Triumph of Failure*. Dublin.

Dué, C. (2006) *The Captive Woman's Lament in Greek Tragedy*. Austin.

Duffy, N. and Dorgan, T. (ed.) (1999) *Watching the River Flow: A Century of Irish Poetry*. Dublin.

Dunleavy, J. E. and Dunleavy, G. W. (1991) *Douglas Hyde: A Maker of Modern Ireland*. Berkeley.

Dunn, F. (1996) *Tragedy's End: Closure and Innovation in Euripidean Drama*. Oxford.

Dunne, T., Coolahan, J.Manning, M., and Ó Tuathaigh, G. (eds.) (2008) *The National University of Ireland, 1908–2008: Centenary Essays*. Dublin.

Dunraven, E. (1875) *Notes on Irish Architecture*. 3 vols., ed. M. Stokes. London.

Dwan, D. (2008) *The Great Community: Culture and Nationalism in Ireland*. Dublin.

Dyer, G. P. and Gaspar, P. P. (1992) 'Reform, the new technology and Tower Hill, 1700–1966' in Challis 1992: 398–606.

Easterling, P. (1997a) 'Form and performance', in Easterling 1997b: 151–77.

Easterling, P. (ed.) (1997b) *The Cambridge Companion to Greek Tragedy*. Cambridge.

Eglinton, J. (1899) 'What should be the subjects of a national drama?', Eglinton et al. 1899: 9–13.

Eglinton, J. et al. (eds.) (1899) *Literary Ideals in Ireland*. London.

Eliot, T. S. (1919) 'Kipling redivivus', *Athenaeum*, 9 May: 297–8.

Eliot, T. S. (1923) 'Ulysses, order, and myth', *The Dial* 75: 480–3.

Ellmann, R. (1982) *James Joyce*. 2nd edn. Oxford.

Ellmann, R. (1988) *Oscar Wilde*. Oxford.

Enenkel, K. A. E. and Ottenheym, K. A. (eds.) (2018) *The Quest for an Appropriate Past in Literature, Art and Architecture*. Leiden.

English, R. and Walker, G. (eds.) (1996) *Unionism in Modern Ireland: New Perspectives on Politics and Culture*. Basingstoke and New York.

Enright, D. J. and de Chickera, E. (eds.) (1962) *English Critical Texts*. London.

Enright, T. (1988) 'George Thomson: a memoir', in Thomson 1988: 117–50.

Evans, R. (2007) 'Perspectives on post-colonialism in South Africa: the Voortrekker monuments' classical heritage', in Hardwick and Gillespie 2007: 141–56.

Evans-Wentz, W. Y. (1911) *The Fairy-Faith in Celtic Countries*. London and New York.

Fahy, T. (ed.) (1919) *M. Minucii Felicis Octavius*. Dublin.

Fahy, T. (1963) *New Testament Problems*. Dublin.

Falconer, R. (2019) 'Heaney and Virgil's underworld journey', in Harrison, Macintosh, and Eastman. Oxford: 180–204.

Falkner, T. M. (1995) *The Poetics of Old Age in Greek Epic, Lyric, and Tragedy*. Norman and London.

Fallon, P. (1990) *Collected Poems*, ed. B. Fallon. Manchester.

Fallon, P. (2004) *The Georgics of Virgil*. Oldcastle.

Fallon, P. (2006) *Virgil:* Georgics: *A New Translation*. Oxford.

Farrell, J. (2012) 'Calling out the Greeks: dynamics of the elegiac canon', in Gold 2012: 11–24.

Farrington, B. (1919) 'The text of Shelley's translation of the *Symposium* of Plato', *Modern Language Review* 14: 325–6.

Ferguson, M. C. (1868) *The Story of the Irish Before the Conquest. From the Mythical Period to the Invasion under Strongbow*. London.

Ferguson, S. (1853) 'Clonmacnnoise, Clare, and Arran', *Dublin University Magazine* 41: 79–94, 492–505.

Ferguson Smith, M. (2001) *Lucretius:* On the Nature of Things, rev. edn. Indianapolis.

Ferriter, D. (2004) *The Transformation of Ireland 1900–2000*. London.

Ferriter, D. (2009) *Occasions of Sin*. London.

Finn, C. (2004) *Past Poetic: Archaeology in the Poetry of W. B. Yeats and Seamus Heaney*. London.

Finneran, R. J., with J. Curtis and A. Saddlemyer (eds.) (2007) *W. B. Yeats: The Tower (1928): Manuscript Materials*. Ithaca NY.

Fischer, S. R. (2012) *Islands: From Atlantis to Zanzibar*. London.

Fitzgerald, W. (1995) *Catullan Provocations. Lyric Poetry and the Drama of Position*. Berkeley.

Fitzgerald, M. and Finneran, R. J. (eds.) (2003) *The Collected Works of W. B. Yeats: Vol. VIII: The Irish Dramatic Movement*. New York.

Fitzpatrick, D. (2001) 'Commemoration in the Irish Free State: a chronicle of embarrassment', in McBride 2001: 184–203.

Fitzpatrick, D. (2012) 'Synge and modernity', in Cliff and Grene 2012: 121–51.

Fitzpatrick, L. (2009a) 'The utopian performative in post-ceasefire Northern Irish theatre', in Fitzpatrick 2009b: 175–88.

Fitzpatrick, L. (ed.) (2009b) *Performing Violence in Contemporary Ireland*. Dublin.

Fitzpatrick, L. (2018) *Rape on the Contemporary Stage*. London.

Flanagan, F. (2015) *Remembering the Revolution. Dissent, Culture, and Nationalism in the Irish Free State*. Oxford.

Flower, R. (1946) *The Irish Tradition*. Oxford.

Foldy, M. (1997) *The Trials of Oscar Wilde: Deviance, Morality and Late-Victorian Society*. New Haven.

Foley, I. (1992) 'History's moral guardians alerted', *Fortnight* 305: 36–7.

Foley, M. (2016) '"The Irish folly": the Easter Rising: the press; the people; the politics', unpublished paper delivered to *Reflecting the Rising* at the Dublin Institute of Technology: 1–13. https://arrow.dit.ie/aaconmuscon/19/ (accessed 20 August 2018).

Foley, T. (ed.) (1999) *From Queen's College to National University: Essays on the Academic History of QCG/UCG/NUI, Galway*. Dublin.

Forbes, C. A. (1946) 'Ezra Pound and Sextus Propertius', *Classical Journal* 42: 177–9.

Ford, A. (2001) 'Martydom, history and memory in early modern Ireland', in McBride 2001a: 43–66.

Fordonski F. (2004) 'William Butler Yeats and the Irish coinage', *Numismatics International Bulletin* 39: 77–83.

Forrester, H. (2006) 'The other Percy Metcalfe', *The Medal* 49: 22–35.

Foster, J. W. (1977) 'Certain set apart: the western island in the Irish Renaissance', *Studies: An Irish Quarterly Review* 66.264: 261–74.

Foster, R. F. (1988) *Modern Ireland 1600–1972*. London.

Foster, R. F. (2003a) *W. B. Yeats: A Life. Vol. I: The Apprentice Mage, 1865–1914*. Oxford.

Foster, R. F. (2003b) *W. B. Yeats: A Life. Vol. II: The Arch-Poet, 1915–1939*. Oxford.

Frank, T. (1922) *Vergil. A Biography*. New York.

Fraser, T. G. and Jeffery, K. (eds.) (1993) *Men, Women and War*. Dublin.

Frazer, R. M. (1971) 'The κλισμός of Achilles, *Iliad* 24. 596–8', *Greek, Roman and Byzantine Studies* 12.3: 295–301.

Freitag, B. (2013) *Hy Brasil: the Metamorphosis of an Island. From Cartographic Error to Celtic Elysium*. Amsterdam and New York.

Friedlander, B. (2010) 'Radio broadcasts', in Nadel 2010: 115–24.

Friel, B. (1981) *Translations*. London.

Froude, J. A. (1868) *Short Studies on Great Subjects*. London.

Fumerton, P. (2006) *Unsettled: The Culture of Mobility and the Working Poor in Early Modern England*. Chicago.

Furr, L. Reilly (1930) 'The nationality of Vergil', *Classical Journal* 25: 340–6.

Gale, M. R. and Scourfield, D. H. (eds.) (2018) *Texts and Violence in the Roman World*. Cambridge.

Gallagher, J. (ed.) (1945) *Caesar: De Bello Gallico I (1–29) Helvetian War*. Dublin.

Gardner, A. T. (1965) *American Sculpture: A Catalogue of the Collection of the Metropolitan Museum of Art*. New York.

Garrigan Mattar, S. (2004) *Primitivism, Science, and the Irish Revival*. Oxford.

Garrod, H. W. (1912) 'Vergil', in Gordon 1912: 146–66.

Garvin, J. (1973) 'Sweetscented manuscripts', in O'Keeffe 1973: 54–61.

Garvin, T. (2004) *Preventing the Future: Why Ireland was Poor for so Long*. Dublin.

Gathercole, P. (2007) 'Aeschylus, the Blaskets and Marxism: interconnecting influences on the writings of George Thomson', in Luce, Morris, and Souyoudzoglou-Haywood 2007: 43–54.

Genet, J. and Cave, R. A. (eds.) (1991) *Perspectives of Irish Drama and Theatre*. Gerrards Cross.

Geue, T. (2017) *Juvenal and the Poetics of Anonymity*. Cambridge.

Geurst, J. (2010) *Cemeteries of the Great War by Sir Edwin Lutyens*. Rotterdam.

Gibbons, L. (1991) 'Challenging the canon: revisionism and cultural criticism', in Deane 1991: 561–8.

Gleeson, D. T. (2013) *The Green and the Grey. The Irish in the Confederate States of America*. Chapel Hill.

Gleitman, C. (1994) '"Isn't it Just like Real Life?": Frank McGuinness and the (re)writing of stage space', *Canadian Journal of Irish Studies* 20: 60–73.

Gnarra, I. E. (2004), 'Barbara', in Jestice 2004: 106.

Goek, S. (2014) 'The poetics of cultural naturalism: Thomas MacDonagh's *Literature in Ireland* (1916)', *Aigne* 6: 22–36.

Goff, B. (ed.) (2005) *Classics and Colonialism*. London.

Goff, B. (ed.) (2009) *Euripides:* Trojan Women. London.

Goff, B. and Simpson, M. (eds.) (2011) *Thinking the Olympics: The Classical Tradition and the Modern Games*. London.

Gold, B. K. (ed.) (2012) *A Companion to Roman Love Elegy*. Malden and Oxford.

Goldsmith, O. (1769) *The Roman History, from the Foundation of the City of Rome to the Destruction of the Western Empire*, 2 vols. London.

Golway, T. (2015) *Irish rebel: John Devoy and America's Fight for Irish Independence*. Dublin.

Gordon, G. S. (ed.) (1912) *English Literature and the Classics*. Oxford.

Gosden, C. and Marshall, Y. (1999) 'Cultural biography of objects', *World Archaeology* 31: 169–78.

Gould, J. P. (1973) 'Hiketeia', *Journal of Hellenic Studies* 93: 74–103.

Gráinséir, S. (2018) 'Irish legal heritage: marital rape', *Irish Legal News*, 21 September: https://irishlegal.com/article/irish-legal-heritage-marital-rape (accessed 5 December 2019).

Grant, D. (2005) 'Owen McCafferty', in Bull 2005: 151–7.

Grayson, R. S. and McGarry, F. (eds.) (2016) *Remembering 1916: The Easter Rising, the Somme and the Politics of Memory in Ireland*. Cambridge.

Graziosi, B. and Greenwood, E. (eds.) (2007) *Homer in the Twentieth Century: Between World Literature and the Western Canon*. Oxford.

Green, P. (2005) *The Poems of Catullus. A Bilingual Edition*. Berkeley.

Greene, D. (1966) 'Robert Atkinson and Irish studies', *Hermathena* 102: 6–15.

Greer, A. (1999) 'Sir James Craig and the construction of Parliament Buildings at Stormont', *Irish Historical Studies*: May 31: 373–88.

Gregg, S. (2007) *Ismene*. Unpublished script.

Gregory, A. (1920) *Visions and Beliefs in the West of Ireland Collected and Arranged by Lady Gregory: with Two Essays and Notes by W. B. Yeats*. New York and London.

Gregory, J. (1991) *Euripides and the Instruction of the Athenians*. Michigan.

Gregory, J. (2002) 'Euripides as social critic', *Greece & Rome* 49: 145–62.

Gregory, J. (ed.) (2005) *A Companion to Greek Tragedy*. Malden and Oxford.

Grene, N. (1971) *The Synge Manuscripts in the Library of Trinity College, Dublin: A Catalogue Prepared on the Occasion of the Synge Centenary Exhibition 1971*. Dublin.

Grene, N. (1975) *Synge: A Critical Study of the Plays*. London and Basingstoke.

Grene, N. (ed.) (2000) *Interpreting Synge: Essays from the Synge Summer Schoool 1991–2000*. Dublin.

Grene, N. and Morash, C. (eds.) (2016) *The Oxford Handbook of Modern Irish Theatre*. Oxford.

Grethlein, J. (2010) *The Greeks and their Past. Poetry, Oratory and History in the 5th Century BCE*. Cambridge.

Grieve, S. (1923) *The Book of Colonsay and Oronsay*, 2 vols. Edinburgh.

Griffin, D. J. and Pegum, C. (2000) *Leinster House*. Dublin.

Grosjean, P. (1963) 'Virgil of Salzburg', in Ryan 1963: 73–85.

Haddon, A. C. and Browne, C. R. (1891–3) 'The ethnography of the Aran Islands, County Galway', *Proceedings of the Royal Irish Academy* 2: 768–830.

Hall, E. (2008) *The Return of Ulysses: A Cultural History of Homer's* Odyssey. London.

Hall, E. (2010) 'British refractions of the 1857 "mutiny" through the prism of ancient Greece and Rome', in Hall and Vasunia 2010: 33–49.

Hall, E. (2019) 'Paving and pencilling: Heaney's inscriptions in J. W. Mackail's translation of the *Aeneid*', in Harrison, Macintosh, and Eastman 2019: 223–43.

Hall, E. (forthcoming) 'The original Brexit drama: Shakespeare's *Cymbeline*', *Journal of the Historical Association*.

Hall, E. and Stead, H. (2015) 'Introduction', in Stead and Hall 2015: 1–19.

Hall, E. and Stead, H. (2016) 'Between the party and the ivory tower: Classics and Communism in 1930s Britain', in Movrin and Olechowska 2016: 3–31.

Hall, E. and Stead, H. (2020) *A People's History of Classics*. London.

Hall, E. and Vasunia, P. (eds.) (2010) *India, Greece and Rome 1757–2007*. London.

Hardie, P. R. (2014) *The Last Trojan Hero: A Cultural History of Virgil's* Aeneid. London.

Hardie, P. R. (ed.) (2016) *Augustan Poetry and the Irrational*. Oxford.

Hardwick, L. (2002) 'Classical texts in post-colonial literatures: consolation, redress and new beginnings in the work of Derek Walcott and Seamus Heaney', *International Journal of the Classical Tradition* 9.2: 236–56.

Hardwick, L. (2003) *Reception Studies*. Oxford.

Hardwick, L. (2005) 'Reconfiguring classical texts: aspects of the postcolonial condition', in Goff 2005: 107–17.

Hardwick, L. (2016) 'Voices of trauma: remaking Aeschylus' *Agamemnon* in the twentieth century', in Constantinidis 2016: 280–303.

Hardwick, L. and Gillespie, C. (eds.) (2007) *Classics in Post-Colonial Worlds*. Oxford.

Hardwick, L. and Stray, C. (eds.) (2008) *A Companion to Classical Receptions*. Oxford.

Harlos, A., Harlos, N., and Poppe, E. (eds.) (2016) *Adapting Text and Styles in a Celtic Context: Interdisciplinary Perspectives on Processes of Literary Transfer in the Middle Ages; Studies in Honour of Erich Poppe*. Münster.

Harris, J. and Sidwell, K. (eds.) (2009) *Making Ireland Roman: Irish Neo-Latin Writers in the Republic of Letters*. Cork.

Harris, S. C. (2002) *Gender and Modern Irish Drama*. Bloomington.

Harris, S. C. (2009) 'Her blood and her brother: gender and sacrifice in Frank McGuinness' *Carthaginians*', in Boltwood 2009: 111–28.

Harrison, S. J. (2008) 'Virgilian contexts', in Hardwick and Stray 2008: 113–26.

Harrison, S. J. (ed.) (2009) *Living Classics: Greece and Rome in Contemporary Poetry in English*. Oxford.

Harrison, S. J. (2019) 'Heaney as translator: Horace and Virgil', in Harrison, Macintosh, and Eastman 2019: 244–62.

Harrison, S. J. (forthcoming) 'Roman traces: Michael Longley and Latin poetry', in Tyler (forthcoming).

Harrison, S. J., Macintosh, F., and Eastman, H. (eds.) (2019) *Seamus Heaney and the Classics: Bann Valley Muses*. Oxford.

Harvey, B. (1991) 'Changing fortunes on the Aran Islands in the 1890s', *Irish Historical Studies* 27.107: 237–49.

Haughton, H. (2007) *The Poetry of Derek Mahon*. Oxford.

Havel, V. (1990) *Disturbing the Peace: A Conversation with Karel Hvížďala*, trans. P. Wilson. New York.

Haverty, M. (1991) 'The Aran Isles; or a report of the excursion of the Ethnological Section of the British Association from Dublin to the western islands of Aran in September 1857', in B. and R. Ó hEithir 1991: 43–6. 1st publ. 1859.

Hayes, S. (ed., trans.) (1853) *Adventures of Donnchadh Ruadh MacConmara, A Slave of Adversity*. Dublin.

Heaney, S. (1983) 'Forked tongues, céilís and incubators', *Fortnight* 197: 18–21.

Heaney, S. (2002a) *Finders Keepers: Selected Prose 1971–2001*. London.

Heaney, S. (2002b) 'The Struga address and two poems', *Irish Pages* 1 (Inaugural Issue: Belfast in Europe): 114–17.

Heaney, S. (2002c) *A Keen for the Coins*. Hickory.

Heaney, S. (2004) *The Burial at Thebes: A Version of Sophocles' Antigone*. New York.

Heaney, S. (2009) 'Title Deeds: translating a classic', in Harrison 2009: 122–39.

Heaney, S. (2016) Aeneid *Book VI: A New Verse Translation, Bilingual Edition*. New York.

Heavey, M. See Ní Éimhthigh, M.

Henigan, J. (2016) *Literacy and Orality in Eighteen Century Irish Song*. London and New York.

Henry, P. (1951) *An Irish Portrait*. London.

Henry, R. M. (ed., comm.) (1905) *Livy. Book XXVI*. London.

Henry, R. M. (1920) *The Evolution of Sinn Féin*. Dublin and New York.

Henry, R. M. and Dougan, T. W. (eds.) (1934) *Tusculanarum disputationum libri V. Vol. II*. Cambridge.

Herren, M. W. (ed.) (1988) *The Sacred Nectar of the Greeks: The Study of Greek in the West in the Early Middle Ages*. King's College London Medieval Studies 2. London.

Herrero de Jáuregui, M. (2011) 'Priam's catabasis: traces of the epic journey to Hades in *Iliad* 24', *Transactions of the American Philological Association* 141: 37–68.

Heyworth, S., Fowler, P. G., and Harrison, S. J. (eds.) (2007) *Classical Constructions: Papers in Memory of Don Fowler, Classicist and Epicurean*. Oxford.

Higgins, P. (2010) *A Nation of Politicians: Gender, Patriotisms, and Political Culture in Late Eighteenth-Century Ireland*. Madison.

Higgins, R. and Uí Chollatáin, R. (eds.) (2009) *The Life and After-life of P. H. Pearse. Pádraic Mac Piarais: Saol agus Oidhreacht*. Dublin.

Highet, G. (1957) *Poets in a Landscape*. New York.

Hill, J. (1998) *Irish Public Sculpture*. Dublin.

Hillan-King, S. and McMahon, S. (eds.) (1996) *Hope and History: Eyewitness Accounts of Life in Twentieth-century Ulster*. Belfast.

Hillers, B. (1995) 'The odyssey of a folktale: *Merugud Uilix Meic Leirtis*', *Proceedings of the Harvard Celtic Colloquium* 12: 63–79.

Hillers, B. (2003) 'In fer fíamach fírglic: Ulysses in Medieval Irish Literature', *Proceedings of the Harvard Celtic Colloquium* 16: 15–38.

Hingerty, K. (1993) 'Kennelly's vengeance for women', *Cork Examiner*, 14 June: 2.

Hirson, B. (2001) *The Cape Town Intellectuals: Ruth Schechter and her Circle, 1907–1934*. Maitland, Cape Town.

Holdeman, D. and Levitas, B. (eds.) (2010) *W. B. Yeats in Context*. Cambridge and New York.

Holland, K. (2016) 'Marital rape remains extremely difficult to prosecute' *The Irish Times* 26 July: https://www.irishtimes.com/news/social-affairs/marital-rape-remains-extremely-difficult-to-prosecute-1.2734172 (accessed 5 December 2019).

Hooley, D. (1988) *The Classics in Paraphrase: Ezra Pound and Modern Translators of Latin Poetry*. Selinsgrove.

Hopper, K. (2009) *Flann O'Brien: A Portrait of the Artist as a Young Post–modernist*, 2nd edn. Cork.

Horner, W. B. (1993) *Nineteenth Century Scottish Rhetoric. The American Connection*. Carbondale.

Hoskins, J. (2006) 'Agency, biography and objects', in Tilley, Keane, Küchler, Rowlands, and Spyer 2006: 74–84.

Houlbrook, C. (2018) *The Magic of Coin-Trees from Religion to Recreation: The Roots of a Ritual*. New York.

Howe, K. R. (2000) *Nature, Culture, and History: The 'Knowing' of Oceania*. Honolulu.

Hubbard, M. (1974) *Propertius*. London.

Huber, W., Fagan, P., and Borg, R. (eds.) (2014) *Flann O'Brien: Contesting Legacies*. Cork.

Hughes, B. (ed.) (2016) *Eoin MacNeill: Memoir of a Revolutionary Scholar*. Dublin.

Hume, D. H. (1996) 'Empire Day in Ireland, 1896–1962', in Jeffery 1996: 149–68.

Hunt, H. (1979) *Abbey Theatre*. New York.

Hussey, C. (1950) *The Life of Sir Edwin Lutyens*. London.

Hutchinson, J. (1987) *The Dynamics of Cultural Nationalism. The Gaelic Revival and the Creation of the Irish Nation State*. London.

Hyde, D. (1903) *Songs Ascribed to Raftery*. Dublin.

Impens, F. (2017) ' "Help me please my hedge-school master": Virgilian presences in the work of Seamus Heaney', *Irish University Review* 47.2: 251–65.

Impens, F. (2018) *Classical Presences in Irish Poetry After 1960: The Answering Voice*. London.

Irwin, L. (ed.) (1998) *Explorations: Centenary Essays*. Limerick.

Jacques [pseudonym for John Rice] (1920) 'Two plays at the Abbey: old Greek and modern Russian', *Irish Independent*, 8 March: 4.

James, C. L. R. (2001) *The Black Jacobins: Toussaint L'Ouverture and the San Domingo Revolution*. London.

Janan, M. (2001) *The Politics of Desire: Propertius IV*. Berkeley.

Jarman, N. (1997) *Material Conflicts: Parades and Visual Displays in Northern Ireland*. Oxford.

Jarman, N. and Bryan, D. (1998) *From Riots to Rights: Nationalist Parades in the North of Ireland*. Belfast.

Jebb, R. C. (1887a) *The Oedipus Tyrannus of Sophocles As Performed at Cambridge November 22–26, 1887*. Cambridge.

Jebb, R. C. (1887b) *The Oedipus Tyrannus of Sophocles As Performed at Cambridge November 22–26, 1887*. Cambridge, with annotations by W. B. Yeats. National Library of Ireland MS 40,568/224.

Jeffery, K. (1993) 'The Great War in modern Irish history', in Fraser and Jeffery 1993: 136–57.

Jeffery, K. (ed.) (1996) *An Irish Empire? Aspects of Ireland and the British Empire*. Manchester.

Jeffery, K. (2000) *Ireland and the Great War*. Cambridge.

Jenkins, I. (1983) 'Is there life after marriage? A study of the abduction motif in vase paintings of the Athenian wedding ceremony', *Bulletin of the Institute of Classical Studies* 30: 137–45.

Jenkinson, B. (2008) *An tAthair Pádraig Ó Duinnín—Bleachtaire*. Dublin.

Jenkinson, B. (2011) *Duinnín Bleachtaire ar an Sceilg*. Dublin.

Jestice, P. G. (ed.) (2004) *Holy People of the World. A Cross-Cultural Encyclopaedia*. Vol. 1. Santa Barbara.

Johnson, C. (ed.) (2000) *The Collected Works of W. B. Yeats: Vol. X: Later Articles and Reviews*. New York.

Jones, R. C. (1997) '"Talking amongst ourselves": language, politics and Sophocles on the Field Day stage', *International Journal of the Classical Tradition* 4.2: 232–46.

Jordan, A. J. (2000) *The Yeats-Gonne-MacBride Triangle*. Westport.

Joy, J. (2009) 'Reinvigorating object biography: reproducing the drama of object lives', *World Archaeology* 41: 540–56

Joyce, J. (1914) *Dubliners*. London.

Joyce, J. (1959) 'Oscar Wilde: the poet of Salome', repr. in Mason and Ellmann 1959: 201–5. 1st publ. 1909.

Joyce, J. (1992) *A Portrait of the Artist as a Young Man*, ed. Seamus Deane. London. 1st edn. 1916.

Joyce, J. (1992) *Ulysses*, with an introduction by Declan Kiberd. London. 1st edn. 1922.

Joyce, P. W. (1910) *English as we speak it in Ireland*. Dublin.

Kaiser, B. M. (ed.) (2015) *Singularity and Transnational Poetics*. London.

Kakridis, J. Th. (1949) *Homeric Researches*. Lund.

Kane, R. J., Betham, W., and Downes, G. (1836–40) 'June 11, 1838', *Proceedings of the Royal Irish Academy* 1: 193–205.

Kanigel, R. (2012) *On an Irish Island*. New York.

Kearney, R. (1985) 'Myth and motherland', in Deane, Heaney, Kearney, Kiberd, Paulin, and Donoghue 1985: 61–80.

Keaveney, A. (1999) 'Classics in Victorian Galway', in Foley 1999: 326–43.

Keith, A. (2008) *Propertius: Poet of Love and Leisure*. London.

Kelly, Aaron (2008) *Twentieth-Century Irish Literature*. London.

Kelly, Adrian (2002) *Compulsory Irish: Language and Education in Ireland 1870s–1970s*. Dublin.

Kelly, F. (2016) 'Enda Kenny urges politicians to follow example of 1916 rebels', *The Irish Times*, 26 March: https://www.irishtimes.com/news/politics/enda-kenny-urges-politicians-to-follow-example-of-1916-rebels-1.2587595 (accessed 10 May 2019).

Kelly, J. and Schuchard, R. (eds.) (1994) *The Collected Letters of W. B. Yeats. Volume III. 1901–1904*. Oxford.

Kelly, W. K. (ed.) (1854) *Erotica. The Elegies of Propertius, the Satyricon of Petronius Arbiter, and the Kisses of Johannes Secundus. Literally translated, and accompanied by poetical versions from various sources. To which are added, the Love Epistles of Aristaenetus. Translated by R. Brinsley Sheridan and Mr. Halhed*. London.

Kelsall, M. (1975) 'Synge in Aran', *Irish University Review* 5.2: 254–70.

Kendell, T. (ed.) (2009) *The Oxford Handbook of British and Irish War Poetry*. Oxford.

Kenna, S. (2014) *16 Lives. Thomas MacDonagh*. Dublin.

Kenneally, M. (ed.) (1988) *Cultural Contexts and Literary Idioms in Contemporary Irish Literature*. Gerrards Cross.

Kennedy, B. (1989–90) 'Paul Henry: an Irish portrait', *The GPA Irish Arts Review Yearbook*: 43–54.

Kennedy, J. and Wheeler, G. (1999) *Parliament Buildings, Stormont: The Building, its Setting, Uses and Restoration, 1922–1998*. Belfast.

Kennedy-Andrews, E. (2000) 'Conflict, violence and "the fundamental interrelatedness of all things"', in Peacock and Devine 2000: 73–99.

Kennelly, B. (2006) *When Then is Now: Three Greek Tragedies*. Tarset.

Kenny, P. (2004–5) 'Manuscript material from the library of W. B. Yeats and George Yeats', National Library of Ireland, Collection List No. 96: Dublin.

Keymer, T. (2014) 'Novel designs: manipulating the page in English fiction, 1660–1780', in Parrinder, Nash, and Wilson 2014: 17–49.

Kiberd, D. (1979) 'Writers in quarantine? The case for Irish studies', *The Crane Bag* 3.1: 9–21.

Kiberd, D. (ed.) (1992) *James Joyce, Ulysses: Annotated Student's Edition*. London.

Kiberd, D. (1993) *Synge and the Irish Language*, 2nd edn. London.

Kiberd, D. (1995) *Inventing Ireland. The Literature of the Modern Nation*. Cambridge MA.

Kiberd, D. (2000a) *Irish Classics*. London.

Kiberd, D. (2000b) 'Synge's *Tristes Tropiques*: the Aran Islands', in Grene 2000: 82–110.

Kiberd, D. (2005) 'Thomas MacDonagh (1878–1916)', in Roche 2005b: 29–37.

Kiberd, D. (2009) 'Patrick Pearse: Irish modernist', in Higgins and Uí Chollatáin 2009: 65–80.

Kiberd, D. and Mathews, P. J. (eds.) (2015) *A Handbook of the Irish Revival. An Anthology of Cultural and Political Writings 1891–1922*. Dublin.

Kilmer, J. (1916) 'Poets marched in the van of Irish revolt', *New York Times Magazine*, 7 May: 3–4.

King, L. and Sisson, E. (eds.) (2011) *Ireland, Design and Visual Culture: Negotiating Modernity 1922–1992*. Cork.

Kirkpatrick, K. and Farago, B. (eds.) (2016) *Animals in Irish Literature and Culture*. New York.

Knatchbull, T. (2009) *From a Clear Blue Sky*. London.

Knight, D. R. and Sabey, A. D. (1984) *The Lion Roars At Wembley. The British Empire Exhibition 1924–1925*. London.

Kopytoff, I. (1986) 'The cultural biography of things: commoditization as process', in Appadurai 1986: 64–91.

Korff, A. (1994) 'The artist's eye', in Waddell, O'Connell, and Korff 1994: 269–88.

Krappe, A. H. (1941) 'Irish earth', *Folklore* 52.3: 229–36.

Lalor, J. F. (1895) *The Writings of James Fintan Lalor*. Dublin.

Larmour, D. (2016) *The Arena of Satire: Juvenal's Search for Rome*. Norman.

Larmour, G. (2016) *They Killed the Ice Cream Man*. Newtownards.

Larmour, P. (1987) *Belfast: An Illustrated Architectural Guide*. Belfast.

Latham, S. (ed.) (2010) *James Joyce*. Dublin and Portland.

Lawless, E. (1897) *Grania: The Story of an Island*, 2nd edn. London.

Lawless, E. (1899) 'Leaves from a diary', *The Nineteenth Century* 46.272: 603–12.

Lawson, J. (1758) *Lectures Concerning Oratory*. Dublin.

Leaf, W. (ed.) (1900–2) *The* Iliad, 2 vols. London.

Leaney E. and Lunney, L. (2009) 'Dillon, Thomas Patrick', in McGuire and Quinn 2009: http://dib.cambridge.org/viewReadPage.do?articleId=a2620 (accessed 5 December 2019).

Leerssen, J. (1986) *Mere Irish and Fíor-Ghael: Studies in the Idea of Irish Nationality, its Development and Literary Expression Prior to the Nineteenth Century*. Amsterdam.

Leerssen, J. (1996) *Remembrance and Imagination: Patterns in the Historical and Literary Representation of Ireland in the Nineteenth Century*. Cork.

Lehman, A. C. (1940) *The Flahertys of Aran*. London.

Leland, T. (1764) *A Dissertation on the Principles of Human Eloquence*. Dublin.

Lennon, J. (2008) *Irish Orientalism: A Literary and Intellectual History*. Syracuse.

Levi-Strauss, C. (1963) *Totemism*, trans. R. Needham. London.

Liebregts, P. (1993) *Centaurs in the Twilight: W. B. Yeat's Use of the Classical Tradition*. Amsterdam.

Liebregts, P. (2010) 'The Classics', in Nadel 2010: 171–80.

Lloyd, M. (2004) 'The politeness of Achilles: off-record conversation strategies in Homer and the meaning of "*Kertomia*"', *Journal of Hellenic Studies* 124: 75–89.

Lloyd, M. (2011) 'Playboy of the ancient world? Synge and the Classics', *Classics Ireland* 18: 52–68.

Lohmann, D. (1970) *Die Komposition der Reden in der Ilias*. Untersuchungen zur Antiken Literatur und Geschichte, eds. H. Dörrie and P. Moraux. Berlin.

Lojek, H. H. (2004) *Contexts for Frank McGuinness' Drama*. Washington DC.

Long, M. (2014) *Assembling Flann O'Brien*. London.

Long, M. (2015) 'Absolute nonabsolute singularity: Jacques Derrida, Myles na gCopaleen and fragmentation', in Kaiser 2015: 95–114.

Long, M. (ed.) (2018) *The Collected Letters of Flann O'Brien*. Victoria TX.

Longley, E. (1986) *Poetry in the Wars*. Newcastle upon Tyne.

Longley, M. (1969) 'Strife and the Ulster poet', *Hibernia* 33/21: 11.

Longley, M. (ed.) (1971a) *Causeway: The Arts in Ulster*. Belfast and Dublin.

Longley, M. (1971b) 'Introduction', in Longley 1971a: 7–9.

Longley, M. (1979) *The Echo Gate*. London.

Longley, M. (1991) *Gorse Fires*. London.

Longley, M. (1994) 'The empty holes of spring: some reminiscences of Trinity & two poems addressed to Derek Mahon', *Irish University Review* 24.1: 51–7.

Longley, M. (1995a) 'Memory and acknowledgement', *Irish Review* 17–18: 153–9.

Longley, M. (1995b) *The Ghost Orchid*. London.

Longley, M. (1997) 'Two Peace Poems and a few thoughts about them', *Assoçião Brasileira de Estudos Irlandeses* 11–12: 1.

Longley, M. (2000) *The Weather in Japan*. London.

Longley, M. (2004) 'An interview with Margaret Mills Harper', *Five Points* 8: 56–7. http://www.webdelsol.com/Five_Points/issues/v8n3/ml.htm (accessed 5 December 2019).

Longley, M. (2006) *Collected Poems*. London.

Longley, M. (2009) 'Lapsed classicist', in Harrison 2009: 97–113.

Longley, M. (2015) *One Wide Expanse: Writings from the Ireland Chair of Poetry*. Dublin.

Longley, M. (2017) *Sidelines: Selected Prose 1962–2015*. London.

Loraux N. (1986) *The Invention of Athens. The Funeral Oration in the Classical City*. Cambridge MA.

Lotringer, S. (1999) *More & Less*, trans. Y. Shafir. Cambridge MA.

Loxley, D. (1990) *Problematic Shores: The Literature of Islands*. Basingstoke.

Luce, J. V. (1969) 'Homeric qualities in the life and literature of the Great Blasket Island', *Greece & Rome* 16.2: 151–68.

Luce, J. V., Morris, C., and Souyoudzoglou-Haywood, C. (2007) *The Lure of Greece: Irish Involvement in Greek Culture, Literature, History and Politics*. Dublin.

Lynam, E. W. (1914) 'The O'Flaherty country', *Studies: An Irish Quarterly Review* 3.10: 13–40.

Lynch, P. J. (1899) 'Caherconree, County Kerry', *Journal of the Royal Society of Antiquaries of Ireland* 9.1: 5–17.

Lynd, R. (1912) *Rambles in Ireland*. London.

Lyne, R. O. A. M. (1987) *Further Voices in Vergil's Aeneid*. Oxford.

Lysaght, P. (2009) 'Thomson, George Derwent (Seoirse Mac Tomáis)', in McGuire and Quinn 2009: http://dib.cambridge.org/viewReadPage.do?articleId=a8537 (accessed 5 December 2019).

Macalister, R. A. S. (1921) *Ireland in Pre-Celtic Times*. Dublin.

Macalister, R. A. S. (1928) *The Archaeology of Ireland*. London.

Macalister, R. A. S. (ed., trans.) (1941) *Lebor Gabála Érenn: The Book of the Taking of Ireland. Volume Four*. Dublin.

Macalister, R. A. S. and MacNeill, J. (eds.) (1916) *Leabhar Gabhála: The Book of the Conquests of Ireland: The Recension of Micheál O'Cléirigh. Part 1*. Dublin.

Mac Amhlaigh, L. (2008) *Foclóirí agus Foclóirithe na Gaeilge*. Dublin.

Mac Annraoi, R. (ed.) (2016) *An Cogadh Mór. Altanna as an* Leader *le 1914–19. Pádraig Ó Duinnín*. Dublin.

Mac Aonghusa, P. (1999) 'Comhra ar bharr aill Dhún Chaoin', in Ó hUiginn and Mac Cóil 1999: 99–123.

MacBain, A. (1885) *Celtic Mythology and Religion*. Inverness.

Mac Cárthaigh, E. (2009) 'Dinneen, Patrick Stephen (Ó Duinnín, Pádraig Stiabhna)', *Dictionary of Irish Biography*. Vol. III D–F. Cambridge: 328–30.

Mac Cóil, L. (2003) 'Irish: one of the languages of the world', in Cronin and Ó Cuilleanáin 2003: 127–47.

Mac Conghail, M. (1987) *The Blaskets: A Kerry Island Library*. Dublin.

Mac Conghail, M. (2009) *Aghaidheanna Fidil agus Púicíní: Seoirse Mac Tomáis in Éirinn 1923–1934*. Dublin.

MacDiarmid, L. (2005) *The Irish Art of Controversy*. Dublin.

MacDonagh, T. (1902) *Through the Ivory Gate*. Dublin.

MacDonagh, T. (1906) *The Golden Joy*. Dublin.

MacDonagh, T. (1911) 'Ancient Irish poetry', *Irish Review* 1.2: 84–7.

MacDonagh, T. (1913a) *Lyrical Poems*. Dublin.

MacDonagh, T. (1913b) *Thomas Campion and the Art of English Poetry*. Dublin.

MacDonagh, T. (1914) 'Antigone and Lir', *Irish Review* 4.37: 29–32.

MacDonagh, T. (1916) *Literature in Ireland: Studies Irish and Anglo-Irish*. Dublin.

MacDonough, P.J. (1904) 'Ireland's poet and dramatist visits Notre Dame', *Notre Dame Scholastic* 37: 276.

Mac Góráin, F. (2013) 'The Shepherd's Jubilee: a Dublin eclogue from 1701', *Vergilius* 59: 81–110.

MacGregor, A. A. (1972) *An Island Here and There*. Bath.

Macintosh, F. (1994) *Dying Acts: Death in Ancient Greek and Modern Irish Tragic Drama*. Cork.

Macintosh, F. (2005) 'Conquering England: Ireland and Greek tragedy', in van Zyl Smit 2005: 323–36.

Macintosh, F. (2008) 'An Oedipus for our times? Yeats's version of Sophocles' *Oedipus Tyrannus*', in Revermann and Wilson 2008: 524–47.

Macintosh, F. (2011) 'Irish *Antigone* and burying the dead', in Mee and Foley 2008: 90–103.

Macintosh, F. (2016) 'Writing a new Irish *Odyssey*: Theresa Kishkan's *A Man in a Distant Field*', in McConnell and Hall 2016: 123–33.

Mackail, J. W. (1896) *Latin Literature*. London.

Mac Laghmhainn, S. [G. Thomson] (1929) *Breith Bháis ar Eagnuidhe: Trí Cómhráidhte d'ár Cheap Platón (Apologia, Critón, Phaedon)*. Dublin.

Macleod, C. W. (ed.) (1982) *Homer,* Iliad *Book XXIV*. Cambridge.

MacLochlainn, A. (2002) 'Father Dinneen and his dictionary', *Studies: An Irish Quarterly Review* 91: 68–77.

Mac Mathúna, S. (2008) 'National University of Ireland, Galway', in Dunne, Coolahan, Manning, and Ó Tuathaigh 2008: 63–86.

Mac Mathúna, S. and Ó Corráin, A. (eds.) (2007) *Celtic Literatures in the Twentieth Century*. Moscow.

MacNeice, L. (1949) *Holes in the Sky: Poems 1944–1947*. New York.

MacNeice, L. (2007) *The Strings are False: An Unfinished Autobiography*, 2nd edn., with an introduction by D. Mahon. London.

MacNeice, L. (2010) *Letters*, ed. J. Allison. London.

MacNeill, E. (1911–15) 'Clare Island survey: place-names and family names', *Proceedings of the Royal Irish Academy. Section B: Biological, Geological, and Chemical Science* 31: 1–42.

MacNeill, E. (1919) *Phases of Irish History*. Dublin.

MacNeill, E. (1935) *Early Irish Laws and Institutions*. Dublin.

MacNeill, E. (1981) *Celtic Ireland*, introduction with new notes by D. Ó Corráin. Dublin. 1st edn. 1921.

Mac Philibín, L. (1942) *P. Vergili Maronis. Aeinéid. Leabhar II*. Dublin.

Mac Tomáis, S. *See* Thomson, G.

Mahaffy, J. P. (1874) *Social Life in Greece: From Homer to Menander*. London.

Mahaffy, J. P. (1875) *Social Life in Greece: From Homer to Menander*. 2nd edn., revised and enlarged. London.

Mahaffy, J. P. (1912–13) 'On the origins of learned academies in modern Europe. An address delivered to the Academy, November 30, 1912', *Proceedings of the Royal Irish Academy* 30: 429–44.

Mahon, D. (1972) *Lives*. London.

Mahon, D. (1999) *Collected Poems*. Oldcastle.

Mahon, D. (2009) *Sextus and Cynthia. After Sextus Propertius, c. 50–c. 16 BC*, with drawings by Hammond Journeaux. Oldcastle.

Mahon, D. (2011) *Raw Material*. Oldcastle.

Mantena, R. S. (2010) 'Imperial ideology and the uses of Rome in discourses on Britain's Indian Empire', in Bradley 2010: 54–73.

Marcus, P. L. (1970) 'Old Irish myth and modern Irish literature', *Irish University Review* 1.1: 67–85.

Martel, E.-A. (1897) *Irlande et Cavernes Anglaises*. Paris.

Martin, A. (2016) 'Easter Rising commemorations in the early Irish State', *History Ireland* 24.2: 42–4.

Martin, C. P. (1935) *Prehistoric Man in Ireland*. London.

Martin, F. X. (1967) '1916: myth, fact, and mystery', *Studia Hibernica* 7: 7–126.

Martin F. X. and Byrne, F. J. (eds.) (1973) *The Scholar Revolutionary: Eoin MacNeill, 1867–1945, and the Making of the New Ireland*. Shannon.

Martin, M. (1703) *A Description of the Western Islands of Scotland*. London.

Martin, R. P. (1989) *The Language of Heroes: Speech and Performance in the* Iliad. Ithaca NY.

Martin, R. P. (2007) 'Homer among the Irish: Yeats, Synge, Thomson', in Graziosi and Greenwood 2007: 75–91.

Martindale, C. and Thomas, R. F. (eds.) (2006) *Classics and the Uses of Reception*. Oxford.

Mason, E. and Ellmann, R. (eds.) (1964) *The Critical Writings of James Joyce*. New York.

Mason, T. H. (1950) *The Islands of Ireland: Their Scenery, People, Life and Antiquities*, 3rd edn. London. 1st edn. 1936.

Mathews, A. C. (2007) 'Essays and poems', *Irish Pages* 4.2: 43–71.

Maume, P. (1995) *D. P. Moran*. Dublin.

Maume, P. (1999) *The Long Gestation: Irish Nationalist Life 1891–1918*. Dublin.

Maume, P. (2009) 'Rice (Ryce), John ("Jacques")', in McGuire and Quinn 2009: http://dib. cambridge.org/viewReadPage.do?articleId=a7654 (accessed 24 March 2016).

Maxwell, J. (2000) 'Bank holiday Monday', in *An Crann/The Tree* 2000: 132–3.

McBride, I. (ed.) (2001a) *History and Memory in Modern Ireland*. Cambridge.

McBride, I. (2001b) 'Introduction', in McBride 2001a: 1–42.

McBride, L. W. (ed.) (1999) *Images, Icons and the Irish Nationalist Imagination*. Dublin.

McBryde, M. (1998) *The Irish Wolfhound: Symbol of Celtic Splendor*. Dorking.

McCafferty, O. (2008) *Antigone By Sophocles: In a version by Owen McCafferty*. London.

McCall, P. (1894) *In the Shadow of St. Patrick's*. Dublin.

McCarthy, J. (1903) *Ireland and her Story*. New York.

McCarthy, M. (ed.) (2004) *Ireland's Heritage: Critical Perspectives on Memory and Identity*. Aldershot.

McCauley, L. T. (1972) 'Summary of the proceedings of the Committee', in W. B. Yeats, *Coinage of Saorstát Éireann, 1928* (Dublin, 1928), repr. in Cleeve 1972: 25–39.

McCone, K. (1990) *Pagan Past and Christian Present in Early Irish Literature*. Maynooth.

McConnell, J. and Hall, E. (eds.) (2016) *Ancient Greek Myth in World Fiction since 1989*. London.

McCormack, W. J. (2005) *Blood Kindred: W. B. Yeats: The Life, the Death, the Politics*. London.

McCourt, J. (2014) 'Myles na gCopaleen: a portrait of the artist as a Joyce scholar', in Huber, Fagan, and Borg 2014: 110–25.

McDonagh, M. (2001) *The Lieutenant of Inishmore*. London

McDonagh, T. (1916) *Literature in Ireland. Studies Irish and Anglo-Irish*. Dublin.

McDonald, M. (1996) 'Seamus Heaney's *Cure at Troy*: politics and poetry', *Classics Ireland* 3: 129–40.

McDonald, M. and Walton, J. M. (eds.) (2002) *Amid Our Troubles: Irish Versions of Greek Tragedy*. London.

McDonald, P. (1998–9) 'An interview with Michael Longley', *Thumbscrew* 12.

McDonald, P. (2000) 'Lapsed classics: Homer, Ovid, and Michael Longley's poetry', in Peacock and Devine 2000: 33–50.

McDonald, P. (2019) "'Weird brightness' and the riverbank: Seamus Heaney, Virgil, and the need for translation', in Harrison, Macintosh, and Eastman 2019: 160–79.

McElduff, S. (2006) 'Fractured understandings: towards a history of classical reception among non–elite groups', in Martindale and Thomas 2006: 180–91.

McElduff, S. (2011) 'Not as Virgil has it: parodying the *Aeneid* in 18th century Ireland', *International Journal of the Classical Tradition* 18: 226–45.

McElduff, S. (2014) 'Irish literature', in Thomas and Ziolkowski 2014: I.668–9.

McGarry, F. (2010) *The Rising: Ireland Easter 1916*. Oxford.

McGarry, F. (2016) *The Abbey Theatre Rebels of 1916: A Lost Revolution*. Dublin.

McGarry, K., Redmill, D., Edwards, M., Byrne, A., Brady, A., and Taylor, M. (2017) 'Punishment attacks in post-ceasefire Northern Ireland: an emergency department perspective', *Ulster Medical Journal* 86.2: 90–3.

McGarry, P. (1993) '"Women" a little too static', *Irish Press*, 3 June: 13.

McGuinne, D. (2010) *Irish Type Design: A History of Printing Types in the Irish Character*. 2nd edn., with a foreword by H. D. L. Vervliet. Dublin.

McGuinness, F. (1988) Carthaginians *and* Baglady. London.

McGuinness, F. (1996) *Plays 1*. London.

McGuinness, P. (ed.) (2000) *Symbolism, Decadence and the* Fin de siècle: *French and European Perspectives*. Exeter.

McGuire, J. and Quinn, J. (eds.) (2009) *Dictionary of Irish Biography*. Cambridge.

McKay, S. (2008) *Bear in Mind These Dead*. London.

McKay, S. (2016) 'Soldier dolls in Belfast' [Diary], *London Review of Books* 38.8: 38–9.

McKenna, B. (2015–16) '"The Silent Ambassadors": Yeats, Irish coinage and the aesthetics of a national material culture', *Yeats Eliot Review* 31: 21–38.

McKittrick, D., Kelters, S., Feeney, B., and Thornton, C. (2007) *Lost Lives: The Stories of the Men, Women, and Children who Died as a Result of the Northern Ireland Troubles*. Edinburgh and London.

McMahon, T. G. (2008) *Grand Opportunity. The Gaelic Revival and Irish Society, 1893–1910*. Syracuse NY.

McNeillie, A. (2001) *An Aran Keening*. Dublin.

McNeillie, A. (2014) 'The Dublin end: anecdotes of Brendan Behan on Árainn', *Irish University Review* 44.1: 59–77.

M.D. [= Myles Dillon?] (1929), '[Review of] *Oidiopus i gColón*', *Studies: An Irish Quarterly Review* 18/71: 531.

Mee, E. B. and Foley, H. P. (eds.) (2011) *Antigone on the Contemporary World Stage*. Oxford.

Mesev, V., Downs, J., Binns, A., Courtney, R. S., and Shirlow, W. (2008) 'Measuring and mapping conflict-related deaths and segregation: lessons from the Belfast "Troubles"', in Sui 2008: 83–101.

Mesev, V., Shirlow, P., and Downs, J. (2009) 'The geography of conflict and death in Belfast, Northern Ireland', *Geographies of Peace and Armed Conflict/Annals of the Association of American Geographers* 99.5: 893–903.

Messenger, J. (1964) 'Literary vs. scientific interpretations of cultural reality in the Aran Islands of Eire', *Ethnohistory* 11.1: 41–55.

Meyer, K. (ed., trans., comm.) (1886) *Meregud Uilix Maicc Leirtis: The Irish* Odyssey. London.

Meyer, K. (1895–7) *The Voyage of Bran, son of Febal, to the Land of the Living*, with an essay by Alfred Nutt, 2 vols. London.

Meyer, K. (1999) *Meregud Uilix Maicc Leirtis; The Wandering of Ulixes Son of Laertes*. Cambridge ON, available online at http://www.yorku.ca/inpar/ulixes_meyer.pdf (accessed 5 December 2019). 1st publ. 1886.

Meyer, R. T. (1952) 'The Middle Irish *Odyssey*: folktale, fiction or saga?', *Modern Philology* 50: 73–8.

Meyer, R. T. (1961) 'The Middle-Irish *Odyssey* and Celtic folktale', *Papers of the Michigan Academy of Science, Arts and Letters* 46: 553–61.

Mhac an tSaoi, M. (1990) 'Brollach', in Ó Coigligh 1990: vi–vii.

Mhac an tSaoi, M. (1993) 'Pádraig de Brún agus an Ghaeilge: Saol agus saothar in aisce?', in Ó Fiannachta 1993: 140–60.

Michael, T. and Judkins, M. (2016) *2017 Standard Catalog of World Coins, 1901–2000*. Iola.

Miles, B. (2011) *Heroic Saga and Classical Epic in Medieval Ireland*. Cambridge.

Millar, F. (1993) *The Roman Near East, 31 B.C.–A.D. 337*. Cambridge MA.

Mills, S. (1997) *Theseus, Tragedy and the Athenian Empire*. Oxford.

Mohr, T. (2015) 'The political significance of the coinage of the Irish Free State', *Irish Studies Review* 23: 451–79.

Mommsen, T. (1866) *The History of Rome*. Vol. IV, trans. W. P. Dickson. London.

Moran, D. P. (2006) *The Philosophy of Irish Ireland*. Reprinted with Introduction by Patrick Maume. Dublin. 1st edn. 1905.

Moran, J. (2017) 'Class during the Irish Revolution: British Soldiers, 1916 and the Abject Body', in Pierse 2017: 153–67.

Moran, P. (2015a) 'Greek dialectology and the Irish origin story', in Moran and Warntjes 2015b: 481–512.

Moran, P. and Warntjes, I. (eds.) (2015b) *Early Medieval Ireland and Europe: Chronology, Contacts, Scholarship. Festschrift for Dáibhí Ó Cróinín*. Studia Traditionis Theologiae 14. Turnhout.

Morash, C. (1997) 'Augustine... O'Brien... Vico... Joyce', in Clune and Hurson 1997: 133–42.

Morgan, A. (1988) *James Connolly: A Political Biography*. Manchester.

Morris, E. (2004) 'Devilish devices or farmyard friends? The Free State coinage debate', *History Ireland* 12: 24–8.

Morris, E. (2005) *Our Own Devices. National Symbols and Political Conflict in Twentieth-Century Ireland*. Dublin.

Mossman, J. (2005) 'Women's voices', in Gregory 2005: 352–65.

Mould, D. D. C. Pochin (1972) *The Aran Islands*. Newton Abbot.

Moulden, J. (2006) *The Printed Ballad in Ireland: Guide to the Popular Printing of Songs in Ireland 1760–1920*. Diss. Galway.

Movrin, D. and Olechowska, E. (eds.) (2016) *Classics and Class: Greek and Latin Classics and Communism at School*. Warsaw and Ljubljana.

Mullen, P. (1934) *Man of Aran*. London.

Müller, N. (1999) 'Kodewechsel in der irischen Übersetzungsliteratur: exempla et desiderata', in Poppe and Tristram 1999: 73–86.

Murphet, J., McDonald, R., and Morrell, S. (eds.) (2014) *Flann O'Brien and Modernism*. London.

Murphy, A. (2017) *Ireland, Reading and Cultural Nationalism, 1790–1930: Bringing the Nation to Book*. Cambridge.

Murphy, P. (2010) *Nineteenth-Century Irish Sculpture: Native Genius Reaffirmed*. New Haven and London.

Murphy, R. E. (1996) 'W. B. Yeats, the Christ Pantokrator, and the Soul's History (The Photographic Record)', *Yeats: An Annual of Critical and Textual Studies* XIV: 69–117.

Murray, C. (1991) 'Three Irish *Antigones*', in Genet and Cave 1991: 115–29.

Murray, C. (ed.) (1999) *Brian Friel. Essays, Diaries, Interviews: 1964–1999*. London and New York.

Murray, D. (2016) 'Padraic Colum: patriot propagandist for the poets' revolution', *Éire- Ireland* 51.3–4: 104–23.

Murray, G. (2006) *The Trojan Women of Euripides*. Stilwell.

Nadel, I. B. (ed.) (2010) *The Cambridge Companion to Ezra Pound*. Cambridge.

Nagy, G. (2010) 'Ancient Greek elegy', in Weisman 2010: 13–45.

Naiden, F. S. (2006) *Ancient Supplication*. Oxford.

National University of Ireland (2008) *A Century of Scholarship: Travelling Students of the National University of Ireland*. Dublin.

Naughton, A. (2011) '*Nádúir-Fhilíocht na Gaedhilge* and Flann O'Brien's Fiction', in Baines 2011: 83–97.

Naughton, A. (2013) 'More of your fancy kiss-my-hand': a further note on Flann O'Brien's *Nádúir-Fhilíocht na Gaedhilge*', *Parish Review* 1: 15–30.

Neilands, C. (1991) 'Irish broadside ballads: performers and performances', *Folk Music Journal* 6: 209–22.

Neill, W. J. V. (1998) 'Place visions and representational landscapes: "reading" Stormont in Belfast and the Palast der Republic in Berlin', *Planning, Practice and Research* 13. 4:1–16.

Newell, K. B. (2011) *New Conservative Explications. Reasoning with Some Classic English Poems*. Cambridge.

Newman, S. (1998) 'Seoirse Mac Tomáis agus Ollscoil na nDaoine', in Irwin 1998: 318–32.

Nic Congáil, R. (ed.) (2012) *Codladh Céad Bliain: Cnuasach Aistí ar Litríocht na nÓg*. Dublin.

Nice, L. (2005) *Place and Memory in the Poetry of Michael Longley and Seamus Heaney*. Diss. York.

NicGhabhann, N. (2015) *Medieval Ecclesiastical Buildings in Ireland, 1789–1915*. Dublin.

Ní Chéilleachair, M. (ed.) (2000) *Seoirse Mac Tomáis, 1903–1987*, Ceiliúradh an Bhlascaoid 4. Dublin.

Ní Dhomhnaill, N. (1999) 'Tidal Surge 1990–1999', in Duffy and Dorgan 1999: 219–25.

Ní Éimhthigh [Heavey], M. (1940) *Caesar: De Bello Gallico II*. Dublin.

Ní Éimhthigh [Heavey], M. (1941) *Bun Chúrsa Ceapadóireachta Gréigise*. Dublin.

Ní Éimhthigh [Heavey], M. (1942) *Graiméar Gréigise. Cuid 1: Deilbh-eolaidheacht. Cuid 2: Coimhréir*, 2 vols. Dublin.

Ní Éimhthigh [Heavey], M. (1955) 'Leacht na bhFáltach i mBaile Átha na Ríogh', *Galvia: Irisleabhar Chumann Seandáluíochta is Staire na Gaillimhe* 2: 4–6.

Ní Éimhthigh, M. and Seán Seártan (1947) *Prós-cheapadóireacht Laidne .i. 'Bradley's Arnold'*. Dublin.

Ní Mhurchú, S. and Kelly, P. (2002) 'Translations into Irish of Greek drama and other works concerning Greece', in McDonald and Walton 2002: 87–100.

Ní Shéaghdha, N. (1989) 'Irish scholars and scribes in eighteenth-century Dublin', *Eighteenth-Century Ireland* 4: 41–54.

Noble, G., Poller, T., Raven, J., and Verrill, L. (eds.) (2007) *Scottish Odysseys: Archaeology of Islands*. Stroud.

Norris, D. (2012) *A Kick against the Pricks*. Dublin.

Norris, M. (1998) 'A walk on the Wild(e) side', in Valente 1998: 19–33.

Norstedt, J. A. (1980) *Thomas MacDonagh. A Critical Biography*. Charlottesville.

North, M. (ed.) (2001) *The Waste Land: T. S. Eliot*. New York.

North, M. A. and Hillard, A. E. (1904) *Latin Prose Composition for the Middle Forms of Schools*. 5th edn. London. 1st edn. 1895.

O'Brien, C. C. (1972) *States of Ireland*. New York.

O'Brien, E. (2009) 'The force of law in Seamus Heaney's Greek translations', in Fitzpatrick 2009: 31–45.

O'Brien, F. (1968) *The Best of Myles: A Selection from Cruiskeen Lawn*. London.

O'Brien, F. (1976a) *Further Cuttings from Cruiskeen Lawn*. London.

O'Brien, F. (1976b) *The Various Lives of Keats and Chapman and The Brother*. London.

O'Brien, F. (1977) *The Hair of the Dogma: A Further Selection from Cruiskeen Lawn*. London.

O'Brien, F. (1999) *Flann O'Brien at War: Myles na gCopaleen, 1940–1945*. London.

O'Brien, H. (1834) *The Round Towers of Ireland, or the Mysteries of Freemasonry, of Sabaism, and of Budhism, for the first time unveiled*. London.

O'Brien, M. (2008) *The Irish Times: A History*. Dublin.

Ó Brolcháin, C. (1994) 'Flann, Ó Caoimh agus Suibhne Geilt (Flann, O'Keeffe and Mad Sweeney)', *Irish Studies Review* 3: 31–4.

Ó Buachalla, B. (1979) 'Ó Corcora agus an hidden Ireland', in Ó Mórdha 1979: 109–37.

Ó Buachalla, B. (2004) *Dánta Aodhagáin Uí Rathaille: Reassessments*. Irish Texts Society, Subsidiary Series 15. London.

Ó Buachalla, S. (1980) *A Significant Irish Educationalist: The Educational Writings of P. H. Pearse*. Dublin.

Ó Buachalla, S. (1984) 'Educational policy and the role of the Irish language from 1831 to 1981', *European Journal of Education* 19.1: 75–92.

Ó Cadhain, M. (1971) 'Irish prose in the twentieth century', in J. E. Caerwyn Williams 1971: 137–51.

Ó Cathail, T. (ed.) (1940) *P. Vergili Maronis Aeneidos. Liber V*. Dublin.

Ó Cathaoir, E. (2018) *Soldiers of Liberty. A Study of Fenianism 1858–1908*. Dublin.

Ó Ciosáin, N. (2004–6) 'Print and Irish, 1570–1900: an exception among the Celtic languages?' *Radharc* 5–7: 73–106.

Ó Coigligh, C. (ed.) (1990) *An Odaisé*. Dublin.

Ó Conaire, B. (ed.) (2004) *Aistí ag Iompar Scéil: In Ómós do Shéamus P. Ó Mórdha*. Dublin.

Ó Conaola, D. (1992) *Misiún ar Muir: Sea Mission*, trans. G. Rosenstock. Inishere.

Ó Concheanainn, T. (ed.) (1956) *Virgil: Aenéis IX*. Dublin.

Ó Concheanainn, T. (1971) *Virgil: Aeinéid IX. Aistriúchán*. Dublin.

Ó Concheanainn, T. (2004) 'Mairéad Ní Éimhigh: Margaret Heavey', in Ó hUiginn and Mac Cóil 2004: 9–27.

Ó Conluain, P. and Ó Céileachair, D. (1976) *An Duinníneach*. Dublin. 1st edn. 1958.

O'Connell, F. W. and Henry, R. M. (eds.) (1915) *An Irish Corpus Astronomiae: being Manus O'Donnell's Seventeenth-Century Version of the Lunario of Geronymo Cortès*. London.

O'Connell, J. W. (1994) 'And here's John Synge himself, that rooted man', in Waddell, O'Connell, and Korff 1994: 261–7.

O'Connor, C. and Regan, J. (eds.) (1987) *Public Works: The Architecture of the Office of Public Works, 1831–1987*. Dublin.

O'Connor, R. (ed.) (2014a) *Classical Literature and Learning in Medieval Irish Narrative*. Cambridge.

O'Connor, R. (2014b) 'Irish narrative literature and the classical tradition, 900–1300', in O'Connor 2014a: 1–22.

Ó Cuív, B. (1973) 'The linguistic training of the medieval Irish poet', *Celtica* 10: 114–40.

Ó Cuív, S. (1954) 'Materials for a bibliography of the Very Reverend Peter Canon O'Leary 1839–1920', Supplement to *Celtica* 2.2: 3–39.

O'Curry, E. (1861) *Lectures on the Manuscript Materials of Ancient Irish History*. Dublin.

Ó Direáin, M. (1984) *Selected Poems*, trans. T. Mac Síomóin and D. Sealy. Newbridge.

O'Donoghue, B. (2019) 'Heaney, Yeats, and the language of pastoral', in Harrison, Macintosh, and Eastman 2019: 147–59.

O'Donovan, D. (1995) *God's Architect: A Life of Raymond McGrath*. Bray.

O'Donovan Rossa, J. (1898) *Rossa's Recollections 1838 to 1898*. Mariner's Harbor NY.

O'Dwyer, F. (1987) 'The architecture of the Board of Public Works 1831–1923', in O'Connor and Regan 1987: 10–16.

O'Faoláin, S. (1940) *An Irish Journey*. London.

O'Faoláin, S. (1947) *The Irish: A Character Study*. London.

O'Farrelly, A. (2010) *Smaointe ar Árainn*, ed. and trans. R. Nic Congáil. Dublin. 1st edn. 1902.

Officer, D. (1996) 'In search of order, permanence and stability: building Stormont, 1921–32', in English and Walker 1996: 130–47.

Ó Fiaich, T. (1972) 'The great controversy', in Ó Tuama 1972: 63–75.

Ó Fiaich, T. (1985) 'Virgil's Irish background and departure for France', *Seanchas Ard Mhacha: Journal of the Armagh Diocesan Historical Society* 11: 301–18.

Ó Fiannachta, P. (1988a) 'Fuíoll léinn Sheoirse Mhic Tomáis, I, II', in Ó Fiannachta 1988c: 162–82.

Ó Fiannachta, P. (1988b) 'Fuíoll léinn Sheoirse Mhic Tomáis, III', in Ó Fiannachta 1988d: 157–89.

Ó Fiannachta, P. (ed.) (1988c) *An Aoir/Léachtaí Cholm Cille* 18. Maynooth.

Ó Fiannachta, P. (ed.) (1988d) *Irisleabhar Mhá Nuad*. Maynooth.

Ó Fiannachta, P. (1989a) 'Fuíoll léinn Sheoirse Mhic Tomáis, III', in Ó Fiannachta 1989b: 76–102.

Ó Fiannachta, P. (ed.) (1989b) *Irisleabhar Mhá Nuad*. Maynooth.

Ó Fiannachta, P. (ed.) (1993) *Maigh Nuad agus an Ghaeilge/Léachtaí Cholm Cille* 23. Maynooth.

O'Flaherty, J. T. (1825) 'A sketch of the history and antiquities of the southern islands of Aran, lying off the west coast of Ireland: with observations on the religion of the Celtic nations, pagan monuments of the early Irish, Druidic rites, &c', *Transactions of the Royal Irish Academy* 14: 79–139.

O'Flaherty, T. (1934) *Aranmen All*. London and Dublin.

Ó Flannghaile, T. (ed.) (1897) *Eachtra Ghiolla an Amaráin*. Dublin.

Ó Foghludha, R. (ed.) (1908) *Eachtra Ghiolla an Amaráin agus gearra-thuairisc ar ré shaoghail a úghdair*. Dublin.

Ó Foghludha, R. (ed.) (1952) *Éigse na Máighe*. Dublin.

O'Halloran, C. (2004) *Golden Ages and Barbarous Nations: Antiquarian Debate and Cultural Politics in Ireland, c. 1750–1800*. Cork.

Ó hÉigeartaigh, C. and Nic Gearailt, A. (2014) *Sáirséal agus Dill 1947–1981: Scéal Foilsitheora*. Indreabhán.

Ó hEithir, B. and R. (eds.) (1991) *An Aran Reader*. Dublin.

O'Higgins, L. (2017) *The Irish Classical Self: Poets and Poor Scholars in the Eighteenth and Nineteenth Centuries*. Oxford.

O'Hogan, C. (2014) 'Reading Lucan with scholia in medieval Ireland: *In Cath Catharda* and its sources', *Cambrian Medieval Celtic Studies* 68: 21–49.

O'Hogan, C. (2018) 'Irish versions of Virgil's *Eclogues* and *Georgics*', in Braund and Torlone 2018: 399–411.

Ó hUiginn, R. and Mac Cóil, L. (eds.) (1999) *Bliainiris 2000*. Ráth Chairn.

Ó hUiginn, R. and Mac Cóil, L. (eds.) (2004) *Bliainiris 2004*. Ráth Chairn.

Ó hUiginn, R. and Ó Catháin, B. (eds.) (2009) *Ulidia 2: Proceedings of the Second International Conference on the Ulster Cycle of Tales*. Maynooth.

O'Keeffe, T. (ed.) (1973) *Myles: Portraits of Brian O'Nolan*. London.

O'Kelly, E. (1993) 'Hecuba meets the New Man', *The Sunday Independent*, 6 June: 9L.

O'Leary, P. (1994) *The Prose Literature of the Gaelic Revival, 1881–1921: Ideology and Innovation*. University Park PA.

O'Leary, P. (2004) *Gaelic Prose in the Irish Free State 1922–1939*. Dublin.

O'Leary, P. (ed.) (2013) *Queen of the Hearth. Patrick S. Dinneen*. With an Introduction and Notes by Philip O'Leary. Dublin.

Ó Lúing, S. (1980) 'Seoirse Mac Tomáis—George Derwent Thomson', *Journal of the Kerry Archaeological and Historical Society* 13: 149–72.

Ó Lúing, S. (ed.) (1988) [*Seoirse Mac Tomáis*] *Gach Órlach de mo Chroí: Dréachta*. Dublin.

Ó Lúing, S. (1989) *Saoir Theangan*. Dublin.

Ó Lúing, S. (1991) *Kuno Meyer 1858–1919: A Biography*. Dublin.

Ó Lúing, S. (1996) 'George Thomson', *Classics Ireland* 3: 141–62, repr. in Ó Lúing 2000: 161–73.

Ó Lúing, S. (2000) *Celtic Studies in Europe and Other Essays*. Dublin.

O'Malley-Younger, A. (2016) 'A terrible beauty is bought: 1916, commemoration and commodification', *Irish Studies Review* 24:4: 455–67.

Ó Maonaigh, C. (1962) 'Scríbhneoirí Gaeilge an seachtú haois déag', *Studia Hibernica* 2: 182–208.

Ó Mórdha, S. (ed.) (1979) *Scríobh* 4. Dublin.

Ó Muirithe, D. (1980) *An tAmhrán Macarónach*. Dublin.

Ó Murchú, S. (2012) 'Idir *Laethanta Gréine* agus *Na Mairbh a d'Fhill*: Súil sceabhach ar an bhfoilsitheoireacht do dhaoine óga i mblianta tosaigh an Ghúim', in Nic Congáil 2012: 23–43.

O'Neill, J. (2001) *At Swim Two Boys*. London.

O'Nolan, K. (1968) 'Homer and the Irish hero tale', *Studia Hibernica* 8: 7–20.

O'Nolan, K. (1969) 'Homer and Irish narrative', *Classical Quarterly* 19: 1–19.

O'Nolan, K. (1970) 'Homer, Virgil and Oral Tradition', *Béaloideas* 37–8: 123–30.

O'Nolan, K. (1973) 'The use of formula in storytelling', *Béaloideas* 39–41: 233–50.

Ó Nualláin, C. (1973) *Óige an Dearthár: .i. Myles na gCopaleen*. Dublin.

O'Rahilly, T. F. (ed.) (1927) *Measgra Dánta: Miscellaneous Irish Poems*. Cork.

O'Rahilly, T. F. (1946) *Early Irish History and Mythology*. Dublin.

O'Reilly, A. F. (2004) *Sacred Play: Soul-journeys in Contemporary Irish Theatre*. Dublin.

O'Reilly, F. (1926) *The Problem of Undesirable Printed Matter: Suggested Remedies: Evidence of the Catholic Truth Society of Ireland*. Dublin.

O'Rourke, D. (2016) 'The madness of elegy: rationalizing Propertius', in Hardie 2016: 199–217.

O'Rourke, D. (2018) 'Make war not love: *militia amoris* and domestic violence in Roman elegy', in Gale and Scourfield 2018: 110–39.

Ó Searcaigh, C. (2009) *Light on Distant Hills*. New York.

Ó Searcaigh, C. and Mc Grath N. (2002) *Challenging our Conformity. On the Side of Light*. Dublin.

Ó Síocháin, P. A. (1990) *Aran: Islands of Legend*, 4th edn. Dublin. 1st edn. 1962.

Ó Síocháin, S. (ed.) (2009) *Social Thought on Ireland in the Nineteenth Century*. Dublin.

Ó Súilleabháin, D. (1988) *Cath na Gaeilge sa Chóras Oideachais 1893–1911*. Dublin.

Ó Súilleabháin, M. (1933) *Fiche Blian ag Fás*. Dublin, trans. M. Llewelyn Davies and G. Thomson (1933) *Twenty Years a-Growing*. London.

O'Sullivan, A. (2007) 'The western islands: Ireland's Atlantic islands and the forging of Gaelic Irish national identities', in Noble, Poller, Raven, and Verrill 2007: 172–90.

O'Sullivan, M. (1997) *Brendan Behan's Life*. Dublin.

Ó Tuama, S. (ed.) (1972) *The Gaelic League Idea*. Cork.

Ó Tuathaigh, G. (2008) 'The position of the Irish language', in Dunne, Coolahan, Manning, and Ó Tuathaigh 2008: 33–43.

Paige, D. D. (1971) (ed.) *The Selected Letters of Ezra Pound 1907–1941*. New York.

Parker, G. (ed.) (2017) *South Africa, Greece, Rome: Classical Confrontations*. Cambridge.

Parker, M. (2019) 'Speaking truth to power: Seamus Heaney's *The Burial at Thebes*, and the poetry of redress', in Harrison, Macintosh, and Eastman 2019: 98–120.

Parrinder, P., Nash, A., and Wilson, N. (eds.) (2014) *New Directions in the History of the Novel*. London.

Pašeta, S. (2016) *Irish Nationalist Women 1900–1918*. Cambridge.

Passaretti, B. (2014) 'Classical languages and cultural memory in Brian Friel's *Translations*', *Lingue antiche e moderne* 3: 181–202.

Paul, C. E. (2010) 'Ezra Pound', in Holdeman and Levitas 2010: 148–57.

Paul, C. E. and Harper, M. M. (eds.) (2008) *The Collected Works of W. B. Yeats: Vol. XIII: A Vision (1925)*. New York.

Paulin, T. (1985) *The Riot Act: A Version of* Antigone *by Sophocles*. London.

Paulin, T. (1996) *Writing to the Moment: Selected Critical Essays 1980–1996*. London.

Paulin, T. (2002) '*Antigone*', in McDonald and Walton 2002: 165–70.

Peacock, A. J. (1988) 'Prolegomena to Michael Longley's Peace poem', *Éire–Ireland* 23: 60–74.

Peacock, A. J. and Devine, K. (eds.) (2000) *The Poetry of Michael Longley*. Gerrards Cross.

Pearse, P. (1898) *Three lectures on Gaelic Topics*. Dublin.

Pearse, P. (1909) 'An English Censorship in Ireland', *An Claidheamh Soluis*, 28 August: 9–10.

Pearse, P. (1912) *Some Aspects of Irish Literature*. Dublin.

Pearse, P. (1915) *How Does She Stand? Three Addresses*. Dublin.

Pearse, P. (1916a) *The Sovereign People*. Dublin.

Pearse, P. (1916b) *The Separatist Idea*. Dublin.

Pearse, P. (1916c) *The Murder Machine*. Dublin.

Pearse, P. (1916d) *The Spiritual Nation*. Dublin.

Pearse, P. (1916e) 'From a Hermitage II, June 1913', in Pearse 1917–22: 149–55.

Pearse, P. (1917–22) *Collected Works of Pádraic H. Pearse. Vol. 3: Political Writings and Speeches*. Dublin.

Pearse, P. (1924) *Collected Works of Pádraic H. Pearse. Songs of the Irish Rebels and Specimens from an Irish Anthology; Some Aspects of Irish Literature; Three Lectures on Gaelic Topics*. Dublin.

Pelletier, M. (2012) 'Field Day revisits the classics: Tom Paulin's *The Riot Act*', in Dubost 2012: 83–93.

Percy, C. and Ridley, J. (eds.) (1988) *The Letters of Edwin Lutyens to his Wife Lady Emily*. London.

Pierse, M. (ed.) (2017) *A History of Irish Working-Class Writing*. Cambridge.

Pinkerton, J. (1787) *Dissertation on the Origin and Progress of the Scythians and Goths, Being an Introduction to the Ancient and Modern History of Europe*. London.

Pitman-Wallace L. (2019) 'A door into the dark: staging *The Burial at Thebes*', in Harrison, Macintosh, and Eastman 2019: 69–84.

Pittock, M. G. (1994) *Poetry and Jacobite Politics in Eighteenth-Century Britain and Ireland*. Cambridge.

Pogorzelski, R. (2016) *Virgil and Joyce: Nationalism and Imperialism in the* Aeneid *and* Ulysses. Madison.

Poppe, E. (1995) 'The classical epic from an Irish perspective', in Calder and Poppe 1995: 1–40.

Poppe, E. (2004) 'Imtheachta Aeniasa: Virgil's *Aeneid* in medieval Ireland', *Classics Ireland* 11: 74–94.

Poppe, E. (2014) '*Imtheachta Aeniasa* and its place in medieval Irish textual history', in O'Connor 2014a: 25–39.

Poppe, E. (2016) 'The Epic Styles of *In Cath Catharda: imitatio, amplificatio*, and *aemulatio*', in Harlos, Harlos, and Poppe 2016: 1–20.

Poppe, E. and Tristram, H. L. C. (eds.) (1999) *Übersetzung, Adaptation und Akkulturation im insularen Mittelalter*. Münster.

Porter, J. (2006a) 'What is "classical" about classical antiquity?', in Porter 2006b: 1–66.

Porter, J. (ed.) (2006b) *The Classical Traditions of Greece and Rome*. Princeton.

Potts, D. L. (2011) *Contemporary Irish Poetry and the Pastoral Tradition*. Columbia MO and London.

Pound, E. (1915) 'The non-existence of Ireland', *The New Age* 16.17: 451–3.

Powell, A. (ed.) (1990) *Euripides, Women, Sexuality*. London.

Powell, D. (1971) 'An annotated bibliography of Myles Na Gopaleen's (Flann O'Brien's) "Cruiskeen Lawn" commentaries on James Joyce', *James Joyce Quarterly* 9: 50–62.

Powell, J. G. F. (1990) 'Two notes on Catullus', *Classical Quarterly* 40.1: 199–206.

Power, M. (1978) 'Flann O'Brien and classical satire: an exegesis of *The Hard Life*', *Éire-Ireland* 13: 87–102.

Power, P. (1935) *Aran of the Saints: A Brief Introduction to the Island's Antiquities*, 2nd edn. Dublin. 1st edn. 1926.

Prescott, J. (1954) 'Joyce's "Stephen Hero"', *Journal of English and Germanic Philology* 53: 214–23.

Prút, L. (2005) *Athbheochan an Léinn nó Dúchas na Gaeilge? Iomarbhá idir Pádraig de Brún agus Domhnall Ó Corcora, Humanitas 1930–31*. Dublin.

Putnam, M. C. J. (2010) 'Virgil and Seamus Heaney', *Vergilius* 56: 3–16.

Putnam, M. C. J. (2012) 'Virgil and Heaney: "Route 110"', *Arion* 19.3: 79–108.

Quinn, B. (1986) *Atlantean: Ireland's North African and Maritime Heritage*. London.

Quinn, B. (2005) *The Atlantean Irish: Ireland's Oriental and Maritime Heritage*, 2nd edn. Dublin.

Rabel, R. J. (1997) *Plot and Point of View in the* Iliad. Ann Arbor.

Rabinowitz, N. S. (1993) *Anxiety Veiled: Euripides and the Traffic in Women*. Ithaca NY.

Rankin, E. and Schneider, R. M. (2017) ' "Copy Nothing": classical ideals and Afrikaner ideologies at the Voortrekker Monument', in Parker 2017: 141–212.

Rankin Russell, R. (2003) 'Inscribing cultural corridors: Michael Longley's contribution to reconciliation in Northern Ireland', *Colby Quarterly* 39.3: 221–40.

Raskin, J. (2009) *The Mythology of Imperialism: A Revolutionary Critique of British Literature and Society in the Modern Age*. New York.

Redfield, J. M. (1994) *Nature and Culture in the* Iliad: *The Tragedy of Hector*, 2nd edn. Durham NC and London. 1st edn. 1975.

Redman, T. (2010) 'Pound's politics and economics', in Nadel 2010: 249–63.

Remoundou-Howley, A. (2011) '*Antigone* stopped in Belfast: Stacey Gregg's *Ismene*', *New Voices in Classical Reception Studies* 6: 53–72.

Renan, E. (1970) *The Poetry of the Celtic Races and Other Studies by Ernest Renan*. Translated, with Introduction and Notes, by William G. Hutchison. Port Washington and London. 1st edn. 1896.

Revermann, M. and Wilson, P. (eds.) (2008) *Performance, Iconography, Reception: Studies in Honour of Oliver Taplin*. Oxford.

Richard, C. (1994) *The Founders and the Classics. Greece, Rome and the American Enlightenment*. Cambridge MA.

Richards, S. (1991) 'Polemics on the Irish past: the 'return to the source' in Irish literary revivals', *History Workshop* 31: 120–35.

Richardson, N. (1993) *The* Iliad: *A Commentary. Volume VI: books 21–24*, ed. G. S. Kirk. Cambridge.

Riggs, P. (ed.) (2005) *Dinneen and the Dictionary*. Irish Texts Society Subsidiary Series 16. London.

Riggs, P. (2016) 'Revising and Rising – An Irishwoman's Diary on Fr Dinneen's dictionary and 1916', *The Irish Times*, 30 December: https://www.irishtimes.com/opinion/revising-and-rising-an-irishwoman-s-diary-on-fr-dinneen-s-dictionary-and-1916-1.2920371 (accessed 9 December 2019).

Riley, K. (2019) ' "The Forewarned Journey Back": *katabasis* as *nostos* in the poetry of Seamus Heaney', in Harrison, Macintosh, and Eastman 2019: 205–22.

Riley, K., Blanshard, A. J. L., and Manny, I. (eds.) (2018) *Oscar Wilde and Classical Antiquity*. Oxford.

Robinson, C. (2005) 'Cavafy, sexual sensibility and poetic practice: Reading Cavafy through Marc Doty and Cathal O Searcaigh', *Journal of Modern Greek Studies* 23: 261–79.

Robinson, L. (1924) Letter to Lady Gregory (23 Dec.). Lennox Robinson papers, Berg Collection, New York Public Library.

Robinson, M. (1992) 'Douglas Hyde (1860–1949): the Trinity connection', *Hermathena, Quartercentenary Papers*: 17–26.

Robinson, T. (1986) *Stones of Aran: Pilgrimage*. Gigginstown, Mullingar.

Robinson, T. (1995) *Stones of Aran: Labyrinth*. Dublin.

Roche, A. (1988) 'Ireland's *Antigones*: tragedy north and south', in Kenneally 1988: 221–50.

Roche, A. (2005a) 'Kennelly's rebel women', in Dillon and Wilmer 2005: 149–68.

Roche, A. (ed.) (2005b) *The UCD Aesthetic: Celebrating 150 Years of UCD Writers*. Dublin.

Rolfe, A. and Ryan, R. (eds.) (1992) *The Department of Industry and Commerce, Kildare Street, Dublin*. Dublin.

Roling, B. (2018) 'Phoenician Ireland: Charles Vallancey (1725–1812) and the oriental roots of Celtic culture', in Enenkel and Ottenheym 2018: 750–70.

Rolleston, T. W. (1911) *Myths and Legends of the Celtic Race*. New York.

Rolston, B. (1991) *Politics and Painting: Murals and Conflict in Northern Ireland*. Rutherford NJ.

Rolston, B. (2003) *Drawing Support 3: Murals and Transition in the North of Ireland*. Belfast.

Roman, L. (2014) *Poetic Autonomy in Ancient Rome*. Oxford.

Rosenbloom, P. (2006) 'Empire and its discontents: *Trojan Women, Birds*, and the symbolic economy of Athenian imperialism', in Davidson, Muecke, and Wilson 2006: 245–71.

Ross, I. (2013) *Oscar Wilde and Ancient Greece*. Cambridge.

Rothery, S. (1991) *Ireland and the New Architecture, 1900–1940*. Dublin.

Rouse, P. (2009) 'Ó Briain, Liam', in McGuire and Quinn 2009, available online at: http://dib.cambridge.org/viewReadPage.do?articleId=a6277 (accessed 5 December 2019).

Rudd, N. (1994) *The Classical Tradition in Operation*. Toronto.

Ruffell, A. (2005) 'Searching for the IRA "disappeared": ground-penetrating radar investigation of a churchyard burial site, Northern Ireland', *Journal of Forensic Sciences* 50.6: 1430–5.

Rushe, D. (1993) 'Passionate, lyrical Kennelly', *Irish Independent*, 3 June: 6.

Ryan, J., SJ (ed.) (1963) *Irish Monks in the Golden Age*. Dublin and London.

Ryan, R. (1992) 'Architectural appraisal', in Rolfe and Ryan 1992: 37–46.

Ryan, S. P. (1961) 'W. B. Yeats and Thomas MacDonagh', *Modern Language Notes* 76.8: 715–19.

Said, E. (1994) *Culture and Imperialism*. New York.

Santino, J. (2001) *Signs of War and Peace: Social Conflict and the Use of Public Symbols in Northern Ireland*. Basingstoke.

Saunders, T. (2012) 'Classical antiquity in Brian Friel's *Translations*', *Nordic Irish Studies* 11: 133–51.

Sayers, W. (2012) 'The deflation of the medieval in Joyce's *Ulysses*', *This Year's Work in Medievalism* 27: https://www.fabula.org/actualites/the-year-s-work-in-medievalism-27-2012_59178.php (accessed 5 December 2019).

Schein, S. L. (1984) *The Mortal Hero: An Introduction to Homer's* Iliad. Berkeley.

Schmuhl, R. (2011–12) 'A Trip to the Archives?', *Notre Dame Magazine* (Winter): 1–5.

Schmuhl, R. (2016) *Ireland's Exiled Children. America and the Easter Rising*. Oxford.

Schork, R. J. (1997) *Latin and Roman Culture in Joyce*. Gainesville.

Schork, R. J. (1998) *Greek and Hellenic Culture in Joyce*. Gainesville.

Scull, M. (2019) *The Catholic Church and the Northern Ireland Troubles, 1968–1998*. Oxford.

Seaford, R. A. S. (2014) 'Thomson, George Derwent (1903–1987)', in *Oxford Dictionary of National Biography*. https://doi.org/10.1093/ref:odnb/61301 (accessed 5 December 2019).

Shaw, G. B. (1970–4) *The Bodley Head Shaw*. London.

Sheaff, N. (1984) 'The harp re-strung', *Irish Arts Review* 1.3: 37–43.

Shouldice, F. (2015) *Grandpa the Sniper: The Remarkable Story of a 1916 Volunteer*. Dublin.

Siggins, L. (2014) 'Guidebook by Aran expert explores mysteries of Dún Aonghasa's past', *The Irish Times*, 21 July: 4.

Sikorska, L. (ed.) (2010) *History is Mostly Repair and Revenge: Discourses of/on History in Literature in English*, Studies in Literature in English 1. Frankfurt am Main and New York.

Silk, M., Gildenhard, I., and Barrow, R. (2014) *The Classical Tradition: Art, Literature, Thought*. Chichester.

Simmons, R. H. (2010) 'Deconstructing a father's love: Catullus 72 and 74', *Classical World* 104.1: 29–57.

Sisson, E. (2004) *Pearse's Patriots: St Enda's and the Cult of Boyhood*. Cork.

Sisson, E. (2010) ' "A note on what happened": experimental influences on the Irish stage: 1919–1929', *Kritica Kultura* 15: 132–48.

Skelton, T. and Gliddon, G. (2008) *Lutyens and the Great War*. London.

Skinner, M. B. (ed.) (2007) *A Companion to Catullus*. Malden and Oxford.

Skoie, M. (2002) *Reading Sulpicia: Commentaries 1475–1990*. Oxford.

Smyth, G. (1998) *Decolonialisation and Criticism. The Construction of Irish Literature*. London and Sterling VA.

Smyth, G. (2000) 'The politics of hybridity: some problems with crossing the border', in Bery and Murray 2000: 43–55.

Sonnenschein, E. A. (1892) *A Greek Grammar for Schools, Based on the Principles and Requirements of the Grammatical Society*. Volume 1. London.

Sonnenschein, E. A. (1894) *A Greek Grammar for Schools, Based on the Principles and Requirements of the Grammatical Society*. Volume 2. London.

Stanford, W. B. (1951) 'Ulysses in the Medieval Troy Tale', *Hermathena* 78: 67–83.

Stanford, W. B. (1976) *Ireland and the Classical Tradition*. Dublin and Totowa NJ.

Stanford, W. B. and McDowell, R. B. (1971) *Mahaffy: A Biography of an Anglo-Irishman*. London.

Starkie, W. (1953) *In Sara's Tents*. London.

Stead, H. and Hall, E. (eds.) (2015) *Greek and Roman Classics in the British Struggle for Social Reform*. London.

Steele, K. (2010) 'Maud Gonne', in Holdeman and Levitas 2010: 119–28.

Steele, K. and de Nie, M. (eds.) (2014) *Ireland and the New Journalism*. Basingstoke.

Stein, G. (2013) *Paris, France*. New York. 1st edn. 1940.

Stephens, S. and Vasunia, P. (eds.) (2010) *Classics and National Cultures*. Oxford.

Stewart, B. (2000) 'On the necessity of de-Hydifying Irish cultural criticism', *New Hibernia Review/Iris Éireannach Nua* 4: 23–44.

Stewart, B. (2010) 'A short literary life of James Joyce', in Latham 2010: 19–44.

Stocker, M. (2015) 'Coining New Zealand: projecting nationhood and money' in Stupples 2015: 145–68.

Stokes, W. (1868) *The Life and Labours in Art and Archaeology of George Petrie*. London.

Stokes, W. (ed. and trans.) (1899) 'The Bodleian *Amra Choluimb Chille*', *Revue Celtique* 20: 404–5.

Storey, Mark (ed.) (1988) *Poetry and Ireland Since 1800: A Source Book*. London.

Storey, Mervyn (2010) Private Members Business, Northern Ireland Assembly, 22 November 2010: https://www.theyworkforyou.com/ni/?id=2010–11–22.4.1&s=%22Pro testant+State%22+speaker%3A13867#g4.3 (accessed 10 May 2019).

Stormont Papers (1921–72) *Fifty Years of Northern Ireland Parliamentary Debates Online*. http://stormontpapers.ahds.ac.uk/index.html (accessed 23 May 2019).

Stray, C. (1998) *Classics Transformed: Schools, Universities, and Society in England, 1830–1960*. Oxford.

Stupples, P. (ed.) (2015) *Art and Money*. Cambridge.

Sturgis, M. (1995) *Passionate Attitudes: The English Decadence of the Eighteen Nineties*. London.

Sui, D. Z. (ed.) (2008) *Geospatial Technologies and Homeland Security*. Dordrecht.

Sullivan, J. (1965) *Ezra Pound and Sextus Propertius: A Study in Creative Translation*. London.

Sullivan, M. R. (1969) 'Synge, Sophocles, and the unmaking of myth', *Modern Drama* 12: 242–53.

Summerson, J. (1980) *The Classical Language of Architecture*, revised and enlarged edn. London.

Sweeney, J. (2018) 'Drama: new play explores human dilemma of the hunger strike', *The Irish News*, 26 April: https://www.irishnews.com/arts/2018/04/26/news/drama-new-play-norah-explores-human-dilemma-of-the-hunger-strike-1310217/ (accessed 5 December 2019).

Sweetman, R. (1974) *Fathers Come First*. London.

Symons, A. (1919) *Cities and Sea-Coasts and Islands*. New York.

Synge, J. M. (1966) *Collected Works. Volume II: Prose*, ed. A. Price. London.

T. [= Torna?] (1928) '[Review of] *Sofoícléas: Aintioghoiné* ... [and] *Rí Oidiopús. Dráma le Sofoícléas*', *Studies: An Irish Quarterly Review* 17.66: 325–7.

Taaffe, C. (2008) *Ireland Through the Looking-Glass: Flann O'Brien, Myles na gCopaleen and Irish Cultural Debate*. Cork.

Taaffe, C. (2011) 'Plain People and Corduroys: the citizen and the artist', in Baines 2011: 112–26.

Taplin, O. (1992) *Homeric Soundings: The Shaping of the* Iliad. Oxford.

Teevan, C. (1998) 'Northern Ireland: Our Troy? Recent versions of Greek tragedies by Irish writers', *Modern Drama* 41: 77–89.

Thackery, W. M. (1843) *The Irish Sketch Book of 1843*. London.

Thomas, Richard F. (2001) 'The *Georgics* of resistance: from Virgil to Heaney', *Vergilius* 47: 117–47.

Thomas, R. F. and Ziolkowski, J. M. (eds.) (2014) *The Virgil Encyclopedia*. 3 vols. Malden.

Thomas, Ronald E. (1977) *The Latin Masks of Ezra Pound*. Epping.

Thomson, G. (ed.) (1932a) *Aeschylus: The Prometheus Bound*. Cambridge.

Thomson, G. (ed.) (1932b) *Alcéstis, le hEuripides*. Dublin.

Thomson, G. (ed.) (1933) *Prométheus fé Chuibhreach, le h–Aeschylus*. Dublin.

Thomson, G. (1944) 'The Irish language revival', *Yorkshire Celtic Studies* 3: 3–12.

Thomson, G. (1946) *Marxism and Poetry*. London.

Thomson, G. (1988) *Island Home: The Blasket Heritage*. Dingle.

Thomson, G. [Mac Tomáis, S.] and Ó Fiannachta, P. (1967) *Mise Agaistín .i. Aistriúchán Gaeilge ar Sancti Augustini Confessionum Libri i–x*. Maynooth.

Thomson, G. [Mac Tomáis, S.] and Ó Lúing, S. (ed.) (1988) *Gach Órlach de mo Chroí: Dréachta*. Dublin.

Thrall, W. F. (1917) 'Vergil's *Aeneid* and the Irish *Imrama*: Zimmer's theory', *Modern Philology* 15: 449–74.

Tierney, M. (1963) 'What did the Gaelic League accomplish? 1893–1963', *Studies: An Irish Quarterly Review* 52.208: 337–47.

Tierney, M. (1980) *Eoin MacNeill: Scholar and Man of Action, 1867–1945*, ed. F. X. Martin. Oxford.

Tilley, C., Keane, W., Küchler, S., Rowlands, M., and Spyer, P. (eds.) (2006) *Handbook of Material Culture*. London.

Titley, A. (1991) *An tÚrscéal Gaeilge*. Dublin.

Titley, A. (2005) 'Turning inside and out: translating and Irish 1950–2000', *The Yearbook of English Studies* 35: 312–22.

Titley, A. (2014–15) 'Patrick Dinneen: lexicography and legacy', *Studies: An Irish Quarterly Review* 103: 485–98.

Tóibín, C. (2007) 'The mystery of Inis Meáin', *The Guardian*, 12 May.

Toomey, D. (1997a) 'Labyrinths: Yeats and Maud Gonne', in Toomey 1997b: 1–40.

Toomey, D. (ed.) (1997b) *Yeats and Women*, 2nd edn. Basingstoke.

Torrance, I. (2013) *Metapoetry in Euripides*. Oxford.

Townsend, S. L. (2016) 'Porcine pasts and bourgeois pigs: consumption and the Irish counterculture', in Kirkpatrick and Farago 2016: 55–72.

Tracy, R. (1993) '"Intelligible on the Blasket Islands": Yeats's *King Oedipus*, 1927', *Éire-Ireland* 28.2: 116–28.

Trench, R. (2010) *Bloody Living: The Loss of Selfhood in the Plays of Marina Carr*. Bern.

Trusted, M. (ed.) (2007) *The Making of Sculpture. The Materials and Techniques of European Sculpture*. London.

Turner, R. (1921) '*The Evolution of Sinn Féin* by R. M. Henry', *American Historical Review* 26: 523–5.

Turpin, J. (2000) *Oliver Sheppard 1865–1941, Symbolist Sculptor of the Irish Cultural Revival*. Dublin.

Twiddy, I. (2012) *Pastoral Elegy in Contemporary British and Irish Poetry*. London.

Tyler, D. (1963) 'Milles, Yeats and the Irish coinage', *Michigan Quarterly Review* 22: 273–80.

Tyler, M. (2005) *A Singing Contest: Conventions of Sound in the Poetry of Seamus Heaney*. New York and Abingdon.

Tyler, M. (ed.) (forthcoming) *The Imaginary Oarsman: Essays on the Poetry of Michael Longley*. Syracuse NY.

Tymoczko, M. (1992) '"The Broken Lights of Irish Myth": Joyce's knowledge of Early Irish literature', *James Joyce Quarterly* 29: 763–74.

Tymoczko, M. (1994) *The Irish Ulysses*. Berkeley.

Tzamalis, A. (1980) *The Coins of Modern Greece 1928–1980* (Τα Νομίσματα της νεώτερης Ελλάδας 1928–1980). Athens.

Ua Ceallaigh, S. (1921) *Ireland: Elements of her Early Story from the coming of Ceasair to the Anglo-Norman Invasion*. Dublin.

Ua Duinnín, P. (1901a) *Amhráin Eoghain Ruaidh Uí Shúilleabháin*. Dublin.

Ua Duinnín, P. (1901b) *Cormac Ua Conaill*. Dublin.

Ua Duinnín, P. (1903) *Duan na Nollag*. Dublin.

Ua Duinnín, P. (1905) *Muinntir Chiarraidhe roimh and droch-shaoghal*. Dublin.

Ua Duinnín, P. (1919) *Spiorad na Saoirse. Aisling Draoidheachta ar an mBliadhain 1916*. Dublin.

Ua Duinnín, P. (1922) *Teachtaire ó Dhia. Dráma bhaineas leis an ndroch-shaoghal*. Dublin.

Ua Duinnín, P. (1927) *Foclóir Gaeidhilge agus Béarla. An Irish-English Dictionary Being a Thesaurus of the Words, Phrases and Idioms of the Modern Irish Language with Explanations in English*. Dublin.

Ua Duinnín, P. (1929) *Aistí ar litridheacht Ghréigise is Laidne*. Dublin.

Ua Duinnín, P. (ed.) (1931) *Aenéis Bhirgil. Leabhar a h-aon: maille le brollach, míniughadh is foclóir*. Dublin. 3rd edn., 1938.

Ua Duinnín, P. and O'Donoghue, T. (eds.) (1911) *Dánta Aodhagáin Uí Rathaille. The Poems of Egan O'Rahilly with Introduction, Notes, Translation and Indexes*, 2nd edn. Dublin.

Ua Súilleabháin, S. (1991) 'Máistir ar an teanga', *Feasta* 50.1: 29–31.

Uden, J. (2015) *The Invisible Satirist: Juvenal and Second-Century Rome*. Oxford.

Uí Chollatáin, R. (2003) 'Literature reviews in *An Claidheamh Soluis*: a journalistic insight to Irish literary reviews in the revival period 1899–1932', *Proceedings of the Harvard Celtic Colloquium* 23: 284–98.

Uí Laighléis, G. (2004) 'An Gúm: scéal agus scéalaíocht', in Ó Conaire 2004: 185–206.

Uí Laighléis, G. (2007) 'An Gúm: the early years', in Mac Mathúna and Ó Corráin 2007: 199–216.

Uí Laighléis, G. (2017) *Gallán an Ghúim: Caidreamh an Stáit le Scríbhneoirí na Gaeilge: Máirtín Ó Cadhain, Seosamh Mac Grianna agus Seán Tóibín*. Dublin.

Unsworth, M. (2002) 'Epic battle to save classical studies at Queen's', *The Irish Times* 29 August. https://www.irishtimes.com/news/epic-battle-to-save-classical-studies-at-queen-s-1.1093509?fbclid=IwAR0IHXL68JMkT-GsypXeLSICIiyAUXWWYWt6tBnOWthxe27 cdqZzcU14prk (accessed 5 December 2019).

Usher, M. D. (1996) 'The strange case of Dr. Syntax and Mr. Pound', *Classical and Modern Literature* 16.2: 95–106.

Usher, S. (1999) *Greek Oratory. Tradition and Originality*. Oxford.

Vale, L. (1992) 'Designing national identity: post-colonial capitols as intercultural dilemmas', in Al Sayyad 1992: 316–24.

Valente, J. (ed.) (1998) *Quare Joyce*. Ann Arbor.

Vance, N. (1997) *The Victorians and Ancient Rome*. Oxford.

van Ert, G. (1994) 'Empty air: Ezra Pound's World War Two radio broadcasts', *Past Imperfect* 3: 47–72.

van Wie, P. D. (1999) *Image, History, and Politics: The Coinage of Modern Europe*. Lanham.

van Zyl Smit, B. (ed.) (2005) *A Handbook to the Reception of Greek Drama*. Chichester.

Vasunia, P. (2013) *The Classics and Colonial India*. Oxford.

Vendler, H. (2002) 'Seamus Heaney and the *Oresteia*: "Mycenae Lookout" and the usefulness of tradition', in McDonald and Walton 2002: 181–97.

Volsik, P. (2009) '"That dark permanence of ancient forms": negotiating with the epic in Northern Irish poetry of the troubles', in Kendell 2009: 669–83.

Waddell, J. (1991–2) 'The Irish Sea in prehistory', *Journal of Irish Archaeology* 6: 29–40.

Waddell, J. (1994) 'The archaeology of the Aran Islands', in Waddell, O'Connell, and Korff 1994: 75–135.

Waddell, J., O'Connell, J. W., and Korff, A. (eds.) (1994) *The Book of Aran*. Newtownlynch, Kinvara.

Wade, A. (ed.) (1954) *The Letters of W. B. Yeats*. London.

Wakeman, W. F. (1862) 'Aran – pagan and Christian', *Duffy's Hibernian Magazine* 1: 460–71, 567–77.

Wall, E. (2011) *Writing the Irish West: Ecologies and Traditions*. Notre Dame.

Wallace, C. (2001) 'Tragic destiny and abjection in Marina Carr's *The Mai, Portia Coughlan and By the Bog of Cats…*', *Irish University Review* 31.2: 431–49.

Wallace, N. (2015) *Hellenism and Reconciliation in Ireland: From Yeats to Field Day*. Cork.

Walsh, B. (2007) *The Pedagogy of Protest. The Educational Thought and Work of Patrick H. Pearse*. Oxford.

Walshe E. (1997a) 'Sodom and Begorrah, or Game to the Last: inventing Michael Mac Liammóir', in Walshe 1997b: 150–69.

Walshe E. (ed.) (1997b) *Sex, Nation and Dissent*. Cork.

Walshe E. (2011) *Oscar's Shadow*. Cork.

Wäppling, E. (1984) *Four Irish Legendary Figures in At Swim-Two-Birds: A Study of Flann O'Brien's Use of Finn, Suibhne, the Pooka and the Good Fairy*. Stockholm.

Ward, G. Kingsley and Gibson, E. (1995) *Courage Remembered*. London.

Warner, M. (1985) *Monuments and Maidens: The Allegory of the Female Form*. New York.

Warren, R. (ed.) (1989) *The Art of Translation*. Boston MA.

Weinstein, L. (2006) 'The significance of the Armagh dirty protest', *Éire-Ireland* 41.3–4: 11–41.

Weisman, K. (ed.) (2010) *The Oxford Handbook of the Elegy*. Oxford.

Welch, R. (ed.) (1996) *The Oxford Companion to Irish Literature*. Oxford.

Westropp, T. J. (1895) 'Aran Islands', *Journal of the Royal Society of Antiquaries* 5.3: 250–74.

Wheatley, C. J. (1999) *Beneath Iërne's Banners: Irish Protestant Drama of the Restoration and Eighteenth Century*. Notre Dame.

Whelan, Y. (2002) 'The construction and destruction of a colonial landscape: monuments to British monarchs in Dublin before and after independence', *Journal of Historical Geography* 28.4: 508–33.

Whelan, Y. (2003) *Reinventing Modern Dublin: Streetscape, Inconography and the Politics of Identity*. Dublin.

White, A. MacBride and Jeffares, A. N. (1993) *The Gonne-Yeats Letters 1893–1938*. New York.

White, J. (1973) 'Myles, Flann and Brian', in O'Keeffe 1973: 62–76.

White, L. W. (2009a) 'De Brún, Pádraig (Browne, Patrick)', in McGuire and Quinn 2009, available online at: http://dib.cambridge.org/viewReadPage.do?articleId=a2457 (accessed 20 August 2018).

White, L. W. (2009b) 'MacDonagh, Thomas', in McGuire and Quinn 2009, available online at: http://dib.cambridge.org/viewReadPage.do?articleId=a5168 (accessed 20 August 2018).

Whitty, S. (1911) 'Aras of the seas', *Celtic Review* 7.25: 10–15.

Wilde, O. (1986) *De Profundis*. London. 1st edn. 1905.

Wilde, W. (1872) *Lough Corrib, its Shores and Islands*, 2nd edn. Dublin.

Wilding, L. A. (1952) *Latin Course for Schools: Part 1, Vol. 1*. London.

Wilkins, J. (1990) 'The state and the individual: Euripides' plays of voluntary self-sacrifice', in Powell 1990: 177–94.

Wilkinson, L. P. (1969) *The Georgics of Virgil: A Critical Survey*. Cambridge.

Willett, S. J. (2005) 'Reassessing Ezra Pound's Homage to Sextus Propertius', *Syllecta Classica* 16: 173–220.

Williams, H. (2013) 'Sterne's manicules: hands, handwriting and authorial property in Tristram Shandy', *Journal for Eighteenth-Century Studies* 36: 209–23.

Williams, J. E. Caerwyn (ed.) (1971) *Literature in Celtic Countries*. Cardiff.

Williams, J. H. C. (2001) *Beyond the Rubicon. Romans and Gauls in Republican Italy*. Oxford.

Williams, M. (2016) *Ireland's Immortals: A History of the Gods of Irish Myth*. Princeton.

Wills, C. (2009) *Dublin 1916: The Siege of the GPO*. London.

Wills, G. (1992) *Lincoln at Gettysburg. The Words that Remade America*. New York.

Wilmer, S. (2007) 'Finding a post-colonial voice for Antigone: Seamus Heaney's *Burial at Thebes*', in Hardwick and Gillespie 2007: 228–42.

Wilmer, S. (2017) 'Greek tragedy as a window on the dispossessed', *New Theatre Quarterly* 33.3: 277–87.

Wilson, G. and McCreary, A. (1990) *Marie: A Story from Enniskillen*. London.

Wilson, J. H. (1804) *Swiftiana*. 2 vols. Dublin.

Winter, J. (1995) *Sites of Memory, Sites of Mourning: The Great War in European Cultural History*. Cambridge.

Wolf, N. (2012) 'Grammars in search of a corpus: pre-revival guides to the Irish language', *Australasian Journal of Irish Studies* 12: 8–24.

Wood, J. (1999) 'Folklore studies at the Celtic dawn: the rôle of Alfred Nutt as publisher and scholar', *Folklore* 110: 3–12.

Wyke, M. (2002) *The Roman Mistress*. Oxford.

X. Z. (1916) 'Poets of the Insurrection, I, Thomas MacDonagh', *Studies: An Irish Quarterly Review* 5.18: 179–87.

Yeates, P. (2001) 'The Dublin 1913 lockout', *History Ireland* 9: 31–6.

Yeats, W. B. (1898) 'The Celtic element in literature', *Cosmopolis*, June, repr. in Yeats 1961a: 173–88.

Yeats, W. B. (1899) 'The theatre', in Fitzgerald and Finneran 2003: 147–51.

Yeats, W. B. (1903) 'An Irish National Theatre', in Fitzgerald and Finneran 2003: 32–5.

Yeats, W. B. (1904a) 'The Dramatic Movement', in Fitzgerald and Finneran 2003: 40–51.

Yeats, W. B. (1904b) 'First principles', in Fitzgerald and Finneran 2003: 52–67.

Yeats, W. B. (1924) 'Editorial', *To-morrow* I.1 (August). 1.

Yeats, W. B. (1925) *A Vision (1925)*, in Paul and Harper 2008.

Yeats, W. B. (1926a) Manuscript of 'Sophocles' King Oedipus'. National Library of Ireland MS 12589 (31, Fol. 51V; SB30).

Yeats, W. B. (1926b) Letter to Augusta Gregory (18 December), Berg Collection, New York Public Library.

Yeats, W. B. (1927) 'The censorship and St. Thomas Aquinas', *Irish Statesman* 11: 47–8.

Yeats, W. B. (1928) *Sophocles' King Oedipus*. London.

Yeats, W. B. (1931a) 'Talk on *Oedipus the King* to be broadcasted from Belfast September 8', National Library of Ireland MS 30,109.

Yeats, W. B. (1931b) 'Oedipus the King', in Johnson 2000: 219–23.

Yeats, W. B. (1933) 'Plain man's *Oedipus*', in Johnson 2000: 244–5.

Yeats, W. B. (1937) *A Vision*. Dublin.

Yeats, W. B. (1938) *On the Boiler*. Dublin.

Yeats, W. B. (1957) *The Variorum Edition of the Poems of W. B. Yeats*, eds. P. Allt and R. K. Alspach. New York.

Yeats, W. B. (1960) *The Senate Speeches of W. B. Yeats*, ed. D. R. Pearce. Bloomington.

Yeats, W. B. (1961a) *Essays and Introductions*. London.

Yeats, W. B. (1961b) *The Collected Poems of W. B. Yeats*. London.

Yeats, W. B. (1966a) *Autobiographies*. London.

Yeats, W. B. (1966b) *The Variorum Edition of the Plays of W. B. Yeats*, ed. R. K. Alspach. New York.

Yeats, W. B. (1972) 'What we did or tried to do', in W. B. Yeats, *Coinage of Saorstát Éireann* (Dublin, 1928), repr. in Cleeve 1972: 9–20.

Yeats, W. B. (1997) *The Collected Letters of W. B. Yeats. Volume II 1896–1900*, eds. W. Gould, J. Kelly, and D. Toomey. Oxford.

Yeats, W. B. (2000) *Later Articles and Reviews*, ed. C. Johnson. New York.

Yeats, W. B. (2003) *The Speckled Bird*, ed. W. H. O'Donnell, new edn. Basingstoke and New York.

Younger, K. (2001) *Irish Adaptations of Greek Tragedies: Dionysus in Ireland*. Lewiston.

Younger, K. (2006) 'Irish Antigones: burying the colonial symptom', *Colloquy* 11: 148–62.

Zimmer, H. (1889) 'Keltische Beiträge II', *Zeitscrhift für deutsches Altertum* 33: 129–220, 257–338.

Zuckerberg, D. (2018) *Not All Dead White Men: Classics and Misogyny in the Digital Age*. Cambridge, MA.

Index

Abbey Theatre, Dublin 8, 221–3, 225, 228, 330
  The Arrow 221
  Euripides' *Trojan Women* 255–60
  Waking the Nation (2016) commemoration
    programme 267
abjection 173–92
abortion 246, 267, 335–6
Ab Urbe Condita (Livy) 200–1
Acton, Eileen 102
Adelphi Theatre 230
Adorno, Theodor 32–3
Adventures of Ulysses (Lamb) 212
Aegospotami, battle of 46–7
Aeneid (Virgil) 97, 114 n. 77, 123–4, 133–4, 140,
    141 n. 8, 199, 208, 273, 278–80, 281
  Heaney's translation of Book 6 8, 9–10,
    316, 345
  and *Merugud Uilix Maicc Leirtis* 210
  statesman simile 144–6
Aeschines 109–10
Aeschylus 109–10
  Oresteia 8, 330
  Prometheus Bound 93–4, 105, 110, 113 n. 73,
    121, 125
'After a Year' (MacDonagh) 77–8
'After the Wake' (Behan) 245–6
Agricola (Tacitus) 31, 122
AIDS 262–3
aisling (vision) poems 271
Albert Memorial, Dublin 354, 370, 371
Alcestis (Euripides) 93–4, 120–1, 126
Alexander the Great 169
Alexander Romance (Meyer) 211
Alexiou, Margaret 92, 112
'All of These People' (Longley) 323–4
'Altera Cithera' (Longley) 299–302
American Civil War 55
American Declaration of Independence
    (1776) 55
'Among School Children' (Yeats) 229, 232
Amra Choluim Chille 408–9
Anabasis (Xenophon) 130
Anderson, Alexander 107
Andrews, J. M. 388–9
Anglo-Irish war (1919–22), *see* Irish War of
    Independence

Annals of the Four Masters 210
Antigone (McCafferty) 332, 339–43, 344
Antigone (Sophocles) 1 n. 2, 8, 10, 129, 218
'Antigone and Lir' (MacDonagh) 66
Antigone myth 326–45
  Gregg's *Ismene* 19–20, 332–8, 344
  Heaney's *The Burial at Thebes* 1 n. 2, 8, 10,
    330–2, 336, 342 n. 102, 344
  Humphreys's *Norah* 344–5
  McCafferty's *Antigone* 332, 339–43, 344
Aosdána 251
Apology (Plato) 93, 105, 109, 120, 128
Aquinas, St Thomas 228
Aran Islands 18, 179–81
  enshrinement as heritage 186–8
  Inis Meáin 190
  Inis Mór 181–2, 185, 186, 188, 191
  racial categorization 184–6
  rockscape 183–4
  ruins 181–2
Aran Islands, The (Synge) 191–2
Aran Island writing 18
  Fir Bolg 173–92
Aranmen All (O'Flaherty) 188
Arbois de Jubainville, Henri d' 191
architecture 5–6, 43, 352–3
Ariel (Carr) 265
Aristotle 126, 211, 410
Arkins, Brian 78, 116 n. 85, 295, 394
Arnold, Matthew 39, 76, 147
Arnold, Thomas Kerchever: *Latin Prose
    Composition* 95, 115
Arrow, The (Abbey Theatre journal) 221
Ars Amatoria (Ovid) 168, 294
Ars Poetica (Horace) 16 n. 43
Artaud, Antonin 182 n. 63
Arts Council, The (An Chomhairle
    Ealaíon) 267
Ashton, Robert 271, 275–7
Atkinson, George 349, 365
Atkinson, Robert 22, 35, 36, 161–2
At Swim-Two-Birds (O'Brien) 157, 166,
    169, 247
At Swim, Two Boys (O'Neill) 12, 247–9
Augustine of Hippo, St 93, 157
Axelos, Michael 403

Babington, Charles 177
Bagley, Richard Blair 101
Baker, Herbert 352–3
Ballad of Reading Gaol, The (Wilde) 245
ballads 269–75
    classical mythology in 269–70
    Dido in 271–4
    hedge schoolmaster songs 271–2
Ballagh, Robert 251
Banim, Mary 182
Bank of Ireland, College Green,
        Dublin 353 n. 12
'Bann Valley Eclogue' (Heaney) 9
Banville, John 311
'Barbara' (MacDonagh) 13, 68–9, 75 n. 54
Barbara, St 68
bardic poetry 37–8
Barlow, Jane 183
Barton, Dunbar Plunket 355, 363
Bataille, Georges 177
Battle of Aughrim, The, or the fall of Monsieur
        St. Ruth (Ashton) 271, 275–7
Béal Bocht, An/The Poor Mouth (na
        gCopaleen) 157
Beaufort, Louise 179 n. 40, 181
Beckett, Samuel 37
Behan, Brendan 12, 181, 245
    'After the Wake' 245–6
    'Do Sheán Ó Súilleabháin'/'To Seán
        O'Sullivan' 245
    The Quare Fella 245
    and Wilde 245–6
Belfast Agreement, *see* Good Friday Agreement
Belfast Newsboys' Club 205
Belfast News Letter 378
Belfast Summer School in Latin and Classical
        Greek 15
Belfast Workers' Educational Association 205–6
Bell for Mister Loss, The (Fallon) 178
Bellum Africanum 110
Beltaine (Irish Literary Theatre journal) 220, 229
Belvedere College 212
Benjamin, Walter 186–7, 188
Bergin, Osborn 41–2
Berkeley, George 35
Bernal, Martin 29
Betham, William 177, 185–6
Blair, Hugh: *Lectures on Rhetoric and*
        Belles-Lettres 53
Blasket Islands 14, 39, 91, 211
Blomfield, Reginald 362 n. 58
blood sacrifice 257 n. 12
Bloody Sunday 277 n. 42, 287, 326–7
    in *The Burning Balaclava* 19, 282, 285–6
Blythe, Ernest 104, 113

Boland, Eavan 10
Bond, Rendal 377
'Bonnán Buí, An'/'The Yellow Bittern'
        (Mac Giolla Ghunna) 69–70
Book of Ballymote, The 207
Boucicault, Dion 159
Bradley, George 124
    Latin Prose Composition 95, 115
Breathnach, Micheál
    Bun-chúrsa Laidne/Foundation Course
        in Latin (Longman) 135
    Gramadach na Laidne/Latin Grammar
        (Sonnenschein) 135
Brenton, Howard 22–3, 31–2
Brereton, Peter 273
Brewer, Ethel 182, 183, 186
Brexit 1
British Association 180, 185
British Empire Exhibition (1924) 402–3, 403*f*
British Legion 364
Brother, The 158
Browne, C. R. 180, 181, 184
Bruton, John 365
Buachaillín Buidhe, An (Sallow Boy), *see* de
        Siúnta, Earnán
'Buchenwald Museum' (Longley) 312
Burial at Thebes, The (Heaney) 1 n. 2, 8, 10,
        330–2, 336, 342 n. 102, 344
burial rites 331
Burke, Edmund 43, 44–5, 53
Burke, Oliver 181
Burnet, John: *Early Greek Philosophy* 230
Bury, John Bagnell: *A History of Greece* 87, 136
Bushe, Paddy 251
'Butchers, The' (Longley) 307
Butte Independent, Montana 46 n. 13
Byrne, T. J. 357, 358, 363
By the Bog of Cats (Carr) 265

Caesar, Julius
    De Bello Gallico 20–1, 95, 96, 109 n. 52, 114, 131
    as love poet 275
Campbell, Charles, 2nd Baron Glenavy 359
Campbell, Lawrence 370, 372
Campbell, Patrick, 3rd Baron Glenavy 167
Campion, Thomas 76
Cantos (Pound) 292
'Caoineadh Airt Uí Laoghaire'/'The Lament for
        Art O'Leary' 330
Carey, James J. 20–1
Carleton, William 276
Carlisle, Earl of 355
Carr, Marina 42
    Ariel 265
    By the Bog of Cats 265

Hecuba 12, 263–6, 267
Phaedra Backwards 265
Carson, Edward 201, 248
Carthaginians (McGuinness) 19–20, 268–9, 271,
    272, 274, 277–86, 287
  The Burning Balaclava 19, 281–3, 285–6
  class and gender 282–3
  Dido 19, 268–9, 271, 274, 277–8, 281–2
  history and memory 285–6
  quizzes 283–5
  rejection of epic and high tradition 278–81
Casement, Roger 62, 243–4
Casson, Stanley 401
Catechism of Cliché 158
Cathleen ni Houlihan (Yeats) 257
Catholic Bulletin 402
Catholic University of Ireland 96: *see also*
    University College Dublin (UCD)
Catullus 74*f*
  Catullus Gaelach/Gaelic Catullus 98–9
  MacDonagh and 13, 50, 69–78, 72*f*
  O'Brien and 157
'Catullus to Himself' (MacDonagh) 70
Cavafy, Constantine 249–50
Cavanaugh, Rev. John W. 218, 219
Cavan orphanage fire 160
'Ceasefire' (Longley) 10–11, 302, 307, 308–25, 342
  Iliad and 314–23
  reception 309–13
  the Troubles 308–9
'Celt and Saxon' (Davis) 147
Celtic nature poets 39
Celtic Revival 206–7, 213, 350, 357
Celtic Society, UCC 148–9
Cenotaph, Dublin
  permanent cenotaph for Collins, Griffith, and
    O'Higgins, Dublin 6, 7 n. 20, 349, 350,
    351–2, 367–72, 369*f*, 371*f*
  temporary cenotaph for Collins, Griffith, and
    O'Higgins, Dublin 6, 7 n. 20, 349, 350, 351,
    365–8, 366*f*
Cenotaph, Whitehall 382, 386
censorship
  English 221–2
  Yeats and 224–6, 228, 229
Cesaire, Aimé 29
Challenge of Socialism, The (Farrington) 196
Chekov, Anton 258
Chomhairle Ealaíon, An (The Arts
    Council) 267
Christmas Carol, A (Dickens) 138
Cicero 44, 96, 110
  Catilinarian Orations 132
  De Amicitia 132
  De Senectute 96, 132, 165

Pro Archia Poeta 132, 164
Pro Lege Manilia 132
Pro Murena 199
  Philippic Orations 96, 131
Civilization of Greece and Rome, The
    (Farrington) 195–6
Civil War (1922–23) 102 n. 16, 266, 351
  see also Cenotaph, Dublin
Claidheamh Soluis, An/*The Sword of Light*
    (Gaelic League newspaper) 96, 222
Clarke, Austin 164
Clarke, Thomas 139
Classical Association of Ireland 205–6
Classical Association of Northern Ireland 15
cló Gaelach, see Gaelic typeface
Clongowes Wood College 212
Clontarf, battle of 45
coinage 6–7, 390–1, 393–406
  barnyard set 8, 393, 394, 395*f*
  British imperial coinage 397, 398–9
  commissioning 396–400
  Eurozone 393
  Greek coins 398*f*
  Metcalfe and 399, 400, 400*f*, 403–4, 405
  Milles and 399–400, 401*f*
  Morbiducci and 399, 400, 401*f*
  and national identity 405–6
  other uses 404–5
  reception 401–4
Coinage Act (1826) 397
Coinage Act (1926) 7, 393
Colleen Bawn, The (Boucicault) 159
Collins, John Henry 381 n. 25
Collins, Michael 6, 7 n. 20, 58 n. 50, 102, 349,
    350, 365
Columba, St 408–9
Colum, Padraig/Padraic 60, 61–2, 77, 179
Committee on Evil Literature 224
Confessions (Augustine) 93
Connacht Tribune 110–11
Connaught Telegraph 45–6
Connolly, James 194, 220, 391
Connor, Jerome 399
Connor, Peats Mhíchíl 87
Conradh na Gaeilge/The Gaelic League,
    see Gaelic League, The
Conrad, Joseph 28
Conroy, Bishop George Michael 182 n. 62
Cooley, Thomas 353 n. 12
Corkery, Daniel 3, 13, 22, 38, 39–41, 89
Cork Examiner 262
Cormac Ua Connaill (Dinneen) 138
'Cornelia' (Longley) 298, 299
Cosgrave, W. T. 351, 356, 358, 359, 363, 365,
    385, 390

Costello, John 369, 372
Countess Cathleen, The (Yeats) 218, 226
Country Life 183
Craigavon Burial Bill 385–6
Craig, Edward Gordon 223
Craig, James (Lord Craigavon) 6, 375, 376, 381, 382, 385–6, 388–9
    burial at Stormont 376, 385–6, 387f, 388
Critias (Plato) 128–9
Crito (Plato) 93, 105, 109, 120, 128, 129
Cronin, Anthony 156
'Cross of Sacrifice' (Blomfield) 362 n. 58
Crotty, Derbhle 265
Cruiskeen Lawn column (na gCopaleen) 17–18, 21 n. 48, 138, 156–70
    classics and medieval Irish
        tradition 163–6, 169
    cló Gaelach 17, 21 n. 48, 166
    code-switching 164, 165
    cultural, social, and literary allusions 160–3
    as marginalia 165–9
    politicization of 159–60
Cúchulainn 42, 44, 48: see also Death of Cúchulainn, The (Sheppard)
Cumann Buan-Choimeadta na Gaeilge/Society
    for the Preservation of the Irish
    Language 212
Cumann na mBan/Irish Women's
    Council 152, 260
Cumann na nGaedheal 102, 349, 351, 365, 367
Cumont, Franz 233
Cure at Troy, The (Heaney) 8, 330
Curry, Eugene 180
Cusack, Michael 213
Customs House, Dublin 5, 353–4, 353 n. 12, 380–1, 382–3
    symbolism of statues 383
Cynegirus (Athenian soldier) 45

Dáil Eireann 140 n. 18, 224, 247, 351–2, 353–4, 356, 365, 367, 369, 412
Dalkey Archive, The (O'Brien) 157
Dalton, Seamus 107 n. 42
Danesfort, Lord 402
d'Arbois de Jubainville, Henri d', see Arbois de Jubainville, Henri d'
Dares Phrygius 208
Daughters of Ireland/Inghinidhe na hÉireann 152, 260
Davies, John Fletcher 101
Davis, Thomas 39, 45, 46, 58–9, 147, 248
Day-Lewis, Cecil 8 n. 24
De Amicitia (Cicero) 132
Dean, Rev. Brett 379–80

Death of Cúchulainn, The (Sheppard) 6, 349–50, 351, 390
De Bello Gallico (Caesar) 20–1, 95, 96, 109 n. 52, 114, 131
de Bhaldraithe, Tomás 110 n. 55
de Brún, Rt Rev. Msgr Pádraig 13–14, 21, 22, 38 n. 33, 85–91, 99
    Aintioghoiné: Dráma le Sofoicléas/Antigone:
        A play by Sophocles 86, 129
    'Ars Scribendi' 88–9
    Beathaí Phlútairc/Plutarch's Lives 87, 129
    'Dán molta na hAittiche. As Oidiopús i
        gColón, dráma le Sofoicléas'/'Poem in
        Praise of Attica. From Oedipus at Colonus,
        a play by Sophocles' 129
    elegies 87
    Iliad, translation of 87, 89, 127
    Íodhbairt Ifigéine: Dráma le Euripides/The
        Sacrifice of Iphigenia: A play by
        Euripides 86, 126
    An Odaisé (Odyssey) 87, 89, 127–8, 412
    Oidiopús i gColón: Dráma le Sofoicléas/
        Oedipus at Colonus: A play by Sophocles 86, 90–1, 129–30
    Rí Oidiopús: Dráma le Sofoicléas/Oedipus Rex:
        A play by Sophocles 86, 87, 130
    Stair na Gréige/History of Greece
        (Bury) 87, 136
    Tús Laidne trí Laidin Eaglasta/Beginning Latin
        through Ecclesiastical Latin 87–8
De Burger (Afrikaans newspaper) 195
decadence 238–9
'Decade of Centenaries' programme
    (Department of Culture, Heritage and the
    Gaeltacht) 2
Declaration of Independence 195
decorum
    funeral rituals 10, 321, 323, 324, 343–5
    manners 321–2
de Hindeberg, Piaras 115
De Lingua Latina (Varro) 73
Demosthenes 53, 57, 96, 129
Demosthenes and Cicero (Plutarch) 96
Dempsey, Thomas 101
De Profundis (Wilde) 239, 240, 245
De Rerum Natura (Lucretius) 73, 75, 199
Derrig, Thomas 111 n. 59
De Senectute (Cicero) 96, 132, 165
de Siúnta, Earnán: Airgead Beo: Cnuasach
    Gearrscéalta as Seanchas na Gréige/
    Quicksilver: Short Stories from the Greek
    Tradition 134
de Valera, Éamon 116, 351, 364, 367, 390
Devane, Richard 224

Devlin, Bernadette 326–7, 328
Devlin, Joseph 201, 376, 380 n. 22, 381 n. 26
Devoy, John 55
Dialectic of Enlightenment (Adorno and
        Horkheimer) 32–3
Dialogues of the Gods (Lucian) 97, 128
Dickens, Charles 138
Dido and Aeneas (Purcell) 278
Dillon, John Blake 45
Dillon, Myles 87 n. 23
Dillon, Thomas 105–6
Dinneen, Rev. Patrick (Pádraic/Pádraig Ua
        Duinnín) 3, 8, 9, 13, 21, 22, 138–55, 410
    Aenéis Bhirgil/Virgil's Aeneid 97, 133
    *Aistí ar Litridheacht Ghréigise is Laidne/Essays
        on Greek and Latin Literature* 97,
        136, 148–50
    'Ban-churadh Ghaelach'/'A Gaelic heroine' 152
    'Béasa is teanga dúthchais'/'Native customs
        and language' 154–5
    Celtic origins of Virgil 146–50
    comparison of Dublin with Troy 254
    Cormac Ua Connaill 138
    'Grá tíre agus a mhalairt'/'Love of country and
        its opposite' 152–4
    on Homer 140
    Irish–English dictionary and thesaurus 138
    and land dispossession 148–9
    and Maecenas 150–1
    The Queen of the Hearth 140, 152
    in *Ulysses* 138
    and Virgil 140, 141–6, 150–5
Dinnsenchas 210
Dirrane, Bridget 18, 188, 190
Disciple, The (Wilde) 245
dissent, aesthetics of 238–42
*Dissertatio De Crure Fracto/Treatise on
        a Broken Leg* 164–5
*Dissertation on the Principles of Human
        Eloquence, A* (Leland) 52–3
divorce 246, 263, 267
Dobbs, Arthur 353 n. 12
Dodds, Eric Roberston 16, 193–4
Doody, Patrick 49 n. 22
'Do Sheán Ó Súilleabháin'/'To Seán O'Sullivan'
        (Behan) 245
Douglas, Lord Alfred 237, 240
Dreaming of the Bones, The (Yeats) 180
Dublin Drama League 11–12
    and Euripides' *Trojan Women* 255–60, 256f
Dubliners, The (Joyce) 180, 216
Dublin Theatre Festival (2019) 266
Dudley-Edwards, Ruth 53
Duffy, Charles Gavan 45

Dún Aonghasa/Dun Aengus, Inis Mór 181–2,
        185, 191
Dunraven, Earl of 182

Eachtra Giolla an Amaráin (McNamara) 274
Earp, Hobbs and Miller, Manchester 377
'Easter 1916' (Yeats) 64, 295–6
Easter Poets 62: *see also* Casement, Roger;
        Connolly, James; MacDonagh, Thomas;
        Pearse, Patrick; Plunkett, Joseph
Easter Rising (1916) 2, 102, 195
    classical influences on 43–59, 60–1
    memorial 349–50
    New York Time report 60–1
    see also Easter Poets
Echo Gate, The (Longley) 294, 299,
        302–5, 307
Eclogues (Virgil) 8–9, 140, 142
education system 97–8
    baptism barrier 263 n. 35
    and British Empire 30–2
    Irish-language university education 100–19
    Leaving Certificate 103, 116, 117
    and slavery 49 n. 23
    Thomson on education 92–3
Eglinton, John (pseudonym of William
        Kirkpatrick Magee) 66
Electric Light (Heaney) 9
elegies 291–307
    de Brún 87
    Longley 297–306, 313
    Propertius 295–302
    Sulpicia 11, 305–6
    Tibullus 302–6
    Yeats 295–7
11 September 2001 attack 311
Elgee, Jane Francesca 45
Eliot, T. S. 20, 27–8, 34, 41
Elizabeth I, Queen of England 142
Empire Day (1922) 268
empires: and Ireland 27–30
'End of a Naturalist' (Heaney) 298 n. 30
Enneads (Plotinus) 7
epic, domestication of 32–4
Epistolae (Pliny) 275 n. 30
Epitome of Roman History (Florus) 199
Epitome of Roman History (Justin) 280 n. 52
Epódanna Oráit/Horace. Epodes
        (Ó Rioghardáin) 132
Epodes (Horace) 132
Eriu (journal) 211, 212
Essay on the Antiquity of the Irish Language, An
        (Vallancey) 19
Euclid 97

Euripides 109, 157
  Alcestis 93–4, 120–1, 126
  Heracles 157, 247 n. 39
  Iphigenia in Aulis 86, 126, 265
  Iphigenia in Tauris 126
  Phoenician Women 340
  Trojan Women 11–12, 126, 254–67
Eurozone 393
Evans-Wentz, W. Y. 181–2
Evening Press, The 245
Evolution of Sinn Féin, The (Henry) 16, 17,
  197–9, 204–5
Exon, Charles 101
Exploded View, An (Longley) 297–302, 307

Fahy, Thomas 101–2, 109, 112–13, 115
Fairytale of Katmandu (documentary) 250–1
Fallon, Padraig 178
Fallon, Peter 8, 43, 140 n. 15
famine, see Great Famine
Fanon, Frantz 29
Farrington, Benjamin 16, 194–6
Faul, Fr Denis 324 n. 71
Ferguson, Mary 183
Ferguson, Samuel 180, 183
Ferriter, Diarmuid 246–7
Fianna Fáil 349–50, 351, 352
Fianna warriors 37
Fiche Bliain ag Fás/Twenty Years A-Growing
  (Ó Súilleabháin) 91, 105, 108
Field Day Anthology of Irish Literature 267 n. 49
Filí na Máighe 41
'Filíocht na Gaeilge: A Cineál'/'Irish Poetry: its
  nature' (Corkery) 38, 41
Fine Gael 352
Fir Bolg 18
  and abjection 173–92
  on Aran 179–86
  and Aran Islands ruins 181–2
  enshrinement as heritage 186–8
  myth 175–9, 183, 186, 191
  origins of 178
  racial categorization 184–6
Fitzgerald, F. Scott 42
Fitzgibbon, Viscount 371 n. 100
Flaherty, Robert 181, 190
Florus 199
Foley, John Henry 6, 43, 371
Foras Feasa ar Éirinn/History of Ireland
  (Keating) 269
forgiveness 322–3
Foster, Roy 139 n. 12, 296 n. 24, 366
Founding Fathers, America 44
Four Courts, Inns Quay, Dublin 5, 353 & n. 12, 382
Fox, Charles James 43

Freedom Park, Pretoria 5
French, Viscount, of Ypres and High Lake 355
Friel, Brian 137–8, 142, 144, 152, 153
Froude, John Anthony 147, 184
'Funeral Oration of Pericles, The'
  (Thucydides) 12–13, 54, 96, 130
funeral rituals 10, 321, 323, 324, 343–5
Furr, Leonora Reilly 146

Gaelic American 62
Gaelic Journal 212
Gaelic League, The/Conradh na Gaeilge 35, 36,
  83, 102, 138, 139
  Aran Islands and 180
  An Claidheamh Soluis/The Sword of
    Light 96, 222
  and Gaelic typography 142
'Gaelic Prose Literature' (Pearse) 48
Gaelic Revival 46, 83–5, 98, 99, 216, 366–7
Gaelic typeface/cló Gaelach 17, 21 n. 48, 142–4,
  143f, 166
Gallagher, John 146
Gandon, James 353 n. 12, 382
Garden of Remembrance, Rotunda Gardens,
  Parnell Square 349, 350, 351, 352
Geilt, Suibhne 126
General Post Office (GPO), Dublin 5, 58, 353
  & n. 12, 374, 382–5, 384f, 389–90, 392
  The Death of Cúchulainn statue 6, 349–50,
    351, 390
  neoclassicism of 254, 382–5, 389–90
  symbolism of statues 383, 385, 390
Genet, Jean 250
George I, King of England 5 n. 15
George II, King of England 5
Georgics (Virgil) 8, 122–3, 140, 144 n. 38, 150–1
Gettysburg address 12–13, 54, 55–6
Gettysburg, battle of 55–6
Ghost Orchid, The (Longley) 10–11, 302, 305,
  307, 308–25, 342
Gifford, Muriel 77: see also MacDonagh, Muriel
  (née Gifford)
Giraldus Cambrensis 147
'Glanmore Eclogue' (Heaney) 9
Glendining, George 371 n. 100
Gods and Fighting Men (Gregory) 161–2
Gogarty, Oliver St John 221
Golden Joy, The (MacDonagh) 67, 69 n. 36, 75–6
Goldsmith, Oliver 43
Gonne, Maud 11, 220, 254, 260, 266,
  295, 296–7
  and coinage 402
  as Hecuba 257–8
Good Friday Agreement (Belfast
  Agreement) 325, 340

Gough, Viscount 355
Grattan, Henry 43, 354, 380, 382–3
Great Famine (1845–9) 7, 226–7, 331
Great War Stone 358, 359–60, 361*f*
Greek funeral orations (*epitaphioi*) 57–8
Gregg, Stacey 10, 19–20, 332–8, 344
Gregory, Lady Augusta 161–2, 180, 222,
    257, 330
Grey, John 355
Grey, Kruger 404
Griffith, Arthur 6, 7 n. 20, 102, 220, 349,
    350, 365
Gúm, An/The Scheme 83–99
    Book Committee 89 n. 32
    Publications Committee 84–5, 86
    Thomson and 94
    translation scheme 83–5, 98, 99
Guthrie, Tyrone 228
Gwynn, Edward John 36
Gwynn, Stephen 355

Ha'aretz (Israeli newspaper) 311
Haddon, A. C. 180, 181, 184
Hales, Seán 102 n. 16
Hall-Edwards, John 45
Hully, E. J. *Notes on the History, Literature and
    Civilisation of Rome* 136
Haly, Joseph 272
'Hamilcar Barca' (Casement) 62
Hanly, Daithi 349
'Happy Prince, The' (Wilde) 242
Hastings, Warren 44–5
Havel, Václav: definition of hope 311
Hayes, Brian 251
Healy, Cahir 381 n. 24
Heaney, Seamus 22, 33, 42, 178, 192, 312, 333
    Aeneid 6 8, 9–10, 316, 345
    and Aeschylus 8
    The Burial at Thebes 1 n. 2, 8, 10, 330–2, 336,
        342 n. 102, 344
    The Cure at Troy 8, 330
    Electric Light 9
    'End of a Naturalist' 298 n. 30
    Human Chain 9–10
    'A Keen for Coins' 8, 393
    'Mycenae Lookout' poems 330
    reworking of Mac Giolla Ghunna's 'An
        Bonnán Buí' 70 n. 40
    Seeing Things 9
    and Sophocles 1 n. 2, 8
    The Spirit Level 330
    Station Island 9
    and Troubles 9
    'Valediction' 298 n. 30
Hearn, William E. 101

Heavey, Margaret (Mairghréad Ní
    Éimhthigh) 13, 14, 102–4, 106, 107, 109,
    113–17, 118 & n. 96, 119
    *Bun-Chúrsa Ceapadóireachta Gréigise/
        Foundation Course in Greek Prose
        Composition* (North and Hillard) 95,
        114, 134
    Graiméar Gréigise/Greek Grammar
        (Sonnenschein) 95, 114, 116 n. 86, 135
    *Prós-Cheapadóireacht Laidne/Latin Prose
        Composition* (Bradley's Arnold) 95, 115,
        116 n. 86, 135
    translation of *De Bello Gallico* 109 n. 52,
        114, 131
    translation of *Georgics* 144 n. 38
    unpublished translations in NUIG
        archive 122–3
Hecuba (Carr) 12, 263–6, 267
hedge schools 137, 271–2, 280 n. 52
Henderson, Thomas 379
Henry, Paul 206
Henry, Robert Mitchell 16–17, 193,
    196–206, 217
    The Evolution of Sinn Féin 16, 17,
        197–9, 204–5
    and Gaelic Society 203–4
    and Irish Volunteers 17, 197
    on post-Easter Rising executions 204–5
    and QUB 206
    rifle practices 197
    and Sinn Féin 196–206
Heracles (Euripides) 157, 247 n. 39
Heraclitus of Ephesus 230, 232
Hermesianax 294
Herodotus 45, 57, 94, 109, 126, 230, 318
Hidden Ireland, The (Corkery) 38, 40, 41
Higgins, Charles 185, 188
Hillard, Rev. A. E. 95, 114, 134
    *Latin Prose Composition for the Middle
        Forms of Schools* 20
Historia de excidio Troiae (Dares Phrygius) 208
History of England (Macaulay) 142
History of Ireland/Foras Feasa ar Éirinn
    (Keating) 269
Hogan, John 6
Hollow Men, The (Eliot) 28
'Homage to Sextus Propertius' (Pound) 291–2,
    293, 296, 301–2
Homer 109, 140
    The Iliad 11, 94, 126–7, 142, 211, 263, 314–23
    Longley and 10–11, 311–13
    The Odyssey 13–14, 32–4, 50, 94, 127–8, 200,
        210–11, 312
Home Rule for Ireland 194
homoeroticism 243, 250

homophobia 241, 244
homosexuality 12, 237–53
  decriminalization of 246–7
  dissent, aesthetics of 238–42
  Pearse 242–4
  see also *Carthaginians* (McGuinness)
Horace 110, 293
  Ars Poetica 16 n. 43
  Epodes 132
  MacDonagh and 49, 75–6
  Odes 76, 132, 140–1
Horkheimer, Max 32–3
House of Parliament, Dublin 353 n. 12, 354
Hughes, Francis 331, 344
Human Chain (Heaney) 9–10
Humanitas (journal) 88–9
Humphreys, Gerard 10, 344–5
hunger strikes 188, 329, 331, 344–5
Hyde, Douglas 36, 65, 138, 139, 147
Hyde-Lees, George 230, 296
Hynes, John 107

'Ice-Cream Man, The' (Longley) 313
Idylls (Theocritus) 94, 130
Iliad, The (Homer) 11, 34, 126–7, 211, 314–23
  Carr and 263
  de Brún's translation 87, 89, 127
  decorum/funeral rites 321, 323, 324
  father as suppliant 317–21
  father's katabasis 316–17
  Longley's 'Ceasefire' and 314–21, 325
  translations of 13–14, 94,142
'Image from Beckett, An' (Mahon) 298 n. 32
'Image from Propertius, An'
  (Longley) 297, 298–9
immram narratives 190 n. 116, 210
Imperial War Graves Commission 350, 358
imperialism 27–32
  British Empire Exhibition (1924) 402–3, 403*f*
  British imperial coinage 397, 398–9
  classical literary approaches in times of
    conflict 27–30
  Latin teaching/language and 30–2
  Portland stone as imperial symbol at
    Stormont 380–2, 386, 389
  and racial purity 27–8
  in Virgil 9
Importance of Being Oscar, The
  (Mac Liammóir) 244
Imtheachta Aeniasa (first Irish language
  translation of Virgil) 38, 144
'In First Century Ireland' (Pearse) 243
Inghinidhe na hÉireann (Daughters of
  Ireland) 152, 260

Inis Meáin 190
Inis Mór 186, 188
  Dún Aonghasa/Dun Aengus 181–2,
    185, 191
INLA (Irish National Liberation Army)
  324 n. 71, 391
'Intellectual Future of the Gael, The' (Pearse) 48
In the Shadow of the Glen (Synge) 220, 259
Iphigenia in Aulis (Euripides) 86, 126, 265
Iphigenia in Tauris (Euripides) 126
IRA (Irish Republican Army) ceasefire 309–10,
  311, 312: *see also* New IRA;
  Provisional IRA
Iraq War 331
Irish bardic poetry 140–1
Irish Citizen Army 195, 197
Irish classicism 37–42
Irish Free State 206, 260, 351
  early years' classical translations into
    Irish 83–99
  and memorials/architecture 353
  new coinage 6
Irish Free State Constitution Act (1922) 213
Irish Historical Society, Dublin 206
Irish Historical Studies (journal) 206
Irish Independent, The 228, 251, 258–60, 262
Irish Institute of Hellenic Studies, Athens 405
Irish Journal of Medical Science 184
Irish Labour Party 194
Irish language: Greek, Latin, and 34–7
  classics taught through 100–19
  revival of, *see* Gaelic Revival
  tension with Greek and Latin 34–42, 156–70
  translation into, *see* Gúm, An/The Scheme
    see also de Brún, Pádraig; Dinneen, Patrick
    (Pádraic/Pádraig Ua Duinnín); Heavey,
    Margaret (Mairghréad Ní Éimhthigh);
    Ó Searcaigh, Cathal; Thomson, George
    (Seoirse Mac Tomáis/Seoirse Mac
    Laghmainn)
Irish Literary Revival 33–4, 35, 36, 42, 62–4,
  137–41, 408
'Irishman in England, The' (Dodds) 194
Irish nationalism 193–6
Irish National Liberation Army (INLA)
  324 n. 71, 391
Irish National Theatre Society 260
Irish National War Memorial 349, 350, 351,
  355–65, 361*f*, 362*f*
Irish *Odyssey,* see *Merugud Ulix Maicc Leirtis*
Irish Patriot Party 382
Irish Press, The 262–3, 386
Irish Republican Brotherhood 139, 197, 202
Irish Review, The 66, 70, 77

Irish Revival, *see* Celtic Revival; Gaelic Revival;
    Irish Literary Revival
Irish Self-Government Alliance 73, 74*f*
Irish Statesman, The 228
Irish Texts Society 139 n. 14
Irish Times Digital Archive 159
Irish Times, The 108–9, 185, 228, 250, 251,
    266 n. 47, 301, 357
    Cruiskeen Lawn column 17–18, 21 n. 48,
        138, 156–70
    on Irish National War Memorial 364
    publication of 'Ceasefire' 309–11
Irish Volunteers (I.V.) 17, 195, 197, 200,
    202, 260
Irish War of Independence 351
Irish Women's Council/Cumann na mBan
    152, 260
Ismene (Gregg) 19–20, 332–8, 344
I.V., *see* Irish Volunteers (I.V.)

James, Henry 29
Jameson, Andrew 355, 358
Jebb, Richard Claverhouse 7, 222, 225, 226
J&H Baird (printing firm) 272, 273
Johnson, Samuel 40
Johnston, Francis 353 n. 12, 383
Jordan, Wayne 8 n. 21
Journal of the Ivernian Society 97
Joyce, James 42, 49 n. 26, 192
    The Dubliners 180, 216
    and *Merugud Uilix Maicc Leirtis* 212–13
    and Modernism 3
    and *The Odyssey* (Homer) 33–4
    'Oscar Wilde: The Poet of Salome' 241
    *A Portrait of the Artist as a Young
        Man* 178, 216
    and Sinn Féin 212–16
    Stephen Hero 216
    Ulysses 16, 17, 20, 29–30, 33, 39, 46–7, 138,
        166, 170, 178, 212–16, 217
    and Wilde 12, 241–2
Joynt, Maud 130
Justin 280 n. 52
Juvenal 124, 200

Keating, Geoffrey 140, 269
'Keen for Coins, A' (Heaney) 8
Kelsall, Malcolm 189–90
Kennelly, Brendan 12, 152 n. 70, 261–3, 266–7
Kenny, Enda 392
Kiberd, Declan 20, 21, 22, 27–42, 44, 58, 75,
    186–7, 413, 417
Killeen, James Frank (Prionsias Ó
    Cillín) 113–14, 132

Kilmer, Joyce 60, 61*f*
'Kindertotenlieder' (Longley) 299
King's Inns Library 207
Kinsella, Thomas 70 n. 40
Kipling, Rudyard 27, 28
Kishkan, Theresa 189 n. 110
Knatchbull, Nicholas 313 n. 24
Knatchbull, Timothy 313 n. 24, 323
Krappe, Alexander 183

Lalor, James Fintan 199
Lamb, Charles and Mary 212
'Lament for Art O'Leary, The'/'Caoineadh Airt
        Uí Laoghaire' 330
language and culture movement 138–9
language revival movement, *see* Gaelic Revival
language textbooks 134–6
    Greek 134–5
    Latin 135–6
Larmour, John 313, 376–7, 378
Lawless, Emily 189, 190
Lawson, John: *Lectures Concerning Oratory*
        (Lawson) 52–3
Leader, The 138, 139
Leask, Harold 367, 368
'Leda and the Swan' (Yeats) 224
Legion of Mary 35
Lehman, Agnes 183–4
Lehmann, Paul 103
Leinster House, Dublin 349, 353, 354, 367
Leland, Thomas 52–3
Levi-Strauss, Claude 401
Liberators, The (Balkan play) 257
Lieutenant of Inishmore (Martin
        MacDonagh) 188 n. 105
Life of Theseus (Plutarch) 386–8
Light on Distant Hills (Ó Searcaigh) 252
Lincoln, Abraham 12–13, 54, 55–6
Literary and Historical Society, University
        College Dublin 156
*Literature in Ireland. Studies Irish and
        Anglo-Irish* (MacDonagh) 49, 64, 65–6,
        76, 78 n. 63
Livy 110, 132, 200–1
Long Kesh (Maze) prison 329 n. 20,
        345 n. 119, 391
Longley, Michael 291–325
    'All of These People' 323–4
    'Altera Cithera' 299–302
    'Buchenwald Museum' 312
    'The Butchers' 307
    'Ceasefire' 10–11, 302, 307, 308–25, 342
    'Cornelia' 298, 299
    decorum and manners 321–2

Longley, Michael (*cont.*)
   The Echo Gate 294, 302–5, 307
   and elegy 291
   An Exploded View 297–302, 307
   The Ghost Orchid 10–11, 302, 305, 307,
      308–25, 342
   'The Helmet' 312
   and Homer 10–11, 311–13
   'The Ice-Cream Man' 313
   'An Image from Propertius' 297, 298–9
   'Kindertotenlieder' 299
   'The Oar' 312–13
   'Oliver Plunkett' 307
   'The Parting' 312
   'Partisans' 312
   'Peace' 294, 302–5
   'Poppies' 312
   and Propertius 293–4, 297–302
   refusal (*recusatio*) poems 296, 299–300
   'Remembering the Poets' 293, 294
   'Skara Brae' 299
   'Sulpicia' 305–6
   and Tibullus 302–6
   and the Troubles 10–11, 300–1, 308–9
   The Weather in Japan 293, 294
   'Wounds' 307
   'Wreaths' 299, 307
L'Ouverture, Toussaint 29
'Love Not War' (Mahon) 292
Lucan 208
Luce, A. A. 36
Lucian of Samosata 96
   Dialogues of the Gods 97, 128
   Vera Historia 96, 128
Lucretius 50, 73, 75, 199
Luibhéid, Colm 116 n. 85
Lutyens, Edwin 353 n. 9, 363, 382
   Irish National War Memorial 349, 350, 357,
      358, 359–60, 364
Lynam, E. W. 186
Lynch, John 199
Lynd, Robert 183
Lyrical Poems (MacDonagh) 50, 67, 69–72, 75

McAlesse, Mary 267, 408
Macalister, R. A. S. 173, 176 n. 16
Macaomh, An (magazine) 53, 66
Mac Aonghusa, Proinsias 108
MacArthur, William 203–4
Macaulay, Thomas Babington 142
MacBride, John 260
McBride, Seán 354
McCafferty, Owen 10, 332, 339–43, 344
Mac Cárthaigh, Rev. Seán 132
McCarthy, Justin 43

McCartney, Robert: sisters' quest for
      justice 332, 334
Mac Cóil, Liam 21
Mac Conghail, Muiris 107
Mac Craith, Seán 21
   Stair na Rómha/History of Rome 136
MacDonagh, John 69–70
McDonagh, Martin 188 n. 105
MacDonagh, Muriel (née Gifford) 71 n. 45
MacDonagh, Thomas 3, 13, 22, 58, 60–79,
      180, 410–11
   'After a Year' 77–8
   'Antigone and Lir' 66
   'Barbara' 13, 68–9, 75 n. 54
   biographical details 65
   and Catullus 13, 50, 69–78, 72*f*
   'Catullus to Himself' 70
   and classical themes 64
   and Easter Rising 62
   The Golden Joy 67, 69 n. 36, 75–6
   and Horace 49, 75–6
   Irish literature *v.* Greek and
      Latin 49–50, 65–9
   *Literature in Ireland. Studies Irish and
      Anglo-Irish* 49, 64, 65–6, 76, 78 n. 63
   Lyrical Poems 50, 67, 69–72, 75
   *Metempsychosis: Or a Mad World: A Play in
      One Act* 64 n. 19, 69
   'Notes for a lecture on ancient Irish
      literature' 66
   'Of a Greek Poem' 50, 67, 69
   Pagans 69
   and Plotinus 69 n. 36
   Poetical Works of Thomas MacDonagh 71–2
   'The Quest' 67
   Songs of Myself 71 n. 45
   Through the Ivory Gate 50, 64 n. 19
   Yeats and 64, 75
McElderry, Robert Knox 101
MacEntee, Seán 352, 369
Mac Fhinn, Eric 106, 108 n. 48
MacFhirbhisigh, Dubhaltach 175–6, 185–6
Mac Giobúin, Rev. Cathal 21, 130
Mac Giolla Eoin, Art 21
   Iphigenia in Tauris 126
Mac Giolla Ghunna, Cathal Buí 69–70, 73
Mac Giollarnáth, Proinnsias 118
McGrath, Raymond 349, 350, 369–70,
      371, 372
McGuinness, Frank 178, 192
   Carthaginians 19–20, 268–9, 271, 272, 274,
      277–86, 287
McGuinness, Martin 340–1, 343
McGurk, Patrick 322–3
Mac Hale, John (Seán Mac Héil) 21, 127

Mackail, John William 76 n. 57
McKee, Lyra 1 n. 4
MacKenna, Stephen 7
McKittrick, David 309
Mac Laghmainn, Seoirse, *see* Thomson, George
Mac Liammóir, Micheál 24
McMahon, Thomas 314, 323
Mac Mathúna, Séamus 107
McNamara, Donncha Rua 274
MacNeice, Louis 63 n. 13, 179, 186
MacNeill, Eoin 18, 49 n. 23, 138, 180, 188
    and Gaelic League 139
    and Irish Volunteers 202
    and Pearse 202
    Phases in Irish History 175–6
    and Sinn Féin 203
Mac Philibín, Rev. Liam 21, 141 n. 28, 144
    Aenéis Bhirgil/Virgil's Aeneid 133
Macrobius 280 n. 52
Mac Tomáis, Seoirse, *see* Thomson, George
Madden, Frederick 270
Madden, John 116 n. 85
'Madonna of Slieve Dun, The' (Robinson) 224
Maecenas 150–1
Magdalene laundries 263
Magill magazine 252
Maguire, Thomas 101
Mahaffy, John Pentland 22, 35, 36, 162, 177,
    185–6, 194–5, 239
Mahon, Derek 292, 294, 298 n. 32
Manchester Guardian, The 401
Man in a Distant Field, A (Kishkan) 189 n. 110
Man of Aran (film) 181, 190
Manship, Paul 399, 401f
Marathon, battle of 45
Marcus Aurelius 4, 5 n. 15
Martel, Édouard-Alfred 182
Martinelli, Rt Rev. Sebastian 219
Mason, T. H. 173
Mathews, Aidan Carl 178
Maudling, Reginald 327
Mausoleum, Halicarnassus 353
Maxwell, John 313, 314, 315–16
Maze (Long Kesh) prison 329 n. 20,
    345 n. 119, 391
Mellows, Liam 102 & n. 16
memorials 349–73
    Albert Memorial 354, 370, 371
    British monarchy 370–1
    classicism and political idealism 373
    classicism and politics 352–5
    The Death of Cúchulainn (Sheppard) 6,
        349–50, 351, 390
    Garden of Remembrance, Rotunda Gardens,
        Parnell Square 349, 350, 351, 352

Irish National War Memorial 349, 350, 351,
    355–65, 361f, 362f
    partisan contexts 351–2
    permanent cenotaph for Collins, Griffith, and
        O'Higgins, Dublin 6, 7 n. 20, 349, 350,
        351–2, 367–72, 369f, 371f
    temporary cenotaph for Collins, Griffith, and
        O'Higgins, Dublin 6, 7 n. 20, 349, 350, 351,
        365–8, 366f
Merrion Square (Dublin) Bill debate 356
*Merugud Cleirech Choluim Chille/The Wandering
    of Colum Cille's Clerics* 207
*Merugud Uilix Maicc Leirtis/The Wanderings of
    Ulysses son of Laertes* 17, 204, 206–13, 216
Messenger, John 180
Metamorphoses (Ovid) 132
Metcalfe, Percy
    and British Empire Exhibition 402–3, 403f
    and coinage 399, 400, 400f, 403–4, 405
*Metempsychosis: Or a Mad World: A Play in One
    Act* (MacDonagh) 64 n. 19, 69
Meyer, Kuno 17, 49–50, 180, 206–12, 216
    *Eine irische Version der Alexandersage/An
        Irish version of the Alexander
        Romance* 211
Mhac an tSaoi, Máire 86, 87, 89
Miller, Malcolm 377
Milles, Carl 399–400, 401f
Mise Éire (Pearse) 153
Mitchel, John 53–4
Mommsen, Theodor 147
Monck, Nugent 222
Moran, David Patrick 139
Moran, Zozimus 270, 273, 275
Morbiducci, Publio 399, 400, 401f
Morgan, Lady 277
Mould, Daphne Pochin 184
Mountbatten, Louis 313
Mountford, James: *Latin Prose Composition* 115
mourning 285–6, 344, 359
Mulcahy, J. B. 46 n. 13
Mulchrone, Kathleen 104 n. 27
Mulholland, Carolyn 8, 393, 394f
Mullen, Pat 181, 190
murals 391
Murder Machine, The (Pearse) 49 n. 23
Murphy, Rev. James W. H. 36
Murray, Gilbert 221, 257
'Mycenae Lookout' poems (Heaney) 330
myths
    Antigone myth 326–45
    classical mythology in Irish ballads 269–70
    Cúchulainn 42, 44, 48: see also *Death of
        Cúchulainn, The* (Sheppard)
    Fir Bolg 175–9, 183, 186, 191

na gCopaleen, Myles
  An Béal Bocht/The Poor Mouth 157
  Cruiskeen Lawn column 17–18, 21 n. 48, 138,
    156–70, see also O'Brien, Flann;
    O'Nolan, Brian
National Gallery, Dublin 354
National Museum, Dublin 367
National University of Ireland (NUI) 100 n. 1, 117
National University of Ireland, Galway (NUIG)
    14, 100 n. 1 see also Queen's College, Galway;
    University College Galway (UCG)
Nation Once Again, A (Davis) 45, 46, 248
Nation, The (newspaper) 45
nativism movement 162–3
Natural History Museum, Dublin 354, 367
Nelson's column, Dublin 5
Nemean Odes (Pindar) 109 n. 52, 123
neoclassicism 254, 374–92
  GPO 254, 382–5, 389–90
  political icons 389–91
  Stormont 375–82
Nesbitt, William 101
New IRA 1 n. 4
New York Times, The 60–1, 62 n. 5, 226, 228,
    230, 263
Ní Chianáin, Neasa 250–1
ní Chonaill, Eibhlín Dubh 330
Nicomachean Ethics (Aristotle) 126
Nic Shiubhlaigh, Máire 260
Ní Dhomhnaill, Nuala 309–10
Ní Éimhthigh, Mairghréad, see Heavey, Margaret
    (Mairghréad Ní Éimhthigh)
9/11 2001 attack 311
Noh theatre 223
Nolan, Frank 48–9
'Non-existence of Ireland, The'
    (Pound) 296
Norah (Humphreys) 344–5
Norris, David 12, 246–7, 251–3
Northern Ireland Executive 340
Northern Ireland Parliament Building,
    see Stormont, Belfast
Northern Irish Troubles 291–345
  Heaney and 9, 312, 330–2, 344, 345
  Longley and 10–11, 300–1, 308–13, 323–5
North, M. A. 20, 95, 114, 134
  Latin Prose Composition for the Middle Forms
    of Schools 20
'No Second Troy' (Yeats) 11, 254, 286, 295
Notre Dame, Indiana 218–20
Notre Dame Scholastic (college newspaper) 218,
    219, 220
NUIG (National University of Ireland, Galway),
    see National University of Ireland,
    Galway (NUIG)

NUI (National University of Ireland),
    see National University of Ireland (NUI)
Nutt, Alfred 210

'Oar, The' (Longley) 312–13
Ó Baoighill, Rev. Micheál 21, 133
Ó Briain, Liam 105–6, 107, 108–9, 112
O'Brien, Conor Cruise 10, 327–8, 332–3
O'Brien, Flann 170
  At Swim-Two-Birds 157, 166, 169, 247
  The Dalkey Archive 157, see also na
    gCopaleen, Myles; O'Nolan, Brian
O'Brien, William Smith 355
Ó Buachalla, B. 139 n. 14
Ó Cadhain, Máirtín 37
Ó Cadhlaigh, Cormac 13, 95–6, 131
O'Casey, Sean 224
Ó Cathail, Tomás 114 n. 77, 133
  Oráid: Ódanna IV/Horace: Odes IV 132
  P. Vergili Maronis Aeneidos 133
Ó Catháin, Seán 21
  Ódanna Horáis/The Odes of Horace 132
Ó Ciardha, Séamus 131
  Aenéis Bhirgil/Virgil's Aeneid 133–4
Ó Cillín, S. P., see Killeen, James Frank
    (Prionsias Ó Cillín)
Ó Conalláin, Domhnall/Dónall 131, 132
  Aenéis Bhirgil/Virgil's Aeneid 133–4
Ó Concheanainn, Tomás 95
  Aeinéis IX 134
  Aistriúchán ar Virgil Aeinéid IX/Essays on
    Virgil, Aeneid IX 133–4
Ó Conchúir, Pádraig 87
O'Connell, Daniel 6, 53 n. 34, 355
O'Connell, Rev. F. W. 204
Ó Cuív, Shán 96
Odes (Horace) 76, 132, 140–1
Ó Direáin, Máirtín 181, 191
Ó Domhnaill, Maoghnas 13, 20, 96
  Óráidí Chicero in aghaidh Chaitilína/Cicero's
    Speeches against Catiline 132
  Prós-Cheapadóireacht Laidne do na
    Meadhon-Rangaibh/Latin Prose
    Composition for Intermediate Classes
    (North and Hillard) 135
  Tosach Laidne/Beginning Latin 135
Ó Donnchadha, Torna/Tadhg 98
O'Donovan, John 126–7, 180
O'Donovan Rossa, Jeremiah 55
  Pearse's funeral oration for 12–13, 43, 50–2,
    53, 54, 57, 58, 410
Ó Dubhthaigh, Fiachra S.: Nótaí ar Stair,
    Litríocht agus Saíocht na Róimhe/Notes on
    the History, Literature and Civilisation of
    Rome (Hally) 136

O'Duffy, Eimar 69
Odyssey, The (Homer) 13–14, 50, 94, 127–8, 200, 210–11, 312
   Adorno and Horkheimer and 32–3
   Joyce and 33–4
Oedipus at Colonus (Sophocles) 86, 90–1, 129–30
Oedipus at Colonus (Yeats) 228, 231–2, 234
Oedipus Rex/Oedipus Tyrannus (Sophocles) 7, 86, 87, 130, 218–19
Oedipus the King (Yeats) 7, 8, 218, 223, 224–7, 234
'Of a Greek Poem' (MacDonagh) 50, 67, 69
O'Faoláin, Seán 164
O'Farrelly, Agnes 185
Ó Fiannachta, Pádraig 112
   Mise Agaistín/Confessions 93
O'Flaherty, J. T. 179
O'Flaherty, Liam 181, 190
O'Flaherty, Tom 181, 188
Ó Flathartaigh, Máirtín 109, 112
O'Higgins, Kevin 6, 7 n. 20, 224, 356, 365–6
O'Higgins, Laurie 3, 15, 163 n. 36
O'Higgins, Tom 160, 247
Ó hOdhráin, Micheál
   Cúrsa Laidine dár Ré Féin III/Latin Course for Our Own Time III 136
   Sleachta as saothar Óivid/Excerpts from the Work of Ovid 133
O'Hussey, Bonaventura 22 n. 53
Oifig an tSoláthair/Stationery Office 85, 111 n. 63
Ó Laoi, Pádraic 21, 131
Oldham, C. H. 201
O'Leary, Art, see 'Caoineadh Airt Uí Laoghaire'/'The Lament for Art O'Leary'
O'Leary, Rev. Peter (Peadar Ua Laoghaire) 13, 21, 84, 128, 138, 163
   Aesop a tháinig go h-Éirinn/Aesop came to Ireland 134
   Catilína: Cúntas ar chogadh Chatilína ó Chaius Salustius Crispus/Cuiiline: An account of the war of Catiline by Caius Salustius Crispus 133
   Lúcián/Lucian 97
   Papers on Irish Idiom together with a Translation into Irish of Part of the First Book of Euclid 134
'Oliver Plunkett' (Longley) 307
Olivier, Laurence 228
Ó Lochlain, Colm 372
Ó Máille, Pádraig 102 & n. 16
Ó Máille, Tomás 102 n. 15, 104
Ó Mathghamhna, Domhnall 13, 122, 132
   An Tarna Philippica/The Second Philippic 96, 131

Démostenés agus Cicero/Demosthenes and Cicero 96, 129
Inis Atlaint/The Island of Atlantis 96, 128–9
Óráid Caointe Phericléis/The Funeral Oration of Pericles 96, 130
Saoghal-ré na nGracchi/The Lives of the Gracchi 96, 129
Scéalta a Filí na Rómha/Stories from the Poets of Rome (Pease) 96, 134
Ó Meachair, Pádraig 130, 132
Omeros (Walcott) 410
Ó Moghráin, Pádraig: Foras Feasa ar Stair na Rómha/Foundation of Knowledge on the History of Rome (Pelham) 136
'On Being Asked for a War Poem' (Yeats) 295–6
O'Neill, Fr George 62 n. 8, 71
O'Neill, Jamie: At Swim, Two Boys 12, 247–9
O'Nolan, Brian 17–18, 157, 158, 169, 170, 414: see also na gCopaleen, Myles; O'Brien, Flann
O'Nolan, Kevin 14, 158
On the Boiler (Yeats) 220, 230, 233
'On the necessity for de-Anglicising Ireland' (Hyde) 147
Ó Nualláin, Feargus: Laidean tré Ghaedhilg 135
O'Rahilly, Thomas 104, 177–8
Ó Raifeartaigh, Tarlach 116 n. 86, 125 n. 106
   Cúrsa Clarendonach Laidne, An/The Clarendon Latin Course (Clendon and Vince) 135
oral poetry tradition 14
Orangeism 201, 276, 308, 343
Ó Rathaille, Aogán 138, 140, 142–3
oratory, classical 50
Oresteia (Aeschylus) 8, 330
Ó Riain, Seán: Virgil: Aeinéid VI 134
origin legends, medieval 173–4
Ó Rinn, Liam/Uilliam 104, 128
Ó Rioghardáin, Flaithrí 280 n. 52
   Epódanna Oráit/Horace. Epodes 132
Ó Ríordáin, Seán 98
'Oscar Wilde: The Poet of Salome' (Joyce) 241
Ó Searcaigh, Cathal 12, 249–52
O'Shea, William 55
Ó Súilleabháin, Eoghan Ruadh 138, 140
Ó Súilleabháin, Muiris 91, 94, 105, 108
Ó Súilleabháin, Paulinus/Pól 116 n. 85, 132
   Nuachúrsa Laidne/New Latin Course 135
Otto, Walter Friedrich 103
Ovid 132–3, 275, 291
   Ars Amatoria 168, 294
   Metamorphoses 132
   Tristia 109 n. 52, 123, 133, 293
Owen, Wilfred 305

Pacino, Al 228
paedophilia 12, 249, 252–3
Pagans (MacDonagh) 69
Paisley, Ian 329, 340, 343
Pantheon, Rome 353
Parke, Edward 353 n. 12
Parnell, Charles Stewart 355
Parry, Milman 91
'Partisans' (Longley) 312
Paulin, Tom 10, 326, 332–3
    The Riot Act 326, 327, 328–9, 330, 344
Pausanias 387
'Peace' (Longley) 294, 302–5
Peace People (formerly Women for Peace),
    Belfast 303, 304
Peace Process 330, 338, 341
Pearce, Edward Lovett 353 n. 12
Pearse, Patrick 3, 6, 22, 42, 58, 65, 138, 188,
    194–5, 408
    and Abbey Theatre 222
    in America 55–7
    and blood sacrifice 257 n. 12
    on coinage 399
    on Davis 58–9
    Emmet Commemoration address 54
    funeral oration for O'Donovan Rossa 12–13,
        43, 50–2, 53, 54, 57, 58, 410
    and Gaelic League 139, 180
    and Greek funeral orations 57–8
    and homosexuality 242–4
    'In First Century Ireland' 243
    Irish literature *v.* classical literature 47–8, 63
    and MacNeill 202
    Mise Éire 153
    The Murder Machine 49 n. 23
    and Proclamation of the Irish
        Republic 384, 385
    The Separatist Idea 51 n. 29
    sexuality of 12
    Some Aspects of Irish Literature 47–8, 63
    The Sovereign People 53–4
    Three Lectures on Gaelic Topics 48
    and Wilde 242
Pearse, Willie 69
pederasty 249, 252–3
Pelham, H. F.: *Outlines of Roman History* 136
Petrie, George 180, 182, 191
Pfeiffer, Rudolf 103
Phaedo (Plato) 93, 105, 109, 120, 128
Phaedra Backwards (Carr) 265
Pharsalia (Lucan) 208
Phases in Irish History (MacNeill) 175–6
Philoctetes (Sophocles) 8, 330
Philosophy of Irish Ireland, The (Moran) 139
Phoblacht, An/The Republic (newspaper) 94

Phoenician Women (Euripides) 340
Pindar 109 n. 52, 123
Plain People of Ireland 158, 167
Plato
    Apology 93, 105, 109, 120, 128
    Critias 96, 128–9
    Crito 93, 105, 109, 120, 128, 129
    Phaedo 93, 105, 109, 120, 128
    Symposium 94, 129
Playboy of the Western World, The
    (Synge) 222, 259
Plays for Dancers (Yeats) 223
Pliny the Younger 275 n. 30
Plotinus 7, 69 n. 36, 230
Plough and the Stars, The (O'Casey) 224
Plunkett, Joseph 50 n. 27, 69, 188
Plunkett, Oliver 307
Plutarch 84, 109, 129
    Demosthenes and Cicero 96
    Life of Theseus 386–8
    Lives of the Gracchi 96, 129
Poems of the Irish Revolutionary Brotherhood 62
Poetical Works of Thomas MacDonagh 71–2
Poetics (Aristotle) 211, 410
Pokorny, Julius 182 n. 65
Pollack, Hugh 268
Pope, Alexander 142
'Poppies' (Longley) 312
popular culture 268–87
    classical mythology in Irish ballads 269–70
    Dido in 271–4
    Rome as model 275–7
    Virgil as love poet 275
    see also *Carthaginians* (McGuinness)
Portland stone
    GPO, Dublin 389
    as imperial symbol at Stormont 380–2,
        386, 389
Portrait of the Artist as a Young Man, A
    (Joyce) 178, 216
Pound, Ezra 11, 291–3, 398
    Cantos 292
    'Homage to Sextus Propertius' 291–2, 293,
        296, 301–2
    and Italian fascism 292–3
    'The Non-existence of Ireland' 296
Power, Albert 399
Prehistoric Aegean, The (Thomson) 39
Pro Archia Poeta (Cicero) 132, 164
Proclamation of the Irish Republic 58, 260,
    384, 385
Pro Lege Manilia (Cicero) 132
Prometheus Bound (Aeschylus) 93–4, 105, 110,
    113 n. 73, 121, 125
Pro Murena (Cicero) 199

Propertius 11, 164, 291–3, 294
  Longley and 293–4, 297–302
  Yeats and 11, 293, 295–7
Provisional IRA 324 n. 71
Punch magazine 401
Purcell, Henry 278
Purgatory (Yeats) 233–4
Pyrrhus 46–7

Quare Fella, The (Behan) 245
Queen of the Hearth, The (Dinneen) 140, 152
Queen's College, Galway 100 n. 1, 101
Queen's University, Belfast (QUB) 15, 195
'Quest, The' (MacDonagh) 67
Quinn, Bob 29

Radió na Gaeltachta 251
Raftery, Anthony 38
Rambles in Ireland (Lynd) 183
rape 262–3, 264, 267, 335–6
reception studies 15, 16
Recollections (O'Donovan Rossa) 55
recusatio (refusal) poems 296, 299–300
Red Branch 243
Redmond, John 200
Rehm, Albert 103
Reinhardt, Max 223
'Remembering the Poets' (Longley) 293, 294
Renan, Ernest 88, 147
Resurrection, The (Yeats) 230–1, 232
Revolutionary Dáil (1919–22) 83–4
RIA (Royal Irish Academy) 179
Rice, John (pseudonym Jacques) 258–60, 266
Riot Act, The (Paulin) 326, 327, 328–9, 330, 344
Robinson, Lennox 224, 225
Robinson, Mary 267
Rockwell College 65
Romans in Britain, The (Brenton) 22–3, 31–2
Rough Magic company 266
'Route 110' (Heaney) 9–10
Royal Courts of Justice, Belfast 381
Royal Dublin Society 354
Royal Hospital, Kilmainham 382
Royal Irish Academy (RIA) 179
Royal Society of Antiquaries 186
Rudimenta Grammaticae Hibernicae
  (O'Hussey) 22 n. 53

St Enda's School, Rathfarnham, Dublin 48–9, 65
Salkeld, Cecil 224
Sallust 133
Samhain (magazine) 221, 226
Sandford, Philip 101
Sartre, Jean-Paul 257
Satires (Juvenal) 200

Saturnalia (Macrobius) 280 n. 52
Saville Report (2010) 327
Scaliger, Julius Caesar 298
School of Irish Learning 211, 212
Séadna (O'Leary) 163
Seártan, Seán: *Prós-Cheapadóireacht Laidne/*
  Latin Prose Composition (Bradley's
  Arnold) 95, 115, 116 n. 86, 135
'Second Coming, The' (Yeats) 234
Second Lebanese War 311
Seeing Things (Heaney) 9
'Selfish Giant, The' (Wilde) 242
Separatist Idea, The (Pearse) 51 n. 29
Shakespeare Association of America 311
Shaw, George Bernard 221–2, 225
Sheppard, Oliver
  and coinage 399
  The Death of Cúchulainn 6, 349–50, 351, 390
Shewing Up of Blanco Posnet, The
  (Shaw) 221–2, 225
Shields, Arthur 260
Shiel(s), John 271
Sinn Féin 16, 195, 340–1
  Henry and 196–206
  Joyce and 212–16
  MacNeill and 203
'Sixteen Dead Men' (Yeats) 64 n. 19
'Skara Brae' (Longley) 299
slavery 31, 49 n. 23, 56, 254, 255, 320 n. 53
  Fir Bolg 173, 175–7, 183, 186, 190
Smirke, Robert 361
Smith, Andrew 116 n. 85
Smith, R. Ingelby 386
Smyllie, R. M. 161, 166 n. 49
Social Life in Greece from Homer to Menander
  (Mahaffy) 239
Society for Irish Historical Studies 206
Society for the Preservation of the Irish
  Language/*Cumann Buan-Choimeadta na*
  Gaeilge 212
Socrates 237
Some Aspects of Irish Literature (Pearse) 47–8, 63
Somme, Battle of (1916) 2 n. 5
Sommer, Ferdinand 103–4
Songs of Myself (MacDonagh) 71 n. 45
Sonnenschein, E. A. 203
  Greek Grammar 95, 114–15, 135
  Latin Grammar 135
Sophocles 233
  Antigone 1 n. 2, 8, 10, 129, 218
  reception of 326–45
  Oedipus at Colonus 86, 90–1, 129–30, 228–9
  Oedipus Rex/Oedipus Tyrannus 7, 86, 87, 130,
    218–23, 337
  Philoctetes 8, 330

Sovereign People, The (Pearse) 53–4
Speckled Bird, The (Yeats) 189 n. 110
Speranza (Lady Jane Wilde) 240
Spirit Level, The (Heaney) 330
Stanford, W. B. 14–15, 16, 63 n. 15, 394
Starkie, Walter 175
Star, The 92–3, 104
States of Ireland (O'Brien) 327–8
Station Island (Heaney) 9
Stationery Office/Oifig an tSoláthair 85,
    111 n. 63
Statius 208
statues 6
    The Death of Cúchulainn 6, 349–50,
      351, 390
    equestrian statues 4–5
    symbolism of Customs House statues 383
    symbolism of GPO statues 383, 385, 390
    symbolism of Stormont statues 378, 390
'Statues, The' (Yeats) 7 n. 19
Stein, Gertrude 407
Stephen Hero (Joyce) 216
Sterne, Laurence 169
Stern, Ludwig Christian 211
Stoffel, Rev. Nicholas J. 218
Stormont (Northern Ireland Parliament
    Buildings), Belfast 5–6, 374, 375–82, 375*f*,
    379*f*, 384, 385–90, 391–2
    Craig, burial of 376, 385–6, 387*f*, 388
    Portland stone as imperial symbol 380–2
    symbolism of statues 378, 390
Strabane Chronicle 45
Stroux, Johannes 103
Stuart, Francis 224
Studies: An Irish Quarterly Review 62 n. 8
Sulpicia 11, 305–6
'Sulpicia' (Longley) 305–6
Sunday Independent 262
Sweetman, Rosita 178–9
Swift, Jonathan 199
Sword of Light, The/An Claidheamh
    Soluis 96, 222
Symons, Arthur 189
Symposium (Plato) 94, 129
Synge, Rev. Alexander 184 n. 77
Synge, John Millington 14, 18, 180
    The Aran Islands 191–2
    The Playboy of the Western World 222, 259
    In the Shadow of the Glen 220, 259
    Yeats' advice to 75
Syrian refugee crisis 265

Tacitus 31, 122
textbooks 31
    Greek language 134–5

Irish language 85, 93, 95, 97–8, 109, 110, 114,
    115, 125–36
    Latin language 135–6
Thebaid (Statius) 208
Theocritus 94, 130
Thermopylae, battle of 45
Third Home Rule Bill (1912) 2
Thompson, D'Arcy Wentworth 101
Thomson, George (Seoirse Mac Tomáis/Seoirse
    Mac Laghmainn) 13, 14, 91–5, 99, 100,
    104–13, 118–19, 211, 408
    Alcéstis le h-Eurípidés/Alcestis by
      Euripides 93–4, 120–1, 126
    Breith Báis ar Eagnuidhe: Trí Cómhráidhte d'ár
      cheap Platón (Apologia, Criton,
      Phaedón)/Sentence of Death on a Sage:
      Three Dialogues written by Plato (Apology,
      Crito, Phaedo) 105, 109, 120, 128
    on education 92–3
    'An lá féile'/'The festival' (Theocritus,
      Idyll 15) 94, 130
    in Galway 109–13
    and An Gúm 94
    Mise Agaistín/Augustine, Confessions 93
    Notes on Greek Syntax 111 n. 63, 121
    The Prehistoric Aegean 39
    Prométheus fé Chuibhreach le
      h-Aeschylus/*Prometheus Bound by*
      Aeschylus 93–4, 110, 113 n. 73, 121, 125
    report to Academic Council (1933) 120–1
    'An seana-shaol Gréagach: Scéalta ó stair
      Herodotus'/'Life in ancient Greece: Stories
      from Herodotus' 94
    'An Suimpóisiam'/*Symposium* 94
    Tosnú na Feallsúnachta/The Beginning of
      Philosophy 94–5, 121, 136
    Tosnú na Sibhialtachta/The Beginning of
      Civilization 94–5
    translations 93, 94, 105, 126, 127, 129, 130
    'Tús na Sibhialtachta san Eoraip'/'The
      Beginning of Civilization in
      Europe' 110–11
Thornely, Arnold 376, 389
'Thought from Propertius, A' (Yeats) 295, 296–7
Three Lectures on Gaelic Topics (Pearse) 48
Through the Ivory Gate (MacDonagh) 50,
    64 n. 19
Thucydides 57, 200, 388
    Funeral Oration of Pericles 12–13, 54, 96, 130
    Peloponnesian War 12–13, 54, 96, 130
Tibullus 11, 291, 293, 294, 302–6
Tierney, Michael 92 n. 42, 104, 115 n. 82,
    118, 176
Timaeus 280 n. 52
Tóibín, Rev. Tomás 131

To-morrow (journal) 224
Tone, Wolf 51
Tower, The (Yeats) 227, 231, 232
Tragedian in Spite of Himself, A (Chekov) 258
Transactions (RIA) 179
Translations (Friel) 137–8, 142, 144, 152, 153
Trinity College Dublin (TCD) 35–6, 194–5, 202
Tristia (Ovid) 109 n. 52, 123, 133, 293
Tristram Shandy (Sterne) 169
Trojan Women (Euripides) 11–12, 126
    and Irish sexual politics 254–67
Trojan Women (Kennelly) 12, 152 n. 70,
    261–3, 266–7
Troyennes, Les (Sartre) 257
Truth about Kathmandu, The
    (documentary) 251
Tuatha Dé Danann 178
Twenty Years A-Growing/Fiche Bliain ag Fás
    (Ó Súilleabháin) 91, 105, 108
Tyrrell, R.Y. 162

Ua Briain, Mícheál: *Trialacha Laidne don
    Mhacléighinn/Latin Tests for Students* 135
Ua Duinnín, Pádraic/Pádraig,
    see Dinneen, Patrick
Ua Laoghaire, Peadar, *see* O'Leary, Peter (Peadar
    Ua Laoghaire)
Ua Nualláin, Tomás: *Leabhar Aristodeil dá
    nglaetar Béasgna Nichomhach/The Book of
    Aristotle entitled Nicomachean Ethics* 126
Ulster Architectural Heritage Society, The 376
Ulster Defence Association (UDA) 322 n. 57
Ulster Solemn League and Covenant 391
Ulster unionism 6, 374–6, 388, 391
Ulster Volunteer Force (UVF) 309 n. 4
Ulster Volunteers 197
Ulysses (Joyce) 16, 17, 20, 29–30, 33, 39, 46–7,
    138, 166, 170, 178, 212–16, 217
'Ulysses, Order and Myth' (Eliot) 34
unionism, *see* Ulster unionism
United Irish League 39, 201
United Irishman (newspaper) 216, 220
University College Cork (UCC) 95, 148–9
University College Dublin 65, 95–6, 156
University College Galway (UCG) 65, 86, 93
    Classics through Irish 100–19
    early 20th-century professors 101–2
    unpublished Irish translations of classical
        texts archive 122–4
University College Galway Act (1929) 104
use/abuse of classics 27–42
UVF *see* Ulster Volunteer Force (UVF)

'Valediction' (Heaney) 298 n. 30
Vallancey, Charles 19

Varro 73
Velleius Paterculus 110
Vera Historia (Lucian) 96, 128
Verres, Gaius 44
Virgil 110, 293
    Celtic origins of 146–50
    Eclogues 8–9, 140, 142
    Eliot on 28
    Georgics 8, 122–3, 140, 144 n. 38, 150–1
    imperialism in 9
    in Irish 141–6
    and Irish history 150–5
    as love poet 275
    see also *Aeneid* (Virgil)
'Virgil: Eclogue IX' (Heaney) 9
Virgil of Salzburg, St 144
Vision, A (Yeats) 223, 230, 231, 233
vision (*aisling*) poems 271
Vitruvius 360
Voortrekker Monument, Pretoria 5, 353
Voyage of Bran, Son of Febal, The 210

#WakingtheFeminists (#WTF)
    movement 12, 267
Walcott, Derek 410
Walls of Athens, The (O'Duffy) 69
*Wanderings of Ulysses son of Laertes/Merugud
    Uilix Maicc Leirtis* 17, 204, 206–13, 216
War of Independence 86, 105 n. 36, 214, 266,
    351, 381
Waste Land, The (Eliot) 28, 34
Weather in Japan, The (Longley) 293, 294
Wellington Testimonial 361, 362f, 372
Westropp, Thomas 180
Weyman, Carl 103
Whitman, Walt 239–40
Whitty, Sophia St John 189
Wilde, Lady Jane (Speranza) 240
Wilde, Oscar 12, 237–53
    The Ballad of Reading Gaol 245
    Behan and 245–6
    De Profundis 239, 240, 245
    The Disciple 245
    and Douglas 237, 240
    'The Happy Prince' 242
    Joyce and 12, 241–2
    'The Selfish Giant' 242
    and Socrates 237
    trial of 239
Wilde, William 177, 180, 182, 184–6
Wilding, L. A.: *Latin Course for Schools* 20, 31
Wild Irish Girl, The (Lady Morgan) 277
Wild Swans at Coole, The (Yeats) 295–7
'Wild Swans at Coole, The' (Yeats) 296
Wilkinson, L. P. 151

William III, King of England 4–5
Wilson, Gordon 314, 322, 323
Women for Peace, *see* Peace People (formerly
    Women for Peace), Belfast
Woolf, Virginia 166
Wormell, D. E. W. 115 n. 83
'Wounds' (Longley) 307
'Wreaths' (Longley) 299, 307
#WTF (#WakingtheFeminists) movement 12, 267

Xenophon 57, 130

Yeats Theatre 221
Yeats, W. B. 7, 180, 189, 330, 408
    'Among School Children' 229, 232
    astrology 233
    Cathleen ni Houlihan 257
    and Celtic stereotype 174 n. 7
    and censorship 224–6, 228, 229
    and coinage 393, 395–6, 397, 398, 399–400
    comparison of Dublin with Troy 254
    The Countess Cathleen 218, 226
    dark roads 228–34
    The Dreaming of the Bones 180
    'Easter 1916' 64, 295–6
    and elegy 291
    and Herodotus 230
    and Irish Literary Revival 33–4
    'Leda and the Swan' 224
    and MacDonagh 64, 75

and national theatre 220–1
'No Second Troy' 11, 254, 286, 295
and obscurantism 223–8
Oedipus at Colonus 228, 231–2, 234
and Oedipus story 218–34
Oedipus the King 7, 8, 218, 223, 224–7, 234
'On Being Asked for a War Poem' 295–6
On the Boiler 220, 230, 233
Plays for Dancers 223
and Plotinus 7, 230
and Propertius 11, 293, 295–7
Purgatory 233–4
The Resurrection 230–1, 232
and Romanticism 3
'The Second Coming' 234
'Sixteen Dead Men' 64 n. 19
The Speckled Bird 189 n. 110
'The Statues' 7 n. 19
'A Thought from Propertius' 295, 296–7
The Tower 227, 231, 232
A Vision 223, 230, 231, 233
'The Wild Swans at Coole' 296
The Wild Swans at Coole 295–7
'Yellow Bittern, The'/'An Bonnán Buí' (Mac
    Giolla Ghunna) 69–70
Young Ascanius, The 274 n. 27
Young Ireland 39, 201

Zeitschrift fur celtische Philologie 211
Zimmer, Heinrich 180, 210